YUCATÁN PENINSULA

LIZA PRADO & GARY CHANDLER

Contents

YUCATÁN PENINSULA

Gulf of Mexico

Bahía de Campeche

Ciudad del Carmen

Laguna de Términos

○ Alvarado

180

San Andrés Tuxtla

Coatzacoalcos

145D Acayucan

Minatitlán

Cárdenas

VILLAHERMOSA

TABASCO

Comalcalco

187

180

180

10

186

180

VERACRUZ

185

195

Presa Netzahualcoyotl

PALENQUE Palenque

199 TONINÁ

Ocosingo

PLAN DE AYUTLA

Fronter Coroza

YAXCHILÁN

BONAMPAK

CARRETERA FRONTERIZA

OAXACA

190 **TUXTLA GUTIÉRREZ**

San Cristóbal de las Casas

Comitán

Monte Azules Biosphere Reserve

190 Juchitan

200

CHIAPAS

Arriaga

Tonalá

Puerto Arista

Golfo de Tehuantepec

200

El Triunfo Biosphere Reserve

Presa La Angostura

Parque Nacional Lagunas de Montebello

190

La Trinitaria

Pijijiapán

Ciudad Cuauhtémoc

Mapastepec

211

Huehuetenango

1

Huixtla

PACIFIC OCEAN

Tapachula

DISCOVER

Yucatán Peninsula

On the northern coast of the Yucatán Peninsula is a place called Uaymitún, where just a thin strip of land separates the ocean from a swampy coastal lagoon. But the swamp is not just a swamp—climbing a roadside tower, you discover it's also home to thousands of flamingos, their bright pink feathers a stark contrast to the gray-green surroundings. Behind you are the emerald waters of the Gulf of Mexico, a favorite spot for windsurfers and kiteboarders. To the east is a small Maya ruin. To the south is the great colonial city of Mérida, and just down the road is the spot where scientists believe a meteorite smashed into the earth 65 million years ago, wiping out the dinosaurs and ushering in the age of humankind. Uaymitún is not a major tourist destination—except for the flamingos, it hardly rates a mention. But that's just it: The Yucatán has so much history, culture, and natural wonder, even a dusty roadside town is rich with stories and possibilities.

It's hard to exaggerate the number and variety of attractions here: stunning Maya ruins, vibrant colonial cities, wildlife-watching, a web of caves and underground rivers, and ideal conditions for kiteboarding and sportfishing.

Clockwise from top left: hibiscus flower; beach camping; *poc-chuc,* a traditional Yucatecan dish; Tulum fishing boat; diving in Cozumel's crystalline water; Uayma's ornate church.

For divers, there are world-famous reefs at Isla Cozumel and eerie inland cenotes. And if you're looking for a beach vacation . . . well, you know you've come to the right place.

The Yucatán is also a place of many stories. Maya hieroglyphics tell complicated tales of gods, kings, and conquest. The exploits of its pirates and buccaneers are still the subject of fairy tales and feature films. The colonial era was rife with the boom and bust of products like henequen and chicle. The Maya have suffered unspeakable exploitation, but not passively—in the Caste War, they nearly drove European settlers off the peninsula for good. More recent is the remarkable story of Cancún, which in a matter of decades was transformed from a mosquito-infested sandbar into one of the world's top resort destinations.

The Yucatán Peninsula is all this, and even more—a place of endless mystery and beauty, fun and fascination. Enjoy!

Clockwise from top left: Tulum, the only Maya ruin with its very own white-sand beach; shopping at Mérida's Mercado Municipal; Chichén Itzá; morning bike ride in Mérida.

10 TOP
EXPERIENCES

1 Dive in Cozumel: Famous for its pristine reef, plunging walls, ornate coral formations, and rich sea life, Cozumel is truly a world-class dive destination. Dives like Palancar and Santa Rosa Wall will leave you breathless (page 117).

2 **Journey back in time at Maya ruins:** Explore sprawling stone temple cities, built over 1,000 years ago and then mysteriously abandoned, at spectacular sites like Chichén Itzá (page 275), Cobá (page 226), Uxmal (page 361), Calakmul (page 411), and Palenque (page 429).

3 **Relax on Caribbean beaches:** The Yucatán boasts Mexico's finest beaches: long stretches of powdery white sand, edged with coconut trees, facing a turquoise sea. Favorites include Playa Delfines in Cancún (page 44), Playa Norte on Isla Mujeres (page 73), and Tulum's southern beaches (page 209).

4 **Spot diverse wildlife:** The Yucatán Peninsula boasts an array of wildlife, including howler monkeys, jaguars, turtles, and countless fish and birds. Some nature and wildlife reserves, like Calakmul, double as must-see archaeological sites (page 30).

<<<

13

5 **Go cenote hopping:** Cenotes are usually translated as sinkholes, which doesn't do justice to these stunning limestone pools, filled with crystalline water. Some are enclosed caverns, just a shaft of sunlight knifing down to the aquamarine surface (page 33).

6 **Snorkel with whale sharks:** The world's largest fish, whale sharks congregate along Mexico's gulf coast in summer. You can snorkel with these gentle giants on guided tours from Isla Mujeres (page 77) and Isla Holbox (page 88).

7 **Catch Mérida's music and dance performances:** A colonial gem, Mérida hosts free cultural events every day and night—literally. On Sundays the streets are closed and performers fete happy crowds (pages 321 and 322).

8 **Take a flamingo tour:** American flamingos are the largest and pinkest of all flamingos. Tens of thousands call the Yucatán home. The best places to observe them are Río Lagartos (page 304) and Celestún (page 341), on a guided boat tour.

9 **Explore Campeche's city walls:** Centuries ago, Campeche built massive walls and bulwarks around the city center as protection against pirate attacks. Today, those same structures have been ingeniously repurposed as museums and raised walkways (page 393).

10 **Savor Yucatecan cuisine:** This is Mexican food like you've never eaten—a rich and colorful amalgam of Maya, Middle Eastern, and traditional Mexican flavors. Try dishes like *cochinita pibil* and *poc-chuc*, topped with face-on-fire habanera hot sauce (page 27).

Planning Your Trip

Where to Go

Cancún

Cancún has two parts: The **Zona Hotelera** (Hotel Zone) has the city's top resorts and nightclubs, plus miles of beautiful beaches. But if you don't mind hopping a bus to the beach, **downtown** has cheaper food and lodging, plus some unexpectedly cool bars and cafés. Most travelers visit **Isla Mujeres,** a sliver of an island offshore from Cancún, as a day trip, but nice hotels and a mellow ambience make it a tempting place to stay. **Isla Holbox** is even smaller, with sand roads and virtually no cars. The beaches aren't glorious, but the tranquility is sublime.

Isla Cozumel

Cozumel's pristine **coral reefs** and crystalline water attract divers the world over; fewer people realize the island also has a scenic **national park,** numerous beach clubs, a tournament golf course, and even an important **Maya ruin.** Beat the cruise ship crowds by heading to the east side's isolated beaches and dramatic surf. Most people arrive by ferry—it's just a half-hour ride from Playa del Carmen—but there's also an airport with international arrivals.

The Riviera Maya

Stretching 130 kilometers (81 miles) from Cancún to Tulum, the Riviera Maya has megaresorts and boutique bed-and-breakfasts, busy cities and quiet towns, great reef diving and jaw-dropping cenotes (freshwater sinkholes). **Playa del Carmen** has the area's largest selection of hotels, food, nightlife, and services; try **Puerto Morelos**

a *calesa* (horse-drawn carriage) in Izamal, a colonial town outside of Mérida

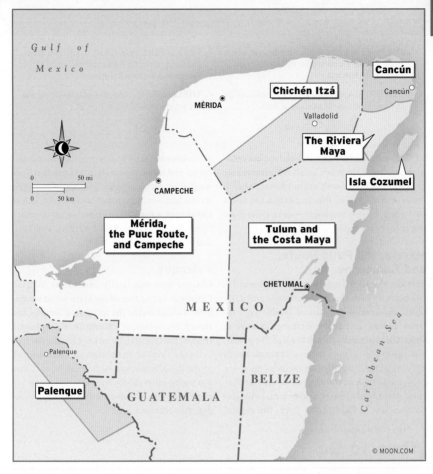

and **Akumal** for something a bit smaller, or isolated clusters of beachfront hotels like **Tankah Tres** and **Soliman Bay** for even more R&R.

Tulum and the Costa Maya

Tulum is justly famous for its stunning beaches, boho-chic bungalows, and namesake **Maya ruin,** with a dramatic view of the Caribbean. An hour from Tulum, **Cobá** boasts the second-tallest Maya pyramid and a lovely forest setting teeming with birds. Directly south of Tulum is the pristine **Sian Ka'an Biosphere Reserve** and beyond that the isolated towns of the **Costa Maya.**

There's a lovely freshwater lagoon, **Bacalar,** with an equally pleasant like-named town that is growing in popularity with independent travelers. Just south is **Chetumal,** the busy state capital and gateway to Belize.

Chichén Itzá

Chichén Itzá is one of the most impressive and recognizable of all Maya ruins, especially its iconic main pyramid. There also is a nighttime sound and light show, and interesting villages and cenotes are nearby. The adjacent town of Pisté is unmemorable—better to base yourself

If You Have...

- **ONE WEEK:** Visit Cancún, Isla Cozumel, or Isla Holbox; take a side trip to Valladolid and the ruins of Chichén Itzá.

- **TEN DAYS:** Add Mérida and the Puuc Route; go to Campeche City for a couple of days.

- **TWO WEEKS:** Add Tulum, the Riviera Maya, and Cobá ruins; join a one-day excursion in the Sian Ka'an Biosphere Reserve.

- **THREE WEEKS:** Add the Costa Maya, the Río Bec region, and Palenque.

in Valladolid, a charming and convenient colonial city. **Ek' Balam** is a small but remarkable archaeological site with an impressive stucco frieze. On the coast, **Río Lagartos** has tours into a neighboring biosphere reserve to see huge colonies of flamingos.

Mérida, the Puuc Route, and Campeche

Mérida, the Yucatán state capital, is a beautiful colonial city with excellent museums and daily music and dance performances. Doable day trips from Mérida include the flamingo reserve at **Celestún,** the mellow beach town of **Progreso,** and the lovely colonial town of **Izamal.** South of Mérida, the **Puuc Route** includes must-see Maya ruins such as **Uxmal** and myriad smaller sites, plus caves, cenotes, and colonial villages. Farther south, **Campeche City,** the capital

of Campeche state, boasts a gorgeous colonial center and impressive walls and forts that once warded off pirate attacks. Southern Campeche state is home to numerous Maya sites, including **Calakmul,** a massive city now buried deep in a forest reserve that's home to parrots, monkeys, and even jaguars.

Palenque

Chiapas isn't technically part of the Yucatán Peninsula, but no tour of the Maya world is complete without seeing the intriguing temples and superb inscriptions at **Palenque.** From there, a series of lovely waterfalls makes a terrific day trip, as do the ruins of **Yaxchilán** and **Bonampak** in the Río Usumacinta valley. Palenque is also a jumping-off point for trips into the Lacandón rainforest, with its rich ecology and reclusive indigenous communities.

When to Go

Considering weather, prices, and crowds, the best times to visit the Yucatán Peninsula are from **late November to mid-December** and from **mid-January to early May.** You'll avoid the intense heat from June to August, the rain (and possible hurricanes) in September and October, and the crowds and high prices around the winter holidays.

The big caveats with those periods are spring break (March/April) and Semana Santa (the week before Easter), when American and Canadian students, and then Mexican tourists, turn out in force and prices spike temporarily.

Be aware that certain attractions are only available (or recommendable) during specific months, whether snorkeling with whale sharks (June-September) or visiting Chichén Itzá on the spring or fall equinoxes. Even many year-round activities like sportfishing, kiteboarding, and bird-watching are better or worse according to the season. Ocean diving, for instance, is optimal in the spring and early summer when tropical storms are rare and visibility is best.

street scene in downtown Campeche City

Before You Go

Passports and Visas

American and Canadian travelers are required to have a valid passport to travel to and from Mexico. **Tourist visas** are issued upon entry; you technically are allowed up to 180 days, but agents often issue just 30 or 60 days. If you want to stay longer, request the time when you present your passport. To extend your visa, visit the immigration office in Cancún, Chetumal, or Merida.

Vaccinations

No special vaccines are required for travel to the Yucatán Peninsula, but it's a good idea to be up to date on the **standard travel immunizations,** including hepatitis A, MMR (measles-mumps-rubella), tetanus-diphtheria, and typhoid.

Transportation

Cancún International Airport (CUN) is far and away the most common and convenient entry point to the region; airports at Mérida, Cozumel, Chetumal, Campeche, and Palenque are secondary options. An excellent network of **buses, shuttles,** and **ferries** covers the entire region, though a rental car makes a world of difference in more remote areas like the Costa Maya and the Río Bec region.

What to Pack

Bring to the Yucatán Peninsula what you would to any beach or tropical destination: light cotton clothing, hat, sunscreen, sunglasses, flip-flops, and so forth. Beach buffs should bring two or even three **swimsuits,** plus **snorkel gear** if you have it. **Water shoes** come in handy wherever the beach is rocky, while **sneakers** and **bug repellent** are musts for the Maya ruins. A light sweater and a rain jacket also come in handy during the winter and rainy seasons. Finally, it's always smart to bring an extra pair of glasses or contacts, prescription medications, birth control, and a travel clock. If you do leave anything behind, no worries—there's a Walmart in all the major cities.

The Best of the Yucatán

See and do a little of everything in the Yucatán Peninsula in just two weeks with this itinerary. With beaches to enjoy, ruins to explore, museums to visit, cenotes to snorkel in, and cities to discover, this is a trip for travelers with plenty of energy and a hankering to see it all. Renting a car for the entire trip will give you added speed and flexibility and ensure you have time to enjoy every stop. If a rental car is out of your budget, most of the route can be done easily enough by bus. A good compromise is to rent a car for a few key days.

Day 1

Arrive in Cancún but head south to **Playa del Carmen,** which is a better base for exploring the Riviera Maya. (**Puerto Morelos, Akumal, Tankah Tres,** and **Soliman Bay** also are good choices if you prefer something smaller.) If you plan to get in some serious diving, consider heading directly to **Isla Cozumel** to save yourself the ferry ride the next day. That, or just fly straight there!

Day 2

Spend your first full day underwater in the Riviera Maya. Just about every town along the coast has a dive shop (usually several) offering **snorkeling and diving tours** on the ocean reef. The waters in front of **Puerto Morelos** and **Akumal** have less boat traffic than Playa del Carmen. Or take the plunge in one of the Riviera Maya's myriad **cenotes,** either at a park like **Dos Ojos** or on your own at a site like **Jardín del Edén.**

Day 3

Head inland. Get an early start and go straight to **Chichén Itzá,** getting there as close to opening time as possible. That way you'll have a jump on the big tour buses and can enjoy these magnificent ruins with fewer people to weave around. Budget at least three hours here. Check into a

palapas on the beach

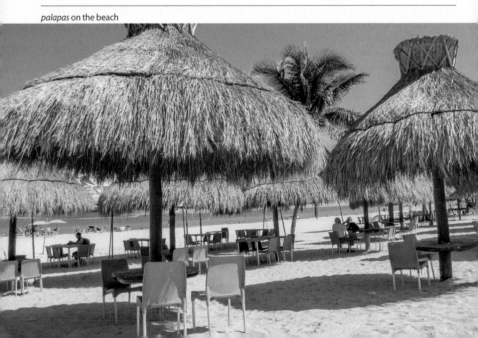

A Family Affair

The Yucatán Peninsula is an excellent family destination, with plenty to see and do for kids and parents, and good hotels and restaurants help take the stress out of traveling en masse. Here are a few recommended stops:

CANCÚN

Isla Mujeres: Super-calm water, a turtle farm, an ecopark, plus a ferry ride there and back—what's not to love?

Isla Holbox: Snorkel with whale sharks, gentle giants that congregate here June-September. Visit Punta Cocos on a dark spring or summer night, when bioluminescent plankton create an otherworldly glow as you walk or paddle through them.

Parque Las Palapas: Downtown Cancún's main plaza, where kids can run around and munch on chocolate-filled churros.

El Rey Archaeological Zone: Hundreds of beefy iguanas make this a fun stop for kids, even if they're lukewarm about piles of old rocks. (Hint: The iguanas love bananas!)

ISLA COZUMEL

Playa Chen Río: This protected ocean beach on Cozumel's east side is deserted midweek and busy with local families on weekends.

Parque Punta Sur: A scenic natural reserve with a nice beach and fantastic snorkeling, plus a maritime museum and a lighthouse you can climb.

Planetario de Cozumel: This state-of-the-art planetarium is a nice place to cool off and enjoy films about the universe, Maya cosmology, and more.

Butterfly Sanctuary: Stroll through a protected garden filled with butterflies, some with no qualms about landing on visitors!

THE RIVIERA MAYA

Ruta de los Cenotes: From the main highway, this 20-kilometer (12-mile) forest road winds past numerous cenotes, some busy and commercialized, others delightfully quiet and remote.

Xcaret: This huge ecopark is an all-day excursion, with snorkeling, tubing, an aquarium, and a fun evening show.

Croco Cun Zoo: Charming little zoo near Puerto Morelos where you can see, pet, and even hold animals (including babies).

TULUM AND THE COSTA MAYA

Dos Ojos Cenote: Great cenote snorkeling for all ages, either with a guide or on your own.

Xel-Há: A family-friendly ecopark built around a natural inlet, with easy-to-access snorkeling, tubing, and other aquatic fun.

Cobá: Renting bikes or hiring bike taxis makes visiting these ruins especially fun for kids, while the thick forest provides cool shade and a chance to spot birds and insects.

Punta Laguna Spider Monkey Reserve: A great family outing where you'll spot not only spider and howler monkeys, but a slew of birds, tropical vegetation, and more.

Mayá Lost Mayan Kingdom: This Maya-themed waterpark in Mahahual has zip lines, a lazy river, and heart-stopping waterslides.

Laguna Bacalar: Explore this beautiful lagoon by kayak to enjoy its remote beaches, mangrove forests, and great bird-watching. A fort-turned-museum has pirate exhibits and cannons to clamber on.

CHICHÉN ITZÁ

Chichén Itzá: Impressive ruins with several family-friendly hotels nearby. Cenote Sagrado Azul, just east of town, is a sure hit.

Valladolid: Charming colonial city, with several impressive cenotes nearby for swimming.

Río Lagartos: Fishing village with fun boat tours of the neighboring biosphere reserve, home to thousands of pink flamingos and nice beaches too.

MÉRIDA, THE PUUC ROUTE, AND CAMPECHE

Mérida: A city tour on an open-air double-decker bus is fun and easy, while older kids may appreciate the museums and outdoor dance performances.

Loltún Caves: Take a guided tour of the largest cave in the Yucatán, with huge stalagmites and stalactites, rock carvings dating to 1600 BC, and ancient handprints on the walls.

Izamal: A charming colonial town, painted in mustard yellow. *Calesas,* horse-pulled buggies, are a fun way to see the sights.

Campeche City: The city's colorful colonial center is enclosed by massive stone walls and forts that not only have interesting museums but also make for great exploring.

PALENQUE

Aluxes Ecoparque Palenque: Families and school groups are the target audience at this conservation park and animal rehab center, with leafy pathways and a chance for close-up glimpses of rescued animals such as jaguars and alligators.

Campeche City's central plaza is a colonial beauty.

nearby hotel, have lunch, and spend the afternoon cooling off at **Cenote Sagrado Azul.** In the evening, head back to Chichén Itzá for its high-tech **sound and light show.**

Day 4

Get up early and head straight to **Mérida,** one of Mexico's great colonial cities. Go to the **anthropology museum** or the **modern art museum,** the market, or just visit the church, the murals in the government buildings, and the plaza. See what's happening that evening—there's a free cultural performance every night of the year.

Day 5

You can spend this day in a couple of different ways. There are a number of great day trips from Mérida, including a **flamingo tour** in the town of **Celestún,** or visiting the colonial town of **Izamal** and swimming in cenotes near **Cuzamá.** Then again, if you especially love the

Maya ruins, you won't want to miss those along the **Puuc Route.** For this option, get an early start and visit **Uxmal** first—it is the biggest and the best of the sites here, and you don't want to shortchange your time there. Afterward, cross the road to the **Choco Story Uxmal,** an engaging museum about the history of chocolate, which dates to the ancient Maya. Time permitting, visit one or two of the smaller Puuc ruins. Check into a hotel in **Santa Elena** and wind down with a relaxed evening in the town's central plaza.

Day 6

Drive to the beautiful colonial town of **Campeche City** this morning. Check into a hotel and pick a few sights to take in. The **museums** along the **city walls** and at **El Palacio Centro Cultural** or **Fuerte de San Miguel** are especially good. Many evenings in the central park, there's also a spectacular **sound and light show,** a multimedia celebration of Campeche's history.

Day 7

Start early for the long drive to **Palenque.** Check into your hotel and have dinner at **Don Mucho** in the jungle neighborhood of El Panchán. If you're up for it, stay late for live music and fire dancers.

Day 8

Spend the day visiting **Palenque archaeological zone.** Be sure to leave time for the terrific on-site **museum.**

Day 9

Stay another day in Palenque to see some of the nearby attractions. If you still haven't gotten enough of the Maya ruins, consider booking an all-day tour to **Yaxchilán** and **Bonampak.** Or visit the impressive waterfalls at **Misol-Há** and **Agua Azul** for a bit of outdoorsy fun.

Day 10

Get an early start for the long drive to the **Río Bec region** in southern Campeche, home to impressive Maya ruins and a rich biosphere reserve. Arrive in time to visit the striking frieze at **Balamkú ruins.** At dusk, check out the **Volcán de Murcielagos,** a rushing cloud of three million bats that emerge from a huge sinkhole every evening. Stay overnight near the entrance to the **Calakmul Biosphere Reserve.**

Day 11

Wake up early and spend the morning exploring **Calakmul ruins,** the crown jewel of southern Campeche's Maya sites, located deep in the same-named **biosphere reserve.** Afterward, head toward the town of **Xpujil.** Depending on your time and energy, visit one of the many small Maya ruins clustered along Highway 186, such as **Becán** or **Chicanná.** Check in to a hotel in Xpujil, or if your budget permits, at one near the highway.

Day 12

Drive to **Tulum,** where you can treat yourself to a beachside bungalow on one of Tulum's glorious beaches. Along the way, stop for lunch on **Laguna Bacalar** to enjoy the view of its brilliant turquoise waters.

Day 13

Spend a **beach day** on Tulum's quiet and dreamy southern beaches. If you get restless, get some snorkeling in at the great nearby **cenotes** of **Gran Cenote** or **Car Wash.** If you're tired of the car, walk to **Tulum ruins,** dramatically overlooking the turquoise Caribbean Sea. Be sure to take your bathing suit for a dip in the ocean from the site's small beach.

Day 14

Take a tour of the **Sian Ka'an Biosphere Reserve,** an ideal place for fishing, bird-watching, and snorkeling—a perfect way to end your vacation.

Maya carving at Palenque's on-site museum

Ecoadventures

Lazing on a beach or contemplating museum displays is all right, but some travelers crave a little more action. The Yucatán has plenty to offer active travelers, including kiteboarding, fly-fishing, kayaking, and mountain biking. This tour is a workout for the eyes too, taking you to some of the peninsula's most stunning (and little-visited) natural areas, from tangled mangrove forests to limestone caverns filled with the clearest, bluest water you've ever seen. The only thing this tour doesn't include is snorkeling or diving on the coast, which are covered in a list of their own.

Day 1

Ease into things by spending a day **stand-up paddling (SUPing)**. It's challenging but fairly easy to master, and especially rewarding in the Riviera Maya's warm, clear water. **Playa del Carmen, Isla Mujeres,** and **Cozumel** are all great places to start. Farther afield, **Xpu Há, Tulum,** and **Mahahual** are fine alternatives.

Day 2

Kayaking is another low-key, easy-to-learn activity that's perfect for exploring the region's rich mangrove forests. The **Sian Ka'an Biosphere Reserve, Laguna Bacalar,** and **Isla Holbox** all have fascinating kayak tours that include paddling through mangrove canals, spotting birds, and locating hidden beaches and lost Maya ruins.

Day 3

Today's the day for pushing yourself. Why not try **kiteboarding**? **Isla Blanca** and **Cozumel** are good for both, with perfect wind, forgiving surf for beginners, and some surprisingly challenging spots for the more advanced. If you want to head inland, **Isla Holbox** and **Progreso** also have first-rate kiting opportunities.

Kiteboarding is a popular sport in many of the region's beach towns.

Classics of Yucatecan Cuisine

Like many regions of Mexico, the Yucatán Peninsula has a cuisine all its own. The base is recognizably Mexican, but the dishes are strongly influenced by traditional Maya ingredients and techniques, with dashes of Caribbean and Middle Eastern flavors. Some popular menu items include:

- **Cochinita Pibil:** pork that has been marinated in achiote, Seville orange juice, peppercorn, garlic, cumin, salt, and pepper, wrapped in banana leaves, and baked. It's typically served on weekends.

- **Dzoto-bichay:** tamale made of *chaya* (a leafy vegetable similar to spinach) and eggs. It comes smothered in tomato sauce.

- **Empanizado:** slices of pork or chicken that has been breaded and fried, often served with salad, rice, and beans.

- **Panucho:** handmade tortilla stuffed with re-fried beans and covered with shredded turkey, pickled onion, and slices of avocado. Like a *salbute* plus!

- **Papadzules:** hard-boiled eggs chopped and rolled into a corn tortilla with a creamy pumpkin-seed sauce.

- **Poc-chuc:** slices of pork that have been marinated in Seville orange juice and coated with a tangy sauce. Pickled onions are added on the side.

- **Salbute:** handmade tortilla covered with shredded turkey, pickled onion, and slices of avocado.

- **Sopa de Lima:** turkey-stock soup prepared with shredded turkey or chicken, fried tortilla strips, and juice from *lima,* a lime-like citrus fruit.

cochinita pibil

You can find Yucatecan dishes just about anywhere, from hole-in-the-wall taco joints to gourmet restaurants—discovering them is half the fun! For a sure bet, check out **La Habichuela** (downtown Cancún), **Quesadillas Tierra del Sol** (downtown Cancún), **Mercado Municipal** (Isla Mujeres), **La Candela** (Isla Cozumel), **La Gran Chaya** (Pisté), **La Palapita de los Tamales** (Valladolid), **El Atrio del Mayab** (Valladolid), **La Chaya Maya** (Mérida), **Kinich** (Izamal), **El Príncipe Tutul-Xiu** (Maní), and **La Olla de la Pagoda** (Campeche City).

Day 4

You may want to spend a second day kiteboarding—few people master it in a day! Otherwise, dig out your sneakers and rent a **mountain bike.** Both **Tulum** and **Laguna Bacalar** have fun and moderately challenging rides, pedaling through the jungle to little-visited Maya ruins and remote beaches.

Day 5

You must be getting tired by now. Spend the day **fishing,** either trolling in the ocean or fly-fishing in the region's vast coastal flats. **Cozumel** is ideal for the former, and for the latest craze: spearfishing. **Sian Ka'an** and **Xcalak** are world-class fly-fishing spots, brimming with tarpon, permit, bonefish, and snook.

Day 6

Get up bright and early to be at **Cobá archaeological zone** at opening. Of all the Maya ruins, this one is the best for **bird-watching.** It's not uncommon to spot toucans and parrots. Cobá also is an impressive ruin, with the second-highest pyramid in the Yucatán Peninsula, affording awesome views of the countryside. You can rent bikes near the entrance and explore the ruins on wheels. A short distance away is the **Punta Laguna monkey reserve,** a perfect place to visit after a late lunch.

Day 7

Drive to **Mérida.** If you get an early start, you'll have time to stop at the beautiful colonial town of **Izamal** or the **cenotes of Cuzamá,** where you'll take a horse-drawn cart through abandoned henequen fields, then descend ladders into underground caverns for a cool swim.

Day 8

Take a day trip to **Celestún** and take a **flamingo tour.** You can get there on your own

or book a tour with one of Mérida's many tour operators. Head back to Mérida and check out a museum and one of the free nightly cultural performances.

Day 9

Spend the next day visiting some of the **caves** (*grutas*) along the **Puuc Route** south of Mérida. **Calcehtok** is the most adventuresome, with local guides offering 1- to 5-hour tours of this huge cave system. The longest tours go about four kilometers (2.5 miles) and reach a tiny chamber where human bones were left from ancient Maya ceremonies. Nearby, **Aktun Usil** offers a look in a sacred Maya cave, with hieroglyphics, cave paintings, rock carvings, and even handprints, in silhouette on the ceiling high above. Not far away, **Loltún caves** are much tamer, with paths and lighting, but fascinating nonetheless. Then make your way back to **Cancún, Cozumel,** or **the Riviera Maya** for your final night in the region.

Day 10

Spend your last day enjoying the Yucatán's other great natural wonder: the **beach.** The beaches in **Cancún, Cozumel, Isla Mujeres,** and **Playa del Carmen** all have plenty to keep you active—swimming, SUPing, kayaking, parasailing, volleyball, soccer, and more.

Pyramids and Palaces

For many people, the Maya ruins are the Yucatán Peninsula's greatest attraction, with their massive pyramids and palaces and remarkable artistic and astronomical features. Few visitors have time to visit every site in a single trip; here is a description of each chapter's best Maya ruins to help you decide which ones to add to your itinerary—and which to save for next time. To dig a little deeper, pair ruin hopping with a visit to one of the excellent **Maya museums** in **Cancún, Chetumal, Mérida,** and **Campeche City.**

Cancún and Isla Cozumel

- **El Rey, San Miguelito, and Yamil Lu'um:** These small ruins are found right in Cancún's Zona Hotelera. El Rey is the largest and best preserved of the group, and is home to hundreds of iguanas—almost as interesting to see as the structures themselves.

- **San Gervasio:** Isla Cozumel's main archaeological site has several modest temples connected by forest paths. Dedicated to the goddess of fertility, Ixchel, San Gervasio was an important pilgrimage site for ancient Maya women.

El Castillo in Chichén Itzá, as seen from the Group of a Thousand Columns

Tulum and the Costa Maya

- **Tulum:** Perched on a bluff overlooking the turquoise Caribbean Sea, Tulum's ruins are the subject of innumerable postcards. Come early, as the site is often mobbed by day-trippers from nearby resorts.

- **Cobá:** With the second-tallest pyramid on the peninsula (42 meters/138 feet), Cobá offers a great view of the countryside. Nestled in a forest near several small lakes, it is also a good place to spot birds and butterflies.

- **Kohunlich:** Located in southern Quintana Roo, Kohunlich is best known for a series of imposing stucco masks. Nearby is a unique all-inclusive luxury resort with guided trips in the surrounding forest and lagoons.

Chichén Itzá

- **Chichén Itzá:** Named one of the New Seven Wonders of the World, this site has the largest ball court of any Maya ruin and a pyramid recognizable the world over. Scores of tours head

there from Cancún, but getting to the site early lets you enjoy this fascinating locale without the crowds. Don't miss the gorgeous sound and light show in the evening.

- **Ek' Balam:** Near the city of Valladolid, Ek' Balam boasts one of the best-preserved stucco friezes in the Maya world and an all-embracing view from atop its main pyramid. Nearby cenotes provide a great place to cool off afterward.

Mérida, the Puuc Route, and Campeche

- **Uxmal:** This may be the chapter's most beautiful site, with intricate palaces and a massive pyramid with rounded corners—a must-see.

- **The Puuc Route:** The Ruta Puuc is a series of four smaller ruins near Uxmal. Kabah and Labná are especially memorable, including beautiful archways and facades decorated with scores of identical rain-god masks. A round-trip bus from Mérida hits all four plus Uxmal, but visiting by car will give you the freedom to appreciate them longer.

spider monkeys

The Yucatán Peninsula is best known for its Maya ruins and beautiful beaches, but it also has some terrific places and opportunities to spot wildlife, including several biosphere reserves and extensive wetlands.

Sian Ka'an Biosphere Reserve: This sprawling coastal reserve south of Tulum is home to an astounding array of wildlife, including dolphins, howler monkeys, crocodiles, sea turtles, and hundreds of bird species. Harder to spot, but still there, are manatees, tapirs, and even jaguars.

Calakmul Biosphere Reserve: Home to a massive Maya ruin as well as to howler and spider monkeys that hang out in the treetops. If you're lucky, you might spot a puma or jaguar as well.

Ría Lagartos Biosphere Reserve and Ría Celestún Biosphere Reserve: These huge estuaries are the best place to observe American flamingos, which nest and feed here by the tens of thousands, plus ibis, herons, and myriad other species.

Isla Holbox: Come here to snorkel with whale sharks, gentle giants that congregate just offshore between June and September. You can also book a kayak or motorboat tour to visit the island's bird-rich lagoons anytime of the year.

Isla Cozumel: Cozumel's protected coral reef system teems with sponges, sea turtles, rays, eels, and countless tropical fish. Divers can get up close and personal, but even snorkelers get an eyeful in these pristine waters. The island's ecology department also welcomes visitors on nighttime excursions to find and protect sea turtle nests (May-September) and to release hatchlings back to the sea (August-November).

Punta Laguna Spider Monkey Reserve: This small reserve north of Cobá is home to several families of rambunctious *monos arañas* (spider monkeys). A small lagoon has canoes to go looking for crocodiles.

Akumal: Yucatec Maya for "Place of the Turtle," Akumal is the center for turtle preservation along the Riviera Maya. Guides here lead snorkelers through turtle feeding grounds in Akumal Bay. A local organization also organizes monthlong volunteer opportunities to help with sea turtle and reef monitoring.

Xcalak Reef National Park: Xcalak sees far fewer visitors than elsewhere, and its reef is accordingly pristine, with rich, colorful coral structures and large schools of fish, including silvery tarpon.

- Near the Puuc Route, other remarkable sites include the neatly organized **Mayapán;** the little-visited **Oxkintok,** with two impressive caves nearby; and **Dzibilchaltún,** with its first-rate museum and intriguing main temple.

- **Edzná:** A peaceful site, Edzná's Temple of Five Stories looks over a small acropolis and broad main plaza. It's located in the Chenes region, less than an hour's drive from Campeche City, but you still may be the only one there.

- **Calakmul:** Located in Campeche's Río Bec region, Calakmul was one of the most powerful Maya cities in its time and contains arguably the largest known Maya pyramid. What's more, the site is ensconced in a biosphere reserve where you can spot monkeys and tropical birds.

- **Becán and Chicanná:** Also in the Río Bec region, Becán's many structures include two huge pyramids and an impressive multiroom palace, while Chicanná has gorgeously decorated temples and residential buildings.

- Other excellent sites in southern Campeche include **Balamkú, El Hormiguero,** and **Río Bec;** the last can be difficult to reach, however.

Palenque

- **Palenque:** This is the all-time favorite ruin of many travelers, thanks to its elegant design, intricate carvings, and superlative museum. Much of what archaeologists know about the Maya calendar, hieroglyphics, and astronomy emerged from studies conducted here.

- **Bonampak and Yaxchilán:** Sister cities located along the Guatemalan border, Bonampak and Yaxchilán are commonly reached on tours from Palenque. The former contains brilliantly colored murals, while the latter has beautifully carved stone panels and monoliths.

view of the Temple of the Count in the Palenque archaeological zone

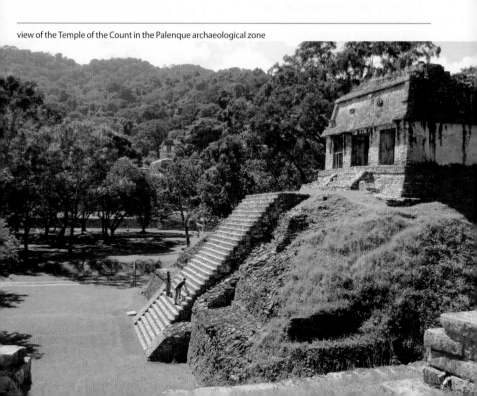

Best Diving and Snorkeling

The Yucatán Peninsula's underwater treasures are as compelling as its terrestrial ones. The region includes the world's second-longest coral reef, the longest known underground river system, and the Northern Hemisphere's largest coral atoll. Below are some of the top spots to get underwater.

Cancún, Isla Holbox, and Isla Mujeres

- **Snorkel with whale sharks** in the waters between **Isla Holbox** and **Isla Mujeres**. The gentle giants congregate there between June and September. Guided tours are available from either island.

- Dive or snorkel among hundreds of lifelike statues at **Museo Subacuático de Arte (MUSA)**, a remarkable underwater museum located between Cancún and Isla Mujeres. Three "galleries" range 4-8 meters deep, all teeming with fish and slow-growing coral.

Isla Cozumel

- **Isla Cozumel**'s crystal-clear water, vibrant coral reef, and first-rate dive operators make it a premier underwater destination. It's especially suited for expert divers, with challenging wall, deep, wreck, and drift dives, including **Palancar, Santa Rosa Wall,** and **Paraíso.**

- Snorkelers should check out **Parque Punta Sur and Chankanaab,** which also have nice beach areas.

The Riviera Maya and Tulum

The **Riviera Maya** is dotted with hundreds of eerily beautiful **cenotes** (freshwater caverns and sinkholes) offering out-of-this-world snorkeling and diving for novices and experts alike. **Tulum**'s dive shops specialize in cenote dives and cave diving courses, while snorkelers can grab their gear

scuba divers and snorkeler swimming by Isla Cozumel

A hole in the ground plus a staircase equals a cenote in the Yucatán.

and spend the day cenote hopping. Favorites include:

- **Jardín del Edén** and **Cenote Cristalino** are lovely open-air cenotes, with cool, clear water, dramatic rock faces, and lush vegetation.

- **Siete Bocas** and **Verde Lucero** are two especially memorable spots on the Ruta de los Cenotes (Cenotes Route), a dirt roadway that extends several miles into the jungle and winds past various cenotes.

- **Dos Ojos,** north of Tulum, is a network of stunning stalagmite-filled caverns, with a well-run operation offering full-service underwater tours.

- **Car Wash** and **Gran Cenote** are two lovely cenotes, among several others, located west of Tulum. Each has stairs leading to the water's edge, and platforms for accessing the water.

For an ocean experience, **Puerto Morelos** is famous for its well-preserved coral reef. A local cooperative takes travelers on rewarding snorkeling tours, while local dive shops offer excellent reef dives.

The Costa Maya

- **Mahahual** and **Xcalak,** two small towns near the Belize border, have dive shops offering snorkeling and diving on the nearby coral reef. There's also fantastic snorkeling and diving right from the shore, including at night.

- **Banco Chinchorro** is the largest coral atoll on this side of the planet, and it boasts spectacular underwater life. Getting there can be a bear—2-3 hours each way—but the massive and pristine coral structures are worth the effort. Dive shops in Mahahual and Xcalak offer tours.

Cenote Hopping

The Yucatán Peninsula is dotted with hundreds of cenotes—pools of shimmering blue water fed by a vast underground freshwater river system. Some look like large ponds, others are deep sinkholes, and still others occupy gaping caverns or have dramatic rock formations. Many cenotes are open to the public, and their cool, clear water is perfect for swimming, snorkeling, and scuba diving. Facilities range from simple restrooms and snorkel rental to full-service "cenote parks" with guided tours. Some favorites include:

The Riviera Maya

- **Ruta de los Cenotes:** Sure, some spots along the "Cenote Route" are tourist traps, but others are sublime, such as Siete Bocas, a huge, eerie cavern filled with shimmering water, and Verde Lucero, a gorgeous open-air pool teeming with freshwater turtles and fish.

- **Jardín del Edén:** The best and biggest of a cluster of cenotes near Playa Xpu-Há, with a large cavern that forms a dramatic overhang.

- **Cenote Cristalino:** Next to Jardín del Edén, Cristalino also has an overhanging cliff but a smaller swimming area.

- **Cenote Azul:** A set of three cenotes near Playa Xpu-Há with impossibly clear waters and a small cliff for jumping into one of them.

- **Cenote Manatí:** Near Tankah Tres, this is actually a series of connected cenotes and lagoons that wind inland through a tangled scrub forest.

Near Tulum

- **Dos Ojos:** A cenote park with rentals, guides, and spectacular caverns.

- **Gran Cenote:** Lovely cavern with natural arches and stalactite formations; east of Tulum on the road to Cobá.

- **Car Wash:** Just past Gran Cenote, this innocuous-looking cenote has stunning rock formations below the surface.

cooling off at Cenote Yokdzonot, just west of Chichén Itzá

- **Choo-Ha:** One of four dramatic cenotes near Cobá, with a high domed ceiling and iridescent blue water.

Chichén Itzá

- **Cenote Yokdzonot:** This little-known gem near Chichén Itzá is all the more rewarding for being operated by a cooperative of enterprising local women.

- **Cenote de Hacienda San Lorenzo Oxman:** A beautiful and accessible cenote, with stairs, a rope swing, and even a restaurant and pool at the top.

- **Cenote X'Canché:** A pretty 12-meter-deep (39-foot) cenote, 1.5 kilometers (0.9 mile) down a forest path from the Ek' Balam ruins.

- **Cenotes Agua Dulce:** This collection of four lovely cenotes includes two with deep turquoise water that's great for swimming.

- **Cenote Sak' Aua:** Like a sunken doughnut, this remote cenote has a flat, rocky center encircled by teal-blue water and high overhanging cliffs.

Mérida, the Puuc Route, and Campeche

- **Cenotes de Cuzamá:** Getting to these three cenotes via horse-drawn cart is half the fun. Two have slippery ladders leading down to their cool azure waters.

- **Ruta Anillo de los Cenotes:** A set of 10 gorgeous cenotes dot the landscape near Homún. Follow the signs to DIY or hire a *mototaxi* to guide you to each.

- **Cenote Kankirixché:** North of Uxmal, this is considered one of the peninsula's prettiest cenotes. It's easy to see why, with its cool turquoise water, dangling tree roots, and a roof bristling with stalactites.

- **Grutas de X'tacumbilxuna'an:** This massive cavern was used for centuries by local Maya for collecting water, and is the subject of a famous drawing by 19th-century explorer-artist Frederick Catherwood.

Cancún

Cancún is a big, beautiful contradiction. For many people, it has all the makings of the ultimate vacation destination: five-star hotels, thick white sand, impossibly blue waters, and a nightlife that never stops.

Others chafe at Cancún for seeming more American than Mexican, a place where you need never speak a word of Spanish, never eat at a restaurant you couldn't find at a mall back home, and never convert your dollars into pesos.

Both perspectives are true, but one-sided. It's hard not to cringe at those loud tourists who don't bother to explore—or even care about—any part of Mexico beyond their beach chairs. Yet those who pooh-pooh Cancún are also selling the city short. Cancún is a working,

Highlights

Look for ★ to find recommended sights, activities, dining, and lodging.

★ **Playa Delfines:** Located at the far southern end of the Zona Hotelera, this is one of the few spots with unobstructed views and a refreshing mix of foreign and local visitors (page 44).

★ **Cancún Nightlife:** You don't have to be on spring break to enjoy Cancún's nightclubs—but it helps! If the all-night-every-nightclub scene isn't for you, head downtown for wine bars and cocktail lounges (page 50).

★ **Museo Subacuático de Arte (MUSA):** This remarkable "museum" on the ocean floor has two sites featuring hundreds of statues made of material designed to promote coral growth, so they only get more interesting as time passes (pages 46 and 71).

★ **Isla Contoy:** Go island-hopping on this popular day trip from Isla Mujeres. A morning boat ride is followed by snorkeling on a rich coral reef, hiking and bird-watching, and digging into a fresh fish barbecue on the beach (page 73).

★ **Playa Norte:** Isla Mujeres's best beach has virtually no waves, just soft white sand lapped by glassy turquoise water (page 73).

★ **Whale Shark Feeding Grounds:** Get goggles-to-gills with the world's biggest fish (page 88).

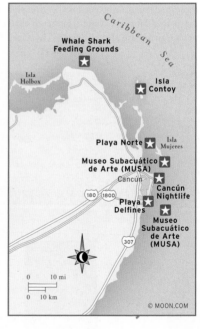

Caribbean Sea

Whale Shark Feeding Grounds ★

Isla Holbox

Isla Contoy ★

Playa Norte ★ — Isla Mujeres

Museo Subacuático de Arte (MUSA) ★

Cancún

Cancún Nightlife ★

180 180D

Playa Delfines ★

Museo Subacuático de Arte (MUSA) ★

307

0   10 mi

0   10 km

© MOON.COM

breathing city that's vital to Mexico's economy and imbued with a fascinating history and plenty of "real" Mexican culture for those willing to seek it out. And contrary to impressions, Cancún has accommodations and services for visitors of all budgets and tastes. Why not take advantage of both sides of Cancún? The resorts, beaches, and nightclubs will blow your mind—don't miss them! But be sure not to overlook Cancún's more subtle side, too, from live music in a downtown wine bar to munching on *elote* (corn on the cob) sold from a cart in the city's pleasant central square.

And when you need to, just get away. A 15-minute ferry ride delivers you to the slow-paced Isla Mujeres, a sliver of sand surrounded by breathtaking blue waters. Farther north and even more laid-back is Isla Holbox, which has no cars, no banks, and no post office—it's a world away from Cancún yet reachable in a morning.

PLANNING YOUR TIME

A week will do just fine in Cancún, allowing time enough to get your tan on plus take a day trip or two, such as to Isla Mujeres or one of the nearby Maya ruins. Ten days gives you time to explore deeper and farther, turning a day trip to Isla Mujeres or the Maya ruins into an overnighter, or venturing north to the remote Isla Holbox. Isla Mujeres and Isla Holbox are small but wonderfully relaxing; if either is your main destination, budget three or four days to experience them fully, but don't be surprised if you end up staying longer.

You don't *need* to rent a car to enjoy Cancún, Isla Mujeres, and Isla Holbox, especially if you don't plan on moving around much; all can be navigated easily by bus, ferry, taxi, and foot. That said, having a car makes many excursions easier, quicker, and more fun, especially if you've got kids in tow. Rather than booking a crowded and expensive tour to, say, Chichén Itzá, you can drive there yourself, arriving before the big groups and then hitting a second ruin or an out-of-the-way cenote on the way home. With the relatively low price of rental cars, and the region's well-maintained roads and highways, it's certainly worth considering.

ORIENTATION

Cancún's Zona Hotelera lies on a narrow white-sand island in the shape of a number 7. The 7's short upper arm leads directly into downtown Cancún, while the longer one (13 kilometers/8 miles) connects to the mainland near the airport. The elbow of the 7 is Punta Cancún, the fast-beating heart of the Zona Hotelera's nightlife; it includes all the major nightclubs, plus several resorts, hotels, restaurants, and shopping malls. The rest of the resorts and several more malls, restaurants, and water sports agencies are spread along the two arms, especially the southern one. The far southern tip of the 7 is called Punta Nizuc and has a few hotels, plus Cancún's largest archaeological site (El Rey). Busy Boulevard Kukulcán runs the entire length of the 7, and most addresses in the Zona Hotelera are simply a kilometer marker. Finally, the huge lagoon that's enclosed by the mainland and the Zona Hotelera is called Laguna Nichupté, and is a popular spot for fishing, waterskiing, and boating.

Downtown Cancún is on the mainland and is divided into numbered *super manzanas* (square blocks, or SM for short). Avenida Tulum is downtown's main thoroughfare; west of Avenida Tulum is Parque Las Palapas (downtown's central plaza), and beyond that Avenida Yaxchilán. East of Avenida Tulum is Avenida Nader. Most of downtown Cancún's hotels, restaurants, and music venues are on or around Parque Las Palapas, Avenida Yaxchilán, and Avenida Nader, primarily in SMs 22-25.

Isla Blanca is a thin peninsula just north of downtown Cancún. It's bordered by the white-sand beaches of the Caribbean on one

---

Previous: golf-cart taxi on Isla Holbox; Playa Delfines, at the southern end of Cancún's Zona Hotelera; conch shells.

Cancún

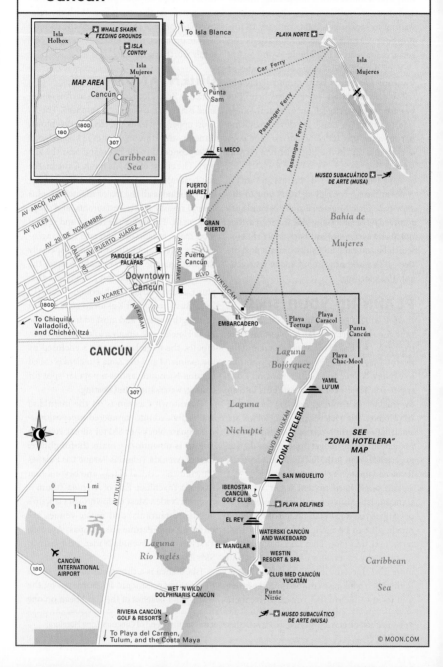

Isla Holbox

WHALE SHARK FEEDING GROUNDS

ISLA CONTOY

MAP AREA

Cancún

Isla Mujeres

Caribbean Sea

180   180D

307

To Isla Blanca

PLAYA NORTE

Car Ferry

Isla Mujeres

Punta Sam

Passenger Ferry

Passenger Ferry

EL MECO

PUERTO JUÁREZ

GRAN PUERTO

MUSEO SUBACUÁTICO DE ARTE (MUSA)

Bahía de

Mujeres

AV ARCO NORTE

AV TULES

AV 20 DE NOVIEMBRE

CALLE 107

AV PUERTO JUÁREZ

Puerto Cancún

AV BONAMPAK

PARQUE LAS PALAPAS

Downtown Cancún

BLVD KUKULCÁN

AV XCARET

180D

AV KABAH

To Chiquilá, Valladolid, and Chichén Itzá

EL EMBARCADERO

Playa Tortuga

Playa Caracol

Punta Cancún

CANCÚN

Playa Chac-Mool

Laguna Bojórquez

YAMIL LU'UM

307

Laguna

Nichupté

BLVD KUKULKÁN

ZONA HOTELERA

SEE "ZONA HOTELERA" MAP

0   1 mi
0   1 km

SAN MIGUELITO

IBEROSTAR CANCÚN GOLF CLUB

PLAYA DELFINES

AV TULUM

EL REY

EL MANGLAR

WATERSKI CANCÚN AND WAKEBOARD

WESTIN RESORT & SPA

Laguna Río Inglés

Caribbean

CLUB MED CANCÚN YUCATÁN

Sea

CANCÚN INTERNATIONAL AIRPORT

180

WET 'N WILD/ DOLPHINARIS CANCÚN

Punta Nizúc

MUSEO SUBACUÁTICO DE ARTE (MUSA)

RIVIERA CANCÚN GOLF & RESORTS

To Playa del Carmen, Tulum, and the Costa Maya

© MOON.COM

Escape the Crowds

Valladolid street scene

So you booked a trip to Cancún because the flights were cheap, the lodging was easy to arrange, and the beaches sounded great. But you are still the sort of traveler who likes to go where the masses generally don't. We hear you. Here are some places within striking distance of Cancún for the traveler who wants something a little different.

- **Isla Blanca:** The beaches and resorts in Cancun's hotel zone are so famous that no one thinks to looks elsewhere. Too bad for them—Isla Blanca, just north of Cancun, is another long strip of lovely white-sand beaches, and there's hardly a soul (or condo) in sight (page 45).

- **El Meco Ruins:** Most visitors to Cancún aren't looking for archaeological sites, so the area's Maya ruins are rarely busy. El Meco is the least visited of the bunch, yet it boasts the tallest pyramid and loads of iguanas. It's located just north of town; city buses can get you there in minutes (page 40).

- **Ruta de los Cenotes:** Travelers often forget that just beyond Cancún's manicured resorts is dense jungle and amazing natural sights. South of town, this well-marked jungle road winds past numerous cenotes—freshwater sinkholes found in stalactite-filled caverns or shimmering pools encircled by lush vegetation (page 148).

- **El Corchal:** The entire Yucatan Peninsula is a haven for birds, and Cancún is no different. At this little-known wetlands reserve, local guides takes visitors on canoeing trips to see flamingos, toucans, and more (page 90).

- **Valladolid:** Mexico is filled with charming colonial cities. Valladolid is a perfect example, with quiet streets, colorful facades, and centuries-old churches. It's a great escape from the hustle and bustle of Cancún, and just two hours away by bus (page 289).

side, and the huge saltwater Chacmochuch Lagoon on the other. It's virtually uninhabited, limited to a handful of private homes—both Maya huts and modern behemoths—plus a kiteboarding school and a rustic beach club.

There's only one road on the peninsula; it begins as a paved street just north of the Isla Mujeres ferry terminals and quickly becomes a rutted sand road that leads almost to the very tip of the peninsula.

Sights

ARCHAEOLOGICAL ZONES

Cancún has three notable archaeological sites, two in the Zona Hotelera and a third north of town on Isla Blanca, near the Isla Mujeres ferry. None compare in size or wow factor to the Yucatán Peninsula's major sites, but they are still worth visiting, and the Zona Hotelera ones can be easily combined with a day at the beach.

El Rey Archaeological Zone

At the southern end of the Zona Hotelera, across from Playa Delfines, **Ruínas El Rey** (Blvd. Kukulcán Km 17.5, 8am-5pm daily, US$2.75) consists of several platforms, two plazas, and a small temple and pyramid, all arranged along an ancient 500-meter (1,640-foot) roadway. The ruins get their name (Ruins of the King) from a skeleton found during excavation and believed to be that of, well, a king. The ruins date from the late Postclassic period (AD 1200-1400); there's limited signage, though it is available in English and Spanish. El Rey also is home to hundreds of iguanas, some quite beefy, which makes a visit here all the more interesting. Last visitors are admitted at 4:30pm.

Yamil Lu'um Archaeological Zone

Lodged between the Park Royal Cancún and the Westin Lagunamar Ocean Resort, **Yamil Lu'um** (Blvd. Kukulcán Km 12.5, 8am-5pm daily, free) consists of two small temples built between AD 1200 and 1550: **Templo del Alacrán** (Temple of the Scorpion) and **Templo de la Huella** (Temple of the Handprint); unfortunately, neither the scorpion nor the handprint that gave the temples their names is visible anymore. The temples were built on Cancún's highest point, suggesting they were used as watchtowers or navigational aids. The ruins can be reached through the Park Royal (nonguests may need to ask permission) and are visible from the beach at Playa Marlin.

El Meco Archaeological Zone

Archaeologists think **El Meco** (Av. López Portillo s/n, 8am-5pm daily, US$2.75) was a major gateway to and from Isla Mujeres—fitting considering it's located just north of the modern-day ferry terminal at Puerto Juárez. The ancient city started out as a fishing village in AD 300 but grew to be a thriving port town, building the tallest pyramid along this part of the coast before collapsing abruptly around AD 600. It was reoccupied four or five centuries later, probably as an outpost for the powerful Chichén Itzá kingdom, before being abandoned in the 16th century. The site is smaller than El Rey but the structures are more substantial.

San Miguelito Archaeological Zone

Located on the grounds of the Museo Maya de Cancún, **San Miguelito** (Blvd. Kukulcán Km 16.5, tel. 998/885-3842, 9am-6pm Tues.-Sun., free with museum admission fee) was one of several Maya communities that occupied the present-day Zona Hotelera during the late Postclassic period around AD 1200 until the arrival of European explorers in the late 1500s. San Miguelito was apparently quite populous, though relatively few structures remain today—most were built of wood and palm and have long since disappeared. Most coastal Maya cities depended on fishing and maritime trade, and domination of the region likely shifted among them over the centuries. At that time, the long coastal island was covered in high sand dunes and dense mangrove forests, which served as a barrier against hurricanes and erosion; that natural protection has been mostly destroyed with the construction of Cancún's hotel strip.

El Rey Archaeological Zone

ADMINISTRATIVE BUILDING

GRAN PLAZA

STRUCTURE 3

STRUCTURE 5

PALACE

PYRAMID-TEMPLE

STRUCTURE 7

PLAZA

SCALE NOT AVAILABLE

© MOON.COM

To Entrance

MUSEUMS
Museo Maya de Cancún
Housed in a stark white modern building, **Museo Maya de Cancún** (Blvd. Kukulcán Km 16.5, tel. 998/885-3843, www.inah.gob.mx, 9am-6pm Tues.-Sun., US$3.50 including museum and archaeological site) has hundreds of Maya artifacts in bright, airy display rooms; vases, bowls, and masks figure prominently. Two permanent exhibition rooms are dedicated to finds from Quintana Roo and the greater Maya world, respectively, while a third room hosts temporary exhibits. Introductory signage is in Spanish and English, though many individual displays lack English translations. The San Miguelito archaeological site is also on the grounds. The entrance fee includes admission to the ruins, though the site itself closes at 4:30pm daily.

PARQUE LAS PALAPAS
Parque Las Palapas is a typical Mexican plaza, where locals congregate most nights and tourists have a chance to enjoy Cancún's quotidian side. The plaza doesn't have the

grand cathedral and government buildings found in Mexico's older colonial cities—remember, Cancún isn't even 50 years old—but it's still a place for adults to chat with friends, for teenagers and couples to circle about, and for youngsters to chase balls and ride electric cars in the spacious central square. Dozens of stands and street carts sell *helado* (ice cream), *churros* (strips of fried dough sprinkled with sugar), *elote* (corn on the cob served with chile and mayo), and knick-knacks of all sorts. The music and neon lights can be a bit much for some, but just as often there's an interesting performance in the plaza's huge *palapa*-roofed stage, whether live music or traditional dance. Along the edges of the main park are smaller squares, some used for art expositions, others favored by young bohos for plucking guitars and engaging in the occasional drum circle.

Beaches

ZONA HOTELERA

The beaches in Cancún are among the most spectacular in the world. Looking at online images, it's easy to think they're digitally enhanced—the sand couldn't be *so* white, or the sea *so* turquoise blue. But a combination of clear Caribbean water, a shallow, sandy seafloor, and a high bright sun makes for a gorgeous sight. At high noon, even picture-perfect web pages don't compare to the living picture show that is Cancún's coastline.

Be aware that the surf along the Zona Hotelera's long, east-facing arm, though beautiful, can be heavy, and drownings and near-drownings do occur. There are lifeguards near all public access points, and colored flags (green is safe, yellow is caution, red is closed) for reference. But nothing is more important than common sense: Don't swim if the conditions (or your own condition) aren't suitable. The beaches along the short, north-facing leg are much calmer. For really calm waters head to Isla Mujeres, where there are no waves and the water in places is only waist deep more than 75 meters (250 feet) from shore. The Laguna Nichupté is not recommended for swimming because of pollution and crocodiles.

Playa Caracol

Playa Caracol (Blvd. Kukulcán Km 8.5) has a small stretch of beach right at the public access point, but it's not too pleasant and often very crowded. The beach is much better just east of there, in front of the Fiesta Americana Coral Beach, but you have to cut through the hotel to get there, and the hotel lounge chairs take up most of the beach.

Playa Gaviota Azul

The pathway to **Playa Gaviota Azul** (Blvd. Kukulcán Km 10), a huge, beautiful beach, is between the City nightclub and Forum by the Sea mall, and it extends well north and south of there (merging with Playa Chac Mool just to the south) with plenty of room to set up a towel and umbrella. Parking can be tricky here—better to arrive by bus or taxi—but you've got plenty of eating and shopping options, if you need a break from the sun. If you're interested in a beach club, **Mandala Beach** (Blvd. Kukulcán Km 8.5, tel. 998/883-3333, www.mandalabeach.com, 10am-6pm daily, US$40 pp) is open to the public and has beach beds, a swimming pool, full bar and restaurant service, and a DJ. It can be a scene, but that's pretty much the point. Adults only.

Playa Marlín

Playa Marlín (Blvd. Kukulcán Km 12.5) is a clean, attractive beach with an access point between Plaza Kukulcán mall and the police and fire station. There's plenty of parking on

Zona Hotelera

Bahía de Mujeres

THE ROYAL CANCÚN
ALL SUITES RESORT

↑ To Isla
Mujeres

PARASAIL
CANCÚN

MARINA
CAPTAIN HOOK

SEE DETAIL

Playa
Caracol

Punta
Cancún

SCUBA
CANCÚN

EL EMBARCADERO/
LA TORRE ESCÉNICA/
TEATRO CANCÚN

BEACHSCAPE KIN HA
VILLAS & SUITES

CHARTER FISHING CANCÚN

CANCÚN
NIGHTLIFE

LOBSTER DINNER
CRUISE/ AQUATOURS
MARINA

LAVANDERÍA
EXPRESS

LA PALAPA
BELGA

Downtown
Cancún

LE NATURA/NATURA HOSTEL/
FARMACIA DEL AHORRO

THE SURFIN'
BURRITO

LAGUNA SUITES
GOLF & SPA

Laguna
Bojórquez

360 SURF
SCHOOL

Playa Chac-Mool

**ZONA
HOTELERA**

LE BLANC
SPA RESORT

LORENZILLO'S

Plaza
Flamingo

Caribbean
Sea

TACUN

La Isla
Shopping
Village

PARK ROYAL CANCÚN

YAMIL LU'UM

INTERACTIVE AQUARIUM

ELEFANTA/
THAI LOUNGE

WESTIN LAGUNAMAR

Laguna
Nichupté

EL FISH FRITANGA

POLICE/FIRE STATION/CASA CONSULAR

Playa Marlín

Plaza Kukulcán

Caribbean

CASA TURQUESA
BOUTIQUE HOTEL

Sea

CANCÚN TARPON
FISHING

PUERTO MADERO

THE RITZ-CARLTON

0   0.5 mi

HARRY'S

0   0.5 km

FRED'S HOUSE

Playa Ballenas

MARRIOTT
CANCÚN RESORT

AQUAWORLD

PARADISUS CANCÚN

HOTEL RIU PALACE
LAS AMÉRICAS

Plaza Caracol

CANCÚN
NIGHTLIFE

GRAND OASIS CANYON

SELECTO SÚPER
CHEDRAUI

GRAND FIESTA
AMERICANA
CORAL BEACH

SOLO
BUCEO

MUSEO MAYA DE CANCÚN

SAN MIGUELITO

CONVENTION
CENTER

PALAZZO

CONGO BAR

ECO-LAUNDRY

MANDALA

IBEROSTAR CANCÚN
GOLF CLUB

PLAYA
DELFINES

DADYO

THE CITY

CARLOS N'
CHARLIE'S

COCOBONGO

Playa
Gaviota
Azul

SEÑOR FROG'S

© MOON.COM

BLVD KUKULCÁN

AV TULUM

307

Caribbean
Sea

307

Beach Access

Look for these signs in the Zona Hotelera for public access to the beach.

There's a notion that high-rise hotels have monopolized Cancún's best beaches, but this is only partly true. While most hotels *do* front prime real estate, all beach areas in Mexico are public (except for military zones). Hotels cannot, by law, prohibit you or anyone else from lying on a towel and enjoying the sun and water. Many high-end hotels subvert this by making it difficult or uncomfortable for nonguests to use "their" beaches: Very few maintain exterior paths, and others spread guest-only beach chairs over the best parts. (In the hotels' defense, they also typically do a good job of keeping their areas clear of trash and seaweed, which can mar otherwise beautiful beaches.) If your hotel has a nice beach area, you're all set. If not, typically you can just walk through a hotel lobby to the beach—as a foreigner, you are very unlikely to be stopped. (Sadly, locals are likely to be nabbed if they do the same thing.) But even that is unnecessary: Cancún maintains several public access points marked with prominent blue and white signs along Boulevard Kukulcán. The area right around the access point is often crowded, but you can walk a couple hundred meters in either direction to have more breathing room. One public access point—Playa Delfines, at the southern end of the hotel zone—has no nearby hotels and is used by a refreshing mix of Mexican and foreign beachgoers.

the road parallel to the beach, and the mall has restaurants just a few steps away.

Playa Ballenas

Playa Ballenas (Blvd. Kukulcán Km 14.5) is a long, pretty beach, with an access path between the Hard Rock and Secrets The Vine resorts. There is no food or drink service on the beach, but look for a few small shops selling water and snacks on the frontage road rear the public access point.

TOP EXPERIENCE

★ Playa Delfines

Located at the far southern end of the Zona Hotelera, **Playa Delfines** (Blvd. Kukulcán Km 17.5) is at the bottom of a bluff, so you can't see it from the road. But once parked, or off the bus (there is a stop directly in front), you're treated to a panoramic view of the beach and ocean, unobstructed by hotels. There are rows of fixed *palapa* umbrellas and plenty of open sand if you brought your own. Perhaps best of all is the mix of people you'll find here: independent travelers, local families, even some surfers if the swell is high. (Take care swimming here, as the waves and tide can be strong.) The beach is across the road from El Rey ruins, which makes a nice side trip. There is no food or drink service, but there are restrooms and outdoor showers on-site.

ISLA BLANCA BEACHES

Isla Blanca's white-sand beaches are wild and mostly untouched—all to say, perfect! Accessing them, though, can be a bit tricky. Though the land between the road and the beach is virtually undeveloped, it is almost entirely privately owned and fenced off. There are occasional breaks between fences, but fortunately a great beach club makes hunting down those openings unnecessary.

Isla Blanca Cabañas (formerly Pirata Morgan, Carr. Cancún-Isla Blanca Km 9, tel. 998/112-1227, dariorock2004@gmail.com, 9am-5pm daily, US$2) is an old-school beach club with a handful of small *palapas* on the sand, a rustic restaurant serving up fresh fish and cold beers, and miles and miles of beach. If you can't tear yourself away from the beach at the end of the day, there are basic *cabañas* (US$50 s/d) where you can spend the night. Each has screen walls to let in the sea breeze at night, cement floors, and private bathrooms; electricity is available 6pm-11pm only. A cab ride from downtown Cancún runs around US$14 each way.

Sports and Recreation

While relaxing by the pool or on the beach is more than enough sports and recreation for many of Cancún's visitors, there *are* a number of options for those looking for a bit more action. From golf and fishing to scuba diving and kiteboarding (and a whole bunch of things in between), Cancún has something for everyone.

BEACH ACTIVITIES

Parasailing (*paracaídas* in Spanish) can be booked as a traditional one-person ride (with takeoff from the shore) or a two-person ride, in which you can take off from the boat or the water. Prices and duration are fairly uniform: US$55-60 per person for a 10-12-minute ride. Look for independent operators on the beach, especially on Playa Tortugas (Blvd. Kukulcán Km 6.5), Playa Chac-Mool (Blvd. Kukulcán Km 10), Playa Ballenas (Blvd. Kukulcán Km 14.5), and Playa Delfines (Blvd. Kukulcán Km 17.5). Or sign up at **Parasail Cancún** (Playa Tortugas, Blvd. Kukulcán Km 6.5, toll-free Mex. tel. 800/220-5681, toll-free U.S./Can. tel. 800/247-1641, www.parasailcancun.com, 8am-8pm Mon.-Fri., 8am-4pm Sat.-Sun.) or **Aquaworld** (Blvd. Kukulcán Km 15.2, tel. 998/689-1013, www.aquaworld.com.mx, 7am-8pm daily).

WaveRunners are rented on the same beaches where parasailing is pitched. Prices average US$45-55 for 30 minutes; one or two people can ride at a time.

SNORKELING AND SCUBA DIVING

Cancún doesn't compare to Cozumel, Isla Mujeres, or really anywhere along the Riviera Maya for snorkeling and diving. Its coral and other sealife are less plentiful and far less healthy. That said, if you enjoy modern art, an underwater sculpture museum provides a special treat. Or consider arranging a snorkeling or diving trip in a cenote, the otherworldly freshwater caves that dot the coast south of Cancún. If you're really hankering for some bubbly, we recommend booking a trip with a shop in Isla Mujeres or Puerto Morelos, both easy to reach from Cancún. (Cozumel is harder to do as a day trip, requiring a trip to

Playa del Carmen and a ferry ride to Cozumel from there...and back again.)

Snorkeling

For the best open-water and cenote snorkeling, book a trip with one of the dive shops listed below. All offer guided snorkeling trips in addition to diving, and are invariably better than the "jungle trips" hawked around Cancún, even for beginners.

★ MUSEO SUBACUÁTICO DE ARTE (MUSA)

Two popular snorkeling sites are Cancún's Nizuc and Punta Sam reefs, where installations of the Subaquatic Museum of Art (MUSA, 998/206-0182, www.musacancun. org) are located. Created by six artists, the sites contain more than 500 life-sized statues of everyday people, from nuns to tribal leaders. Breathtaking exhibits in and of themselves, the works were created from a special cement that promotes coral and sealife formation. A third MUSA installation is located near Isla Mujeres, at Manchones reef, which is best for divers.

Scuba Diving

A number of shops offer fun dives as well as certification courses at all levels. Hotels with their own dive shop may offer special rates to guests, but not necessarily.

Solo Buceo (Hyatt Ziva Cancún Hotel, Blvd. Kukulcán s/n, tel. 998/260-4995, toll-free U.S./Can. tel. 800/348-3639, www. solobuceo.com, 9am-4:30pm daily) is a friendly shop with a strong reputation for service. Two-tank reef dives run US$90, while two-tank cenote trips cost US$195, including lunch; prices include all gear including wetsuit. Open-water certification classes (US$420, 3-4 days) can also be arranged.

Scuba Cancún (Blvd. Kukulcán Km 5, tel. 998/849-7508, www.scubacancun.com. mx, 7am-8pm daily) was founded in 1980 and is still run by the same family. It offers the standard selection of dives, including one-tank (US$62), two-tank (US$77), and two-tank cavern and Cozumel dives (US$165 and US$180, respectively); all prices include equipment except wetsuit (US$10, recommended for cavern trips). Snorkel trips are offered in Cancún (US$39), Cozumel (US$125), and nearby cenotes (US$92). Trips can sometimes get crowded—ask about the size of your group before you book.

Aquaworld (Blvd. Kukulcán Km 15.2, tel. 998/689-1013, www.aquaworld.com.mx, 7am-8pm daily) is Cancún's biggest, most commercialized water sports outfit, of which scuba diving is only a small part. Come here if you're looking for activities for the whole family, divers and nondivers alike, all in one spot. Otherwise, head to smaller shops for more personalized attention.

KITEBOARDING

Ikarus (tel. 998/874-4246, www. kiteboardmexico.com) is a full-service kiteboarding school on the lagoon side of Isla Blanca, just north of Cancún. Conditions for learning to kiteboard don't get much better than this: steady wind, kilometers of flat water with few boats or other obstacles, and water never more than waist deep. Private classes are US$80-95 per hour, while groups are US$65 per hour per person (3 hours, maximum 3 people). Equipment is included for students or can be rented separately (US$50-75 for two hours). Classes are held November-May, when the conditions are best. Simple lodging also is offered (US$7-8 pp hammock, US$7-15 pp tent, US$25 pp tent with bed, US$75 s/d). There's a restaurant and free Wi-Fi too.

WATERSKIING, WAKEBOARDING, SURFING, AND SUP

Waterski Cancún and Wakeboard (Marina Manglar, Blvd. Kukulcán Km 19.8, cell tel. 998/874-4816, www.waterskicancun. com, by appointment only) has three slalom courses and a number of ski sites at the

1: kiteboarding; 2: dive tanks; 3: parasailing at the beach

southern end of Laguna Nichupté. Free-skiing and wakeboarding costs US$200 per hour, while the slalom courses are US$60 for 15 minutes. All equipment is included, except carbon skis.

360 Surf School (Blvd. Kukulcán Km 9.8, cell tel. 998/241-6443, www.360surf schoolcancun.com, by appointment only) offers popular surfboarding classes on Playa Chac-Mool. Classes are geared toward beginners but can be tailored to any level. One-on-one classes run US$140 for 90 minutes; group lessons cost US$100 per person for 120 minutes (3 people maximum). Family packages and multiday packages also are offered. Surfing classes include surf equipment, Lycra tops, drinking water, and use of surfboard after the lesson. Stand-up paddleboard (SUP) classes also are offered one-on-one (US$140) and in small groups (US$75-100 per person, up to 8 students); each class is about two hours. Equipment rentals—bodyboards, short boards, longboards, fun boards, and paddle-boards—also are available (US$15-65 per 24 hours). Look for the informational kiosk on the main drag, next to the Surfin' Burrito.

FISHING

More than a dozen species of sport fish ply the waters off Cancún, including blue and white marlin, blackfin tuna, barracuda, dolphin dorado, wahoo, grouper, and more. For those more interested in fly-fishing and light-tackle tours, there's no need to look past the Zona Hotelera's lagoon, which is home to tarpon, snook, snapper, barracuda, and jack.

Charter Fishing Cancún (Blvd. Kukulcán Km 6.5, cell tel. 998/200-3240, www.charterfishingcancun.com, by appointment only) offers excellent customer service on its small fleet of boats. Private charters range US$530-950 (4-8 hours); "shared" trips cost US$135-155 per person (4-6 hours). All trips include bait, tackle, ice, drinks (beer, soda, and water), and fishing licenses. Round-trip transportation to/from your hotel—anywhere between Cancún and Playa del Carmen—is included for private charters only.

Cancún Tarpon Fishing (Blvd. Kukulcán Km 13.5, cell tel. 998/126-6640, toll-free U.S./Can. tel. 866/607-2246, www.cancuntarponfishing.com, by appointment only) specializes in fly-fishing and light-tackle tours, all in the Zona Hotelera's lagoon, Laguna Nichupté, and just north near Isla Blanca. Trips are geared for one to two people and last anywhere from four to six hours. They include an experienced guide, equipment, box lunch, and soft drinks. Service is top-notch.

SWIMMING WITH DOLPHINS

Located within Ventura Park, **Dolphinaris Cancún** (Blvd. Kukulcán Km 25, tel. 998/881-3030, toll-free U.S. tel. 855/203-9863, www.dolphinaris.com) offers dolphin interaction programs that include "fin shaking" and receiving a "kiss" (US$99, 1 hour), as well as swimming with and getting a foot push from them (US$149, 1 hour). For those toying with the idea of working with dolphins, visitors also can help out as Trainers for the Day (US$199, 8 hours). Free shuttle transportation is provided within the Zona Hotelera.

Interactive Aquarium (La Isla Shopping Village, Blvd. Kukulcán Km 12.5, tel. 998/206-3311, www.interactiveaquariumcancun.com, 9am-8pm daily, US$15) has a modest number of tanks, including touch tanks where visitors can handle rays, starfish, and sea cucumbers. Its raison d'être, however, is the interactive dolphin program where activities range from receiving a "kiss" and getting a "foot push" (US$109-159, 45-60 minutes) to a couples-only program (US$199, 75 minutes) that includes a review of the anatomy and physiology of dolphins.

ECOPARKS AND WATER PARKS
Ecoparks

Despite the deluge of advertising you'll see for ecoparks like Xcaret, Xel-Há, Xplor, and Garrafón, none are actually in Cancún. Garrafón is the closest, situated on the southern end of Isla Mujeres. The others are 60-90 minutes south of Cancún, nearer to Playa del Carmen and Tulum. You can buy tickets at the gates, though most people buy them online or at their hotels so bus transportation is included in the cost; discounted park tickets also are popular giveaways for taking part in a time-share presentation.

Water Parks

In Ventura Park, on the southern end of the Zona Hotelera, **Wet n' Wild** (Blvd. Kukulcán Km 25, tel. 998/881-3030, toll-free U.S. tel. 855/203-9863, www.wetnwildcancun.com, 9:30am-5pm daily, US$48 adult, US$42 child) is a small but classic water park with a handful of twisting, slippery slides, high-speed water toboggans, and family-size inner tubing. It's a great way to cool off, especially if you're traveling with kids (or want to channel your own inner five-year-old). The all-inclusive plan includes all slides, meals, and drinks, though, oddly enough, not the inner tubes. BYO towel too. Check for online specials.

GOLF

Iberostar Cancún Golf Club (Blvd. Kukulcán Km 17, tel. 998/881-8016, http://golf.iberostar.com, US$199/99 public/hotel guests, US$149/49 public/guests after 2pm) is considered one of the finer courses in the region. This 18-hole par 72 course hugs Laguna Nichupté and boasts a great view of the Maya ruins of El Rey from the 16th hole. Alligators also are rumored to be in one of the water hazards, so consider leaving those water-bound balls behind. Food and drinks (including tequila shots and beer) are included.

Riviera Cancún Golf & Resorts (Blvd. Kukulcán Km 26, tel. 998/848-7777) is a challenging 18-hole par 72 golf course designed by Jack Nicklaus. Located on the southern end of the Zona Hotelera, it's a narrow course winding its way through low jungle and mangroves, with a distant view of the Caribbean. Greens fees are US$180 and drop to US$149 after 2:30pm. Rates include a golf cart, snacks, and drinks. There's also a driving range on-site.

If you feel like a short, easy (and cheap) round of golf, there are two par 3 courses in the Zona Hotelera: **Paradisus Cancún** (Blvd. Kukulcán Km 16.5, tel. 998/881-1100, www.melia.com, 7am-1pm last tee-off, US$45 greens fees, US$10 club rentals) and **Grand Oasis Cancún** (Blvd. Kukulcán Km 16, tel. 998/885-0867, www.grandoasiscancunresort.com, 8am-2:30pm last tee-off, US$35 greens fees including clubs).

SPECTATOR SPORTS

Bullfights

Though more often used as a concert venue, the **Plaza de Toros** (Av. Bonampak at Av. Sayil, tel. 998/884-8372, www.plazadetoroscancun.com.mx) still hosts bullfights throughout the year. Admission prices depend upon the headliner but typically run US$8-20. Tickets can be purchased online (www.superboletos.com) or at the box office.

Baseball

Baseball (*béisbol* in Spanish) is huge in Mexico, particularly in the north, where there are as many baseball diamonds as soccer fields. While still not having the pull in the Yucatán as it does elsewhere, it is a sport on the rise. The local team, **Tigres de Quintana Roo** (Quintana Roo Tigers), is one of the 16 teams that make up Mexico's professional baseball league, the Liga Mexicana de Béisbol (www.lmb.com.mx). You can catch a game March-September at the **Estadio Beto Avilá** (Av. Xcaret s/n, behind Walmart, tel. 998/887-3113, US$2-10).

Soccer

Arriving in Cancún from Mexico City in 2007, **Atlante** (www.atlantefc.mx) is the city's first professional *fútbol* team. Atlante won both the Mexican League's championship and the Apertura Championship in its first year in residence. The following season Atlante won the CONCACAF Champions League, earning it a spot in the 2009 FIFA Club World

Cup. The team plays at the **Estadio Andrés Quintana Roo** (Av. Mayapán s/n, US$10-40), west of the baseball stadium, August-May.

SPAS AND GYMS

Many hotels and resorts have spas, but the following are some of the best that are open to the public. Reservations are strongly encouraged.

Spas don't get much better, or bigger, than the 40,000-square-foot **Gem Spa** (Gran Fiesta Americana Coral Beach, Blvd. Kukulcán Km 9.5, tel. 998/881-3200, www. coralbeachcancunhotel.com, 10am-10pm daily). There are dozens of available treatments, many using precious stones of the Maya, Asian/South Pacific, and Baltic regions. Obsidian, amber, amethyst, and even diamond dust are used to soothe and smooth your body and mind.

Bamboo (Plaza Teramar, Blvd. Kukulcán Km 8.5, tel. 998/883-0106, www.cancun-spa-relax.com, 9am-9pm daily) is a simple day spa offering everything from facials and massages to mani-pedis and haircuts. Service is excellent and prices are reasonable, making it a popular spot.

Downtown, **Spa Xbalamqué** (Hotel Xbalamqué, Av. Yaxchilán 31, tel. 998/887-7853, 10am-8pm Mon.-Sat.) offers a full line of massages, facials, and body wraps, plus Reiki, crystal therapy, and *temascal* treatments. The spa's entrance is on Calle Jazmines, around the corner from the main hotel entrance. Prices are very reasonable, most ranging US$30-50.

TOURS
Aerial Tours and Views

AeroSaab (Playa Del Carmen Airport, 20 Av. Sur near Calle 1, tel. 998/865-4225, www.aerosaab.com, 7am-7:30pm daily) offers scenic full-day tours from Cancún, running to Cozumel, Chichén Itzá, Isla Holbox, Chetumal, Mérida, and as far as Palenque, with time to visit the area. Trips are in five-seat or six-seat Cessna airplanes and run US$93-796 per person, plus airport fees. Most trips require a minimum of 2-4 people.

If you prefer to stay *somewhat* grounded, board **La Torre Escénica** (Scenic Tower, El Embarcadero, Blvd. Kukulcán Km 4.2, tel. 998/849-5582, 9am-9pm daily, US$15 during the day, US$18 at night), an 80-meter (262.5-foot) tower with a rotating passenger cabin, affording a beautiful 10-minute view of this part of the coastline. A brief history of the region is played over the audio system. **Note:** Admission to this site is included in the Xcaret ticket; show your Xcaret wristband—it must still be on your wrist!—for free entry.

Entertainment and Events

Cancún is justly famous for its raucous nightclubs, pulsing with lights and music and packed with revelers of all ages every night of the week. The club scene is especially manic during spring break, July, August, Christmas, and New Year's, but you can count on finding a party no matter when you visit. And those with quieter tastes will be happy to learn there's more to Cancún's nightlife than clubs, including a nice mix of lounge bars, theaters, and cinemas.

★ NIGHTLIFE

Cancún's most popular nightclubs are within walking distance of each other in the **Zona Hotelera,** at Punta Cancún. Downtown, meanwhile, has some great cocktail bars and nightclubs specializing in Latin music.

Cuncrawl (Mex. cell tel. 984/165-0699, toll-free U.S. tel. 800/975-4349, www. cuncrawl.com, US$80 pp) does fun guided bar/club crawls in the heart of Cancún's Zona Hotelera, hitting three different clubs (they vary by night) with VIP entrance and seating, unlimited drinks, and bottle service, over the course of five hours.

Nightclubs
ZONA HOTELERA
Nightclubs in the Zona Hotelera charge US$60-80 admission with open bar included. Most clubs are open every day, from around 10pm until 4am or later. Special events, like ladies night or bikini parties, vary by the day, club, and season; check the clubs' websites or Facebook pages for the latest info and deals. Discounted tickets also are occasionally sold at concierge desks.

CocoBongo (Blvd. Kukulcán Km 9.5, tel. 998/883-2373, toll-free Mex. tel. 800/841-4636, www.cocobongo.com) is a spectacular club featuring live rock and salsa bands, flying acrobats, and impersonators ranging from Beetlejuice to Freddie Mercury. For dancing, hit the main floor; for free-flowing drinks, reserve a seat in the VIP section.

The City (Blvd. Kukulcán Km 9, tel. 998/883-3313, www.mandalatickets.com) is a megaclub with three levels and a total capacity of 6,000 (and allegedly the world's biggest disco ball). Be sure to take a whirl on the movable dance floor, which descends from the 3rd floor to the center of the club below. Open Friday only.

Palazzo (Blvd. Kukulcán Km 9, tel. 998/848-8380, www.mandalatickets.com) books big-name DJs and draws raucous crowds. The interior has a sleek Vegas-like look, huge chandeliers, and a VIP section. Open Wednesday and Saturday only.

Mandala (Blvd. Kukulcán Km 9, tel. 998/883-3333, www.mandalanightclub.com) is an upscale club with indoor and outdoor areas for partying. There's plenty of VIP seating in case you want to splurge on a private table (and better service).

Dady-O (Blvd. Kukulcán Km 9.5, tel. 998/883-3333, http://dadyocancun.com) is, well, the daddy of Cancún's nightclubs, with seven different "environments," including

laser shows, swimsuit contests, and theme parties on five different levels.

DOWNTOWN
Grand Mambo Café (Plaza Hong Kong, 2nd Fl., Av. Xcaret at Av. Tulum, tel. 998/884-4536, 9:30pm-3am Wed.-Sat., US$10 cover, US$3.50-8 open bar, free before 11pm) is Cancún's biggest Latin music club, and popular with locals, tourists, and expats alike. Live Latin music—mostly salsa, cumbia, and bachata—doesn't start until midnight, but the crowds arrive earlier than that, spinning to recorded rhythms.

A popular gay nightclub, **11:11 Club Cancún** (Av. Tulum at Calle Claveles, tel. 998/135-2243, www.1111gayclubcancun.com, 10:30pm-6am Thurs., 9pm-6am Fri.-Sat., US$5-7 cover) features drag shows, go-go dancers, and DJs spinning pop and electronica until breakfast. There are drinks sold by the liter plus open-bar specials too. Look for the rainbow signage on the building.

Bars and Live Music
Several of the major nightclubs feature live rock music and even big-name concerts, most notably Palazzo and CocoBongo, while the lounges and bars tend toward DJs or recorded music. Downtown, you'll find smaller venues filled with locals.

ZONA HOTELERA
Congo Bar (Blvd. Kukulcán Km 9.5, tel. 998/883-0563, www.congobar.com.mx) is about as lively as a bar can get without being called a club. Music is upbeat and drinks are plentiful. A conga line inevitably forms at some point (or points) and usually heads out the door and onto the street for a quick spin.

Old standbys **Carlos n' Charlie's** (Forum by the Sea, Blvd. Kukulcán Km 9, tel. 998/883-1862, www.carlosandcharlies.com) and **Señor Frog's** (Blvd. Kukulcán Km 9.5, tel. 998/883-5644, www.senorfrogs.com) both open at noon for meals and stay open until 3am for drinking, dancing, and general mayhem.

Downtown Cancún

Authentic Cancún

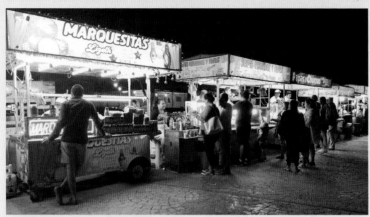

Food carts are perfect for a late-night snack in Parque Las Palapas.

It's easy to assume that Cancún, with its high-rise resorts and spring break ethos, has little to offer in the way of "authentic" culture. In fact, it's a rich and bustling Mexican city like any other, with plenty of culturally rich outings for those interested in finding them. Here are a few leads for having a locals' experience in Cancún:

- Spend an evening at **Parque Las Palapas,** Cancún's central plaza, where locals go for live music, a place for kids to romp around, and food carts galore. Try *elote*—a corn cob on a stick, slathered with butter or mayo, parmesan cheese, and chili powder (page 41).

- **Plaza de Toros,** Cancún's bullring, does have occasional bullfights—but it's better known as a nightspot. Grab some beers and snacks while taking in the scene in the many surrounding watering holes (page 54).

- Every city has an area that suddenly "pops"; in Cancún, that's **Avenida Nader,** with a crop of new bars and restaurants serving up creative drinks, high-end meals, and a hipster vibe (page 56).

- Nothing is more Mexican than shopping for produce at a local market. Head to **Mercado 23** to be wowed by the array of tropical fruits and vegetables, and to enjoy the sounds, smells, and bustle of a working market (page 60).

- Movies are a favorite outing for many Mexicans, including midweek. Treat yourself to a cushy reclining chair, waiter service, and even a glass of wine at one of Cancún's **Cinépolis VIP theaters** (page 54).

- Catch a show at **Teatro Cancún,** which brings live acts from around the country, from music and dance to comedy and theater (page 54).

DOWNTOWN

Nomads (Av. Nader 78, tel. 998/898-3192, www.nomadscancun.com, 3pm-2am daily) is a hipster restaurant with a killer cocktail bar. The place itself feels like an old-world pub—wood-panel ceilings, brick walls, mismatched tile floors. Outside, a breezy patio has towering trees and twinkling lights. Thursday means open bar for just US$17. Look for the huge black duckling standing guard at the entrance.

Mixologists at **Amarula con Acento Tropical** (Av. Nader at Calle Huachinango, tel. 998/884-8046, 9pm-3am Wed.-Sat.) serve up strong cocktails with a tropical flair: chili-rimmed glassware, floating seashells, anise stars, and bright flowers on top. Set in an old Cancún house, the bar has a 1920s-meets-hacienda style with art deco flair, tropical woodwork, and arches here and there. Head to the patio for cozy seating under the stars.

It may be the bullring but the **Plaza de Toros** (Av. Bonampak at Av. Sayil, www.plazadetoroscancun.com.mx) also is a nightlife hot spot. Bars encircle the structure, selling cheap beer and finger food, many blasting Mexican rock and classics. A couple of food trucks park outside on weekends should you need something heftier to soak up your drinks. Most bars are open 3pm-3am daily.

On the southern end of Parque Las Palapas, **La Terraza del Vino** (Alcatraces 29, cell tel. 998/166-7273, 6pm-2am Tues.-Sun.) is a pleasant open-air wine bar that books live guitar soloists most nights starting at 9pm.

La Taberna (Av. Yaxchilán at Punta Nicchehabi, tel. 998/887-5433, www.lataberna.com.mx, 2pm-4am daily) is a locals' sports bar with lots of big-screen TVs and drink and food specials every night of the week. Free appetizers often come with each round of drinks.

THE ARTS
Theater

Teatro Cancún (El Embarcadero, Blvd. Kukulcán Km 4, tel. 998/849-5580, www.teatrodecancun.com.mx, ticket office on ground level 9am-9pm Mon.-Sat.) stages shows of all sorts, from music and dance to comedy and theater, both amateur and professional, mostly in Spanish. Ticket prices vary, but typically run US$5-30.

Teatro Xbalamqué (Hotel Xbalamqué, Av. Yaxchilán 31, www.teatroxbalamque.com, tel. 998/204-1028) stages experimental and one-act theater performances in a small space inside the hotel of the same name. Most shows are in Spanish; check the theater's website for showtimes. Tickets are typically US$5-10.

Cinema

Cancún has three convenient movieplexes, two in the Zona Hotelera and one downtown, both offering the latest American and Mexican releases. Most Hollywood movies are subtitled, but be aware that those made for kids, and even teenagers, are likely to be dubbed. Look for "DOB" (for *doblado*, or "dubbed") or "SUB" for (*subtitulada*, or "subtitled") to be sure. Ticket prices average around US$3.50, and US$5 for IMAX screenings; early shows may be discounted, and there's two-for-one Tuesday at the Cinemex.

In the Zona Hotelera, look for **Cinemex** at La Isla Shopping Village (Blvd. Kukulcán Km 12.5, 999/242-2126, www.cinemex.com), as well as **Cinépolis IMAX** at Puerto Cancún (Blvd. Kukulcán Km 1, 552/122-6060, www.cinepolis.com), the latter the only movie theater with IMAX screenings.

Downtown, there's a **Cinépolis** at Plaza Las Américas (Av. Tulum at Av. Sayil, tel. 998/884-0403, www.cinepolis.com). At the same location, there's also a **Cinépolis VIP**—a real treat—with reclining leather seats and wait service, plus a menu including sushi, baguette sandwiches, cappuccinos, and cocktails. Tickets are sold at a separate window, and cost around US$7.

FESTIVALS AND EVENTS

Taking place the last Saturday and Sunday of each month, **Manos Mágicas** (literally, magic hands) is an artisanal market held in the Jardín del Arte (across from Oasis Palm Hotel, Blvd. Kukulcán Km 4.5, 4pm-10pm). Dozens of local artisans showcase their textiles, paintings, jewelry, and more alongside organic foods and treats. At 6pm, live music and ballet *folklórico* (traditional Mexican folk dancing) are featured on a stage set up at the far end of the park.

Puerto Vallarta and Acapulco have long been Mexico's top destinations for gay travelers, but organizers of the **Cancún International Gay Festival** are working to put Cancún on the list. Inaugurated in 1995 and typically held in May, the festival includes beach parties, sunset cruises, city tours, and more.

The **Concurso Municipal de Artesanías,** a citywide handicraft competition, is held every August in Cancún's Palacio Municipal. In addition to showcasing the city's best artisans, participants also sell their work. Look for the large white tents—and the crowds—on Avenida Tulum.

Shopping

Cancún has six major malls, a handful of open-air markets, and hundreds of independent shops, so you can buy just about anything. Most mall and independent shops accept credit cards, but plan on paying cash at the markets.

OPEN-AIR MARKETS

Mercado 28 (Av. Sunyaxchen at Av. Xel-Há, 8am-8pm daily) is a large open-air market featuring a wide variety of Mexican handicrafts: ceramics from Tonalá, silver from Taxco, hammocks from Mérida, *alebrijes* (wooden creatures) from Oaxaca, and handwoven shirts from Chiapas. You'll also find a fair share of T-shirts, key chains, coconut monkeys, and the like. A handful of restaurants in the center of the market offer traditional Mexican fare.

Adjacent to Mercado 28, **Plaza Bonita** (Av. Sunyaxchen at Av. Xel-Há, 9am-8pm daily) is a multilevel shopping center built to look like a colonial village—bright courtyards, fountains, greenery, and all. Folk art here is a bit more expensive than that in the market next door, but the quality is usually better.

On weekend evenings, stroll through **Parque Las Palapas** and **Parque Los Artesanos,** both great spots to pick up local handicrafts, Chiapanecan clothing, bohemian jewelry, and art.

MALLS

The **Puerto Cancún Marina Town Center** (Blvd. Kukulcán Km 1, 10am-10pm daily) is the newest and swankiest of the area malls.

Modern and sleek, the open-air facility is home to high-end boutiques, international chain stores, and Cancun's only IMAX theater. Though it's just a two-minute walk from the main drag along a landscaped walkway, a shuttle takes mall-goers back and forth.

Plaza Caracol (Blvd. Kukulcán Km 8.5, 8am-9pm daily) is the best place in the Zona Hotelera to get beach essentials, with good brands and decent prices on bathing suits, flip-flops, sunglasses, sunscreen, and more. You can also grab a cup of Starbucks and good cheap grub at several small eateries.

Forum by the Sea (Blvd. Kukulcán Km 9, 10am-11:30pm daily) is a horseshoe-shaped mall with three floors opening onto the airy main lobby. It's home to Hard Rock Cafe—you can't miss the huge guitar out front—a good steak house, and various kitschy shops selling all manner of tourist souvenirs. The 3rd floor was under renovation when we passed through but has a balcony with a spectacular view of the beach and ocean, which is great for photo ops.

An open-air mall, **La Isla Shopping Village** (Blvd. Kukulcán Km 12.5, www.laislacancun.com.mx, 10am-10pm daily) is set around an artificial river, with wide shady passageways, a variety of international chain stores, and a food court featuring crepes, tacos, Italian, and more. The mall opens onto the lagoon, where there's a small marina and a nice boardwalk with half a dozen sit-down restaurants and a couple of water sports kiosks. A newer section called Fashion Harbour houses various luxury

Black Coral: A Disappearing Treasure

Despite its name, living black coral is not black at all, but a rich blue-green. It's only when the shell is stripped and the skeleton polished that the namesake color emerges. Black coral belongs to a family of coral whose shells are semiflexible, and colonies grow into beautiful tree-like formations that bend and sway in ocean currents. It's the world's slowest-growing coral, adding just 1-2 *hundredths of a millimeter* per year. (That's 200 times slower than human fingernails.) Black coral is among a handful of coral species discovered at extreme depths—300 meters (984 feet) down, and more—far deeper than previously thought possible for coral. And perhaps most remarkable of all was the finding, in 2009, that a colony of black coral near Hawaii is over 4,000 years old, making it the oldest known marine organism. Vast colonies of black coral once populated Cozumel's waters, and the island was for many years the center of black coral collection and trade. That's less true today, thanks partly to stricter regulation but also to the fact that the island's black coral is so diminished that the species is becoming endangered. Still, black coral retains a certain cachet, and its collection continues. Buying jewelry, souvenirs, and other items made with it only supports its demise—please resist!

shops. La Isla is also home to the popular Interactive Aquarium and has a five-screen movie theater.

Plaza Kukulcán (Blvd. Kukulcán Km 13, 10am-10pm daily) is an everyday mall with knickknack shops and teen clothing stores, though it boasts a swanky section called Luxury Avenue selling fine watches, jewelry, and couture clothing. There's also a full-on grocery store on the 2nd floor, which is especially convenient for visitors staying on the south end of the Zona Hotelera.

You don't have to go to the Zona Hotelera for your mall fix. **Plaza Las Américas** (Av. Tulum at Av. Sayil, 9am-10pm daily) stretches almost a block and includes dozens of mid- to upscale shops, an arcade, and two movie theaters.

Food

Cancún has dozens of excellent restaurants—the finest are in the Zona Hotelera, mostly in the high-end resorts and along the west (lagoon) side of Boulevard Kukulcán. Be aware that eating out in the Zona Hotelera can be shockingly expensive, similar to prices at top restaurants in major U.S. cities. There are a handful of Zona Hotelera gems, with great food at reasonable prices, and, of course, there are plenty of fast-food restaurants too. For something more authentic but still affordable, downtown Cancún is the place to go. The streets surrounding Parque Las Palapas and Avenida Nader have restaurants for all tastes and budgets, from fine dining to tasty street food, plus a number of great little cafés and sandwich shops.

ZONA HOTELERA
Mexican

The Surfin' Burrito (Blvd. Kukulcán Km 9.8, tel. 998/883-0083, 24 hours daily, US$5-8) is a hole-in-the-wall serving up a huge variety of burritos—pick your tortilla, protein (beef, chicken, or seafood), choice of salsas, and toppings. Rice and beans are a given. Wash it down with a mammoth one-liter margarita (US$7) or fruit smoothie (US$4). Delivery is available.

Easy to miss, ★ **Tacun** (Blvd. Kukulcán Km 11.5, tel. 998/593-3638, 8am-10pm daily, US$6-10) is a roadside taco joint at heart, and one of the few places in the Zona Hotelera serving good, genuine Mexican food at reasonable prices. Try a taco sampler platter with shrimp, beef, chicken, and *al pastor* tacos, served piping hot with a variety of fresh salsas. The staff and ambience are friendly. Look for it across from the Flamingo Mall. Cash only.

Seafood

A hidden gem, **El Fish Fritanga** (aka Pescadillas, Blvd. Kukulcán Km 12.6, tel. 998/840-6216, 11am-10:30pm daily, US$5-15) offers tasty home-style seafood at great prices. If you can't choose a dish, try the *pescadillas* or grilled nurse shark tacos, both house classics. The restaurant faces the lagoon and is below street level, making it easy to miss— look for the blue awning next to a Domino's Pizza sign.

★ **Fred's House** (Blvd. Kukulcán Km 14.7, tel. 998/840 6466, www.fredshouse restaurant.com, 1pm-midnight daily, US$22-45) is a lovely lagoon-side restaurant specializing in seafood dishes. Share an impressive iced shellfish tower featuring six varieties of crustaceans and then move on to any number of tartares, carpaccios, or sashimi. If you prefer your seafood hot, try one of the pasta dishes or wood-grilled entrees. For a memorable dinner, reserve a patio bungalow at sunset. Fred's is located across from the JW Marriott.

The nautical-themed **Lorenzillo's** (Blvd. Kukulcán Km 10.5, tel. 998/883-1254, www. lorenzillos.com.mx, 1pm-midnight daily, US$18-48) is known as one of the best lobster houses in town. Live lobster is kept in an adapted rowboat tank at the entrance—select the one you want, weigh it on an old-time scale, and before you know it, dinner is on. (All of the lobster comes from the restaurant's lobster farm off Isla Blanca, just north of the Zona Hotelera). Ask for a table on the lagoon-side patio for a chance to see crocs.

Steak Houses

Puerto Madero (Blvd. Kukulcán Km 14.1, tel. 998/885-2829, www.puertomadero restaurantes.com, 1pm-1am daily, US$20-55) is a longtime favorite serving carefully prepared meats in huge Argentinean portions. Choose a table in the warehouse-style dining room (a nod to the Puerto Madero shipyard in Argentina) or on the open-air patio with views of the lagoon. The menu includes salads, pastas, and excellent seafood, in addition to the many cuts of beef, some of which serve two. Prices are high, but you're sure to leave full.

Harry's (Blvd. Kukulcán Km 14.2, tel. 998/840-6550, www.harrys.com.mx, 1pm-1am daily, US$24-75) specializes in best-of-the-best beef, expertly prepared (some cuts are dry-aged for up to four weeks) and cooked in blazing-hot broilers. There's also a long menu of sashimi, oysters, ceviche, tartare, and other seafood dishes, plus excellent wine and cocktails. The bill comes with a cotton candy fluff. It's a memorable and worthwhile splurge for steak lovers.

Other Specialties

Hidden in a small hotel, **La Palapa Belga** (Royal Cancún, Calle Quetzal 13, tel. 998/883-5454, www.lapalapabelga.com, 3pm-10:30pm Mon.-Sat., US$12-20) has been serving fine French-Belgian cuisine for two decades. It's worth searching out both for its views across the lagoon to the Zona Hotelera and its delicious food like beef tartare and escargot de Bourgogne. Reservations are recommended on weekends.

Le Natura (Blvd. Kukulcán Km 9.8, tel. 998/252-6799, 8am-11pm daily, US$5-9) is a casual bistro serving an amazing variety of whole foods and juices. The juice and smoothie menu alone is 33 items long (who knew a juice combo of carrots, beets, spinach, and celery could taste so good?); the breakfast menu includes fruit and yogurt plates, egg dishes, and comfort food like waffles and pancakes; and lunch and dinner is just as varied with salads, bagel sandwiches, pastas, seafood, and Mexican classics. There are lots of vegetarian options too.

For a change of pace, **Elefanta** and **Thai Lounge** (La Isla Shopping Village, Blvd. Kukulcán Km 12.5, tel. 998/176-8070, www. elefanta.com.mx, 6:30pm-1am daily, US$12-34) are sister restaurants serving quality Indian and Thai food, respectively. The ambience at both is quite chic, despite being in a mall; the Thai Lounge has private cabañas on stilts overlooking the lagoon and stays open late as a bar-lounge.

Groceries

Numerous mini-marts along Boulevard Kukulcán sell chips, water, sunscreen, and other beach basics. Most are open from 7am to midnight.

For a more complete grocery experience, head to the upscale **Selecto Súper Chedraui** (Blvd. Kukulcán Km 9, tel. 998/830-0866, 7am-11pm daily), a three-story supermarket featuring organic foods, gourmet wines and cheeses, a sushi bar, and a popular prepared food section. Not as fancy but still well stocked is Soriana Super (Blvd. Kukulcán Km 13, 7am-11pm daily) on the 2nd floor of Plaza Kukulcán shopping mall.

DOWNTOWN
Mexican

★ **Quesadillas Tierra del Sol** (Margaritas near Tulipanes, tel. 998/271-0111, 8am-midnight daily, US$2-4) serves up hefty quesadillas (and *sopes, panuchos,* and *salbutes*) made with Oaxacan cheese and your choice of dozens of stuffings, from chorizo to *nopales* (cactus). Two will satisfy a decent appetite, four could push you over the edge. Fresh, fruity *aguas* help wash it down. Order at the register and they'll call your number.

Just a couple of blocks from the bus station, **Taquería Coapeñitos** (Av. Nadar 25, tel. 998/253-0360, 2pm-2am Mon.-Wed., 2pm-3am Thurs.-Sat., noon-midnight Sun., US$2-4) sells some mean street tacos. The kitchen is open, so you can watch your tacos being prepped while you wait. Be sure to hit up the fixins' bar for a variety of salsas, pickled onions, and lime. Beers are cheap too.

La Habichuela (Parque Las Palapas, Calle Margaritas 25, tel. 998/884-3158, www. lahabichuela.com, 1pm-midnight daily, US$10-26) is a longtime favorite for Yucatan cuisine. The seafood is especially tasty—try

the giant shrimp in tamarind sauce or *cocobichuela*, the house specialty, with big chunks of lobster and shrimp in a sweet curry sauce. For dessert, ask for a Maya coffee flambé: Chiapanecan coffee made with cinnamon, brandy, and *Xtabentún* (a regional liqueur made with anise, rum, and fermented honey).

Combine Disneyland and the Mexican Revolution and you might get **Pericos** (Av. Yaxchilán 61, tel. 998/884-0821, noon-1am daily, US$7-15), a classic Cancún family restaurant. *Bandito* waiters sport bandoliers, the bar has saddles instead of stools, and kids may get a rubber chicken on their plate instead of taquitos. Low-key it is not, but Pericos has a solid reputation for serving good grilled meats and seafood in a fun, boisterous atmosphere. Live marimba and mariachi starts at 8pm most nights.

On the north end of Parque Las Palapas is a set of **food stalls** (7am-midnight daily, US$1.50-4) selling cheap Mexican and Yucatecan eats—tacos, quesadillas, tostadas, and *salbutes*. It's perfect if you're looking for some good street food or are on a tight budget.

Seafood

Pescaditos (Av. Yaxchilán 69, 11am-midnight daily, US$5-9) is the sort of restaurant you'd expect to see on the beach, complete with reggae music, a handful of tables, and a sign made from an old surfboard. And like the best beach shacks, this place will wow you with simple, tasty seafood dishes. The ceviche, beer-battered shrimp, and fish tacos are all outstanding, and very well priced. Wash it down with a frosty beer or homemade *limonada.*

Sitting among several open-air eateries, **El Cejas** (Mercado 28, Av. Sunyaxchen at Av. Xel-Há, tel. 998/887-1080, 8am-8pm daily, US$3-6) is bustling most days for good reason—fresh seafood and ambience. Live marimba music is in the air, colorful *papel picado* (decorative paper) sways overhead, and a combo of tourists and locals fill the seats. Service can be painfully slow but the dishes—freshly fried fish, grilled shrimp, ceviche of all sorts—are worth the wait.

Pescado Con Limón (Mercado 28, Av. Sunyaxchen at Av. Xel-Há, tel. 998/887-2436, 11am-7pm daily, US$5-11) may be a little short on ambience—its plastic tables and chairs face the Mercado 28 parking lot—but the seafood is as fresh and good as it comes, an open secret among locals and expats. For a sure thing, try a shrimp dish or one of the fried-fish platters. The tip is typically included (and somewhat hidden) in the bill.

Other Specialties

★ **Sirena Morena** (Av. Nader 66, tel. 998/887-9774, 8am-10pm Mon.-Sat., US$4-6) is where it's at for veggie fans. The menu is all organic and all vegetarian and includes sandwiches and salads, egg dishes, even mushroom risotto and *pozole* (spicy soup made with hominy). There are lots of gluten-free and vegan options too. Tables are in a garden setting with shabby-chic flair. Look for the entrance down a small alley next to a natural food shop.

El Tigre y El Toro (Av. Nader between Calles Mero and Rubia, tel. 998/898-0041, 6pm-12:30am Mon.-Sat., 6pm-11:30pm Sun., US$8-15) is a trendy outdoor restaurant specializing in wood-fired pizza. The thin-crust pies are topped with items like prosciutto and burrata, lobster, and Argentinean sausage. Gourmet salads and homemade pastas round out the menu. This is a casual spot that doubles as a special (pizza) night out.

Rolandi's Pizzeria Cancún (Av. Cobá 12, tel. 998/884-4047, 1:30pm-12:30am daily, US$9-22) is an institution, with sister restaurants in Isla Mujeres, Playa del Carmen, and Cozumel. The food here—and at all of them—is consistently good; choose among thin-crust pizzas, calzones, and great homemade pastas. Pocket bread, warm and inflated, and a dish of olive oil come with every order. Sit on the veranda, which is draped in ivy that blocks out street noise.

La Parrilla (Av. Yaxchilán 51, tel. 998/287-8118, www.laparrilla.com.mx, noon-2am daily, US$7-28) is one of the most popular of the restaurant-bars on this busy street, grilling a variety of delicious beef fillets, plus shrimp and lobster brochettes, chicken, fajitas, and tacos—the fiery spit in front is for *taquitos al pastor,* a Mexican classic. The breezy street-side eating area is comfortable and casual and good for families. There's also live mariachi music every night starting at 8pm.

Ceviche is a popular seafood dish on beaches in Mexico.

Light Fare

Get a tasty baguette sandwich at ★ **Ty-Coz Baguettería** (Av. Tulum at Av. Uxmal, tel. 998/884-6060, 8am-10pm Mon.-Sat., 8am-8pm Sun, US$2-5), a cozy eatery tucked behind the Comercial Mexicana supermarket opposite the bus terminal. The menu includes French- and German-inspired baguette sandwiches and *cuernos* (croissants). Most run around US$3, but you can always order the *económica* baguette with ham, salami, and cheese for just US$1.25. If you don't want to head downtown for a sandwich, visit its **Zona Hotelera branch** (Blvd. Kulkulcán Km 9, 6am-9pm daily).

Rooster (Av. Nader 114, tel. 998/884-4252, 8am-10pm daily, US$2.50-6) is a cool-cat café serving up good breakfast dishes, fresh deli sandwiches, and a variety of coffee drinks and smoothies. Seating is either in a cozy corner or on a leafy terrace. Tables fill up fast, so arrive early or take your eats to go.

Groceries

Chedraui (Blvd. Kukulcán at Av. Tulum) and **Comercial Mexicana** (Av. Tulum at Av. Uxmal) are huge supermarkets with everything from produce and in-house bakeries to pharmacies and beach supplies. Both are open 7am-11pm daily and have ATMs just inside their doors.

Just a couple of blocks from the bus station, **Mercado 23** (Calles Ciricote and Cedro, three blocks north of Av. Uxmal via Calle Palmeras, 6am-6pm daily) has stands of fresh fruits and vegetables. The selection is somewhat limited, but the produce is the freshest around.

DINNER CRUISES

For couples, the **Columbus Lobster Dinner Cruise** (Aquatours Marina, Blvd. Kukulcán Km 6.5, toll-free Mex. tel. 800/727-5391, toll-free U.S. tel. 866/393-5158, www.thelobsterdinner.com, US$89-109 dinner with open bar, no children under 14, departs at 5:30pm and 8:30pm nightly) offers a change of pace, serving three-course dinners aboard a Spanish-style galleon. The ship cruises the Laguna Nichupté for 2.5 hours, accompanied by live jazz.

If you're traveling with kids, the **Galleon of Captain Hook** (Marina Captain Hook, Blvd. Kukulcán Km 5, tel. 998/849-4931, www.capitanhook.com, US$70-95 adult with open bar, US$35-51 child, departs at 7pm nightly, 3.5 hours) offers dinner plus a costumed crew and tales of pirate conquest while cruising the open sea. Be aware that a "surcharge"—US$14 adult, US$5 kid—is added to the bill. It covers travel insurance, security and, of all things, diesel fuel.

Accommodations

Cancún has scores of hotels, varying from backpacker hostels to ultra-high-end resorts. They're also divided by their location: the Zona Hotelera and downtown. The Zona Hotelera has spectacular views, easy access to the beaches, swimming pools, and excellent restaurants, but prices are higher and you won't get much "authentic" interaction with local people. Downtown Cancún has a variety of food, shopping, and services (from Walmart to laundries) at generally lower prices, but staying downtown also means driving or taking a bus to the beach and foregoing ocean-view rooms.

ZONA HOTELERA
Under US$100

Just steps from both the nightclubs and the beach, **Natura Hostel** (Blvd. Kukulcán Km 9.5, tel. 998/883-0585, cancunhostelnatura@gmail.com, US$30 pp dorm with a/c, US$65 s/d with a/c and shared bath, US$75 s/d with a/c) is as good as it gets in Cancún, location-wise. The rooms themselves are tiny but clean, many with colorful murals. Mattresses are on the thin side but bunks have privacy curtains, personal fans, and lights. There's also a rooftop lounge with a common kitchen, pool table, and enviable views of the lagoon. The hostel is located above the like-named restaurant.

Set on Laguna Nichupté, **El Manglar** (Blvd. Kukulcán Km 19.8, tel. 998/885-1808, www.villasmanglar.com, US$90-100 s/d with a/c) has simple and spacious rooms, each with cable TV, air-conditioning, a king-size bed, and two couches that double as twin beds. There's a well-maintained pool on-site and beach access nearby at Playa Delfines. With the marina next door, it's especially popular with people who enjoy fishing, waterskiing, and wakeboarding.

US$100-200

With just 30 suites, **Casa Turquesa Boutique Hotel** (Blvd. Kukulcán Km 13.5, tel. 998/193-2260, www.casaturquesa.com, US$143-210 with a/c, US$420 suite with a/c) is a welcome change of pace from the massive resorts lining Boulevard Kukulcán. Units are spacious and spotless, if somewhat dated in style (at the time of research, they were being updated); ocean views and whirlpool tubs more than make up for the old-school prints. Works of art also are featured throughout the property—paintings and sculptures from notable artists, mostly from Mexico. The hotel itself is perched above the beach, making for spectacular views from the pool. Service is warm and personalized.

An excellent value, **Beachscape Kin Ha Villas & Suites** (Blvd. Kukulcán Km 8.5, tel. 998/891-5400, www.beachscape.com. mx, US$144 s/d with a/c, US$230-413 suite with a/c) is a comfortable, low-key resort on a beautiful beach on the upper arm of the Zona Hotelera. Its one-, two-, and three-bedroom suites have fully equipped kitchens, living and dining areas, and ocean-view terraces; there also are a handful of standard hotel rooms. In addition to that huge beach, the property has a large (and rather plain) pool, restaurant-bar, and children's play area. Though lacking the style and ambience of Cancún's top resorts, Beachscape Kin Ha can hardly be beat for location and value. Coin-op laundry, an exercise room, and Wi-Fi (reception area only) are available.

US$200-400

★ **Grand Fiesta Americana Coral Beach** (Blvd. Kukulcán Km 9.5, tel. 998/881-3200, www.coralbeachcancunhotel.com, US$329-349 junior suite with a/c, US$649-849 master suite with a/c) is an elegant hotel offering spacious and comfortable suites, all with spectacular ocean-view balconies. It features a series of infinity pools, lush and manicured gardens, and one of the calmest beaches of the Zona Hotelera. The hotel has five restaurants and cafés, a luxurious spa, a kids club, and activities ranging from yoga to Jet Skis.

Marriott Cancún Resort (Blvd. Kukulcán Km 14.8, tel. 998/881-2000, toll-free U.S./Can. tel. 888/236-2427, www.marriott. com, US$219-282 s/d with a/c, US$302-402 suite with a/c) has over 400 rooms, all with private terraces and amenities like flat-screen TVs and wireless Internet. Its eight eateries include an Argentinean steak house, a sushi restaurant, and a Thai restaurant. There's also a full-service spa, illuminated outdoor tennis courts, and a gym with separate men's and women's saunas. The hotel's main drawback is the pool, which is well maintained but small for the size and caliber of the resort; fortunately, it's just steps from the Caribbean.

Located alongside the Pok-ta-Pok golf course, **Laguna Suites Golf + Spa** (Paseo Pok-ta-Pok No. 3, tel. 998/891-5252, toll-free U.S./Can. tel. 866/760-1843, www. lagunasuites.com.mx, US$152 s/d with a/c, US$168-188 pp all-inclusive, children under 16 stay free) has just 47 rooms, allowing for genuinely personalized service without the hubbub of a large beachfront resort. There's a small pool and a chic *palapa* lounge, plus free hourly shuttles to three nearby sister resorts—the Sunset Royal, Sunset Marina, and Ocean Spa—where you can enjoy the pool, beach, restaurants, and amenities like any other guest. It's a great option if you don't mind a little resort hopping.

Over US$400

The Ritz-Carlton (Blvd. Kukulcán Km 13.9, tel. 998/881-0808, toll-free U.S/Can. tel. 800/542-8680, www.ritzcarlton.com, US$707-837 s/d with a/c, US$927-987 suite with a/c) is unparalleled in its elegance. Fine art, chandeliers, and marble floors greet you the moment the white-gloved porter opens the door. All rooms have stunning ocean views and boast features like feather beds, downpour shower-heads, and twice-daily housekeeping. Other high-end features include a full-service spa and gym, tennis courts, the Culinary Center (a gorgeous kitchen where guests can take cooking classes), and a well-maintained beach. The only hiccups are the unremarkable pools—nice enough but nothing special—an odd oversight given the luxuriousness of the rest of the hotel.

All-Inclusive Resorts

The Royal Cancún All Suites Resort (Blvd. Kukulcán Km 4.5, toll-free Mex. tel. 800/020-1761, toll-free U.S./Can. tel. 888/721-4431, US$155-173 pp all-inclusive) is a quiet re-sort well suited for families. It's on the short, north-facing part of the Zona Hotelera, so the beach has virtually no waves—a big difference from the east-facing beaches, and a relief for parents with young children. There's also a kids club and lots of free sports gear, such as snorkeling equipment, sailboats, golf clubs, and bikes. The spacious units have been re-cently updated (all have two bedrooms and a full kitchen). Guests enjoy access to the prop-erty's all-inclusive sister resorts, the Royal Sands in Cancún and the Royal Haciendas in Playa del Carmen.

Located at the southernmost tip of the Zona Hotelera, **Club Med Cancún Yucatán** (Blvd. Kukulcán Km 20.6, tel. 998/881-8200, toll-free U.S. tel. 888/932-2582, www.clubmed.com, US$270 pp all-inclusive) is a secluded re-sort with a huge offering of activities—from paddleboarding and waterskiing to flying trapeze and golfing. The Mini Club keeps the little ones happy and busy all day long with ac-tivities like tennis and cooking lessons. There also are three good restaurants and a handful of bars—enough variety to keep most guests happy.

Hotel Riu Palace Las Américas (Blvd. Kukulcán Km 8.5, tel. 998/881-4300, www.riu.com, US$199-302 pp all-inclusive) is an adults-only hotel with 350-plus suites that, while not as elegant as the Victorian-style common areas indicate, are quite nice. Each has a separate sitting area, a minibar that's re-stocked daily, and standard amenities like sat-ellite TV and in-room safes; most rooms also have ocean views. Beds are ultra-firm—ask for a foam topper if that's an issue. The resort's beach is narrow but well maintained; there are also three infinity pools, endless water activi-ties, five restaurants, and several bars.

The luxurious, adults-only ★ **Le Blanc Spa Resort** (Blvd. Kukulcán Km 10, tel. 998/881-4740, toll-free Mex. tel. 800/681-5338, toll-free U.S. tel. 888/702-0913, www.leblancsparesort.com, US$380-466 pp all-inclusive) offers all the amenities a vacation-ing couple could want: infinity pools, à la carte gourmet restaurants, a fully equipped gym and spa, Pilates and spinning classes, unlimited golf, bars and lounges, and yards and yards of white-sand beach. There's even butler service. The guest rooms are minimal-ist chic with whirlpool tubs. All have views of the Caribbean or the lagoon.

DOWNTOWN
Under US$50

★ **Mayan Monkey** (Av. Nader 3, tel. 998/217-5332, www.mayanmonkey.com, US$11-15 pp dorm with a/c, US$80 s/d with a/c) is a four-story, mid-century modern af-fair. Dorms are airy and bright, with custom wood bunks that have individual lights, two outlets, privacy curtains, thick mattresses, and big built-in lockers; all have en suite bathrooms. There are cozy common areas on every level but the rooftop is where's it at, with a pool with great city views, a bar, and an open-air restaurant. Best of all? The rate includes breakfast and dinner.

Moloch Hostel (Margaritas 54, tel. 998/884-6918, www.moloch.com.mx, US$11 dorm with a/c, US$29/34 s/d with a/c) a/c) is a low-key hostel with mini-split air conditioners in all the rooms, including the dorms (8am-8pm only), and an inviting pool in back. Dorms are a bit cramped, but the beds are good; private rooms are larger and would even work for families. There's a fully equipped communal kitchen, as well as continental breakfast, a TV lounge, Wi-Fi, and a computer station. It's located a block from both the bus station and Parque Las Palapas.

A social place, **Hostel Ka'beh** (Calle Alcatraces at Calle Claveles, tel. 998/892-7902, www.hostelkabeh.com, US$19 dorm with a/c, US$44 s/d with a/c) has welcoming lounge areas and daily activities like clubbing trips, movie nights, and barbecue nights. Breakfast—oatmeal, pancakes, eggs, waffles, PB&J—is self-service and available 24/7. There's also a common kitchen and a huge lending library of travel guides. Dorms are mixed and comfortable enough; ask for a bed in the new section—they're away from the hubbub so you can actually get some shut-eye. Private rooms are located across the street and are even quieter. There's a two-night minimum during the high season.

US$50-100

Half a block from the bus station, ★ **Selina Cancún** (Av. Tulum 75, toll-free Mex. tel. 800/ 953-0822, www.selina.com, US$18-20 pp dorm with a/c, US$34 s/d with shared bath and a/c, US$60 s/d with a/c, US$75 suite with a/c) is an artful hotel-hostel with boho-hipster style. Murals, Talavera tiles, and tropical woods accent most rooms and common areas, including a fully equipped kitchen, movie screening room, and library. Outdoors, there's an expansive garden with a pool, lounge, and bar/restaurant; many nights a DJ is working the tunes. There's a gorgeous co-working space too.

Cancún International Suites (Calle Gladiolas at Av. Alcatraces, tel. 998/884-1771, cancuninternationalsuites@gmail.com, US$65 s/d with a/c) has large, comfortable rooms with a hacienda-like feel. Rooms combine warm colors, wood furniture, and high ceilings with modern amenities like glass showers, flat-screen TVs, and Wi-Fi. The downtown location, just a half block from Parque Las Palapas, is perfect. A rooftop lounge has superb views.

Located on a quiet stretch of Avenida Nader, **Hotel & Suites Nader** (Av. Nader near Av. Cobá, tel. 998/884-1584, www.suitesnadercancun.com, US$54 s/d with a/c, US$63-75 suite with a/c and kitchenette) is a comfortable and modern hotel. Rooms are somewhat sparse but have updated amenities like flat-screen TVs, silent air-conditioning, and free Wi-Fi. The owners are often on-site, which makes for warm, personalized service. Discounts are often offered if you reserve by phone.

Over US$100

Bougainvillea and a gurgling fountain welcome you to **Hotel El Rey del Caribe** (Av. Uxmal at Nader, tel. 998/884-2028, www.elreydelcaribe.com, US$170 s/d with a/c and kitchenette), an eco-friendly hotel two blocks east of the bus terminal. Rooms are clean and comfortable (those in the newer section are more spacious, with lovely wood floors), but it's the verdant tropical garden with hammocks, a pool, and an outdoor dining area that really sets El Rey apart. The hotel employs solar heating, rainwater recovery, and organic waste composting. Breakfast is included.

Information and Services

TOURIST INFORMATION

Downtown, the **City Tourist Office** (Av. Nader at Av. Cobá, tel. 998/887-3379, www.fonatur.gob.mx, 9am-4pm Mon.-Fri.) is a bustling office with staffers who happily provide information on city and regional sights. English is spoken.

Note: Be aware that booths with "Tourist Information" signs along Avenida Tulum and Boulevard Kukulcán are in fact operated by **time-share companies,** offering free tours and other goodies in exchange for attending a sales presentation.

Casa Consular (Blvd. Kukulcán Km 13, tel. 998/840-6082, www.casaconsular.org, 9am-3pm Mon.-Fri) has helpful staffers who act as liaisons between international travelers and their consular representatives. The office also offers advice to those travelers needing to contact Mexican authorities with everything from immigration issues to theft. English is spoken. Look for it next to the fire station in the Zona Hotelera.

There are also a few publications that are worth picking up: *Cancún Tips* (www.cancuntips.com.mx) is a free tourist magazine with general information about Cancún and nearby sights; both *Restaurante Menu Mapa* and *Map@migo* have maps, restaurant menus, reviews, and discount coupons; and *Agenda Cultural* has listings of Cancún's upcoming cultural events, exhibitions, and workshops. This last one can be hard to find—ask at the tourist office.

EMERGENCY SERVICES

There are several recommended private hospitals within a few blocks of each other in downtown Cancún. All have emergency rooms and English-speaking doctors and are open 24 hours daily: **Hospitén Cancún** (Av. Bonampak s/n, south of Av. Nichupté, tel. 998/881-3700, www.hospiten.

com), **AmeriMed Hospital** (Av. Tulum at Av. Nichupté, behind Las Américas mall, tel. 998/881-3400, www.amerimedcancun.com), and **Hospital Galenia** (Av. Tulum at Av. Nizuc, tel. 998/891-5200, www.hospitalgalenia.com).

For meds in the Zona Hotelera, try any of the malls or head to **Farmacia del Ahorro** (Blvd. Kukulcán Km 9.5, tel. 998/892-7291, 24 hours). Downtown, **Farmacias Similares** (Av. Tulum near Calle Crisantemos, tel. 998/898-0190, 24 hours) is a reliable national chain.

The **police department, fire station,** and **ambulance** all can be reached by dialing toll-free 060 or 066 anytime. In the Zona Hotelera, all three are located in the same building next to Plaza Kukulcán (Blvd. Kukulcán Km 12.5). Downtown, the main police station (Av. Xcaret at Av. Kabah, tel. 998/884-1913, 24 hours) faces the Carrefour supermarket, and there's a small office on Parque Las Palapas, near the food stalls, which is usually open 24 hours.

MONEY

You'll have no problem accessing or exchanging your money in Cancún. ATMs are ubiquitous, including at all the shopping malls, and give the best exchange rate. Many resorts will exchange dollars and euros, or simply accept them directly as payment. Ditto for many tour operators and even restaurants, especially in the Zona Hotelera. The exchange rate may be awful, however.

If you need an actual bank, head to **Plaza Caracol** (Blvd. Kukulcán Km 8.5), where you'll find Bancomer, HSBC, and Banamex. All have ATMs that accept foreign cards and are open roughly 9am-4pm Monday-Friday.

Downtown, the most conveniently located banks are on Avenida Tulum between Avenida Cobá and Avenida Uxmal: **Bancomer** (Av.

Tulum 20, 8:30am-4pm Mon.-Fri.) and **Citi-Banamex** (Av. Tulum 19, 9am-4pm Mon.-Fri., 10am-2pm Sat.).

MEDIA AND COMMUNICATIONS
Post Office
The **post office** (Av. Sunyaxchen at Av. Xel-Há, tel. 998/834-1418, 8am-4pm Mon.-Fri., 9am-12:30pm Sat.) is located in front of Mercado 28. There is no post office in the Zona Hotelera, though your hotel may mail postcards for you.

Internet and Telephone
Wi-Fi is offered by most hostels, hotels, and resorts, whether for free or at a small cost, and some have computers available for those without a laptop or mobile device of their own. Malls, restaurants, and even the Mexican government is following suit: Most Mexican cities, Cancún among them, have public Wi-Fi in their main plazas. If all else fails, you can get online at a few *cibercafes*, which are located downtown. Most have Skype-enabled computers too.

Recommended Internet cafes include **Cyber Café Uxmal** (Av. Uxmal near Margaritas, no phone, 24 hours daily, US$0.75 per hour) near the bus station, and **Papelería Internet** (Margaritas near Gladiolas, 8am-10pm daily, US$0.60 per hour), facing Parque Las Palapas.

Newspapers
There are a handful of newspapers for local and regional news: In Spanish, *Novedades Quintana Roo* (www.sipse.com/novedades) is the state's oldest newspaper, centrist in coverage; *¡Por Esto!* (www.poresto.net) is a left-of-center paper with Quintana Roo and Yucatán versions; and *Diario de Yucatán*

(www.yucatan.com.mx) is more conservative and covers the entire region. The Cancún version of the *Miami Herald Tribune* is a good English-language alternative.

LAUNDRY AND STORAGE
Downtown, **Lavandería Las Palapas** (Parque Las Palapas, Alcatraces near Gladiolas, 7am-9pm Mon.-Fri., 7am-8pm Sat.) will do your laundry for US$3.50 per three kilos (6.6 pounds); same-day service is available if you drop off before 9am.

In the Zona Hotelera, **Eco-Laundry** (Kukulcán Km 9.5, tel. 998/883-4315, 9am-8pm Mon.-Sat., 9am-2pm Sun.) offers same-day laundry service for US$2.50 per kilo (2.2 pounds). With similar prices, **Lavandería Lumi Express** (Blvd. Kukulcán Km 8, tel. 998/883-3874, www.lumiexpress.com.mx, 8am-8pm Mon.-Sat., 9am-5pm Sun.) also offers self-service machines. Pickup and drop-off is available.

At the bus station, near the second-class departure area, **Guarda Equipaje** (tel. 998/884-4352, ext. 2851, 6:30am-10pm daily) will store luggage for US$0.50-1 per hour, depending on the size.

Storage lockers (US$6 per 24 hours) also can be rented in Terminal 3 at Cancún International Airport; they are big enough to hold carry-on bags only. Look for the lockers as you exit customs.

INSTRUCTION
The welcoming **Centro Cultural La Pitahaya** (Av. Yaxchilán near Av. Uxmal, cell tel. 998/118-0099, 4pm-11pm Mon.-Fri., prices vary) offers a wide range of workshops in theater, music, art, and even jewelry design. If you're going to be in town for a month or longer, consider checking out the offerings.

Getting There and Around

GETTING THERE
Air

The **Cancún International Airport** (CUN, Hwy. 307 Km 22, tel. 998/848-7200, www.cancun-airport.com) is 20 kilometers (12.4 miles) south of Cancún. Most international flights arrive and depart from Terminals 3 and 4, which have taxi, bus, and car rental desks. All have ATMs or money exchange kiosks. In general, Terminal 2 is used for domestic flights; Terminal 1 is reserved for charter flights. A free shuttle ferries travelers between the terminals.

The following airlines serve Cancún International Airport:

- **Aeromar** (toll-free Mex. tel. 800/237-6627, www.aeromar.com.mx)

- **Aeroméxico** (Av. Cobá at Av. Bonampak, tel. 998/884-1186, toll-free U.S. tel. 800/237-6639, www.aeromexico.com)

- **AeroTucán** (toll-free Mex. tel. 800/640-4148, www.aerotucan.com)

- **Air Canada** (toll-free Mex. tel. 800/719-2827, toll-free U.S./Can. tel. 888/247-2262, www.aircanada.com)

- **Alaska Airlines** (toll-free Mex. tel. 800/654-5669, toll-free U.S./Can. tel. 800/252-7522, www.alaskaair.com)

- **American Airlines** (toll-free Mex. tel. 800/904-6000, toll-free U.S./Can. tel. 800/433-7300, www.aa.com)

- **Cubana de Aviación** (Av. Tulum 232, tel. 998/887-7210, airport tel. 998/886-0355, www.cubana.cu)

- **Delta** (toll-free Mex. tel. 800/266-0046, toll-free U.S. tel. 800/241-4141, www.delta.com)

- **Frontier Airlines** (toll-free U.S. tel. 801/401-9000, www.frontierairlines.com)

- **InterJet** (toll-free Mex. tel. 800/011-2345, toll-free U.S. tel. 866/285-9525, www.interjet.com.mx)

- **JetBlue** (toll-free Mex. tel. 800/861-3372, toll-free U.S. tel. 800/538-2583, www.jetblue.com)

- **MAYAir** (airport tel. 998/881-9413, toll-free Mex. tel. 800/962-9247, toll-free U.S./Can. tel. 844/622-0800, www.mayair.com.mx)

- **Southwest Airlines** (toll-free Mex. tel. 800/083-1179, toll-free U.S. tel. 800/435-9792, www.southwest.com)

- **Spirit Airlines** (toll-free Mex./U.S./Can. tel. 801/401-2222, www.spiritair.com)

- **United Airlines** (toll-free Mex. tel. 800/900-5000, toll-free U.S./Can. tel. 800/864-8331, www.united.com)

- **VivaAerobus** (toll-free Mex. tel. 818/215-0150, toll-free U.S. tel. 888/935-9848, www.vivaaerobus.com)

- **Volaris** (tel. 551/102-8000, toll-free U.S. tel. 855/865-2747, www.volaris.com)

Bus

Buses leave Cancún's clean and modern **bus terminal** (Av. Tulum at Av. Uxmal) for destinations in the Yucatán Peninsula and throughout the interior of Mexico.

Combi

Combis, public shuttle vans, run between Cancún and Playa del Carmen. They queue up directly across Avenida Tulum from the bus terminal, near the Comercial Mexicana, and depart every 10-15 minutes 24 hours a day (US$2, 1 hour). For slightly more, **Playa Express** has larger, air-conditioned shuttles, departing on roughly the same schedule from the parking lot in front of the bus terminal (US$2.25, 50 minutes). Both services make stops along the way, including Puerto Morelos (US$1.25, 30 minutes).

Cancún Bus Schedule

Cancún's bus station (tel. 800/702-8000) is located downtown at Avenidas Tulum and Uxmal. Departures listed below include both first- and second-class service; in many cases, second-class buses take significantly longer for only marginal savings.

DESTINATION	PRICE	DURATION	SCHEDULE*
Cancún Int'l Airport	US$4	25 mins	every 30 mins 4:30am-11pm
Chetumal	US$21-27	5-6 hrs	every 30-90 mins 12:30am-11:59pm
Chichén Itzá	US$15	4 hrs	8:45am or take any Pisté bus
Chiquilá (Isla Holbox)	US$6.75	3-3.5 hrs	five departures 7:40am-2pm
Mahahual	US$12-23	4.5 hrs	6:50am and 4:45pm
Mérida	US$14-32	4-4.5 hrs	every 30-60 mins 1am-11:59pm
Pisté	US$7.50-15	3.5-4.5 hrs	8:45am and every 30-60 mins 12:30pm-11:30pm
Playa del Carmen	US$2-4	1 hr	every 15-30 mins 12:30am-10:30pm
Puerto Morelos	US$1.75	45 mins	every 15-30 mins 6am-10pm
Tulum	US$4.50-11	2.5 hrs	every 45-90 mins 5:30am-11:15pm
Valladolid	US$8-11	2-3.5 hrs	every 60-90 mins 4am-8pm

*Schedules are subject to change.

GETTING AROUND
To and from the Airport

Cancún's airport is served by taxi, shuttle, and bus. The authorized airport taxi service, Yellow Transfers (toll-free Mex. tel. 844/373-6983, www.yellowtransfers.com), has booths inside the airport terminals. It offers taxi and shuttle service, including luxury class and for the disabled, anywhere on the coast. Fares are fixed and prominently displayed at the airport and online (where rates are sometimes discounted). Rates to the Zona Hotelera or downtown are the same; private taxis and shuttles run US$44-66 (4-8 people), while shared shuttles are US$18 per person. Yellow Transfers offers round-trip service at a discount, or you can hire an ordinary taxi; you'll end up paying roughly the same. Service along the coast includes Playa del Carmen (US$90-171) and Tulum (US$152-375).

ADO provides bus service from stops just outside each terminal. Tickets can be purchased at ADO booths inside the airport or at kiosks located at each bus stop. Comfortable, air-conditioned buses leave every 30 minutes for downtown Cancún (8:15am-12:30am daily, US$4, 25 minutes) and every 30 minutes for Playa del Carmen (12:30am-11:59pm daily, US$9.50, 1 hour); the latter stops in Puerto Morelos (US$6, 25 minutes) along the

Driving Distances from Cancún

LOCATION	DISTANCE	LOCATION	DISTANCE
Airport	20 km (12.4 mi)	Playa del Carmen	68 km (42.5 mi)
Akumal	105 km (65 mi)	Puerto Aventuras	87 km (54 mi)
Bacalar	320 km (199 mi)	Puerto Morelos	36 km (22.5 mi)
Campeche	485 km (301.5 mi)	Punta Allen	182 km (109 mi)
Chetumal	382 km (237.5 mi)	Tulum	130 km (81 mi)
Chichén Itzá	178 km (110.5 mi)	Valladolid	158 km (98 mi)
Cobá	173 km (107.5 mi)	Xcalak	411 km (255.5 mi)
Mahahual	351 km (218 mi)	Xcaret	74 km (46 mi)
Mérida	320 km (199 mi)	Xel-Há	122 km (76 mi)
Paamul	82 km (51 mi)	Xpu-Há	101 km (63 mi)

way. There also are eight daily departures for Mérida (2:05pm-9:15pm, US$19-34, 3.5-4.5 hours). For other destinations, take any bus to Cancún or Playa del Carmen and transfer. ADO's airport buses do not enter Cancún's Zona Hotelera.

Bus

Frequent buses (US$0.75) run between downtown Cancún and the Zona Hotelera—you'll rarely have to wait more than five minutes for one to pass. The buses are red and have "R-1," "Hoteles," or "Zona Hotelera" painted on the front, and stop along Avenida Tulum, at the bus station, and near most major hotels, beaches, and ferry ports.

Taxi

You'll have no trouble finding a taxi around town or in the Zona Hotelera—they're everywhere tourists are. Before getting into one, however, make sure to agree upon a price—meters aren't used, and drivers sometimes overcharge. As of this writing, the rate around downtown is US$2.50, from downtown to the Isla Mujeres ferries US$3.50, and from downtown to the Zona Hotelera US$10-20, depending on the destination. Rates within the Zona Hotelera jump dramatically and depend on

how far you're going. Ask your concierge for specific rates, but expect to pay US$8-20.

Car

Although you won't need a car to visit Cancún proper, renting one is a great way to visit the nearest archaeological sites (i.e., Tulum, Cobá, Ek' Balam, and Chichén Itzá) without being part of a huge tour group. A rental also makes exploring the Riviera Maya a little easier, though buses cover that route fairly well. Driving in the Cancún area is relatively pain-free—unexpected speed bumps and impatient bus drivers are the biggest concerns.

Most international car rental companies, and a few local ones, have offices at the airport (some are right at the terminal, others in a purpose-built rental center a few miles away) as well as in select resorts and at offices downtown and in the Zona Hotelera. Various sizes and types of vehicles are available, from SUVs to Volkswagen Bugs (optimistically dubbed VW sedans); prices with insurance and taxes start at around US$32 a day. The best rates are online; you also can sometimes get discounted rates by spending half a day in a time-share presentation. Commonly used companies include:

- **America Car Rental** (Cancún Airport,

tel. 998/253-6100; Flamingo Plaza, Blvd. Kukulcán Km 11.5, tel. 998/883-0160, www.america-carrental.com)

- **Avis** (Cancún Airport, tel. 998/886-0221; La Isla Shopping Village, Blvd. Kukulcán Km 12.5, tel. 998/883-1436, www.avis.com)

- **Easy Way** (Cancún Airport, toll-free Mex. tel. 800/327-9929, toll-free U.S./Can. tel. 877/640-3279, www.easywayrentacar.com)

- **Hertz** (Cancún Airport, tel. 999/999-8040; La Isla Shopping Village, Blvd. Kukulcán Km 12.5, tel. 999/118-040, www.hertz.com)

- **National** (Cancún Airport, tel. 998/277-2796; La Isla Shopping Village, Blvd. Kukulcán Km 12.5, tel. 998/176-8117, www.nationalcar.com)

- **Thrifty** (Cancún Airport, tel. 998/886-0333; Westin Resort & Spa, Blvd. Kukulcán Km 20, tel. 998/885-0086, www.thrifty.com)

Parking lots in the Zona Hotelera are in the shopping centers: La Isla Shopping Village, Forum by the Sea, Plaza Kukulcán, Plaza Caracol, and Puerto Cancún Marina Town Center. Rates are typically US$1 for the first hour and US$0.50 for each additional hour. Downtown, it's easiest—and relatively safe—to park on the street or in the public lots around Parque Las Palapas.

Travel Agencies

Most travelers handle their travel and hotel bookings online, but there are still a handful of travel agencies in Cancún for anyone who finds a need for their service—look especially on Avenidas Tulum and Uxmal. Worth noting is **American Express** (Plaza Las Americas, Av. Tulum at Av. Sayil, tel. 998/881-4000, 9am-5pm Mon.-Fri., 9am-1pm Sat.), which has special services for cardholders.

Isla Mujeres

Just 8 kilometers (5 miles) long and no more than 0.4 kilometers (0.25 mi) wide, Isla Mujeres is a sliver of land fringed by white-sand beaches amid the turquoise sea. It actually was one of the first places in the Mexican Caribbean to have hotels and other tourist developments, but attention quickly shifted to Isla Cozumel and then Cancún proper. It may have been a blessing in disguise: As those areas exploded, rushing to build high-rise hotels and ports for cruise ships, Isla Mujeres developed more slowly, attracting backpackers and bohemians while remaining pretty much what it always was—a quiet, picturesque fishing community.

Of course, even slow change adds up, and today Isla Mujeres is a well-established tourist destination. Thousands of day-trippers come from Cancún to shop, eat, and relax on the island's calm beaches. While still popular with backpackers, Isla Mujeres now also attracts midrange and upscale travelers

with a solid selection of boutique hotels and bed-and-breakfasts.

Despite higher hotel prices and T-shirt shops, golf carts, and sometimes pushy tour operators, Isla Mujeres remains at its core a mellow tropical island with a friendly and laid-back population. Passersby greet one another, people stroll in the middle of the street, and many businesses close for long lunches. Add to that beautiful beaches and numerous options for snorkeling, biking, and other outdoor excursions, and it's no wonder so many visitors find themselves extending (and re-extending) their time here.

The precise origin of the name Isla Mujeres (Island of Women) is unknown, though not for lack of theories. Some say the name comes from the days of pirates trolling the Caribbean; they allegedly kept their female captives on Isla Mujeres while they ransacked boats sailing along the coast. Another more likely story is that the island served as

Isla Mujeres

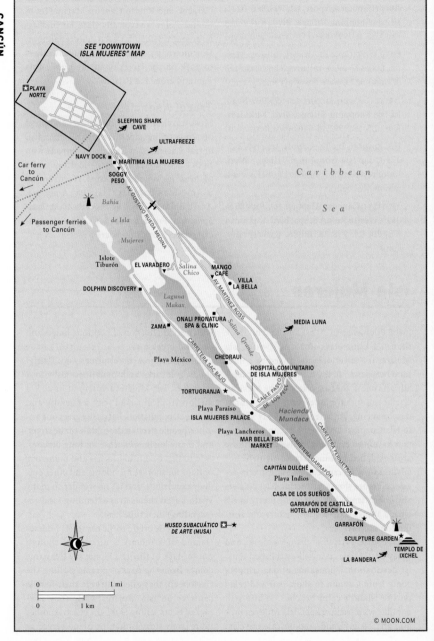

SEE "DOWNTOWN ISLA MUJERES" MAP

★ PLAYA NORTE

SLEEPING SHARK CAVE

ULTRAFREEZE

Car ferry to Cancún

NAVY DOCK ■ ▼ MARÍTIMA ISLA MUJERES

SOGGY PESO

Bahía

↙ Passenger ferries to Cancún

de Isla

Mujeres

Islote Tiburón

EL VARADERO ▼ *Salina Chico*

MANGO CAFÉ ▼

VILLA LA BELLA ●

DOLPHIN DISCOVERY ■

Laguna Makax

AV GUSTAVO RUEDA MEDINA

AV MARTÍNEZ ROSS

Salina Grande

ZAMA ■

ONALI PRONATURA SPA & CLINIC ■

MEDIA LUNA

CARRETERA SAC BAJO

Playa México

CHEDRAUI ■

HOSPITAL COMUNITARIO DE ISLA MUJERES

CALLE PASEO DE LOS PECE

TORTUGRANJA ★

Playa Paraíso
ISLA MUJERES PALACE

Haciénda Mundaca

Playa Lancheros
MAR BELLA FISH MARKET

CARRETERA GARRAFÓN

CARRETERA PERIMETRAL

CAPITÁN DULCHÉ ■
Playa Indios

CASA DE LOS SUEÑOS

GARRAFÓN DE CASTILLA HOTEL AND BEACH CLUB

GARRAFÓN ★

MUSEO SUBACUÁTICO DE ARTE (MUSA) ★

SCULPTURE GARDEN ★

TEMPLO DE IXCHEL

LA BANDERA

Caribbean

Sea

0   1 mi
0   1 km

© MOON.COM

a stopover (or secondary site) for Maya pilgrims on their way to Isla Cozumel to worship Ixchel, the female goddess of fertility. When Spanish explorers landed here, they reportedly found a large number of female-shaped clay idols and named the island after them.

ORIENTATION

The town of Isla Mujeres (known as the *centro,* or center) is at the far northwestern tip of the island; at just eight blocks long and five blocks deep, it is very walkable. This is where most of the hotels, restaurants, shops, and services are. There is no main street per se, although Avenida Hidalgo intersects with the town *zócalo* (central plaza) and has a bustling pedestrian-only section. Avenida Rueda Medina is the busy street that runs along the south side of the *centro* past the ferry piers and continues all the way to the island's other end, becoming Carretera Punta Sur at Garrafón (and therefore also known as Carretera Garrafón). The road that runs along the north side of the island is Avenida Martínez Ross as it leaves the downtown area, becoming Carretera Perimetral partway down the island.

SIGHTS

Hacienda Mundaca

A dilapidated estate, **Hacienda Mundaca** (Av. Rueda Medina at Carr. Garrafón Km 3.5, no phone, 9am-4pm daily, US$1) is not interesting enough to visit, but is just historical enough that tourism folks (including guidebook authors) can't just ignore it. It was built by a 19th-century retired slave trader, Antonio Mundaca, to woo a local woman. Legend has it that when she rejected his advances, Mundaca went crazy, holing up in the estate until it crumbled around him . . . and that's pretty much where things stand today: You'll find a small home, the platforms of a Maya ruin, two caged crocs, a lagoon, and lots and lots of mosquitoes.

Tortugranja

A modest sea turtle sanctuary on the island's southwestern shore, **Tortugranja** (Carr. Sac Bajo 5, tel. 998/877-0595, 9am-5pm daily, US$3) makes for an interesting stop on your golf-cart tour of the island. The one-room cement structure contains several enclosures with sea turtles of different ages and species. The tank of just-hatched *tortuguitas* is always a hit; please respect the rules (and huge signs) and refrain from touching or picking them up. Small aquariums along the walls also contain sea anemones, sea horses, lionfish, and the deadly rockfish, among others. Outside there are three tanks with more turtles as well as a large fenced-in area of the ocean that is home to a nurse shark. During the nesting season (May-October), one section of sand is fenced off, and eggs collected from nests are transplanted here for protection.

Between July and November, travelers may be able to accompany the center's workers to look for fresh sea turtle nests on the island's eastern shore and relocate eggs to protected areas, and, until October and November, help release hatchlings into the sea. Both activities take place in the evening several nights a week, typically starting around 9pm, but are not formal tours. Those interested should inquire at the center; having basic Spanish skills (and possibly your own vehicle) will make participating much easier. There's no charge, but a tip is customary.

★ Museo Subacuático de Arte (MUSA)

Underwater sculpture is nothing new, but there's never been a project as ambitious—or as gorgeous, frankly—as the **Museo Subacuático de Arte** (MUSA, www.musacancun.org). British sculptor Jason de Caires Taylor, along with four Mexican sculptors (Karen Salinas Martínez, Roberto Díaz Abraham, Rodrigo Quiñones Reyes, and Salvador Quiroz Ennis) and one Cuban artist (Elier Amado Gil), created hundreds of life-size statues of everyday people—garbagemen, pregnant women, wizened tribal leaders, and more—and sank them in two separate sites; one is near Cancún's Nizuc reef (approximately 12 feet deep), the other

Downtown Isla Mujeres

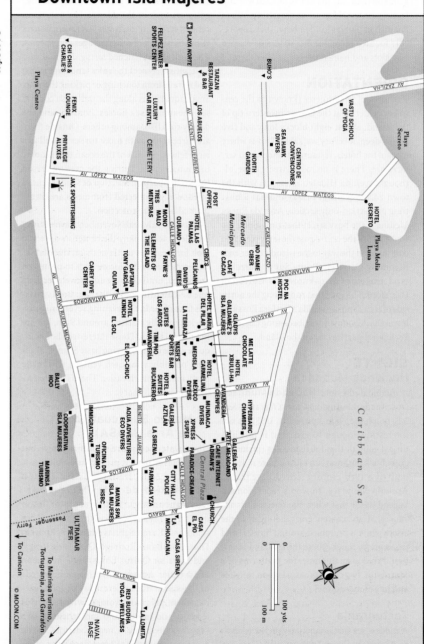

CHI CHIS &
CHARLIE'S

FELIPEZ WATER
SPORTS CENTER

Playa Centro

FENIX
LOUNGE

PRIVILEGE
ALUXES

JAX SPORTSFISHING

AV LÓPEZ MATEOS

LUXURY
CAR RENTAL

CEMETERY

AV VICENTE GUERRERO

PLAYA NORTE

TARZAN
RESTAURANT
& BAR

LOS ABUELOS

BUHO'S

NORTH
GARDEN

CENTRO DE
CONVENCIONES

SEA HAWK
DIVERS

VASTU SCHOOL
OF YOGA

AV ZAZIL-HA

Playa
Secreto

Playa Media
Luna

HOTEL
SECRETO

AV LÓPEZ MATEOS

AV CARLOS LAZO

POST
OFFICE

TRES
MALO

MENTIRAS

MONO

QUBANO

CALLE HIDALGO

HOTEL LAS
PALMAS

FAYNE'S

ELEMENTS OF
THE ISLAND

CIRO'S

PELICANOS

DAVID'S

Mercado
Municipal

CAFÉ
& CACAO

NO NAME
CIBER

AV MATAMOROS

AV GUSTAVO RUEDA MEDINA

CAPTAIN
TONY GARCIA

OLIVIA'S

CAREY DIVE
CENTER

AV MATAMOROS

HOTEL
KINICH

EL SOL

SUITES
LOS ARCOS

LA TERRAZA

TIM PHO
LAVANDERIA

EL POC-CHUC

NASH'S
SPORTS BAR

HOTEL &
SUITES
BUCANEROS

MEDISLA

BIKES

HOTEL MARIA
DEL PILAR

GLADYS
GALDAMEZ

ISLA MUJERES

AV ABASOLO

POC NA
HOSTEL

ME LATTE
CHOCOLATE

HOTEL
CARMELINA

HOTEL
XBULU-HA

LAVANDERIA

CIENPIES

MÉXICO
DIVERS

AV MADERO

MUNDACA
DIVERS

HYPERBARIC
CHAMBER

GALERIA DE
ARTE MEXICANO

Caribbean Sea

BALLY
HOO

COOPERATIVA
ISLA MUJERES

IMMIGRATION

AQUA ADVENTURES
ECO DIVERS

OFICINA DE
TURISMO

HSBC

MARINSA
TURISMO

ULTRAMAR
PIER

Passenger Ferry

To Cancún

GALERIA
AZTLAN

LA SIRENA

BENITO JUAREZ

AV MORELOS

MAYAN SPA
ISLA MUJERES

AV ALLENDE

XPRESS
SUPER

PARADICE-CREAM

FARMACIA YZA

CAFE INTERNET
ADRIAN'S

CALLE HIDALGO

Central Plaza

CITY HALL/
POLICE

AV BRAVO

LA
MICHOACANA

CASA SIRENA

RED BUDDHA
YOGA + WELLNESS

NAVAL
BASE

CHURCH

CASA
EL JIO

LA LOMITA

0   100 yds

0   100 m

To Marinsa Turismo,
Tortugranja, and Garrafón

© MOON.COM

near Isla Mujeres's Manchones reef (approximately 24 feet deep). Striking for their lifelike quality, the figures were made from a special cement that will promote coral and other sealife, eventually forming an artificial reef system. Most dive shops offer dive and snorkeling trips to both sites.

Templo de Ixchel and Sculpture Garden

At the far southern tip of the island, a crumbling Maya temple stands on a cliff overlooking the sea. Its original function is unknown: The location suggests it was an observation post or even an astronomical observatory, but most experts believe it was related to Ixchel, the Maya goddess of the moon, fertility, weaving, and childbirth, possibly as a secondary pilgrimage site after Isla Cozumel. Whatever its history, the temple was abandoned long before Francisco Hernández de Córdoba first reported its existence in 1517.

The temple alone isn't too exciting, as time and weather have all but destroyed it. But a visit here also includes pondering a dozen or so multicolored modern sculptures lining the path to the ruins as well as enjoying an oceanside trail past the ruins that continues to the very tip of the island—the easternmost point of Mexico, in fact—before looping back along the craggy waterfront to the entrance. It's a decent side trip, with some fine photo ops along the way.

Admission to the Ixchel ruins is included in the ticket price to Garrafón park; all others must pay US$1.50 (9am-5pm daily).

★ Isla Contoy

Peeking out of a crystal-clear sea and dotted with saltwater lagoons, mangroves, and coconut palms, Isla Contoy is home to over 150 species of birds, including herons, brown pelicans, frigates, and cormorants, and is a preferred nesting ground for three different species of endangered sea turtles. The island was decreed a national park in 1998, and its only structures are a three-story viewing tower, a visitors center, and a small museum; a few trails allow for appreciating the otherwise pristine island environment. Just 24 kilometers (14 miles) north of Isla Mujeres, Isla Contoy is a popular and rewarding outing for nature buffs and average day-trippers alike.

Various tour operators on Isla Mujeres offer the same basic trip for a standard price (US$75-100, including the park entrance fee): Depart around 9am with a 30-45-minute stop for snorkeling along the way, then three hours to explore the island or just relax, including lunch on the beach (typically freshly grilled fish or chicken). Boats head back around 3pm, reaching Isla Mujeres at 4pm.

Recommended operators include **Captain Tony García** (Av. Matamoros near Av. Benito Juárez, tel. 998/877-0229, captaintonys@ hotmail.com), a friendly English-speaking guide with over 25 years' experience whose house doubles as his office, and **Cooperativa Isla Mujeres** (end of Av. Madero at Pier 7, cell tel. 998/198-0893, www.islamujerestours. mx, 7am-7pm daily).

BEACHES

TOP EXPERIENCE

★ Playa Norte

Playa Norte (North Beach) is a long, undulating strip of sand on the northern edge of Isla Mujeres. Its fine white sands descend ever so slowly into a gorgeous turquoise sea—you can wade almost a hundred yards out and still be only waist deep. The long, shallow shelf means Playa Norte has virtually no waves, adding to the beach's tranquility. It's a favorite spot for visitors of all ages: couples sunning themselves and sipping margaritas, backpackers on colorful beach towels, kids frolicking in the calm water, and older travelers relaxing under huge umbrellas.

You can rent beach chairs and umbrellas at a number of spots along Playa Norte, including **Buho's** (end of Av. Carlos Lazo, no phone, US$4.50 chair, US$4.50 umbrella); **Chi Chis & Charlie's** (southwestern end of Playa Norte,

Island Murals

Mercado Municipal on Isla Mujeres

It's impossible to miss the massive ocean-themed murals dotting Isla Mujeres, their vibrant, colorful designs adorning seawalls, hotel exteriors, even city hall. They extend up to a half block long or several stories high, and range from highly realistic to psychedelic to abstract modern to urban street art. The murals are the work of various artists belonging to **PangeaSeed** (www. pangeaseed.org), a nonprofit organization that uses education and "artivism" to promote marine conservation worldwide. In 2014, Isla Mujeres became one of several communities selected for the group's "Sea Walls for Oceans" mural project; others are in Florida, New Zealand, Vietnam, Sri Lanka, and elsewhere. Of course, Mexico was once a muralist's mecca, the birthplace and inspiration of world-famous painters like Diego Rivera, José Orozco, and David Siqueiros. The murals in Isla Mujeres are not only gorgeous and impactful, but are a refreshing revival of the art form, connecting the greats of the early 20th century to contemporary street artists like Banksy and Shepard Fairey.

no phone, US$12 chair and umbrella); **Tarzan Restaurant & Bar** (end of Av. Guerrero at Playa Norte, tel. 998/877-0679, US$11.50 chair and umbrella); and **Fenix Lounge** (end of Av. Rueda Medina, tel. 998/274-0073, www. fenixisla.com, US$12 chair and umbrella, US$25 beach bed).

Tarzan Restaurant & Bar (end of Av. Guerrero at Playa Norte, tel. 998/877-0679) also rents snorkel gear (US$10/day), single and double kayaks (US$15-20/hour), Hobie Cats (US$45/hour), and stand-up paddleboards (US$12.50/hour) and can arrange snorkel tours (US$30 pp, 2 hours). **FeliPez Water**

Sports Center (end of Av. Hidalgo at Playa Norte, tel. 998/593-3403) rents the same gear at similar prices.

Playa Centro

Around the corner from Playa Norte, Playa Centro (aka Playa Sol) is also lovely, with deeper water and a wider beach than Playa Norte's. One end of the beach is packed with fishing boats, while the other is cordoned off for use by guests at a nearby resort and day-trippers from Cancún. That said, there's still a large section in the middle where you can stretch out a towel. Lounge chairs and umbrellas also can be rented here for US$10-15 for the day.

Playa Secreto

East of Playa Norte (around the *other* corner), Playa Secreto sits on a wide lagoon facing a resort hotel. The water is calm, shallow, and clear, making it a perfect spot for children. This is a popular place for locals, especially on weekends, when extended families come with coolers filled with food and drinks to enjoy a day off.

Other Beaches

Zama (Carr. Sac Bajo s/n, tel. 998/877-0739, www.zamaislamujeres.com, 10am-6pm daily) is a small beach club on the island's calm southwest shore that's a popular wedding spot, if that gives you an idea of how pretty it is. You can relax in a comfy beach bed on the well-tended beach or in a hammock in the shady garden. The sand is a bit thin and there's seagrass in the shallows, but you can swim comfortably from the long pier or in one of the two appealing mosaic-tiled pools. The classy open-air restaurant is reasonably priced and has everything from burritos to shrimp dishes, plus a kids menu (US$5-20). There's no admission or minimum consumption, but they charge US$10 for use of the lounge chairs, US$25 for the beach beds.

Capitán Dulché (Carr. Sac Bajo s/n, tel. 998/355-0012, www.capitandulche.com, 10am-6pm Mon.-Wed., 10am-8pm Thurs.-Sun., US$15) is a beach club with a relaxed marina feel. It's divided into three sections—a well-tended beach with calm waters and *palapa* shade, a wide grassy area with antique anchors and thick tow chains, and a modern beachfront restaurant (US$8-17) with a solid menu of international dishes. Be sure to check out the bar that also happens to be housed in a repurposed sailboat. There's a small nautical museum on-site, too—good if you're interested in model sailboats. Admission is applied as credit towards food and drinks. Poolside cabanas and oceanfront *palapas* also can be rented (US$17-23, including towels and two drinks).

SPORTS AND RECREATION
Scuba Diving

Beginner divers will appreciate the calm waters and vibrant sealife on Isla Mujeres's western side, while the east side presents more challenging options for advanced divers, with deeper water (up to 40 meters/131 feet), more varied terrain, and even a couple of shipwrecks. Favorite sites include La Bandera (a reef dive), Media Luna (a drift dive), Ultrafreeze (a shipwreck, in notoriously chilly water), and the famous Sleeping Shark Cave—a deep cave known to attract sharks, where they fall into a strangely lethargic and nonaggressive state. Explanations for this last phenomenon vary: Salinity of the water, low carbon dioxide, and underwater currents are some theories. Unfortunately, overfishing (and overdiving) has disrupted the slumber party, and there's only a 50-50 chance, at best, of seeing sharks on any given day. When sharks are seen, they're typically nurse sharks these days. September seems to be the best month to spot them, but you just never know.

Isla Mujeres's dive shops charge fairly uniform rates: US$65-70 one tank, US$80-90 two tanks. Gear and marine park admission is sometimes included; otherwise, an additional US$10-20 per day is tacked on. The Sleeping Shark Cave and deep dives run a little higher, and most shops offer multi-dive specials. Open-water certification courses cost around US$395, including equipment and materials.

Aqua Adventures Eco Divers (Av. Juárez at Calle Morelos, cell tel. 998/322-8109, www.diveislamujeres.com, 9am-7pm Mon.-Sat., 10am-6pm Sun.) goes the extra mile to provide friendly, professional service.

Carey Dive Center (Av. Matamoros near Av. Rueda Medina, tel. 998/877-0763, www.careydivecenter.com, 8am-8pm daily) is a recommended dive shop that enjoys lots of repeat customers.

México Divers (Av. Madero at Av. Hidalgo, tel. 998/877-1117, www.mexicodivers. com, 8am-8pm daily) is a popular dive shop with a youthful vibe.

Mundaca Divers (Av. Madero 10, tel. 998/877-0607, www.mundacadivers islamujeres.com, 8am-8pm daily) has been in business for more than 35 years, making it one of the longest standing and well-respected operations in the region.

Sea Hawk Divers (Av. Carlos Lazo at Av. López Mateos, tel. 998/877-1233, www. seahawkislamujeres.com, 9am-8pm daily) is a recommended dive shop owned and run by island locals Ariel and Bonnie Barandica. Sea Hawk has a half-dozen comfortable rooms and studios attached to the dive shop, which are often included as part of dive packages.

Snorkeling

Isla Mujeres's western side has calm water and extensive coral reefs that make for excellent snorkeling, though relatively few spots are accessible from the shore. Snorkeling tours can be booked at **dive shops** or with the **Cooperativa Isla Mujeres** (end of Av. Madero at Pier 7, cell tel. 998/198-0893, www. islamujerestours.com.mx, 7am-7pm daily). Most operators take snorkelers to El Farito (The Lighthouse) and other spots near the northern end of the island, where the coral is decent but somewhat trafficked; tours run around US$25-35 per person. Dive shops are more likely to take you to less-visited spots.

You can also arrange to snorkel at **Museo Subacuático de Arte** (MUSA), the remarkable underwater sculpture park near Manchones reef, at the southern end of the island. Dive shops and other operators charge around US$40-45 per person for a trip combining MUSA and one other spot.

Yet another option is to take a trip to **Isla Contoy** (US$75-100 pp), which includes snorkeling on Ixlanche reef in addition to exploring the island. Boats depart Isla Mujeres around 9am and return at 4pm.

Snorkel on your own at **Garrafón de Castilla Hotel and Beach Club** (Carr. Punta Sur Km 6, tel. 998/877-0107, 10am-5pm daily, US$3.50), at the southern tip of the island. The club itself is pretty desultory, but you can explore over 300 meters (894 feet) of coral reef, including the part used by its much-hyped neighbor, Garrafón. Snorkel gear rents for US$5, and lockers and towels can be rented for around US$1.50 each.

TOP EXPERIENCE

Whale Shark Tours

Snorkeling with whale sharks, the world's largest fish, is an experience you won't soon forget. These gentle giants congregate along the northeastern tip of the Yucatán Peninsula mid-May-mid-September and typically measure 6-7.5 meters (20-25 feet) and weigh more than 10 tons. (They're known to grow upwards of 18 meters, or nearly 60 feet, though such behemoths are rare here.) From Isla Mujeres, whale shark tours leave around 8am for a 60-90-minute boat ride northwest past Isla Contoy toward Isla Holbox (where such tours first became popular). Once in the feeding grounds, you'll see the huge sharks trolling along the surface, feeding on krill. The boat is maneuvered nearby the shark, and a guide plus two guests slip overboard and swim alongside. The sharks are surprisingly fast, despite their languid appearance, and you have to kick hard to keep up and get a good look at their sleek spotted bodies and massive gaping mouths. The smaller your group, the more chances you'll have to get into the water, though most people welcome the short breathers between turns. Rules also require that boats not linger with any one shark more than 30 minutes; in all, each guest can expect to have 2-4 chances to jump in. Lunch and beverages are included. Boats typically return to Isla Mujeres by 3pm.

Cooperativa Isla Mujeres (end of Av. Madero at Pier 7, cell tel. 998/198-0893, www.

1: Playa Norte on Isla Mujeres; 2: shopping for *artesanía* on Isla Mujeres; 3: brown pelicans on Isla Contoy; 4: Garrafón's seaside walkway islamujerestours.com.mx, 7am-7pm daily) handles most whale shark tours, charging around US$125 per person. Most **dive shops** in Isla Mujeres also offer whale shark tours, charging around US$150 per person. Always confirm the departure times, how long the tour will last, and whether lunch and water are provided.

Swimming with Dolphins

Dolphin Discovery (end of Carr. Sac Bajo, toll-free Mex. tel. 800/727-5391, toll-free U.S. tel. 866/393-5158, www.dolphindiscovery. com, US$109-199 adult, US$89-119 child) offers various dolphin interaction programs on the island's calm western shore, as well as ones with manatees and sea lions. Garrafón, a nearby sister park with snorkeling, zip lines, and more, has packages combining Dolphin Discovery programs with admission to Garrafón, a good option if you'd like to make a day of it. Most visitors come from Cancún on Dolphin Discovery's private ferry (included in the price), though no transport is provided for guests staying on Isla Mujeres. Reservations required.

Ecoparks

Built on a bluff at the southern end of Isla Mujeres, **Garrafón** (Carr. Garrafón Km 6, tel. 998/849-4748, toll-free U.S. tel. 866/393-5158, www.garrafon.com, 10am-6pm daily, US$89-189 adult, US$59-99 child) is a combo ecopark and water park. There's snorkeling, kayaking, zip-lining, an interactive dolphin program (conducted at Dolphin Discovery, a nearby sister park), and, of course, just relaxing on the beach or by the pool. Ferry service to and from Cancún is included, as well as admission to Templo de Ixchel, a tiny Maya ruin.

Sportfishing

Cooperativa Isla Mujeres (end of Av. Madero at Pier 7, cell tel. 998/198-0893, www. islamujerestours.com.mx, 7am-7pm daily) offers *pesca deportiva* (sportfishing) at reasonable prices. Boats typically carry up to six people for the same price, and prices include nonalcoholic drinks, sandwiches, and bait. Two trips are usually available, depending on the season: Pesca Mediana (US$330, 4 hours) focuses on midsize fish, including snapper, grouper, and barracuda; and Pesca Mayor (US$500, 6 hours) goes after large catch such as marlin and sailfish. Reserve directly at the pier. **Sea Hawk Divers** (Av. Carlos Lazo at Av. López Mateos, tel. 998/877-1233,

Snorkeling with whale sharks is a one-of-a-kind experience.

www.seahawkislamujeres.com, 9am-8pm daily) offers comparable services and prices.

JAX Sportfishing (JAX Bar and Grill, Av. López Mateos at Av. Rueda Medina, tel. 998/877-1254, www.jaxsportfishing.com, US$950) has an experienced English-speaking captain and offers all-day charters for a maximum of four anglers, ensuring highly personalized service.

Spas

Just one block from the ferry terminal, **Mayan Spa Isla Mujeres** (Av. Morelos near Av. Rueda Medina, tel. 998/257-4614, www.themayanspaislamujeres.com.mx, 10am-8pm Mon.-Sat.) is a small family-owned spa offering top-rated massages and body treatments. It's nothing fancy, but it's welcoming and professional.

Onali Pronatura Spa & Clinic (Calle Cayo Ratón s/n, tel. 998/240-5524, 10am-6pm Mon.-Sat.) is a full-service spa offering a wide range of massages, body treatments, and facials in a serene setting near the Salina Grande lagoon.

Yoga

Red Buddha Yoga + Wellness (Av. Juárez 22, tel. 984/159-5508, www.redbuddhayoga.com, US$7.50 class) is an upscale yoga studio and spa offering a cozy indoor studio and breezy thatch-roofed studio for instruction. Vinyasa, hatha, power, yin, and slow flow are among the classes offered. Body treatments like massages, reiki, and acupuncture are also available.

Vastu School of Yoga (Calle Zazil-Ha 118, tel. 866/719-2138, www.vastuyoga.com, US$15 class) offers yoga instruction in a breezy *palapa* studio at Na Balam Hotel. Classes are held daily at 9am, 11am, and 6pm; Monday and Thursday, there's also a class at 7:15pm. Workshops and private sessions also are available.

Yoga classes at **Poc Na Hostel** (Av. Matamoros near Av. Lazo, tel. 998/877-0090) are open to the public every morning at 9am. The price—US$5—can't be beat.

ENTERTAINMENT AND EVENTS

Isla Mujeres's nightlife ranges from beach bars to sports bars. Fortunately, the town is small enough that you can wander about until you find the scene that suits you best.

Bars

On the pedestrian walkway, **Tres Mentiras** (Av. Hidalgo s/n, no tel., 5pm-1am daily) is a colorful little restaurant-cantina serving up creative cocktails, many made with mezcal. Combos like kiwi with ginger beer, pineapple with coriander and jalapeño, even popcorn are commonplace. (You also can get a pint of locally made craft beer.) It's popular with just about everyone, so get here on the early side if you want a seat. There's live music on weekends.

Sitting pretty on Playa Norte, **Fenix Lounge** (end of Av. Rueda Medina, tel. 998/274-0073, www.fenixisla.com, 11am-11pm Mon.-Sat., 11am-8pm Sun) is a classic beach club that transforms into a lively bar scene around sunset. A changing lineup of DJs typically keeps the crowd happy, either on the dance floor or at their seats. Sundays bring salsa dancing and occasional live music.

Nash's Sports Bar (Av. Hidalgo s/n, tel. 998/705-9005, 9am-midnight daily) is a dive bar with at least eight TVs tuned to the big game of the day pretty much every day. A favorite of American expats, you'll find cheap buckets of beer, wings, and a friendly crowd. Nash himself is often on-site, checking in on guests

Soggy Peso (Av. Gustavo Rueda Medina, tel. 998/274-0050, www.soggypeso.net, 9am-8pm daily) is a favorite for daytime drinkin' Americans, open early and closed not long after sunset (the view, by the way, is terrific here). The vibe is casual and jocular, and every day there's a different special from the kitchen: Hot Wings Wednesdays, BBQ Sundays, and so forth. It's located south of the center, on the waterfront.

Live Music

La Terraza (Av. Hidalgo at Av. Abasolo, tel. 998/236-3879, 11am-midnight daily, no cover) has great live salsa, cumbia, and other Latin dance music most nights after 10pm. Drinks here are excellent—try the watermelon and jalapeño margarita for something with a kick—and the food isn't bad, but it's the music and lively atmosphere that draw folks in, night after night.

Fayne's (Av. Hidalgo 12, tel. 998/877-0525, 5pm-midnight daily, no cover) features live nightly music, mostly Caribbean but with a smattering of rock and reggae acts as well. The high *palapa* roof and spacious bar area make it equally suited for dancing or just chilling out. Thursday-Sunday are the busiest nights, often with two bands starting as early as 6pm; otherwise, things get hopping around 10:30pm.

SHOPPING

It's easy to be put off by the onslaught of kitschy souvenir shops that greet you as soon as you step off the ferry. But fear not: Isla Mujeres has a number of genuinely good specialty stores, especially for Mexican *artesanía*, if you keep your eyes open.

Located in a Caribbean clapboard house, **Galería Aztlán** (Av. Hidalgo at Av. Madero, cell tel. 998/110-3782, 9am-9pm Mon.-Sat.) sells gorgeous Mexican masks from every corner of the country. The owners, transplants from Mexico City, also design specialty T-shirts and religious art.

Mono Malo (Av. Hidalgo between Avs. Lopez Mateos and Matamoros, no phone, www.monomalo.com.mx, 2pm-10pm daily) specializes in original high-end T-shirts, most inspired by Mexican skeleton art, revolution heroes, and *lucha libre* (wrestling) stars. Check out the website to shop the store's entire line.

Galería de Arte Mexicano (Parque Central, Av. Guerrero 3, tel. 998/877-1272, 10am-8pm daily) has fine Talavera pottery as well as an extensive selection of silver jewelry. The prices are somewhat higher here than elsewhere, but so is the quality.

Specializing in beachwear, **Gladys**

Galdamez's Isla Mujeres (Abasolo 40, cell tel. 998/147-1115, ggaldamez59@hotmail.com, 9am-6pm Mon-Fri., noon-6pm Sat.) sells everything from swimsuits and cover-ups to flip-flops and seashell jewelry. The shop makes custom bathing suits for women—choose from a huge variety of patterns or bring your own.

La Sirena (Av. Morelos near Av. Hidalgo, tel. 998/877-0223, 10am-6pm Mon.-Sat.) is a tiny shop that's jam-packed with high-quality folk art from all over Mexico: textiles from Chiapas, masks from Guerrero, skeleton art from Mexico City, and *alebrijes* (wooden creatures) from Oaxaca.

FOOD

Seafood is the specialty in Isla Mujeres, even more so than in Cancún. In fact, much of the lobster and fish served on the Riviera Maya is caught near Isla Mujeres, so it stands to reason that it's freshest here.

Mexican

Don't be put off by its garish mural with fluorescent fish: **El Poc-Chuc** (Calle Abasolo at Av. Juárez, tel. 998/152-2613, 7:30am-10:30pm Tues.-Sun., US$3-8) serves up delicious Mexican food, especially for breakfast. The setting is old-school, with plastic tables and chairs crammed into a tiny dining room. Service is fast, though, which makes rubbing elbows (literally) with your neighbor no big deal.

La Lomita (Av. Juárez near Av. Allende, tel. 998/826-6335, 9:30am-10:30pm daily, US$5-9), a brightly painted restaurant frequented by locals, offers tasty Mexican fare. *Comida corrida*—a two-course lunch special with drink—is offered daily and often includes chiles rellenos, tacos, and stews. Ceviche, grilled whole fish, and other seafood meals also are featured at reasonable prices.

Though somewhat sterile in decor, the verdant outdoor café **North Garden** (Av. Carlos Lazo 14, tel. 998/151-6130, 7am-5pm daily, US$5-8) serves excellent Mexican dishes with flair: tostadas topped with ahi tuna, chicken tacos with pineapple and guacamole, sizzling chicken fajitas. There's also a good variety of salads, if you're hankering for something lighter. Drinks—both alcoholic on nonalcoholic—are not to be missed. The basil mint lemonade is a fan favorite.

Mercado Municipal (Av. Guerrero at Av. Matamoros, 6am-4pm daily, US$2-4) has a handful of simple eateries that serve good cheap meals. On Sunday, *cochinita pibil* (slow-roasted pork marinated in achiote sauce and wrapped in banana leaves) is offered at a handful of stands. Get there by 9am to enjoy some before it sells out.

Seafood

Bally Hoo (Av. Rueda Medina near Av. Abasolo, cell tel. 998/214-5805, 6am-10pm daily, US$5-11) may be stuck behind a gas station, but the Baja-style breaded fish tacos are to die for, and well worth any necessary searching. The fish-and-chips are great, too, and if you've got an appetite, the fish fillet or shrimp dishes are filling. Cold beers and margaritas are the perfect accompaniment.

★ **Mar Bella Fish Market** (Perímetral Poniente 80, cell tel. 998/577-8318, noon-8pm daily, US$12-40) is a swanky seafood restaurant, set on a gorgeous beach halfway down the island, that sells everything by the kilo. There's no menu. Instead, diners peruse the fresh fish and seafood on offer (all beautifully displayed on ice or in tanks) and are given suggestions of possible made-to-order dishes. Service is tops.

Los Abuelos (Av. Guerrero s/n, tel. 998/156-5689, 1pm-10pm Mon.-Sat., US$5-9) is a family-run restaurant serving up all manner of seafood dishes. The specialties are coconut shrimp and grilled lobster tail but the menu features everything from ceviche to fried fish. Takeout is available and a popular option for picnicking, especially because Playa Norte is just a half block away.

Other Specialties

Upscale but homey, ★ **Olivia** (Av. Matamoros between Calle Juárez and Av. Rueda Medina, tel. 998/877-1765, www.olivia-isla-mujeres.

com, 5pm-9:45pm Mon.-Sat., US$7-18) serves up the best Mediterranean cuisine on the island. Owned by an Israeli couple who pooled their families' recipes and opened shop, the menu is a phenomenal amalgam of specialties from Morocco, Greece, Bulgaria, and Turkey. Seating is either in the *palapa*-roofed dining room or in the lush garden courtyard. Reservations are recommended. Cash only.

A farm-to-table eatery, ★ **Café & Cacao** (Av. Matamoros s/n, tel. 503/475-5596, 9am-1pm and 6pm-9:30pm daily, US$6-11) serves gorgeous and creative meals, many of which are vegan and gluten-free. The menu is seasonal and almost entirely organic. Breakfasts range from granola bowls to free-range egg dishes, while dinner often features lionfish and edible flowers. There's also freshly made baked goods (the quinoa bread is to die for), homemade cheeses, and a variety of coffee, teas and freshly pressed juices.

Qubano (Av. Hidalgo between Avs. Matamoros and Mateos, cell tel. 998/214-2118, noon-10pm Mon.-Sat., US$10-15) is a colorful place with a tasty selection of Cuban sandwiches, burgers, and salads. Favorites include the Tostón (plantain slices stuffed with chicken, pork, or *picadillo*), the Cuban (grilled ham, pork, and cheese), and the goat-cheese-stuffed burger. Snag a table and enjoy a Cuban coffee while you wait, or take your eats to go.

In a clapboard house facing the lagoon, with fishing boats crowded next to it, **El Varadero** (Calle de Septiembre s/n, tel. 998/877-1600, 1pm-8pm Tues.-Sun., US$10-19) doesn't really evoke the famous white-sand beach east of Havana that it's named for, but good food—and even better mojitos—have a way of trumping geography. Dig into classic Cuban fare while sitting at aluminum tables on an outdoor patio decorated with shipping buoys. Find it at the mouth of Laguna Makax, near Puerto Isla Mujeres.

Cafés

Located partway down the island, ★ **Mango Café** (Carr. Perimentral at Calle Payo Obispo, tel. 998/274-0118, 7am-3pm Tues.-Wed., 7am-9pm Thurs.-Mon., US$6-14) has a cheerful bohemian exterior that practically begs a closer look. You'll be glad you did: Dishes like coconut French toast and eggs Benedict with chaya and portabella mushrooms, plus drinks like ginger lemonade and bottomless organic coffee, make this small eatery an island favorite—and that's just breakfast!

Serving up organic products, **Elements of the Island Café** (Av. Juárez between López Mateos and Matamoros, cell tel. 998/117-8651, www.elementsoftheisland.com, 7:30am-1pm Thurs.-Tues., US$4-6) serves up hearty and healthy meals. Breakfasts are especially popular, with homemade bread and marmalade, and cappuccinos to die for.

Me Latte Chocolate (Av. Guerrero 8, tel. 998/236-3879, 7am-6pm Mon.-Sat., US$2.50-6) sells a mouthwatering array of freshly made baked goods, fruit cups, sandwiches, and salads—all to go. There are also loads of smoothies and coffee drinks on offer. It's perfect when you're running to catch the ferry or for a picnic lunch on the beach.

Sweets

La Michoacana (Av. Bravo at Av. Hidalgo, 9am-11pm daily, US$1-2.50) offers homemade *aguas, paletas,* and *helados* (juices, Popsicles, and ice cream). Choose from seasonal fruits including passion fruit, watermelon, pineapple, and mamey. Of course, chocolate- and vanilla-flavored treats are available, too.

Try **ParadICE-CREAM** (Av. Hidalgo at Av. Morelos, 10am-10pm daily, US$2-6) for terrific handmade gelato.

Groceries

For a big supermarket, head to **Chedraui** (www.chedraui.com.mx, 7am-8pm daily), about halfway down the island, across from the baseball diamond. To get there, simply follow Avenida Gustavo Rueda Medina; the supermarket will be on your right, just before a sharp bend known as "devil's curve."

Xpress Super (Av. Morelos 5, www.sanfranciscodeasis.com.mx, 7am-10pm Mon.-Sat., 7am-9pm Sun.) is the island's longtime local grocery store, facing the central plaza.

Mercado Municipal (Av. Guerrero at Av. Matamoros, 6am-4pm daily) has a good selection of fruits, vegetables, and meats, a *tortillería,* plus fresh-squeezed juices sold by the liter.

ACCOMMODATIONS

Isla Mujeres has a wide variety of lodging options, from youth hostels to upscale boutique hotels. Most budget and midrange places are in the *centro,* while higher-end resorts occupy secluded areas farther down the island (which may mean you'll need to rent a golf cart to get around).

Under US$50

Isla Mujeres's longtime backpacker haven, ★ **Poc Na Hostel** (Av. Matamoros near Av. Lazo, tel. 998/877-0090, www.pocna.com, US$6.50 pp camping, US$10 pp dorm, US$11 pp dorm with a/c, US$23 s/d with shared bath, US$27 s/d with a/c) is a labyrinth of rooms, courtyards, and common areas, just steps from the island's best beach. Dorms have 4-9 bunks each and, like the private rooms, have cement floors and whitewashed walls. There's foosball, table tennis, and TV in the various common areas, plus a dining room with basic food service. The hostel hosts live music most nights starting at 9:30pm. The drawbacks are no kitchen access and a serious risk of never leaving.

Hotel Maria del Pilar (aka Posada Mary Pili, Calle Abasolo 15, tel. 998/877-0071, US$45 s/d) is a small, well-located hotel with tidy rooms, most with TVs, air-conditioning, and mini fridges, plus Wi-Fi and a shared outdoor kitchen. Bikes and snorkel gear are available for rent. It's a fine choice for budget travelers who want some of the conveniences of a hostel without the scene.

Hotel Carmelina (Av. Guerrero 4, tel. 998/877-0006, US$25-40 s/d with a/c) is a reliable budget choice. It has a slightly residential-motel feel (the family who runs it lives on the ground floor, and another room houses a manicure shop), but the rooms are clean, albeit small. Each also has a mini fridge, TV, and Wi-Fi.

US$50-100

The charming ★ **Casa El Pío** (Av. Hidalgo near Av. Bravo, tel. 998/229-2799, www. casaelpio.com, US$85-100 s/d with a/c) is a five-room boutique-ish hotel with minimalist decor accented with artful touches and splashes of color. Rooms are spacious and comfortable, with good beds, separate seating areas, balconies (two with ocean views), and Wi-Fi; each also has a mini fridge and a coffeemaker. There's a small mosaic-tile plunge pool for cooling off. Adults only; reservations are highly recommended.

Hotel Kinich (Av. Juárez near Av. Matamoros, tel. 998/888-0909, US$75-90 s/d, US$130 suite) is a great find: Rooms are simple but elegant with warm wood furnishings, muted colors, and Mexican wall art from Guadalajara. All rooms have quiet air-conditioning, cable TV, and Wi-Fi, and more than half of them have king-size beds. Two gorgeous suites occupy the top floor—modern one-bedroom apartments with state-of-the-art kitchens, outdoor whirlpool tubs, and views of town. Continental breakfast is provided. The only downer: The hotel is in a four-story building with no elevator.

Hotel Xbulu-Ha (Av. Guerrero between Avs. Abasolo and Madero, tel. 998/877-1783, www.islamujeres.biz, US$50-60 s/d with a/c, US$70-80 suite with kitchenette and a/c) offers bright and airy rooms with modern amenities like cable TV, mini-split air conditioners, and safety deposit boxes. The beds are double sized—something to consider if you plan on sharing. Suites are larger versions of the standard rooms, with fully equipped kitchenettes and king-size beds. Wi-Fi and beach towels and chairs are included in the rate. The hotel is just one block from the Caribbean.

Hotel & Suites Bucaneros (Av. Hidalgo near Av. Madero, tel. 998/877-1228, www.bucaneros.com, US$85-94 s/d with a/c, US$94 d/t with a/c and kitchenette) has 20 comfortable rooms, all with modern bathrooms, air-conditioning, and Wi-Fi, plus continental breakfast. The budget rooms are quite small, though not uncomfortable, while larger ones have small equipped kitchens (hot plate or gas stove, mini fridge, and toaster) and in some cases a sofa bed, balcony, and separate dining area. The location couldn't be more central, but that also means it can be noisy at night.

US$100-200

Elements of the Island (Av. Juárez between Avs. López Mateos and Matamoros, cell tel. 998/117-8651, www.elementsoftheisland.com, US$114 s/d with a/c) has three lovely studio apartments, each with fine wood furnishings, flowing white curtains, and bursts of color. All rooms have king-size beds and basic kitchenettes, plus Wi-Fi and TVs with DVD players. Guests pass through a leafy courtyard with a gurgling fountain to access the rooms, which are behind the hotel's recommended restaurant. Common spaces include a sundeck with a hot tub, lounge chairs, and hammocks. Kind and attentive owners provide excellent service.

Simple and well located, **Suites Los Arcos** (Av. Hidalgo near Av. Abasolo, tel. 998/877-1343, US$104-126 s/d with a/c) has large, colorful rooms with gleaming bathrooms and heavy wood furnishings. All have a small fridge, microwave, and coffeemaker, plus TV, air conditioner, and Wi-Fi. Four of the 12 rooms have balconies—two overlook the pedestrian walkway and are great for people-watching (but can be noisy), while the others face the opposite direction and are huge and sunny.

A colonial-style home turned boutique inn, ★ **Casa Sirena** (Av. Hidalgo near Av. Bravo, no phone, www.casasirenamexico.com, US$139-159 s/d with a/c) has just six rooms, all sumptuously appointed with teak furnishings, Tiffany lamps, stone-tiled bathrooms, and extras like iPod docks and laptop-size safes; some rooms also boast beautiful Talavera tile floors. A full Mexican breakfast—*huevos divorciados, enfrijoladas,* chicken enchiladas—is served daily (except Sunday) on the small, leafy patio. There's an evening happy hour (Monday-Saturday) hosted by the gregarious owner, who serves up potent cocktails on the rooftop terrace. Other features include two plunge pools (one with Venetian glass tiles), a sundeck with almost 360-degree views of the Caribbean, and Wi-Fi. Online reservations are required; adults only.

The adults-only **Villa La Bella** (Carr. Perimetral s/n, tel. 998/888-0342, www. villalabella.com, US$175 s/d with a/c, US$185 suite, US$240 honeymoon suite with a/c) is run by an amiable American couple who give warm, personalized service to all their guests. There are just six units: three bright pool-front rooms with whimsical decor, two 2nd-floor *palapa*-roofed units with hanging beds (but no air-conditioning), and a colorful honeymoon suite with fantastic ocean views from its two terraces. There also is a well-maintained pool. A gourmet breakfast is included (except Monday) and served in the open-air lounge, where you can also score cocktails and ice-cold beer.

Hotel Las Palmas (Av. Guerrero near Av. López Mateos, cell tel. 998/877-0043, www. laspalmasonisla.com, US$60-130 s/d with a/c, US$140-170 penthouse) is a homey hotel run by a friendly mother-daughter team from Canada. Rooms are small but tastefully decorated, with creature comforts like good water pressure, pillow-top beds, and full-length mirrors. There's lots of common space for relaxing and socializing, including a rooftop lounge with hammocks, a shared kitchen, and a plunge pool. Most guests enjoy the camaraderie, but those seeking seclusion may find it overly hostel-like. Guests enjoy complimentary use of snorkel gear and coolers (first come, first served). There's a five-night minimum in high season.

Over US$200

Hotel Secreto (Sección Rocas 11, tel. 998/877-1039, www.hotelsecreto.com,

US$231-281 suite with a/c) is a classy glass and stucco hotel that's good for couples who want a quiet getaway without having to go down-island. The beach here isn't swimmable (Playa Norte is a short walk away), but there are gorgeous views from the rooms and the hotel's long, narrow infinity pool. Rooms have native stone floors, plasma TVs, pillow-top mattresses, and huge private balconies. Upkeep can be lacking, but not egregiously. Continental breakfast is included, and there's a small gym.

★ **Casa de los Sueños** (Carr. Garrafón s/n, tel. 998/888-0370, toll-free U.S. tel. 877/372-3993, www.casasuenos.com, US$217-399 s/d with a/c, US$599 presidential suite) is a boutique hotel with 10 immaculate rooms. Located on a bluff at the southern end of the island, the hotel has gorgeous views, including from the large infinity pool. There's no beach, but a large pier does well for swimming, sunbathing, and spa treatments, while the hotel's excellent restaurant-bar is on the water's edge. Bikes, kayaks, and snorkel gear are available for exploring. Full breakfast is included (and served until noon!).

All-Inclusive

Privilege Aluxes (Av. Lopez Mateos at Gustavo Rueda Medina, tel. 998/848-8470, toll-free U.S. tel. 877/635-5293, www. privilegehotels.com, US$243-347 s/d with a/c, US$157-189 pp all-inclusive) is a resort offering both all-inclusive and B&B options. The beach club is lovely and a highlight for most travelers, despite having to walk across the street to get there. The hotel's pool is sleek and clean (though oddly chilly), and rooms, though somewhat sterile in decor, are large and comfortable. It's a good option if you're looking for a resort experience in downtown Isla. Adults only.

Isla Mujeres Palace (Carr. Sac Bajo s/n, tel. 984/873-4960, toll-free U.S. tel. 800/986-5632, www.palaceresorts.com, US$240-278 pp all-inclusive) is an upscale, couples-only all-inclusive resort with just 62 rooms and an exclusive getaway vibe. Suites have king-size beds and muted modern decor. There are only two restaurants, but they are good ones, with international cuisine, including a full offering of ceviches. The beach and pool areas are lovely, though noise from neighboring beach clubs can be irritating.

Apartments and Private Homes

If you feel like lingering for a while in Isla Mujeres—and who doesn't?—consider booking an apartment or private home. There are a surprising number available, both in town and down island, running the gamut in size and price, and available by the week or month. Check out the options at agencies like **Lost Oasis** (www.lostoasis.net) and **Isla Beckons** (www.islabeckons.com), which specialize in Isla Mujeres. Or, of course, there's always **Vacation Rentals by Owner** (www.vrbo.com) and **Airbnb** (www.airbnb.com).

INFORMATION AND SERVICES

Tourist Information

The **Oficina de Turismo** (Av. Rueda Medina 130, tel. 998/877-0307, www.islamujeres.gob.mx, 9am-4pm Mon.-Fri.) sometimes has maps and useful information.

The English-language website www.islamujeres.info has concise and accessible descriptions of various aspects of Isla Mujeres, including activities, tours, taxis, ferry schedules, and history, plus a Q&A section frequented by longtime expats.

Soul de Isla Mujeres (www.souldeisla.com) also has information and recommendations about Isla Mujeres, from restaurants to wedding planners. Also try www.isla-mujeres.net for information about visiting Isla.

MapChick Isla Mujeres (www.cancunmap.com, US$15) is a fantastic professional-quality color map of Isla Mujeres. It is extremely detailed, including annotated listings of almost every restaurant, hotel, and point of interest on the island. It is available at a handful of Isla's restaurants and hotels, and also can be ordered online.

Emergency Services

MEDISLA (Av. Abasolo 40, tel. 998/688-4364, 24-hour tel. 998/845-2370, dr.asalas@hotmail.com, 9am-3pm and 4pm-9pm Mon.-Sat.) is the office of Dr. Antonio Salas, who is highly recommended by islanders for nonurgent medical needs. English and basic German are spoken.

The **Hospital Comunitario de Isla Mujeres** (Av. Rueda Medina at Calle Paseo de los Peces, tel. 998/877-0117, 24 hours) is a small but modern hospital equipped to handle walk-in consultations, emergencies, and surgeries. It also has a hyperbaric chamber for diving-related injuries.

Isla Mujeres's primary **hyperbaric chamber** (tel. 998/877-0819, 9am-4pm daily), or *cámera hiberbárica* in Spanish, is on the pedestrian-only extension of Avenida Morelos, just north of the *zócalo*.

Farmacia YZA (Av. Benito Juárez at Calle Morelos, tel. 998/999-0234, 24 hours) has sunscreen, bug repellent, and toiletries in addition to medications.

The **police station** (tel. 998/999-0051, 24 hours) is on the central plaza.

Money

HSBC has a bank and ATMs across from the UltraMar pier (Av. Rueda Medina between Avs. Madero and Morelos, tel. 998/877-0005, 9am-5pm Mon.-Fri.) and an ATM only at Xpress Super grocery store on the central plaza.

Media and Communications

Like many cities in Mexico, Isla Mujeres has **free public Wi-Fi** in the central plaza, available to anyone with a computer or mobile device. Most hotels offer Wi-Fi to guests, too.

There are two Internet cafés in town: **Café Internet Adrian's** (An. Morelos s/n, no tel., 8am-10pm daily, US$1 per hour), facing the central plaza; and **No Name Ciber** (Av. Matamoros near Av. Carlos Lazo, no tel., 9am-9pm, US$0.75 per hour) near Poc Na Hostel.

The **post office** (Av. Guerrero at Av. López Mateos, tel. 998/877-0085) is open 9am-5pm Monday-Friday, and 9am-12:30pm Saturday.

Ferries to Isla Mujeres

Various passenger ferries (and also a car ferry) leave for Isla Mujeres from Cancún every day. Those leaving from the Zona Hotelera are more expensive and take longer but may be more convenient. There's also a vehicle ferry. **Note:** During the high season, additional departures are occasionally offered.

ZONA HOTELERA

El Embarcadero
UltraMar (Blvd. Kukulcán Km 4, tel. 998/881-5890, www.ultramarferry.com, US$14/19 one-way/round-trip, 30 minutes). **Departure:** 9:15am, 10:30am, 11:45am, 1pm, 2:15pm, 4:30pm, 6:15pm, and 8:45pm. **Return:** 9:45am, 11am, 12:15pm, 1:30pm, 4pm, 5:15pm, 6:45pm, 8pm, and 9:15pm.

Playa Tortugas
UltraMar (Blvd. Kukulcán Km 7, tel. 998/881-5890, www.ultramarferry.com, US$14/19 one-way/round-trip, 30 minutes). **Departure:** hourly 9am-6pm, 7:15pm, and 8:30pm. **Return:** hourly 9:30am-5:30pm, 6:45pm, 8pm, and 9:15pm.

Playa Caracol
UltraMar (Blvd. Kukulcán Km 9.5, tel. 998/881-5890, www.ultramarferry.com, US$14/19 one-way/round-trip, 30 minutes). **Departure:** 9am, 10:15am, 11:30am, 12:45pm, 2pm, and 4:45pm. **Return:** 9:45am, 11am, 12:15pm, 1:30pm, 4pm, 5:15pm.

DOWNTOWN

To get to either of the passenger ferries in downtown Cancún, take the red R-1 bus (US$0.75) on Boulevard Kukulcán or Avenida Tulum; continue past the downtown bus terminal and north out of the city. **Gran Puerto** is easily located by its tall observation tower. (Be aware that you may be approached by people dressed in UltraMar uniforms who are in fact selling time-shares here.) **Puerto Juárez** is two blocks past Gran Puerto. It's the original Isla Mujeres ferry pier, but the boats and waiting area are older. The vehicle ferry at **Punta Sam** is located on Avenida López Portillo, about five kilometers (3 miles) north of Gran Puerto. On Isla Mujeres, the car ferry pier is a few hundred meters south of the passenger piers, past the naval dock.

Gran Puerto
UltraMar (Av. López Portillo s/n, tel. 998/881-5890, www.ultramarferry.com, US$8/15 one-way/round-trip, 15 minutes) boats feature comfy seats in an air-conditioned cabin and an open-air deck, with televisions playing a short promotional program on Isla Mujeres. There's often live music on the open deck. **Departure:** every 30 minutes 5am-9:30pm, then hourly until 11:30pm. **Return:** every 30 minutes 5:30am-9pm, then hourly 10pm-midnight.

Puerto Juárez
Marinsa Turismo (Av. López Portillo s/n, tel. 998/478-0011, www.marinsaturismo.com, US$8/15 one-way/round-trip, 45 minutes) utilizes traditional vehicle ferryboats to transport people; the trip takes longer than its competitors but, if you're not in a rush, it's a beautiful ride. **Departure:** every hour 6:15am-9:15pm. **Return:** every hour 7:15am-10:15pm.

Punta Sam (vehicle ferry)
The lumbering vehicle ferry to Isla Mujeres is run by **Marítima Isla Mujeres** (Av. López Portillo s/n, tel. 998/878-4171, www.maritimaislamujeres.com, 45-60 minutes). Rates are according to vehicle: US$15 for cars, US$26 for SUVs and vans, US$5 for motorcycles or mopeds, and US$4.75 for bicycles. Rates include the driver only—each additional passenger costs US$2. Arrive about an hour early to get in line; tickets go on sale 30 minutes prior to departure. **Departure:** 7:15am, 9am, 11am, 1pm, 5:30pm, and 8:15pm Mon., 7:15am, 9am, 11am, 1pm, 3pm, 5:30pm, and 8:15pm Tues.-Sat., and 11am, 3pm, and 8pm Sun. **Return:** 6am, 8am, 10am, noon, 4:15pm, and 7:15pm Mon., 6am, 8am, 10am, noon, 2pm, 4:15pm, and 7:15pm Tues.-Sat., and 10am, 2pm, and 7pm Sun.

Laundry and Storage

Lavandería Cienpies (Av. Vicente Guerrero at Av. Madero, no phone, 7am-9pm Mon.-Sat., 7am-2pm Sun.) will wash, dry, and fold for US$4 per four kilos (8.8 pounds).

Tim Pho Lavandería (Av. Juárez at Abasolo, no phone, 8am-8pm Mon.-Sat., 8am-2pm Sun.) offers same-day service with a two-hour wait. Loads cost US$4.50 per four kilos (8.8 pounds).

Storage lockers (US$5 per 24 hours) are available at the Ultramar ferry pier; they are big enough to hold carry-on bags only. If it's really early or late in the day and there's no staffer around, ask for help from the parking lot attendant, just east of the pier.

GETTING THERE

A number of ferries ply the turquoise waters of the Bahía de Mujeres (Bay of Women) between Isla Mujeres and various mainland ports in and around Cancún. There is no direct ferry service from Isla Cozumel, however, and despite having an airstrip, no regular air service either.

Passenger Ferries

Passenger-only ferries leave for Isla Mujeres from Cancún in the Zona Hotelera and from Puerto Juárez, about three kilometers (1.9 miles) north of downtown Cancún. If you are just visiting for the day, reconfirm the return times and remember that service to the Zona Hotelera ends earlier than service to Puerto Juárez.

Car Ferries

A vehicle ferry operates from Punta Sam, about eight kilometers (5 miles) north of Cancún past Puerto Juárez.

GETTING AROUND

Isla Mujeres is a small and mostly flat island. In town you can easily walk everywhere. Buses and taxis are available for exploring farther afield, but definitely consider renting a golf cart, moped, or bike for more flexibility and independence.

Taxi

Isla Mujeres has many more taxis than seem necessary—in town, it feels more likely that you'd be hit by a taxi than have trouble finding one. Out of town, you shouldn't have to wait too long for a taxi to pass, either, and Garrafón, Dolphin Discovery, and Playa Lancheros all have fixed taxi stands. From downtown, rates are US$2.50 around town (including the beaches) and US$4-6 elsewhere on the island. Official rates are posted wherever taxis line up, including the ferry terminal and Punta Sur. Taxis are per trip, not per person, and drivers may pick up other passengers headed the same direction. You can also hire a taxi to give you a private driving tour of the island for US$15 per hour. **Note:** Taxi fares double after dark until 6am.

Golf Cart, Moped, and Bicycle Rental

Most rental operations on the island share the same fixed rates: golf carts US$12-15 per hour, US$35-40 per day (store hours), and US$45-60 for 24 hours; mopeds US$6 per hour, US$15 per day, US$20 for 24 hours; and bicycles (including lock but often not helmet) US$7-10 per day, US$10-13 for 24 hours.

Note: Isla Mujeres has a regular occurrence of serious accidents involving tourists driving mopeds. Riding double is a major culprit: Mopeds are much harder to control with two people riding instead of one. Poor roads and wet and windy conditions also are dangerous, not to mention unpredictable. Better to rent a bike or golf cart, or at least separate mopeds.

Agencies right at the ferry pier sometimes charge slightly more than those a few blocks away. Solid choices include **Ciro's** (Av. Guerrero near Av. Matamoros, tel. 998/877-0568, 9am-5pm daily), **El Sol** (Av. Juárez between Avs. Abasolo and Matamoros, tel. 998/877-0791, 9am-5pm daily), **Luxury Car Rental** (Av. Hidalgo near Playa Norte, tel. 998/877-0392, 8am-6pm daily), **Pelícanos** (Av. Matamoros near Av. Guerrero, no phone, 8am-5pm daily), and **David's Bikes**

(Av. Matamoros near Av. Guerrero, no tel., 8am-8pm Mon.-Sat., 8am-5pm Sun.).

Isla Mujeres Golf Cart Rentals (cell tel. 998/857-5266, www.islamujeres golfcartrentals.com) is a convenient service that makes renting a golf cart easy. Rates are slightly higher than you'd pay normally, but you can reserve and pay online, the cart can be delivered to your hotel, and someone even comes by every day or two to fill the gas tank. Four- and six-seat carts are available; there are discounts for longer rentals.

Isla Holbox

At the northeastern tip of Quintana Roo, where the Caribbean Sea mingles with the Gulf of Mexico, and completely within the Yum Balam Reserve, sits Isla Holbox (hole-BOASH). Once reasonably obscure, Holbox is hitting the radar of independent travelers, which may spell big changes in the future. For now, the town of Holbox is a fishing village with sand roads, golf carts instead of cars, no hospital, and no post office. You'll find brightly painted homes, *palapa*-roofed hotels, and Italian and Argentinean expats who have opened bed-and-breakfasts and small restaurants. The water here is emerald—not the clear turquoise of Cancún and Tulum—and while the sand is coarser, the beach is loaded with seashells and is no less scenic. Holbox is well known as a place to snorkel with behemoth but harmless whale sharks—present June-September—and also has great opportunities for bird-watching, kayaking, and sportfishing. Above all, Holbox offers a sense of peace and tranquility hard to find on Mexico's Caribbean coast. The island's growing popularity, though, means its vibe is changing. What direction it goes—bohemian chic, big eco-business, or something altogether different—remains to be seen.

Indigenous Maya inhabited Holbox for centuries but abandoned the island more than 300 years before the first Europeans arrived. The name of the island and town is a matter of some dispute. Some say *holbox* is derived from a Maya term meaning "black water" and is a reference to the island's natural springs, whose dark depths make the water appear black. A more popular, albeit fantastical, story is that the pirate Francisco de Molas buried a treasure on the island and cut off the head of his African bodyguard so that his ghost would watch over the spot for eternity. De Molas was promptly killed by a snakebite, but the disembodied head of his bodyguard has appeared occasionally to islanders, trying to divulge the treasure's location but succeeding only in scaring everyone away. By this latter account, the island originally would have been called *poolbox* (black head), and was altered later by European settlers.

Storms are serious business on this low, flat island, which is regularly buffeted by tropical conflagrations. In fact, the town was originally located farther west but was destroyed by a hurricane and rebuilt in its current location about 150 years ago. *Nortes* are fall and winter storms that sweep down the Gulf coast bringing rain and turbid seas. *Maja' che* is the Maya name for sudden winds that can knock over trees; they are most common in April and May. During major storms, the entire island is evacuated.

SIGHTS

TOP EXPERIENCE

★ Whale Shark Feeding Grounds

From June to September, large numbers of whale sharks—the world's largest fish, typically measuring 6-7.5 meters (20-25 feet) and weighing more than 10 tons—congregate in shallow waters about 16 kilometers (10 miles)

Isla Holbox

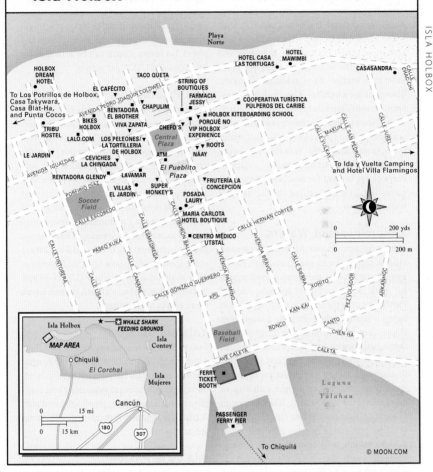

Playa Norte

HOTEL CASA LAS TORTUGAS
HOTEL MAWIMBI
CASASANDRA
CALLE CHACCHI

HOLBOX DREAM HOTEL
TACO QUETA
STRING OF BOUTIQUES
EL CAFÉCITO
To Los Potrillos de Holbox, Casa Takywara, Casa Blat-Ha, and Punta Cocos
AVENIDA PEDRO JOAQUÍN COLDWELL
CHAPULIM
FARMACIA JESSY
COOPERATIVA TURÍSTICA PULPEROS DEL CARIBE
CALLE MAKUN
CALLE SAN PEDRO
CALLE JUBEL
RENTADORA EL BROTHER
HOLBOX KITEBOARDING SCHOOL
TRIBU HOSTEL
BIKES HOLBOX
VIVA ZAPATA
CHEFO'S
PORQUÉ NO VIP HOLBOX EXPERIENCE
CALLE VULKAY
LALO.COM
LOS PELEONES/ LA TORTILLERIA DE HOLBOX
Central Plaza
ROOTS
To Ida y Vuelta Camping and Hotel Villa Flamingos
LE JARDIN
ATM
NÁAY
CEVICHES LA CHINGADA
El Pueblito Plaza
AVENIDA IGUALDAD
RENTADORA GLENDY
LAVAMAR
FRUTERÍA LA CONCEPCIÓN
PORFIRIO DÍAZ
VILLAS EL JARDIN
SUPER MONKEY'S
POSADA LAURY
Soccer Field
CALLE ESCOBEDO
CALLE ESMERDEGA
CALLE TIBURON BALLENA
MARIA CARLOTA HOTEL BOUTIQUE
CENTRO MÉDICO UTSTAL
CALLE HERNAN CORTES
0   200 yds
0   200 m
PASEO KUKA
CALLE CANANE
CALLE LISA
CALLE GONZALO GUERRERO
AVENIDA PALOMINO
AVENIDA BRAVO
CALLE SIERRA
XOHITO
PEZ VOLADOR
AH KAN HOC
CALLE TINTORERA
XPI
KAN-KAI
CANTO
CHEN-HA
RONCO
CALETA
AVE CALETA
Baseball Field
Laguna Yalahau
FERRY TICKET BOOTH
PASSENGER FERRY PIER
To Chiquilá

WHALE SHARK FEEDING GROUNDS
Isla Holbox
MAP AREA
Isla Contoy
Chiquilá
El Corchal
Isla Mujeres
Cancún
0   15 mi
0   15 km
180
307

© MOON.COM

east of Holbox village. Despite their size, the sharks are completely harmless, eating plankton, krill, and other tiny organisms, much like baleen whales. Snorkeling with whale sharks is a unique and (to some) nerve-wracking experience. The captain pulls the boat alongside a shark—at Holbox they tend to feed on the surface—and two guests and a guide slip into the water with life jackets, masks, snorkels, and fins. The water tends to be murky (it's all the sealife in the water that attracts the sharks in the first place), and

the sharks are surprisingly fast. Still, you get a good view of these enormous, gentle animals, with their tiny eyes, bizarre shovel mouths, and dark spotted skin. It's best to be on a small tour—since you go in two by two, you'll get more time in the water. Tours cost around US$130 per person, last 4-6 hours, and typically include snorkel gear, a life preserver, a box lunch, and nonalcoholic beverages. Some trips also include a stop on the way back for snorkeling or to visit the island's inland lagoons and mangrove forest.

Playa Norte

Playa Norte is Holbox's scenic main beach, extending eastward along the island's long, north-facing shore; it is broad and flat, with white sand, and dotted with stands of tangled dune grass. The number of homes and hotels along the beach grows every year, and most have lounge chairs available to guests. There also are a handful of beach clubs (10am-6pm)—mostly restaurants with lounge chairs, umbrellas, and hammocks—open to the general public at no cost as long as you eat something (meals US$8-15). Whether you bring your own towel or set up at an establishment, Playa Norte is great for beachcombing, shell collecting, and sunbathing the farther you walk from town.

Bioluminescent Waters

During the summer months, the waters around Holbox are filled with plankton—tiny, harmless organisms that are a major food source for whale sharks and other animals. Around **Punta Cocos,** a particular variety of plankton light up when touched, forming a blue-green fluorescent glow around anything passing through the water—a fish, a hand, a paddle. It's otherworldly, to say the least. Mid-May through mid-August is the best time of year to check it out; try to go on a night with little or no moon for the best viewing. It's easy enough to see it on your own: Punta Cocos is located at the western end of Avenida Coldwell, about a 20-30-minute walk from the central park, along the beach. Tour operators also offer excursions (1 hour, US$15-20 per person), which include transportation and a guide.

El Corchal

Near Solferino, a village along the road to the Chiquilá, sits **El Corchal,** a 2,000-hectare (4,942 acres) swath of mangroves and protected wetlands. A local ecotourism initiative leads canoe tours through the area (cell tel. 998/165-7105, pepecorcho05@gmail.com, US$35 pp)—ask for Pepe Quintal Olivar, the founder and experienced guide. Visitors glide past *corcho* trees, their thick roots curiously growing above the waterline, and see and learn about the myriad birds that inhabit the area, including flamingos, toucans, woodpeckers, and quail. If you're lucky, you might even see turtles and small crocs. Tours last about 3-4 hours. Lunch can be arranged for an additional US$10 per person.

Isla Pájaros

Located in Yalahau Lagoon, Isla Pájaros (Bird Island) is a wildlife sanctuary and the permanent home to some 150 species of birds, including frigate birds, white ibis, double-crested cormorants, roseate spoonbills, and boat-billed herons. In addition, between May and September up to 40,000 flamingos nest on Holbox before their long winter migration to South America. Environmental restrictions mean you can't simply wander on Isla Pájaros, but two observation towers and walkways make spotting birds easy. Most tour operators offer bird-watching trips here (US$17-30 pp), usually by *lancha* (motorboat), though kayak tours also can be arranged.

Yalahau Spring

Said to have been used by pirates to fill their water barrels, Yalahau Spring is an *ojo de agua* (natural spring) on the edge of the mainland. Today, it is a picturesque swimming hole complete with a large *palapa,* picnic area, and pier. A trip here typically is combined with a stop at Isla Pájaros.

Isla de la Pasión

Just 15 minutes from town by boat, Isla de la Pasión is a tiny deserted island just 50 meters (164 feet) wide. It's known for its white-sand beach and beautiful emerald waters that are perfect for a relaxing day. There are trees and a large *palapa* for shade. Be sure to bring plenty of water and snacks—there are no services on the island.

Street Art: Murals

Walking around Holbox, it's impossible to miss the gorgeous and dramatic murals that dot the island. They're the product of two

Bug Patrol

Isla Holbox's famous whale sharks may weigh 10 tons and have mouths that measure five feet across, but it's the island's itty-bitty residents that pack the meanest bite. Mosquitoes, sand flies, and *tábanos* (horseflies) can be fierce, particularly in the summer and after heavy rains. Bring bug repellent and use it liberally, day and night. Another tip: Always dry off and reapply repellent immediately after swimming— horseflies love skin that's moist, especially with seawater.

projects: *Soñando por Holbox* (Dreaming for Holbox) and the *Festival Internacional de Arte Público* (International Festival of Public Art). The prior was a Kickstarter project that funded two of the murals; the latter funded the rest. Both projects involved artists from Mexico and beyond who met with islanders and explored the island for inspiration. Ask at your hotel for a map of the murals.

SPORTS AND RECREATION

There is a lot to do on Holbox, and various excursions can be arranged through your hotel or local tour operators or done on your own. Most of Holbox's tour operators offer the full gamut of excursions, at comparable prices. Recommended outfits include **Cooperativa Turística Pulperos del Caribe** (Av. Igualdad near Calle Sierra, tel. 984/875-2021), **Turística Moguel** (tel. 984/875-2028, www.holboxislandtours.com), and **VIP Holbox Experience** (Av. Igualdad near Av. Bravo, tel. 984/875-2107, http://vipholbox.com).

Snorkeling

Besides swimming with whale sharks, the best place to snorkel on Isla Holbox is **Cabo Catoche,** a coral reef in about 2-4 meters (6.5-13 feet) of water at the far eastern end of the island. The water isn't as clear as in the Riviera Maya, but the reef here is pristine and

the animal life abundant, including stingrays, moray eels, nurse sharks, sea stars, and conch. Because it is so far from town, tours cost around US$75 per person (minimum 4 people). Alternatively, a stop at Cabo Catoche can be combined with another outing, such as an island tour or a whale shark excursion.

Wind Sports

Holbox's steady winds and shallow, nearly waveless coastal waters make it ideal for wind sports, particularly kiteboarding and windsurfing. The strongest winds are September-March, while July and August tend to have lighter, novice-friendly breezes. **Holbox Kiteboarding School** (Av. Igualdad s/n, tel. 984/875-2129, www.holboxkiteboarding.com, 8am-1:30pm and 5:30-8pm daily) offers all-level courses in several languages. Instruction prices, including gear, range US$57 per hour per person (group lessons, 3 students maximum) to US$72 per hour (private lessons). Rentals also are available. Lessons are offered November to May only.

Kayaking and Paddleboarding

Paddling is a great way to see the interior lagoons of the island, and especially for spotting birds. A fun and challenging option is to hire a golf-cart taxi to drive you and your kayak or paddleboard—balanced on the back—to the main inlet where you can put in. From there it's possible to wend through the lagoons to the other side of the island, then paddle along the shore to the main ferry dock, passing Isla Pájaros along the way. Several shops and hotels rent kayaks (US$10-15/hour), while **Explora Holbox** (tel. 998/304-6005) offers recommended group tours starting at US$35 per person. For customized trips, contact **Andrés Limón** (tel. 984/875-2220, kayak_holbox@hotmail.com), a popular local guide. Paddleboards can be rented through **Holbox Kiteboarding School** (Av. Igualdad s/n, tel. 984/875-2129, www.holboxkiteboarding.com, 8am-1:30pm and 5:30pm-8pm daily) for US$20 per hour.

Bird-Watching

Holbox has more than 30 species of birds, including herons, white and brown pelicans, double-crested cormorants, roseate spoonbills, and American flamingos (the brightest pink of the five flamingo species). Most hotels can arrange a standard bird-watching excursion (US$17-30 pp, 4 hours, minimum 4 people), which generally includes taking a motorboat or kayaks through the mangroves to Isla Pájaros and the flamingo nesting grounds at Punta Mosquita. More specialized bird-watchers may want to contact **Juan Rico Santana** (aka El Karateca, tel. 984/875-2347 or cell tel. 984/100-9132), a certified birder who leads many of the hotel trips, but also often arranges separate, more focused trips tailored to your interests.

Fishing

Holbox is an excellent spot for **sportfishing**, yet it's still relatively unknown. A deep-sea fishing excursion costs US$375-450, depending on duration. It typically includes gear, bait, drinks, and lunch. A coastal fishing tour with a local fisherman, going after smaller and more plentiful catch, lasts 4-5 hours and costs around US$140-190. Local tour operators, and most hotels, can help you organize either trip.

Holbox also has great **fly-fishing**, with 100-plus-pound giant tarpons cruising the coastal waters, and smaller juveniles plying the interior lagoons, along with snook and jack. **Holbox Tarpon Club** (tel. 984/875-2144) offers personalized tours, running US$420 per boat (8 hours, lunch included, maximum 2 anglers per boat).

Horseback Riding

Los Potrillos Holbox (across from airport, Av. Pedro Joaquin Coldwell s/n, tel. 984/129-9995) offers horseback riding tours into the interior of the island, along the beach, or both. Most tours last approximately 1.5 hours and cost US$25 per person.

Yoga

Hotel Casa Las Tortugas (Av. Igualdad s/n, cell tel. 984/252-2565, www.holbox casalastortugas.com, US$10) offers hatha yoga sessions at 8am Monday-Friday in its gorgeous beachfront yoga studio; all classes are led by certified instructors. English is spoken.

Just a block from the central plaza, **Amaité Hotel & Spa** (end of Calle Tiburón Ballena s/n, tel. 984/875-2217, www.amaitehotelholbox.com, US$10) offers oceanfront yoga at 9am every day in its breezy *palapa*-roof studio.

ENTERTAINMENT AND EVENTS
Festivals and Events
FESTIVAL DE SAN TELMO

Most of Holbox's residents live by fishing, and the island has over 400 fishing boats and numerous fishing cooperatives. It's no surprise, then, that San Telmo, the patron saint of fishermen, is celebrated here with fervor. The party lasts for two weeks in mid-April, with food stands, live performances, and special events, including a popular sportfishing tournament. The festival ends on April 19 when fishermen and their families participate in a huge boat procession followed by general revelry in the decked-out main square.

FESTIVAL DE LA VIRGEN DE FATIMA

In mid-May, Holbox celebrates the Virgin of Fatima, the community's official patron saint. Held just a month after the San Telmo blowout, this festival is more austere, with religious processions and more folksy music and other performances. That said, it's still a party.

SHOPPING

Holbox isn't exactly a shopper's paradise, but there is a **string of boutiques** along Avenida Igualdad (just east of the central plaza) selling everything from handcrafted jewelry to whale shark magnets. Most are open 9am-8pm every day.

If you're into shells, **Lalo.com** (Calle Canane near Av. Pedro Joaquín Coldwell, tel.

Pirates of the Caribbean

For most of the colonial era, pirates were a major and constant threat to ships and port towns throughout the Yucatán Peninsula. They launched attacks throughout the region, creating virtual pirate colonies. Some of the region's more notorious and colorful nemeses include:

- **Francisco de Molas:** Said to have lived on present-day Isla Holbox for nearly four decades, attacking ships that approached looking for drinking water. The story goes that Molas had an African slave help him bury his treasure, then killed him so that his ghost would watch over the spot. Islanders say a wailing disembodied head haunts the island, and that the name Holbox is an alteration of the Maya term *poolbox*, or black head.

- **Henry Morgan and Jean Lafitte:** Pirates who used Isla Cozumel as a refuge and a base to launch attacks on the Yucatecan mainland and various Caribbean islands. Lafitte is said to have often used the island's safe northern harbors to hide from pursuers.

- **Pierre de Sanfroy:** A French corsair who occupied Cozumel's small village for several weeks in 1579, making the church his home, including sleeping on the altar, and harassing the local townspeople.

- **Lorencillo:** Born Laurent de Graff, the French buccaneer is best known for attacking Campeche City in 1685 with a pirate army of 700 men and holding the city ransom for two months. According to legend, he was captured in Valladolid after being lured there by a woman he captured on a ship. Held in the Ex-Convento San Bernardino, he was rescued by his crew before authorities could jail or execute him.

- **Peg Leg:** Cornelius Jol was one of the first privateers known to use a wooden prosthetic—and to go by the now-iconic pirate name. Technically an admiral in the Dutch navy, Peg Leg terrorized Spanish and Portuguese ships and ports, including a 10-ship assault on Campeche City in 1663.

Other notable pirates who sailed Yucatán's waters and who figure in the region's lore include Sir Francis Drake, John Hawkins, Michel de Grammond, and Jacobo Jackson.

984/875-2118) is jam-packed with beautifully polished *conchas* from around the world (plus a coconut monkey or two). The owner, *maestro* Lalo, lives below the shop—just ring his bell, and he'll open up the shop.

El Pueblito Plaza (Calle Tiburón Ballena near Porfirio Díaz) is as close as you'll get to a mall in these parts. Located just off the central plaza, it has a handful of boutiques, eateries, and even an ATM.

FOOD

There are only a handful of restaurants on Isla Holbox, so anyone staying more than two days could easily sample them all. It wouldn't even take much effort either, as virtually all face the central plaza or are less than a couple blocks off it. A quick stroll around the plaza lets you whet your appetite while sizing up the options.

Mexican and Seafood

★ **Taco Queto** (Av. Pedro Joaquín Coldwell near Av. Palomino, 6pm-midnight daily, US$3-8) is a classic Mexican restaurant, down to the plastic chairs and tables, the tarp, and the spit of *al pastor* meat prominently placed at the front of the joint. As the name suggests, the specialty is street tacos, but the burritos are huge and delicious, too—jam-packed with meat, chicken, or beans, and doused in *crema*. Come hungry—the portions are hearty.

Chapulim (Calle Tiburón Ballena near Av. Coldwell, cell tel. 984/137-6069, 6pm-10pm Mon.-Sat., US$15-30) serves gourmet meals, mostly seafood-based, in an artful locale. There is no menu. Instead, there are four main entrees and a signature cocktail offered each night, using fresh, seasonal ingredients found on the island. Almost best of all is the personalized service—the chef himself, Erik Winckelmann, visits with each table to describe the entrees and answer questions.

Viva Zapata (Av. Igualdad between Calle Tiburón Ballena and Calle Esmedregal, tel. 984/875-2362, www.vivazapataholbox.com, 10am-11:30pm daily, US$7-22) is a sand-floored *palapa* restaurant near the central plaza. It's all about seafood here, with dishes made from locally caught fish, shrimp, octopus, and other seafood. There's also a kids menu with tasty treats like fish burgers and quesadillas. Come early to beat the crowd, or order a beer and kick back at the swing bar while you wait for a table.

A locals' fave, **Las Panchas** (Calle Esmedregal near Av. Coldwell, tel. 984/120-8354, 8am-11am and 1pm-7pm daily, US$6-15) is a simple, open-air restaurant serving fresh seafood. The menu is classic: ceviche, cocktails, tacos, fish prepared seven different ways. The cost, given the high quality and big portions, is tough to beat. Come early for a seat—a line often forms during the dinner rush.

Ceviches La Chingada (Calle Esmedregal near Av. Porfirio Díaz, tel. 984/876-4439, 9am-6pm daily, US$2-7) is little more than a food stand on a side street: a handful of plastic tables on a dirt lot, the chef working furiously in the open kitchen, the waiter running to and fro. Yet the ceviche is so fresh, so perfectly tangy, and the stream of customers so steady, you'll find yourself waiting for a seat. But it goes fast. And whatever the wait, you'll find it was worth it.

International

La Tortilleria de Holbox (central plaza, tel. 984/875-2443, 8am-4pm daily, US$5-8) is a breakfast favorite with great fresh-brewed coffee to go along with omelets, yogurt and fresh fruit, and more—all with friendly service. For lunch, the Spanish tortilla is definitely the way to go, plus it feeds two.

Decked out with kitschy Mexican wrestling memorabilia, **Los Peleones** (central plaza, Calle Tiburón Ballena between Avs. Porfirio Díaz and Igualdad, no phone, 6:30pm-11pm daily, US$10-25) is a small 2nd-floor restaurant overlooking the central plaza. It specializes in classic Italian dishes, including great handmade pasta and seafood. Grab a table on the balcony for the best view and sea breeze.

Often bustling, ★ **Roots** (Av. Porfirio Díaz near Av. Bravo, tel. 984/241-5953, 4pm-11:30pm daily, US$7-10) specializes in thin-crust pizza with loads of Mexican-style toppings, all prepped in a wood-fired oven. Try the Poblana with chicken mole or the Oaxaqueña with grasshoppers and mushrooms. And the lobster tail pizza? An absolute treat. The restaurant itself is on a big open-air lot, the tables made of repurposed cable spools and the chairs upholstered barrels. If there's a wait, check out the trampoline or slackline. Even better, give the Hula-Hoops a whirl. There's live music on weekends too.

Light Fare and Sweets

It's all about huge salad bowls at ★ **Náay** (Calle Porfirio Díaz near Av. Bravo, tel. 984/157-9220, www.naayholbox.com, 1pm-8pm daily, US$6-8), where customers can either create their own (including one protein, one grain, one topping, and dressing) or choose a house specialty like curry chicken or falafel mint on a bed of spinach. All meals include freshly made iced tea or an *agua fresca* (fruit-based drink). Enjoy your salad at a communal table or take it to go in a rentable glass container.

El Cafécito (Av. Pedro Joaquín Coldwell near Av. Palomino, tel. 984/136-0232, 8:30am-3pm daily, US$4-8) is a cozy café just steps from the central plaza. Diners enjoy croissant and focaccia sandwiches, hummus platters, lasagna, and—the pièce de résistance—giant crepes with fillings like Nutella, caramel and nuts, and fruit.

An artisanal French bakery, **Le Jardin** (Calle Lisa near Av. Pedro Joaquín Coldwell, 8am-12:30pm daily, US$2-5) specializes in simple breakfasts made with homemade breads like croissants, brioche, and baguettes. Diners order at the register and take a seat under the *palapa*-roofed dining room.

Come early to be sure to get a meal—once the bread runs out (and it does), the place closes for the day.

Porqué No (Av. Igualdad near Av. Bravo, cell tel. 984/130-9133, noon-11:30pm daily, US$2-5) specializes in artisanal gelato. Flavors change periodically but include varieties like Oreo, pomegranate, coconut, and pistachio.

Groceries

Supplies ebb and flow in Isla Holbox, so you might have to go to more than one store to find everything you're looking for.

The souped-up **Super Monkey's** (Calle Tiburón Ballena near Calle Escobedo, 6am-midnight daily) has a decent selection of canned and packaged food, bug repellent, sunscreen, and toiletries.

For late-night munchies, check out **Chefo's** (central plaza, 24 hours daily).

The best selection of fruits and vegetables on the island is at **Frutería La Concepción** (Calle Escobedo near Av. Palomino, cell tel. 984/129-1240, 7am-10pm daily). You'll also find eggs, honey, and spices. Delivery is available.

ACCOMMODATIONS

For most travelers, Holbox's most appealing accommodations are its beachfront bungalows; they vary in style, amenities, and price, but all offer simple rest and relaxation in a peaceful seaside setting. Alternatively, hotels in town offer comfortable rooms at more accessible rates, and you're still just a short distance from the beach. Be aware that rates typically rise during whale shark season (mid-May-mid-September).

Under US$50

Holbox's best budget choice is ★ **Tribu Hostel** (Av. Pedro Joaquín Coldwell s/n, tel. 984/875-2507, www.tribuhostel.com, US$16-18 pp dorm, US$50 s/d, US$80 s/d with a/c). Set in two-story *palapa*-roofed buildings with polished wood floors, each room is named after one of the world's tribes—Maori, Huli, Woodabe, and so forth—and is decorated

accordingly. Dorms have 3-5 bunks apiece, fans, en suite bathrooms, and private balconies. Sheets and big lockers (BYO lock) are included. Private rooms are similarly outfitted but smaller. Common areas are first-rate: a fully equipped kitchen, an outdoor dining room, a rooftop lounge with lots of hammocks and stellar views, and a bar with swings for seats. Wi-Fi, laundry, yoga, kayaks, and Spanish classes also are offered.

Though the mosquitos can be a problem (bring bug repellent), **Ida y Vuelta Camping** (Calle Plutarco Elias Calles between Róbalo and Chacchi, tel. 984/875-2358, www.holboxhostel.com, US$10 pp hammock, US$10 pp camping, US$13 pp dorm, US$39 s/d bungalow with shared bath, US$44 s/d *cabaña*, US$52 s/d suite with shared kitchen, US$60 house) has a good range of options, from hammock and tent sites to a fully equipped house. The most popular choices are the garden bungalows, which have sand floors, screened windows, and shared bathrooms, and the *cabañas*—wood-plank cabins on stilts, each with two basic rooms with private bathrooms. Breakfast is included at the on-site restaurant. Free Wi-Fi.

Located on a quiet residential street, **Posada Laury** (Paseo Kuka near Av. Palomino, tel. 984/875-2133, US$44 s/d with a/c) offers stark rooms with unexpected creature comforts: air-conditioning, cable TV, and mini fridges, plus hot water and decent beds, too. It's a great deal, especially considering it's just two blocks from the central plaza. If you want to check in and there's no staff onsite, go around the corner to the nearest house on Avenida Palomino, where the owner lives (look for the "Posada Laury" sign above the doorbell).

US$50-100

Located about half a mile west of the central plaza, **Casa Blat-Ha** (Calle Caguama at Calle Charral, tel. 984/807-8490, cell tel. 984/137-6721, www.casablatha.com, US$69 s/d) is a small B&B with a welcoming off-the-grid boho feel. It has 12 simple and clean rooms

that are set in two buildings: the main one, where the rooms have ocean views and private balconies, and a building across the sand road, which has smaller, dark rooms with air-conditioning and king-size beds. The main building also has a cozy lounging area, a rooftop meditation and yoga center, an organic garden, and a vegetarian kitchen where continental breakfast is served. The beach is just a block away.

One of the best deals on the island, **Villas El Jardín** (Calle Esmedregal near Calle Escobedo, tel. 984/875-2326, reservaciones@villaseljardin.com, US$85 1-bedroom apartment with a/c) is a three-story bungalow hotel offering modern one-bedroom apartments. All have thick beds, downpour shower heads, well-equipped kitchenettes, and terraces or balconies. Details like hand-painted throw pillows and tropical wood accents make units homey. Daily maid service keeps them gleaming. The only bummer? Wi-Fi is accessible in common areas only.

Maria Carlota Hotel Boutique (Paseo Kuka near Calle Tiburón Ballena, cell tel. 983/111-5483, maria.carlota.hotelboutique@gmail.com, US$83-105 s/d with a/c) offers 18 sleek windowless rooms (read: dark and quiet) with low-lying beds that "float" above the polished cement floors (read: creative bed stands). Tropical wood and beautiful lighting add lots of personality. Rooms open onto a narrow interior garden that leads to a small reception area. The hotel is located on a quiet neighborhood street.

US$100-250

★ **Hotel Mawimbi** (Av. Igualdad s/n, tel. 984/875-2003, www.mawimbi.net, US$180-220 s/d with a/c, US$260 s/d with a/c and kitchenette, US$300 suite with a/c) offers modern rooms and comfortable bungalows with a touch of boho flair. Guatemalan bedspreads, colorful tiles, and shell accents all lend an artistic touch, while quiet

air-conditioning and free Wi-Fi keep you cool and connected. The shady garden has plenty of lounge chairs and hammocks, and is just steps from one of the island's best-kept stretches of beach. The low-key Italian owners maintain a friendly, welcoming atmosphere and offer recommended island excursions. There also is a good restaurant on-site, El Barquito, serving complimentary continental breakfast.

About a 10-minute walk from town, **Casa Takywara** (Av. Pedro Joaquín Coldwell s/n, cell tel. 984/141-3381, www.casatakywara.com, US$144-155 s/d with a/c and kitchenette) offers six spacious and lovely units in a circular three-story building. All have fully equipped kitchenettes (down to blenders and lime presses) and share wood-floored porches. The oceanfront, just steps away, has plenty of lounge chairs, hammocks, and other places to relax. Continental breakfast is delivered to rooms daily. Service is friendly and efficient.

Holbox Dream Hotel (Av. Pedro Joaquín Coldwell s/n, tel. 984/875-2433, www.holboxdream.com, US$90-124 s/d with a/c, US$134-142 deluxe s/d with a/c) is a refreshing alternative to the deserted-isle getaways that make up most of Holbox's hotels. Standard rooms are comfortable and modern, with air-conditioning, good mattresses, stone basin sinks, and balconies with partial ocean views; deluxe rooms are bigger, with mini fridges, security boxes, and better balcony views, plus some even have whirlpool tubs. There's Wi-Fi in all the rooms. The hotel also has a well-maintained beach, two small and inviting pools, and a restaurant that is perfect for leisurely meals.

Over US$250

★ **CasaSandra** (Calle Igualdad s/n, tel. 984/875-2171, www.casasandra.com, US$260-298 s/d with a/c, US$337-469 suite with a/c) is one of Holbox's most exclusive boutique hotels, though it still maintains the welcoming feel of a home. The main building looks like a Swiss ski lodge (it houses ocean-view rooms, the library, and a restaurant), but it also has a

1: getting around Isla Holbox by golf cart;
2: beachfront oasis

handful of smaller *palapa*-roofed buildings more in style with their island neighbors. Rooms are shabby-chic in decor and have features like claw-foot tubs and original art. Outside, guests can relax on the well-tended beach or by the large pool. A full breakfast is included in the rate.

Hotel Villas Flamingos (Paseo Kuka s/n, tel. 984/875-2167, www.villasflamingos.com, US$240-280 s/d with a/c, US$350-490 suite with a/c) is one of the nicest places to stay on the beach. Units are modern with boho flair: conch shell showerheads, coconut lamps, bamboo accents, and gorgeous mosaic tile bathrooms. All rooms have air-conditioning, private balconies, and ocean views (some partial, some dramatically expansive), and some even have private plunge pools and whirlpool tubs. There is a well-tended pool just feet from the ocean, as well as a high-end restaurant/bar. Full breakfast is included in the rate.

INFORMATION AND SERVICES

While Holbox is making it onto more travelers' radars, there still is no bank (though there is one bank-affiliated ATM) and no post office. Also, note that hours of operation on the island are decidedly flexible—"open all day" usually means "closed for a couple of hours in the middle of the day for lunch."

Tourist Information

There is no tourist information office in Holbox, but https://the.holboxeno.com and www.holboxisland.com are good sources of information and listings.

Emergency Services

Centro Médico Utstal (Av. Tiburón Ballena s/n, tel. 984/875-2158, cell tel. 984/121-2332, 9am-9pm daily) offers basic health services, including X-rays and routine lab work. For more advanced medical attention, head to Cancún or Mérida; in emergencies, consider taking an air taxi.

Farmacia Jessy (Av. Igualdad near Av. Bravo, no phone, 9am-3pm and 5pm-10pm

Mon.-Fri., 9am-3pm Sat.-Sun.) usually has a moderate selection of medications and basic toiletries.

Money

There is **no bank** on Isla Holbox, but there is one **Bancomer ATM** on the 2nd floor of the city hall (central plaza, Av. Porfirio Díaz s/n). There also are two **unaffiliated ATMs** in El Pueblito Plaza (Calle Tiburón Ballena near Porfirio Díaz) that charge an arm and a leg in fees. **Note:** The ATMs on the island often run out of money, so plan accordingly.

Though more hotels, restaurants, and tour operators are accepting credit cards, don't count on using plastic; be sure to **bring enough cash** for the length of your stay (plus an extra day or two, in case you decide to extend your visit).

Media and Communications

The days of Internet cafes are long gone on this little island. Instead, you'll find free Wi-Fi in your hotel—often in common areas only—and in a handful of restaurants and cafés.

Laundry

Just half a block from the central plaza, **Lavamar** (Av. Porfirio Díaz near Calle Esmedregal, 9am-6pm Mon.-Sat.) does a good job of washing, drying, and folding clothes; it charges US$0.80 per kilo, with a 3-kilo (6.5 pounds) minimum. Same-day service is available for a small additional charge.

GETTING THERE
Car, Ferry, Bus, Taxi, and Shuttle

To get to Holbox, you first need to get to the small coastal village of Chiquilá. There are buses from Cancún, Playa del Carmen, Valladolid, and Mérida. If you're driving, take old Highway 180 (not the *autopista*) to El Ideal, about 100 kilometers (62 miles) west of Cancún. Turn north onto Highway 5 and follow that about 140 kilometers (87 miles) to Chiquilá, passing though the town of Kantunilkín. (There are shortcuts from both Mérida and Cancún, but they follow smaller, less-maintained roads.) You'll have to leave your car in Chiquilá. Several families run small overnight parking operations, charging around US$5 per 24 hours; ask about weekly rates.

Ferries are operated by two companies: **9 Hermanos** (cell tel. 984/120-8655) and **Holbox Express** (tel. 984/875-2029). Holbox Express has a newer fleet with cushy seats, TVs, and floor-to-ceiling windows, while 9 Hermanos's boats are well maintained but no-frills. That said, the ride is so short that it doesn't really matter much which one you take. Between the two, boats leave Chiquilá for Isla Holbox (US$7 adult, US$4.50 child, 25 minutes) starting at 6am and run every 30 minutes from 7:30am until 8:30pm with the last boat leaving at 9:30pm. Returning boats leave Holbox at 5am and run every 30 minutes from 6:30am to 8:30pm. Going to Holbox, it's a good idea to get to the dock a half hour early, as boats occasionally leave ahead of schedule. Private boatmen also make the trip in either direction for approximately US$60-65 for up to six people; ask at the dock. **Note:** Private boats are prohibited from ferrying passengers to/from Holbox after dark.

From Chiquilá, **second-class buses** to Cancún (US$6.75, 3.5 hours) leave the dock parking area at 5:45am, 7:45am, 1:45pm, 2:15pm, and 3:15pm; the 1:45pm departure continues to Cancún International Airport (US$12.50, 4.5 hours). Two daily buses head straight to Playa del Carmen at 2:45pm and 4:15pm (US$11, 2.5 hours). To Mérida, there are two departures at 5:30am and 4:45pm (US$11, 7 hours); this bus also stops in Valladolid (US$5, 2.5 hours). All buses wait for the ferry arriving from Holbox. **Note:** For other destinations on the Riviera Maya, take a bus to Cancún or Playa del Carmen and transfer there.

Taxis also often are available at the dock to take travelers door-to-door to Cancún (US$70), Cancún International Airport (US$100), Playa del Carmen (US$120), and Valladolid (US$75); fares are often negotiable

so be sure to agree on a price before you step into the car.

Chiquilá Shuttle (cell tel. 984/135-6451, www.chiquilashuttle.com) also provides private van service to/from Chiquilá and Cancún International Airport for US$115 (max 6 people) to US$125 (max 9 people). Shared van service is also available for US$17 per person with four daily departures. Advance reservations are required.

If you'd prefer someone else deal with transportation logistics (you are on vacay, after all), consider using **Balleneros Tour & Travel** (cell tel. 999/236-1524, ballenerosholboxgmail.com). It provides door-to-door service to/from Holbox and Cancún (US$34 per person), Cancún International Airport (US$34 per person), and Playa del Carmen (US$37 per person). The cost includes a taxi to/from your hotel in Holbox, ferry tickets, and pickup/drop-off on the mainland.

Air

If you've got the money and the stomach for itty-bitty planes, **AeroSaab** (tel. 998/873-0501, www.aerosaab.com) offers a full-day tour to Isla Holbox departing from several regional cities, including Cancún, Playa del Carmen, and Cozumel. Using Cessna airplanes, the trip begins with a scenic flight up the coast to Holbox, followed by a tour of Isla Pájaros and Yalahau Spring, lunch, and a chance to explore the village and beach (US$178-202 pp, minimum 4 people). Overnight trips and/or whale shark excursions also can be arranged.

For air taxi service, try **Flights Holbox** (cell tel. 984/136-8852, www.flights-holbox.com). The cost depends on the size of the plane and the destination. To Cancún International Airport, rates run US$470 (max 5 passengers) to US$1,090 (max 13 passengers). Check the website for last-minute deals, sometimes running as low as US$50 per person.

GETTING AROUND

Holbox is very easy to get around on foot. Even the farthest hotels are no more than a

30-minute walk from town, and it's very safe day or night. The only time you may really need a lift is when you're lugging your bags between the pier and your hotel.

Taxi

Golf carts serve as the island's taxis (some are even painted in yellow-and-black checkers). A ride from the pier into town is US$1.50-3 per person or US$3-5 per person to the hotels farther down the beach. They are almost always parked on the plaza, or your hotel can call one.

Golf Cart

Though you really don't need a golf cart to get around Holbox, you may enjoy the convenience of one. Rates, though not cheap, are relatively uniform: US$15 per hour, US$30 for 4 hours, US$50 for 12 hours, and US$75 for 24 hours.

Recommended outfits include **Rentadora Glendy** (Av. Porfirio Díaz at Av. Morelos, tel. 984/875-2093, www.holboxglendytours.com, 7am-11pm daily) and **Rentadora El Brother** (Calle Tiburón Ballena at Av. Igualdad, tel. 998/875-2018, 8am-10pm daily).

Bicycle

Other than walking, the easiest—and most affordable—way of getting around town is by bike. **Bikes Holbox** (Av. Coldwell near Calle Esmedregal, tel. 984/212-5941, 8am-6:30pm Mon.-Sat.) rents bikes (no helmets, no locks) for US$1.50 per hour or US$10 per 24 hours. Delivery is available.

Isla Cozumel

All around Isla Cozumel, the Caribbean Sea glitters a hundred shades of blue. Beneath the waves, pristine coral reefs make for spectacular diving and snorkeling, the island's number one draw.

San Miguel de Cozumel—usually just called Cozumel, since it's the only city on the island—is where the ferries from Playa del Carmen arrive. It's also where cruise ships, as many as 30 per week in the high season, arrive; it's then that the waterfront promenade becomes a human river, flowing slowly down a channel of jewelry stores, souvenir shops, and open-air restaurants.

Just a few blocks from the promenade, another Cozumel emerges— a small, friendly community where old folks sit at their windows and

Highlights

Look for ★ to find recommended sights, activities, dining, and lodging.

★ **San Gervasio:** Smack-dab in the middle of the island is Cozumel's best and biggest Maya ruin, thought to be dedicated to Ixchel, the goddess of fertility (page 107).

★ **Playa Chen Río:** A rocky arm on Cozumel's east side forms a calm natural pool (page 116).

★ **Santa Rosa Wall:** Sit back and enjoy the ride at one of Cozumel's marquee dive sites, where a strong current whisks you past a long wall that's home to various sealife (page 119).

★ **Palancar:** This massive dive site has something for everyone: shallows, winding ravines, and natural arches (page 120).

★ **Parque Punta Sur:** Snorkel the colorful ocean reef, or stay above water on the long curving beaches of this scenic nature reserve. There's also a small maritime museum, a Maya ruin, and a lighthouse (page 124).

Caribbean Sea

★ ISLA COZUMEL

San Miguel de Cozumel

San Gervasio ★

Playa ★ Chen Río

Santa Rosa Wall ★

Parque Punta Sur ★

Palancar ★

0   5 mi
0   5 km

© MOON.COM

dogs sleep in the streets. In spring, masses of orange *framboyán* (poinciana) flowers bloom on shade trees in the plaza, and festivals and religious celebrations are widely attended.

Cozumel's interior—including an important Maya ruin—and its eastern shore are yet another world, lacking even power lines and telephone cables. Heavy surf makes much of the eastern shore too dangerous for swimming, but you easily can spend a day beachcombing or relaxing on the unmanicured beaches and lunching at small restaurants overlooking the sea.

As Mexico's third-largest island, it shouldn't be surprising to discover that Cozumel is so multifaceted. But it's hard not to marvel at how stark the differences are. Come for the diving and snorkeling, but leave time to experience a side of Cozumel you may not have expected.

HISTORY

Cozumel has been inhabited since 300 BC and was one of three major Maya pilgrimage sites in the region (the others were Chichén Itzá and Izamal in Yucatán state). The name is derived from the island's Maya name, *Cuzamil* (Land of Swallows). The height of its pre-Hispanic occupation was AD 1250-1500, when Putún people (also known as the Chontol or Itzás, the same group who built Chichén Itzá's most famous structures) dominated the region as seafaring merchants. Capitan Don Juan de Grijalva arrived on the island in 1518 and dubbed it Isla de Santa Cruz, marking the beginning of the brutal dislocation of the native people by Spanish explorers and conquistadors. It eventually was overrun by British and Dutch pirates who used it as a base of operations. By the mid-1800s, however, the island was virtually uninhabited. The henequen, chicle, and coconut-oil booms attracted a new wave of people to the Quintana Roo territory

(it didn't become a state until 1974), and Cozumel slowly rebounded, this time with a mostly Mexican mestizo population.

Cozumel benefitted mightily from the worldwide popularity of Jacques Cousteau's early underwater films (which were not filmed there, contrary to legend, but inspired others that were) and later, of course, the establishment of Cancún in the 1970s.

PLANNING YOUR TIME

Don't let the cruise ship hubbub on Avenida Rafael Melgar turn you off from the town altogether. Beside the fact that most of the hotels, dive shops, banks, and other services are here, the town itself has much to offer, including a pleasant central plaza and a great museum. Budget a day or two to rent a car and explore the rest of the island, including the beach clubs, Maya ruins, family-friendly ecoparks, and the wild beaches and deserted coastline of Cozumel's eastern side.

ORIENTATION

The town of San Miguel de Cozumel (aka "downtown Cozumel") is located on the west side of the island. The main passenger ferry arrives here, across from the central plaza.

Avenida Benito Juárez is one of the main streets in downtown Cozumel, beginning at the central plaza, crossing town, and becoming the Carretera Transversal (Cross-Island Highway). The highway passes the turnoff to the San Gervasio ruins before intersecting with the coastal road. The coastal road follows Cozumel's eastern shore, which is dotted with a few beach clubs and restaurants. Rounding the southern tip, the road heads north along the west shore before becoming Avenida Rafael Melgar and returning to the central plaza. Continuing north, the road passes turnoffs to the airport and a country club before turning to dirt and eventually dead-ending.

Previous: Cozumel's famous coral reef; Isla de la Pasión; painted maracas.

Isla Cozumel

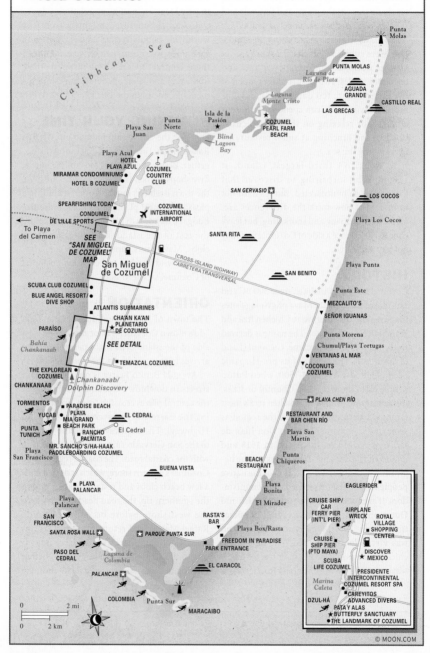

Caribbean Sea

Punta Molas
PUNTA MOLAS
Laguna de Río de Plata
AGUADA GRANDE
LAS GRECAS
CASTILLO REAL
Laguna Monte Cristo
COZUMEL PEARL FARM BEACH

Playa San Juan
Punta Norte
Isla de la Pasión
Blind Lagoon Bay

Playa Azul HOTEL
PLAYA AZUL
MIRAMAR CONDOMINIUMS
HOTEL B COZUMEL
COZUMEL COUNTRY CLUB

SAN GERVASIO
LOS COCOS
Playa Los Cocos

SPEARFISHING TODAY
CONDUMEL
DE LILLE SPORTS
COZUMEL INTERNATIONAL AIRPORT
SANTA RITA

To Playa del Carmen

SEE "SAN MIGUEL DE COZUMEL" MAP
San Miguel de Cozumel

(CROSS-ISLAND HIGHWAY)
CARRETERA TRANSVERSAL
SAN BENITO
Playa Punta
Punta Este

SCUBA CLUB COZUMEL
BLUE ANGEL RESORT/ DIVE SHOP
ATLANTIS SUBMARINES
CHA'AN KA'AN PLANETARIO DE COZUMEL

MEZCALITO'S
SEÑOR IGUANAS
Punta Morena
Chumul/Playa Tortugas

PARAÍSO
Bahía Chankanaab
SEE DETAIL
TEMAZCAL COZUMEL

VENTANAS AL MAR
COCONUTS COZUMEL

THE EXPLOREAN COZUMEL
CHANKANAAB
Chankanaab/ Dolphin Discovery

PLAYA CHEN RÍO

TORMENTOS
YUCAB
PARADISE BEACH
PLAYA MIA GRAND BEACH PARK
EL CEDRAL
RANCHO PALMITAS
El Cedral
RESTAURANT AND BAR CHEN RÍO
Playa San Martín

PUNTA TUNICH
MR. SANCHO'S/HA-HAAK PADDLEBOARDING COZUMEL
Playa San Francisco
BUENA VISTA
Punta Chiqueros
BEACH RESTAURANT
Playa Bonita

PLAYA PALANCAR
Playa Palancar
El Mirador

SAN FRANCISCO
SANTA ROSA WALL
RASTA'S BAR
Playa Box/Rasta

PASO DEL CEDRAL
Laguna de Colombia
PARQUE PUNTA SUR
FREEDOM IN PARADISE PARK ENTRANCE

PALANCAR
EL CARACOL

COLOMBIA
Punta Sur
MARACAIBO

0 | 2 mi
0 | 2 km

EAGLERIDER
CRUISE SHIP/ CAR FERRY PIER (INT'L PIER)
AIRPLANE WRECK
ROYAL VILLAGE SHOPPING CENTER
CRUISE SHIP PIER (PTO MAYA)
DISCOVER MEXICO
SCUBA LIFE COZUMEL
PRESIDENTE INTERCONTINENTAL COZUMEL RESORT SPA
Marina Caleta
DZUL-HÁ
CAREYITOS ADVANCED DIVERS
PATA Y ALAS
BUTTERFLY SANCTUARY
THE LANDMARK OF COZUMEL

© MOON.COM

Sights

PARQUE BENITO JUÁREZ

Downtown Cozumel's central plaza has long maintained a surprisingly peaceful atmosphere, despite the mass of humanity that disembarks at the nearby ferry pier and cruise ship ports. It's been a place where locals and tourists come to stroll about, enjoy live music and dancing on weekends, and snack at food vendors. The city municipal building, which occupies most of the plaza's east side, houses an airy commercial center on the ground floor and civic offices above. A recent M$95 million renovation to the plaza removed the central kiosk—an upset to many locals—and replaced it with a ground-level water fountain that children often play in during the day. In the evenings, the fountain is roped off for a "Luz y Sonido" show, where the water "dances" in time to classical music and is lit by a colorful lights. Shows typically start at 8pm and make for great photo ops.

MUSEO DE LA ISLA DE COZUMEL

The town's small but excellent museum, **Museo de la Isla de Cozumel** (Av. Rafael Melgar at Calle 6, tel. 987/872-1434, 8am-4pm daily, US$4), is on the waterfront in a turn-of-the-20th-century hotel building. Well-composed exhibits in English and Spanish describe the island's wildlife, coral reefs, and the fascinating, sometimes tortured, history of human presence here, from the Maya pilgrims who came to worship Ixchel, the fertility goddess, to present-day survivors of devastating hurricanes. The museum also has a small bookstore and a library. For a good photo op head to the terrace, which has a great view of the main drag, ferry pier, and—on a clear day—Playa del Carmen. It's also home to a popular restaurant (7am-11pm Mon.-Sat., 7am-3pm Sun., US$7-18) serving mostly Mexican fare.

COZUMEL PEARL FARM BEACH

Located on a remote private island on Cozumel's northern shore, the **Cozumel Pearl Farm Beach** (cell tel. 987/564-8698, www.cozumelpearlfarm.mx, US$110 adult, US$85 child ages 6-12, free age 5 and under) is a fun place to spend a day and learn about these unique nature-made jewels. The six-hour trip includes touring the farm's facilities to learn how pearls form and how they are farmed and harvested, followed by snorkeling around the underwater installations. Lunch on the beach is included (burgers, chips, and drinks), plus time for relaxing in hammocks and "speed snorkeling"—snorkeling while being tugged by a boat. Camping overnight is possible too, including gear and meals (US$225 adult, US$175 child ages 6-12, free age 5 and under). Boat transportation is provided from the Aqua Safari Pier (Av. Rafael Melgar near Calle 5).

PATAS Y ALAS BUTTERFLY SANCTUARY

Pata y Alas Butterfly Sanctuary (Carr. Costera Sur Km 6.8, tel. 987/869-0504, toll-free US tel. 866/732-8375, 9:30am-4pm Mon.-Sat., US$4) is a small site inside the Palmar Snorkel Beach Club dedicated to the protection and documentation of the butterflies in Cozumel. Visitors stroll through a protected garden while a variety of colorful butterflies flits about here and there, landing on tropical flowers and sometimes on guests. Keep your eyes peeled for caterpillars munching on foliage. Staffers are on hand to answer questions.

PLANETARIO DE COZUMEL

The Cha'an Ka'an Planetario de Cozumel (Av. Claudio Canto between Avs. Rafael Melgar and 65, tel. 987/857-0867, www.

San Miguel de Cozumel

© MOON.COM

planetariodecozumel.org, 9:30am-6:30pm Mon.-Fri., 11:30am-7pm Sat., free) is a state-of-the-art planetarium with an observatory for viewing the skies (US$3/2 adult/child) and a domed planetarium with 3-D shows ranging from Maya astrology to the coral reefs (Fri.-Sat. only, US$8/7 adult/child); screenings are in English and Spanish. There are also educational exhibits on subjects like the biodiversity of Cozumel and water conservancy. It's a good stop for families traveling with children.

DISCOVER MEXICO

Discover Mexico (Carr. Costera Sur Km 5.5, tel. 987/857-2820, www.discovermexico. org, 8am-4pm Mon.-Sat., US$26 adult, US$19 child) boasts hundreds of enthusiastic reviews from visitors, but we're hard-pressed to understand the appeal. Exhibits include a video on Mexican history, scale models of various iconic Mexican structures (the cathedral in Mexico City, the pyramid at Chichén Itzá, etc.), a gallery of Mexican folk art, tequila tasting, and, of course, plenty of opportunities for eating, drinking, and shopping. The center's tour guides are peppy and well informed, and Mexican art never fails to impress, but the overall experience is too gimmicky to be truly satisfying.

ARCHAEOLOGICAL ZONES

Isla Cozumel played a deeply significant role in the Maya world as a vital port of trade and, more importantly, as one of three major destinations of religious pilgrimages (the others were Izamal and Chichén Itzá, both in Yucatán state). The island's primary site—known as San Gervasio today—was dedicated to Ixchel, the Maya goddess of fertility as well as of the moon, childbirth, medicine, and weaving. Archaeologists believe that every Maya woman was expected, at least once in her lifetime, to journey to Cozumel to make offerings to Ixchel for fertility—her own, and that of her family's fields. Cozumel's draw was powerful, as inscriptions there refer to places and events hundreds of miles away.

Over 30 archaeological sites have been discovered on the island, though only four are easily accessible, and only San Gervasio can properly be called a tourist attraction. San Gervasio is certainly not as glorious as ruins found on the mainland, but it's worth a visit all the same.

★ San Gervasio

The area around **San Gervasio** (Cross-Island Hwy. Km 7.5, 8am-4pm daily, US$8) was populated as early as AD 200 and remained so after the general Maya collapse (AD 800-900) and well into the Spanish conquest. In fact, archaeologists excavating the ruins found a crypt containing 50 skeletons along with numerous Spanish beads; the bodies are thought to be those of 16th-century Maya who died from diseases brought by the conquistadors.

Today's visitors will find a modest ruin whose small square buildings with short doors are typical of those found elsewhere on the island. This style, known as *oratorio,* almost certainly developed in response to climatic imperatives: Anything built here needed to withstand the hurricanes that have pummeled Cozumel for millennia.

San Gervasio has three building groups that are accessible to the public—Las Manitas, Plaza Central, and Murciélagos; all are connected by trails that follow the same ancient causeways used by the city's original inhabitants. A fourth building group, El Ramonal, is not yet open to the public.

Entering the site, you'll come first to the building group named after the structure **Las Manitas** (Little Hands), for the red handprints still visible on one of its walls. This structure is thought to have been the home of one of San Gervasio's kings, Ah Huneb Itza, and the inner temple was likely a personal sanctuary. Just east of Las Manitas is **Chi Chan Nah;** consisting of two rooms, it is the smallest structure in San Gervasio. The exact purpose of this building is unknown, though it is theorized that it was used for rituals.

Bearing left, the trail leads to the **Plaza Central,** a large courtyard surrounded by nine low structures in various states of decay; it is believed that the structures were made taller with wood extensions. The Plaza Central served as the seat of power in San Gervasio's latest era, from AD 1200 onward. At the northwest side of the Plaza Central is the somewhat precarious-looking **El Arco** (The Arch), which served as an entrance to this section of the city.

At 0.5 kilometer (0.3 mile) from the Plaza Central is the **Murciélagos** (Bats) building group, containing the site's largest and most important structure: **Ka'na Nah** (Tall House). Also dating to San Gervasio's later era, this was the temple of the goddess Ixchel, and in its heyday would have been covered in stucco and painted red, blue, green, and black.

Finally, on the northeastern edge of San Gervasio rests **Nohoch Nah** (Big House), a boxy but serene temple. With an interior altar, the temple might have been used by

Downtown Cozumel

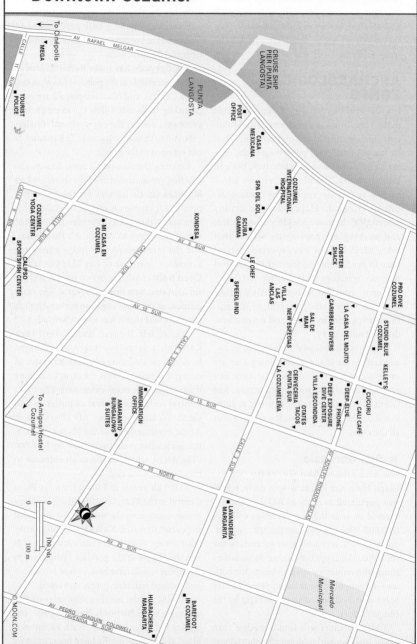

To Cinepolis →

AV. RAFAEL MELGAR

CALLE 11 SUR

MEGA

TOURIST POLICE

PUNTA LANGOSTA

CRUISE SHIP PIER (PUNTA LANGOSTA)

POST OFFICE

CASA MEXICANA

SPA DEL SOL

COZUMEL INTERNATIONAL HOSPITAL

KONDESA

SCUBA GAMMA

CALLE 9 BIS

CALLE 9 SUR

COZUMEL YOGA CENTER

CALIPSO SPORTSFISH CENTER

MI CASA EN COZUMEL

AV. 5 SUR

CALLE 7 SUR

LE CHEF

SPEEDL@ND

VILLA LAS ANCLAS

NEW ESPECIAS

LOBSTER SHACK

PRO DIVE COZUMEL

LA CASA DEL MOJITO

CARIBBEAN DIVERS

SAL DE MAR

STUDIO BLUE COZUMEL

KELLEY'S

AV. 10 SUR

CALLE 5 SUR

CERVECERIA PUNTA SUR

VILLA ESCONDIDA

OTATES TACOS

LA COZUMELEÑA

DEEP EXPOSURE DIVE CENTER

PHONET

DEEP BLUE

CUCURU

CALI CAFÉ

To Amigos/Hostel Cozumél

IMMIGRATION OFFICE

AMARANTO BUNGALOWS & SUITES

AV. 15 SUR

CALLE 3 SUR

AV. ADOLFO ROSADO SALAS

AV. 20 NORTE

0   100 yds
0   100 m

LAVANDERIA MARGARITA

AV. 25 SUR

Mercado Municipal

HURACHERIA MARGARITA

BAREFOOT IN COZUMEL

AV. PEDRO JOAQUIN COLDWELL (AVENIDA 30 SUR)

© MOON.COM

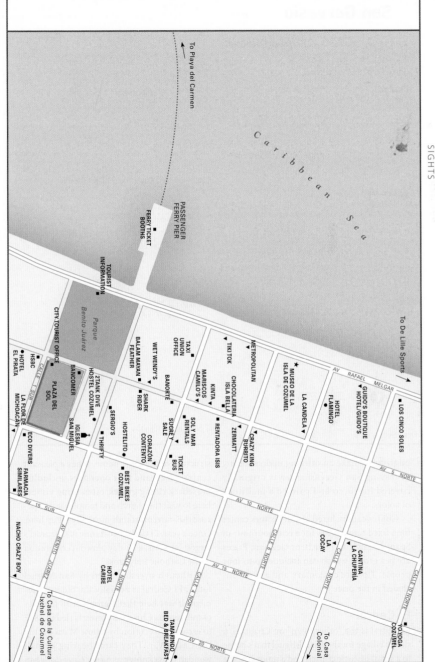

To Playa del Carmen

Caribbean Sea

To De Lille Sports

PASSENGER
FERRY PIER

FERRY TICKET
BOOTHS

TOURIST
INFORMATION

CITY TOURIST OFFICE

Parque
Benito Juarez

HSBC
HOTEL
EL PIRATA

LA FLOR DE
MICHOACAN

PLAZA DEL
SOL

BANCOMER

2TANK DIVE
HOSTEL COZUMEL

IGLESIA
SAN MIGUEL

THRIFTY

SERGIO'S

BALAM MAYAN
FEATHER

WET WENDY'S

TAXI
UNION
OFFICE

BANORTE

SHARK
RIDER

HOSTELITO

CORAZON
CONTENTO

BEST BIKES
COZUMEL

TIKI TOK

CHOCOLATERIA
ISLA BELLA

KINTA

MARISCOS
CAMILO'S

SUGRE Y
SALE

METROPOLITAN

ZERMATT

SOL Y MAR
RENTALS

RENTADORA ISIS

TICKET
BUS

MUSEO DE LA
ISLA DE COZUMEL

LA CANDELA

CRAZY KING
BURRITO

HOTEL
FLAMINGO

GUIDO'S BOUTIQUE
HOTEL/GUIDO'S

AV. RAFAEL MELGAR

LOS CINCO SOLES

AV 5 NORTE

AV 10 NORTE

LA
COCAY

CANTINA
LA CHUPERIA

ECO DIVERS

FARMACIA
SIMILARES

AV 15 SUR

AV BENITO JUAREZ

NACHO CRAZY BOY

CALLE 1 SUR

HOTEL
CARIBE

CALLE 2 NORTE

CALLE 4 NORTE

AV 15 NORTE

CALLE 6 NORTE

CALLE 8 NORTE

CALLE 10 NORTE

TAMARINDO
BED & BREAKFAST

To Casa de la Cultura
Ixchel de Cozumel

AV 20 NORTE

To Casa
Colonial

YOYOGA
COZUMEL

San Gervasio

EL RAMONAL

MURCIÉLAGOS

NOHOCH NAH

KA'NA NAH

EL ARCO

Plaza Central

CHI CHAN NAH

LAS MANITAS

VISITOR CENTER

P

To Cross-Island Highway

0   100 yds
0   100 m

© MOON.COM

pilgrims to make an offering upon entering or leaving San Gervasio. It was originally covered in stucco and painted a multitude of colors.

Guides can be hired at the visitors center for a fixed rate: US$25 for a one-hour tour in Spanish, English, French, or German. Prices are per group, which can include up to four people. Tips are customary and are not included in the price.

El Cedral

El Cedral is the "other town" on Cozumel, a sleepy village south of San Miguel that's home to a small historic church and a modest Maya structure of the same name. It has a pleasant central plaza, and tour operators, including horseback riding guides, often bring visitors here to visit the church and temple, and to peruse the souvenir stands normally set up here. Once a year, El Cedral hosts one of Cozumel's largest festivals, a 10-day blowout celebration of the Catholic holy cross.

Although overshadowed by San Miguel today, El Cedral is actually the older settlement. It was here that a group of 18 families of indigenous Christian converts fled in 1847 to escape persecution by fellow Maya during the Caste War. They came bearing a small wooden cross known as *Santa Cruz de Sabán*

(Holy Cross of Sabán) and founded their church and village alongside a Maya temple that they discovered just inland from their landing site. The group was led by Casimiro Cárdenas, whose descendants still serve as caretakers, or *mayordomos,* of the temple and church; there's a statue of Don Casimiro in the central plaza.

El Cedral is famous for its **Fiesta de la Santa Cruz** (Festival of the Holy Cross), which begins in late April and culminates on May 3. The celebration includes food, music, dance, performances, rodeos, and fireworks aplenty, and even some traditions of distant Maya origin. The party is open to everyone, including tourists, and makes for a fun and fascinating outing if your visit happens to coincide with it.

A well-marked turnoff just south of Playa San Francisco leads five kilometers (3.1 miles) to the village. El Cedral's **Maya ruin** (8am-5pm daily, free) is tiny and underwhelming, though it still bears a few traces of the original paint and stucco. The church is directly adjacent and contains the original wooden cross borne by El Cedral's founders.

El Caracol

Located inside **Parque Punta Sur** (Carr. Costera Sur Km 27, tel. 987/872-0914, www.cozumelparks.com, 9am-4pm Mon.-Sat., US$14 adult, US$8 child under 12), El Caracol is a small, conch-shaped structure that dates to AD 1200. It's believed to have been a lighthouse where Maya used smoke and flames to lead boats to safety. Small openings at the top of the structure also acted as whistles to alert Maya to approaching tropical storms and hurricanes. Admission to the reserve includes access to this small site.

Castillo Real

Castillo Real is a partially excavated site with a temple, two chambers, and a lookout tower. It is believed to have been a Maya watchtower to protect against approaching enemies. It's located on the remote northeastern corner of the island, along the sand road leading to Punta Molas. The road is quite treacherous, such that even ATVs and motorcycles can have trouble making it. Ask at the tourist office for the latest before making any plans to head up there.

Beaches and Beach Clubs

Cozumel isn't famous for its beaches, but it is not without a few beautiful stretches of sand. The best swimming beaches are on the protected southwestern coast, with soft white sand and calm azure waters. The finest stretches are occupied by large beach clubs, which have conveniences like lounge chairs, umbrellas, restrooms, restaurants, and water sports; a few even have swimming pools. Most beach clubs charge either a cover or a minimum consumption, but neither is exorbitant. The clubs cater to cruise shippers and range from peaceful and low-key to boisterous and loud. Independent travelers are perfectly welcome too, of course.

Beaches on Cozumel's east side are wild and picturesque, with virtually no development

beyond a few small restaurants. The surf can be fierce here, though a few sheltered areas have good swimming and are popular with locals. The municipal government has been steadily improving the road on the east side, including adding signs, stairways, and parking, but it remains a far different experience from the west-side beach clubs.

NORTHWESTERN COZUMEL
Isla de la Pasión

One of Cozumel's loveliest beaches is **Isla de la Pasión** (tel. 987/872-6941, www.islapasion.com.mx, US$70 pp via catamaran, US$90 pp via speedboat), a privately owned island and beach club just off Cozumel's north shore.

Although aimed squarely at cruise ship passengers, anyone can sign up for a package tour, which includes a buffet, open bar, and free beach activities. The beach is gorgeous—one of Corona's commercials was filmed here—and the island is covered, oddly, with wispy pine trees. (Scientists believe their seeds were washed or blown from the Atlantic coast of the United States.) The price is a bit steep, but the main bummer is you only get four hours at the beach. Tours leave from the Puerta Maya pier by catamaran or speedboat.

It's possible, though not easy, to visit Isla de la Pasión on your own; the beach itself is public, after all, and you can stay as long as you like. From the northern end of Avenida Rafael Melgar, a dirt road continues 5 kilometers (3.1 miles) past a water treatment plant to the port at Bahia Ciega. (The road isn't bad, but drive carefully, as your vehicle's insurance is probably void here.) At the port, ask around for a fisherman to take you across (around US$15, 20 minutes). Be sure to arrange a time for him to return, and cross your fingers he's got a good memory; otherwise, you'll be left begging a ride with a tour group. Bring food, water, and an umbrella—you won't be allowed to use the beach club facilities, but there's plenty of beach on which to lay out a towel.

SOUTHWESTERN COZUMEL

The majority of beach clubs are clustered on Playa San Francisco, a three-kilometer (1.9-mile) stretch of white-sand beach that begins just south of Secrets Aura Cozumel resort. Another beach, Playa Palancar, is farther south, near the tip of the island, and has a beach club of the same name.

Paradise Beach

Paradise Beach (Carr. Costera Sur Km 14.5, tel. 987/689-0000, www.paradise-beach-cozumel.com, 9am-sunset daily, US$10 minimum consumption) has a gorgeous pool and a spacious, picture-perfect beach that's dotted with palm trees. Oddly, they charge US$3 for beach chairs and US$18 for use of the water

sports gear, such as kayaks, trampoline floats, paddleboards, and snorkel gear. Nevertheless, it's a lovely and not-too-raucous place to spend a day at the beach.

Playa Mia

Playa Mia Grand Beach Park (Carr. Costera Sur Km 14.25, tel. 987/872-9040, www.playa-mia.com, 9am-6pm daily, US$30/25 adult/child, US$45/35 adult/child with buffet, US$60/50 adult/child with buffet and drinks) is big and busy without being obnoxious. The beach is decent, though often very crowded, and there's an excellent beachside pool. There's also a small water park with two additional pools with features like water cannons and sprays as well as a pair of 61-meter-long (200-foot) waterslides. The restaurant-buffet area is cool and pleasant, thanks to a high-peaked, circus-like tent. And there's certainly no shortage of activities: volleyball, table tennis, a kids' play structure, floating obstacle course, an underwater sculpture park, snorkeling, and more.

Mr. Sancho's

Though you can pay as you go at **Mr. Sancho's** (Carr. Costera Sur Km 15, tel. 987/120-2220, www.mrsanchos.com, 8am-5pm Mon.-Sat., US$55 adult, US$40 teen, US$35 child), it's known best for its all-inclusive packages. It has a decent Mexican restaurant, fairly mellow ambience, and plenty of extras, from snorkeling to massage. There's also a floating aquatic park with trampolines, water tubes, climbing walls, and more (US$12 pp extra). The beach is a bit narrow, meaning the lounge chairs are squeezed pretty tight, but it's a lovely spot all the same, and a great option for a no-brainer beach day with kids.

Playa Palancar

With a calm atmosphere to match the tranquil turquoise waters, **Playa Palancar** (Km 19.5, cell tel. 987/118-5154, www.buceopalancar.

1: ancient archway at San Gervasio archaeological zone; **2:** Playa Chen Río

com.mx, 8am-5pm daily, no cover or minimum consumption) is just the place to relax in a hammock or hunker down with a book while digging your toes into the thick white sand. Playa Palancar has gotten busier over the years, now with music and even parasailing, but it's still the mellowest of Cozumel's main beach clubs. And there happens to be great diving and snorkeling at nearby Palancar and Columbia reefs; an on-site dive shop offers fun dives (US$65/90 one/two tanks) and guided snorkeling trips (US$35-45, 60-90 minutes), with daily departures at 9am, noon, and 2pm. Snorkel gear can be rented separately (US$10), but there's not much to see close to shore. A *palapa*-roofed restaurant serves classic Mexican seafood and a wide range of drinks (US$8-20). The club is 750 meters (0.5 mile) off the main road.

SOUTHEASTERN COZUMEL

The east side of the island has a wild and windswept coastline dotted with beaches facing the open ocean. The surf here can be quite rough, and only a few beaches are safe for swimming.

Parque Punta Sur

As the name suggests, **Parque Punta Sur** (Carr. Costera Sur Km 27, tel. 987/872-0914, www.cozumelparks.com, 9am-4pm Mon.-Sat., US$14 adult, US$8 child under 12) covers Cozumel's southern point, but the entrance is on the east side, and the ambience and appeal is certainly akin to that of the eastern beaches. It is an important natural reserve that happens to have a fine beach and outstanding snorkeling. Because it faces south, the surf tends to be light. There's a small eatery, plus restrooms, a changing area, and a kiosk renting snorkel gear.

Playa Box (Playa Rasta)

Playa Box (pronounced *boash,* Yucatec Maya for head) is also known as Playa Rasta for the two reggae-themed bars—**Freedom in Paradise** (no phone, www.bobmarleybar.

com, 9am-sunset daily, US$7-13) and **Rasta's Bar** (same hours and menu)—that occupy it and share a kitchen. It's just past Punta Sur, where the road turns north along Cozumel's eastern shore. It's a rocky stretch of coastline with only a few sandy inlets and the two restaurant-bars blasting reggae at each other. It's not really the best place to spend the day—unless you like rambling on rocks and have a serious craving for jerk chicken.

El Mirador

Spanish for "The Lookout," this is the best place to appreciate Isla Cozumel's dramatic ironshore formations, including a natural arch and exposed huge bulges of the black jagged stone. Ironshore is formed when waves, wind, and especially microscopic organisms erode the ancient limestone cap that underlies much of the island. Be very careful walking on the ironshore—it can be sharp and slippery. Wear water shoes or Teva-style sports sandals to help you stay upright!

Playa Bonita and Punta Chiqueros

Playa Bonita is another picturesque curve of sand with plenty of room to lay out a towel and soak in the sun. Heavy surf usually makes swimming here inadvisable, but it's beautifully dramatic. The northern end of the beach is Punta Chiqueros, where a small **beach restaurant** (no phone, 10am-5pm daily, US$7-18) serves hamburgers, fresh fish, and other standards. It's also the home of tacky tropical drinks—rum punch served in pineapples with mini-umbrella décor or massive margaritas served in half-gallon-size martini glasses.

Playa San Martín

A wooden stairway leads from the road down to the sand at this long, scenic, windswept beach. There are a handful of permanent *palapa* umbrellas near the stairway that are popular with couples and families, but otherwise you're likely to have the beach virtually to yourself.

Sea Turtles of the Yucatán

sea turtle hatchlings waiting to be released into the sea

All eight of the world's sea turtle species are endangered due to a combination of antiquated fishing practices, habitat destruction, and a taste for turtle products. Four turtle species—hawksbill, Kemp's ridley, green, and loggerhead—nest on the shores of the Yucatán Peninsula, and until fairly recently were a common supplement to the regional diet. Turtles make easy prey, especially females clambering on shore to lay eggs. They are killed for their meat, fat, and eggs, which are eaten or saved for medicinal purposes, as well as for their shells, which are used to make jewelry, combs, and other crafts.

Various environmental organizations collaborate with the Mexican government to protect sea turtles and their habitats; they maintain strict surveillance of known nesting beaches to stop poaching and have developed breeding programs, too. This, in combination with laws that prohibit the capture and trade of sea turtles or their products, has tremendously increased awareness about their protection.

On Isla Cozumel, travelers can volunteer to monitor nests (US$25-40, 3 hrs) and to release hatchlings into the sea (US$20, 1 hr). Nesting season runs May-September, and during that period volunteers join biologists on nighttime walks of Cozumel's beaches, locating and marking new nests and helping to "search and rescue" baby turtles who are stuck in nests and need help reaching the water. From August to November, volunteers release hatchings, typically at sundown, by encouraging the tiny turtles to move toward the water (without touching them) and scaring off birds in search of an easy meal. Reservations are required; ages 10 and over are preferred.

The island's Ecology Department, **Dirección Municipal de Ecología y Medio Ambiente,** (Calle 11 at Av. 65, tel. 987/872-5795, ecologia@islacozumel.gob.mx) monitors Cozumel's sea turtles and manages volunteer opportunities. It maintains a **visitors center** (9:30am-2pm and 3:30pm-5:30pm daily May-Nov. only) in a small trailer, usually parked on the roadside near Playa San Martín on the eastern side of the island. Inside are a handful of aquariums, Plexiglas-enclosed nests, and more. Call for more information or to reserve a spot on upcoming beach walks and hatchling releases. Donations are appreciated. Spanish is useful but not required.

Similar volunteer opportunities also are available in Akumal at the **Centro Ecológico Akumal** (CEA, tel. 984/875-9095, www.ceakumal.org) as well as on Isla Mujeres at **Tortugranja** (Carr. Sac Bajo 5, tel. 998/877-0595).

★ Playa Chen Río

The best place to swim on the east side of the island is **Playa Chen Río** (1 kilometer/0.6 mile south of Coconuts Bar), where a rocky spit blocks the waves, forming a huge natural pool, and lifeguards are on duty on weekends. Quiet during the week, it's lively and bustling most Sundays, when local families turn out in force. **Restaurant and Bar Chen Río** (no phone, 11am-6pm daily, US$8-20) is located here, but it's a bit pricey for the quality so it's not uncommon to see families picnicking with coolers and even small grills.

Chumul (Playa Tortugas)

About six kilometers (3.7 miles) south of the Carretera Transversal intersection is Chumul, also known as Playa Tortugas, a broad, beautiful beach on the north side of the Ventanas al Mar hotel. The scenic, windswept beach is good for surfing—and has nesting turtles May-November—but it is often too rough for swimming or snorkeling. Still, it makes a good place to watch the wild and crashing waves.

A few steps away is **Coconuts Cozumel** (tel. 987/107-7110, www.coconutscozumel. com, 9:30am-sunset daily, US$7-18). Set on a dramatic palm-studded bluff—the only piece of elevated land on the island, in fact—the tables are arranged for diners to enjoy fabulous views of the beach below and the Caribbean beyond. Classic beach fare is served—ceviche, tacos, nachos—along with plenty of cold beer. Live music starts at 2pm.

Punta Morena

This scenic and little-used stretch of beach has a small restaurant with restrooms. Like elsewhere on the eastern shore, swimming here can be hazardous because of heavy surf and rocky outcrops, but it's still a nice place to relax or search for shells on the beach.

Mezcalitos and Señor Iguanas

These two low-key restaurants—**Mezcalito's** (tel. 987/876-0914, www.mezcalitos.com, 9am-6:30pm daily) and **Señor Iguanas** (no phone, 8am-6pm Mon.-Sat., 9am-6pm Sun.)—are located side by side, right where the Carretera Transversal hits the coast. Longtime Cozumel institutions, they have similar menus (ceviche, fried fish, hamburgers, US$8-15), drinks (beer, margaritas, and tequila shots, US$2.50-6), and services (beachside chairs, hammocks, and *palapas*, free if you buy something from the restaurant). Boogie boards also are available for rent at Señor Iguanas (US$6 for 2 hours)—a lot of fun if you can handle the rough surf.

NORTHEASTERN COZUMEL

Cozumel's northeastern shoulder is its long-lost coast, the wildest and least visited part of the island. The 25-kilometer (15.5-mile) stretch from the Carretera Transversal north to Punta Molas includes coastal dunes, scrub forest, and deserted beaches, plus the ancient Maya site of **Castillo Real** at around the 22-kilometer (14-mile) mark. This untended coast also is the final resting spot of a shockingly large amount of trash and jetsam, an ugly reminder of civilization in the one place on the island it ought to be easy to forget.

The road itself is a challenge—four-wheel drive is essential to avoid becoming mired in deep sand—and hurricanes and other storms can render it impassable. The area also is at the center of a bitter, on-again off-again land dispute and is occasionally closed without warning. Naval police patrol the area, too, on the lookout for both drug traffickers and turtle poachers.

If you do go, be aware that there are no facilities whatsoever, or any other people most of the time. If you plan to camp, take plenty of water and food, a flashlight, extra batteries, bug repellent, and a mosquito net. Remember, too, that most car insurance policies (including all policies sold by rental agencies on the island, regardless of the vehicle) specifically exclude this and other dirt roads from coverage.

Sports and Recreation

SCUBA DIVING

Cozumel is one the world's best (and best-known) places to scuba dive and snorkel, so it's no surprise that the island is home to dozens of dive shops—more than 100 at last count. Virtually all offer diving, snorkeling, and all levels of certification courses; there are a handful of dive "resorts," too, which offer packages that include lodging, diving, gear, and sometimes food.

Rates can vary considerably from shop to shop, and season to season, so be sure to clarify all the details up front. For most of the year, a two-tank fun dive costs US$80-95, plus US$18-30 per day if you need gear. Low-season rates can be significantly lower, and often include gear rental. PADI open-water certification courses (3-4 days) generally cost US$420-500, including all equipment and materials. Most shops also offer advanced courses, Nitrox and night diving, and multi-dive packages. All divers also must pay US$2 per day for marine park admission and to support Cozumel's hyperbaric chambers and marine ambulance; ask if the fees are included in a shop's rates or charged separately.

TOP EXPERIENCE

Dive Sites

Cozumel's coral reef—and the world-class diving and snorkeling it provides—is the main reason people come to the island. The reef was designated a national marine reserve more than two decades ago, and the waters have thrived under the park's rigorous protection and cleanup programs. Dozens of dive and snorkeling sites encircle the island, and the 1,000-meter-deep (3,281-foot) channel between Cozumel and the mainland provides spectacular drift and wall dives. Here is a list of some of the most popular dives, though by no means all the worthwhile ones.

AIRPLANE WRECK

A 40-passenger Convair airliner lies on Cozumel's seabed, about 65 meters (213 feet) from the shore near El Cid hotel. Sunk in 1977 for the Mexican movie production of *Survive II*, the plane has been broken into pieces and strewn about the site by years of storms. The site itself is relatively flat, though with parrot fish, damselfish, and a host of sea fans and small coral heads, there's plenty to see. With depth ranges of 3-15 meters (10-49 feet), this is a good site for snorkelers.

PARAÍSO

Just south of the international pier, and about 200 meters (656 feet) from shore, lies Paraíso, an impressive three-lane coral ridge. Medium-size coral—mostly brain and star—attract sergeants major, angelfish, grunts, squirrel fish, and snappers; ask your guide about the

Dive Insurance

Although diving and snorkeling accidents are relatively rare on Cozumel, especially among beginning divers, you might consider purchasing secondary accident and/or trip insurance through the **Divers Alert Network** (DAN, toll-free U.S. tel. 800/446-2671, 24-hour emergency Mex. tel. 919/684-9111, accepts collect calls, www.diversalertnetwork.org), a highly regarded international nonprofit medical organization dedicated to the health and safety of snorkelers and recreational divers. Dive accident plans cost just US$30-75 per year, including medical and decompression coverage and limited trip and lost equipment coverage. More complete travel insurance—not a bad idea in hurricane country—and life and disability coverage are also available. To be eligible for insurance, you must be a member of DAN (US$35 per year).

How to Choose a Dive Shop

There are more than 100 dive shops on Isla Cozumel, and scores more at Isla Mujeres, Playa del Carmen, Cancún, Tulum, and elsewhere. Choosing just one—and then placing all your underwater faith into its hands—can be daunting.

Safety should be your number one concern in choosing a shop. Fortunately, the standards in Cozumel and the Riviera Maya are almost universally first-rate, and accidents are rare. Still, don't dive with a shop that doesn't ask to see your certification card or logbook. Also ask how long the shop has been in business, how much experience the dive guides have, how long the captain and crew have been with the shop, and how many divers per guide will be on the tour. "Cattle boats" are a sign of shops trying to maximize profits; even if they're not unsafe, they often make for a less enjoyable experience due to the sheer number of people around you in the water.

Equipment is another crucial issue. You should ask to inspect the shop's equipment, and the dive shop should be quick to comply. Although few casual divers are trained to evaluate gear, a good dive shop will appreciate your concern and be happy to put you at ease.

The most important equipment is not what's on the rack but what you actually use. On the day of your dive, get to the shop early so you can **double-check your gear.** Old equipment is not necessarily bad, but you should ask for a different BCD, wetsuit, or regulator if the condition of the one assigned to you makes you uneasy. Learn how to check the O-ring (the small rubber ring that forms the seal between the tank and the regulator), and do so before every dive. You also should attach your regulator and open the valve, to listen for any hissing between the regulator and the tank, or in the primary and backup mouthpieces. If you hear any, ask the dive master to check it and, if need be, change the regulator. Arriving early lets you do all this before getting on the boat—ideally before leaving the shop—so you can swap gear if necessary.

There are some specific **questions** you should ask about a shop's practices. Has their air been tested and certified? Do they carry radios and oxygen? Does the captain always stay with the boat? Above all, be vocal and proactive about your safety, and remember, there are no stupid questions.

Finally, **logistics** can be a determining factor between two equally good dive shops. Items like: How is bottom time determined? How advanced are the other divers on your trip? (Some dive shops let you dive your own tank—as long as your computer safely allows—while others make

endemic splendid toadfish. This also is a good site for night dives because of its proximity to hotels, which means less time on the boat in the dark. Depth ranges 5-13 meters (16-43 feet). Snorkeling is decent near the shore, but be very careful of boat traffic.

DZUL-HÁ (AKA THE MONEY BAR)

Located off the old coastal road (Km 6.5), Dzul-Há is a good spot for DIY snorkeling, with small coral heads and sea fans that support blue tangs, parrot fish, and queen angels. Steps lead into the ocean, where depths range 3-10 meters (10-33 feet), with boundary ropes for added safety. You can rent snorkel gear on-site for US$15. Plan to have lunch here; the restaurant has huge portions and a full bar fronting a small beach.

TORMENTOS

At this site divers can see about 60 coral heads, each decorated with an assortment of sea fans, brain and whip corals, and sponges. The site is known for its many crevices and overhangs; keep your eyes peeled for hidden-away invertebrates like flamingo tongue shells, arrow crabs, black crinoids, and, of course, lobster (especially at the north end of the site). Definitely bring your camera to this one. Depth ranges 5-15 meters (16-49 feet).

YUCAB

A perfect drift dive, Yucab has archways, overhangs, and large coral heads—some as tall as three meters (10 feet)—that are alive with an incredible array of creatures. Lobsters, octopus, scorpionfish, banded coral shrimp, and

Dive sites, here we come!

everyone surface as soon as the first diver's tank hits 700 psi.) Also does the shop provide pickup/drop-off at your hotel? Is it a one- or two-tank excursion? And, if you're short of time or get seasick easily, how far are the dive sites from the dock?

Feeling free to ask questions or raise concerns (of any sort at any time) is a crucial factor in safe diving. That's where a dive shop's **personality** comes in. Every dive shop has its own culture or style, and different divers will feel more comfortable in different shops. Spend some time talking to people at a couple of different dive shops before signing up. Try to meet the person who will be leading your particular dive—you may have to come in the afternoon when that day's trip returns. Chances are one of the shops or dive masters will click with you.

butterfly fish can almost always be found. Photographers have a field day here. Try maneuvering behind some of the large formations—they block the current, giving you a chance to really enjoy the scenery. Depth ranges 5-15 meters (16-49 feet).

PUNTA TUNICH

Punta Tunich usually has a strong 1.5-knot current, which makes it a challenging but rewarding drift dive. The site itself has a white-sand bottom with a gentle downward slope that ends in a drop-off. Along the way, the reef is dotted with finger coral and elephant ear sponges. Divers regularly encounter eagle rays, barracuda, sea horses, bar jacks, and parrot fish. The depth ranges 5-18 meters (16-59 feet). Punta Tunich tends to be less crowded than other areas.

★ SANTA ROSA WALL

Santa Rosa Wall is a spectacular and iconic Cozumel dive—a must-see for intermediate and expert divers. With a sensational drop-off that begins at 22 meters (72 feet), Santa Rosa is famous for its tunnels, caves, and stony overhangs. Ask to start your dive on the northern end, where there are a series of swim-throughs that lead to the shallows. You're sure to see loads of sealife along the way: translucent sponges, mammoth sea fans, file clams, horse-eyed jacks, fairy basslets, gray angelfish, black groupers. The site has strong currents and depths ranging 5-27 meters (16-89 feet).

PASO DEL CEDRAL

A strip reef lined with small corals such as disk and cactus, this site attracts large schools of fish that include blue-striped grunts and snapper, and also is a good spot to see nurse and reef sharks, southern stingrays, and turtles. The current is strong but the visibility is good. Experienced divers should check out the adjacent wall. Depths range 10-20 meters (33-66 feet).

★ PALANCAR

This breathtaking five-kilometer-long (3.1-mile) dive spot is actually made up of five different sites—Shallows, Garden, Horseshoe, Caves, and Bricks. It's known for its series of enormous coral buttresses. Some drop off dramatically into winding ravines, deep canyons, and passageways; others have become archways and tunnels with formations 15 meters (49 feet) tall. The most popular site here is Palancar Horseshoe, which is made up of a horseshoe-shaped series of coral heads at the top of a drop-off. All sites are teeming with reef life but can also get packed with divers and snorkelers—book an early-morning trip to avoid the crowds. Depths range 5-40 meters (16-131 feet).

COLOMBIA

Colombia is another dive that is really two sites in one. Head to Colombia Shallows for gorgeous coral, abundant marinelife, and longer bottom time, or test your maneuvering skills at Colombia Deep, full of tall pillars separated by passageways, channels, and swim-throughs. Larger creatures—sea turtles, groupers, nurse sharks, and southern stingrays—are commonly seen here. The site is recommended for experienced divers. Depths range 5-40 meters (16-131 feet).

MARACAIBO

At the island's southern tip, Maracaibo is a deep buttress reef interspersed with tunnels, caves, and vertical walls. It's known for its immense coral formations as well as for the possibility of spotting large animals—sharks (blacktip and nurse) as well as turtles and eagle rays. Maracaibo is a deep-drift dive with strong currents, occasional up- and downdrafts, and rough surface conditions; it is recommended for advanced divers only. Descend slowly to maintain control. Depths range 30-40 meters (98-131 feet).

Dive Shops

Cozumel's diver safety record is good, and there are many competent outfits in addition to those listed here. Consider this list a starting point, to be augmented by the recommendations of trusted fellow divers, travelers, locals, and expats. Most important, go with a shop you feel comfortable with, not just the cheapest, the cheeriest, or the most convenient. Dive shops are generally open 8am-8pm daily, closing during those business hours only if no one's around to run the shop during a dive trip.

- **Blue Angel Dive Shop** (Carr. Costera Sur Km 2.2, tel. 987/872-0188, www.blueangelresort.com)
- **Careyitos Advanced Divers** (Marina Caleta, cell tel. 987/117-6187, www.careyitosadvanceddivers.com)
- **Caribbean Divers** (Calle 3 between Avs. Rafael Melgar and 5, tel. 987/872-1145, cdivers@prodigy.net.mx)
- **Deep Blue** (Calle Rosado Salas at Av. 10 Sur, tel. 987/872-5653, www.deepbluecozumel.com)
- **Deep Exposure Dive Center** (Av. 10 Sur between Calles 3 Sur and Rosado Salas, tel. 987/872-3621, toll-free U.S. tel. 866/670-2736, www.deepexposuredivecenter.com)
- **Eco Divers** (Av. 10 at Calle 1 Sur, tel. 987/872-5628, www.ecodiverscozumel.com)
- **Scuba Gamma** (Calle 5 near Av. 5 Sur, tel. 987/878-4257, www.scubagamma.net)
- **Scuba Life Cozumel** (Marina Fonatur, tel. 987/118-8226, www.scubalifecozumel.com)

1: Cozumel's colorful coral reef; **2:** fishing boat; **3:** the road into Parque Punta Sur

- **Scuba Tony** (no storefront, tel. 987/876-1171, U.S. tel. 405/698-2318, www.scubatony.com)
- **Studio Blue Cozumel** (Calle Rosado Salas between Avs. 5 and 10 Sur, tel. 987/872-4330, www.studioblue.com.mx)

SNORKELING

Snorkelers have plenty of options in Cozumel, from cheap-and-easy snorkeling tours to renting gear and exploring on your own, right from shore.

Most dive shops offer snorkeling as well as diving trips, usually visiting 2-3 sites for a half hour each (US$55-65 pp). Snorkelers often go out with a group of divers and either snorkel in the same general location or go to a nearby site while the divers are underwater. This can mean some extra downtime as divers get in and out of the water, but the advantage is that you typically go to better and less crowded sites.

For a quick and easy snorkeling tour, stop by one of the booths that flank the ferry pier. These trips are somewhat less expensive (though with larger groups) and can be booked right as you disembark from the ferry. Most offer two tours daily at around 11am and 2pm; some use a glass-bottom boat for extra pizzazz. The standard trip (US$50, including equipment) lasts 2-3 hours, visiting two or three sites and spending 30-45 minutes snorkeling at each one.

There are several terrific snorkeling spots near town and just offshore where you don't need a boat or a guide at all. Cozumel's boat drivers are careful about steering clear of snorkelers, but even so, do not swim too far from shore, look up and around frequently, and stay out of obvious boat lanes. If you plan to do a lot of snorkeling, especially outside of established snorkeling areas, consider bringing or buying an inflatable personal buoy. Designed for snorkelers, they are brightly colored and have a string you attach to your ankle or to a small anchor weight, alerting boat drivers of your presence. Also be aware of the current, which typically runs south to north and can be quite strong.

KITEBOARDING

Kiteboarding has quickly and thoroughly morphed from a novelty act to one of the most popular beach sports worldwide. Cozumel is no exception, with a dedicated cadre of kiteboarders and a growing number of options for travelers who want to learn or practice the sport.

De Lille Sports (Playa Casitas, Av. Rafael Melgar s/n, tel. 987/103-6711, www.delillesports.com) is operated by Cozumel native Raul de Lille, a former Olympic-level windsurfer and now one of Mexico's top kiters and instructors. Raul doesn't come cheap, but he's an outstanding instructor, not least for his calm demeanor and excellent English. Private lessons are US$125 per hour or US$500 per day. An intensive three-day introductory kiteboarding course includes 15 hours of instruction and costs US$900 per student (maximum 2 students per instructor); it also can be broken into modules depending on your time and previous experience. Kiteboarding rentals are US$150 per day for a full kit. For experienced kiters, de Lille offers clinics on kite control, tricks, and other specialties, plus adventuresome tours like downwinding the entire island. Look for the De Lille stand under the Shaka Snack Bar.

Another locally run option is **Cozumel Kiteboarding** (no storefront, tel. 987/876-1558, www.cozumelkiteboarding.com). The shop offers kiting excursions around the island (4 hours, US$250-350 for 1-2 people), including to the little-visited northern lagoons: Río de Plata, Monte Cristo, and Blind Bary. Kiteboarding instruction for beginners and more experienced students also is offered.

STAND-UP PADDLING

Stand-up paddling (or SUPing) is the sport du jour in Cozumel and around the world, and for good reason: It's fun and easy to learn yet challenging to master. It's also a unique way to experience Cozumel's rich coastline and extraordinarily clear waters. The glassy waters on Cozumel's western shore are perfect for the sport, which involves standing upright on an oversized surfboard-like board and using a long paddle to cruise around. Fitness buffs appreciate the full-core workout SUPing provides, while the elevated perspective allows you to see surprisingly well into the surrounding water—significantly better than in a kayak, in fact. It's not uncommon to see fish, rays, even sea turtles and dolphins swimming below and around you. Numerous resorts have SUP boards available for guests, and a handful of agencies offer instruction, rentals, and tours.

De Lille Sports (Playa Casitas, Av. Rafael Melgar s/n, tel. 987/103-6711, www.delillesports.com) is operated by windsurfing and kiteboarding legend (and Cozumel native) Raul de Lille, but he's big on SUPing too, even designing his own line of boards. The sports complement each other well: If there's not enough wind for kiting, it's probably perfect for SUPing, and vice versa. The agency offers private and group lessons, plus tours in remote areas of the island. SUP instruction runs US$60 per student (2-3 hours, maximum 8 students), while high-quality SUP rentals are US$25 per hour or US$85 per day.

Based out of Mr. Sancho's beach club, **Ha-Haak Paddleboarding Cozumel** (Carr. Costera Sur Km 15, cell tel. 987/800-3022, www.supcozumel.com, 8am-4pm daily) offers friendly one-on-one instruction (US$35/hour) as well as paddleboard rentals (US$35/hour or US$60/day). It also has a variety of tours that depart from different parts of the island, depending on the weather (US$60, 1.5 hours). All guides are bilingual.

SURFING

Owned and operated by professional surfer Nacho Gutierrez, **Cozumel Surfing** (no storefront, tel. 987/111-9290, www.cozumelsurfing.com, price varies) provides beginner surf lessons to adults and children of all ages. Instruction is given on the east side of the island in either a private or group setting. Classes typically begin with a 30-60-minute lesson on land to learn and practice the basics of surfing. Then it's straight to the water

for two separate 75-minute sessions alongside Nacho and his team. Snacks and drinks are provided, and rentals are available.

KAYAKING

Cozumel's calm, clear waters make it a nice place to kayak. Most **all-inclusive resorts** and some **beach clubs** have a handful of kayaks available for guests to use (free to US$12/hour). If you plan to swim or snorkel along the way—a great way to enjoy little-visited spots on the reef—be sure the kayak has a small anchor to prevent it from floating away.

SPORTFISHING AND SPEARFISHING

Cozumel boasts good deep-sea fishing year-round. It's one of few places anglers can go for the grand slam of billfishing: hooking into a blue marlin, a white marlin, a sailfish, and a swordfish all in a single day. It also has plentiful tuna, barracuda, dorado, wahoo, grouper, and shark. For an extra challenge, jump out of the boat and give spearfishing a try.

Albatros Charters (tel. 987/872-7904, toll-free U.S. tel. 888/333-4643, www.albatroscharters.com, US$500 for 4 hours, US$600 for 6 hours, US$700 for 8 hours) has a variety of boats, each able to carry at least six anglers. Trips include hotel pickup and drop-off, beer and soda, snacks, bait, and gear. Other recommended outfits include **Aquarius Fishing** (tel. 987/869-1096, toll-free U.S. tel. 800/371-2924, www.cozumelflatsfishing.com) and **Tres Hermanos Fishing Charters** (tel. 987/107-2030, www.cozumelfishing.com).

Spearfishing Today (Puerto de Abrigo, Carr. Costera Norte Km 1.5, tel. 987/876-0862, www.spearfishingtoday.com, US$250-850 for 2-6 people) gets rave reviews for its excellent service and wide variety of spearfishing excursions, from mellow first-timer and family tours to private "deep blue" outings for intermediate and advanced hunters. Half-day trips include gear, instruction, refreshments, and complimentary fish cleaning at the end of the tour. Although Cozumel is known for its currents, most trips head to the calmer protected waters at the island's north end (and outside the marine park, of course).

ECOPARKS AND WATER PARKS

★ Parque Punta Sur

Parque Punta Sur (Carr. Costera Sur Km 27, tel. 987/872-0914, www.cozumelparks.com, 9am-4pm Mon.-Sat., US$14 adult, US$8 child under 12) is a massive natural reserve on the southern tip of Cozumel. The park spans thousands of acres of coastal dunes, beaches, mangroves, and wetlands, and extends well out into the ocean, including large areas of coral reef. Its home to a vast array of land and sea creatures, including 30 types of seabirds and some huge crocodiles that live in the park's large inland lagoons. There's a small Maya ruin known as El Caracol, which dates to AD 1200 and is believed to have been used for navigation, plus the park's famous lighthouse (which you can climb for great views) and a small but rewarding maritime museum. At the park's long, lovely beach—about a kilometer past the lighthouse—there are beach chairs, restrooms, a small eatery, and a shop to rent snorkel gear and kayaks. The snorkeling here is outstanding, including sea fan "forests" that wave gently in the current.

Most visitors arrive on package tours, but it's perfectly easy to visit independently; there's even a separate area away from the volleyball nets and buffet lines for people arriving on their own. You'll need a car or to hire a cab (US$15 from downtown) and be sure to arrive no later than 1pm in order to take full advantage of all the park has to offer.

Chankanaab

Some nine kilometers (5.6 miles) south of town, **Chankanaab** (Carr. Costera Sur Km 9, tel. 987/872-0914, www.cozumelparks.com, 8am-4pm daily, US$21 adult, US$14 child under 12) is a national park that operates mainly as a beach club and water park; that is to say, more Xcaret than Punta Sur. A visit here includes sunbathing by the pool,

snorkeling in the ocean, relaxing in a hammock, and watching the sea lion shows (included in the ticket price); there is also a zip line course, a crocodile sanctuary, replicas of various Maya ruins, and a small tequila "museum" (i.e., a bar with a hacienda feel, old photos, and a small agave patch). **Dolphin Discovery** (toll-free Mex. tel. 800/727-5391, toll-free U.S. tel. 866/393-5158, www.dolphindiscovery.com) has a facility within the park, with various interactive programs with dolphins, manatees, and sea lions, for an additional fee. Reserve in advance or right upon arrival, as they fill up fast. Chankanaab also has a fully equipped dive shop on-site, plus two thatch-roofed restaurants, a handful of gift shops, lockers, and restrooms. Chankanaab may be a bit commercialized for independent travelers—consider Punta Sur instead—but it's a great option for families looking for an easy all-day option.

GOLF

Jack Nicklaus designed the par-72 championship course at **Cozumel Country Club** (Carr. Costera Norte Km 6.5, tel. 987/872-9570, www.cozumelcountryclub.com.mx, 6:30am-6pm daily), located at the far end of the northern hotel zone. Greens fees are US$99 before 8am (and all day Sunday), US$125 until 1:30pm, and US$89 afterwards. Carts are required and included in the rate. In addition to the slightly rolling, moderately challenging course, the club has a driving range, putting and chipping areas, overnight bag storage, a retail shop, and lessons from PGA golf pros. Book online for a discount.

SPAS

Spa del Sol (Calle 5 between Avs. 5 and Rafael Melgar, tel. 987/872-6474, www.spadelsolcozumel.com, 9am-7pm Mon.-Sat., 10am-2pm Sun.) provides a variety of traditional and holistic treatments in its quaint downtown location. Almost a dozen types of massages are offered, including Swedish, Thai, and Aquasana (a treatment performed in open water). Acupuncture, Reiki, and ear

Parque Punta Sur

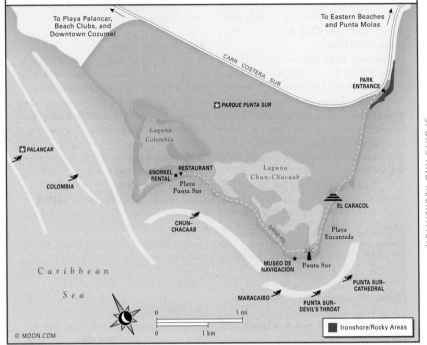

To Playa Palancar, Beach Clubs, and Downtown Cozumel

To Eastern Beaches and Punta Molas

CARR. COSTERA SUR

PARK ENTRANCE

⭐ PARQUE PUNTA SUR

Laguna Colombia

⭐ PALANCAR

COLOMBIA

SNORKEL RENTAL

RESTAURANT

Playa Punta Sur

Laguna Chun-Chacaab

EL CARACOL

CHUN–CHACAAB

SAND RD.

Playa Encantada

Caribbean

Sea

MUSEO DE NAVIGACION

Punta Sur

PUNTA SUR–CATHEDRAL

MARACAIBO

PUNTA SUR–DEVIL'S THROAT

0   1 mi
0   1 km

Ironshore/Rocky Areas

© MOON.COM

candling, among other alternative treatments, also are performed regularly. One-hour treatments run US$60-80. Walk-ins are very welcome, and shorter and longer sessions are available, too.

Barefoot in Cozumel (Calle 3 between Avs. 25 and 30, tel. 987/878-4662, www.barefootincozumel.com, 9am-7pm daily by appointment only, US$60/85 per 60/90 minutes) is the one-woman business of U.S. certified massage therapist Sally Hurwitch. She offers a popular Ashiatsu massage, which is administered using her feet to help clients who suffer from chronic back pain. Swedish massages as well as energy treatments, such as Reiki, are also offered.

Temazcal Cozumel (Xcan-Ha Reserve, tel. 987/876-3565, experiencia.cozumel@gmail.com, US$80) provides a traditional Maya steam lodge experience. It's a favorite practice of health- and spiritual-minded folks of all stripes, and especially popular in the region. Temazcal Cozumel has a lovely spot to experience this unique treatment, a leafy retreat well inland from Cozumel's busy western shore. A session here begins by addressing the cardinal directions before entering the low, circular brick hut, where a guide leads guests through additional exercises and visualizations, related to ancient Maya beliefs as well as one's own experiences—all intended to further the cleansing and mind-opening process. Afterward, you can take a dip in a nearby freshwater cenote and relax in a hammock with a fresh-made juice.

FITNESS

EGO (Calle 11 at Av. 5, tel. 987/872-4897, 5:30am-11pm Mon.-Fri., 6am-6pm Sat.) is a full-service gym complete with free weights, weight machines, cardio machines (plus personal trainers to help), and a slew of classes including Pilates, yoga, spinning, and kickboxing. Monthly membership is US$35, while visitors pay a mere US$5 per visit. All that, plus air-conditioning!

Cozumel Yoga Center (Av. 5 between Calles 9 and 9 Bis, tel. 987/869-1055, www.yogacozumel.com, US$5-8) offers a wide variety of yoga classes—26 styles at last count. Yoga and meditation workshops as well as teacher trainings are also a regular part of the programming. Classes are held either in the studio, in an oceanfront *palapa,* or on the beach.

Yo Yoga Cozumel (Av. 15 at Calle 10, tel. 987/113-5283, info@yoCozumel.com, US$5) offers early-morning and late-afternoon instruction in a variety of yoga practices, including flow, Ashtanga, and aerial. Classes are held either in a small studio, on the rooftop, or on the beach. Prices are suggested—the studio encourages students to pay what they can, whether it's more or less than what's listed.

TOURS AND CLASSES
Horseback Riding
Located on the inland side of the highway across from Nachi-Cocom beach club, **Rancho Palmitas** (Carr. Costera Sur Km 16, cell tel. 987/118-3032, palmitas_ernesto@hotmail.com, 8am-4pm daily) offers two horseback tours. A 2.5-3-hour tour (US$40 pp) includes stops at a cavern with a cenote, the archaeological site of El Cedral, and a few unexcavated Maya ruins. A shorter 1.5-hour tour (US$35 pp) leads to the cavern only. Call to set up a tour or just drop in—the last excursion leaves at 3pm.

ATV Excursions
Though catering to cruise ship passengers, **Wild Tours** (Av. 95 at Calle 11, tel. 987/872-5876, toll-free U.S./Can. tel. 888/497-4283, www.wild-tours.com) offers ATV excursions to everyone. Tours include off-roading through the jungle, visiting a cenote and inland cave, exploring isolated Maya ruins, relaxing and snorkeling at Playa Uva's beach club, even a 45-minute ride in a high-speed jet boat (US$70-90 adult, US$95-115 child with adult, 4 hours).

Submarine Tour
Atlantis Submarines (Carr. Costera Km 4, tel. 987/872-5671, toll-free Mex. tel. 800/715-0804, www.atlantissubmarines.com, US$105 adult, US$65 child) offers 40-minute underwater excursions near Chankanaab national park, including to Felipe Xicotencatl, a 154-foot-long minesweeper sunk to promote the coral reef's health. The sub has oversized portholes with low seats in a long row down the center. Staff members describe what you're seeing outside. The sub dives as deep as 80 feet; you're sure to see lots of tropical fish and coral formations, and, if you're really lucky, a shark or sea turtle. It's pretty pricey considering how short the actual tour is, but it's a memorable way for youngsters and nondivers to admire Cozumel's marine riches.

Cooking Classes
Josefina's Cocina Con Alma (tel. 987/105-5300, www.cozumelchef.com, US$80 adult, US$70 teen 13-17, US$30 child 6-12, by appointment only) is a small cooking school offering private bilingual instruction in Yucatecan and classic Mexican dishes. Classes begin with a field trip to the market to select fresh ingredients, and then it's straight to the kitchen to learn to create a preselected meal. Dishes offered range from *cochinita pibil* (pork marinated in orange juice, achiote, and other spices and baked in banana leaves) and *sopa de lima* (a citrus-based soup with shredded turkey and fried tortilla strips) to *chiles en nogada* (poblano peppers stuffed with meat or cheese and topped with a walnut-based cream sauce and pomegranate seeds) and tamales (seasoned meat, cheese, or vegetables stuffed in a cornmeal dough and wrapped in corn husks). Afterward, students enjoy their creations at a sit-down meal. Chef Josefina gets rave reviews for her expertise and warm manner.

Entertainment and Events

NIGHTLIFE

Most of the partying on Cozumel happens during daylight hours, when cruise ships disgorge thousands of tourists eager to stretch their legs and see some new faces. Beach clubs can get raucous, and many bars in town are open before lunch. Still, there are enough locals, expats, and overnight visitors to support a cadre of lounges and nightclubs. Most places don't charge a cover; if they do, it's on select nights, such as when there's a live band.

Bars and Breweries

At long last, Cozumel's first craft brewery! **Cerveceria Punta Sur** (Av. 10 between Av. Rosado Salas and Calle 3, tel. 987/119-2879, www.cerveceriapuntasur.com, 2pm-11pm Tues.-Sun.) serves up a changing variety of homemade brews, though the IPA is a local fave. Pints and flights run US$3-5. The tasting room has a mid-century modern-meets-Mexico look, and a kitchen serves wood-fired pizza, empanadas, and salad.

Pitched as a "Husband Day Care Center," **Kelley's** (Av. 10 between Calles 1 and Rosado Salas, tel. 987/878-4738, 9am-midnight daily) is an outdoor sports bar with nine HDTVs and a monster projection screen airing major sporting events, including pay-per-view. There's Guinness on tap plus weekly food specials like all-you-can-eat barbecue, twelve-for-six wings, and dollar taco day.

Set in a 102-year-old clapboard house, **Cantina La Chupería** (Av. 10 at Calle 8, cell tel. 984/132-6224, 1pm-2am daily) has a classic Mexican dive bar feel: dim lighting, traditional Talavera tiles, long family-style wood tables. It's no-frills except for the drinks—a full line of craft beer, domestic and foreign, is the poison of choice here. Mezcal cocktails give the taps a run for their money. Open late, this is an after-hours hot spot.

La Casa del Mojito (Av. 5 near Calle 3, tel. 987/111-4124, 4pm-midnight Mon.-Sat.) is a Cuban restaurant-bar that—surprise!—serves some of the best mojitos on the island. Mojitos come in a variety of flavors but the classic—fresh mint, crushed ice, lots of rum—packs a punch. Sit at the bar or grab a table and order *tostones* to go with your drinks.

Nightclubs and Live Music

Tiki Tok (Av. Rafael Melgar between Calles 2 and 4, tel. 987/872-5704, 11am-3am Mon.-Sat., no cover) sports a hodgepodge of beach-isle decor, from Polynesian lamps to Jamaican carved masks and figures. There's a dance floor, plenty of tables, and nice sea views. A live band gets the crowd moving to salsa and bachata Friday and Saturday nights, starting around 9:30pm. The bar is popular during the day with cruise shippers, and at night with locals.

Wet Wendy's (Av. 5 Norte between Av. Benito Juárez and Calle 2, tel. 987/872-4970, www.wetwendys.com, 10am-midnight Mon.-Sat., noon-10:30pm) is a classic expat island bar, with Monday Night Football, bacon burgers, and a jocular atmosphere. There's live music most nights too. But more than anything, Wet Wendy's is famous for its huge handcrafted margaritas: potent creations that look more like sundaes than cocktails and range from mango and ginger to peanut butter-chocolate and cucumber-jalapeño.

Metropolitan (Av. Rafael Melgar between Calles 2 and 4, cell tel. 987/119-6823, 7pm-4am Wed.-Sun.) is a bouncing 2nd-floor club with long, high tables and music and dancing most nights. Thursdays and Fridays often bring specials like US$5 open bar and US$1.50 beers.

THE ARTS
Cultural and Music Performances

Every Sunday evening, the city hosts an **open-air concert** in the central plaza. Locals and expats come out to enjoy the show—put on a clean T-shirt and your nicest flip-flops, and you'll fit right in. Concerts typically last two hours, beginning at 7pm in the summer, 8pm in the winter. Simple food stands selling homemade flan, churros, and other local goodies set up around the park on these nights. **Casa de la Cultura Ixchel de Cozumel** (Av. 50 between Av. Benito Juárez and Calle 2, tel. 987/872-1471, 9am-5pm Mon.-Fri.) hosts free concerts, movies, and art exhibits year-round. If you'll be on the island for an extended stay, a variety of classes—dance, art, music, drama, creative writing—also are offered, with a wide selection for children.

Cinema

You can catch relatively recent releases at **Cinépolis** (Av. Rafael Melgar between Calles 15 and 17, tel. 987/869-0799, www.cinepolis. com.mx, US$3.75 adult, US$2.25 child, US$2.25 adult before 3pm), which is located in the Chedraui shopping center. All day Wednesday, tickets are US$2.25.

FESTIVALS AND EVENTS
Carnaval

Cozumel is one of the few places in Mexico where Carnaval is celebrated with vigor. Held in February, the one-night celebration centers on a parade of floats and dance troupes, all decked out in colorful dress, masks, and glitter. Entire families come to participate and watch. Spectators dance and cheer in the streets as the floats go by, and many join the moving dance party that follows the floats with the largest speakers. Eventually the parade ends up in the center of town, where more music, dancing, and partying continue late into the night. Typically, the weekends leading up to the party are filled with musical performances and events—such as the crowing of the king and queen of Carnaval—in the central plaza.

Festival de El Cedral

Residents of the village of El Cedral celebrate their namesake festival beginning in late April and culminating on May 3, the Day of the Holy Cross. Traditionally, the festival entails daily prayer sessions and ends with a dance called the *Baile de las Cabezas de Cochino* (Dance of the Pigs' Heads). The festival, started by a survivor of the Caste War to honor the power of the cross, has morphed over the years into a somewhat more secular affair, with rodeos, dancing, music, and general revelry.

Rodeo de Lanchas Mexicanas

Every May, Cozumel hosts a popular sportfishing tournament known affectionately as the Mexican Boat Rodeo (tel. 987/564-0405, www.rodeodelanchasmexicanas. com). Prizes range from cash to luxury cars. Anglers from all over Mexico participate—including nearly 200 boats—and international anglers are welcome as long as they register their boats in Mexico. The tournament is timed to coincide with the arrival of big game to Cozumel's waters; tuna, dorado, marlin, and sailfish are often among the fish caught.

Fiesta de San Miguel Arcángel

You'd be forgiven for not knowing that the main town on Cozumel is officially called San Miguel. Hardly anyone, local or tourist, calls it that, preferring just Cozumel instead. One story, among many, is that the city got its name when construction workers unearthed a centuries-old statue of the winged saint on September 29, the very day Saint Michael the Archangel is traditionally celebrated. San Miguel was designated the town's patron saint, and every year September 29 is marked with a citywide celebration, including special masses and religious processions, a rodeo, food stands, music, and general revelry, mostly in and around the central square and San Miguel church.

Festival de Aves

Held in late October or early November, the **Festival de Aves** (Festival of Birds, tel. 987/872-4689, cozumelbirdingclub@gmail. com) is a three-day event that brings birders to the island to sneak a peek at or learn more about the almost 350 species of birds found in Cozumel. Bird-watching outings are the highlight of the event, but bird-related conferences, workshops, and exhibits also are quite interesting.

Gran Fondo Cozumel

The Italian-born international bicycle racing craze that is *Il Gran Fondo* made its Cozumel debut in 2014, with over 400 riders participating in the inaugural event. By 2017, it had grown to over 2,500 riders. Like all Gran Fondo races, Cozumel's features a mass start, individual chip timing, and an atmosphere that's both jocular and competitive. The main 100-mile Gran Fondo takes riders twice clockwise around the island; a "Medio Fondo" option is 50 miles and just one lap. A "King of the Wind" medal is given to the racer with the fastest intermediate time along the 19-kilometer section from Punta Sur to Mezcalitos, infamous for punishing "Maya winds." Gran Fondo New York (www.gfnycozumel.com) has good information about the race.

Ironman Cozumel

Ironman Cozumel (www.ironman.com) is one of two qualifying events in the Ironman series to be held in Mexico (the other is in Los Cabos). It features a course that's as beautiful as it is grueling. The swim (3.8 kilometers/2.4 miles) is certainly the most distinctly *cozumeleño* part, starting and ending at Chankanaab, with gorgeous underwater vistas, and scuba divers and sea creatures observing from below. The bike ride (180 kilometers/112 miles) entails three laps around the island, with lovely sea views but crosswinds strong enough to topple unwitting racers. The run is oddly uninspired—three laps between downtown and the airport—although the sunsets there are spectacular. Ironman Cozumel is usually held in late November and typically attracts around 2,800 triathletes.

Cozumel Scuba Fest

Every June, hundreds of divers from around the world converge on Cozumel for the annual **Cozumel Scuba Fest** (www. cozumelfest.com), a six-day celebration of the island's unique underwater wonderland. The marquee event typically is the "Jean Michel Cousteau Route," a four-day, nine-dive circuit that retraces signature dives made by Jean Michel's famous father. The festival also includes dive competitions, lectures, film screenings, equipment demos and sales, gala events, and plenty of impromptu carousing in venues throughout the island. Many hotels and dive shops offer special packages for what is arguably the premier diving festival in the Americas.

Shopping

Shopping in Cozumel is aimed straight at cruise ship passengers—and it's no wonder, since they tend to spend a lot of money quickly. Avenida Rafael Melgar is where most of the action is, with a succession of marble-floored shops blasting air-conditioning to entice sweaty passersby in for a refreshing look around. For better prices and more variety, head inland a block or two.

AVENIDA MELGAR

Populated with a mix of high-end jewelry shops and souvenir chain stores, Avenida Melgar has the highest prices in town for items that, on the whole, can be found back home. None of the shops are open to bargaining—at least when there is a cruise ship in port—so if you're looking for a deal, head inland a couple of blocks. In fact, unless you find something you absolutely can't live without, you're uniformly better off shopping elsewhere on the island.

The one exception to this rule is **Los Cinco Soles** (Av. Rafael Melgar at Calle 8, tel. 987/872-9004, www.loscincosoles.com,

8am-8pm daily). A labyrinth of rooms at the northern end of Avenida Melgar, it's filled with high-end Mexican folk art from every state in the country: pre-Columbian replicas, *barro negro* pottery, colorful *rebosos* (shawls), hand-carved furniture, silver jewelry, handmade wood toys, alabaster sculptures, wool rugs, and more. The prices are higher than others in town, but it's reflected in the quality. It's definitely worth a stop, if only to admire the artisanship.

CENTRAL PLAZA AND BEYOND

Aquatic Performance (Calle 1 between Avs. 85 and 90, tel. 987/869-8116, www.cozumelscubarepair.com, 8:30am-5pm Mon.-Fri., 8:30am-1pm Sat.) is a highly recommended shop selling and renting snorkel and dive equipment. It also repairs dive equipment, often with 24-hour turnaround times, and provides loaners if needed. If you plan to return to Cozumel to dive, long-term storage of equipment is available for US$120 per year and includes a complete regulator servicing.

Plaza del Sol has souvenirs and keepsakes of all kinds.

Though pricey, **Pro Dive Cozumel** (Calle Rosado Salas at Av. 5, tel. 987/872-2420, 9am-9pm daily) is centrally located and has a great selection of snorkel and dive equipment—perfect if you've forgotten your mask or lost a fin.

Sergio's (Av. Benito Juárez between Avs. 5 and 10, tel. 987/872-7632, 10am-8pm daily) is a longtime mom-and-pop shop that specializes in high-end jewelry made from silver from Taxco, Mexico's silver mining capital. Most of the items are made by local artisans, which means you'll find unique and beautiful pieces of jewelry. Unlike other shops, there's no pressure to buy, though prices are nonnegotiable. If you don't find what you're looking for here, head to its second location one block east on Avenida Juárez between Avenidas 10 and 15 (same phone and hours).

Cucuru (Av. 10 near Av. Rosado Salas, no tel., 1pm-9pm Tues.-Sun.) is a lovely little shop selling gorgeous and wearable Mexican *artesanía*—shawls, dresses, purses—much of it from Chiapas and Oaxaca. There's also handmade jewelry for sale, made by local artisans. The staff is friendly and helpful and the items well priced. The name of the shop is a nod to a traditional Mexican lullaby.

If you're in the market for a pair of traditional leather sandals, check out **Huaracheria Margarita** (Av. 30 at Calle 3, no phone, 10am-8pm Mon.-Sat., 10am-2pm Sun.). Among the colorful jellies and flip-flops, you'll find rows and rows of handmade huaraches, many brought from the mainland. The leather inventory is well priced, especially considering the craftsmanship that goes into making each sandal.

Calipso Sportsfish Center (Calle 9 Bis. s/n, tel. 987/872-4105, 9am-2pm and 4pm-7pm Mon.-Fri., 10am-5pm Sat.) is a small shop specializing in fishing gear—everything from bait and tackle to clothing and flags to high-end fishing poles. There are no rentals, unfortunately.

Balam Mayan Feather (Av. 5 at Calle 2, tel. 987/869-0548, 10am-10pm daily) trades in a unique and dying art: selling oil paintings created on the feathers of regional birds. Most feathers depict scenes of traditional villages or ancient Maya people, but there is a decent variety beyond that, including tropical flowers and sealife. If you're lucky, an artist will be working on a new feather painting while you're browsing—feel free to watch. Prices range US$30-150.

Artists can be found demonstrating their skills and plying their wares in Cozumel's plazas.

SHOPPING CENTERS

Located in a yellow building on the east side of the main plaza, **Plaza del Sol** (Av. 5 Norte between Av. Benito Juárez and Calle 1, 9am-8pm Mon.-Sat., 11am-5pm Sun.) houses a labyrinth of small souvenir shops selling everything from T-shirts to silver jewelry. You'll have to poke around a bit to find items worth buying, but a little perseverance will go a long way, especially if you're on a tight budget.

Punta Langosta (Av. Rafael Melgar between Calles 7 and 11, 9am-8pm daily) is downtown Cozumel's biggest shopping center. The modern open-air building is home to air-conditioned jewelry stores, knickknack shops, and fancy ice cream stands. It's a decent place to window-shop, especially if you want to buy a memento but aren't sure exactly what you'd like.

Located across from the Puerto Maya and TMM International piers, **Royal Village Shopping Center** (Carr. Sur Km 4.5, tel. 987/857-0457, 9am-6pm Mon.-Sat.) is squarely aimed at cruise ship travelers. Shops are higher-end and international—think Swarovski, Zingara, Harley-Davidson. There's also a Hard Rock Café.

Every weekend, a *mercado artesanal* (crafts market, Av. 10 between Av. Benito Juárez and Calle 1, 5pm-9pm Fri.-Sun.) is held behind Plaza del Sol. Handcrafted items, all locally made, are sold: jewelry, candles, clothing, soaps and lotions, decorative knickknacks. Live music plays and food stands pop up, making it a festive place to shop or just take in the scene.

Food

Cozumel's food scene is steadily improving, with an ever-increasing variety and quality of restaurants. Like most islands, it has terrific seafood, always served fresh, everywhere from gourmet restaurants to simple eateries. (You may be surprised to learn, though, that much of the catch actually comes from around Isla Mujeres because the waters around Cozumel are protected.) The island's popularity with Americans, especially hungry divers, means you'll never want for steak, pizza, or big breakfasts either.

MEXICAN AND YUCATECAN

★ **Otates Tacos** (Av. 15 between Calles Rosado Salas and 3, tel. 987/120-1076, noon-4am Sun.-Thurs., noon-5am Fri.-Sat., US$2-6) is a bustling taco joint serving authentic Mexican grub at nearly street-cart prices. Tacos are just the beginning, served piping hot on tiny corn tortillas; the quesadillas, *tortas* (Mexican-style sandwiches), and *pozole* (pork and hominy soup) are all terrific,

and the guacamole is rave-worthy. Service is fast and friendly, with menus in Spanish and English.

Kinta (Av. 5 between Calles 2 and 4 Norte, tel. 987/869-0544, www.kintarestaurante.com, 5pm-11pm daily, US$8-17) is a chic bistro serving gourmet Mexican dishes and knockout cocktails. Seating is indoors in a modern, welcoming space or outdoors in a leafy tropical garden. The menu is seasonal but often includes specialties like *chile relleno*, a poblano chile stuffed with ratatouille and Chihuahua cheese, and *peskado,* catch of the day baked in a pumpkin-sesame seed crust and smothered in a spicy *mole verde* sauce. Be sure to try the margarindo—an unforgettable tamarind-based margarita. Reservations are recommended.

Kondesa (Av. 5 between Calles 5 and 7, tel. 987/869-1086, www.kondesacozumel.com, 5pm-11pm daily, US$8-18) may well be Cozumel's classiest restaurant, with its sister restaurant, Kinta, its closest competition. Seating is in a lush garden with tables under a high *palapa*, on a central wooden platform, or right under the stars. The menu has some classic Mexican and Mediterranean dishes, but is mostly contemporary fusion. The guacamole trio and lionfish cakes are popular appetizers and go well with the restaurant's creative cocktails, including mojitos and sangria. The catch of the day is always flavorful and inventive, while homemade churros and coffee make a perfect dessert.

Crazy King Burrito (Av. 5 at Calle 4, tel. 987/102-6638, 11am-7pm Mon.-Sat., US$2.50-9.50) is a tiny family-run eatery serving up massive burritos, stuffed with classics like chicken, meat, and beans. If you're looking for something different, try one of the shrimp combos or brave the California, which features chicken strips, french fries, beans, cheese, and lettuce, all smothered in ranch dressing. Take your meal to go or grab a seat at one of the street-front tables.

The breezy *palapa*-roofed **La Candela** (Av. 5 at Calle 6 Norte, tel. 987/878-4471, 8am-11pm Mon.-Sat., US$4-9) offers an extensive lineup of Mexican and traditional Yucatecan dishes in a cafeteria-style setting. Check out what's steaming behind the glass window cases, find a seat, and then place your order with your waitperson. Lunch specials typically include soup or pasta, a main dish, and a drink (US$5-6).

Opened in 1962, **La Cozumeleña** (Av. 10 Sur at Calle 3, tel. 987/872-0189, 7am-3pm daily, US$3-7) is a longtime favorite with local families and professionals, serving classic dishes in a quiet air-conditioned dining area. For breakfast, try *chilaquiles* (fried tortilla strips, scrambled eggs, and chicken doused in green or red salsa) or eggs with *chaya*. Lunch specials include a main dish, like fish tacos or baked chicken, and a drink. There's a bakery next door for dessert-on-the-go afterward.

SEAFOOD

Mariscos Camilo's (Av. 5 between Calles 2 and 4, tel. 987/872-6161, 11am-9pm Mon.-Sat., 11am-8pm Sun., US$8-16) is a small place offering an abundance of fresh seafood: ceviche, shrimp cocktail, lobster tail, fried fish, grilled fish, soups, tacos, salads, and even seafood sandwiches—you name it, they've probably got it. Popular with locals and expats.

Lobster Shack (Calle 3 near Av. Rafael Melgar, tel. 987/869-0812, 11am-10pm Mon.-Sat., US$7-18) is exactly what it sounds like: a hole-in-the-wall serving lobster goodness. Think po'boys, burritos, and bowls all featuring lobster purchased directly from the fishermen. Steak and shrimp are also offered, just in case. Can't decide? Try the Cozumel Box (US$15), which features three half po'boys of lobster, steak, and shrimp with a side of chips and coleslaw and a drink.

Spacious **La Conchita del Caribe** (Av. 65 between Calles 13 and 15, tel. 987/872-5888, 11am-8pm daily, US$6-13) is another locals' favorite and a great off-the-beaten-path option. Whole fish served grilled or fried is the house specialty—choose your own out of a cooler by the counter and pay according to size. Beyond fresh fish, the menu is rife with shrimp, octopus, squid, and conch, almost all swimming earlier in the day. Takeout is also available.

OTHER SPECIALTIES

Sal de Mar (Calle 3 between Avs. 5 and 10, tel. 987/872-2708, www.saldemarczm.com, 1pm-11pm Mon.-Sat., 4pm-10pm Sun, US$11-17) serves creative Mediterranean fusion dishes with Asian, Mexican, and American twists. Think lobster mac n' cheese or thin-crust pizza with chorizo, miso, and chipotle toppings. The setting is "welcoming hipster," with a mid-century modern design and trees growing through the middle of the restaurant. Service is excellent.

La Cocay (Calle 8 between Avs. 10 and 15, tel. 987/872-5533, www.lacocay.com, 5:30pm-11pm daily, US$15-22) offers Mediterranean cuisine with flair. The menu changes seasonally, but expect to see dishes like fish of the day with Cajun spice and mango sauce and blue-cheese-filled phyllo dough rolls with black cherry sauce. Seating is in a candlelit

dining room or on the breezy garden patio—perfect for a special night out.

★ **Le Chef** (5 Av. near Calle 5, tel. 987/878-4391, noon-11pm Mon.-Sat., US$7-15) is a cozy bistro serving gourmet baguettes, pasta dishes, and salads. The most popular item is the lobster bacon sandwich, a hefty and flavorful dish packed with fresh lobster meat; order a salad and it's plenty for two. Seating is in a whimsical dining room or in a breezy back patio.

Founded in 1978, **Guido's** (Av. Rafael Melgar between Calles 6 and 8, tel. 987/872-0946, www.guidoscozumel.com, 11am-11pm Mon.-Sat., 3pm-9:30pm Sun., US$13-25) is a bit pricey but worth every peso, serving unique Italian dishes like brick-oven-baked lasagna, homemade pastas, memorable seafood dishes (like prosciutto-wrapped sea scallops served with risotto and citrus beurre blanc sauce), and excellent desserts. The leafy courtyard setting makes a meal here all the more worthwhile.

New Especias (Calle 3 between Avs. 5 and 10, tel. 987/869-7947, 6pm-11pm Thurs.-Tues., US$15-28) is a longtime go-to restaurant that serves up excellent Italian dishes along with friendly service. Favorites include smoked salmon with asparagus fettucine and filet mignon with peppercorn sauce. A plate of complimentary bruschetta comes with every meal. Seating is either in a dimly lit dining room or on a breezy balcony with street views.

LIGHT FARE

Tiny, bright, and welcoming, ★ **Cali Café** (Av. Rosado Salas between Avs. 10 and 15, tel. 987/872-6275, 8am-8pm Tues.-Fri., 9am-8pm Sat.-Sun., US$3-6) serves up a tasty menu of vegetarian and vegan dishes. Plant-based tacos, burgers, scrambles, and bowls form the basis of the offerings; ask about the protein of the day. A remarkable menu of fresh-squeezed juices and smoothies make this a good place for a midday stop as well.

Corazón Contento (Av. 10 at Calle 2, tel. 987/872-0838, 7am-2pm Mon.-Sat., US$3-6) has a peaceful and welcoming ambience befitting its name (Contented Heart). A home converted into a restaurant, service is friendly, with great bottomless coffee and simple breakfast and lunch specials. Watch out: The bread basket is charged per item, and the chocolate-filled croissants are almost impossible to resist!

Nacho Crazy Boy (Av. 20 Sur between Av. Benito Juárez and Calle 1, 8am-11pm Mon.-Sat., 10am-2pm Sun., US$2-3) serves outstanding juices and smoothies right from the patio of the owner's modest house. Fruits fresh from the market are squeezed and blended on the spot by Nacho Crazy Boy himself, an earnest and interesting guy who makes time for conversation with customers.

SWEETS

A display case of beautiful French pastries greets you at **Sucré y Sale** (Calle 2 between Avs. 5 and 10, tel. 987/115-5968, 8am-10pm daily, US$3-5), a cozy café just a block from the sea. Everything is freshly made, from the tarts and chocolate gateau to the baguette sandwiches and quiche. It's a perfect place for a cappuccino, a light meal, or an indulgent hour.

Rave reviews keep the small **Chocolateria Isla Bella** (Av. 5 between Calles 2 and 4, tel. 987/111-8462, noon-8pm Mon.-Sat., US$2 per chocolate) hopping. A mother-daughter team creates exquisite handmade chocolates in a variety of flavors, including vanilla bean, TLC (tequila, lime, and coconut), and a luscious triple dark chocolate. New creations and holiday specials are announced on the restaurant's Facebook page, as well as special events such as truffle-making classes.

At **Zermatt** (Av. 5 Norte at Calle 4, tel. 987/872-1384, 7am-9pm Mon.-Sat., US$1-2.50) you may have to jostle with locals for a crack at the island's best traditional Mexican baked goods. Be sure to grab a tray and tongs to make your selections—and maybe consider

---

1: *huevos rancheros,* a classic Mexican breakfast;
2: Cozumel's Mercado Municipal

getting a little something extra for the stray pooch that is often hanging around out front.

La Flor de Michoacán (Calle 1 near Av. 10, 9am-11pm daily, US$1-2) serves cool treats, including *aguas* (fruit drinks), *helados* (ice cream), and *paletas* (Popsicles).

GROCERIES

Whatever groceries you need, you'll find them and more at **MEGA** (Av. Rafael Melgar at Calle 11, tel. 987/872-3658, 7am-11pm daily), the island's largest supermarket.

For a traditional market experience, Cozumel's **Mercado Municipal** (Av. 25 between Calles 1 and Rosado Salas, 7am-3pm daily) has stalls brimming with colorful produce, freshly butchered chickens, eggs, cheeses, spices, and more, all at reasonable prices.

Accommodations

DOWNTOWN COZUMEL
Under US$50

One block from the central plaza, **Hostelito** (Av. 10 between Av. Benito Juárez and Calle 2 Norte, tel. 987/869-8157, www.hostelcozumel.com, US$15 dorm, US$18-20 dorm with a/c, US$40 s/d with a/c, US$50-60 suite with a/c and kitchenette) is a stylish hostel with a large coed dorm packed with 20 bunks, lockers, and fans. Groups of four or more should ask about the air-conditioned dorm with private bathroom—at US$18-20 per head, it's a steal. Private doubles have air-conditioning and TVs. There also are a couple of spacious suites with kitchenettes and lots of natural light. A fully equipped rooftop kitchen is available to all, as is a great lounge, solarium, and a pool.

2Tank Dive Hostel Cozumel (Av. Juárez between Avs. 5 and 10, tel. 987/872-6601, www.divehostel.com, US$11-15 dorm with a/c, US$30-34 s/d with a/c) is a modern place aimed at budget travelers who are more interested in diving than partying. Dorms and private rooms are sparse and windowless but beds are comfortable enough and the air-conditioning runs full blast at night. There's a clean common kitchen, a comfortable lounge, and most importantly, a full-service dive shop with knowledgeable staffers. Fun dives and lots of PADI courses are offered. Guests receive a US$10 discount on their room rate per day if they dive with the shop.

Though a long way from downtown, **Amigos Hostel Cozumel** (Calle 7 between Avs. 25 and 30, tel. 987/872-3868, www.cozumelhostel.com, US$12 dorm, US$45 s/d/t) is a great option for budget travelers looking for a peaceful stay. The hostel's sprawling property has a well-tended pool, a fully equipped communal kitchen, an open-air game room (with a pool table), and lots of hammocks and lounge chairs. There are two mixed dorms with four bunks apiece and en suite bathrooms. There's also one private room with a kitchenette that sleeps three comfortably. All units have air-conditioning, but it's only turned on May-October (10pm-8am).

Hotel Caribe (Calle 2 Norte between Avs. 15 and 20, tel. 987/872-0325, US$45-50 s/d with a/c) has a small, appealing pool in a leafy central garden—a rare and welcome feature in the ranks of budget hotels. Rooms are plain but clean, with one, two, or three beds, decent bathrooms, and old-school air conditioners. Service can be ambivalent, but you can't argue with the value.

Located a half block from the central plaza, **Hotel El Pirata** (Av. 5 near Calle 1, tel. 987/872-0051, US$45-55 s/d with a/c) is a solid budget option. Rooms are modern in decor and have thick beds, flat-screen TVs, and mini-split air conditioners. More expensive rooms have partial views of the park. Wi-Fi is available in the lobby. The only bummer is that guests must climb a steep set of stairs to access rooms—a challenge for some.

US$50-100

★ **Mi Casa en Cozumel** (Av. 5 between Calles 7 and 9, tel. 987/111-9512, www.micasaencozumel.com, US$55 s/d, US$70 s/d with a/c, US$85 suite with a/c and kitchenette, US$165 penthouse) is a terrific boutique hotel and architectural gem—the curves of the spiral staircase and interior walls are counterbalanced by triangular patios and angled nooks occupied by whirlpool tubs. All nine units have contemporary Mexican decor, private balconies or patios, mini fridges, and TVs; one has a kitchenette. All but one unit has air-conditioning, though all were designed for natural ventilation and are quite comfortable with fans only. The split-level penthouse is stunning, with full kitchen, outdoor hot tub, front and rear patios, and great views. The hotel's towering structure is equally impressive, but could be difficult for guests who have trouble climbing stairs. Breakfast is included and is served in a cozy ground-floor dining area. Weekly rates are available.

Updated in 2017, **Tamarindo Bed and Breakfast** (Calle 4 between Avs. 20 and 25 Norte, tel. 987/120-9995, www.tamarindobedandbreakfast.com, US$20 pp dorm, US$60-70 s/d with a/c, US$85-95 suite with a/c and kitchenette) is a beautiful B&B owned by a friendly U.S.-Mexican couple who live on-site. The hotel has seven units bordering a large, leafy garden, including an artful eight-bed dorm with en suite bathroom and *palapa* roof. Each private room is slightly different from the other, from two boxy hotel-type rooms to whitewashed suites with lots of windows and tasteful murals. All integrate traditional Mexican textiles into the décor. Full breakfast is included in the rate and is served on a rooftop patio. There's also a small but well-equipped communal kitchen.

Amaranto Bungalows & Suites (Calle 5 between Avs. 15 and 20 Sur, cell tel. 987/106-6220, www.amarantobedandbreakfast.com, US$65 s/d bungalow with a/c, US$65 s/d suite, US$75 s/d suite with a/c) offers seclusion and privacy within easy walking distance from downtown. The shining stars are the suites, in a three-story tower, each with a sitting area and 360-degree views; the lower unit has air-conditioning, high ceilings, and a modern feel, while the upper one has a *palapa* roof that offers a bird's-eye view. There also are three thatch-roofed bungalows with modern bathrooms and beachy decor. Each room has either a king-size or two queen-size beds, mini fridge, microwave, cable TV, and security box. There's a plunge pool and Wi-Fi runs throughout the entire place. Amaranto doesn't have a full-time attendant, so it's best to reserve in advance.

Hotel Flamingo (Calle 6 between Avs. Rafael Melgar and 5 Norte, tel. 987/872-1264, toll-free U.S. tel. 800/806-1601, www.hotelflamingo.com, US$87-105 s/d with a/c, US$230 penthouse) offers classy, well-priced rooms with modern furnishings, mosaic tile bathrooms, and colorful Guatemalan decor, all in a quiet north-of-center location. Rooms have mini-split air conditioners, electronic safes, and cable TV. Three common areas provide lots of extra outdoor space for guests—a rooftop solarium with lounge chairs and whirlpool tub, a shady midlevel area with hammocks, and a garden courtyard with tables and chairs. Families might consider the penthouse, a two-bedroom apartment with full-size kitchen, private whirlpool tub, and even a rooftop grill.

Located in the heart of San Miguel, **Villa Escondida** (Av. 10 Sur between Calles 3 Sur and Rosado Salas, tel. 987/120-1225, www.villaescondidacozumel.com, US$90 s/d with a/c) is an adults-only B&B with just four guest rooms. Each is modern—if a bit sparse—in style, with comfortable beds and spacious bathrooms. All look onto a well-tended garden with an inviting swimming pool, lounge chairs, hammocks, and Wi-Fi. A full breakfast, from pancakes to *chilaquiles,* is served on the hotel terrace. Complimentary bicycles and snorkeling gear also are available to guests.

Over US$100

★ **Villa Las Anclas** (Av. 5 Sur between Calles 3 and 5, tel. 987/872-5476, www. hotelvillalasanclas.com, US$110 1-bedroom apartment) is a great option for those who want a little home away from home. Seven pleasantly decorated apartments open onto a leafy, private garden, each with a fully equipped kitchenette, living room, and loft master bedroom accessed by spiral stairs. Using the sofas as beds, the apartments can accommodate up to four people while still not feeling overcrowded. All units also have air-conditioning and Wi-Fi. There's also a mosaic tile pool plus an outdoor area for grilling and hanging out.

Guido's Boutique Hotel (Av. Rafael Melgar between Calles 6 and 8 Norte, tel. 987/872-0946, www.guidosboutiquehotel. com, US$110-130 1-bedroom apartment) is less a hotel and more do-it-yourself apartments, but the location, amenities, and price make Guido's an outstanding option. Masters have king beds, while juniors have queens; all are spacious, with full-size kitchens, stylish decor, and satellite TV and Wi-Fi. Each has a small balcony overlooking the street and ocean—traffic can get noisy but the views are priceless. The hotel is located just north of the center, above Guido's Restaurant, one of the island's best. There's no formal reception, so reserve ahead.

Casa Mexicana (Av. Rafael Melgar between Calles 5 and 7, tel. 987/872-9080, toll-free U.S. tel. 877/228-6747, www. casamexicanacozumel.com, US$160-167 s/d with a/c) is a modern beauty with a soaring interior courtyard and gorgeous views of the Caribbean from the oceanside rooms. Rooms are spacious and bright, with good beds and quiet air-conditioning, though less inspired than the building itself. There's a small infinity pool overlooking the water on one end of the lobby (though, admittedly, it's a little strange to take a dip so close to the front desk). Rates include buffet breakfast.

A long walk from town but worth every step, **Casa Colonial** (Av. 35 between Calles 8 and 10, U.S. tel. 954/525-1539, www.casa-colonial-cozumel.com, US$1,075/week with a/c) has four fully equipped Mexican-style villas. All are two stories with two bedrooms, 2.5 bathrooms, a living room, a dining room, a modern kitchen, cable TV, Wi-Fi, and even a washer and dryer. And unlike many longer-term rentals, you still get daily maid service and complimentary concierge service. All

words of wisdom at the bottom of the pool at Hotel B Cozumel

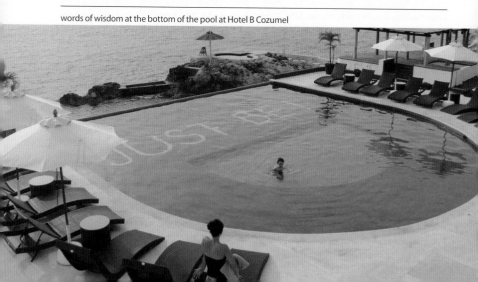

villas face a lush courtyard with a large pool and hot tub. Dive rinse tanks are available, too.

NORTHWESTERN COZUMEL
Under US$200

Maya stelae decorate the facade of **Condumel** (Zona Hotelera Norte Km 1.5, tel. 987/872-0892, www.condumel.com, US$142 1-bedroom apt), an old-school but very agreeable oceanfront condo complex a 15-minute walk from downtown. Ten spacious one-bedroom apartments have king-size beds, Wi-Fi, fully equipped kitchens, and daily maid service. Oversized sliding-glass doors offer awesome views of the Caribbean and incoming airplanes. The coast here is ironshore, so there's just a small patch of sand; steps and a ladder make swimming and snorkeling easy.

Miramar Condominiums (Zona Hotelera Norte Km 3.4, toll-free U.S. tel. 866/564-4427, www.cozumelvillas.com/miramar, US$170-250 1-bedroom condo, US$240-250 2-bedroom condo) is a well-maintained complex with units varying in style, though all are updated and very comfortable. There's a fabulous infinity pool overlooking the Caribbean and entry points to the ocean that make snorkeling easy. The staff does a good job of making guests feel welcome—from fresh flowers upon arrival to concierge services like booking rental cars. There's no on-site beach, which is a drawback, but if you enjoy exploring the island, this is a great place to stay. It's especially suitable for families and those traveling in small groups.

Over US$200

Hotel Playa Azul (Zona Hotelera Norte Km 4, tel. 987/869-5160, www.playa-azul.com, US$202 s/d with a/c, US$255-310 suite with a/c) caters mostly to golfers—guests pay no greens fees at Cozumel Country Club—but has packages for divers and honeymooners as well. Medium-size rooms and spacious suites all have fairly modern furnishings, large bathrooms, and excellent ocean views from balconies and terraces; master suites have private outdoor whirlpool tubs, too. Full breakfast is included in the rates. The pool is clean and attractive, but the beach (already small) can get crowded with day-trippers visiting the hotel's beach club.

Oozing cool, **Hotel B Cozumel** (Zona Hotelera Norte Km 2.5, tel. 987/872-0300, www.hotelbcozumel.com, US$279-336 s/d with a/c, US$423-538 suite with a/c) is a boutique hotel that combines mid-century aesthetic with traditional Mexican decor. Rooms have clean lines and lots of natural light, and feature gorgeous Mexican folk art. All have a balcony or patio and the amenities you'd expect—silent air-conditioning, cable TV, and Wi-Fi. Most have ocean views, too. Outdoors, there's a breezy restaurant, a great half-moon pool, a whirlpool tub, plus lots of sandy areas with hammocks and beach chairs. The main thing missing is a beach; the waterfront is mostly ironshore, so the hotel has done its best to create plenty of entry points to the water. Customer service can be hit or miss.

SOUTHWESTERN COZUMEL
Under US$200

A laid-back dive resort, **Blue Angel Resort** (Carr. Sur Km 2.2, tel. 987/872-0819, www.blueangelresort.com, US$706-976 s/d with a/c for four nights plus daily diving) provides all the amenities a diver could want: a reputable dive shop, reliable boats, an on-site dock, and drying racks and lockers for gear. The rooms themselves are modern but basic; all have great ocean views and private balconies. There's also an open-air restaurant, a well-tended pool, and plenty of shady places to sit back and relax. The only thing really missing is a beach. If you can live with that, this a perfect place to stay awhile. There's a four-night minimum.

Scuba Club Cozumel (Carr. Sur Km 1.5, tel. 987/872-0853, toll-free U.S. tel. 844/792-6976, www.scubaclubcozumel.com, US$140 pp all-inclusive) is an old-school dive hotel with great packages, an on-site dock, and drying racks for your gear. Rooms are basic—clean and bare-bones (good beds and a balcony yes, cable TV and updated amenities no). There's a small pool and a sandy area on the water. Meals are typically included in the rate and are served in a bustling dining room with plastic tables and chairs. It's not exactly a tropical getaway, but it's perfect if you'll be underwater most of the time anyway.

Over US$200

★ **Presidente InterContinental Cozumel Resort Spa** (Carr. Sur Km 6.5, tel. 987/872-9500, toll-free U.S. tel. 800/593-5447, www.intercontinental.com, US$223-440 s/d with a/c, US$520-1,357 suite with a/c) may well be the best resort in Cozumel, with sleek mid-century modern rooms with high-end amenities, views, and niceties like twice-daily maid service and turndown service. While balconies face either the tropical gardens or turquoise ocean, all roads lead to a mellow and welcoming pool scene and a great beach—despite the ironshore—with plenty of access points for snorkelers and shore divers. A well-regarded dive shop, three restaurants, and a full-service spa round out this elegant hotel.

The Explorean Cozumel (Carr. Sur Km 7.5, tel. 443/310-8137, www.explorean.com, US$264-366 pp all-inclusive) is a small hotel nestled in the low forest behind its sister resort, the Fiesta Americana. Guests enjoy the amenities of both—pools, restaurants, spas, oceanfront relaxation—with the added benefit of newer facilities and more personalized service. The biggest plus is that the Explorean integrates daily excursions into the rate: snorkeling and paddleboarding, catamaran trips, tours of San Gervasio ruins and Parque Sur. Guides are knowledgeable and professionally

trained, bringing a different (and welcome) adventure each day.

The Landmark of Cozumel (Carr. Sur Km 6.5, tel. 987/869-5130, www. thelandmarkresortofcozumel.com, US$503 1-bedroom condo, US$503-608 2-bedroom condo, US$755-818 3-bedroom condo) is a condo-hotel with spacious 1-, 2-, and 3-bedroom "residences." All are modern in style and amenities (think granite countertops and washer/dryers) and have balconies with sweeping ocean views. Daily maid service is included. There's a well-tended pool and guests enjoy access to the VIP area of the Money Bar Beach Club, with a small sandy section, hammocks, lounges, and direct access to the Dzul-Há, one of the best DIY snorkel sites on the island.

SOUTHEASTERN COZUMEL

The only hotel on the east side of the island, **Ventanas al Mar** (south end of Playa Tortugas, tel. 984/267-2237, www. ventanasalmar.com.mx, US$145 s/d with kitchenette and a/c, US$228 s/d suite with kitchenette and a/c) is run almost entirely on wind and solar power. It has 14 large rooms and two suites, all with high ceilings and private patios or decks, all with marvelous ocean views. The décor is a bit dated but suits the hotel's isolated feel. There's also a heart-shaped pool, which is a huge plus because the ocean is often too rough for swimming. There's a popular restaurant and beach club next door but not much else (including no ATM or grocery stores). Some guest rent cars for easy access to the rest of the island while many embrace the isolation, spending a week or more without going to town at all. Rates include full breakfast; Wi-Fi is in the lobby only. Children 12 and over only.

Information and Services

TOURIST INFORMATION

The **city tourist office** (Plaza del Sol, Av. 5 Norte between Av. Benito Juárez and Calle 1, tel. 987/869-0212, 8am-3pm Mon.-Fri.) is located on the central plaza. It also has **information booths** with interactive displays in the central plaza (8am-2pm and 4pm-9pm Mon.-Sat., 9am-2pm Sun.), the international pier (8am-3pm daily), and at the Puerta Maya pier (8am-3pm daily). English is spoken at all locations.

There are numerous websites with news, tips, maps, special deals, discussion groups, and other information about Cozumel, including www.thisiscozumel.com, www.cozumelinsider.com, www.cozumelmycozumel.com, www.cozumeltoday.com, and even www.cruiseportinsider.com.

EMERGENCY SERVICES

Costa Med (Calle 1A Sur at Av. 50, tel. 987/872-9400, toll-free Mex. tel. 800/900-1133, toll-free U.S. tel. 855/301-4111, www.costamed.com.mx, 24 hours daily) accepts many foreign insurance plans, though the prices tend to be high.

Cozumel International Hospital (Calle 5 between Avs. Rafael Melgar and 5 Sur, tel. 987/872-1430, www.sssnetwork.com, 24 hours daily) specializes in diver-related medical treatment, though nondiving ailments also are regularly treated.

For meds, try **Farmacia Similares** (Calle 1 Sur at Av. 15 Norte, tel. 987/869-2440, 9am-10pm Mon.-Sat., 9am-2pm Sun.). Mexico now requires a prescription for many antibiotics; this pharmacy has an on-site *consultorio* (doctor's office), open roughly the same hours.

The **tourist police** (Calle 11 Sur near Av. Rafael Melgar, 8am-11pm daily) are stationed in a kiosk near Punta Langosta, though officers often can be found patrolling the central plaza.

The **police station** (Palacio Municipal, Calle 13 between Avs. 5 and Rafael Melgar, tel. 987/872-0092, 24 hours) can be reached toll-free at 066.

MONEY

Accessing your money is not difficult in Cozumel, especially near the central plaza. **HSBC** (Av. 5 Sur at Calle 1, 9am-5pm Mon.-Fri.), **Bancomer** (Av. 5 Sur between Av. Juárez and Calle 1, 8:30am-4pm Mon.-Fri.), and **Banorte** (Av. 5 Norte between Av. Juárez and Calle 2, 9am-5pm Mon.-Fri.) all have ATMs and exchange foreign cash.

MEDIA AND COMMUNICATIONS

Cozumel's **post office** (Av. Rafael Melgar at Calle 7, no phone, 9am-4pm Mon.-Fri., 9am-1pm Sat.) is next to Punta Langosta shopping center.

There are a handful of Internet cafés where you can get online and make international phone calls. **Phonet** (Calle Rosado Salas near Av. 10, no phone, 9am-9pm daily) is a quiet, reliable place charging US$1 per hour for Internet use and US$0.35 per minute for calls to the United States, Canada, and Europe. Another option is **Speedl@nd** (Calle 5 near Av. 5, tel. 987/878-4390, 9am-midnight Mon.-Sat., 10am-11pm Sun.), which charges US$0.50 per hour for Internet, US$0.20 per minute for calls to the United States and Canada, and US$0.20-0.40 for calls to Europe.

LAUNDRY AND STORAGE

Lavandería Margarita (Av. 20 between Calle 3 and Av. Rosado Salas, cell tel. 987/112-5740, 7am-9pm Mon.-Sat., 8am-4pm Sun.) charges US$7.75 per load to wash and dry up to eight kilos (17.5 pounds). There also are self-service machines (US$1.75/washer, US$1.25/dryer per 10 min.); detergent, fabric softener, and dryer sheets are sold separately.

Getting There and Around

GETTING THERE

Air

Cozumel International Airport (CZM, tel. 987/872-2081, www.asur.com.mx) is approximately three kilometers (1.9 miles) from downtown. The airport has an ATM in the departures area, currency exchange at arrivals, and a few magazine stands and duty-free shops. The **airport taxi cooperative** (tel. 987/872-1323) provides private and shared transport to the center and to resorts along the western coast. Prices vary by destination. Private taxis are US$7-25 per person, while shared transport costs US$5-7 per person and utilizes 10-person shuttles or Suburbans; departures are every 5-20 minutes. A taxi stand near the exit sells tickets and has prices prominently displayed.

Airlines servicing Cozumel International Airport include:

- **Air Canada** (toll-free Mex. tel. 800/719-2827, toll-free U.S./Can. tel. 888/247-2262, www.aircanada.com)

- **American Airlines** (toll-free Mex. tel. 800/904-6000, toll-free U.S./Can. tel. 800/433-7300, www.aa.com)

- **Delta** (toll-free Mex. tel. 800/266-0046, toll-free U.S. tel. 800/241-4141, www.delta.com)

- **InterJet** (toll-free Mex. tel. 800/011-2345, toll-free U.S. tel. 866/285-9525, www.interjet.com.mx)

- **MAYAir** (airport tel. 998/881-9413, toll-free Mex. tel. 800/962-9247, toll-free U.S./Can. tel. 844/622-0800, www.mayair.com.mx)

- **United Airlines** (toll-free Mex. tel. 800/900-5000, toll-free U.S./Can. tel. 800/864-8331, www.united.com)

- **Volaris** (tel. 551/102-8000, toll-free U.S. tel. 855/865-2747, www.volaris.com)

Bus

Ticket Bus (Calle 2 at Av. 10 Sur, tel. 987/869-2553, 8am-9pm Mon.-Sat., 9:30am-7pm Sun.) sells tickets for ADO buses leaving from Playa del Carmen at no extra charge, a handy service for when you're ready to move on.

Ferry

Passenger ferries to Playa del Carmen (30 minutes) leave from the passenger ferry pier across from the central plaza. **UltraMar** (tel. 998/293-9092, www.ultramarferry.com, US$13), **Mexico Water Jets** (tel. 987/872-1588, www.mexicowaterjets.com, US$13), and **Barcos Caribe** (tel. 987/869-2079, www.barcoscaribe.com, US$7) compete for customers during the day (although there are a few time slots when only one boat leaves, making it an easy choice). The boats are equally fast, though UltraMar's tend to be newer. The ferry ticket booths are opposite each other partway down the pier, with the time of the next departure displayed prominently. The ticket seller may try to sell you a round-trip ticket, but there's no savings in doing so; better to buy a *sencilla* (one-way ticket) and wait to see which company's ferry is departing when you're ready to leave. Between the three companies, there are ferries every 45-60 minutes 5:45am-10pm daily.

Car ferries operated by **Transcaribe** (tel. 987/872-7683, www.transcaribe.net) depart the international pier in Cozumel for the Calica dock south of Playa del Carmen at 6am, 11am, 4pm, and 8:30pm Monday-Saturday and at 9am, 5pm, and 9pm on Sunday. Returning ferries leave Calica at 4am, 8am, 1:30pm, and 6pm Monday-Saturday and at 7am, 11:30am, and 7pm on Sunday. The trip takes about 1.25 hours and costs US$25 for a passenger car including driver, and US$3.50 per additional passenger. Reservations are available online, by phone, or at the pier, and are strongly recommended.

GETTING AROUND

In town, you can walk just about anywhere or else grab a public van, or *combi,* circulating on various routes between the city center and outskirts (US$0.75, every 10-25 minutes 6am-8pm, less frequently on Sunday). However, the powerful taxi union has succeeded in quashing any and all efforts to start public bus service out of town and around the island. It is a shame, really, because it would be so easy and convenient to have a fleet of buses making loops around the island, or even just up and down the western shore. Until that changes (don't hold your breath), you'll need a car, moped, or bike to explore the rest of the island on your own.

Bicycle

A bike can be handy for getting to beach clubs and snorkel sites outside of town. Traffic on Avenida Rafael Melgar can be heavy south of town, but once clear of that, the roadway is relatively unhurried.

A highly recommended biking outfit is **Rent A Bike Cozumel** (no storefront, tel. 987/113-1082, www.rentabikecozumel.com,

US$20-50/day), which has a wide variety of bicycles, from beach cruisers and mountain bikes to hybrids and road bikes. All rentals include a helmet and lock; road bikes also include an emergency repair kit. Extras like lights and saddlebags also can be rented. Bikes are brought to your hotel or location of choice; rates go down the longer you rent. Reserve in advance, especially during the high season.

If you want a last-minute rental, consider renting a bicycle from **Best Bikes Cozumel** (Av. 10 between Av. Juárez and Calle 2, tel. 987/126-0503, www.bestbikescozumel.com, 9am-6pm daily, US$8.50-18/day), which offers a variety of bikes, including helmet and lock. Snorkel gear is also rented.

Taxi

Taxis are everywhere—you can easily flag one down on Avenida Rafael Melgar, near the main passenger pier, and around the plaza. If you want to be picked up at a specific place and time, call the **taxi union office** (Calle 2 between Avs. 5 and 10, tel. 987/872-0041, 24 hours daily). Cabs typically charge US$3 around town and US$5 from the center to the airport, for up to four people. For hotels and beach clubs on the western shore south of town, you'll pay US$12-25, depending on

Mopeds are convenient for getting around town.

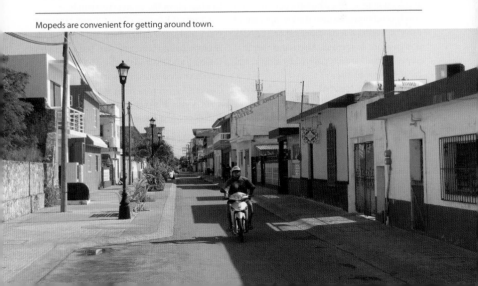

the distance. Fares to the east side are a bit more, US$13.50-35, while San Gervasio costs US$50-60, including wait time. A trip around the island, including stops, runs around US$130 for four hours. Most taxi stands have the current fares prominently displayed; always agree on a price before getting into a taxi.

Car and Moped Rental

Renting a car is a nice way to get out of downtown and see the rest of the island. It is virtually impossible to get lost, and you can visit all the main spots in a day or two.

If you do decide to rent some wheels, go to the agency yourself—don't let one of the friendly guys at the pier lead you there. They are *comisionistas,* freelancers who earn hefty commissions for bringing tourists to particular shops, which then pass the cost on to you. Shop owners go along begrudgingly; if they decline the "service," the same freelancers will actively steer future tourists away from the shop, saying it's closed, burned down, fresh out of cars—you get the idea.

Excluding commissions, rental cars in Cozumel start at around US$45-65 for a compact car, including insurance and taxes. Mopeds rent for around US$25-35 per day. Be aware that scooters account for the majority of accidents here, as speed bumps, potholes, and windy conditions can upend even experienced drivers; having a second person on the back is even more dangerous. Also remember that unpaved roads are not covered by most rental car insurance plans.

Rentadora Isis (Av. 5 Norte between Calles 2 and 4, tel. 987/872-3367, www.rentadoraisis.com.mx, 8am-6:30pm daily) consistently has the island's best rates, and friendly service to boot; its Internet specials often are good, too. Another good local option is **Sol y Mar Rentals** (Calle 2 near Av. 5 Norte, tel. 987/869-0545, 7am-8pm daily).

International companies have newer fleets, and sometimes have better rates if you book online. Try **Avis** (airport, tel. 987/872-0219, www.avis.com), **Hertz** (airport, tel. 987/869-8184, www.hertz.com), or **Thrifty** (Av. Juárez at Av. 10 Norte, tel. 987/869-8090, airport, tel. 987/869-2957, www.thrifty.com).

Motorcycle Rental

To explore the island in style, head to **Eaglerider** (Palmar Plaza, Carr. Costera Sur Km 3.8, tel. 987/857-0106, toll-free U.S. tel. 888/900-9901, www.eaglerider.com, US$169/day), which rents several types of Harley-Davidson motorcycles, from Sportsters to Road Kings to Electra Glides.

Highways and Road Conditions

The distance around the island—on paved roads, and including the northwestern arm that dead-ends after Cozumel Country Club—is approximately 93 kilometers (58 miles). Driving without stopping, it takes a little under two hours to circumnavigate the island. If doing this, consider going counterclockwise so there's nothing between your vehicle and the ocean, especially on the east side. Biking around the island is possible but challenging, given the strong crosswinds.

Cozumel has three **PEMEX gas stations** (7am-midnight daily). Two are in town on Avenida Benito Juárez (at Avs. Pedro Joaquin Coldwell and 75), and the third is four kilometers (2.5 miles) south of town on the Carretera Costera Sur, across from Puerta Maya, the main cruise ship pier.

Note: Most streets are one-way in town; if you're driving, be aware that *avenidas* (avenues) run north-south and have the right-of-way over *calles* (streets), which run east-west. Once you leave town, there is a single road that circles the entire island.

The Riviera Maya

Cancún may be the name everyone recognizes, but for many people—especially repeat visitors—the best of Mexico's Caribbean coast is the Riviera Maya.

Stretching more than 130 kilometers (81 miles) south from Cancún to Tulum, the Riviera Maya is home to fast-growing cities like Playa del Carmen, low-key towns like Puerto Morelos, and tiny beachfront settlements like Tankah Tres. It boasts megaresorts and tiny bed-and-breakfasts and is flanked by the world's longest underground river on one side and the world's second-longest coral reef on the other. And, of course, the Riviera Maya has the same spectacular beaches Cancún is famous for.

Highlights

Look for ★ to find recommended sights, activities, dining, and lodging.

★ **Snorkeling Puerto Morelos's Coral Reef:** Go snorkeling where the reef is still healthy, the water uncrowded, and the price unbeatable (page 150).

★ **Playa del Carmen's Quinta Avenida:** Ever growing yet still walkable, Playa's 5th Avenue has block after block of tempting restaurants, hipster boutiques, and lively bars (page 161).

★ **Xcaret:** Xcaret is the region's most ambitious ecopark—a safe, active, family-friendly place, with tubing and snorkeling, an aquarium, and an end-of-the-day extravaganza (page 164).

★ **Laguna Yal-Ku:** A long elbow of water fed by freshwater cenotes and flowing into the sea, this lagoon is a snorkeler favorite for its colorful fish and jumble of underwater rocks (page 188).

★ **Playa X'cacel:** Just off the highway down an easy-to-miss sand road, this glorious stretch of white-sand beach is home to a sea turtle nesting area protected from development (page 196).

Previous: beach at Playacar, just south of Playa del Carmen. **Above:** turtle at Akumal; one of the Riviera Maya's myriad tropical flowers.

The Riviera Maya

EL MECO

Cancún
180
EL REY
307

1800

To Valladolid
and Chichén Itzá

Caribbean

Sea

Siete
Bocas
CROCO
CUN ZOO
Boca
del Puma
RUTA DE
LOS CENOTES
SNORKELING
CORAL REEF

Puerto Morelos

Verde
Lucero
LOS COLIBRIS
MAYAN JUNGLE SPA
JARDÍN BOTÁNICO
"DR. ALFREDO
BARRERA MARÍN"

To Selvática,
Cenotes Zapote Ecoparque,
and Leona Vicario

Punta Maroma

307

Punta Bete/
Playa Xcalacoco
Isla
Cozumel

Passenger
Ferry

QUINTA AVENIDA
San Miguel
de Cozumel

XPLOR
Playa del Carmen

DELPHINUS
RIVIERA MAYA
XCARET

Car Ferry

CALICA PIER

Paamul

Cenote
Cristalino
Puerto Aventuras

Jardín del Edén

Cenote Azul
Xpu-Há

LAGUNA YAL-KU

Aktun
Chen
Half Moon Bay

Akumal
Aventuras Akumal

To Cobá and
Valladolid
PLAYA X'CACEL

307

Dos Ojos
XEL-HÁ

Gran
Cenote
El Pit
Soliman Bay

Yax Kin
Cenote Manatí

Calavera
Tankah Tres

Tulum
TULUM

To the Costa Maya
and Chetumal
To Punta Allen and Sian
Ka'an Biosphere Reserve

0   5 mi
0   5 km

© MOON.COM

There's plenty to see and do, much of it do-it-yourself: Go snorkeling in freshwater cenotes and lagoons, help release newly hatched sea turtles into the sea, explore little-visited Maya ruins, or spend the day at a family-friendly ecopark. For party hounds, Cancún still has a lock on over-the-top nightspots, though Playa del Carmen has several of its own, and there are plenty of lounge bars, beach clubs, and resort nightclubs where visitors can kick back or cut loose.

PLANNING YOUR TIME

You'll probably want to pick a home base (or two) for your time here and make day trips from there. Playa del Carmen is the area's only big city, with all the expected urban amenities, including nightlife. (It's also the gateway to Isla Cozumel.) Puerto Morelos and Akumal are smaller but still have a decent selection of hotels and restaurants. If isolation is more important than convenience, the Riviera Maya has some secret getaways, like Xpu-Há and Tankah Tres. If you have a week or more, consider spending half your time in the northern section—around Playa del Carmen, for example—and then move farther south to enjoy Akumal, Tankah Tres, and even Tulum.

A rental car isn't absolutely necessary but will certainly make exploring the Riviera Maya a lot easier. Cheap public shuttles zip up and down the coast, but they only stop along the highway, which in most places is about a kilometer (0.6 mile) from the ocean. That leaves you to make the hot, dusty walk up and down the access roads, especially in more unpopulated areas where taxis are uncommon.

Puerto Morelos

Puerto Morelos has largely escaped the mega-development that has swept up and down the Riviera Maya, despite being squeezed between the booming cities of Cancún and Playa del Carmen. It remains, for the most part, a quiet seaside town. Yes, the town fills up with tourists in the high season—and more and more condos and resorts are cropping up—but it is still a place where a substantial part of the local population lives by fishing, where life revolves around the central plaza, and where kids and dogs romp in the streets.

The beach in Puerto Morelos has improved significantly in the last few years, and more and more travelers are spending lazy afternoons in the sun and sand. But Puerto Morelos is best known for the reef system just offshore. Local residents fought tirelessly (and successfully) to have a large section in front of town designated a national reserve, and as a result, the snorkeling and diving are superb. A town cooperative and several local dive shops offer tours of various sorts, most highly recommended and quite affordable. Puerto Morelos also is gaining popularity as a destination for yoga and meditation groups—no surprise given its serene atmosphere—and a growing number of hotels and resorts cater to that market.

Be aware that the low season here is *very* low, and many businesses close in May, September, and/or October.

SIGHTS AND BEACHES
Playa Principal
Over the years, Puerto Morelos has improved its beachfront area considerably, with leafy arbors and palm-shaded benches. The beach itself, however, lacks the creamy white sand found elsewhere in the Riviera Maya, and the same regulations that protect the town's famous coral reef also prevent the removal of seagrass in the shallow areas. Fishing boats also moor on the beach, though there's still plenty of room to lay out a towel, especially toward the northern and southern ends. A popular beach option is **Paradise Beach Club** (end of Calle Plutarco Elías, tel. 998/206-9354, www.myparadise.com.mx, 10am-7pm daily), which rents lounge chairs and umbrellas and offers tasty beach food and well-priced drinks.

The Central Plaza
Puerto Morelos's peaceful central plaza is a highlight of the town, with shaded benches, a basketball court, and a well-maintained play structure for kids, making it a great place to while away the early evening hours, especially for families. Many of Puerto Morelos's best restaurants face the plaza or are just a block away, so you're sure to pass by more than once.

Ruta de los Cenotes
Marked by an enormous mustard-yellow arch on Highway 307, the "Cenote Route" is one of the newest developments along the Riviera Maya, and a sign, for better or worse, that the megaresorts are finally starting to appreciate cenotes. The route is simply a paved road, which begins just south of Puerto Morelos and extends nearly 20 kilometers (12.4 miles) into the scrub forest, passing several cenotes along the way. The most popular stops, at least for tour groups, are cenotes like **Boca del Puma** and **Selvática,** which also have ATV tours, zip lines, roller coasters—you get the picture. But the route also has some true gems: gorgeous and remote cenotes, undeveloped and all but overlooked by the package tours, and well worth the drive to reach them.

Independent travelers will particularly enjoy **Siete Bocas** (Carr. Pto. Morelos-Vallarta Km 15.5, tel. 998/208-9199, 8am-4pm daily, US$15), so named for its seven openings (or "mouths"). Three openings have steep wooden stairways leading straight into the cool, clear water; another is a jumping-screaming-cannonball-entry spot for the

Puerto Morelos

To Dreams Riviera Cancún
Resort and Spa

ABBEY DEL
SOL

VILLAS
CLARITA

HOTEL EDÉN

CASA CARIBE HOTEL/
THE LITTLE MEXICAN
COOKING SCHOOL

MARTINA'S
OASIS SPA   PARADISE
BEACH CLUB

PUERTO MORELOS
LANGUAGE CENTER

WET SET DIVING
ADVENTURES

AV. ANDRES QUINTANA ROO

AV. JAVIER ROJO GOMEZ

AV. NIÑOS HEROES

SALCICCIUM
FOOD TRUCK
VILLAGE

I WANNA PIZZA

Playa Principal

SEE
DETAIL

To Médica Puerto Morelos,
Buenos Dias B&B, Zona Urbana,
Bus Station, and Hwy 307

Central
Plaza

Caribbean

Sea

HUNAB KÚ

AL CHIMICHURRI

DK PUERTO MORELOS

AQUANAUTS
DIVE ADVENTURES

SNORKELING
CORAL REEF

LAYLA GUESTHOUSE/
CHUMUK KANBAL
LEARNING CENTER

CENTRO DE
SALUD

AV. RAFAEL MELGAR

THE
WAREHOUSE
HOSTEL   LA CASA
DEL MAR

SHIPPING
DOCK

To Rancho Sak Ol and
Hotel Marina El Cid
Spa & Beach Resort

0   200 yds
0   200 m

© MOON.COM

Detail:

LAVAPLUS

PUERTO MORELOS
GREEN BIKES

CUATRO COLIBRÍ

LAS
ROBLES

EL
PESQUERO

AV. JAVIER ROJO GOMEZ

AV. NIÑOS HEROES

HOTEL EL MORO

POLICE/ATM   CASA MARTÍN/
ATM

CANCÚN BILLY'S

AV. RAFAEL MELGAR

DIVERSPOINT

SNORKELING TOURS
(LOCAL COOPERATIVE)

FARMACIA SAN JOSÉ OBRERO

FRUIT, VEGETABLE, AND
MEAT STANDS

Central
Plaza

LOS GAUCHOS   ATM

SOUVENIR
SHOPS

EUROPCAR

PUNTA CORCHO

ALMA LIBRE BOOKSTORE/
EL NICHO

more adventurous (the cenote is said to be 492 feet deep); the other three allow sunlight into the underground chamber, lighting the water dramatically, especially around midday. Inside, you can swim or float through the cave, with its spectacular stalagmites and stalactites, often with no one else around (BYO snorkel gear and underwater flashlight; life vests provided).

Just down the road from Siete Bocas is **Verde Lucero** (Carr. Pto. Morelos-Vallarta Km 18, cell tel. 998/224-3731, 8am-5pm daily, US$7.50), an open-air cenote surrounded by huge tropical trees. Completely different from its neighbor but no less dramatic, Verde Lucero is like an enormous swimming hole with clear turquoise water and seemingly no bottom. There's a zip line as well as a thick safety line stretching across the cenote. Look for the freshwater turtles that make their home here. It's popular with locals, especially on weekends.

A good option for those who prefer organized tours is **Cenotes Zapote Ecoparque** (Carr. Pto. Morelos-Vallarta Km 19, tel. 998/100-2406, www.cenoteszapote.com, 8am-5pm, US$35-79). The park consists of three cenotes in a lush and minimally commercialized setting: Zapote, an open cenote with a 14-meter platform for jumping (in diving circles, this cenote is known as "Hells Bells" for the remarkable bell-shaped formations found at 120 feet); Palmas, another open cenote with a 30-meter-long zip line running over it (snorkelers enjoy this cenote for its fish and turtles); and El Abuelo Che Che, an otherworldly domed cenote with crystal-clear water that is surrounded by stalagmites and stalactites. Visitors have the option of tagging on a 500-meter zip line ride over the jungle, a bike tour, as well as lunch. Regardless of the package, admission includes guides who lead visitors through the park, lockers, hammocks, and well-maintained bathrooms and showers. Transportation to and from hotels is available.

Croco Cun Zoo

A small tropical petting zoo, **Croco Cun Zoo** (Hwy. 307, tel. 998/850-3719, www.crococunzoo.com, 9am-5pm daily, US$32 adult, US$22 child 6-12, free 5 and under) is located five kilometers (3.1 miles) north of the Puerto Morelos turnoff. Seventy-five-minute guided tours, offered in English or Spanish, bring visitors up close and personal to all sorts of local creatures. You can feed spider monkeys and white-tailed deer, walk through a crocodile enclosure, be "kissed" by macaws, and hold boas and baby crocs. Though pricey, it's well managed and, for many, a highlight of a trip.

Jardín Botánico "Dr. Alfredo Barrera Marín"

Just south of the Puerto Morelos turnoff is the peaceful **Jardín Botánico "Dr. Alfredo Barrera Marín"** (aka Ya'ax Ché Jardín Botánico, Hwy. 307 Km 320, tel. 998/206-9233, 8am-4pm daily Nov.-Apr., 9am-5pm daily May-Oct., US$6 adult, US$2.50 child), which has four kilometers (2.4 miles) of trails winding through diverse habitat, from tropical forest to mangrove swamp. In addition to hundreds of marked plants, there's a scenic lookout tower, a 130-foot suspension bridge, the remains of a small Maya ruin, and recreations of a modern Maya home and *chicle* camp. Monkeys can be sometimes spotted in the afternoon. Wear long sleeves, pants, and plenty of bug repellent.

SPORTS AND RECREATION
★ Snorkeling

Puerto Morelos's top attraction is snorkeling on the coral reef. Directly in front of the village, around 500 meters (0.3 mile) offshore, the reef here takes on gargantuan dimensions—up to 30 meters (99 feet) wide. Winding passages and large caverns alive with fish and sea flora make for great exploring. And because it's a marine reserve, and fishing and motor traffic are limited, the reef is more pristine here than almost any place along the Riviera. A **local cooperative** (central plaza, Av. Rafael Melgar s/n, cell tel. 998/121-1524, 9am-3pm Mon.-Sat., US$25 pp for 2 hours) offers guided tours of the reef, with boats leaving every 30 minutes—or sooner, if there are four snorkelers—from the municipal pier. The tour includes visits to two snorkeling sites, gear, and a certified guide. The **dive shops** in town also offer snorkeling tours to the town reef and beyond, for slightly higher prices.

Caution: *Do not swim to the reef* from anywhere along the beach. Although it's close enough for strong swimmers to reach, boats use the channel between the reef and the shore, and tourists have been struck and killed in the past.

Scuba Diving

Puerto Morelos has over two dozen dive sites within a 15-minute boat ride, virtually all in protected marine reserve waters. Add to that the nearby cenotes, plus night and wreck diving, and even diving with bull sharks, and folks have plenty to keep them happy and

Cenotes: Then and Now

divers exploring the otherworldly depths of the Riviera Maya's cenotes

Cenotes are intriguing features of the Yucatán Peninsula. These freshwater sinkholes, sometimes hundreds of meters deep, are filled with crystalline fresh water that is fed by underground rivers. Cenotes owe their formation to the massive meteorite that hit the Yucatán Peninsula 65 million years ago. The impact shattered the peninsula's thick limestone cap like a stone hitting a car windshield, and in the millions of years that followed, rainwater seeped into the cracks, carving huge underground caverns and hundreds of kilometers of channels out of the highly soluble limestone. Cenotes are former caverns whose roofs collapsed—cave-ins are extremely rare today, however—and together the channels form the world's longest underground river system.

Cenotes were sacred to Maya, who relied on them for water and viewed them as apertures to the underworld. (The name is derived from the Yucatec Maya word *dz'onot,* meaning "well.") Sacrificial victims were sometimes thrown into their eerie depths, along with finely worked stone and clay items, and archaeologists have learned a great deal about early Maya rituals by dredging cenotes near archaeological sites, most notably Chichén Itzá. Indeed, the name *Chichén Itzá* means "Well of the Itzá," undoubtedly a reference to the ancient city's dramatic cenote.

Today the peninsula's cenotes attract worshippers of a different sort: snorkelers and scuba divers. The unbelievably clear water—100-meter (328-foot) visibility in places—is complemented by what other inland and underground diving environments (such as lakes and flooded mines) lack: stunning stalactites and stalagmites. During early ice ages, water drained from the cenotes, giving time for the slow-growing features to form. When the climate warmed, the cenotes filled with water once again, their depths now forested with dramatic stone spires, pillars, and columns.

Divers with open-water certification can dive in the cenotes. Though "full-cave" diving requires advanced training, most cenote tours are actually "cavern" dives, meaning you are always within 40 meters (130 feet) of an air pocket. It's a good idea to take some open-water dives before your first cenote tour—buoyancy control is especially important in cenotes, and you'll be contending with different weights and finning techniques.

interested. The dive shops in town tend to have small groups and offer a full range of fun dives and certification courses. Prices range US$60-85 for one tank, US$100-120 for two tanks, and US$425-440 for open-water certification. Be sure to ask about any extra fees, like equipment, taxes, and the marine park fee. Shop hours are generally 8am-5pm Monday to Saturday, and reservations are strongly recommended.

Wet Set Diving Adventures (Hotel Ojo de Agua, Av. Javier Rojo Gómez s/n, tel. 998/206-9204, www.wetset.com) is one of the longest-running dive shops around, offering top-to-bottom service and extensive area expertise.

Aquanauts Dive Adventures (Hotel Hacienda Morelos, Av. Rafael Melgar 5, cell tel. 984/126-7966, www. aquanautsdiveadventures.com) is another long-operating dive shop offering personalized service.

Diverspoint (Av. Javier Rojo Gómez s/n, tel. 998/206-9051, www.diverspoint.com) is a small shop run by a friendly Dutch couple. English, Spanish, Dutch, French, and German are spoken.

Sportfishing

The dive shops in Puerto Morelos also offer fishing trips, whether trolling for barracuda or marlin, or dropping a line for "dinner fish" like grouper or snapper. **Wet Set Water Adventures** (Hotel Ojo de Agua, Av. Javier Rojo Gómez s/n, tel. 998/871-0198, www. wetset.com) has been taking visitors fishing for many years; the **local cooperative** (central plaza, Av. Rafael Melgar s/n, no phone, 9am-3pm Mon.-Sat.) does the same. Both charge around US$65-150 per hour, depending on the size of the boat.

Another popular—though pricier—option is the fishing fleet at **Marina El Cid** (Hotel Marina El Cid Spa & Beach Resort, Blvd. El Cid Unidad 15, tel. 998/871-0185, toll-free U.S. tel. 888/870-3010, www.elcidmarinas. com). Trips run US$550-1,100 for 4-8 hours, but the boats tend to be newer and faster. The cost includes captain, crew, fishing license, tackle, ice, and insurance; food and beverages are optional. Taxidermy, filleting, and cooking are offered, too.

Golf

You'll find two Jack Nicklaus courses at **Moon Palace Cancún** (Hwy. 307 Km 36.5, tel. 998/881-6100, www.moonpalacecancun. com, US$303 for 18 holes, US$187 for 9 holes), just 10 minutes north of town. It has three nine-hole courses spanning nearly 11,000 yards. Greens fees include a shared golf cart, snacks, drinks, and round-trip transportation to select hotels; from 2:30pm until closing at 6pm, greens fees are US$187 for as many holes as you can play. There's also a driving range, a practice bunker, and putting and chipping greens.

Tours

ECAB Explorer (cell tel. 998/123-5062, www.ecabexplorer.com) is a small but reliable tour operator run by a longtime Puerto Morelos resident. Tours include not only the main destinations—Chichén Itzá, Cobá, Ek' Balam, Sian Ka'an—but also whale shark snorkeling tours and interesting add-ons like bird-watching and visits with a local family. Groups are small and rates reasonable considering the tours' length and depth: around US$85-135 adult, with discounts for children and groups. Check the website for scheduled outings or to arrange a private tour.

Chumuk Kanbal Learning Center (Layla Guesthouse, Av. Rafael Melgar s/n, cell tel. 998/104-9831, www.laylaguesthouse. com, US$100) offers a popular cenote tour to a little-visited site about 90 minutes from Puerto Morelos. The trip includes a guided nature walk, a visit to a dry cave, a swim in a gorgeous cenote, and a traditional lunch at a local Maya home. Tours run 8:30am-5:30pm and must be booked in advance.

Over 50 visual artists live in the Zona Urbana of Puerto Morelos, located on the west side of the highway. Get an inside look at some of these artists' studios through the **Art Tour of Puerto Morelos** (tel. 998/322-5672, nadjabvd@gmail.com, US$35 for up to 3 people), a three-hour tour of 4-5 workshops led by bilingual guide Nadja Billard. Tours include meeting the artists and learning about their processes. Discounts are available if you provide your own transportation. Tours are held on Thursdays only.

Spas

Ixchel Jungle Spa (Casa Cacahuate B&B, Calle 2 near Calle Vallarta, Zona Urbana, tel. 998/180-5424, www.mayaecho.com, 10am-4pm Tues.-Sat., Sun. by appointment only) is one of several community projects undertaken by Maya Echo, a local nonprofit founded by a longtime expat. Local women provide professional massage and traditional Maya treatments for far less than at ordinary spas. Treat yourself to one of various available treatments, from a four-handed full-body massage (US$80, 1 hour) to a chocolate body wrap and massage (US$60, 1 hour). Group massage or *temascal* (traditional Maya sweat lodge) also can be arranged with advance notice. A cab ride from Puerto Morelos's central plaza runs about US$3.

Martina's Oasis Spa (Av. Andres Quintana Roo at Av. Plutarco Elias, tel. 998/213-4595, www.martinasoasis.com, by appointment only) draws on the considerable skills of its owner, Martina, a licensed massage therapist with an uncanny ability to zero in on the precise source of discomfort and know just how to alleviate it. Prices are reasonable: US$40-85 for facials, manipedis, and so forth; US$65-165 for one- and two-hour massages, including Swedish, Thai, deep tissue, and hot stone; and US$65-125 for Reiki energy treatments. Treatments are also offered off-site.

Set on a jungle plot along the Ruta de los Cenotes, **Los Colibris Mayan Jungle Spa** (Ruta de los Cenotes Km 15, cell tel. 998/105-2016, www.loscolibries.mx, 9am-5pm daily) offers Maya massages, *temascal* sessions, and outdoor bath treatments. Prices range

US$50-90 for 1-2.5 hours. A nice way to end a day of cenote-hopping.

Cooking Classes

The Little Mexican Cooking School (Casa Caribe, Calle Rojo Gómez 768, tel. 998/251-8060, www.thelittlemexicancookingschool.com, 10am-3:30pm Tues.-Fri., US$128 pp, including complimentary recipe book and apron) offers a fun and unique introduction to Mexican cuisine. Class begins with pastries and coffee, followed by an hour-long discussion of regional food and ingredients, and moves to demonstrations and hands-on practice of 7-8 Mexican recipes and drinks. Class ends with a luncheon from the dishes you helped create. Note that the class size is maxed at 18 people, which may be too big for some.

SHOPPING

Mayan Jungle Market (Calle 2 near Calle Vallarta, Zona Urbana, tel. 998/180-5424, www.mayaecho.com, 10am-1pm Sun., Dec.-April only) is held at Casa Cacahuate B&B in the residential part of Puerto Morelos, on the other side of the highway. This cheerful, family-friendly event is facilitated by the nonprofit founded by the bed-and-breakfast's owners. The market features a variety of handicrafts produced by local women, as well as tasty food and drink. A traditional Maya dance is held at 11:30am.

Cuatro Colibrí (Av. Javier Rojo Gómez s/n, cell tel. 998/198-1235, 10am-1pm and 4pm-9pm Mon.-Sat.) specializes in high-end *artesanía* and jewelry from around the country. You'll find everything from *corazónes de latón* (tin hearts) to Huichol-inspired T-shirts. Prices are somewhat higher here, but the quality is tough to beat.

The artisan's market of **Hunab Kú** (Av. Javier Rojo Gómez s/n, 9am-8pm daily) may be your best bet for finding local handicrafts in Puerto Morelos. There are a bunch of stands with colorful blankets, ceramics, hammocks, masks, jipi hats, and shell art. A **string of souvenir shops** (8am-8pm daily)

on the central plaza sell similar items, in case you don't find what you're looking for at the market.

One of the best bookstores on the peninsula, **Alma Libre Bookstore** (central plaza, tel. 998/251-1206, www.almalibrebooks.com, 10am-6pm daily) has a whopping 20,000 titles, new and used, ranging from "beach trash to Plato," in the words of the friendly Canadian owners. There's Maya culture, Mexican cooking, ecology, mysteries, guidebooks, maps, and more—not just in English, but Spanish, French, German, Dutch, Italian, and others. The store's website is an outstanding resource for everything Puerto Morelos, too.

FOOD

Who knows how it happened, but modest little Puerto Morelos is home to an amazing array of restaurants and eateries, from cheerful holes-in-the-wall to international cuisine that draws diners all the way from Cancún and Playa del Carmen.

Mexican and Seafood

Overlooking the central plaza, ★ **Punta Corcho** (Av. Rafael Melgar at Calle Tulum, tel. 998/206-9105, 1pm-11pm daily, US$12-20) is a shabby-chic restaurant serving gorgeous seafood creations, most of them made in a wood-fired oven. Expect dishes liked grilled octopus in adobo sauce, seafood risotto, and lobster ceviche wrapped in banana leaves. The cocktails, many of them made with mezcal, are equally creative—and strong. Reservations are recommended on weekends.

DK Puerto Morelos (Av. Rafael Melgar at Calle Isla Mujeres, cell tel. 998/192-4307, www.dk-puertomorelos.com, 1pm-10:30pm Tues.-Sun., US$4-7) is a hipster eatery with a kitchen set in a converted shipping container and handmade tables spread out on a gravel lot. The menu is Mexican-Asian fusion with a focus on seafood—think octopus tostadas and spicy lionfish with coconut rice. Cocktails

change with the season, but count on drinks with a kick that use premium mezcal. It's a popular spot, especially after the sun sets.

A *palapa*-roofed eatery with sand floors and plastic tables, **El Pesquero** (Av. Rafael Melgar 4, tel. 998/206-9129, 12:30pm-8pm daily, US$6-14) specializes in fresh seafood—everything from *chipachole* soup (a seafood medley of shrimp, fish, octopus, and squid) and ceviche to whole fish and lobster tail. Portions are generous and often include sides like coleslaw, rice, beans, and cucumber salad.

Cancún Billy's (Av. Rafael Melgar s/n, tel. 987/871-0913, 9am-11pm daily, US$5-16) is one of the only beachfront restaurant-bars in town, making it a go-to simply for the views. The food varies from excellent barbecue platters to solid seafood dishes like ceviche, fish tacos, and whole fried fish. Best of all is the atmosphere: It's laid-back and friendly, with live music Thursday-Sunday and karaoke on Wednesday. There's two-for-one draft beer every day.

Other Specialties

★ **Al Chimichurri** (Av. Javier Rojo Gómez s/n, tel. 998/252-4666, 5pm-11pm Tues.-Sun., US$7-21) serves up Uruguayan specialties, with the shining stars being the grilled meats, chicken, and homemade sausage (don't be afraid to ask for extra chimichurri sauce for dipping). Food is served at candlelit tables in an open-air dining room and along the sidewalk, perfect for people-watching. If you have room, finish off your meal with the flambéed apple crepe topped with vanilla ice cream.

Salciccium Food Truck Village (Av. Javier Rojo Gómez s/n, tel. 998/871-0943, www.salciccium.com, 1:30pm-11:30pm Wed.-Mon., US$8-13) is a sit-down restaurant that accesses the kitchens of a handful of food trucks, all surrounding an open-air dining area with picnic tables. Offerings range from lobster po'boys and crepes to gyros and steaks. Take-out is also available—a great option for a sunset picnic on the beach.

On the central plaza, **El Nicho** (Av. Javier Rojo Gómez at Av. Tulum, tel. 998/201-0992,

---

1: shopping in Puerto Morelos; **2:** fish tacos, a Riviera Maya staple www.elnicho.com.mx, 8am-2pm daily, US$3-7) is a buzzing café serving up all manner of egg dishes, creative salads, and fresh panini. Many items are organic and most have healthy twists. Think plates of papaya with bee pollen, chia, and hemp seeds and scrambled eggs with spinach, feta, and pumpkin seeds. Fresh-squeezed juices and to-die-for cappuccinos are a must.

Draped in art, **Las Robles** (Av. Javier Rojo Gómez s/n, tel. 998/380-0568, 7:30am-10pm Mon.-Sat., 7:30am-2pm Sun., US$4-7) is a cute little café featuring a full menu of vegan and vegetarian dishes, much of it organic. Think fruit plates and omelets, big salads and sandwiches…even veggie hot dogs. Come here for a light meal or for a midafternoon break—the smoothies alone are worth a stop.

Considered one of the best pizza joints in town, **I Wanna Pizza** (Av. Javier Rojo Gómez s/n, tel. 984/281-3036, 4pm-11pm Tues.-Sun, US$8-10) lives up to the hype. Pizzas are made in a brick oven, with a soft-on-the-inside-crisp-on-the-outside crust and a range of toppings varying from pepperoni to red onion reduction with prosciutto, mushrooms, and feta cheese. Plastic tables are set up on an outdoor patio with soft lighting and inch-thick tree rounds for plates. Bring bug repellent—the restaurant backs into the mangrove, which can be buggy, especially in the rainy season.

There's great homemade pasta at **Los Gauchos** (Calle Tulum s/n, cell tel. 998/206-9243, 1pm-11pm Wed.-Mon., US$5-15), but don't leave without trying the empanadas: a classic Argentinean snack made of puffy, crispy fried dough stuffed with cheese, olives, or other goodies. At just US$1.50-2.50 apiece, a plate of five or six and a couple of sodas make a great cheap meal for two. Live tango is presented most Friday or Saturday nights starting around 8pm (with plenty of room to join, if you're inclined to dance).

Groceries

Casa Martín (central plaza, 6:30am-10pm daily) has a fairly large selection of canned foods, pastas, snacks, and drinks; there's also a small produce section near the back.

Every Wednesday, **fruit, vegetable, and meat stands** (Calle Tulum near Av. Javier Rojo Gómez, 7am-2pm) set up a half block from the central plaza. Prices are by the kilo.

For a bigger shopping run, head to **Super Chedraui** (Hwy. 307, 7am-11pm daily), located in front of the highway underpass. It's a traditional supermarket with a big produce section, an in-house bakery, and even beach supplies.

ACCOMMODATIONS
Under US$100

Located on the quiet end of the main drag, **The Warehouse Hostel** (Av. Javier Rojo Gómez s/n, U.S. tel. 763/398-9966, thewarehousepuerto@gmail.com, US$12/20 s/d tent, US$16 pp dorm) is a small hostel with a simple eight-bed dorm (think *palapa* roof, wood-plank bunks, and fans) and a lawn for tents (BYO gear). It's not fancy, but hot showers, lockers and linens, Wi-Fi, and a full breakfast make it a deal. Add a pool and an outdoor hangout area and it's a score for budget travelers.

★ **Buenos Dias B&B** (Calle Ciricote at Calle Che Chen, Zona Urbana, tel. 998/255-6950, www.buenosdiaspuertomorelos.com, US$52 s/d with a/c, US$67 studio with a/c) is a family-run hotel in Puerto Morelos's residential area, on the inland side of the highway. Units are modern and spick-and-span with thick beds, Wi-Fi, and powerful air-conditioning. Studios have fully equipped kitchenettes. Common areas include an outdoor kitchen, a shaded terrace, and a well-tended pool. Continental breakfast and bikes are included in the rate. This is an excellent place to experience the non-touristed side of the Riviera Maya.

A 10-minute walk from the central plaza, **Hotel Edén** (Av. Andrés Quintana Roo near Calle Lázaro Cardenas, tel. 998/871-0450, www.puertomoroloseden.com, US$70 1-bedroom apartment with a/c and kitchenette) is rather more austere than its name suggests but is a fine budget option all the same. Decent-sized one-bedroom apartments have cable TV, Wi-Fi, clean hot-water bathrooms, and small but well-equipped kitchenettes. Air-conditioning is in the bedrooms only. Weekly and monthly rates are also available.

Hotel El Moro (Av. Javier Rojo Gómez near the central plaza, tel. 998/871-0159, www. hotelelmoro.mx, US$72 s/d with a/c, US$90-102 suite with a/c and kitchenette) is a homey hotel with spacious units, most with polished cement floors, brightly painted walls, and lots of natural light. There's Wi-Fi throughout most of the hotel, plus a pleasant little pool surrounded by hammocks and lounge chairs toward the back. Continental breakfast is included. Late-night music from nearby restaurants can be a bummer during the winter months; ask for a room facing the interior courtyard for a quiet stay.

Rancho Sak Ol (1 kilometer/0.6 mile south of the central plaza, tel. 998/292-1896, www.ranchosakol.com, US$78-87 s/d, US$87-100 s/d with a/c, US$133 suite, 2-night minimum) is a relaxing *palapa* hideaway located a 15-minute walk south of town. Rooms have hanging beds and private patios with hammocks. A buffet breakfast is included in the rate, and guests can use the well-stocked community kitchen. The beach here is just okay—very clean, with good snorkeling offshore, but boxed in by the cargo ferry on one side and a condo complex on the other. Still, there's enough breathing room so as not to spoil Rancho Sak Ol's quiet, isolated feel. The resort is for adults and teens only, except during the school holidays, when children over the age of three are welcome.

US$100-200

⭐ **Layla Guesthouse** (Av. Rafael Melgar s/n, cell tel. 998/104-9831, www.laylaguesthouse. com, US$130 studio with a/c) has four modern studios with aesthetic flair and homey comforts. Each integrates the outdoors through skylights, a patio or balcony, and even an airy shower. All have a well-equipped kitchenette, plush king-size bed, foldout sofa, flat-screen TV, and details like coffee-table books, fine art, soaking showerheads, and tropical woods. There's a leafy garden plus a 3rd-floor plunge pool overlooking the ocean. The welcoming owners, Robin and Steve, are a wealth of information on the region.

Just down the street, **La Casa del Mar** (Av. Rafael Melgar s/n, cell tel. 998/130-0968, US$130 studio with a/c, US$260 penthouse, 2-night minimum) has eight studios with a modern, airy feel—think white walls, clean lines, and splashes of color. Each unit has a kitchenette and includes use of beach chairs and beach umbrellas. There's also a gorgeous two-bedroom penthouse with full kitchen and ocean views. A small, well-tended pool with teak lounge chairs makes for a great place to unwind.

Occupying a converted hacienda-style house, the relaxing **Casa Caribe Hotel** (Av. Javier Rojo Gómez near Calle Lázaro Cardenas, tel. 998/251-8060, U.S. tel. 512/410-8146, www.casacaribepuertomorelos.com, US$155 s/d with a/c) has four 2nd-floor rooms with whitewashed walls, colorful paintings, and large glass doors opening onto private ocean-view terraces. (A fifth room, on the ground floor, has no views.) The rate includes a delicious full breakfast, served in the hotel's interior patio-garden. Hotel/cooking class packages also can be arranged with the on-site Little Mexican Cooking School.

Abbey del Sol (Av. Niños Héroes 806, tel. 998/871-0127, U.S. tel. 651/690-3937, www. abbeydelsol.com, US$90 s/d with a/c, US$125-135 1-bedroom apartment with a/c) offers nicely appointed units with king-size beds, balconies or private patios, and fully equipped kitchens (in all except one). There's a small pool in the leafy garden and a rooftop patio with *palapa*-shaded hammocks. Complimentary use of bicycles is included. If Abbey del Sol is booked, check its website for availability in its other properties around town.

Villas Clarita (Av. Niños Héroes near Calle Benito Juárez, tel. 984/217-2896, www.villasclaritamexico.com, US$120-175 with a/c) has eight comfortable one- and two-bedroom apartments that open onto two courtyards: One courtyard has a large pool with lots of lounge chairs and tables; the other has an open-air yoga studio and shady garden. Most of the apartments have a hacienda-like feel and feature heavy wood furnishings. (The best units open onto the garden courtyard, though families may like having an apartment right next to the pool.) All units have full kitchens, cable TV, Wi-Fi, purified water, and daily maid service.

Over US$200

Dreams Riviera Cancún Resort and Spa (Hwy. 307 Km 324, tel. 998/872-9200, toll-free U.S. tel. 866/237-3267, www.dreamsresorts.com, US$218-240 s with a/c, US$332-397 d with a/c, US$472-998 suite) is a bustling all-inclusive resort north of downtown Puerto Morelos. It has a South Pacific aesthetic with airy rooms that feature tropical woods and bamboo accents. The amenities are high-end and luxurious; some rooms have their own plunge pool. Outside there are lots of infinity pools and a long, wide beach with plenty of places to relax. Nine restaurants (six à la carte) and a wide variety of activities provide enough options to keep most people happy.

Located south of town, **Hotel Marina El Cid Spa & Beach Resort** (Blvd. El Cid Unidad 15, tel. 998/872-8999, toll-free U.S. tel. 888/733-7308, www.elcid.com, US$282 s with a/c, US$301 d with a/c, US$306-381 suite, US$388 1-bedroom apartment) is Puerto Morelos's first all-inclusive resort—a milestone that didn't please everyone in this tight-knit town. The resort gets high marks from families though, with a kids club, waterslide, and manageable size, though the beach is smallish. There is a full-service spa on-site—including beachfront massage tables—as well as a great gym with floor-to-ceiling windows facing the Caribbean. Rooms have modern, tasteful decor and lots of natural light; ask for one in building 21, 22, or 23, which have ocean views over a gorgeous infinity pool.

INFORMATION AND SERVICES

Although this town sees a good number of tourists, the information services remain somewhat sparse. Check out www.InPuertoMorelos.com and www.puertomorelos.com for up-to-date information on restaurants, bars, and things to do around town.

Emergency Services

Médica Puerto Morelos (Calle Ignacio López Rayón, Col. Pescadores, tel. 998/255-3092 or 998/201-2456, 9:30am-2pm and 4pm-8pm Mon.-Sat.) is the small but well-equipped medical office of Dr. Víctor Ballestros, a Mexico City-trained surgeon and general practitioner. Look for signs leading to his office along the access road, near the highway. English is spoken.

Centro de Salud (no phone, 8am-2pm daily) is a basic medical clinic. It's located just south of the central plaza, on an unmarked connector street between Avenidas Javier Rojo Gómez and Rafaél Melgar.

Farmacia San José Obrero (central plaza, Av. Javier Rojo Gómez, tel. 998/871-0053, 8am-2pm and 4pm-10pm daily) is a mom-and-pop pharmacy selling basic meds and toiletries.

The **police station** (central plaza, Av. Javier Rojo Gómez) can be reached toll-free at 066.

Money

There is no bank in Puerto Morelos, but there are three **ATMs** in town—an HSBC one in front of Casa Martín, a Santander ATM in front of the police station, and a Banco Norte ATM inside the OXXO mini-mart on the west corner of the central plaza. The most reliable one (with the lowest transactions fees), however, is in front of the Super Chedraui supermarket, just off the highway.

Media and Communications

There's **free Wi-Fi** (24 hours) in the central plaza. Most hotels and many cafes also offer Wi-Fi to guests.

Laundry

The bustling **LavaPlus** (Av. Niños Héroes s/n, cell tel. 998/198-4850, 8am-8pm daily) charges US$1.15 per kilo (2.2 pounds). For service in five hours, the rate jumps to US$1.40 per kilo. Coin-operated machines are also available.

GETTING THERE AND AROUND

Puerto Morelos is almost exactly halfway between Cancún (36 kilometers/22 miles, 40 minutes driving) and Playa del Carmen (35 kilometers/21 miles, 35 minutes). The Cancún airport is closer, just 18 kilometers (11 miles, 20 minutes) north of Puerto Morelos. A rental car isn't really necessary around town, but makes exploring the Riviera Maya beyond Puerto Morelos significantly easier.

Europcar (Calle Tulum near Av. Javier Rojo Gómez, tel. 998/206-9372, www.europcar.com.mx, 8am-5pm daily) has a small office just off the main plaza, making it the most convenient option for renting a car. Otherwise, Cancún's airport has a large number of agencies, and you can often find excellent deals online.

Bus

ADO buses pass the Puerto Morelos turnoff on Highway 307 but do not enter town. The northbound stop is right at the turnoff, while the southbound bus stop is across the highway and a block south. Headed north to Cancún (US$1.75, 45 minutes) or south to Playa del Carmen (US$1.65, 45 minutes), second-class buses and *combis* (shared vans) pass every 10-15 minutes 5:30am-10pm daily, and less frequently throughout the night. A handful continue to Tulum, but it may be quicker to go to Playa and transfer. Buses to the Cancún airport (US$5.50, 25 minutes) pass roughly every 30-90 minutes 3:45am-9:15pm daily. Buy your ticket a day in advance, as buses often fill in Playa del Carmen.

Colectivo

Colectivos (shared minivans) make rounds to and from Puerto Morelos Pueblo, across the highway (US$0.50, 10 minutes), every 5-10 minutes 6:30am-10pm daily. Flag one down on the main drag or wait for one to pass the central plaza. *Colectivos* also are a convenient and cheap way to get to the highway, where you can catch a bus or *combi* (shared van) to destinations along the Riviera Maya.

Taxi

Taxis (tel. 998/871-0090) line up day and night at the taxi stand on the northwest corner of the central plaza. Prices are fixed and prominently displayed on a signboard at the taxi stand. A ride around town or to the highway/ADO bus stop costs US$1.50.

Bicycle

Puerto Morelos Green Bikes (Av. Niños Héroes s/n, tel. 998/734-8132, ride@greenbikesrentals.com, US$10 per 24 hours) rents comfortable bikes—even adult trikes—that include a basket, lock, rear rack, blinking lights, and a bell.

Another good option is the dive shop **Diverspoint** (Av. Javier Rojo Gómez s/n, tel. 998/206-9051, www.diverspoint.com), which rents bicycles for US$2 per hour, US$9 per 24 hours, and US$35 per week.

PUNTA BETE AND PLAYA XCALACOCO

It used to be that the only way to find Punta Bete and its main beach, Playa Xcalacoco, was to look for the big Cristal water plant. That's still the best landmark, but a flurry of construction has prompted hoteliers to finally add signs along the highway. The beach here is decent—the sand is clean but coarse, and the shoreline rocky in places—but the snorkeling is good, and the isolation has always been a big plus. It's still a quiet place, but all the new development—including a huge condo complex—may mark a new chapter for this long-overlooked stretch of beach.

Food

Coco's Cabañas (Hwy. 307 Km 296, tel. 998/874-7056, www.cocoscabanas.com, 8:30am-8pm daily, US$6-18) has a small outdoor bar and restaurant that specializes in wood-oven pizzas, though there are lots of seafood dishes as well. It's a bit pricey for the location, but then again you don't often see lobster pizza with hefty portions of prosciutto, arugula, and brie.

Accommodations

★ **Hotel Petit Lafitte** (Hwy. 307 Km 296, tel. 984/877-4000, www.petitlafitte.com, US$204-293 s/d with a/c, US$246-336 s/d bungalow with a/c) offers the comfort of a full-scale hotel on this isolated stretch of beach, including a large pool, plenty of lounge space, and a well-maintained beach area with *palapas* and hammocks. Accommodations are either in the main building, where all the rooms have at least partial ocean views, or in spacious beachfront bungalows. All accommodations have one or two beds, cable TV, air-conditioning, a minibar, and Wi-Fi.

Owned by a Mexican-Swiss couple, **Coco's Cabañas** (Hwy. 307 Km 296, tel. 998/874-7056, www.cocoscabanas.com, US$68-85 s/d with a/c, US$95-106 suite with a/c) has a handful of charming *palapa*-roofed bungalows on a small garden plot. The *cabañas* are comfortable and attractive, with large paintings and artful stonework, plus patios with hammocks. There's a heart-shaped pool next to the open-air restaurant and bar, and the beach is just 30 meters (100 feet) away. Continental breakfast and bicycles are included.

Getting There and Around

From the highway, follow the access road two kilometers (1.2 miles) until it forks at the Viceroy Riviera Maya resort. Bear left to reach the listed hotels and beach.

There is no taxi stand in this tiny community; when guests need one, hotels call cabs from Playa del Carmen or Puerto Morelos. A ride to the airport costs around US$50, to Playa del Carmen US$20.

Playa del Carmen

Playa del Carmen (or Playa for short) has long been a favorite among travelers looking for an alternative to Cancún, a place where boutique hotels and lounge bars outnumber glitzy high-rises and all-night clubs. There also are more opportunities for tourists and locals to interact in Playa, and it's easier to find "authentic" Mexican outlets, especially compared to Cancún's Zona Hotelera. And while Cancún is an American playground, Playa attracts many more Europeans.

But Playa is no longer the small seaside town some remember. Its population has exploded in recent years, with tourist and residential development stretching farther and farther up the coast every year. The main tourist strip, Quinta Avenida (5th Avenue), is still mostly pedestrian, but walking from end to end is no longer the casual jaunt it once was; a bike path along 10 Avenida is a smart and welcome addition. And while lounge bars and beach clubs are still the mainstay of Playa's nightlife, nightclubs like Coco Bongo Playa and Palazzo, both offshoots of famous Cancún clubs, have fanned the fears of the "Cancúnification" of Playa del Carmen.

Playa still has plenty of small hotels and hipster bars, and remains a genuine alternative to Cancún. It has pretty beaches, and the atmosphere remains decidedly mellow, even with all the changes. Playa's location also makes it a convenient base from which to explore the rest of the Riviera Maya and Yucatán Peninsula, whether snorkeling in cenotes, diving on Isla Cozumel, or visiting inland Maya ruins.

SIGHTS AND BEACHES

★ Quinta Avenida

Playa's main pedestrian and commercial drag is Quinta Avenida, or 5th Avenue, which stretches more than 20 blocks from the ferry dock northward. Pronounced KEEN-ta av-en-EE-da, you may see it written as 5 Avenida or 5a Avenida, which is akin to "5th" in English. The southern section, especially near the ferry dock, is packed with typical tourist traps: souvenir shops, chain restaurants, and so forth. North of Avenida Constituyentes, the atmosphere is somewhat more sophisticated, with more bistros, cool bars, and high-end boutiques. The north-south division is less stark than it used to be, with some nice spots opening in the former and plenty of kitsch in the latter. You'll probably walk the length of Quinta Avenida once or twice, and everyone seems to find his or her favorite part.

Museo Frida Kahlo (5 Av. at Calle 8, tel. 984/980-0595, wwwmuseofridakahloriviera-maya.org, 9am-11pm daily, US$12) provides a fascinating look at one of Mexico's most famous painters. The museum contains no original paintings but it outlines, in detail, the defining moments of Kahlo's life: her early life, her debilitating accident, the surgeries, and, of course, her tumultuous relationship with fellow painter Diego Rivera. Copies of her paintings, letters, and photographs are displayed throughout. Knowledgeable guides lead 45-minute tours in English and Spanish; afterward, visitors are welcome to linger and revisit exhibits.

El Acuario de Playa (Plaza Calle Corazón, 5 Av. between Calles 12 and 14, tel. 984/879-4462, www.elacuariodeplaya.com, 11am-7pm daily, US$13.50) is a smallish aquarium showcasing over 200 types of sea creatures, all found regionally. Bilingual guides lead visitors through the exhibits, answering questions along the way; tours last about 30-minutes (there also are educational placards in Spanish and English). There are some touch tanks and an eerily beautiful jellyfish room with row upon row of tanks lit up in purple. Best of all is a glass tunnel that runs through the largest tank, allowing visitors to be surrounded by tropical fish. Look for the entrance on the 2nd floor of the Calle Corazón shopping mall.

Beaches and Beach Clubs

A series of storms and shifting currents have changed the landscape of Playa del Carmen's beaches. Once uniformly gorgeous, they are now thin and rocky in the central section (Calle 4 to Av. Constituyentes) and wide with soft white sand on the bookends (near the ferry terminal and north of Av. Constituyentes). Fortunately, Playa is blessed with clear aquamarine water and mild surf along its entire shore. The state of the beaches, though, is ever changing—it is nature, after all. Online forums are a good way to get the latest info.

All along Playa's coast are numerous beach clubs where, for a small fee or for simply ordering something from the menu, you can make use of the lounge chairs, umbrellas, restrooms, and even swimming pools and changing rooms. If beach clubs aren't your thing, there are several convenient beaches on which to lay out your own towel and umbrella.

BEACH CLUBS

Playa Tukán (end of Calle 28) has two popular beach clubs, both with waiter service, pools, changing areas, lockers, and Wi-Fi; admission includes credit toward food and drinks. **Mamita's Beach Club** (tel. 984/803-2868, www.mamitasbeachclub.com, 8am-6pm daily, US$15-17 lounge chair, US$150-170 sun bed up to 4 people) is one of Playa's best-known beach clubs, with thumping music and a lively atmosphere. It has an adults-only section, including a pool. Topless sunbathing is permitted and common throughout the club. Just down the beach is **Kool** (tel. 984/873-1255, www.koolbeachclub.com.mx, 8am-6pm daily, US$25-68 adult lounge chair, US$13-34 child lounge chair, US$119-270 sun bed up to

Playa del Carmen

307

To Hospiten Riviera Maya,
XCARET, Xplor, Delphinus Riviera Maya,
Car Ferry to Cozumel, and Tulum

45 AV

40 AV

35 AV

CALLE 4

30 AV

30 AV

25 AV

WALMART

DAS BROT

CALLE 8

CALLE 6

CALLE 10

PALACIO MUNICIPAL

EL GALLINERO DU CHOCOLAT

YOGALOFT
FARMACIAS DEL AHORRO

Plaza 28 de Julio
Pelicanos

LA CHANCLA

BANAMEX

COCO BONGO
PLAYA PALAZZO
Plaza Calle Corazón
PURA VIDA BAR

HERTZ

CALLE 14

CALLE 14 BIS

EL ACUARIO DE PLAYA
GANDHI

ARTIK POP

5 AV

TEXTILE MAYA CHIAPAS

CALLE 12

PHANTOM DIVERS

CLUB YEBO

THE ACANTO BOUTIQUE HOTEL & CONDOMINIUMS

CALLE 16 BIS

1 AV NORTE

PLAYA EXPRESS

POST OFFICE

COMISTO CANCUN AND TULUM

LAVANDERIA LOS MECATES

"LAS QUESADILLAS"

HOTEL LUNASOL
PLAYA HOSTEL

YUM K'IIN

EL JAGUAR DORADO

FALAFEL NESSA

FAH

BABE'S NOODLES & BAR

YUCATREK'S

PLAYA DEL CARMEN AIRPORT

AEROSAAB
AIRPORT TERMINAL

U.S. CONSULAR AGENCY

PRIMER PLATO

HOSTEL 3B

CALLE 2

City Park

PARAISO DIVERS
YUCATEK DIVERS

MANNE'S BIERGARTEN
FOOD COURT

HOTEL BARRIO LATINO
EASY WAY

ZENZI

DIVE MIKE

SCUBA PLAYA

LIDO BEACH CLUB

Plaza Paraiso

IMMIGRATION OFFICE

ARTIK POP

AV JUAREZ

CALLE 1 SUR

Paseo del Carmen

TOURIST INFORMATION KIOSK

TERMINAL TURISTICA

PARAISO AZUL'S CASA DE GOPALA

SELINA

CLUB 69

CARBONCITOS

QUINTA AVENIDA

Bike Path

10 AV

PLAYA MAYA

PARAISO BEACH

FUSION

Playa El Faro

SKY DIVE PLAYA

FERRY TICKET BOOTHS

5 AV

LA TARRAYA

Plaza

Playa Principal

PASSENGER FERRY PIER

To Playacar, Aviario Xaman Ha,
Playacar Vacation Rentals,
and Hard Rock Golf Club Riviera Maya

Caribbean Sea

To Cozumel

0   200 yds
0   200 m

© MOON.COM

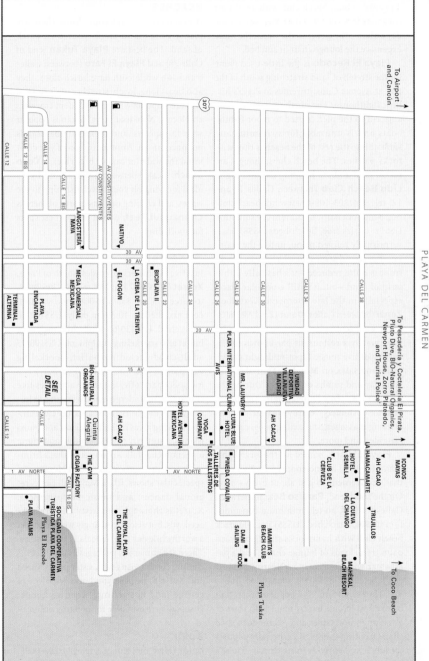

To Airport
and Cancún

307

To Pescadería y Coctelería El Pirata,
Pluto Dive, BIO-Natural Organics,
Newport House, Zorro Plateado,
and Tourist Police

CALLE 12
CALLE 14
CALLE 12 BIS
CALLE 14 BIS
AV CONSTITUYENTES
AV CONSTITUYENTES
30 AV
30 AV
CALLE 20
CALLE 22
CALLE 24
CALLE 26
CALLE 28
CALLE 30
CALLE 34
CALLE 38

LANGOSTERIA MAYA

NATIVO
EL FOGÓN
LA CEIBA DE LA TREINTA
BICIPLAYA II

MEGA COMERCIAL MEXICANA
PLAYA ENCANTADA
TERMINAL ALTERNA

20 AV

15 AV

BIO-NATURAL ORGANICS

PLAYA INTERNATIONAL CLINIC
AVIS
MR. LAUNDRY
LUNA BLUE HOTEL
UNIDAD DEPORTIVA VILLANUEVA MADRID
AH CACAO

SEE DETAIL

CALLE 12
CALLE 14
CALLE 16 BIS

Quinta Alegria
AH CACAO
HOTEL AVENTURA MEXICANA
YOGA COMPANY
TALLERES DE LOS BALLESTROS
PINEDA COVALIN

5 AV

1 AV NORTE
1 AV NORTE

THE GYM
CIGAR FACTORY

ICONOS MAYAS
AH CACAO
LA HAMACAMARTE
HOTEL LA SEMILLA
CLUB DE LA CERVEZA
LA CUEVA DEL CHANGO
TRUJILLOS

PLAYA PALMS
SOCIEDAD COOPERATIVA TURISTICA PLAYA DEL CARMEN
Playa El Recodo

THE ROYAL PLAYA DEL CARMEN

DANI SAILING
KOOL
MAMITA'S BEACH CLUB
Playa Tukán
MAHEKAL BEACH RESORT

To Coco Beach

4 people), a busy beach club with an almost corporate feel. Guests choose their seat for the day online—the closer to the water, the more expensive the lounge chair or sun bed.

Playa El Recodo is the little-used name for the stretch of sand stretching south of the pier at Avenue Constituyentes to Playa's historic lighthouse. The northernmost section, adjacent to the pier, is used to moor fishing boats and is unusable for swimming and sunbathing; the rest of the beach is thin with rocky patches. The beach clubs, though, are set on sand and are hopping day and night. **Lido Beach Club** (between Calles 10 and 12, tel. 984/803-1090, www.lidobeachclub. mx, 8am-8pm daily, minimum consumption US$12, chairs free, beach beds US$8) has a surprisingly refined menu, unlike the plain-Jane fair served at most beach clubs. Its beachfront is quite reduced—it's basically a thin strip of sand—but it's still a popular place, especially in the late afternoon. Next door, **Zenzi** (between Calles 10 and 12, tel. 983/803-5738, www.zenzi-playa.com, 8am-2am daily) is primarily a restaurant-bar known for its variety of live music (5pm-midnight daily), including salsa on Monday, Thursday, and Saturday and samba on Sunday. During the day, there are free lounge chairs and beach beds for customers. Nearby are beach booths offering massages, snorkeling trips, catamaran rides, and more.

Playa El Faro, named for the large lighthouse (or *faro*) at one end, is a lovely beach that's convenient to just about everywhere. On the south end, **Paraíso Beach** (between Calles 6 and 8, no tel., minimum consumption US$10, beach beds US$5) is a laid-back beach club with hammocks strung between palm trees, loads of lounge chairs, and a *palapa* bar with rope swings. Nearby, **Fusion** (Calle 6, tel. 984/873-0374, 10am-10pm Tues.-Sat., 11am-9pm Sun.) is a popular beach club by day and lounge bar by night with rows of low-slung wood tables and Adirondack-style chairs fronting the sea. It's especially popular for lunch and early-evening drinks. There's live music most nights plus fire dancers too.

BEACHES

If beach clubs aren't your thing, there are plenty of spots to claim your own patch of sand. The best are **Playa Tukán** (end of Calle 28) and **Playa El Faro** (between Calles 6 and 16); while both have beach clubs, they also boast long, lovely stretches of open sand and are popular with independent travelers and locals. Note that Playa Tukán is popular with Europeans, and topless sunbathing is not uncommon. Another option, if you don't mind the walk (or taxi or bike ride), is **Coco Beach;** located between Calles 38 and 46, it's ideal for lying on your towel, listening to the waves, and chilling out. Just north of there is **Chunzubul Reef,** one of Playa's best spots for snorkeling.

★ Xcaret

Just five kilometers (3.1 miles) south of Playa, **Xcaret** (Hwy. 307 Km 282, tel. 984/206-0038, toll-free U.S. tel. 855/326-0682, www.xcaret. com.mx, 8:30am-10:30pm daily, US$100/50 adult/child, US$130/65 adult/child including buffet and snorkeling equipment, US$190/95 adult/child including buffet, snorkeling equipment, and one optional activity) is a mega-ecopark offering water activities like snorkeling in underground rivers and swimming with dolphins and sharks; up-close animal viewing areas including jaguar and puma islands, a butterfly pavilion, and an aquarium; a phenomenal folk art museum that's brimming with *artesanía* from around Mexico; and spectacular shows, like a Maya ball game, regional dances, and music performances. Xcaret is thoroughly touristy and prepackaged, yes, but also surprisingly well done and a worthwhile day trip, especially for families. There are numerous packages and prices, including combo visits with sister parks **Xplor** and **Xel-Há;** be sure you know what you're getting (and not getting) when you book. Discounts are available for booking online.

Xplor

Xplor (Hwy. 307 Km 282, tel. 984/206-0038, toll-free U.S. tel. 855/326-06852, www.xplor.

travel, 9am-5pm Mon.-Sat., US$140/70 adult/child) is adjacent to the mother ship and focused on adventure activities. The park has two zip line circuits with seven segments each, including tandem lines and a splashdown in the mouth of a cavern. Other activities include swimming and rafting through caverns bristling with stalactites, and driving amphibious ATVs through the forest and underground passages. Admission includes lockers, showers, buffet lunch, and fresh-made smoothies, water, and snacks. Xplor also offers evening-only admission (5:30pm-11:30pm daily, US$100/50 adult/child), with colored lights and torches lighting up the park and its activities, adding an additional rush.

Aviario Xaman Ha

A short distance inside the Playacar entrance off 10 Avenida, the small bird sanctuary **Aviario Xaman Ha** (Paseo Xaman Ha s/n, tel. 984/873-0593, 9am-5pm daily, US$20 adult, children under 12 free) is home, or a stopover, for more than 60 species of tropical birds, including toucans, flamingos, cormorants, and parrots. Some birds are in enclosures, but many are not, and a stone path meanders through the leafy grounds. It's a pleasant place to spend an hour, though the admission price is ridiculously inflated. If you do go, be sure to bring bug repellent.

SPORTS AND RECREATION
Scuba Diving

Playa del Carmen has decent offshore diving—virtually all drift dives, thanks to prevailing currents—and relatively easy access to Cozumel and inland cenotes. It's a logical base if you want a taste of all three, plus the convenience of being in a major town. However, if diving is the main reason you came, consider basing yourself on Cozumel itself, or closer to the cenotes, such as at Akumal or Tulum. This will save you the time, money, and effort of going back and forth.

Diving prices in Playa del Carmen are reasonable, and fairly uniform from shop to shop. Two-tank reef dives cost US$70-85, Cozumel trips run US$95-165, cenote trips are around US$120-175, and open-water certification courses run US$395-430. Gear is included in the courses but may be charged separately for fun dives (US$15-20/day). Most shops do not include the price of taking the ferry to Cozumel, and additional fees, like marine park and cenote admissions, may also apply.

Dive Mike (Calle 8 between 5 Av. and the beach, tel. 984/803-1228, www.divemike.com, 7am-7:45pm daily) is a friendly, professional, and reasonably priced shop.

Phantom Divers (Av. 1 Norte at Calle 14, tel. 984/879-3988, www.phantomdivers.com, 8am-8pm daily) is one of a handful of locally owned dive shops offering lower-than-average prices.

Pluto Dive (Calle 40 between 5 and 10 Avs., cell tel. 984/151-9046, www.plutodive.com, 9am-7pm Mon.-Sat.) is an Italian-run shop that keeps its trips limited to five divers.

Scuba Playa (Calle 10 between 1 and 5 Avs., tel. 984/803-3123, www.scubaplaya.com, 7:30am-9pm daily) specializes in small groups and offers a six-dive package that includes two tanks apiece in Cozumel, the cenotes, and the reef.

Yucatek Divers (15 Av. between Calles 2 and 4, tel. 984/803-2836, www.yucatek-divers.com, 8am-5pm daily) is a longtime shop with instruction available in several languages. Notably, all fun dives are led by instructors.

Snorkeling

In Playa itself it's best to go snorkeling with a boat tour because the snorkeling off the beach isn't too rewarding. There are also numerous nearby cenotes that make for unique snorkeling, most of which you can visit on your own.

Most of Playa's dive shops offer guided snorkeling tours to excellent sites. Ocean trips cost US$40-50, while cenote trips are US$70-80, all gear included. Be sure to clarify how many reefs or cenotes you'll be visiting and for how long. A wetsuit is strongly recommended, even if it means paying extra

to rent one. Cenotes can be quite cold, while sunburn is a serious concern in the open ocean; wetsuits protect against both, as well as against accidental scrapes and cuts.

Dani Sailing (Calle 28 near the beach, cell tel. 984/136-3363, 9am-6pm daily) offers catamaran trips (US$65) with an hour spent sailing and another hour snorkeling. Or rent snorkel gear (US$12/hour) and a kayak or stand-up paddleboard (US$25/hour) and find a spot of your own. Look for the small shop where Calle 28 hits the beach.

Sociedad Cooperativa Turística Playa del Carmen (Playa El Recodo, end of Calle 14, no phone, 9am-6pm daily) is a local fisherman's cooperative offering snorkeling tours from a kiosk on the beach (US$35/45 pp for one/two sites). Trips typically are to **Moc Che,** a shallow snorkel site on the north end of Playa, and **Inah,** a reef known for its huge coral heads and sea turtle sightings, located about 10 kilometers (6 mi) south of Playa.

Wind Sports

Kiteboarding, sailboarding, and sailing have grown in popularity along the Caribbean, a trickle-down effect from the world-famous wind belt on the Gulf coast. You can catch at least some breeze almost any time of the year, but the strongest, most consistent winds blow November-March.

Dani Sailing (Calle 28 near the beach, cell tel. 984/136-3363, 9am-6pm daily) offers catamaran rentals and tours, with or without snorkeling, as well as kiteboarding rentals and instruction. Prices vary.

Arguably a wind sport, **Sociedad Cooperativa Turística Playa del Carmen** (Playa El Recodo, end of Calle 14, no phone, 9am-6pm daily) offers parasailing—either single or double seated. Rides last 12-15 minutes (US$65 pp).

1: a stand-up paddleboard waiting for a rider; 2: Puerto Morelos's rich coral reef, easily accessible to snorkelers; 3: taking a parasailing ride on the wind

Stand-Up Paddling and Kayaking

Stand Up Paddle Playa del Carmen (tel. 512/822-3692, www.suppdc.com) is a one-man operation offering hour-long lessons for US$65 (US$50 pp for 2 people) at the beach nearest you, with an hour's free rental afterward to practice your skills. There's no fixed storefront, so reservations are recommended; otherwise, look for SUP gear near the pier at Avenida Constituyentes or near Fusion beach bar (end of Calle 6). Rental gear is available (US$30/hour, US$80/half day).

Do-it-all beach sports outfit **Dani Sailing** (Calle 28 near the beach, cell tel. 984/136-3363, 9am-6pm daily) rents kayaks (US$18/hour single, US$23/hour double) and stand-up paddleboards (US$23/hour). Hour-long instructional courses (US$30) are available for anyone new to "SUPing."

Sociedad Cooperativa Turística Playa del Carmen (Playa El Recodo, end of Calle 14, no phone, 9am-6pm daily) also rents stand-up paddleboards for US$25 per hour.

Swimming with Dolphins

With swimming pens set up in the ocean, **Delphinus Riviera Maya** (Hwy. 307 Km 282, toll-free Mex. tel. 800/335-3461, toll-free U.S./Can. tel. 888/526-2230, www.delphinusworld.com, US$99-499) is about as good as it gets for performing dolphins. There are various packages, from 30-minute group interactions to 45-minute one-on-one encounters. Book online to access discounts. Transportation is available for a fee.

Sportfishing

Playa de Carmen has excellent sportfishing and bottom fishing, with plentiful wahoo, dorado, mackerel, snapper, barracuda, and—especially April-June—sailfish and marlin. Trips depend mostly on the size and power of the boat that's used, but a 4-5-hour trip for 1-4 people usually costs US$230-260, including tackle and drinks. Many dive shops offer tours, as does **Sociedad Cooperativa Turística Playa del Carmen** (Playa El

Recodo, end of Calle 14, no phone, 7am-6pm daily).

Golf

Hard Rock Golf Club Riviera Maya (Paseo Xaman-Há s/n, tel. 984/873-4990, toursinfo@ allinclusivecollection.com, 7am-sundown daily) is a challenging 7,144-yard championship course designed by Robert Van Hagge and located in Playacar, the upscale hotel and residential development south of Playa del Carmen proper. Greens fees are US$180 per person, US$96 after 3pm, including cart and all-inclusive food and drinks from the beverage carts that travel the course and at the on-site restaurant; hotel pickup is available for a fee. Reserve at least a day in advance November-January.

Skydiving

Gleaming white beaches and brilliant turquoise seas make the Riviera Maya a spectacular place for skydiving. If you're up for it, **Sky Dive Playa** (Plaza Marina, just south of the ferry dock, tel. 984/873-0192, www.skydive.com.mx, 9am-4pm Mon.-Sat.) has been throwing travelers out of planes at 10,000 feet since 1996. You freefall for 4,500 feet—about 45 seconds—and then the chute opens for a 7-8-minute ride down to a soft landing on the beach. Tandem dives (you and an instructor, US$269) are scheduled every hour; walk-ups are accepted, but reservations are highly recommended. For an additional US$99, a cameraman also can be booked to **freefall** alongside you to record your jump either in an eight-minute video or 50-60 digital photographs.

Tours

YucaTreks (Av. 10 between Calles 10 and 12, tel. 984/803-1265, www.yucatreks.com, 9:30am-2pm Mon.-Fri., 10am-1pm Sat.) offers highly recommended tours to a variety of sites in the region: archaeological zones like Cobá and Chichén Itzá, snorkeling (cenote or reef), whale shark tours, and sailboat excursions. Trips are limited to small groups and

are led by knowledgeable and enthusiastic—and punctual—people. Private tours also can be arranged.

Alltournative (Hwy. 307 Km 287, tel. 984/803-9999, toll-free U.S. tel. 877/437-4990, www.alltournative.com, 9am-7pm daily) offers a variety of conservation-minded full-day tours, including a combination of activities like canoeing, zip lines, ATV riding, and snorkeling, plus visits to the Tulum or Cobá archaeological zone—even to a small Maya village.

AeroSaab (Playa Del Carmen Airport, 20 Av. Sur near Calle 1, tel. 998/865-4225, www. aerosaab.com, 7am-7:30pm daily) offers stunning panoramic flights of the Riviera Maya (US$195-1,064, 4-6 passengers, 15 minutes-2 hours), as well as scenic full-day tours to places like Isla Holbox (US$696-754, 5-6 passengers) and Mérida/Uxmal (US$1,305-1,515, 5-6 passengers). Trips are in 5- and 6-seat Cessna airplanes and typically require a minimum of 2-4 people.

Spas and Gyms

The Gym (Av. 1 near Calle 16 Bis, tel. 984/873-2098, www.thegymplaya.com, 6am-midnight Mon.-Fri., 7am-7pm Sat., 8am-5pm Sun.) is a modern facility offering state-of-the-art equipment and a host of classes, including yoga, Pilates, spinning, and jiujitsu. There are personal trainers on-site. Day passes are US$15; multiday and monthly passes are available.

Yoga Company (Calle 26 between 5 and 10 Avs., tel. 984/803-3295, hours vary Mon.-Sat., US$10/class) is a popular 2nd-floor studio just steps from Quinta Avenida. Instruction focuses on vinyasa yoga, with classes for all levels of students. If you prefer a bigger studio, check out **Yogaloft** (Plaza Pelícanos, Calle 10 between 10 and 15 Avs., tel. 984/803-0352, www.yogaloftplaya.com, hours vary Mon.-Sun., US$13/class), which has two airy and modern studios and a wider variety of classes. Private instruction is available at both studios.

You can get a **massage on the beach** at various locations—look for the white tents and massage tables—for about US$60 per hour.

The recently renovated **Unidad Deportiva Villanueva Madrid** (Av. 10 near Calle 30, no phone, 6am-10pm daily) is Playa del Carmen's public sporting facility, with a gym, tennis and basketball courts, a track, and a soccer field. All have night lighting and are open to the public free of charge, but you need to bring your own gear.

ENTERTAINMENT

Playa del Carmen's nightlife has long been dominated by bars and lounges, as if deliberately leaving the raucous clubs and discotheques to Cancún. While that's still mostly the case, Playa is definitely getting rowdier, with several major nightclubs and the increasingly boisterous cluster of club-like bars at the corner of 1 Avenida and Calle 12.

Lounges and Bars

A hipster little hole-in-the-wall right on Quinta Avenida, **Club de la Cerveza** (5 Av. near Calle 38, tel. 984/147-0635, www. clubdelacerveza.mx, 4pm-2am daily) has a laid-back vibe, knowledgeable bartenders, and the area's best selection of craft beers. Over half the brews are from Mexico, including a few locals like Akumal IPA and Mundo Maya's citrusy ale "The Warrior." There's also tasty bar food and prices that won't kill your buzz.

Fah (5 Av. between Calles 8 and 10, tel. 984/803-1166, www.siestafiestahotelplaya. com, 8am-midnight daily) is an open-air restaurant-bar with seating on the pedestrian walkway and even more near a small stage inside. There's live music most nights; some of the bands are quite good, while others…well, at least they're giving it a go. But there's always a crowd and a fun time to be had, and the food and cocktails are outstanding.

Manne's Biergarten (Calle 4 between Avs. 10 and 15, tel. 984/876-5363, 4pm-1am Wed.-Mon.) is owned by the namesake German transplant who handles much of the customer service himself at this popular bar-restaurant. The bar, the walls, and even the ceiling are crammed with German memorabilia. Come here for tall glasses of German brew and to sample authentic dishes from the homeland: sauerkraut, brats, spätzle, and a great Sunday prime rib special.

La Chancla (Calle 10 at 10 Av., tel. 984/158-1948, 4pm-4am daily) is a locals' favorite, and just hard enough to find to keep it that way. Beer is sold here by the bottle or by the *litro* (liter), and there's good bar food, all at very reasonable prices. There's live rock music occasionally, and always a fun, relaxed atmosphere.

Nightclubs

Coco Bongo Playa (Calle 12 at Av. 10, tel. 984/803-5939, toll-free U.S. tel. 800/841-4636, www.cocobongo.com, 10:30pm-3:30am Mon.-Sat., US$70 including open bar) is an offshoot of the famous nightclub in Cancún. Like the original, Coco Bongo Playa features a slew of celebrity impersonations, from Beetlejuice to Rihanna, plus acrobats, light shows, and multiple DJs to keep everyone dancing. The space here is fairly small, but the crowds can be huge and boisterous—tons of fun, assuming you're not claustrophobic. Check with your hotel concierge about VIP tickets and party-hopper tours; shows begin at 11:30pm.

There are two more clubs nearby, which either benefit from or are overshadowed by the crowds amassing outside Coco Bongo. Directly next door to Coco Bongo is another Cancún offshoot, **Palazzo** (Calle 12 near Av. 10, tel. 984/803-0730, www.palazzodisco. com, 10pm-3am Thurs.-Sat., US$60), a sister club to the City and Palazzo Cancún in the Zona Hotelera. It offers a somewhat more traditional techno nightclub scene, while aiming to inject old-school glamour through its décor and image. **Pura Vida Bar** (Calle 12 between 5 and 10 Avs., no tel., 8pm-3am daily, no cover) is a laid-back bar with a dance floor that gets packed by midnight. Guest DJs and live bands, playing everything from cumbia to funk, keep people spinning. Tuesday and Wednesday are Ladies Nights (free drinks!).

One of Playa's only gay clubs, **Club 69** (off 5 Av. between Calles 4 and 6, tel. 984/876-9466, 9pm-5am Tues.-Sun., US$5) doesn't get interesting until after 1am, and sometimes later. There are regular drag shows and exotic dancers, and, of course, music and dancing. Drinks are so-so and the place could use a good scrub, but it's not bad considering Playa's slim pickings for gay travelers. The entrance is easy to miss—look for the 7-Eleven mini-mart on the west side of Quinta Avenida, then follow the rainbow sign down an alley.

SHOPPING

Playa del Carmen offers some of the best shopping on the Riviera Maya, and Quinta Avenida is (mostly) where it's at. Here you'll find numerous souvenir shops, from small to gargantuan, open all day every day. For something unique, try the following stores.

Artesanía

A hidden gem, **El Jaguar Dorado** (Calle 8 between Avs. 10 and 15, cell tel. 984/147-2705, 10am-8pm Mon.-Sat.) sells whimsical and unique art and textiles. Many of the objects are made on-site; others have been created by cooperatives of artists from the Yucatán and Chiapas. You'll find embroidered masks, handmade dolls, lithographs, T-shirts, bags, and more.

Pineda Covalín (5 Av. between Calles 26 and 28, tel. 984/803-2285, www.pinedacovalin.com, 10am-11pm daily) has gorgeous high-end accessories, including purses, scarves, and wallets, made from silk and other luxurious fabrics printed with traditional Mexican and indigenous images. This is the largest Pineda Covalín store in the Riviera Maya, with smaller shops in the Cancún and Cozumel airports.

Textile Maya Chiapas (5 Av. near Calle 14, no phone, 9am-2am daily) is a huge open-air shop bursting with colorful handicrafts from Chiapas. Piles of handwoven blankets and runners, baskets of handmade wool toys, shelves upon shelves of embroidered clothing, countless traditional garments hanging from the rafters—the abundance and the quality are breathtaking. Prices are fair (and fixed).

A small, colorful shop, **La Hamacamarte** (Calle 38 near 5 Av., tel. 984/873-1338, 9am-9pm Mon.-Sat., 9am-6pm Sun.) specializes in high-end hammocks and hammock spinoffs like hanging chairs and knit bags, all made in the Yucatán. There's also a small selection of handwoven linens and hats.

Specialty Items

Prison Art (5 Av. Benito Juárez and Calle 1, no tel., www.prisonart.com.mx, 9am-10pm daily) sells handmade leather goods that are inspired by tattoo art and created by men and women serving time in Mexican prisons. The shop is an arm of Fundación Proarca, a nonprofit organization that works to support and rehabilitate prisoners as well as to help reintegrate them into society.

Iconos Mayas (5 Av. between Calles 38 and 40, tel. 984/873-3111, www.iconosmayas.com, 9am-10pm daily) sells gorgeous handcrafted jewelry integrating Maya glyphs, mostly in silver. Customers provide the date or name that they'd like represented (e.g., a birth date, their child's name) and choose the jewelry type (e.g., bracelet, necklace), including any semiprecious stones. By the end of the day, a one-of-a-kind piece is ready to wear. All items come with an explanation of each glyph.

Talleres de los Ballestros (5 Av. at Calle 24, tel. 984/803-1923, www.ballesteros.net, 9am-11pm daily) is a well-respected silver shop selling gorgeous items from Taxco, Mexico's silver capital. Jewelry and home décor figure prominently. For more options, check out the like-named **sister shop,** located in the Paseo del Carmen mall (tel. 984/803-3939, 9am-11pm daily). Light haggling is welcome at both stores.

1: Playa's pedestrian-only Quinta Avenida; **2:** moments before the Papantla Flyers perform a ritual ceremony at Xcaret; **3:** traditional Maya costumes at Xcaret; **4:** Xcaret's spectacular end-of-day show

Gandhi (Plaza Calle Corazón, 5 Av. between Calles 12 and 14, toll-free Mex. tel. 800/426-3440, www.gandhi.com.mx, 11am-11pm daily) is an excellent bookshop located on the 1st floor of Calle Corazón shopping center. Come here if you're hankering for a good read that won't run out of battery. Novels, guidebooks, and more are sold in several languages.

With workers rolling cigars at the front of the store, it's tough to walk by **Cigar Factory** (5 Av. at Calle 16, no phone, 10am-11pm daily) without taking a second look. Inside you'll find a good variety of Cuban and Mexican *puros* sold individually (US$7-17) or by the box (US$60-450).

Shopping Centers and Markets

Caminarte (5 Av. between Calles 24 and 34) is an outdoor market held along Quinta Avenida featuring works by local artists; paintings, prints, pottery, and jewelry are among the items you'll find. It's held every Thursday 6pm-11pm.

At the southern end of Quinta Avenida, **Paseo del Carmen** (5 Av. at Calle 1, no phone, www.paseodelcarmen.com, 10am-10pm daily) is a leafy outdoor shopping center with high-end clothing boutiques, jewelry stores, art galleries, and restaurants. Its series of modern fountains make it an especially pleasant place to window-shop or enjoy a nice lunch after a morning at the beach.

What was once a quiet cobblestone street is now **Plaza Calle Corazón** (5 Av. between Calles 12 and 14, no phone, www.callecorazon.com, 10am-10pm), a swanky two-level shopping center with several outdoor lounges. You'll find international boutique shops, gourmet restaurants, even an aquarium.

At Avenida Constituyentes, **Quinta Alegria** (5 Av. s/n, tel. 984/803-2358, www.quintaalegria.com.mx, 10am-11pm daily) is an airy and verdant three-story shopping center with big-name shops like Nike, Levi's, Victoria's Secret, Forever 21, and, of course,

Starbucks. Not exactly a slice of Mexico but a pretty place to shop.

FOOD

Playa del Carmen has restaurants and eateries for all tastes and budgets. Those on Quinta Avenida are pricier, of course—many for good reason, others less so. Cheaper eats tend to be off the main drag.

Mexican

A popular taco place, ★ **El Fogón** (Av. Constituyentes between 25 and 30 Avs., tel. 984/803-0885, 1pm-6am daily, US$3-12) serves up mean plates of grilled food—everything from tacos and fajitas to brochettes and T-bone steaks. There are some options for vegetarians—cheese-based dishes like quesadillas and fondue, mostly. Drinks are cheap and strong, and lines can be long but move fast. Get here early to beat the crowds or head to its second location at Avenida 30 at Calle 6 Bis (same hours).

La Cueva del Chango (Calle 38 near 5 Av., cell tel. 984/147-0271, www.lacuevadelchango.com, 8am-11pm Mon.-Sat., 8am-2pm Sun., US$5-11) means The Cave of the Monkey, but there's nothing dim or primitive about it: The covered dining area has lighthearted décor (and a back patio ensconced in leafy vegetation), while the menu features crepes, empanadas, and innovative items like eggs with *chaya,* cactus, and Oaxacan cheese. It's often packed with Playa's upper crust, though the prices make it accessible to all.

Las Quesadillas (Calle 8 near Av. 20, no tel., 8am-midnight, US$1.50-4) is a friendly, low-key eatery serving simple but tasty *sopes* and quesadillas at red plastic tables, accompanied by *aguas de sabor* (fresh fruity drinks). The tortillas are made by hand and grilled fresh, and fillings are hearty and flavorful. It's a favorite among locals and tourists for an authentic Mexican meal at a very affordable price.

Carboncitos (Calle 4 between 5 and 10 Avs., tel. 984/873-1382, 7:30am-11pm daily,

US$7-30) is a traveler favorite in Playa, serving terrific Mexican food and some things you may be missing from home, such as fresh salads. Prices are a bit inflated but the restaurant gets the little things right, like tasty guacamole and homemade salsas.

Seafood

★ **Pescadería y Coctelería El Pirata** (Calle 40 between 5 and 10 Avs., no phone, 11am-8pm daily, US$10-52 per kg) serves up freshly caught fish, shrimp, octopus, and lobster, all sold by weight and prepared to your liking. Sides are à la carte and include rice, beans, and tortillas. Seating is in the casual dining room or on the sidewalk under big umbrellas. It's a bustling place, especially on weekends; live music is often featured streetside.

A classic beachfront restaurant, **La Tarraya** (Calle 2 at the beach, no phone, noon-9pm daily, US$3-11.50) serves up tasty fish and seafood dishes that are easy on the wallet: think ceviche, shrimp cocktail, and fish tacos for under 10 bucks. The downer? Service can be painfully slow. Prepare to spend a few hours for a simple meal.

Unassuming and off the beaten track, **Langostería Maya** (Av. 30 near Av. Constituyentes, tel. 984/873-1037, www.

langosteriamaya.com, 11am-midnight daily, US$5-16) specializes in super-fresh seafood, including hefty fish and shrimp plates, tasty ceviche, choose-you-own lobster, and great fish tacos. It's a bit of a hike from the center and has a view of a supermarket parking lot, but it is a tasty way to get off Quinta Avenida.

Vegetarian

BÍO-Natural Organics (Av. 10 between Av. Constituyentes and Calle 16, cell tel. 984/267-2208, 8am-11pm daily, US$4-8) specializes in vegan and vegetarian dishes, all organic, with lots of gluten-free options. The menu includes items like quinoa bowls, hummus and baba ghanoush plates, vegetarian paella, and lots of fresh fruits, veggies, and nuts. Look for it behind the Quinta Alegria mall. A **second location** (same hours, same menu) is on Quinta Avenida between Calles 40 and 42.

It's all about wood-fire grilling and roasting at ★ **Zorro Plateado** (5 Av. at Av. CTM, tel. 984/859-0298, 8am-midnight daily, US$5-12). There's steak and seafood, of course, but the inventive menu veers towards vegetables: grilled purple cabbage with bay leaf and orange, baked yucca with quail eggs, grilled cucumber and fish ceviche. Cocktails are equally

La Tarraya

interesting and pack a punch. All menu items are organic and locally sourced. Service is tops.

La Ceiba de la Treinta (Av. 30 at Av. 20, tel. 984/873-1255, 7am-10pm Mon. and Wed., 9am-8pm Tues., 8am-8pm Thurs., 9am-7pm Fri., 8am-4pm Sat., 7am-2pm Sun., US$4-10) is a bustling café serving up all manner of salads, wraps, and sandwiches—almost all vegetarian. Drinks focus heavily on freshly squeezed juices: liter-sized combos integrating seasonal fruit and veggies like beets, spinach, and cactus. Come early or late to guarantee a seat. It's located next to a small health food market.

Nativo (Calle 30 near Av. Constituyentes, tel. 984/873-0758, 7am-1am daily, US$4-10) serves up gigantic plates of Mexican classics and fruit-based meals. The fruit plate is remarkable—a heaping bowl of cut fruit (six types) with granola, yogurt, and honey; one bowl is enough for two. The freshly squeezed juices and smoothies aren't a joke either. Served in one-liter cups, combos include the Alma Grande (*chaya*, pineapple, guava, and orange juice) and Indio Mora (spinach, kiwi, strawberry, and OJ). The restaurant sits in a two-story *palapa*-roofed building, with an airy 2nd floor decked out in dramatic murals. If this place is full, try its sister restaurant a few doors south.

Other Specialties

★ **Falafel Nessya** (Calle 6 between Avs. 10 and 15, cell tel. 984/182-0643, noon-11pm daily, US$4-7) is a hole-in-the-wall serving up some of the best falafel on the coast. The menu is centered on falafel, of course: in a light and fluffy pita with hummus; as a sandwich with fried eggplant, a boiled egg, and hummus; as a "plato completo" with hummus, fresh salad, and homemade potato chips. Be sure to load up at the fixins' bar before grabbing a seat at one of a handful of tables.

The name **Primer Plato** (Av. 15 between Av. Juárez and Calle 1, tel. 984/804-3196, 9am-6:30pm Mon.-Sat., US$3-5) is a reference to the Italian custom of starting a meal with pasta. So it's no surprise that pasta is the specialty here, and it could hardly be fresher—the dough is cut and boiled right before your eyes, from spaghetti to ravioli. The location is out of the way, and there's only limited counter space, but if you love homemade pasta (and who doesn't?), Primer Plato is the real deal, and well worth the trip.

Dubbed by some the "Jungle Restaurant," **Trujillos** (Calle 38 near Av. 1, tel. 984/688-8207, 6pm-1:30am daily, US$9-16) is nestled in a grove of trees along the main drag, a pleasant pocket of nature in a place where signs of greenery are fast disappearing. The menu ranges from organic chicken to baked octopus, plus cocktails like cucumber mezcal.

Although occasionally missing the mark, old-timer **Babe's Noodles and Bar** (Calle 10 between 5 and 10 Avs., tel. 984/879-3569, www.babesnoodlesandbar.com, 5pm-midnight Tues.-Sun., US$8-18) still serves up delicious Thai-fusion meals in a retro-hip bistro setting. Dishes come in half and full orders. Don't miss a chance at ordering the *limonmenta*, an awesome lime-mint slushie. It's not a huge place, so you may have to wait for a table during high season.

A set of repurposed shipping containers serve as Playa's most hipster **food court** (Calle 4 at Av. 10, no tel., 7am-10pm daily, US$2-6). Offerings range from a cool-cat coffee shop and a rooftop bar to a Jamaican eatery and a vegetarian cafe. Come after 4pm—the metal containers can get pretty hot during the day, plus the evening is when locals show.

Sweets

A puff of pink, **El Gallinero du Chocolat** (Av. 20 at Calle 10, cell tel. 984/120-3250, www.elgallineroduchocolat.com, 9am-11pm daily, US$2-7) is a dreamy place for anyone with a sweet tooth. You'll find artisanal chocolates, homemade ice cream, and freshly made baked goods, plus mouthwatering crepes and waffles.

Playa has lots of great bakeries but

German-style **Das Brot** (Av. 20 at Calle 8, tel. 984/801-9391, 8am-1pm and 3:30pm-7pm Mon.-Fri., 8am-2pm Sat., US$1.50-4) is a real standout (the name means "the bread" in German). The cinnamon buns are to die for, especially fresh from the oven in the morning. There are also loafs, tarts, and, of course, hot coffee.

Mexicans make great *paletas* (Popsicles) and Italians make great gelatos, so why not combine the two? **Artik Pop** (Paseo del Carmen and Paseo Corazón malls, tel. 984/167-1942, www.artikpop.com, 10am-10pm daily, US$3-4) does just that. The bars at this bright and welcoming mall kiosk are little works of art, with colorful exteriors and creamy fillings. The hard part is picking a flavor, which range from biscotti to pistachio nut and everything in between.

Chocolate lovers will melt over **Ah Cacao** (5 Av. at Av. Constituyentes, tel. 984/803-5748, www.ahcacao.com, 7:15am-11:30pm daily, US$3-6), a chocolate café where every item on the menu—from coffees to cakes—is homemade from the finest of beans. **Two sister shops** are located nearby, with the same operating hours (Calle 30 near 5 Av., and 5 Av. between Calles 38 and 40).

Groceries

MEGA Comercial Mexicana (Av. 30 at Av. Constituyentes, tel. 984/876-2236, www.comercialmexicana.com, 7am-11pm daily) is a huge supermarket that sells everything from clothes, shoes, and snorkel gear to groceries, prepared food, and booze. If you don't find what you're looking for, head three blocks north to **Walmart** (Calle 8 between Avs. 20 and 25, toll-free Mex. tel. 800/710-6352, www.walmart.com.mx, 7am-midnight daily).

At the far end of Quinta Alegria shopping center, **La Europea** (5 Av. at Av. Constituyentes, 10am-9pm Mon.-Sat., 10am-5pm Sun.) has an excellent selection of wines, beer, and liquors. It also has a high-end deli and a small baked goods section, with freshly made pastries and baguettes.

Playa del Carmen has a huge selection and variety of accommodations, from youth hostels to swanky resorts to condos and long-term rentals. There are a couple of all-inclusives in town, though most are located in **Playacar,** just south of Playa.

Under US$50

A hostel with hipster style, **Hostel 3B** (Av. 10 at Calle 1, tel. 984/803-2901, www.hostel3B.com, US$15-17 dorm with a/c, US$40-45 s/d with a/c) offers clean and comfortable dorms—mixed and female-only—on the southern end of town. Each has custom-designed bunk beds with matching lockers, individual bed lamps, air-conditioning, and muted décor. Two of the private rooms open onto the spacious rooftop lounge with a pool and popular bar—a party zone really, complete with guest DJs on Sundays (don't expect to go to bed early). There's a small but well-equipped galley kitchen and lots of indoor common areas for chilling out. The name "3B" is a reference to the Mexican saying *Bueno, Bonito, Barato* (Good, Pretty, Cheap)—an accurate description for this place.

Opened in 2018, ★ **Selina** (Calle 2 between 5 and 10 Avs., tel. 984/873-2799, www.selina.com, US$9-14 pp dorm with a/c, US$40 s/d with shared bath and a/c, US$53-61 s/d with a/c, US$82 suite) feels more like an upscale resort than a budget hotel. The 389-bed behemoth has a mid-century modern style with Mexican flair—think clean lines with traditional tiles, tropical wood furnishings, and gorgeous murals. Rooms themselves are spacious and airy, with excellent beds, air-conditioning, and strong Wi-Fi. Common areas are just as comfortable and include a huge outdoor lounge with a bar, a well-tended pool, library, movie screening room, yoga deck, fully equipped modern kitchen, even a co-working space.

Enjoy Playa Hostel (Calle 4 between Avs. 15 and 20, cell tel. 984/132-2953, US$10-13 dorm with a/c, US$30 s/d with shared bath and a/c, US$50 s/d with a/c) is a small hostel decked out in murals and colorful furnishings. Dorms have 4-10 beds, all tidy, with big lockers and air-conditioning that runs 9pm-9am only. There's a tiny common kitchen as well as a breezy rooftop lounge and bar where most of the socializing happens (it closes at 11pm). Continental breakfast is included, as is a free tequila shot every evening at 9pm.

Hotel Yum K'iin (Av. 20 between Calles 6 and 8, tel. 984/873-0173, www.hotelyumkiin. com, US$40 s/d with a/c) is a clean, well-located budget alternative. Rooms won't win any awards for charm but are well maintained and perfectly comfortable, all with flat-screen TVs and mini-split air-conditioning. All open onto a long, leafy courtyard. The Wi-Fi is hit or miss—head to the reception area for the best connection.

US$50-100

Hotel Barrio Latino (Calle 4 between Avs. 10 and 15, tel. 984/873-2384, www. hotelbarriolatino.com, US$50-78 with a/c) has charming rooms with mosaic-tile bathrooms, stone-inlaid floors, and private balconies with hammocks. A complimentary continental breakfast is served in a leafy courtyard with a *palapa*-roofed lounge. Be sure to confirm online reservations—the system experiences occasional glitches (which may mean no reservation). Adults only.

Hotel LunaSol (Calle 4 between Avs. 15 and 20, tel. 984/873-3933, www.lunasolhotel. com, US$80-90 s/d with a/c) offers 16 comfortable rooms, all with private balconies or terraces, on spacious, leafy grounds. The rooms are a bit sparse but have nice tile bathrooms, mini fridges, and flat-screen TVs; 2nd-floor rooms have higher ceilings and better light. Though well located for eating out, the hotel also has a fully equipped outdoor kitchen. There's a nice swimming pool and whirlpool tub too.

Wabi Hotel (35 Av. between Calles 4 and 6, tel. 984/147-4898, www.wabihotel.com, US$50-55 s/d with a/c, US$61 suite) is a small hotel offering clean and comfortable rooms that range from modern to shabby-chic in style. Two breezy terraces and an interior garden make good places to relax or to meet other guests. Service is friendly and helpful.

An old-school hotel, **Paraíso Azul's Casa de Gopala** (Calle 2 between Avs. 10 and 15, tel. 984/873-0054, www.casadegopala.com, US$75 s/d with a/c, US$85-140 s/d with a/c and kitchenette) has 19 spacious units, with rustic Mexican furnishings and colorful fabrics, that open onto shared leafy terraces. The comfortable but unremarkable rooms all have air-conditioning, mini fridges, and TVs. Head upstairs for the rooftop solarium with a small, well-kept pool and an enviable view of Playa del Carmen, the Caribbean, and, on a clear day, Cozumel.

US$100-150

A crate full of fresh fruit, eggs, bread, and jam greets you upon arrival at **Newport House** (Av. 10 at Calle 44, tel. 984/859-1557, www.newporthouseplaya.com, US$97-147 1-bedroom apt), a small apart-hotel with stylish one-bedroom apartments. All have king-size beds and fully equipped kitchenettes; the more expensive ones are bigger and have washer-dryers and two balconies. A major plus is the rooftop, with a well-maintained lap pool, cozy lounge chairs, and city views. Located on the far north end of Quinta Avenida, the hotel is in a quiet part of town but close enough to the restaurants, bars, and beach that you'll still feel a part of the action.

The adults-only ★ **Luna Blue Hotel** (Calle 26 between 5 and 10 Avs., tel. 984/873-0990, www.lunabluehotel.com, US$89-115 s/d with a/c, US$125-135 suite) is a leafy oasis, and an excellent value, just off busy Quinta Avenida. Units are tidy and cool, some with pithy travel-related quotes stenciled on the wall, and range from standard hotel rooms to suites with balconies and kitchens. A pleasant garden has colorful Adirondack chairs and a sunken pool, all beneath a canopy of tropical trees. Wi-Fi, beach club passes, purified water, and morning coffee and baked goods are included in the rate.

Tucked into a leafy courtyard, **Club Yebo** (Av. 1 at Calle 14, tel. 984/803-3966, toll-free Mex. tel. 800/681-9510, toll-free U.S./Can. tel. 888/676-4431, www.clubyebo. com, US$65 s/d with a/c, US$85-105 studio with a/c, US$120 1-bedroom apartment with a/c) is a small hotel offering tasteful studios and apartments with modern furnishings and fully equipped kitchens (plus a couple of basic hotel rooms). All have quiet air-conditioning, cable TV, Wi-Fi, and daily maid service. Common areas include a small pool and two *palapa* lounges with hammocks. Each room also comes with a "beach kit," which includes beach chairs, towels, and a cooler—perfect for a DIY beach day.

Hotel Aventura Mexicana (Calle 24 between 5 and 10 Avs., tel. 984/873-1876, www. aventuramexicana.com, US$115-125 s/d with a/c, US$125-143 suite with a/c) has two sections: The adults-only area has deluxe rooms with muted colors, elegant furnishings, and a nicely manicured garden and pool. The original section has colorful rooms with traditional heavy wood furnishings and has a long, thin pool squeezed in the center of the courtyard; it's slightly cheaper and open to families. Guests give both areas top marks. À la carte breakfast is included in the rate, plus there's a yoga studio on-site with daily all-level classes. An all-inclusive food and drink option available is in both sections; typically, children 12 and under enjoy the upgrade for free with a paying adult.

US$150-250

The boutique ★ **Hotel La Semilla** (38 Av. between 1 and 5 Avs., tel. 984/147-3234, www. hotellasemilla.com, US$195-225 s/d with a/c, US$245 suite with a/c) sits on a lush lot, a tropical oasis just steps from Quinta Avenida. Trees and greenery are everywhere—the gorgeous garden patio, windowsills, the rooftop lounge—creating a sense of tranquility. The nine rooms are equally soothing with shabby-chic décor, fine linens, and modern amenities. A full gourmet breakfast and wine hour are included in the rate, both good times to chat with the affable owners and meet other guests. Use of bicycles is complimentary.

Playa Palms (Av. 1 Bis near Calle 14, tel. 984/803-3966, toll-free Mex. tel. 800/681-9510, toll-free U.S./Can. tel. 888/676-4431, www.playapalms.com, US$200-290 s/d with kitchenette and a/c, US$250 1-bedroom suite with kitchenette and a/c) is a classy beachfront hotel, with airy and colorful rooms, kitchenettes, and fine ocean views. A thin pool winds through the leafy interior courtyard; it's picturesque and refreshing, though not practical for actual swimming. Likewise, the beach area is comfortable, but fishing boats typically moor there, making it hard to enjoy the water. Still, the location and amenities made this a popular option.

Playa Maya (on the beach between Calles 6 and 8, tel. 984/803-2022, toll-free U.S./Can. tel. 888/866-2988, www.playa-maya.com, US$180-200 s/d with a/c) is one of the few small hotels in Playa with direct beach access. All 20 rooms are modern and comfortable, many with balconies and ocean views. There's a tiny pool, whirlpool tub, and sundeck, located somewhat awkwardly at the entrance. Steps away, though, is the beach with plenty of lounge chairs, umbrella shade, and waiter service. There's a 4-5-night minimum, varying with the season (shorter stays are possible, depending on the occupancy). Breakfast is included in the rate. Note: The entrance faces the beach, so you may need a porter to help carry bags across the sand.

On a shady street just a block from the beach, **The Acanto Boutique Hotel & Condominiums** (Calle 16 Bis between Avs. 1 and 3, tel. 984/873-1252, toll-free U.S. tel. 888/331-2177, www.acantohotels.com, US$128 s/d with a/c, US$150 studio, US$150-180 1-bedroom condo, US$207-248 2-bedroom condo, US$270-325 3-bedroom condo) is a peaceful place with 21 units, most with modern kitchens, spacious living-dining rooms, and balconies. Each is decked out in dark woods, marble floors, luxurious fabrics, and fine art. A small swimming pool sits in the lush central courtyard, where complimentary continental breakfast is served daily. There's also a rooftop lounge with several grills and a whirlpool tub.

Over US$250

Mahékal Beach Resort (Calle 38 near 5 Av., tel. 984/873-0611, toll-free Mex. tel. 800/836-8942, toll-free U.S. tel. 877/235-4452, www.mahekalplaya.com, US$289-399 s/d with a/c) is a huge yet tranquil resort on the northern end of town. All units are in thatch-roofed one- and two-story bungalows, each with a modern beachy feel. Each features a private terrace with hammocks; there's Wi-Fi and phone but no TV. The resort has four pools and a gorgeous beach. Breakfast and dinner plans are available.

Smack-dab in the middle of Playa del Carmen, the all-inclusive **The Royal Playa del Carmen** (Av. Constituyentes at Av. 1, toll-free U.S./Can. tel. 800/627-5328, www.realresorts.com, US$294-1,230 s, US$184-769 d all-inclusive) is an adults-only Mediterranean-style resort. A winding pool (one of many) runs through the center of its manicured gardens, leading to a beautiful beach. All of the units are suites, which means ocean views, private terraces, and luxurious amenities, with extras like a minibar stocked with top-shelf liquors, soft bathrobes, even umbrellas; some units even open to a semi-private pool. There are a dozen buffet and à la carte restaurants as well as a spa, tennis courts, and lounges. Almost best of all, Playa is right outside your door.

Rental Properties

Playacar has scores of houses for rent, of all sizes and styles. Prices vary considerably, but expect to pay a premium for ocean views and during peak seasons. A number of property-management companies rent houses, including **Playacar Vacation Rentals** (Bahía del Espiritu Santo s/n, tel. 984/873-0418, toll-free U.S. tel. 866/862-7164, www.playacarvacationrentals.com), one of the oldest agencies in the Riviera Maya. Good online alternatives include **AirBnB** (www.airbnb.com) and **Vacation Rentals by Owner** (www.vrbo.com).

INFORMATION AND SERVICES

Tourist Information

There is no tourist information office in Playa, but there's a **tourist information kiosk** on the plaza (5 Av. at Av. Juárez, 8am-8pm Mon.-Sat.) that is stocked with brochures and maps and often is manned by a reasonably knowledgeable staffer.

Other good sources of information include *The Playa Times* (www.theplayatimes.com), a bimonthly newspaper that covers, among other topics, art and culture, area sites, and upcoming events, and www.everythingplayadelcarmen.com, a good place to get a pulse on local trends and hot spots.

Emergency Services

Hospiten Riviera Maya (Hwy. 307 at Paseo Tulum, tel. 984/159-2200, www.hospiten.com, 24 hours daily) is a private hospital offering modern, high-quality medical service at reasonable rates. Many of the doctors have U.S. training and speak English, and are accustomed to treating foreign visitors. It is located along the east side of the highway, near the entrance to Playacar.

Playa International Clinic (10 Av. at Calle 28, tel. 984/873-1755, 24-hr emergency tel. 984/873-1365, www.sssnetwork.com, 9am-8pm daily) offers specialized medical care for recreational and commercial scuba divers. It has a hyperbaric chamber and lab on-site.

Prescriptions are required for many antibiotics now, unlike years past. **Farmacias del Ahorro** (10 Av. at Calle 10, toll-free Mex. tel. 800/711-2222, 24 hrs daily) has a full pharmacy on the 1st floor and a **free walk-in clinic** (9am-3pm and 5pm-10pm Mon.-Fri.) on the 2nd floor, where a doctor can write prescriptions after a short interview or exam.

The **tourist police** (Av. 1 at Calle CTM, tel. 984/877-3340, or 060 from any pay phone) have an office on the north side of town.

Money

Banamex (Calle 12 at 10 Av., 9am-4pm Mon.-Fri.) and **Banorte** (Plaza Pelícanos, 10 Av. between Calles 8 and 10, 8am-4pm Mon.-Fri., 9am-2pm Sat.) are full-service banks with ATMs and foreign exchange. There also are several freestanding **ATMs** around town; use ones that are affiliated with recognizable banks to avoid exorbitant service charges.

Media and Communications

The **post office** (Calle 2 at 20 Av., 8am-4pm Mon.-Fri., 9am-1pm Sat.) is easy to miss—look for the pink-striped building near the *combi* terminal.

Internet cafés have gone from ubiquitous to nearly obsolete. Today, most hotels have free Wi-Fi for guests, as do many restaurants and coffee shops.

Laundry and Storage

At the north end of town, **Mr. Laundry** (10 Av. between Calles 28 and 30, 7am-10pm Mon.-Sat., 8am-5pm Sun.) charges US$1 per kilo with a two-kilo (4.4-pound) minimum. **Lavandería Los Mecates** (Calle 4 near 20 Av., 8am-9pm Mon.-Sat.) charges US$0.70 per kilo and has a three-kilo (6.6-pound) minimum. At both places, rates are for next-day service; same-day service is available for an additional fee.

Luggage storage is available at both bus stations. **Guarda Plus** (6am-10pm daily) charges US$0.30-1 per hour depending on the size of the bag, or US$5 per day.

GETTING THERE

Air

Playa del Carmen has a small airport a few blocks from the ferry pier, but it's used for private and charter flights only. Commercial service is available at Cancún International Airport.

Bus

Playa del Carmen has two bus stations: **Terminal Turística** (aka Terminal Riviera, 5 Av. and Av. Juárez) is in the center of town and has frequent second-class service to destinations along the coast, including Cancún, Tulum, and everything in between; **Terminal Alterna** (Calle 20 between Calles 12 and 12 Bis) has first-class and deluxe service to interior destinations such as Mérida, Campeche, and beyond. There is some overlap, and you can buy tickets for any destination at either station, so always double-check from which station your bus departs.

Combi

Combis (shuttle vans) are an easy way to get up and down the Riviera Maya. In Playa, northbound *combis* line up on Calle 2 near 20 Avenida, with service 24 hours a day (every 10-15 minutes, US$2, 1 hour). For slightly more, **Playa Express** has larger, air-conditioned shuttles, departing from a lot on Calle 2 between 20 and 25 Avenidas (every 10-15 minutes, 24 hrs daily, US$2.25). The final destination of both services is Cancún's main bus terminal (50 minutes), but you can be dropped off anywhere along the highway, including Puerto Morelos (US$1.25, 30 minutes). *Combis* do not enter Cancún's Zona Hotelera, but you can catch a bus there from outside the terminal.

South from Playa del Carmen, ordinary *combis* leave from the same corner around the clock, going as far as the Carrillo Puerto bus station (US$4.50, 2 hours), passing the turnoffs for Puerto Aventuras (US$1.50, 10 minutes), Xpu-Há (US$1.75, 20 minutes), Akumal (US$2, 25 minutes), Tankah Tres (US$2.75, 45 minutes), Tulum Ruins (US$2.25, 50 minutes), and Tulum (US$2.75, 1 hour). To return, flag down a *combi* anywhere along the highway.

Car

If you are driving to Playa del Carmen, look for the two main access roads to the beach—Avenida Constituyentes on the north end of town and Avenida Benito Juárez on the south. Playacar has its own entrance from the highway but can also be reached by turning south on Calle 10 off Avenida Juárez.

Playa del Carmen Bus Schedules

Terminal Turística (5 Av. and Av. Juárez, tel. 984/873-0109, ext. 2501, toll-free Mex. tel. 800/702-8000) is located near the ferry dock and has frequent service along the Caribbean coast and throughout the Yucatán Peninsula. Long-distance buses to other parts of the country use the **Terminal Alterna** (Calle 20 between Calles 12 and 12 Bis, tel. 984/803-0944, toll-free Mex. tel. 800/702-8000).

Most Tulum-bound buses stop at the turnoffs for destinations along the way, including **Paamul** (US$1.25, 15 minutes), **Puerto Aventuras** (US$1.75, 20 minutes), **Xpu-Há** (US$2.25, 25 minutes), **Akumal** (US$2.75, 30 minutes), **Xel-Há** (US$2.85, 45 minutes), and **Dos Ojos** (US$3.25-5.25, 40 minutes).

Most Chetumal-bound buses stop in **Bacalar** (US$10.50-17, 4 hours).

Most Cancún-bound buses stop at **Puerto Morelos** (US$1.75, 35 minutes), but *not* the airport or Cancún's Zona Hotelera.

DESTINATION	PRICE	DURATION	SCHEDULE*
Cancún	US$2-4	1 hr	every 15-30 mins 12:15am-11:40pm
Cancún Int'l Airport	US$9.50	1.25 hrs	every 30-60 mins 3am-10:20pm
Chiquilá (Isla Holbox)	US$13	2.5 hrs	9:25am and 10:15am
Chetumal	US$9-23	4.5 hrs	every 60-90 mins 1:50am-11:58pm
Chichén Itzá	US$11	4 hrs	8am
Chiquilá (Isla Holbox)	US$13	3.5 hrs	9:25am, 10:15am, 10:25am
Cobá	US$5.50-8	2 hrs	9am and 10:30am
Mérida	US$15-30	4.5-5.5 hrs	every 60-90 mins 1:30am-11:59pm
Puerto Morelos	US$1.75	35 min	every 15-30 mins 12:15am-11:40pm
Tulum	US$1.75-5.50	1 hr	every 15-30 mins 1:30am-11:40pm
Valladolid	US$5.75-11	2.5 hrs	every 15-90 mins 1:30am-9:30pm
Xcaret (main entrance)	US$3.50-4	20 mins	8:30am, 9:40am, 9:50am

*Schedules are subject to change.

Ferry

There are three passenger ferries to Cozumel (hourly, 7am-11pm daily, 30 minutes), all leaving from the pier at the end of Calle 1 Sur: **UltraMar** (www.ultramarferry.com, US$9.50 adult, US$6.75 child), **Mexico Water Jets** (tel. www.mexicowaterjets.com.mx, US$9.50 adult, US$5.25 child), and **Barcos Caribe** (www.barcoscaribe.com, US$8 adult, US$4 child). They have almost identical schedules, though UltraMar tends to have newer boats and Cozumel Express tends to be a bit cheaper. The ferry ticket booths are side by side at the foot of the pier, with the time of the next departure displayed prominently. The ticket seller will try to sell you a round-trip ticket, but there's no disadvantage to buying a *sencilla* (one-way ticket) and avoiding the risk of losing your return ticket.

Car ferries operated by **Transcaribe** (tel. 987/872-7688, www.transcaribe.net) depart from the Calica dock south of Playa at 4am, 8am, 1:30pm, and 6pm Monday; 8am, 1:30pm, and 6pm Tuesday-Saturday; and 7am, 11am, and 7:30pm on Sunday. Returning from Cozumel, the ferry leaves from the international pier at 6am, 11am, 4pm, and 8:30pm Monday-Saturday; and 9am, 5pm, and 9pm on Sunday. The trip takes about 1.25 hours and costs US$25 for a car including passengers. Reservations are strongly recommended.

GETTING AROUND

Playa del Carmen is a walking town, although the steady northward expansion is challenging that description. The commercial part of Quinta Avenida now stretches over 44 blocks and keeps getting longer. Bicycles are a great way to get around town—head to Calle 10, which has a bike lane. Cabs also are a good option, especially if you have luggage.

Bicycle

BiciPlaya II (30 Av. at Calle 20, tel. 984/147-0317, biciplaya2@gmail.com, 9am-9pm Mon.-Sat., 10am-4pm Sun.) rents decent bikes by the day (US$5). Another good option is **Playa Encantada** (Calle 12 Bis at 20 Av., tel. 984/803-5602, 7am-9:30pm daily), which rents bicycles for US$10 per day, including lock. A US$25 deposit, or an ID, is required to rent at the latter.

Taxi

Taxis around town cost US$5-8, or a bit more if you use a taxi stand or have your hotel summon one. All taxi drivers carry a *tarifário*—an official fare schedule—which you can request to see if you think you're getting taken for a ride (no pun intended). Prices do change every year or two, so ask at your hotel what

the current rate is, and always be sure to agree on the fare with the driver before setting off.

Car Rental

Playa has myriad car rental agencies, with prices starting around US$32 per day, including insurance. Local chain **Easy Way** (Av. 10 btwn Calles 2 and 4, toll-free Mex. tel. 800/327-9929, toll-free U.S./Can. tel. 877/640-3279, www.easywayrentacar.com) offers well-maintained cars and no-hassle service. Major international agencies like **Avis** (Fiesta Inn, 10 Av. between Calles 26 and 28, tel. 984/688-8154, www.avis.com) and **Hertz** (10 Av. at Calle 14, toll-free Mex. tel. 800/709-5000, www.hertz.com) also are reliable options and often have online specials.

Parking in Playa in the high season can be a challenge, especially south of Avenida Constituyentes. Many hotels have secure parking; there are also parking lots around town, including on Calle 2 at 10 Avenida (8am-10pm daily) and at Calle 14 Bis and 10 Avenida (8am-10pm daily), charging around US$1 per hour or US$12.50 per day.

PAAMUL

What started out as an unassuming trailer park on a beautiful stretch of beach has now become a seaside community all its own. Located about 20 kilometers (12.4 miles) south of Playa del Carmen, Paamul has everything from RVs with elaborate wood and *palapa* structures over them to hotel rooms, a restaurant, and even a dive shop.

Beach

Paamul stretches over a wide, curving beach. It's classically pretty with white sand and turquoise water, perfect for swimming and exploring. Watch your step on the south end of the beach, as its waters harbor prickly sea urchin—consider wearing water shoes.

Snorkeling and Scuba Diving

Scuba-Mex Dive Center (Hwy. 307 Km 85, tel. 984/807-7866, toll-free U.S. tel. 888/871-6255, www.scubamex.com, 8am-5pm daily) is a full-service shop offering fun dives, dive packages, and dive courses at good prices; cenote dives require reservations. If you're just interested in snorkeling off the beach, the shop also rents snorkel gear.

Food

The only eatery in Paamul, **Reefs of Paamul Restaurant and Bar** (Hwy. 307 Km 85, tel. 984/875-1050, 8am-8pm daily, US$6-18) is open-air, modern, and has great views of the Caribbean. It serves up classic Mexican dishes along with a variety of international meals. It's a solid option (despite being the only option!).

For groceries, the very mini **Mini Super Paamul** (7am-8pm Mon.-Sat., 7am-2pm Sun.) sells basic foodstuffs. It's located at the highway turnoff to Paamul.

Accommodations

Sitting on a gorgeous bay all its own is

Paamul Hotel & Cabañas (Hwy. 307 Km 85, tel. 984/875-1050, U.S. tel. 612/597-0888, www.paamul.com, US$12 pp camping, US$50 s/d RVs, US$195 s/d with a/c). From classy hotel rooms to well-kept campsites, it appeals to travelers of all budgets. The hotel rooms are simple and elegant with features like mini fridges and microwaves, quiet air-conditioning, Wi-Fi, and ocean views from private terraces. The tent and trailer spaces are just steps from the Caribbean, have electricity and running water, and share clean hot-water bathrooms. A true find and a perfect getaway, especially considering the on-site restaurant and dive shop.

Information and Services

There are no health, banking, postal, or laundry services in Paamul. The closest town for a full range of services is Playa del Carmen, 20 kilometers (12.4 miles) north.

Puerto Aventuras

Puerto Aventuras is an odd conglomeration of condos, summer homes, and hotels with a marina that's home to a swim-with-dolphins program as well as several restaurants and bars. It's more than a resort but not really a town. Whatever you call it, Puerto Aventuras's huge signs and gated entrance are impossible to miss, located a few minutes north of Akumal on Highway 307.

SPORTS AND RECREATION

Swimming with Dolphins

Dolphin Discovery (Marina, tel. 984/873-5078, toll-free U.S. tel. 866/393-5158, www.dolphindiscovery.com, 9am-5pm daily) offers several dolphin encounter activities; prices vary according to the duration and degree of interaction (US$99-169 adult, US$89 child). The center also has a manatee program (US$59 adult/child) that can be combined with dolphin activities. Programs start

at 9am, 11am, 1pm, and 3pm daily; round-trip shuttle service is available to/from area hotels for US$10 per person.

Snorkeling and Scuba Diving

Some 25 dive sites lie within a 10-minute boat ride from town, each boasting rich coral, abundant sealife, and interesting features such as pillars and swim-throughs.

Aquanauts (Bldg. A, tel. 984/873-5041, toll-free U.S./Can. tel. 877/623-2491, www.aquanautsdiveshop.com, 8am-5pm Mon.-Sat.) is a full-service shop that enjoys lots of repeat guests. The shop offers the full range of dives and courses, including reef dives (US$71/132 one/two tanks) and cenote dives (US$100/140 one/two tanks); equipment rental, other than tanks and weights, is not included. The shop also offers snorkel tours, including one with a stop at the Tulum ruins (US$60-100).

Another great option is **Planet Scuba** (Calle Bahía Xcacel s/n, cell tel.

CEDAM and the Riviera Maya

Maya artifacts have been found in cenotes, probably thrown in as offerings to the gods.

In 1948, a small group of Mexican divers—active frogmen during World War II—created a non-profit organization called Club de Exploración y Deporte Acuáticos de México (Exploration and Aquatic Sports Club of Mexico, or CEDAM). Their mission was to promote ocean conservation and educate others about the sea's treasures and resources.

In 1958, the group set about salvaging the *Mantanceros,* a Spanish galleon that foundered offshore in 1741. It set up camp in present-day Akumal, then just an uninhabited beach owned by a man named Argimiro Arguelles. Arguelles leased CEDAM an old work boat for their project, the SS *Cozumel,* and worked as its captain.

It was this relationship that sealed Akumal's—and arguably, the Riviera Maya's—destiny. Sitting around the campfire one night, Arguelles sold Pablo Bush Romero, one of CEDAM's founders, the bay of Akumal and thousands of acres of coconut palms north and south of it. For the next 12 years, CEDAM continued its work in the rustic and beautiful place—replacing its tents with sturdy *palapa* huts, and using the creaky SS *Cozumel* to carry divers to work sites along the coast.

It wasn't long before the idea of promoting tourism on Mexico's forgotten Caribbean coast arose. In 1968, the group—which had changed the words behind its initials to Conservation, Ecology, Diving, Archaeology, and Museums—donated 5,000 acres of land to the government, including the Cove of Xel-Há, to create a national park. The aim was to open the isolated area to tourists and, in so doing, create jobs for local residents. CEDAM also provided housing, food, electricity, running water, a school for the children, and a first-aid station with a trained nurse.

Based in Akumal for many years, CEDAM grew into an important scientific and conservation organization. It played an active role in the archaeological exploration of the region's cenotes and ocean. The group is no longer in existence, but a small museum in Puerto Aventuras—**Museo Sub-Acuático CEDAM** (Bldg F, no tel.)—showcases CEDAM's work and findings. It was temporarily closed when we passed through but hopefully will reopen soon.

984/182-0227, www.planetscubamexico. com, 8am-6pm daily), which offers specialized cavern (US$150-250/two tanks), cave (US$250/two tanks), and tech (US$300/two tanks) dives. Reef dives (including with bull sharks) and a full line of certification courses are also offered.

Sportfishing

Captain Rick's Sportfishing Center (past Omni Puerto Aventuras Beach Resort, tel. 984/873-5195, toll-free U.S. tel. 888/449-3562, www.fishyucatan.com, office 8am-6pm daily) offers customized trips—trolling, drift fishing, and fly-fishing—utilizing a fleet of a dozen boats, including a 48-foot yacht with room for up to 12 people. You can also arrange time for visiting a deserted beach or Maya ruin, snorkeling on the reef, or just cruising by upscale homes and hotels. Rates are for half day (US$450-695), three-quarter day (US$580-850), and full day (US$690-1,050).

Sailing

Fat Cat (Bldg. E, cell tel. 984/116-3040, www.fatcatsail.com, 8:30am-5pm Mon.-Sat.) offers a spacious, custom-designed catamaran used for half-day excursions (US$110 adult, US$78 child 3-11) that include sailing north toward Bahia Ihna or south toward Xpu-Há—both with good snorkeling in shallow and protected waters. Daily trips leave at 9:30am and 2pm; all include a box lunch.

Golf

Puerto Aventuras Club de Golf (across from Bldg. B, tel. 984/873-5109, 7am-dusk daily, US$62 for 18 holes, US$54-57 for 9 holes) offers a nine-hole, par-36 golf course right in town. The course, designed in 1991 by Tom Lehman, is flat but has two par-5s over a total 2,961 yards (3,255 championship).

FOOD

Buzzing with expats, **Paparazzi** (Bldg. F, tel. 984/873-5651, 8am-5pm daily, US$5-11) is a small Italian restaurant with a whopping menu of pastas, salads, and panini. The main attraction, though, is the thin-crust pizza, made in a brick oven and topped with all manner of yummy goodness—everything from mussels to Nutella. Come early for a seat or take your pie to go.

Café Olé in Puerto Aventuras (Bldg. A, tel. 984/873-5125, 8am-10pm daily, US$7-22) has an extensive international menu with something for just about everyone. It's best known, though, for its filet mignon and homemade desserts like coconut cream pie and dulce de leche cheesecake. A welcoming place, there's karaoke on Tuesday and Thursday nights and live music (by professionals) every night starting at 7pm.

★ **Taquería El Arbolito** (Hwy 307 Km 270, no tel., 5:30am-3pm daily, US$2-4) is a popular roadside eatery selling mouthwatering tacos stuffed with your choice of more than 35 different takes on eggs, chicken, beef, pork, vegetables, and seafood. Order your meal cafeteria-style, make a pit stop at the fixins' bar, and join other diners at plastic communal tables. Look for it on the west side of the highway (or just follow your nose).

If you're cooking for yourself or just want some fresh fruit, check out the outdoor **fruit and vegetable market** (8am-5pm), which is held every Wednesday and Saturday next to the town's kiosk.

Located across from the Omni hotel, **OXXO** (9am-9pm Mon.-Sat., 9am-1pm Sun.) is a convenience store with basic foodstuffs. For serious shopping—and better prices—head to the mega-store **Chedraui** (tel. 984/802-8773, 7am-10pm daily), located directly across Highway 307 from the Puerto Aventuras entrance.

ACCOMMODATIONS

The road into town bumps right into **Omni Puerto Aventuras Beach Resort** (tel. 984/875-1950, toll-free U.S. tel. 888/444-6664, www.omnihotels.com, US$180-270 s/d with a/c), a small resort with the marina on one side and a fine, palm-shaded beach on the other. There are just 30 rooms, all spacious with colorful regional décor, private patios, and hot tubs; ocean-view rooms are particularly nice. The resort's small size and low-key atmosphere make it easy to meet other guests, and nighttime typically finds everyone around the main hot tub/beach bar overlooking the ocean.

Casa del Agua (Punta Matzoma 21, tel. 984/873-5184, www.casadelagua.com, US$262-750 pp) is a beacon of class and charm amid the cookie-cutter commercialism of Puerto Aventuras. What looks like a private home is actually a boutique hotel with a handful of spacious suites. Each has elegant decor, a king-size bed, and luxurious bathrooms and amenities. There is a small sunny pool and private beach as well as complimentary kayaks and snorkeling gear. Daily maid service and a private chef are included in the rate. The per night rate is based on private use of the entire villa (maximum 8 guests). There's a seven-night minimum during Thanksgiving, Christmas/New Year's, and Easter, and a three-night minimum most of the rest of the year.

INFORMATION AND SERVICES
Tourist Information
Located on the main drag, the **Puerto Aventuras Activity Center** (Bahía Xcacel s/n, tel. 984/802-9047, puertoaventuras activitycenter@gmail.com, 9am-3pm and 5pm-7pm Mon.-Sat., 9am-1pm Sun.) offers tourist information on area sites; most staffers speak English. The lounge has free Wi-Fi.

The town website for Puerto Aventuras— **www.puertoaventuras.com**—also is a good source of information.

Emergency Services
There is one pharmacy in town: **Emergency 911 Pharmacy** (Bldg. A, tel. 984/873-5305, 8am-10pm daily, or by telephone 24 hours). Delivery is available.

Money
Puerto Aventuras doesn't have a bank, but there's a **Banamex ATM** in the Omni hotel.

Media and Communications
The **post office** (11am-2:30am Mon.-Thurs.) is in a large kiosk a short distance from the golf club entrance.

The tourist information office, **Puerto Aventuras Activity Center** (Bahía Xcacel s/n, tel. 984/802-9047, puertoaventuras activitycenter@gmail.com, 9am-3pm and 5pm-7pm Mon.-Sat., 9am-1pm Sun.), has free Wi-Fi in its lounge. Most hotels and condos also offer Wi-Fi to guests.

GETTING THERE AND AROUND
Arriving by public transportation, you can take a *combi* from Cancún, Playa del Carmen, or Tulum. Let the driver know where you're going, and he'll drop you off on the side of the highway. From there, it's 500 meters (0.3 mile) into town. Arriving by car, you'll pass through a large control gate, but no one who looks like a tourist is stopped.

You can walk to virtually all restaurants and shops in Puerto Aventuras because they're centered on the main marina. To explore the complex and its beaches a bit more, **Puerto Aventuras Activity Center** (Bahía Xcacel s/n, tel. 984/802-9047, puertoaventurasactivitycenter@gmail.com, 9am-3pm and 5pm-7pm Mon.-Sat., 9am-1pm Sun.) rents golf carts (US$10/hr, US$40/day).

Xpu-Há

This long, picturesque beach has clusters of development on either end and a couple of small hotels and beach clubs in between. It seems only a matter of time before the owners of this enviable stretch of sand give their blessing to a megaresort, but for now it's a gorgeous and peaceful spot where you could easily while away the whole day, or several.

SPORTS AND RECREATION
Beach Clubs
La Playa Xpu-Há (Hwy. 307 Km 264, tel. 984/133-6701, www.laplayaxpuha.com, 10am-7pm Mon.-Wed., 10am-10pm Thurs.-Sun.) is a bustling club with a few rows of lounge chairs and *palapa* shade. There's a full-service restaurant and bar (stick to finger food and beer). On weekends and holidays, there's a US$5 per person "toll" at the entrance, charged by the landowner for upkeep of the access road. You get it back, though, as a credit on restaurant bills over US$10. There's live music on weekends.

Just down the beach, **KSM Beach Club** (Hwy. 307 Km 264, tel. 984/140-2339, 9am-8pm Sun.-Thurs., 9am-2am Fri.-Sat.) has a hipper vibe with more areas to chill out, away from the scene. There's also a hut renting snorkeling gear, kayaks, and paddleboards, and it offers kiteboarding and windsurfing instruction too. A *palapa*-roofed restaurant is a good option for eats and drinks. There's also plenty of parking—though, like La Playa Xpu-Há, there's a US$5 "toll" at the entrance. To get here, look for a narrow dirt road with a small sign, just south of the Catalonia Royal Tulum resort.

Scuba Diving
Bahía Divers (Hwy. 307 Km 265, cell tel. 984/156-9898, www.bahiadivers.com, 8am-4pm Mon.-Sat.) operates out of a collection of huts a short distance down the beach from La Playa Xpu-Há beach club. It offers the full gamut of ocean and cenote dives, plus certification courses, all with the advantage of small groups (6 divers maximum) and personalized service. They also provide transport to and from your hotel. Ocean dives cost US$90 for two tanks, while cenote diving runs US$120 for two tanks, all including gear.

Snorkeling
In addition to the ocean reef, there's great snorkeling in the numerous cenotes along the inland side of Highway 307, including a cluster just north of Xpu-Há. They vary in size, but most are like large ponds, some with high or overhanging limestone walls, and all filled with cool, crystalline water—heaven on a hot day. The cenote floor is often a jumble of stone slabs and in places quite deep; some even have gaping underwater caves that descend out of sight. The cenotes near Xpu-Há are not, however, the huge stalactite-laden caverns you may have seen in photos; for those, head south to Dos Ojos cenote parks, near Tulum.

Half-moon-shaped **Cenote Cristalino** (Hwy. 307, 2 kilometers/1.2 miles north of Xpu-Há, 8am-6pm daily, US$4 adult, US$2.50 child, no rental gear available), much of which is shallow and covered in algae, has a unique section that extends under a deep, overhanging rock ceiling.

Jardín del Edén (formerly Ponderosa Cenote, Hwy. 307, 1.75 kilometers/1 mile north of Xpu-Há, 9am-6pm daily, US$6 adult, US$3.50 child, US$4 mask and snorkel, US$4 life vest) is much larger than most cenotes—almost like a small lake—with a craggy floor that makes for fun snorkeling. At one end, the floor falls away into a deep underwater cave, where you can see divers emerging—or disappearing—into the abyss, their halogen lights piercing the shadows. A six-meter (19.7-foot) cliff is fun to jump off; just be alert for divers who may be coming up. Between cave-diving classes, snorkeling groups, and independent travelers, Jardín del Edén can get busy but is generally big enough to make a stop here worthwhile.

Cenote Azul (Hwy. 307, 1.5 kilometers/0.9 mile north of Xpu-Há, 8:30am-5:30pm daily, US$5 adult, US$2.50 child) is made up of three refreshing pools with teal waters: two small ones toward the front that are teeming with tiny fish and surrounded by thin leafy trees, and one large pool with a section of overhanging rock (great for jumping off of) and walkways along the edges for exploring or easing into or out of the cenote. Snorkel gear rentals also are available (US$2.50 mask and snorkel, US$2.50 life vest).

Kiteboarding and Stand-Up Paddling

A small hut on the beach, **KSM Kiteboarding & Paddle Surfing Center** (Hwy. 307 Km 264, tel. 984/140-2339, 9am-5pm daily) offers kitesurfing instruction to all levels of students (US$80-500, 1-9 hours). Classes include KSM Beach Club entrance fee and all equipment. The shop also rents stand-up paddleboards (US$25 per hour), kayaks (US$20-25 per hour), and snorkel gear (US$15 per hour).

FOOD AND ACCOMMODATIONS

Hotel Esencia (Hwy. 307 Km 265, tel. 984/873-48350, www.hotelesencia.com, US$700 s/d with a/c, US$777-1,544 suite, US$2,395 2-bedroom villa with pool) is a luxurious private estate turned resort. It boasts 38 gorgeous units, including classy garden-view rooms (some with private plunge pools), larger ocean-view suites, and a stunning split-level villa with a private swimming pool. The beach is just steps away and stretches, virtually untouched, for over a mile. Meal plans are available at the hotel's three gourmet restaurants and beach bar, plus there's a full-service spa and health club on-site. Service is impeccable.

Set on a tropical plot near the beach,

Serenity Eco-Luxury Camp (Hwy. 307 Km 264, tel. 984/803-3980, toll-free U.S./Mex. tel. 800/960-7019, https://en.serenitycamp.com, US$205-255 s/d with a/c) is all about glamping: spacious and sturdy tents with wood floors, real beds, nice linens, electricity, air-conditioning, and private bathrooms (yes, even running water); some even have patios with whirlpool tubs. All to say, these are nice hotel rooms with soft walls. The "camp" itself has a U-shaped pool, a cozy fire pit, a restaurant, and a path leading to its beach club, about a five-minute walk away. Check the website for discounts and bring bug repellent.

KSM Beach Club (Hwy. 307 Km 264, tel. 984/140-2339, 9am-8pm Sun.-Thurs., 9am-2am Fri.-Sat., US$5-14) has a relaxed restaurant-bar with a high *palapa* roof, sand floor, tree trunks for chairs, and a bar with swing-style seats. The food is solid—mostly tacos, empanadas, seafood, salads, and nibblers like nachos and fries. The bar is fully loaded, though at US$3, the *chelas* (a combo of beer, lime juice, and hot spices) are tough to pass up.

INFORMATION AND SERVICES

There are no services in Xpu-Há, save what's available to guests at the hotels. For laundry, an ATM, and other services, head to Akumal or Puerto Aventuras.

GETTING THERE AND AROUND

Each of the listings for Xpu-Há has its own access road, marked with large or small signs, and located at or near Kilometer 265 on the main coastal highway (Hwy. 307). Catalonia Royal Tulum resort is the largest and most obvious landmark; the other access roads are within a few hundred yards. La Playa and KSM Beach Clubs, at the southern end of the beach, are the best access points if you're only staying the day, and are located 25 kilometers (15.5 miles) south of Playa.

Akumal

Unreachable by land until the 1960s, Akumal (Yucatec Maya for "Place of the Turtle") is a quiet destination community that has developed on two bays, known as Akumal Bay and Half Moon Bay. It's a very agreeable midrange place with dozens of condominiums and rental homes. The beach in town is quite nice, if you don't mind the boats parked on the sand and paying a small fee to access it; the beach at Half Moon Bay is long and curving with soft white sand, though it's narrow in places. Just offshore, a spectacular portion of barrier reef makes for great diving and snorkeling, and protects Akumal's bays from heavy surf.

A short distance south of Akumal proper is **Aventuras Akumal,** another small bayside development. It doesn't have the townlike feel or activity that Akumal does, but a good condo-hotel and a truly gorgeous beach make this a tempting alternative. Aventuras Akumal has a separate access road from the highway, and walking there along the beach takes about 45 minutes.

SIGHTS AND BEACHES
Beaches
Akumal Bay—the one right in front of town—has a slow-curving shoreline, with soft sand shaded by palm trees. It's a beautiful beach and a turtle habitat, both for feeding and nesting. In 2016, the bay was declared a marine conservation area in order to protect the turtles from the growing number of visitors. The results have been mixed. Once an easily accessible beach and great place for snorkeling, public access now costs US$5; the only way around this is staying at one of the beachfront hotels or cutting through a dive shop. Beachgoers are only allowed to snorkel as part of a guided tour (you can, however, walk south a bit and snorkel on your own). Needless to say, the chain-link fences, throngs of guides pushing snorkeling tours, and guards watching over the water has dampened

a day at this beach. It hard to argue with all of these changes, though, because it's about protecting and saving sea turtles.

Down the road, **Half Moon Bay** is a much more relaxed and typical beachgoing experience. It's a long and wide bay that's nice for swimming and snorkeling with a white-sand beach to match. Turtles are spotted swimming here too (and snorkeling is unrestricted!). It can be rocky underfoot in some places, though—water shoes come in handy.

★ Laguna Yal-Ku
At the mouth of an elbow-shaped lagoon at the north end of Akumal, an endless upwelling of underground river water collides with the tireless flow of seawater. The result is a great place to snorkel, teeming with fish and plants adapted to this unique hybrid environment. Once a secret snorkelers' getaway, **Laguna Yal-Ku** (tel. 984/875-9065, 9am-5pm daily, US$14 adult, US$10 child 4-12, free 3 and under, US$5 apiece for mask, fins, and life vest, US$3 locker) now has a spot in every guidebook and tour group itinerary—come before 10am or anytime on Sunday for the least traffic. That, and a shot at snagging a private picnic area (US$20), complete with *palapa* shade, a table, and chairs. Use a T-shirt or wetsuit instead of sunscreen, as even the biodegradable kind can collect on plants and coral. The lagoon is dotted with 34 intriguing bronze sculptures by Mexican artist Alejandro Echeverría.

Centro Ecológico Akumal
Facing the town basketball court, **Centro Ecológico Akumal** (CEA, Plaza Ukana, tel. 984/875-9095, www.ceakumal.org, 9am-1pm and 2pm-6pm Mon.-Fri.) is a nonprofit founded in 1993 to monitor the health of Akumal's ecosystems, particularly those related to coral and sea turtles. May through October, CEA operates monthlong

Akumal

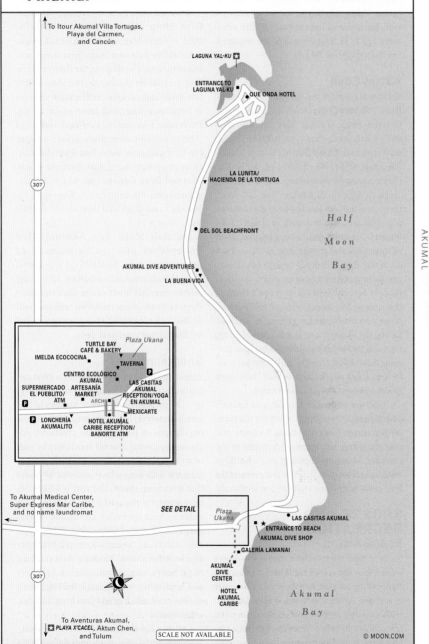

To Itour Akumal Villa Tortugas,
Playa del Carmen,
and Cancún

LAGUNA YAL-KU

ENTRANCE TO
LAGUNA YAL-KU
QUE ONDA HOTEL

307

LA LUNITA/
HACIENDA DE LA TORTUGA

DEL SOL BEACHFRONT

Half

Moon

AKUMAL DIVE ADVENTURES

Bay

LA BUENA VIDA

TURTLE BAY
CAFÉ & BAKERY   *Plaza Ukana*
IMELDA ECOCOCINA
                    TAVERNA
CENTRO ECOLÓGICO
AKUMAL
SUPERMERCADO   ARTESANÍA   LAS CASITAS
EL PUEBLITO/   MARKET   AKUMAL
ATM   RECEPTION/YOGA
            ARCH   EN AKUMAL
                          MEXICARTE
LONCHERÍA
AKUMALITO   HOTEL AKUMAL
                CARIBE RECEPTION/
                BANORTE ATM

To Akumal Medical Center,   SEE DETAIL   Plaza
Super Express Mar Caribe,   Ukana   LAS CASITAS AKUMAL
and no name laundromat   ENTRANCE TO BEACH
                                          AKUMAL DIVE SHOP
                                       GALERÍA LAMANAI

                               AKUMAL
                               DIVE
307   CENTER

                         HOTEL
                         AKUMAL   *Akumal*
                         CARIBE
                                      Bay
To Aventuras Akumal,
PLAYA X'CACEL, Aktun Chen,
and Tulum

SCALE NOT AVAILABLE   © MOON.COM

THE RIVIERA MAYA
AKUMAL

volunteer projects on reef monitoring, sea turtle monitoring, and environmental education. Volunteers stay in the center's dorms, with kitchen and Internet access; the minimum age is 21, and some fees are required. See the website for details.

Aktun Chen

Yucatec Maya for "Cave with an Underground River," **Aktun Chen** (Hwy. 307 Km 107, tel. 984/806-4962, toll-free Mex. tel. 800/099-0875, www.aktun-chen.com, 9:30am-5:30pm daily, last tour 1 hour before closing, US$29-106 adult, US$23-85 child) is certainly that, plus a cenote for swimming and snorkeling, and a canopy/zip line route. You can do all three activities, or just the ones that interest you. The cave tour is a walk of about 0.6 kilometer (0.3 mile) amid a breathtaking array of stalactites and stalagmites; at the end is a 12-meter-deep (39-foot) cenote filled with crystalline water. Lighting and a pathway make it accessible to all. You can't swim in that cenote, but there's another nearby, with stairs and platforms for getting in and out. Lastly, the canopy tour is made up of 10 zip lines and two wobbly suspension bridges, covering a full kilometer (0.6 mile). Between activities, check out the park's small "zoo," with spider monkeys, toucans, and more.

Tours are offered in English and Spanish and last about 90 minutes. Look for the turn-off just across from Aventuras Akumal, and continue three kilometers (1.9 miles) to the entrance. Mosquito repellent and a bottle of water are recommended. You'll encounter the least crowding before 11am and on weekends.

SPORTS AND RECREATION

Scuba Diving

Some of the Riviera Maya's first scuba divers waded into the waves right here at Akumal Bay, and the area has been special to the sport ever since. Akumal's diving is easy and fun, with a mellow current and moderate depths; few profiles go below 20 meters (66 feet). The reef here is predominantly boulder coral, which isn't as picturesque as other types, but it still teems with tropical fish and plant life.

Founded more than 30 years ago, **Akumal Dive Shop** (Akumal Bay, tel. 984/875-9032, toll-free Mex. tel. 800/462-1212, www.akumaldiveshop.com, 8am-5pm daily) was one of the first dive shops in the Riviera Maya. Still located on the beach, the shop offers fun dives and various certification courses in both open-water and cave/cavern diving. Divers can take one- or two-tank reef dives (US$53/100) or cavern dives (US$75-120), or buy dive packages. Note: Fun dives don't include equipment rental. Just down the beach, **Akumal Dive Center** (tel. 984/875-9025, www.akumaldivecenter.com, 8am-5pm) offers the same dives and courses for slightly less.

On Half Moon Bay, **Akumal Dive Adventures** (next to La Buena Vida restaurant, tel. 984/875-9157, www.akumaldiveadventures.com, 8am-5pm daily) offers somewhat lower prices than the other shops (US$40/70 one tank/two tanks) as well as dive and accommodation packages at Del Sol Beachfront hotel next door.

Snorkeling

Snorkeling in **Akumal Bay** offers a great opportunity to see turtles in their natural habitat. The increased number of visitors to this beach, however, led to the adoption of new regulations to protect these creatures, including requiring that all snorkelers be part of an organized tour. Trips are limited to 45 minutes, following a loop outlined by buoys that start from shore. The cost is US$25-50, depending on the outfit (i.e., independent guide vs. tour operator); all include snorkel gear and life vests. Independent guides typically stand near the entrance to the beach but also walk the shores, hawking their services. Note: Snorkeling is prohibited in February and September, which mark the beginning of the turtle nesting and hatching seasons, respectively.

Laguna Yal-Ku (tel. 984/875-9156, caleta_yalku@hotmail.com, 9am-5pm daily, US$14 adult, US$5 child 4-12, free 3 and under, US$5 apiece for mask, fins, and life vest, US$3 locker) is a favorite among many snorkelers for its large area, calm water, and unique mix of fresh- and saltwater ecosystems.

The dive shops also offer **snorkel tours** in the area, which typically last 60-90 minutes. Those along the reef run US$40-50 per person while cenote tours start at US$70 per person.

You also can **rent snorkel gear** at any of Akumal's dive shops for US$14 per day and head out on your own in Half Moon Bay, which has plentiful fish and a decent chance of seeing sea turtles. If you've rented a car, cenote-hopping is another good way to spend the day.

Sailing

Akumal Dive Shop (Akumal Bay, tel. 984/875-9032, toll-free Mex. tel. 800/462-1212, www.akumaldiveshop.com, 8am-5pm daily) offers a popular "Robinson Crusoe" cruise: a five-hour excursion on a catamaran sailboat, with stops for fishing and snorkeling (US$111 adult, US$52 child including lunch and gear). Or try the two-hour Sunset Cruise, which doesn't include snorkeling or fishing, but offers beautiful evening views of the bay (US$53 pp).

Sportfishing

Akumal's dive shops also offer fishing tours year-round. The price, duration, and group size vary considerably based on the season, type of fishing, and boat. That said, expect to pay US$250-300 for a three-hour tour with 2-6 anglers; gear, bait, and license are included. Fishing is excellent year-round, but April-August are when sailfish and marlin are most prevalent.

Yoga

Yoga en Akumal (town arch, 2nd Fl., tel. 984/876-2652, www.facebook.com/pg/YogaEnAkumal) offers a variety of hatha classes for all experience levels in a breezy studio inside the arch at the entrance to town. Sessions are led by certified instructors; they cost US$15 per class, US$45 for four classes, or US$100 for an unlimited month pass; check Facebook for the monthly schedule.

SHOPPING

MexicArte (tel. 984/875-9115, www.mexicarte.shop, 8am-9pm daily) is the small, bright pink shop just inside the arch on your right. The owner hand-selects the best folk art from around the region and country. Prices are high, but so is the quality and artisanship.

Galería Lamanai (tel. 984/875-9055, 8am-9pm daily) offers similar wares, both in quality and price. The shop is located on the beach near Snack Bar Lol Ha.

There is an open-air *artesanía* **market** (8am-6pm daily) behind Plaza Ukana, facing the town basketball court. The items are standard Mexican handicrafts, such as colorful ceramics from Puebla and textiles from Chiapas.

FOOD

In Town

★ **Taverna** (Plaza Ukana, tel. 984/875-9009, www.tavernabylombardi.com, noon-10pm daily, US$7-15) is a high-end Italian restaurant set in a two-story *palapa* with tables inside and out. The menu features a full line of homemade pasta dishes, wood-fired pizza, and fresh seafood. Start with an order of avocado fries (slices of fresh avocado, breaded and fried), an unexpected treat. Craft beers and top-shelf cocktails are also on offer (happy hour is 3pm-5pm daily). There's live music most nights starting at 7pm.

Turtle Bay Café & Bakery (Plaza Ukana, tel. 984/875-9138, www.turtlebaycafe.com, 7am-10pm daily, US$6-19) offers creative comfort food like crab cakes, seafood-stuffed chiles rellenos, and "Black and Bleu" salad. For breakfast, try the famous sticky buns and eggs Benedict. Enjoy your meal surrounded by palm trees, either in the outdoor *palapa*-roofed dining room or on the porch of the main building. Free Wi-Fi is available.

Just outside of the town arch, ★ **Lonchería Akumalito** (no tel., 7am-9pm daily, US$3-5) is a no-frills Mexican

eatery serving everything from pancakes and eggs to hamburgers and enchiladas. Order a fresh *agua* (fruit drink) or smoothie to go with your meal. Seating is at a few outdoor tables with a view of the road. Service is blazing fast. Cash only.

For a fresh, healthy meal, try **Imelda Ecococina** (no phone, 8am-5pm Mon.-Sat., US$4-7). Breakfast options include eggs, omelets, pancakes, and French toast. For lunch, the *comida corrida* (lunch special) comes with a choice of main plate and a side dish or two. Look for it near the town basketball court.

For groceries, the best prices are across from the Akumal turnoff on Highway 307 in **Super Express Mar Caribe** (Av. Gonzalo Guerrero, 7am-11pm daily); look for the store about 100 meters (328 feet) west of the highway. Otherwise, just outside the arch, **Supermercado El Pueblito** (7am-9pm daily) is a pricey market selling basic foodstuffs plus sunscreen and bug repellent. Both markets sell fresh fruit and veggies too, but you may find a better selection at the **farmers market** held Wednesday and Saturday in Plaza Ukana.

Half Moon Bay

A skeleton of a flying serpent greets diners at **La Buena Vida** (beachfront, tel. 984/875-9061, http://labuenavidarestaurant.com, 8am-11pm daily, US$5-15), where clients enjoy the varied menu—from French toast to shrimp ceviche—under *palapa*-shaded tables on the beach. If you've already had a meal, stop in for a drink at the swing-lined bar; happy hour runs 5pm-6pm.

La Lunita Restaurant (Hacienda de la Tortuga, tel. 984/875-9070, lalunita@prodigy. net.mx, 1:30pm-11pm daily, US$14-26) is an intimate bistro serving gourmet Mexican and international dishes, with both small plates or full entrées. Seafood is king here, though there are plenty of options for vegetarians and serious meat eaters. With only a handful of tables,

some overlooking the Caribbean, La Lunita is a perfect place for a romantic dinner—just be sure to make reservations.

Aventuras Akumal

★ **Beached Bikini Bar and Grill** (beachfront, tel. 998/845-4528, www.beachedbikini. com, 11am-last person leaves, US$6-14) is a classic chilled-out beach joint with swing seats at the bar, plastic tables on the beach, and palm tree shade. It's a friendly, jocular place where everyone is treated like a regular. Stick to the basics—nachos, burgers, and ceviche—and you won't be disappointed. Order a mango jalapeño margarita to wash it all down.

ACCOMMODATIONS

Akumal draws many long-term visitors and has a large number of fully equipped condos and villas, in addition to ordinary hotels.

In Town

Hotel Akumal Caribe (reception in the arch at the entrance to town, tel. 984/875-9012, www.hotelakumalcaribe.com, US$189 s/d bungalow, US$215 s/d with a/c, US$230 s/d with a/c and kitchenette) is the oldest hotel in town, and the bungalows show it in their bamboo furnishings and floral prints. Hotel rooms, however, have been updated and feature amenities like sleek espresso furnishings, stainless steel mini fridges, and mini-split air conditioners. They also have balconies with ocean views. The property fronts the town's gorgeous palm tree-laden main beach, plus there's a great pool with a small waterfall. Continental breakfast is included.

On the eastern end of town, ★ **Las Casitas Akumal** (tel. 984/875-9071, toll-free U.S./Can. tel. 800/525-8625, www. lascasitasakumal.com, US$351-398 2-bedroom condo with a/c) has 18 airy condominiums, each with two bedrooms, two baths, a living room, fully equipped kitchen, and private patio. Some have two floors and space for six people, and most feature bright, colorful Mexican artwork. All have ocean views and direct access to a semiprivate section of the

1: Playa X'cacel, just south of Akumal; **2:** getting ready to snorkel in Akumal's Laguna Yal-Ku beach. There's a five-night minimum in the high season.

Half Moon Bay

Del Sol Beachfront (tel. 984/875-9060, toll-free U.S. tel. 888/425-8625, www.akumalinfo.com, US$101-118 s/d with a/c, US$160-252 studio to 3-bedroom condo with a/c) has 16 spacious condos plus 15 smallish hotel rooms, all overlooking a lovely stretch of beach. Condos are decorated in colorful Mexican décor and have long balconies or porches, fully equipped kitchens, separate living and dining rooms, and master bedrooms with king-size beds. Some have whirlpool tubs too. Hotel rooms are comfortable but may feel a bit cramped for longer stays. All units have daily maid service and share a well-tended beach with lounge chairs and *palapa* shades. All that, plus a beachfront pool.

★ **Hacienda de la Tortuga** (tel. 984/875-9068, www.haciendatortuga.com, US$178 1-bedroom condo, US$238 2-bedroom condo) has just 16 units and cultivates a quiet, relaxed atmosphere geared toward couples. Roomy one-bedroom and two-bedroom condos all have huge ocean-view windows, plus a living room, kitchen, king-size bed(s), and air-conditioning in the bedrooms. Each is uniquely decorated, many with fine Mexican artwork and homey touches like a well-stocked bookcase. There's a small pool just steps from the beach, and a well-regarded Mexican restaurant, La Lunita, on-site.

Just a block from Laguna Yal-Ku, **Que Onda Hotel** (tel. 984/875-9101, maribel.ondarte@gmail.com, US$90-105 s/d with a/c, US$180-220 suite) has seven rooms, each lovingly decorated with beautiful fabrics and unique works of art. Two suites are similar in style, can accommodate up to six guests, and include terrific upper-floor views of the Caribbean and Yal-Ku. All face a verdant garden with a pool. The on-site restaurant can get a bit busy, but fortunately it stops receiving guests at 10pm. Use of snorkel gear is included in the rate.

Aventuras Akumal

Villa Las Brisas (tel. 984/875-9263, www.aventuras-akumal.com, US$100 s/d, US$75 studio with a/c, US$150 1-bedroom condo, US$200 2-bedroom condo) has just three units, two of which can be combined to make a two-bedroom condo. All are spacious, spotless, and meticulously furnished, down to a stocked spice rack in the kitchen. The condos have large terraces with hammocks and stunning views; the smaller units have balconies that overlook a tidy garden. With comfortable beds, modern Mexican-style furnishings, and space to stretch out, it's easy to feel at home here. Snorkel gear and kayaks are included in the rate. There's a simple mini-mart at the entrance (8am-4pm Mon.-Sat.), but you'll have to go to Akumal for additional shopping and services. There is free Wi-Fi throughout but only the studio has air-conditioning.

A small all-inclusive resort, **Akumal Bay Beach & Wellness Resort** (Hwy. 307 Km 254, www.akumalbayresort.com, US$274-327 pp all-inclusive) sits on a gorgeous stretch of beach, within easy walking distance of Akumal proper. The restaurant options include an international buffet and à la carte restaurants serving Japanese, Brazilian, and Mexican fare. Rooms are a bit stark in décor but are modern and comfortable and have with stocked mini fridges; daily turn-down service is a nice touch. Best of all are the activities: yoga, meditation, core energetics, snorkeling tours, and free use of stand-up paddleboards, kayaks, bikes, and tennis courts. There's also an on-site spa and a gorgeous oceanfront pool, surrounded by lounge chairs and beach beds.

Outside of Town

Located on the inland side of Highway 307, **Itour Akumal Villa Tortugas** (Hwy. 307 Km 256, cell tel. 984/146-3669, US$42-46 s/d with a/c) is a great little place offering six studios amid a leafy jungle setting. Each unit is a colorful casita with a kitchenette, one or two firm beds, a private patio, air-conditioning, and Wi-Fi; they are spick-and-span, with daily maid service. The grounds include a mosaic-tiled pool and an outdoor lounge area, both surrounded by a well-tended garden. Located three kilometers (1.8 miles) north of Akumal, it's a peaceful place to base yourself, especially if you have a car and don't mind being a few miles from the beach.

Rental Properties

The majority of rooms for rent in Akumal are in privately owned homes and condos, especially along Half Moon Bay. Most are managed and rented by one of various property management companies. Some reliable agencies include **Caribbean Fantasy** (toll-free U.S. tel. 800/523-6618, www.caribbfan.com), **Akumal Villas** (toll-free U.S. tel. 866/535-1324, www.akumalvillas.com,), and **Akumal Rentals** (U.S. tel. 815/642-4580, www.akumal-rentals.com). Reliable online sources for rentals include **Loco Gringo** (www.locogringo.com), **AirBnB** (www.airbnb.com), and **Vacation Rentals by Owner** (www.vrbo.com).

INFORMATION AND SERVICES

Tourist Information

Akumal doesn't have an official tourist office, but it's a small town, and you can probably find what you're looking for by asking the first person you see. If that fails, the folks at **Centro Ecológico Akumal** (CEA, Plaza Ukana, tel. 984/875-9095, www.ceakumal.org, 9am-1pm and 2pm-6pm Mon.-Fri.) are friendly and well informed, and most speak English.

Emergency Services

In a residential neighborhood across the highway form the main town entrance, **Akumal Medical Center** (Av. Gonzalo Guerrero s/n, tel. 984/875-9090, cell tel. 984/806-4616, www.akumaldoctoroncall.com, 24 hours daily) is the medical office of longtime Akumal provider Dr. Néstor Mendoza Gutiérrez.

The **police** can be reached by calling 060.

Money

There is no bank in town, but there is a **Banorte ATM** inside the arch at the entrance. **Supermercado El Pueblito** (7am-9pm daily) also has an ATM.

Media and Communications

Most hotels and condos offer free Wi-Fi to guests, as does **Turtle Bay Café & Bakery** (tel. 984/875-9138, www.turtlebaycafe.com, 7am-10pm daily) in Plaza Ukana.

Laundry

There's an **unnamed laundry** (Av. Gonzalo Guerrero s/n, no tel., 8am-5pm Mon.-Sat.) on the west side of the highway, along the main street. Next-day service costs US$0.50 per kg (2.2 lbs).

GETTING THERE AND AROUND

The turnoff to Akumal is between kilometers 254 and 255 on the main highway. For Aventuras Akumal, the access road is just south of the main Akumal entrance; look for the sign to Hotel Villas DeRosa, as the community itself isn't well signed.

Bus and *Combi*

Combis and second-class buses stop at the Akumal turnoff, but it's a one-kilometer (0.6 mile) walk into town. Likewise, you can manage the center area by foot, but walking to and from Half Moon Bay can be long, hot, and dusty. Consider hiring a cab, which are often parked just outside the town arch.

Combis and second-class buses also stop at the Aventuras Akumal entrance; it's only about 500 meters (0.3 mile) into the community from there.

Car

If you drive into town, there is a small **town parking lot** (7am-4pm daily, US$1/hour) in front of Plaza Ukana. Some shops and restaurants can validate your parking—be sure to bring your receipt. There also are a handful of **public parking lots** just outside the town arch charging US$2.50 per day.

Taxi

Taxis gather near the entrance of Akumal, just outside of the arch. A ride from town to Laguna Yal-Ku costs US$5.

★ PLAYA X'CACEL

For all the breakneck construction along the Riviera Maya, much of the coastline remains virtually untouched, including some gorgeous stretches of white-sand beach. **Playa X'cacel** (Hwy. 307 Km 247.5, 9am-5pm daily, US$1) is one of those, a gently curving band of thick white sand, with only a small parking lot, restrooms, and changing area,

and popular with local residents. X'cacel's pristine state is thanks in part to the fact that sea turtles nest here, and development is restricted by federal law. Along the inland edge of the beach are scores of wood blades with dates on them, marking where and when sea turtles laid eggs; needless to say, do not move the markers or disturb the nests! A small freshwater cenote is located down a slippery path, about 350 meters (0.2 mile) south of the main entrance; due to its popularity, visitors are admitted in waves of 30 people, with swim time limited to just 20 minutes. The turnoff to Playa X'cacel is easy to miss, but it's located 11 kilometers (7 miles) north of Tulum, just south of Chemuyil community.

Tankah Tres and Soliman Bay

Tucked innocuously between Akumal and Tulum, Tankah Tres and Soliman Bay see only a fraction of the tourist traffic that their better-known neighbors do. But that's just the way visitors to this little stretch of coastline prefer it, enjoying excellent snorkeling, diving, and pretty beaches, with a sense of isolation that's hard to find in these parts. The area has three small bays. The scattered hotels, villas, and private homes along their shores were once connected by a U-shaped access road, but development cut the U in half; the southern entrance is still marked Tankah Tres, while the northern entrance has a sign for Soliman Bay.

SIGHTS AND BEACHES
Playa Tankah

The handful of hotels here have nice beachfronts along three sandy bays. If you aren't staying here, consider having a meal at the hotel restaurants of **Blue Sky Tulum** and **Casa Cenote,** which allow nonguests to enjoy the facilities and beach if they order something.

Cenote Manatí
(aka Casa Cenote)

Across from Casa Cenote (and sometimes called by the same name), **Cenote Manatí** (Tankah Tres, 1.5 kilometers/0.9 mile from the southern turnoff, no phone, sunrise-sunset, US$6) is a series of interconnected cenotes and lagoons extending from the road well inland (an underground channel drains into the ocean). The crystal-clear water, winding channels, and tangle of rocks, trees, and freshwater plants along the edges and bottom all make for terrific snorkeling. Look for schools of tiny fish near the surface and some bigger ones farther down. Admission includes a life jacket; snorkel gear rental is available for US$6.

Yax Kin Cenote

Located just north of the Soliman Bay access road, **Yax Kin Cenote** (Hwy. 307 Km 242, cell tel. 998/244-0612, 10am-6pm daily, US$4 adult, US$2.50 child under 10) is a pool of shimmering teal water with a limestone shelf that makes entering the cool water easy (and less stressful for parents of small children). Snorkeling equipment can be rented (US$4) to get a better view of the small fish darting about. Camping (US$10 pp, BYO gear) is permitted in two-story towers located about 50 meters (164 feet) from the cenote.

SPORTS AND RECREATION
Scuba Diving and Snorkeling

There are excellent dive and snorkel sites in and near Tankah Tres and Soliman Bay. Located inside the Tankah Inn, **Tankah Divers Tulum** (Tankah Tres, tel. 984/128-2000, www.tankahdivers.com, hours vary) is a full-service shop offering guided trips (US$50/85 one-tank reef/cenote, US$80/130 two-tank reef/cenote) and all levels of PADI dive instruction. The shop also offers snorkeling excursions (US$40/60 reef/cenote).

FOOD

The restaurant at **Blue Sky Tulum** (Tankah Tres, 1.7 kilometers/1 mile from the southern turnoff, cell tel. 984/202-2185, www.blueskytulum.com.mx, 7:30am-9pm daily, US$10-24) specializes in Italian food, prepared to order, with simple but beautiful presentation. The pizza is famously good, handmade with fresh ingredients and baked in a custom brick oven. Appetizers like ceviche and mains like grilled calamari with vegetables are also worth sampling.

Set in a large palm grove along the curving Soliman Bay, ★ **Chamico's** (Soliman Bay, end of road, cell tel. 984/115-0260, 11am-5pm daily, US$6-15) is a family-run restaurant serving up unbelievably fresh seafood and fish dishes. "Restaurant" is a bit of a stretch, though; it's more like a handful of plastic tables and chairs set under swaying palms, and a Maya-style hut with a couple of open-fire grills and rickety wood tables serves as the kitchen. Meals range from whole grilled fish and lobster tail to fish ceviche and seafood stews.

The restaurant at **Casa Cenote** (Tankah Tres, 1.5 kilometers/0.9 mile from the southern turnoff, tel. 984/115-6996, www.casacenote.com, 8am-9pm daily, US$6-16) has a breezy *palapa*-roofed dining area just steps from the ocean. Stick to beach food like quesadillas or guacamole, or, better yet, come on Sunday afternoon when the hotel hosts a Texas-style barbecue (US$11) that's popular with expats. There's live music on weekends.

the view from Chamico's in Soliman Bay

ACCOMMODATIONS

Tankah Inn (Tankah Tres, 1.1 kilometers/0.6 mile from the southern turnoff, tel. 984/100-0703, www.tankah.com, US$140 s/d with a/c) has five spacious rooms with murals of Maya temples. Each room has a private terrace and ocean views; all feature mini fridges, drinking water, and air-conditioning. A breezy common room has sweeping views of the Caribbean—comfy chairs and tables, lots of board games, and an honor bar make this a popular place to hang out. The beach, with its lounge chairs and hammocks, is a tempting alternative. À la carte breakfast is included, as is use of kayaks and Wi-Fi.

Blue Sky Tulum (Tankah Tres, 1.7 kilometers/1 mile from the southern turnoff, cell tel. 984/202-2185, www.blueskytulum. com.mx, US$289-329 s/d with a/c, US$409-519 suite with a/c) is not in Tulum, regardless of its name. But, it is an excellent small hotel in Tankah, offering 10 breezy rooms with views of the Caribbean or the jungle. Units are simple but elegant with large private terraces and amenities like luxurious linens, high-pressure showers, and, in some, a plunge pool. Turndown service is provided each night; breakfast is provided each morning. There's also a refreshing pool facing the beach, lots of lounge chairs and hammocks for relaxing, and kayaks, snorkel gear, and paddleboards for playing.

A gorgeous boutique hotel, ★ **Jashita** (Soliman Bay, 1.2 kilometers/0.7 mile from the northern turnoff, tel. 984/875-4158, www.jashitahotel.com, US$250 s/d with a/c, US$630-1,750 suite) sits on the curving Soliman Bay. It's an intimate place with elegant rooms that have marble floors, fine hardwoods, basin sinks, and rainfall showerheads—some even have private plunge pools. The common areas are just as sophisticated without losing a sense of hominess; fine art and beautiful furnishings make you feel like you're staying at your most stylish friend's home. There are also three great pools, a yoga studio and spa, a gourmet restaurant, and a breathtaking beach. Use of kayaks, stand-up paddleboards, and snorkel gear is included in the rate, as is breakfast. There's a minimum three-night stay; it's a seven-night minimum December 20-January 10.

If you have camping gear, make a beeline to **Chamico's** (Soliman Bay, end of road, cell tel. 984/115-0260, US$10 pp camping). A basic restaurant is located in a gorgeous palm grove, and tents can be set up at the far end of the beach. Rustic bathrooms are the only bummer, but it seems a small price to pay considering the location—swaying palms, gentle ocean waves, and, on a clear night, an endless array of stars. All to say, a slice of heaven.

INFORMATION AND SERVICES

There are no formal services here, because it's not really a formal town. Head to Tulum for ATMs, medical services, Internet, groceries, and more.

GETTING THERE AND AROUND

The turnoff to the southern portion of Tankah Tres is between kilometers 237 and 238 on the main highway, and marked with a large road sign. Driving south from Cancún, you'll have to overshoot the entrance a short distance until a break in the median (at Dreams Tulum Resort and Spa) allows you to make a U-turn and return to the turnoff; this access road makes a beeline for the shore and then turns abruptly to the left, hugging the beach and passing the listed hotels and sights. The access road to the northern section is a bit farther and is marked with a large sign for Oscar & Lalo's Restaurant, which is actually on the west side of the highway. If you don't have a car, you can ask a *combi* to drop you at either turnoff, but it will not enter Tankah Tres or Soliman Bay itself.

Tulum and the Costa Maya

Tulum has long been favored by travelers who

cringe at the splashy resorts and package tourism found in Cancún (and increasingly in the Riviera Maya).

In that sense, Tulum is a fitting bridge between Quintana Roo's booming northern section and its far-less-traveled south. Tulum has so far managed to avoid the impulse to fill the coast with ever-bigger resorts; prices have certainly gone up, but there are still no megadevelopments here, or even power lines for that matter. Its beaches and *cabañas* remain as idyllic as ever.

If Tulum is the anti-Cancún, you might call southern Quintana Roo, or the "Costa Maya," the non-Cancún. Though fairly close in distance, it's worlds apart by any other measure. Immediately south

Highlights

Look for ★ to find recommended sights, activities, dining, and lodging.

★ **Tulum's Southern Beaches:** Mile after mile of powdery white sand, tranquil turquoise water, cozy bungalows peeking out from behind softly bending palm trees . . . these are the beaches you've been dreaming of (page 209).

★ **Cenotes near Tulum:** Don't miss these eerie and unforgettable limestone caverns, bristling with stalagmites and stalactites and filled with the crystalline water of the world's longest underground river system (page 209).

★ **Cobá Archaeological Zone:** Just an hour from Tulum are the terrific jungle-cloaked ruins of Cobá, where you can climb the Yucatán's second-highest pyramid (page 226).

★ **Cenotes near Cobá:** A visit to Cobá is made even better with a stop at three impressive cenotes a short distance from the ruins (page 232).

★ **Bahía de la Ascensión:** A protected expanse of calm ocean flats and tangled mangrove forests make this a world-class destination for bird-watchers and anglers (page 236).

★ **Banco Chinchorro:** A punishing two-hour boat ride across the open sea is rewarded with spectacular diving on one of the world's largest coral atolls (page 243).

★ **Canal de los Piratas:** Tours of Laguna

Bacalar (available by pontoon, kayak, even SUP) inevitably stop at this lovely natural waterway, a great place for swimming, mud baths, and basking in the sun (page 255).

Previous: Tulum archaeological site overlooking the Caribbean. **Above:** painted *calaveras,* a kind of *artesanía;* sea fans swaying in the currents.

Tulum and the Costa Maya

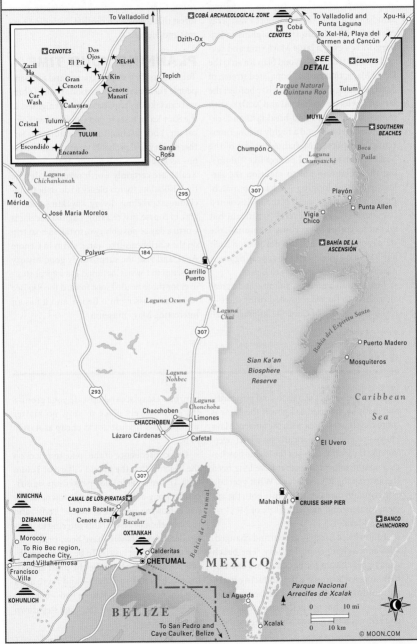

To Valladolid

★ COBÁ ARCHAEOLOGICAL ZONE

To Valladolid and Punta Laguna

Xpu-Há

Cobá

CENOTES

To Xel-Há, Playa del Carmen and Cancún

Dzith-Ox

★ CENOTES

SEE DETAIL

Tepich

Parque Natural de Quintana Roo

Tulum

MUYIL

★ SOUTHERN BEACHES

Santa Rosa

Chumpón

Laguna Chunyaxché

Boca Paila

295

307

Playón

Laguna Chichankanah

Vigía Chico

Punta Allen

To Mérida

José Maria Morelos

★ BAHÍA DE LA ASCENSIÓN

Polyuc

184

Carrillo Puerto

Laguna Ocum

Laguna Chai

Bahía del Espíritu Santo

307

Puerto Madero

Mosquiteros

Sian Ka'an Biosphere Reserve

Caribbean Sea

293

Laguna Nohbec

Laguna Chonchoba

Chacchoben

Limones

CHACCHOBEN

Lázaro Cárdenas

Cafetal

El Uvero

307

KINICHNÁ

CANAL DE LOS PIRATAS

Laguna Bacalar

Laguna Bacalar

DZIBANCHÉ

Cenote Azul

OXTANKAH

Mahahual

CRUISE SHIP PIER

★ BANCO CHINCHORRO

Morocoy

To Río Bec region, Campeche City, and Villahermosa

Calderitas

CHETUMAL

Bahía de Chetumal

MEXICO

Francisco Villa

KOHUNLICH

BELIZE

La Aguada

Parque Nacional Arrecifes de Xcalak

To San Pedro and Caye Caulker, Belize

Xcalak

0   10 mi
0   10 km

© MOON.COM

★ CENOTES

Dos Ojos

El Pit

XEL-HÁ

Zazil Ha

Gran Cenote

Yax Kin

Car Wash

Calavera

Cenote Manatí

Cristal

Tulum

TULUM

Escondido

Encantado

of Tulum is the massive Sian Ka'an Biosphere Reserve, one of the Yucatán's largest and richest preserves, whose bays, lagoons, mangrove stands, and inland forests support a vast array of plants and animals, from dolphins to jaguars; there's even a large Maya ruin and several smaller temples. Beyond Sian Ka'an is the Costa Maya, the sparsely populated stretch of coast reaching down to the Belize border; the largest towns are Mahahual and Xcalak, with numerous small bed-and-breakfasts and seaside hotels in both (and a highly incongruous cruise ship port in Mahahual). Most of the beaches aren't postcard-perfect like Tulum's, but the isolation—not to mention the far-less-expensive lodging—is hard to match. Inland and farther south is the multicolored Laguna Bacalar and several significant but all-but-forgotten Maya ruins. Chetumal, the state capital, isn't much of a destination itself but has some unexpectedly appealing areas nearby, and it is the gateway to Belize.

Less than an hour from Tulum—and a great alternative to the overcrowded ruins there—is the ancient city of Cobá (42 kilometers/26 miles from Tulum), home of the second-tallest known Maya pyramid. Unlike many other ruins, Cobá is ensconced in a thick tropical forest that teems with birdlife, including parrots and toucans.

PLANNING YOUR TIME

Tulum is the first stop, of course, and for many people their main destination. From Tulum you can take day trips or short overnighters to the Sian Ka'an reserve and Cobá archaeological site, both fascinating. To venture any farther south you'll probably want a rental car, as bus service grows infrequent. Mahahual and Xcalak are certainly worth savoring; despite their isolation, there's plenty to do in both, including snorkeling, diving, kayaking, fishing, and, of course, just relaxing. Laguna Bacalar is worth a day or possibly two, to take a boat trip on the Caribbean-like water, swim in Cenote Azul, and visit the surprisingly good history museum in town. Chetumal is a logical stopover for those headed west toward the Río Bec region or crossing into Belize, and it has an interesting Maya museum.

Tulum

Tulum is the subject of a thousand postcards, and justly so. It's hard to know if the name is more closely associated with the ancient Maya ruins—perched dramatically on a cliff overlooking the Caribbean—or the idyllic beaches and oceanfront *cabañas* that have long been the jewel of the Riviera Maya. What's certain is that Tulum manages to capture both the ancient mystery and modern allure of Mexico's Riviera Maya.

Tulum has definitely grown and changed, with more changes on the way. The beach used to be a haven for backpackers and bohemians, with simple *cabañas* facing beautiful untouched beaches. The beaches are still beautiful, but the prices have long since gone through the *palapa* roof, catering more to urban escapists and upscale yoga groups. It's still a lovely place to stay, no matter who you are, it's just not as cheap as it used to be.

One consequence of the spike in prices on the beach is that the inland village of Tulum (aka Tulum Pueblo) has perked up significantly. Long a dumpy roadside town, it now has a growing number of hotels, B&Bs, and recommendable restaurants catering to independent travelers who have been priced out of the beachfront hotels. To be sure, a beachside *cabaña* will always be the most appealing place to stay in Tulum—and there are a handful of bargains still to be had—but staying in town is no longer the huge step down that it once was.

ORIENTATION

The name Tulum is used for three separate areas, which can be confusing. The first is Tulum archaeological zone, the scenic and popular Maya ruins. This is the first part of Tulum you encounter as you drive south from Cancún. A kilometer and a half (1 mile) farther south (and well inland) is the town of Tulum, known as Tulum Pueblo, where you'll find the bus terminal, supermarket, and numerous restaurants, hotels, tour guides, and shops. The third area is Tulum's beachfront hotel zone, or Zona Hotelera. Located due east of Tulum Pueblo, the Zona Hotelera extends for almost 10 kilometers (6 miles) from the Maya ruins to the entrance of the Sian Ka'an Biosphere Reserve, with fantastic beaches and bungalow-style hotels virtually the entire way. There's a walking path, but no road, connecting the Tulum ruins to the upper end of Tulum's Zona Hotelera.

TULUM ARCHAEOLOGICAL ZONE

The Maya ruins of **Tulum** (8am-5pm daily, US$3.50) are one of Mexico's most scenic archaeological sites, built atop a 12-meter (40-foot) cliff rising abruptly from turquoise Caribbean waters. The structures don't compare in grandeur to those of Cobá, Uxmal, or elsewhere, but are interesting and significant nevertheless.

Tulum is the single most frequently visited Maya ruin in the Yucatán Peninsula, receiving thousands of visitors every day, most on package tours from nearby resorts. (In fact, it's second only to Teotihuacán, near Mexico City, as the country's most visited archaeological site.) For that reason, the first and most important piece of advice for independent travelers regarding Tulum is to **arrive early.** It used to be that the tour bus madness didn't begin until 11am, but it creeps earlier and earlier every year. Still, if you're there right at 8am, you'll have the ruins mostly to yourself for an hour or so—which is about all you need for this small site—before the hordes descend. Guides can be hired at the entrance for around US$40 for 1-4 people. Bring your swimsuit if you fancy a morning swim: This is the only Maya ruin with a great little beach right inside the archaeological zone.

History

Tulum was part of a series of Maya forts and trading outposts established along the Caribbean coast from the Gulf of Mexico as far south as present-day Honduras. Its original name was Zamá-Xamanzamá or simply Zamá (derived from *zamal*, or dawn) but was later called Tulum, Yucatec Maya for "fortification" or "city wall," in reference to the thick stone barrier that encloses the city's main structures. Measuring 380 by 165 meters (1,250 by 540 feet), it's the largest fortified Maya site on the Quintana Roo coast (though small compared to most inland ruins).

Tulum's enviable patch of seashore was settled as early as 300 BC, but it remained little more than a village for most of its existence, overshadowed by the Maya city of Tankah a few kilometers to the north. Tulum gained prominence between the 12th and 16th centuries (the Late Postclassic era), when mostly non-Maya immigrants repopulated the Yucatán Peninsula following the general Maya collapse several centuries prior. Tulum's strategic location and convenient beach landing made it a natural hub for traders, who plied the coast in massive canoes measuring up to 16 meters (52 feet) long, laden with honey, salt, wax, animal skins, vanilla, obsidian, amber, and other products.

It was during this Postclassic boom period that most of Tulum's main structures were built. Although influenced by Mayapán (the reigning power at the time) and Central Mexican city-states, from which many of Tulum's new residents had emigrated, Tulum's structures mostly exemplify "east coast architecture," defined by austere designs with relatively little ornamentation and a predominantly horizontal orientation (compared to high-reaching pyramids elsewhere). Ironically, construction in these later eras tended to be rather shoddy, thanks in part to

Tulum Archaeological Zone

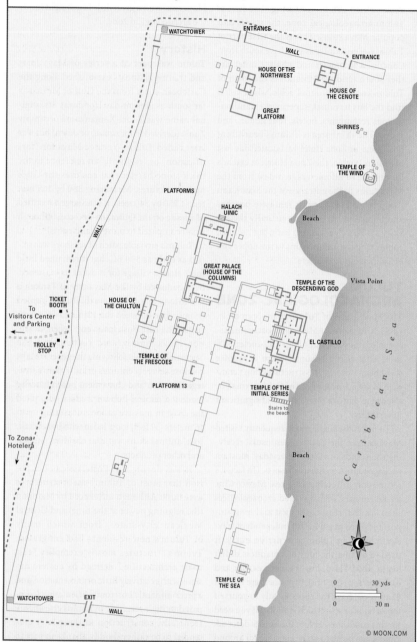

ENTRANCE

WATCHTOWER

WALL

ENTRANCE

HOUSE OF THE NORTHWEST

HOUSE OF THE CENOTE

GREAT PLATFORM

SHRINES

TEMPLE OF THE WIND

PLATFORMS

HALACH UINIC

Beach

GREAT PALACE (HOUSE OF THE COLUMNS)

Vista Point

TEMPLE OF THE DESCENDING GOD

TICKET BOOTH

To Visitors Center and Parking

HOUSE OF THE CHULTÚN

EL CASTILLO

TROLLEY STOP

TEMPLE OF THE FRESCOES

Caribbean Sea

PLATFORM 13

TEMPLE OF THE INITIAL SERIES

Stairs to the beach

To Zona Hotelera

Beach

WATCHTOWER

EXIT

WALL

TEMPLE OF THE SEA

0   30 yds
0   30 m

© MOON.COM

improvements in stucco coverings that meant the quality of underlying masonry need not be as precise. Today, with the stucco eroded away, Tulum's temples appear more decayed than structures at other sites, even those built hundreds of years prior.

The Spanish got their first view of Tulum, and of mainland indigenous society, on May 7, 1518, when Juan de Grijalva's expedition along the Quintana Roo coast sailed past the then brightly colored fortress. The chaplain of the fleet famously described the city as "a village so large that Seville would not have appeared larger or better." Tulum remained an important city and port until the mid-1500s, when European-borne diseases decimated its population. The once-grand city was effectively abandoned and, for the next three centuries, slowly consumed by coastal vegetation. In 1840, Spanish explorers referred to an ancient walled city known as Tulum, the first recorded use of its current name; two years later John Lloyd Stephens and Frederick Catherwood visited Tulum, giving the world its first detailed description and illustrations of the dramatic seaside site. During the Caste War, Tulum was occupied by members of the Talking Cross cult, including the followers of a Maya priestess known as the Queen of Tulum.

House of the Cenote

The path from the ticket booth follows Tulum's wall around the northwest corner to two low corbel arch entryways. Using the second entrance (closer to the ocean), you'll first see the Casa del Cenote. The two-room structure, with a third chamber added later, is less impressive than the gaping maw of its namesake cenote. The water is not drinkable, thanks to saltwater intrusion, but that may not have been the case a half millennium ago; it's unlikely Tulum could have grown to its size and prominence without a major water source, not only for its own residents but passing traders as well. Cenotes were also considered apertures to Xibalba, or the underworld, and an elaborate tomb discovered in the floor

of the House of the Cenote suggests it may have had a ceremonial function as well.

Temple of the Wind

Following the path, the next major structure is the Temple of the Wind, perched regally atop a rocky outcrop overlooking a picturesque sandy cove. If it looks familiar, that's because it appears on innumerable postcards, magazine photos, and tourist brochures. (The view is even better from a vista point behind El Castillo and from the ocean.) The name derives from the unique circular base upon which the structure is built: In Central Mexican cosmology, the circle is associated with the god of the wind, and its presence here (and at other ruins, like San Gervasio on Isla Cozumel) is evidence of the strong influence that Central Mexican migrants/invaders had on Postclassic Maya societies.

Temple of the Descending God

One of Tulum's more curious structures is the Temple of the Descending God, named for the upside-down winged figure above its doorway. Exactly who or what the figure represents is disputed among archaeologists—theories include Venus, the setting sun, the god of rain, even the god of bees (as honey was one of the coastal Maya's most widely traded products). Whatever the answer, it was clearly a deeply revered (or feared) deity, as the same image appears on several of Tulum's buildings, including the upper temple of Tulum's main pyramid. The Temple of the Descending God also is notable for its cartoonish off-kilter position, most likely the result of poor construction.

El Castillo

Tulum's largest and most imposing structure is The Castle, a 12-meter-high (40-foot) pyramid constructed on a rocky bluff of roughly the same height. Like many Maya structures, El Castillo was built in multiple phases. The first iteration was a low, broad platform, still visible today, topped by a long palace fronted by a phalanx of stout columns. The second

Rediscovering the Maya

The Maya ruins of the Yucatán Peninsula were all but unknown in the United States and Europe until well into the 19th century. Although Spanish explorers and colonizers had occupied the peninsula for more than two centuries, conflicts with local Maya and Catholic antipathy for all things pagan probably account for the Spaniards' lack of research or even apparent interest. To be fair, the immensity of the task was surely daunting—by the time the Spanish reached the Yucatán in the early 1500s, the majority of sites had been abandoned for at least 300 years, and in some cases double or triple that. Many were piles of rubble, and those still standing were mostly covered in vegetation. Just getting to the sites was a task in itself.

And so it was an American and an Englishman—diplomat John Lloyd Stephens and artist-architect Frederick Catherwood—who brought global attention to the Maya world. Between 1839 and 1841, they conducted two major explorations of the Maya region, including present-day Yucatán, Chiapas, and Central America, visiting a total of 44 ruins. Stephens kept a detailed account of their travels, making many observations on the nature of Maya civilization that proved remarkably prescient. He correctly surmised that Maya writing contained detailed dynastic and historical accounts, and rejected the prevailing notion that Mesoamerican civilizations were descended from Egyptian or other Old World societies, declaring the mysterious ruins "a spectacle of a people skilled in architecture, sculpture, and possessing the culture and refinement attendant upon those, not derived from the Old World, but originating and growing here without models or masters like the plants and fruits of the soil, indigenous." Meanwhile, Catherwood made incredibly precise drawings of numerous structures, monuments, hieroglyphs, and scenes of peasant life. (Though they've been widely reprinted, you can see a rare collection of original Catherwood prints in Mérida, at the highly recommended museum-gallery Casa Catherwood.)

Stephens and Catherwood published their work in two volumes, both of which were instant sensations in the United States and Europe, awakening immense interest in ancient Maya civilization. Their books now are condensed into a single, very readable volume, *Incidents of Travel in Yucatán* (Hard Press, 2007), available in English and in many bookstores in the Yucatán. It is a fascinating read, not only for the historical value but also as a backdrop for your own travels throughout the region.

phase consisted of simply filling in the center portion of the original palace to create a base for a new and loftier temple on top. In the process, the builders created a vaulted passageway and inner chamber, in which a series of intriguing frescoes were housed; unfortunately, you're not allowed to climb onto the platform to see them. The upper temple (also off-limits) displays Central Mexican influence, including snakelike columns similar to those found at Chichén Itzá and grimacing Toltec masks on the corners. Above the center door is an image of the Descending God. Archaeologists believe a stone block at the top of the stairs may have been used for sacrifices.

Temple of the Frescoes

Though quite small, the Temple of the Frescoes is considered one of Tulum's most archaeologically significant structures. The name owes to the fading but remarkably detailed paintings on the structure's inner walls. In shades of blue, gray, and black, they depict various deities, including Chaac (the god of rain) and Ixchel (the goddess of the moon and fertility), along with a profusion of symbolic imagery, including corn and flowers. On the temple's two facades are carved figures with elaborate headdresses and yet another image of the Descending God. The large grim-faced masks on the temple's corners are believed to represent Izamná, the Maya creator god.

Halach Uinic and the Great Palace

In front of El Castillo are the remains of two

palatial structures: the House of the Halach Uinic and the Great Palace (also known as the House of the Columns). Halach Uinic is a Yucatec Maya term for king or ruler, and this structure seems to have been an elaborate shrine dedicated to Tulum's enigmatic Descending God. The building is severely deteriorated, but what remains suggests its facade was highly ornamented, perhaps even painted blue and red. Next door is the Great Palace, which likely served as residential quarters for Tulum's royal court.

Practicalities

Tulum's massive parking lot and strip-mall-like visitors complex ought to clue you in to the number of tourists that pass through here every day. (Did we mention to get here early?) If this is your first visit to a Maya ruin, don't be turned off by all the hubbub. Tulum is unique for its excessive and obnoxious commercialization; most sites have just a ticket booth and restrooms.

You'll find a small museum and bookshop amid innumerable souvenir shops and fast-food restaurants. The actual entrance and ticket booth are about one kilometer (0.6 mile) from the visitors center; it's a flat, mild walk, but there are also **trolleys** that ferry guests back and forth for US$2 per person round-trip (kids under 10 ride free).

Getting There

The Tulum archaeological zone is a kilometer (0.6 mile) north of Tulum Pueblo on Highway 307. There are two entrances off the highway; the one farther south is newer and better, leading directly to the main parking lot (parking US$6). Arriving by bus or *combi*, be sure to ask the driver to let you off at *las ruinas* (the ruins) as opposed to the town. To return, flag down a bus or *combi* on the highway.

The ruins also can be accessed by foot from Tulum's beach road—from the northernmost spot in the Zona Hotelera, it's about a 500-meter (0.3 mile) walk to the entrance.

BEACHES AND CENOTES
Northern Beaches

The road from Tulum Pueblo hits the coast near the upper end of the Zona Hotelera, which stretches from the archaeological zone down to the entrance of the Sian Ka'an reserve, almost exactly 10 kilometers (6 miles). The area north of the Tulum/Zona Hotelera junction has two easy-to-reach beach areas that are ideal for people staying in town. There is plenty of open space to lay out your own towel as well as a handful of beach clubs if you're looking for lounge chairs and food services.

Playa El Paraíso (Carr. Tulum-Punta Allen, 2 kilometers/1.2 miles north of junction, cell tel. 984/113-7089, www. elparaisohoteltulum.com, 10am-6pm daily) is the most popular beach club on the north end of Tulum. Once little more than a bar and some hammocks, it has morphed into a bustling expanse of lounge chairs, beach beds, and umbrellas (US$10-20/day), with waiters weaving between them and the full restaurant and beach bar. It's busy but still scenic and relaxing.

Directly north of Playa El Paraíso is **Playa Mar Caribe** (Carr. Tulum-Punta Allen, 2.3 kilometers/1.4 miles north of junction), named after the rustic bungalows that have long fronted this portion of beach. Broad and unspoiled, this is a great place to lay out your towel on the soft white sand, which you share with a picturesque array of moored fishing boats. There are few services here—mostly beachfront kiosks—so be sure to bring snacks and plenty of water.

South of Playa El Paraíso, **Pocna Beach Club** (Carr. Tulum-Punta Allen, 1.6 kilometers/1 mile north of junction, cell tel. 984/154-1825, 8am-11pm daily) fronts a quiet stretch of beach with lots of beach beds for lounging (US$25 per four people). Get here early to stake out a spot and to enjoy the all-you-can eat breakfast buffet (US$8 pp) with loads of fresh fruit, breads, freshly squeezed OJ, and, almost best of all, bottomless coffee. There's free parking for clients.

★ Southern Beaches

Tulum's very best beaches—thick white sand, turquoise-blue water, gently bending palm trees—are toward the southern end of the Zona Hotelera. Not surprisingly, Tulum's finest hotels are in the same area, and there are no official public access points. That said, hotels rarely raise an eyebrow at the occasional nonguest cutting through to reach the beach. You can also grab breakfast or lunch at one of the hotel restaurants and cut down to the beach afterward; in some cases, you can even use the lounge chairs.

Aimed at an older crowd, **Ana y José Beach Club** (Carr. Tulum-Punta Allen, 2.4 kilometers/1.5 miles south of junction, cell tel. 998/112-5229, 8am-6pm daily, free) is located about a kilometer (0.6 mile) north of the resort of the same name and is open to guests and nonguests alike. An airy, sand-floored dining area serves mostly seafood, including ceviche, shrimp cocktail, and grilled fish, at decent prices (US$8-14), and there is a full bar (US$3-10). Chaise lounges and four-poster beach beds (US$10-20/day) are arranged a bit too close together, but they are comfy and relaxing nonetheless.

Ziggy Beach (Carr. Tulum-Punta Allen, 3.5 kilometers/2.1 miles south of junction, cell tel. 984/871-1145, 9am-5pm daily, free) is a mellow beach club with rows of thick queen-size beach beds and lounge chairs plus hammocks strung from palm trees. They're free to use if you buy something from the restaurant-bar. (Drinks often come with a complimentary round of chips and salsa, too). The beach, as expected, is gorgeous. Service is personable and efficient.

A popular spot for weddings, **Ak'iin Beach Club** (Carr. Tulum-Punta Allen, 4 kilometers/2.4 miles south of junction, cell tel. 984/113-7293, www.akiintulum.com,

9am-5pm daily, free) is truly a beautiful place. A wood-plank walkway snakes through the leafy property before arriving at the white-sand beach. Along the way, guests pass the restaurant, a spacious high-roofed *palapa* structure with a solid menu of Mexican and international dishes (US$7-12). There's also a two-for-one happy hour 5pm-7pm most days. Like neighboring beach clubs, use of the comfy beach couches, beds, and chairs is complimentary with the purchase of pretty much anything on the menu.

Maxa Camp Beach Club (Carr. Tulum-Punta Allen, 3 kilometers/1.8 miles south of junction, tel. 984/180-7151, www.maxacamp.com, 8am-11pm daily, free) is a bohemian-chic beach club that's part of the Venado Azul glamping site (the expansive tents are on the north side of the property). Beach beds and huge cushions are set up on the sand, with gourmet Maya-inspired meals served in a rustic oceanfront restaurant. Driftwood art, flowing bolts of cloth, and dream catchers abound. Admission is free with purchase of food or drink.

★ Cenotes

Dos Ojos (Hwy. 307 Km 244, tel. 984/108-3312, www.parquedosojos.com, 8am-5pm daily), or "Two Eyes," is a reference to twin caverns that are the largest openings—but far from the only ones—into the labyrinthine river system that runs beneath the ground here. You can snorkel on your own (US$18 pp, US$6 pp snorkel gear), but you'll see a lot more on a guided snorkeling tour (US$30 pp, no reservations required). There is no limit to the amount of time guests can stay; many bring food and drinks and make a day of it (there are hammocks, lockers, and a restaurant on-site too). Visitors also can dive at Dos Ojos (US$29) but must bring their own equipment and guide; the two primary dive "lines" are technically cavern dives, ideal for those new to overhead environments. There are various other cenotes in the Dos Ojos system for much more challenging diving, including **The Pit** (US$29 pp), at 40 meters the deepest

1: House of the Cenote at the Tulum ruins; 2: one of Tulum's picture-perfect beaches; 3: taking a refreshing dip in a cenote; 4: swimming in Cenote Azul dive site and with a spectacular halocline. (Each cenote has a separate entrance fee, from US$29 to $50, which you should confirm with your dive shop.) A rental car will make visiting Dos Ojos more rewarding; the primary visitor area is 4 kilometers (2.5 miles) from the main highway down a dirt road, passing various cenotes along the way, while others lie beyond. Cash only.

One of the only cenotes in the Zona Hotelera that's open to the public, **Cenote Encantado** (aka Cenote Yax Chen, Carr. Tulum-Punta Allen Km 10.5, 8am-sunset) is a winding channel of cool, clear water with freshwater plants along the edges. Measuring about 300 meters (984 feet) in length, it's part of an intricate network of about 100 cenotes on the jungle side of Tulum. Three small hotels—Cabañas y Cenote Yaxchen, Cenote Encantado, and Hotel Maya Cabañas & Cenote—provide easy access (US$2.50 pp) and rent kayaks (US$5-9) and snorkel gear (US$5) to better explore it. Look for schools of tiny fish (and some say baby crocs) in the water as well as herons in the low-hanging trees.

Other favorite cenotes include **Zazil Ha, Car Wash, Gran Cenote,** and **Calavera Cenote** (all west of Tulum on the road to Cobá); **Cristal** and **Escondido** (Hwy. 307 just south of Tulum); **Casa Cenote** (at Tankah Tres); and **Cenote Cristalino, Jardín del Edén,** and **Cenote Azul** (Hwy. 307 just north of Xpu-Há). All can be visited on a tour or independently, and most have snorkel gear for rent (US$4-7). Most are on private or *ejido* (collective) land and charge admission fees, usually US$5-10. If you take a tour, ask if admission fees are included in the rate. Most cenotes are open 8am-5pm daily.

TOURS

Mexico Kan Tours (Av. Tulum between Orion and Centauro, tel. 984/688-5864, www.mexicokantours.com, 7am-10pm Mon.-Sat., 3pm-10pm Sun.) offers excellent excursions throughout the Riviera Maya—kayaking in Sian Ka'an Biosphere Reserve, snorkeling in cenotes, bird-watching and monkey tours, even inland trips to Chichén Itzá and Valladolid. Groups are small—often no more than three or four people—and the company focuses on sustainable travel like offering reusable canteens instead of disposable water bottles and encouraging the use of biodegradable sunblock. Guides are enthusiastic, knowledgeable, and fluent in English and Spanish. Private and custom tours are also offered.

Community Tours Sian Ka'an (Calle Osiris Sur near Calle Sol Ote, tel. 984/871-2202, www.siankaantours.org, 7am-7pm daily) is a co-op offering a variety of tours (US$75-109, 3-7 hours) to the Sian Ka'an Biosphere, a 1.3-million-acre reserve of coastal and mangrove forests and wetlands. Among the most popular outings are the "Muyil" route, which begins with a visit to the Muyil archaeological zone, followed by a boat tour of Muyil and Chunyaxche lagoons, including a chance to jump in and float down a long, mangrove-edged canal; "Mayaking" in Sian Ka'an, a bird- and animal-spotting tour by kayak through the lagoons and mangroves; and a "Chicle" tour, where you learn about the practice of tapping *chicle* (gum) trees, from Maya times to today, followed by a swim in the lagoon.

SPORTS AND RECREATION
Scuba Diving

The reef here is superb, but Tulum's diving claim to fame is the huge and easily accessible network of freshwater cenotes, caverns, and caves, offering truly one-of-a-kind dive environments. Divers with open-water certification can dive in cenotes (little or no overhead) and caverns (no more than 30 feet deep or 130 feet from an air pocket) without additional training. Full-cave diving requires advanced certification, which is available at many of Tulum's shops. If you haven't dived in a while, definitely warm up with some open-water dives before doing a cenote or cavern trip. Buoyancy control is especially important in such environments because of the roof above and the sediment below, diving is complicated by the fact that it's fresh water instead of salt water, and it entails gear you may not be accustomed to, namely thick wetsuits and a flashlight.

Prices for cenotes and caverns are fairly uniform from shop to shop: around US$90-160 for one tank or US$150-190 for two. Be sure to ask whether gear and admission to the cenotes are included. Shops also offer multi-dive packages, cave and cavern certification courses, and hotel packages. As always, choose a shop and guide you feel comfortable with, not necessarily the least expensive one.

If you plan on cave and cavern diving (or want to learn to do either), **Xibalba Dive Center** (Calle Andrómeda between Calles Libra and Geminis, tel. 984/871-2953, www.xibalbadivecenter.com, 9am-7pm daily) has an excellent record for safety and professionalism. It also has an on-site hotel with comfortable rooms, a small swimming pool, and space to dry, store, and repair gear. Good packages are available. Xibalba also fills its own tanks and offers free Nitrox to experienced clients. The shop's name, aptly enough, comes from the Yucatec Maya word for the underworld.

Koox Dive Center (Av. Tulum between Calles Beta and Osiris, tel. 984/141-5502, www.kooxdiving.com, 7:30am-9pm daily) is another reliable option for diving and snorkeling, on the reef and in cenotes.

La Calypso Dive Center (Calle Sagitario at Calle Osiris, cell tel. 984/106-8002, www.lacalypsodive.com, 8:30am-1pm daily) offers highly professional service with a deep nod to customer service.

In the Zona Hotelera, **Mexi-Divers** (Punta Piedra, Carr. Tulum-Punta Allen, 1.5 kilometers/0.9 mile south of junction, tel. 984/807-8805, www.mexidivers.com, 8am-7pm daily) is located opposite Zamas Hotel in the Punta Piedra area and has regularly scheduled snorkeling and diving trips, in the ocean and nearby cenotes.

Snorkeling

Like divers, snorkelers have an embarrassment of riches in Tulum, with great reef snorkeling and easy access to the eerie beauty of the area's many cenotes. **Dive shops in Tulum** offer snorkel trips of both sorts; prices vary considerably, so be sure to ask which and how many reefs or cenotes you'll visit, for how long, and what's included (gear, entrance fees, transport, snacks, etc.). Reef trips cost US$25-45 and visit 1-3 different spots, while cenote trips run US$75-99; snorkel gear can also be rented.

Kiteboarding

Mexican Caribbean Kitesurf (Ahau Tulum, Carr. Tulum-Punta Allen Km 4.4, tel. 984/168-1023, www.mexicancaribbeankitesurf.com, 9am-5:30pm daily) is a friendly shop with IKO-certified instructors and top-of-the-line equipment. Private and group (two people max) instruction is offered by the hour (US$40-50/hour group, US$60-80/hour private). Radio helmets also are provided so students and instructors can easily communicate on the water.

Morph Kiteboarding (Coco Limited Tulum, Carr. Tulum-Punta Allen Km 8, cell tel. 984/114-9524, www.morphkiteboarding.com, 9am-sunset daily) also offers classes to all levels of kiteboarders. Rates are for private classes, though group lessons can be arranged as well: US$240, US$390, and US$468 for three-, five-, and six-hour courses, respectively.

Stand-Up Paddling

Stand-up paddling, or "SUPing," is especially well suited to the calm, clear waters found in much of the Riviera Maya. You can see a surprising amount of sealife doing SUP instead of kayaking, thanks simply to the vantage point.

Pro Kite Tulum (Villa Las Estrellas, Carr. Tulum-Punta Allen Km 8, cell tel. 984/100-5878, www.prokitetulum.com, 9am-5pm daily) offers SUP tours to the Tulum ruins (US$65), a nearby lagoon (US$90), and the reef, including snorkeling (US$95). Instruction is also offered, starting with safety and theory on the beach, graduating to kneeling paddling, and then standing. Private classes are US$60 per hour, while groups of two or three start at US$45 per person per hour. Gear and refreshments are included. Rentals (US$20/hr, US$80/day) also are available. **Mexican Caribbean Kitesurf** (Ahau Tulum, Carr. Tulum-Punta Allen Km 4.4, tel. 984/168-1023, www.mexicancaribbeankitesurf.com, 9am-5:30pm daily) has similar offerings and price points.

A dreamy experience, **SUP Yoga Tulum** (cell tel. 984/134-9721, www.supyogatulum.com, 9am-3:30pm, US$100) offers yoga instruction while floating on paddleboards. The 1.5-hour class is held on a private lagoon or cenote, both in the Sian Ka'an Biosphere Reserve. Afterward, students are welcome to explore and paddle at their leisure. Transportation, post-class paddling, gear, and a light snack are included. No prior paddleboarding experience is required (but expect to get wet!).

Ecoparks

Built around a huge natural inlet, **Xel-Há** (Hwy. 307, 9 kilometers/5.6 miles north of Tulum, tel. 998/883-0524, toll-free U.S./Can. tel. 855/326-2610, www.xel-ha.com, 8:30am-6pm daily, US$90 adult all-inclusive, US$45 child under 12, child under 5 free) is all about water—being in and around it. Activities include snorkeling, tubing, aquatic zip lines, and, for an additional fee, interactive programs with dolphins, manatees, and stingrays. Although it doesn't compare to snorkeling on the reef, there's a fair number of fish darting about, and it makes for a fun, easy intro for children and beginners. Several buffet restaurants are available for breakfast and lunch. An open bar is included. Check the website for online deals and combo packages with sister parks Xcaret and Xplor.

Spas and Gyms

On the jungle side of the road, the luxurious **Yaan Wellness Energy Spa** (Carr. Tulum-Punta Allen Km 10, tel. 984/179-1530, www.yaanwellness.com, 9:30am-9pm daily) offers a wide range of spa services: massages, body treatments, facials, soaking baths—even energy healing and traditional *temascal* (pre-Hispanic sweat lodge) ceremonies. All treatments begin with a "Healing Water Circuit," which integrates purified cenote waters and includes leisurely stops in the sauna, steam room, and hot and cold massage pools. Most services run around US$175 per hour—pricey for sure, but totally worthwhile.

For some, stand-up paddling is a family affair.

Mayan Clay Spa (Carr. Tulum-Punta Allen Km 8.5, tel. 984/807-9376, www.mayanclayspa.com, 9am-6pm daily) offers a memorable and immensely relaxing spa experience that's especially popular with couples and groups. The 1-2-hour clay massages include a full body massage with silky-smooth clay, followed by a hot shower (or a dip in the ocean) and a classic oil massage. The bathhouse treatment lasts a full three hours, and includes a variety of skin-soothing treatments at the spa's jungle location. The leafy open-air setting is lovely, but privacy is not absolute (very Tulum-esque); full nudity is not required but definitely adds to the experience if you're comfortable with it. Leave valuables in your car or hotel, as there's no good place to stow them.

Tulum Jungle Gym (Carr. Tulum-Punta Allen Km 7.5, cell tel. 998/243-4533, www.tulumjunglegym.com, 8am-5pm daily) is certainly one of the more interesting gyms you're likely to encounter. Not only is it right on a gorgeous beach, but the equipment is fashioned from local products, like tree log bench presses and a rope-pull full of rocks. Hour-long classes include the "Jungle Gym Circuit," "Beach Body Bootcamp," and "Booty Bootcamp." All levels are welcome, and no reservations are needed.

Yoga

Yoga Shala Tulum (Carr. Tulum-Punta Allen Km 7.4, cell tel. 984/141-8116, www.yogashalatulum.com, 8:30am-6:30pm Mon.-Sat., 11am-6:30pm Sun.) offers a wide range of yoga instruction in its gorgeous open-air studio. Classes cost US$20 each or US$70 per week for unlimited classes. Look for it on the jungle side of the Zona Hotelera road, alongside its namesake hotel.

Tree Top Yoga Shala (tel. 984/179-1530, www.yaanwellness.com, US$20) offers drop-in yoga classes—vinyasa and hatha, mostly—in an open-air studio at the upscale Yaan Wellness Energy Spa (Carr. Tulum-Punta Allen Km 10). Classes are at 10am and 5pm every day; guided meditation also is offered at 9:15am on Tuesday, Thursday, and Saturday (45 min., US$15).

On the road between the beach and town, Tribal Yoga (Av. Cobá s/n, tel. 984/871-2508, www.tribaltulum.com, 8:30am-7:30pm Mon.-Sat., 10am-11:15am Sun.) is a welcoming studio with huge picture windows overlooking the jungle. Classes are led by a well-trained cadre of instructors and vary from yin to flow. The drop-in rate is US$15; 5- and 12-packs are available at a discount.

ENTERTAINMENT AND SHOPPING
Entertainment
ZONA HOTELERA

Papaya Playa Project (Carr. Tulum-Punta Allen, 1.5 kilometers/1 mile south of junction, cell tel. 984/116-3774, www.papayaplayaproject.com, hours vary) has a regular lineup of live musical acts, plus full-moon parties, bongo drum sessions, and an overall counterculture vibe. Saturday is the main night, but look for schedules online for upcoming events. Papaya Playa is actually a rustic-chic resort, hence all the *cabañas*, but is better known (and better liked, really) as a place to party. Most shows begin around 10pm; cover is US$5-15.

Capturing the essence of boho hipster, Maxa Camp Beach Club (Carr. Tulum-Punta Allen, 6.5 kilometers/4 miles south of junction, tel. 984/180-7151, www.maxacamp.com, 8am-11pm daily, free) is an earthy place with colorful cushions and hammocks, dream catchers, and huge driftwood sculptures. A beach club by day, Maxa transforms into a lounge by evening: movie nights, chilled-out barbecues, DJ dance parties, and general revelry rule.

The lounge bar at La Zebra (Carr. Tulum-Punta Allen, 4.8 kilometers/3 miles south of junction, cell tel. 984/124-0337, www.lazebratulum.com, 8am-10pm daily) serves up shots and mixed drinks, including its signature Zebra negroni, made with tequila and homemade orange and cinnamon bitters.

Most afternoons, a DJ spins acoustic tunes, keeping things chill.

The oceanfront bar at its namesake boutique resort, **Mezzanine** (Carr. Tulum-Punta Allen, 1.3 kilometers/0.8 mile north of junction, tel. 984/131-1596, www.mezzaninetulum.com) is a go-to spot on Friday nights, with cocktails prepped by a master mixologist and a hipster vibe to match.

Gitano (Carr. Tulum-Punta Allen, 3 kilometers/1.8 mile south of junction, tel. 984/745-9068, www.gitanotulum.mx, 6pm-midnight Mon.-Thurs., 6pm-3am Fri., 6pm-1am Sat.-Sun.) is a jungle restaurant-bar known for its mixologists, DJs, and dance floor. It's definitely a scene—down to the beautiful people inside and the velvet ropes keeping out the riffraff. That said, if you like mescal, can clean up nicely, and want to run with the "it" crowd, this is a great option. There's live music on Sunday, Wednesday, and Thursday.

IN TOWN

Just off the main drag, **El Batey** (Calle Centauro Sur between Av. Tulum and Calle Andromeda, tel. 984/745-4571, 8am-2am Mon.-Sat., 5pm-1am Sun.) is a welcoming and often packed bar featuring live jazz, blues, acoustic, and Mexican *bohemia* groups most nights starting at 7:30pm. There's a leafy courtyard in the back where bands set up, an artsy bar in front, and a VW Bug converted into a mojito bar (with drinks made with real sugarcane!).

Encanto Cantina (Av. Tulum between Calles Alfa and Jupiter, tel. 984/871-2019, 5pm-1am daily) is equal parts bar and restaurant, with great Mexican *lotería*-themed flourishes throughout. Snag a spot in the long front area, where the bar is located and the atmosphere is lively. (For meals, the rear garden is sublime—just be sure to bring bug spray.) Music varies from cool electronic jazz to classic rock and occasional live bands, and the staff are known to spontaneously break into dance. There's craft beer and a super-creative cocktail menu featuring fresh fruit and quality tequila and mescal.

The craft beer revolution has hit Tulum, and **Hermana República** (Calle Sol at Calle Centauro, tel. 999/405-1117, 1pm-11pm Mon.-Thurs., 1pm-midnight Fri.-Sat., 1pm-6pm Sun.) is ground zero. Pick from a variety of house brews, from a refreshing pilsner or German wheat to a vanilla porter or in-your-face IPA. Samplers, served on a wood tray cleverly formed in the shape of a hop cone, are a good option for the indecisive, and growlers are available if you can't get enough. Hip industrial-chic décor and tasty cantina-plus eats round out the experience.

Boheme Tulum (Calle Sol between Calles Alfa and Jupiter, U.S. tel. 617/669-8799, bohemetulum@gmail.com, 2pm-midnight Thurs.-Sat.) is an artsy multipurpose compound, housing a cool café-bar, artist workshops, a boutique hotel, and the studios of Radio Tulum. Evenings bring indie films, live music broadcasts with well-known DJs (aka great dance parties), and art show openings. Look online for upcoming events.

Shopping

Tulum's main drag is peppered with *artesanía* and knickknack shops. You'll find everything from T-shirts and magnets to high-end Maya replicas and custom-made jewelry. Consider window-shopping a bit—it won't take long to peruse most of the shops. A couple of standouts include:

Mexik (Av. Tulum between Calles Alfa and Jupiter, tel. 984/871-2136, 9am-9pm Mon.-Sat., 9am-7pm Sun.) has a large selection of quality folk art, from green copper suns to carved wooden angels and masks. Cool T-shirts, jewelry, cards, and more also are sold. There's a sister shop of the same name in the Zona Hotelera (Punta Piedra, Carr. Tulum-Punta Allen, 1 kilometer/0.6 mile south of junction, same hours).

Cabrón (Av. Tulum near Calle Acuario, cell tel. 984/144-4203, www.karaniart.com.mx, 10:30am-9:30pm daily) sells artful T-shirts that celebrate Mexican culture in tongue-in-cheek ways: a storm trooper mask decorated with Maya glyphs, a Batman logo with an ancient bat design, a Day of the Dead skull made from a flurry of flowers. T-shirts aren't cheap (US$18-25) but they are unique, making a great memento or gift.

FOOD

Zona Hotelera

Health food aficionados will need no convincing, but even skeptics may be converted at ★ **Raw Love Café** (Ahau Hotel, Carr. Tulum-Punta Allen, 7.5 kilometers/4.5 miles south of junction, cell tel. 984/130-2013, www.rawlovekitchen.com, 9am-6pm daily, US$4-9), a raw, vegan, organic, gluten-free, sugar-free restaurant. Steps from the beach, there's a great vibe here and a long menu: favorites include the living pizza, maki rolls, fruit smoothies and bowls, and coffee with coconut milk (made daily from fresh coconuts). Cash only.

At the fine-dining spot **Kitchen Table** (Carr. Tulum-Punta Allen, 1.5 kilometers/0.9 miles north of junction, cell tel. 984/188-4924, www.kitchentabletulum.com, 6pm-10pm daily, US$14-31) meals are made from mostly local ingredients and are prepped at a long table in plain view. Pan-fired octopus and the grilled deviled avocado appetizer are perennial favorites, as are cocktails like the tamarind margarita. You'll be ushered from the bar, to your table, to a separate dessert nook; the whole experience is impressive, albeit a bit precious, even for Tulum—come here for a sophisticated meal, not a family gathering or après-beach chill out.

Mexican and Japanese foods may not seem fusible, but the wizards at **Ukami** (Carr. Tulum-Punta Allen, 6.7 kilometers/4 miles south of junction, tel. 984/205-0709, www.ukamitulum.com, 4pm-midnight Wed.-Mon., US$12-20) make it work with items like tuna sashimi tostadas and miso tortilla soup. There's also a lot of straight-up great sushi and sashimi, plus noodle dishes, rice bowls, and more. The presentation is a bit overwrought—like nigiri connect-the-dots—but the flavors, service, and overall experience are superb.

Thai is the specialty at **Mezzanine** (Carr.

Tulum-Punta Allen, 1.3 kilometers/0.8 mile north of junction, cell tel. 984/124-0888, www.mezzaninetulum.com, 7:30am-10pm daily, US$8-26), one of Tulum's chicest hotel restaurants. Curries—red, green, sweet potato, pineapple—and house specialties like crispy-style whole fish and lemongrass soup are among the dishes served in a sleek dining area or on a shaded outdoor patio, both with fine sea views. A full bar—martinis are the thing to order here—and a DJ spinning cool tunes make this a place to linger.

La Zebra (Carr. Tulum-Punta Allen, 4.8 kilometers/3 miles south of junction, cell tel. 984/124-0337, www.lazebratulum.com, 8am-10pm daily, US$10-23) serves up classic Mexican dishes like *cochinita pibil*, chicken in mole sauce, and tamales. For lighter fare, check out the ceviche bar, with everything from fish and shrimp to octopus and tuna (there's even a vegan option). Tables are set up on a lovely beachfront patio and in a *palapa*-roofed dining area; at night, the long entry path is lit by lanterns. Every Tuesday and Friday, the "Chef's Table" tasting menu is offered to just eight diners, served in an intimate dining room set just off the kitchen.

In Town

★ **El Asadero** (Av. Satélite near Calle Sagitario, tel. 984/157-8998, 4:30pm-11pm Mon.-Sat., US$6-18) is the go-to steak house for locals and expats looking for a spectacular meal without breaking the bank. Meat, chicken, and yes, even veggies are grilled in the open kitchen, the flavorful smells wafting throughout the dining room and out to the street-side tables. Try the hearty taco plate with your choice of fillings, cooked to order. All meals come with crispy tortilla chips and a trio of homemade salsas.

An unexpected budget eatery, **Uno: Japanese Noodles** (Calle Jupiter near Av. Tulum, tel. 984/234-4394, 2pm-11pm Thurs.-Tues., US$4-6) is a hole-in-the-wall ramen place with just a handful of tables, inside and out. Big bowls of steaming noodle soup come topped with a hard-boiled egg, seaweed, and fresh seafood like shrimp, octopus, or fish; veggie, chicken, and pork options are also available. If it's too hot outside for soup, opt for one of the many sushi rolls or dumplings with a plate of lightly salted edamame.

Roraima Burgers Tulum (Calle Jupiter near Av. Tulum, cell tel. 984/142-8980, noon-11pm daily, US$5-7) is an appealing open-air eatery serving up a huge variety of burgers and *tortas* (Mexican sandwiches). All are made to order, and come with toppings like bacon, avocado, eggplant, and gouda or brie. Vegan and chicken options are available. Complete your order—and fill your belly—with an order of *papas rústicas* (hand-cut fries) and a freshly squeezed juice.

One of the best breakfast places in town, **Azafrán** (Av. Satélite near Calle Polar, cell tel. 984/129-6130, www.azafrantulum.com, 8am-2pm daily, US$5-11) serves up superb morning meals made with gourmet products: homemade bagels with prosciutto and brie, crepes stuffed with an assortment of fresh fruits, *chaya* omelets, and pâté platters with freshly baked bread. Organic coffee is a must, as is the fresh-squeezed orange juice. The only bummer is that this place gets crowded fast—come early to beat the morning rush.

Taquería El Carboncito (Av. Tulum between Calles Acuario and Jupiter, 6pm-2am Wed.-Mon., US$2-5) serves up sizzling tacos at plastic tables in the driveway of an auto shop that closes in the evening. It's a great place for a cheap, tasty meal, and popular with local families. If there aren't any free tables, cross the street to **Antojitos La Chiapaneca** (Av. Tulum at Jupiter, tel. 984/112-3249, 5:30pm-1am Tues.-Sun., US$2-5), a no-frills taco joint known for its *tacos al pastor* (pork tacos).

★ **Sabor de Mar** (Calle Jupiter at Av. Tulum, tel. 984/116-3187, 11am-9:30pm Tues.-Sun., US$5-10) is a classic Mexican street-side eatery with six or eight tables with vinyl tablecloths and bad lighting. But the seafood here is outstanding, and it's not uncommon to have to wait for a table (it's worth it). Lots of menu items come in towers—literally, food stacked

like a Greek column—with fish, shrimp, avocado, and cucumbers providing most of building material. It's a nice change from the hipster eateries on the beach, and incredibly cheap too.

La Barracuda (Av. Tulum near Calle Luna Norte, tel. 984/160-0325, noon-8pm daily, US$6-13) is another popular, no-frills seafood eatery with plastic tables and chairs. Ceviche and fish soup are the specialties, but the shrimp cocktail and made-to-order fish dishes are tough to resist. Come hungry—portions are generous.

For home-style Mexican cooking, head to **Don Cafeto** (Av. Tulum between Calles Centauro and Orion, tel. 984/871-2207, 7am-11pm daily, US$5-16), serving Mexican staples like mole and enchiladas, plus ceviche plates that are meals unto themselves. On a hot day, try a tall, cold *chayagra,* an uplifting blend of pineapple juice, lime juice, cucumber, and *chaya* (similar to spinach).

Sweets and Groceries

A classic Mexican bakery, **Pan del Carmen** (Av. Tulum near Calle Osiris, 6am-11pm daily, US$0.50-1.50) is a bustling shop offering everything from fresh rolls to chocolate-filled *cuernos* (croissants). Be sure to grab a metal tray and tongs to carry your selections.

La Reyna de Michoacan (Calle Alfa Sur at Calle Sol Ote, no phone, 7:30am-11pm, US$1.50-3) specializes in *paletas* (frozen ice pops), *helado* (ice cream), *aguas* (juices), and *licuados* (smoothies), all made with fresh fruits. There's a huge variety of flavors—from coconut and strawberry to guava and pineapple with chili. It's a perfect stop while strolling about town.

For a supermarket with the basics and then some, head to the **Chedraui** (Av. Cobá s/n, 7am-10pm daily), located between Tulum town and the Zona Hotelera; beyond fresh, dry, and canned food, you'll find a bakery, a beachwear and shoe section, and even home appliances.

On Sunday, check out the **Tianguis Orgánico y Natural** (central plaza,

10am-3pm), a farmers market featuring organic produce, artisanal products, and homeopathic medicines.

ACCOMMODATIONS

Chances are you've come to Tulum to stay in one of the famous beachside bungalow-type hotels. There are many to choose from, each slightly different but most sharing a laid-back atmosphere and terrific beaches. However, some travelers are surprised by just how rustic some of these accommodations are, even those charging hundreds of dollars per night. The root of the matter is that there are no power lines or freshwater wells serving the beach. Virtually all accommodations have salty water in the showers and sinks. Most (but not all) have fans, and electricity may be limited to nighttime hours only. Air-conditioning is available in only a handful of places. At the same time, some hotels use generators to power their restaurants and reception, so it's worth asking for a room away from the generator; nothing is a bigger killjoy than a diesel motor pounding outside your window when the point of coming here was to enjoy the peace and quiet.

If staying on the beach is out of your budget (join the club!), staying in town is a perfectly good alternative. The options have improved significantly, with a crop of new bed-and-breakfasts and boutique hotels to go along with a burgeoning number of hostels and budget digs. The beach is just a short drive or bike ride away, and prices for food, drinks, and laundry are much lower.

Zona Hotelera
UNDER US$100

Fronting a winding cenote, ★ **Cenote Encantado** (Carr. Tulum-Punta Allen Km 10.5, cell tel. 984/142-5930, www.cenoteencantado.com, US$25 pp tent) is, in some ways, a throwback to Tulum's beginnings: a haven for backpackers with boho spirit. The hotel is more like a camping village, with 17 tents set up around the leafy property. Each is set on a platform and has

a bed with sheets, a bedside table, lamp, fan (there's electricity 7:30pm-midnight), Wi-Fi (10am-midnight), even a rug. There's also a clean communal kitchen and a cozy wood-floor lounge for meditating, yoga classes (price varies), and just hanging out; both structures are breezy but enclosed with strong mosquito netting. Open-air showers and dry toilets round out the camping-plus experience. Admission to the cenote also is included; kayaks, paddleboards, and snorkeling equipment are available for rent.

Cabañas y Cenote Yaxchen (Carr. Tulum-Punta Allen Km 10.5, cell tel. 984/209-9837, US$50-70 s/d with shared bathroom) has eight simple *palapa*-roofed cabins on a palm-laden property. Each has a decent bed with mosquito netting, big screened windows, and electricity (5:30pm-2am only). There's also an open-air kitchen with a gas-operated fridge to keep your perishables kicking, as well as a comfortable lounge with Wi-Fi. Admission to Cenote Encantado (in the backyard) is included in the rate, as is use of kayaks.

Santa Fe (Carr. Tulum-Punta Allen, 2.5 kilometers/1.5 miles north of junction, tel. 984/136-5248, US$13 pp tent) is a beachfront restaurant (8am-6pm daily) that welcomes campers on its property. The facilities are very basic—wear your flip-flops in the shower—and there's no electricity after 10pm. (All the better to enjoy the night sky!)

US$100-200

One of the best deals in the hotel zone, **Las Palmas Maya** (Carr. Tulum-Punta Allen Km 8.5, tel. 984/213-1515, www.laspalmasmaya.com, US$130-155 s/d) has large, comfortable rooms and awesome showers (the heat and water pressure can't be beat!). The catch is that it doesn't have air-conditioning and it's on the jungle side of the road. That's a small price to pay, as fans keep the rooms perfectly cool and the beach is literally just steps away. There's also free coffee and a communal kitchen, and wonderful personalized service.

Ahau Tulum (Carr. Tulum-Punta Allen Km 4.4, tel. 984/231-1081, www.ahautulum.

Tulum Town and Zona Hotelera

To Cenote Cristal, Escondido, Muyil Archaeological Zone, Mahahual, and Chetumal

307

HOTEL DON DIEGO DE LA SELVA

JARDIN DE FRIDA

CHAN-CHEN

ZAZILHA

KUKULCAN

ACUARIO NORTE

AVENIDA TULUM

TAURO PTE

LUNA NORTE

PRIV LUNA NORTE

SATURNO NORTE

SECRET GARDEN

LA BARRACUDA

HOSPITAL DE TULUM

RORAIMA BURGERS TULUM

MERCURIO OTE

POSADA LUNA DEL SUR

BUS STATION

MEXIK

LA REYNA DE MICHOACAN

FARMACIA SIMILARES

ENCANTO CANTINA

CABRON

TAQUERIA EL CARBONCITO

SABOR DE MAR

BOHEME TULUM

UNO TULUM

SATURNO OTE

ARIES SUR

LEO SUR

JUPITER SUR

MERCURIO SUR

AEROCUTO

CENTRO DE SALUD TULUM

JAPANESE NOODLES

OMEGA

PLUTON SUR

NEPTUNO OTE

PRIV ALFA SUR

Central Plaza

OSIRIS SUR

BETA SUR

0   300 yds

0   300 m

Caribbean Sea

ZONA HOTELERA

ULTRAMAR SHUTTLE

UKAMI

MORPHI KITEBOARDING

MAXA CAMP BEACH CLUB

COCO TULUM

POSADA LAMAR

CABAÑAS LA LUNA

GITANO

ZIGGY BEACH

PRO KITE TULUM

YOKTE BIKES

YOGA SHALA TULUM

RAW LOVE CAFÉ/ AHAU TULUM/ MEXICAN CARIBBEAN KITESURF

TULUM JUNGLE GYM

AK'IIN BEACH CLUB

TITA TULUM

HOTEL NUEVA VIDA DE RAMIRO

LA ZEBRA

LAS PALMAS MAYA

MAYAN CLAY SPA

YAAN WELLNESS ENERGY SPA/ TREE TOP YOGA SHALA

Cenote Encantado

To Sian Ka'an, El Ultimo Maya, Sol Caribe, Mukan Resort, and Punta Allen

CABAÑAS Y CENOTE IXCHEN

CENOTE ENCANTADO

SUEÑOS TULUM

DOS CEIBAS

TULUM'S SOUTHERN BEACHES

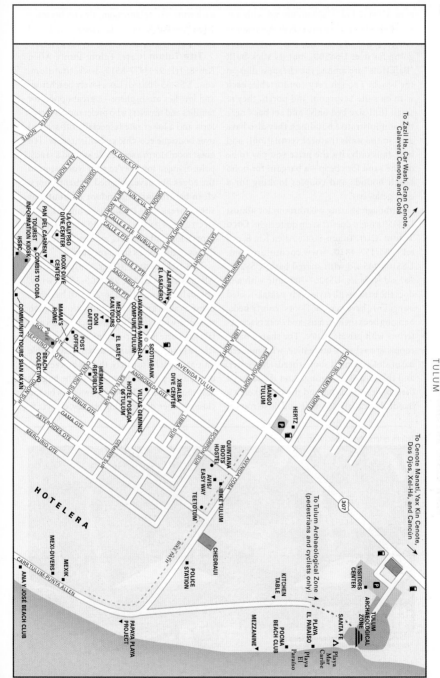

com, US$112 hut, US$246-308 s/d with a/c, US$490-504 suite with a/c) is by no means a budget place—it has stunning rooms, some going for over US$500—but its stick-built "Bali Huts" are among the cheapest digs on the beach. Though very comfortable, each with en suite bathroom and porch, they're small (full-size bed only) and set back near the administrative buildings; they also have gaps in the walls (natural ventilation!) and have fans only. It's the price you pay to be on the sand for cheap—a bargain for boho beach hounds and couples looking for a cozy getaway.

Although sharing a bathroom for almost US$150 a night doesn't seem quite right, **Coco Tulum** (Carr. Tulum-Punta Allen Km 8, cell tel. 984/157-4830, www.cocotulum.com, US$108-145 s/d with shared bath, US$218-267 s/d with a/c, US$267-305 suite with a/c) does the basics with style. Tidy *palapa*-roofed bungalows have cement floors, comfy beds, hanging bookshelves, fans, and sleek black exteriors with private patios. The shared bathrooms are actually quite nice, with modern basin sinks, rainfall showerheads, hot water, and thrice-daily cleaning. And if sharing a bathroom really is beyond the pale, there's a handful of cabañas as well as deluxe rooms,

each with private bathroom, air-conditioning (7pm-7am only), and stellar views. Wind- and solar-powered electricity is available 24 hours.

Tita Tulum (Carr. Tulum-Punta Allen Km 8, tel. 984/877-8513, www.titatulum.com, US$185-205 s/d) has a lovely beachfront and low-key atmosphere—a great option for families and travelers who prefer modest comforts and a lower rate (especially off-season) over boutique eco-chic embellishments. Ten guest rooms form a semicircle around a sandy, palm-fringed lot; they're a bit worn around the edges but have polished cement floors, clean bathrooms, and indoor and outdoor sitting areas, plus fans, Wi-Fi, and 24-hour electricity. Tita is a charming and attentive proprietor, and prepares authentic Mexican dishes in the hotel's small restaurant.

Posada Lamar (Carr. Tulum-Punta Allen Km 6, cell tel. 984/106-3682, www.posadalamar.com, US$156-219 s/d) has eight comfortable and artful bungalows, with salvaged-wood detailing and rich colors and fabrics. There is no air-conditioning, and electricity (wind and solar powered) is available only at night; fortunately, the sea breezes and one fan keep the units cool (and the bugs at bay) most nights. The bungalows are a bit too close together, diminishing privacy, especially

Tulum offers idyllic beachfront hotels.

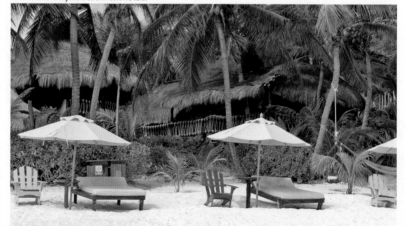

since you often need the windows and doors open, but the beach here is clean and beautiful, with plenty of chairs, beds, and *palapas.* Continental breakfast is included, served every morning on your private terrace.

OVER US$200

Nestled in a jungly plot facing a glorious stretch of beach, **Hotel Nueva Vida de Ramiro** (Carr. Tulum-Punta Allen Km 8.5, tel. 984/877-8512, www.tulumnv.com, US$151-160 s/d, US$211-296 bungalow, US$296-494 suite) has a variety of accommodations, from spacious suites with pillow-top mattresses and ocean views to simple thatch-roof bungalows, including some with kitchenette, and even an adults-only area. (The oldest rooms can be dark, however, and aren't a great value, despite being cheaper.) There's 24-hour clean power, though most units have just fans and sea breezes; a handful of units have air-conditioning 9pm-8am. Complimentary continental breakfast, including a bottomless cup of joe, is served across the street at the hotel's restaurant, Casa Banana.

Artful, spirit-minded decor is nothing new in Tulum, but ★ **Sueños Tulum** (Carr. Tulum-Punta Allen Km 8.5, cell tel. 984/119-3484, www.suenostulum.com, US$290-585 s/d with a/c) takes the theme further than most. Each of the hotel's 13 suites is decorated according to an essential force—Earth, Rain, Moon, Sun, Jungle—and there's Maya imagery inside and out. All units have ceiling fans and air-conditioning (8am-8pm only) and Wi-Fi, and most have ocean views. A small pool is a bonus, even with beaches as gorgeous as these. Located at the far southern end of the hotel zone, Sueños is quiet and isolated, even by Tulum's standards. Continental breakfast is included, as are bikes and flashlights.

Accommodations at the lovely **Cabañas La Luna** (Carr. Tulum-Punta Allen Km 6.5, cell tel. 984/146-7737, U.S. tel. 310/984-5484, www.cabanaslaluna.com, US$178-220 s/d, US$328-595 2- and 4-bedroom villas with a/c) range from cozy beachfront bungalows to spacious split-level villas, but share essential details like bright, artful décor, comfortable mattresses, high ceilings, fans, and 24-hour electricity (some with air-conditioning 7pm-8:30am). The beach is stunning, of course, and the property is big enough for a sense of isolation, yet within walking distance of shops and restaurants in Punta Piedra. There's a three-night minimum stay during the high season.

Dos Ceibas (Carr. Tulum-Punta Allen Km 10, tel. 984/198-5461, www.dosceibas.com, US$210-315 s/d, US$368 suite) has eight comfortable, if a bit bare-bones, units on a beautiful stretch of beach. Units range from a top-floor honeymoon suite to a hotel-type room with a view of the parking lot. Most have polished cement floors, whitewashed walls, and firm beds; all but the two breezy oceanfront rooms have ceiling fans (electricity available at night only). Note: There's only one electrical outlet per room and the Wi-Fi is hit or miss, so prepare to disconnect.

In Town
UNDER US$50

Stunning murals make **Quintana Roots Hostel** (Calle Sol near Av. Cobá, tel. 984/871-2426, www.quintanaroots.com, US$12 pp dorm with a/c, US$30 s/d with shared bathroom, US$40 s/d with a/c) stand out from the street. Inside, there's even more wall art but, more importantly, you'll find a friendly and mellow vibe and lots of common areas, including a well-equipped kitchen and game room. Sleeping units are spread out over a few floors: Dorms are sunny and clean and have bunk beds and quiet air-conditioning, while private rooms are modern and stylish, with details like slate-floor bathrooms and throw pillows. Full breakfast is included in the rate. Another bonus? The on-site dive shop, which offers good package deals.

Jardín de Frida (Av. Tulum near Calle Kukulcán, tel. 984/871-2816, www.fridastulum.com, US$10 pp dorm, US$12 pp dorm with a/c, US$35 s/d, US$50 s/d with a/c, US$65 s/d with kitchenette and a/c) is an artsy hotel with a jungly garden replete with mango and palm trees; a lounge decorated with tapestries, eclectic furnishings, artworks, and an intriguing library; a spacious common kitchen; and lots of outdoor spaces for hanging out. All the units have murals—from jungle scenes to modern art. Dorms have twin beds (no bunks here) and en suite bathrooms. Private rooms are different in style and size but are comfortable and homey. Continental breakfast and Wi-Fi are included in the rate.

Known for its elaborate daily breakfasts, **Mama's Home** (Calle Orion Sur between Calles Venus and Sol Ote., cell tel. 984/137-1393, US$16 pp dorm, US$19 pp dorm with a/c, US$67-80 s/d with a/c) is a popular spot for budget travelers. Two mixed dorms and eight private rooms—all with thick mattresses—open onto a colorful courtyard with Maya-inspired murals, hammocks, and long tables. There's a small communal kitchen plus a living room with a couple of computers for Internet access (there's also Wi-Fi). Weekly themed events like Mojito Demo, Flamenco Night, and Karaoke Night make it easy to meet other travelers.

US$50-100

Tucked into a quiet residential street, ★ **Secret Garden** (Calle Sagitario near Calle Acuario, tel. 984/157-8001, www. secretgardentulum.com, US$50-68 s/d with a/c, US$68 s/d with a/c and kitchenette) offers stylish, comfortable rooms at affordable rates (guests over age 16 only). Units vary in size and layout—some with kitchenettes, some with lofts—but all have artful décor and high-end amenities. Rooms open onto a long, leafy central garden with hammocks and low couches, perfect for relaxing day or night. Service is outstanding, and purified water, fruit, and baked goods are offered daily.

Mango Tulum (Calle Polar Pte. near Av. Cobá, tel. 984/169-9097, www.mangotulum. com, US$55-70 s/d with a/c, US$100 studio with a/c) is a pleasantly sparse hotel with whitewashed walls, polished cement floors, and a spacious garden with mature trees and a pool. Rooms are bright and airy and open onto the garden; some have king-size beds. The studio penthouse is especially spacious and has a fully equipped kitchen and TV. Fresh fruit, coffee, and tea are available in the morning. Mango is located behind the OXXO convenience store on Avenida Cobá.

Hotel Don Diego de la Selva (Av. Tulum s/n, cell tel. 984/114-9744, www. dondiegodelaselva.com, US$70 s/d, US$85-130 s/d with a/c) offers spacious rooms and bungalows with classy, understated decor, comfortable beds, and large glass doors opening onto a shady garden. There's a large pool, and the hotel restaurant serves good French-Mexican cuisine; half-board options are available. The only catch is the location, about a kilometer (0.6 mile) south of the plaza. The hotel rents bikes, but most guests find a rental car indispensable. Wi-Fi and continental breakfast are included.

Wearing many hats, **Boheme Tulum** (Calle Sol between Calles Alfa and Jupiter, U.S. tel. 617/669-8799, bohemetulum@gmail. com, US$62-120 s/d with a/c) is a hipster cultural center and home to Radio Tulum. It's also a boutique hotel with four gorgeous and well-equipped rooms. Each varies in size and décor but has a shabby-chic feel that integrates polished cement, antiques, modern art, and details like a hanging desk and a live tree in the shower (really). There's also a pool and gourmet café on-site. Before booking be sure to ask about the events schedule; some can go until the wee hours of the night.

OVER US$100

Posada Luna del Sur (Calle Luna Sur near Av. Tulum, tel. 984/182-9696, www. posadalunadelsur.com, US$110 s/d with a/c) has compact but pleasant rooms, with whitewashed walls, comfortable beds (king or two twins), and small terraces overlooking a leafy garden. A full à la carte breakfast is included in the rate; it's served in a pleasant rooftop lounge that's a great evening hangout. Service is friendly and accommodating.

On the road to the beach, **Teetotum** (Av. Cobá Sur s/n, cell tel. 984/143-8956, www.

hotelteetotum.com, US$135 s/d with a/c) has a handful of minimalist rooms—ceramic basin sinks, low bed stands—and artful decor throughout, including playful murals in the dining room. All rooms have air-conditioning and Wi-Fi but no TV or telephone. Guests enjoy free continental breakfast and bike rentals, as well as a lovely plunge pool and rooftop sun beds. The on-site restaurant serves a little of everything, from hummus plates to bacon cheeseburgers, with an equally varied (and enticing) drink menu.

A long, thin pool winds its way through **Hotel Posada 06 Tulum** (Calle Andromeda near Calle Geminis, tel. 984/160-0428, www.posada06tulum.com, US$100-130 s/d with a/c), a small hotel in the quiet part of town. Rooms feel fresh and airy, with adobe walls, muted colors, and simple décor; all have small private balconies or patios. The grounds and common areas are equally welcoming and well maintained. Full breakfast is included in the rate and is served at its street-front café. Adults only.

★ **Villas Geminis** (Calle Andrómeda at Calle Gemini, tel. 984/140-4501, www.villasgeminis.com, US$155 s/d with a/c, US$195 studio with a/c, US$185 1-bedroom condo with a/c, US$225 2-bedroom condo with a/c) has spacious rooms, penthouse studios, and one- and two-bedroom condos with modern kitchens and private terraces. All are simple but elegant in décor; some have luxurious outdoor soaking tubs. There's 24-hour security and daily maid service, and the owners and staff are friendly and attentive. The interior courtyard has a nice swimming pool surrounded by a lush garden. Complimentary bicycles are available for guests.

INFORMATION AND SERVICES
Tourist Information
A **tourist information kiosk** (no phone, 9am-4pm Mon.-Fri., 10am-3pm Sat.-Sun.) is located on the central plaza, across from the HSBC bank. The chief attendant is quite knowledgeable, her teenage disciples less so.

You often can glean useful information from the stacks of brochures here. The website www.todotulum.com also offers good information on current goings-on and offerings in Tulum.

Emergency Services
Hospital de Tulum (Av. Tulum between Calles Luna and Acuario Norte, tel. 984/871-2271, www.hospitaldetulum.com, 24 hours daily) is a small private hospital offering emergency and preventative services; it has a bilingual staff. For minor medical issues, Tulum's local clinic, **Centro de Salud Tulum** (Calle Andrómeda between Calles Jupiter and Alfa, tel. 984/871-2050, 24 hours), is a decent option. For serious health problems, head to Cancún.

Farmacia Similares (Av. Tulum at Calle Jupiter Sur, tel. 984/871-2736) is open 9am-11pm Monday-Saturday and 9am-9pm Sunday; it also has a doctor on staff for simple consultations 9am-9pm Monday-Saturday and 9am-3pm Sunday.

The **police** (toll-free tel. 066, 24 hours) share a large station with the fire department, about two kilometers (1.2 miles) from Tulum Pueblo on the road to the Zona Hotelera.

Money
HSBC (Av. Tulum at Calle Alfa, 9am-5pm Mon.-Fri.) has reliable ATMs and will change foreign cash and AmEx travelers checks. If there's a line, **ScotiaBank** (Av. Tulum at Calle Satélite, 8:30am-4pm Mon.-Fri.) is another good option.

Media and Communications
Tulum's **post office** (Calle Orion Sur at Calle Andrómeda Sur) is open 8am-4pm Monday-Friday and 9am-1pm Saturday.

Most hotels offer free Wi-Fi for guests; in the Zona Hotelera, many only offer Wi-Fi in the reception or restaurant areas. In town, **Compunet Tulum** (Av. Tulum near Av. Satélite, 8:30am-7:30pm Sun.-Fri., 8am-2pm Sat., US$1/hour) has flat-screen computers and killer air-conditioning.

Tulum Bus Schedule

Departures from the **bus terminal** (Av. Tulum between Calles Alfa and Jupiter, tel. 984/871-2122) include:

DESTINATION	PRICE	DURATION	SCHEDULE*
Cancún	US$4.50-11	2.5 hrs	every 15-60 mins 3:45am-10pm
Cancún International Airport	US$12.50	2 hrs	five departures 7:10am-3pm
Chetumal	US$8-19	3.5-4 hrs	every 60-90 mins 8:30am-11:50pm
Chichén Itzá	US$7.50	3 hrs	9am and 2:45pm
Cobá	US$3-4.50	45-60 mins	10:10am and 11:35am
Mahahual	US$7.50-10	3 hrs	8:55am and 6:50pm
Mérida	US$8.50-17	4 hrs	nine departures 2:30am-9:40pm
Playa del Carmen	US$2-5.50	1 hr	every 15-90 mins 12:20am-9:55pm
Valladolid	US$5-7	1.5-2hrs	every 30-90 mins 2:30am-10:20pm

*Schedules are subject to change.

Laundry and Storage

Tucked into an alley just off the main drag, **Lavandería Mandala** (Av. Tulum near Av. Satélite, 8am-9pm daily) charges US$1.25 per kilo (2.2 pounds) with a three-kilo (6.6-pound) minimum. Next-day service only.

The **bus terminal** (Av. Tulum between Calles Alfa and Jupiter, tel. 984/871-2122, 24 hours) has luggage storage for US$0.50-1.25 per hour or US$5 per 8-24 hours, depending on the size of the bag.

GETTING THERE
Bus

Tulum's **bus terminal** (Av. Tulum between Calles Alfa and Jupiter, tel. 984/871-2122) is at the south end of town, a block from the main plaza.

Combi

Combis are white collective vans that zip between Tulum and Playa del Carmen all day, every day (US$2.25, 1 hour, every 10 minutes 5am-10pm). They leave more frequently than buses and are handier for intermediate stops, such as Dos Ojos, Akumal, and Xpu-Há. Flag them down anywhere on Avenida Tulum or Highway 307.

Combis also go to Cobá (US$3.50, 1 hour), stopping at cenotes along the way. They leave hourly 8am-6pm Monday-Saturday and every two hours on Sunday. Look for the stop on Avenida Tulum at Calle Osiris Norte. You can also catch them at the intersection of Highway 307 and the Cobá/Zona Hotelera road.

Ferry Shuttle

Ultramar (Carr. Tulum-Punta Allen Km 6.7, tel. 998/881-5898, www.ultramarferry.com) offers shuttle service to its ferry terminal in Playa del Carmen for boats headed to

Cozumel (US$42 pp), and to the Gran Puerto ferry terminal in Cancún for ferries headed to Isla Mujeres (US$62). Shuttles leave at 7:45am, 9:30am, and 6pm daily. The fare includes round-trip shuttle service as well as the round-trip ferry ticket.

Car

Highway 307 passes right through the middle of Tulum Pueblo, where it is referred to as Avenida Tulum. Coming south from Cancún or Playa del Carmen, you'll first pass the entrance to Tulum archaeological site, on your left. A kilometer and a half later (1 mile) you'll reach a large intersection, where you can turn left (east) toward the beach and Zona Hotelera, or right (west) toward Cobá. Continuing straight ahead takes you into Tulum Pueblo, then onward to the Costa Maya.

GETTING AROUND
Bicycle

A bike can be very handy, especially for getting to or from the beach, or anywhere along the now-paved road through the Zona Hotelera.

In the Zona Hotelera, check out **Yokte Bikes** (Carr. Tulum-Punta Allen Km 7.5, cell tel. 984/145-4061, 9am-6pm daily), which rents beach cruisers for US$10 per 24 hours, including helmet, lock, and safety vest. Drop-off and pickup at your hotel is included.

In town, **iBike Tulum** (Av. Cobá Sur at Calle Sol, tel. 984/802-5518, www.ibiketulum. com, 8am-5:30pm Mon.-Sat.) rents a variety of bikes and trikes, including beach cruisers and mountain bikes (US$10-13 per 24 hours), most in top condition. All come with helmet, lock, lights, and roadside assistance. Accident insurance is included.

Beach Shuttle

There is a local *colectivo* (US$0.75) labeled **"Cabañas"** that goes from Tulum town to the arch at the southern end of the Zona Hotelera and back again, every 20-30 minutes 6am-8pm. Another *colectivo* (US$1), labeled **"Ruínas,"** goes from town to the northern end of the Zona Hotelera at 8am, 8:30am, 5:30pm, and 6pm. Both routes start at the corner of a little playground at Calle Sol Ote and Orion Sur. You also can catch both *colectivos* along Avenida Tulum and on the road to and along the beach. Schedules often change, so be sure to confirm the departure and return times.

Car

A car can be very useful in Tulum, especially in the Zona Hotelera, even if you don't plan on using it every day. Renting a car from the airport in Cancún is the easiest and most affordable option for most travelers, especially if you book online and in advance. In Tulum, agencies include **Easy Way** (Av. Cobá near Calle Sol, toll-free Mex. tel. 800/327-9929, toll-free U.S./Can. tel. 877/640-3279, www. easywayrentacar.com), **Avis** (Av. Cobá Sur at Calle Sol Ote, cell tel. 984/871-2937, www.avis. com), and **Hertz** (Hwy. 307 at Av. Cobá, toll-free Mex. tel. 800/709-5000, www.hertz.com).

Taxi

Taxis are plentiful, and fares run about US$3 in town and US$8-12 to get to the Zona Hotelera. In the Zona Hotelera, there's an unofficial taxi stand in Punta Piedra and across from the Mezzanine hotel; rates are roughly the same within the Zona Hotelera or back into Tulum Pueblo. From either area, a ride to Tulum ruins costs about US$5.

Cobá

The Maya ruins of Cobá make an excellent complement—or even alternative—to the memorable but vastly overcrowded ruins at Tulum. Cobá doesn't have Tulum's stunning Caribbean view and beach, but its structures are much larger and more ornate—in fact, Cobá's main pyramid is the second tallest in the Yucatán Peninsula, and it's one of few you are still allowed to climb. The ruins are surrounded by lakes and thick forest, making it a great place to see birds, butterflies, and tropical flora.

★ COBÁ ARCHAEOLOGICAL ZONE

Cobá (8am-5pm daily, US$3.50) is especially notable for its complex system of *sacbeob,* or raised stone causeways, that connected it to other Maya cities near and far. (The term *sacbeob*—whose singular form is *sacbé*—means white roads.) Dozens of such roads crisscross the Yucatán Peninsula, but Cobá has more than any other ancient city, underscoring its status as a commercial, political, and military hub. One road extends in an almost perfectly straight line from the base of Cobá's principal pyramid to the town of Yaxuna, more than 100 kilometers (62 miles) away—no small feat considering a typical *sacbé* was 1-2 meters (3.3-6.6 feet) high and about 4.5 meters (15 feet) wide, and covered in white mortar. In Cobá, some roads were even bigger—10 meters (32.8 feet) across. In fact, archaeologists have uncovered a massive stone cylinder believed to have been used to flatten the broad roadbeds.

History

Cobá was settled as early as 100 BC around a collection of small lagoons; it's a logical and privileged location, as the Yucatán Peninsula is virtually devoid of rivers, lakes, or any other aboveground water. Cobá developed into an important trading hub, and in its early existence had a particularly close connection with the Petén region of present-day Guatemala. That relationship would later fade as Cobá grew more intertwined with coastal cities like Tulum, but Petén influence is obvious in Cobá's high, steep structures, which are reminiscent of those in Tikal. At its peak, around AD 600-800, Cobá was the largest urban center in the northern lowlands, with some 40,000 residents and over 6,000 structures spread over 50 square kilometers (31 square miles). The city controlled most of the northeastern portion of the Yucatán Peninsula during the same period before being toppled by the Itzás of Chichén Itzá following a protracted war in the mid-800s. Following a widespread Maya collapse—of which the fall of Cobá was not the cause, though perhaps an early warning sign—the great city was all but abandoned, save as a pilgrimage and ceremonial site for the ascendant Itzás. It was briefly reinhabited in the 12th century, when a few new structures were added, but had been abandoned again, and covered in a blanket of vegetation, by the time of the Spanish conquest.

Cobá Group

Passing through the entry gate, the first group of ruins you encounter is the Cobá Group, a collection of over 50 structures and the oldest part of the ancient city. Many of Cobá's *sacbeob* initiate here. The primary structure, **La Iglesia** (The Church), rises 22.5 meters (74 feet) from a low platform, making it Cobá's second-highest pyramid. The structure consists of nine platforms stacked atop one another and notable for their round corners. Built in numerous phases beginning in the Early Classic era, La Iglesia is far more reminiscent of Tikal and other Petén-area

Cobá Archaeological Zone

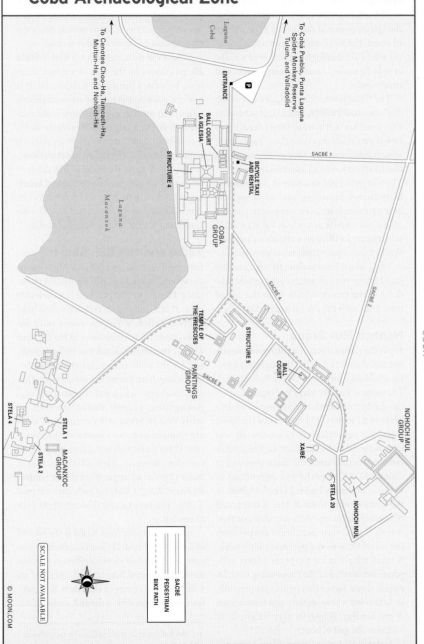

Laguna
Cobá

To Cobá Pueblo, Punta Laguna
Spider Monkey Reserve,
Tulum, and Valladolid

ENTRANCE

To Cenotes Choo-Ha, Tamcach-Ha,
Multun-Ha, and Nohoch-Ha

SACBÉ 1

BALL COURT
LA IGLESIA

STRUCTURE 4

BICYCLE TAXI
AND RENTAL

Laguna
Macanxok

COBÁ
GROUP

SACBÉ 4

SACBÉ 2

TEMPLE OF
THE FRESCOES

STRUCTURE 5

BALL
COURT

PAINTINGS
GROUP

SACBÉ 8

NOHOCH MUL
GROUP

STELA 4

STELA 1

MACANXOC
GROUP

STELA 2

XAIBÉ

STELA 20

NOHOCH MUL

SACBÉ
PEDESTRIAN
BIKE PATH

SCALE NOT AVAILABLE

© MOON.COM

structures than it is of the long palaces and elaborate facades typical of Puuc and Chenes sites. Visitors are no longer allowed to climb the Iglesia pyramid due to the poor state of its stairs, but it is crowned with a small temple where archaeologists discovered a cache of jade figurines, ceramic vases, pearls, and conch shells.

The Cobá Group also includes one of the city's two **ball courts,** and a large acropolis-like complex with wide stairs leading to raised patios. At one time these patios were connected, forming a long gallery of rooms that likely served as an administrative center. The best-preserved structure in this complex, **Structure 4,** has a long, vaulted passageway beneath its main staircase; the precise purpose of this passageway is unclear, but it's a common feature in Cobá and affords a close look at how a so-called Maya arch is constructed.

The Cobá Group is directly opposite the stand where you can rent bicycles or hire bike taxis. Many travelers leave it for the end of their visit, after they've turned in their bikes.

Nohoch Mul Group

From the Cobá Group, the path winds nearly two kilometers (1.2 miles) through dense forest to Cobá's other main group, Nohoch Mul. The name is Yucatec Maya for "big mound"—the group's namesake pyramid rises an impressive 42 meters (138 feet) above the forest floor, the equivalent of 12 stories. (It was long believed to be the Yucatán Peninsula's tallest structure until the main pyramid at Calakmul in Campeche was determined to be some 10 meters higher.) Like La Iglesia in the Cobá Group, Nohoch Mul is composed of several platforms with rounded corners. A long central staircase climbs steeply from the forest floor to the pyramid's lofty peak. A small temple at the top bears a fairly well-preserved carving of the Descending God, an upside-down figure that figures prominently at Tulum but whose identity and significance is still unclear. (Theories vary widely, from Venus to the god of bees.)

Nohoch Mul is one of few Maya pyramids

that visitors are still allowed to climb, and the view from the top is impressive—a flat green forest spreading almost uninterrupted in every direction. A rope running down the stairs makes going up and down easier.

Where the path hits Nohoch Mul is **Stela 20,** positioned on the steps of a minor structure, beneath a protective *palapa* roof. It is one of Cobá's best-preserved stelae, depicting a figure in an elaborate costume and headdress, holding a large ornate scepter in his arms—both signifying that he is an *ahau,* or high lord or ruler. The figure, as yet unidentified, is standing on the backs of two slaves or captives, with another two bound and kneeling at his feet. Stela 20 is also notable for the date inscribed on it—November 30, 780—the latest Long Count date yet found in Cobá.

Xaibé and the Ball Court

Between the Cobá and Nohoch Mul Groups are several smaller but still significant structures. Closest to Nohoch Mul is a curiously conical structure that archaeologists have dubbed **Xaibé,** a Yucatec Maya word for "crossroads." The name owes to the fact that it's near the intersection of four major *sacbeob,* and for the same reason, archaeologists believe it may have served as a watchtower. That said, its unique design and imposing size suggest a grander purpose. Round structures are fairly rare in Maya architecture, and most are thought to be astronomical observatories; there's no evidence Xaibé served that function, however, particularly because it lacks any sort of upper platform or temple. Be aware that the walking path does not pass Xaibé—you have to take the longer bike path to reach it.

A short distance from Xaibé is the second of Cobá's **ball courts.** Both courts have imagery of death and sacrifice, though they are more pronounced here: a skull inscribed on a stone in the center of the court, a decapitated jaguar on a disk at the end, and symbols

1: Cobá ball court; **2:** touring Cobá on two wheels and on foot

of Venus (which represented death and war) inscribed on the two scoring rings. This ball court also had a huge plaque implanted on one of its slopes, with over 70 glyphs and dated AD 465; the plaque in place today is a replica, but the original is under a *palapa* covering at one end of the court, allowing visitors to examine it more closely.

Paintings Group

The Paintings Group is a collection of five platforms encircling a large plaza. The temples here were among the last to be constructed in Cobá and pertain to the latest period of occupation, roughly AD 1100-1450. The group's name comes from paintings that once lined the walls, though very little color is visible now, unfortunately. Traces of blue and red can be seen in the upper room of the **Temple of the Frescoes,** the group's largest structure, but you aren't allowed to climb up to get a closer look.

Although centrally located, the Paintings Group is easy to miss on your way between the more outlying pyramids and groups. Look for a sign for **Structure 5,** where you can leave your bike (if you have one) and walk into the group's main area.

Macanxoc Group

From the Paintings Group, the path continues southeasterly for about a kilometer (0.6 mile) to the Macanxoc Group. Numerous stelae have been found here, indicating it was a place of great ceremonial significance. The most famous of these monuments is **Stela 1,** aka the Macanxoc Stela. It depicts a scene from the Maya creation myth—"the hearth stone appears"—along with a Long Count date referring to a cycle ending the equivalent of 41.9 billion, billion, billion years in the future. It is the most distant Long Count date known to have been conceived and recorded by the ancient Maya. Stela 1 also has reference to December 21, 2012, when the Maya Long Count completed its first Great Cycle, equivalent to 5,125 years. Despite widespread reports to the contrary, there is no known evidence, at Cobá or anywhere, that the Maya believed (much less predicted) that the world would end on that date.

Flora and Fauna

The name Cobá ("Water Stirred by the Wind" in Maya) is surely a reference to the group of shallow lagoons here (Cobá, Macanxoc, Xkanha, and Sacakal). The archaeological site and the surrounding wetlands and forest are rich with birdlife—herons, egrets, motmot, parrots, and the occasional toucan are not uncommon. Arrive early to see the most birds—at the very least you'll get an earful of their varied songs and cries. Later, as the temperature climbs, you'll start to see colorful butterflies, including the large, deep-blue morphidae and the bright yellow-orange barred sulphur.

If you look on the ground, you'll almost certainly see long lines of leaf-cutter ants. One column carries freshly cut leaves to the burrow, and the other marches in the opposite direction, empty-jawed, returning for more. The vegetation decays in their nests, and the fungus that grows on the compost is an important staple of the ants' diet—a few scientists even claim that this makes leaf-cutter ants the world's second species of agriculturists. Only particular types of leaves will do, and the columns can be up to a kilometer (0.6 mile) long.

Practicalities

Cobá's main groups are quite spread apart, and visiting all of them adds up to several kilometers. Fortunately, you can rent a bicycle (US$2.50) or hire a *triciclo* (US$6 for 1 hour, US$10 for 2 hours) at a large stand a short distance past the entryway, opposite the Cobá Group. Whether you walk or ride, don't forget a water bottle, comfortable shoes, bug repellent, sunscreen, and a hat. Watch for signs and stay on the designated trails. Guide service is available—prices are not fixed but average US$40 per group (1.5 hours, up to 6 people). Parking at Cobá is US$2.50.

Cobá is not nearly as crowded as Tulum (and is much larger), but it's still a good idea

Deciphering the Glyphs

Maya glyphs

For years, scholars could not agree whether the fantastic inscriptions found on Maya stelae, codices, and temple walls were anything more than complex records of numbers and dates.

Mayanist and scholar Michael D. Coe's *Breaking the Maya Code* (Thames and Hudson, 2012) is a fascinating account of the decipherment of Maya hieroglyphics. Coe describes how, in 1952, reclusive Russian scholar Yuri Valentinovich Knorosov made a crucial breakthrough by showing that Maya writing did in fact convey spoken words. Using a rough alphabet recorded by Fray Diego de Landa (the 16th-century bishop who, ironically, is best known for having destroyed numerous Maya texts), Knorosov showed that ancient texts contain common Yucatec Maya words such as *cutz* (turkey) and *tzul* (dog).

But Knorosov's findings were met with staunch resistance by some of the field's most influential scholars, which delayed progress for decades. By the mid-1980s, however, decipherment picked up speed; one of many standouts from that era is David Stuart, the son of Maya experts, who went to Cobá with his parents at age eight and passed the time copying glyphs and learning Yucatec Maya words from local playmates. As a high school student he served as chief epigrapher on a groundbreaking exploration in Belize, and at age 18 he received a US$128,000 MacArthur Fellowship (aka "Genius Award") to, as he told Michael Coe, "play around with the glyphs" full-time.

Researchers now know that Maya writing is like most other hieroglyphic systems. What appears at first to be a single glyph can have up to four parts, and the same word can be expressed in pictorial, phonetic, or hybrid form. Depending on context, one symbol can have either a pictorial or phonetic role; likewise, a particular sound can be represented in more than one way. One of David Stuart's great insights was that for all its complexity, much of Maya glyphic writing is "just repetitive."

But how do scholars know what the symbols are meant to sound like in the first place? Some come from the Landa alphabet, others are suggested by the pictures that accompany many texts, still others from patterns derived by linguistic analyses of contemporary Maya languages. In some cases, it is simply a hunch that turns out to be right. If this seems like somewhat shaky scientific ground, it is—but not without a means of being proved.

Hundreds of glyphs have been deciphered, and most of the known Maya texts can be reliably translated. Some archaeologists lament, not unreasonably, that high-profile glyphic studies divert attention from research into the lives of everyday ancient Maya, who far outnumbered the nobility but are not at all represented in the inscriptions. That said, the effort has lent invaluable insight into Maya civilization, especially dynastic successions and religious beliefs.

to arrive as early as possible to beat the ever-growing crowds.

COBÁ PUEBLO

It's fair to say that the town of Cobá, a rather desultory little roadside community, has never regained the population or stature that it had as a Maya capital more than 1,000 years ago. Most travelers visit Cobá as a day trip from Tulum or Valladolid, or on a package tour from resorts on the coast. There are two decent hotels in town, used mostly by those who want to appreciate Cobá's rich birdlife, which means being at the gate right when the site opens at 8am; if you're lucky, the gatekeeper may even let you in early.

Sights

Cobá Pueblo itself doesn't have much in the way of sights—besides the ruins, of course—but a number of small eco-attractions have cropped up, all a short distance from town.

RESERVA DE MONOS ARAÑAS PUNTA LAGUNA

The **Punta Laguna Spider Monkey Reserve** (Otoch Ma'ax Yetel Kooh, cell tel. 985/107-9182, puntalagunamexico@gmail.com, 7:30am-5:30pm daily, US$10) is a federally protected forest that's home to various families of boisterous spider monkeys, as well as smaller groups of howler monkeys—it's estimated that there are up to 800 individual monkeys living in the reserve. There are also numerous bird species as well as coati, white-tailed deer, and even pumas. A short path winds through the reserve, passing a small unexcavated Maya ruin and a large lagoon with a lookout tower and pier where you can rent canoes (US$8.50). There's also a zip line and a place to rappel into a cenote (and climb out on a rope ladder), but it's typically reserved for large groups. Your best chance of spotting monkeys is by going in late afternoon, and by hiring one of the guides near the entrance (US$20, 2-4 people). The reserve (whose official name is Otoch Ma'ax Yetel Kooh, Yucatec Maya for "House of the

Spider Monkey and Puma") is operated by a local cooperative, whose members live in the nearby village and serve as guides; most speak at least some English. Be sure to wear good walking shoes and bring plenty of bug repellent. The reserve is located 18 kilometers (11 miles) north of Cobá, on the road toward Nuevo X'can.

★ CENOTES

If you have a car, a cluster of three well-maintained and well-run cenotes (no phone, 8am-5pm daily) are a great addition to a day spent at Cobá. **Choo-Ha, Tamcach-Ha,** and **Multun-Ha** are southwest of Cobá and are operated jointly (US$5/7/10 for 1/2/3 cenotes); a fourth cenote called **Nohoch-Ha** is a bit farther and requires a separate entrance fee (US$4). Each is slightly different—one has a high roof and platform for jumping, another is wide and low—but all are impressive enclosed chambers bristling with stalactites and filled with cool, crystalline water that's heaven on a hot day. Cement or wooden stairways lead down to the pools; showers and changing areas are available at Choo-Ha. To get there, continue past the Cobá ruins on the road to Tepich and follow the signs.

Food

Approaching town, **El Cocodrilo** (facing Laguna Cobá, tel. 984/137-5711, 8am-7pm daily, US$3-7) is a bustling restaurant with plastic tables and chairs on a small leafy plot facing the lagoon. Dishes are classic Mexican with some Yucatecan faves—*poc-chuc, panuchos, salbutes*—and a handful of sandwiches and tasty vegan options. The freshly squeezed juices and smoothies alone are worth a stop.

With a large raised patio overlooking the lagoon, **La Pirámide** (Calle Principal at Laguna Cobá, tel. 984/206-7018, 8am-5pm daily, US$6-15) is a nice place for breakfast or lunch après-ruins. The restaurant receives

1: Hotel Sac Be; **2:** Choo-Ha, an underground cenote made more accessible with interior lighting

a number of tour groups, and it often has a buffet set up (US$12); otherwise, the menu has grilled fish, chicken, and meat dishes as well as typical Mexican fare.

Accommodations

The simple **Hotel Sac Be** (Calle Principal, tel. 984/144-3006, www.hotelsacbe.com, US$28-33 s/d with a/c) has friendly service and spotless rooms with one or two beds, televisions, Wi-Fi, and a small desk. All have gleaming tile floors and colorful bedspreads. Guests get 10 percent off at the hotel's open-air restaurant; nab a seat on the 2nd floor for the best breeze.

Hacienda Cobá (Calle Principal s/n, tel. 55/5351-3798, www.haciendacoba.com, US$85-95 s/d with a/c) is a small and very pleasant colonial-style hotel, with just six rooms and a relaxing hands-off atmosphere. Rooms are large and airy, with either a king or two queen beds, and tidy bathrooms with basin sinks and walk-in showers. (Hot water is a bit spotty, however.) Its location near the traffic circle at the northeast entrance to town means you can be first at the ruins in the morning. Light continental breakfast is included.

Information and Services

Cobá has neither an official tourist office nor a health clinic. There also are no banks or ATMs—the nearest banking and medical services are in Tulum and Valladolid.

Facing the lagoon, **Farmacia El Porvenir** (Calle Principal s/n, no phone, 9am-1pm and 2pm-9pm Mon.-Sat.) is a small shop selling basic medicines and toiletries.

The **police station** (toll-free tel. 066) is halfway down the main drag, before you hit the lagoon.

Getting There and Around

Except for Hacienda Cobá, you can easily walk to any of the listed businesses in town; the archaeological site is a five-minute walk down the main road, alongside the lagoon.

BUS

A tiny bus station operates out of El Bocadito restaurant (Calle Principal). For the coast, the lone first-class bus departs Cobá at 3:10pm, with stops in Tulum (US$4.50, 1 hour) and Playa del Carmen (US$7.75, 2.5 hours). Second-class buses to the same destinations cost a bit less but take longer; there are five departures from 9:30am to 6pm.

CAR

Getting to Cobá is easiest by car. No matter what direction you're coming from, the roads are smooth and scenic, cutting through pretty farmland and small towns. Keep your speed down, however, as there are innumerable *topes* (speed bumps) and occasional people and animals along the shoulder. Buses ply the same routes, but somewhat infrequently.

Three different roads lead to Cobá; none are named or marked, so they are known by the towns on either end. There are no formal services along any of the roads, save a gas station in the town of Chemax.

The Cobá-Tulum road (45 kilometers/28 miles) is the busiest, cutting southeast to Tulum and the coastal highway (Hwy. 307). The other two roads connect to Highway 180, the main highway between Cancún and Chichén Itzá. The Cobá-Nuevo X'Can road (47 kilometers/29 miles) angles northeast, connecting with Highway 180 about 80 kilometers (50 miles) outside Cancún and passing places like the Punta Laguna monkey reserve along the way. The Cobá-Chemax road (30 kilometers/19 miles) angles northwest to the town of Chemax; from there it's another 20 kilometers (12.4 miles) to Valladolid and Highway 180, connecting to the highway about 40 kilometers (25 miles) from Chichén Itzá.

All three roads, plus the short access road to Cobá, intersect at a large roundabout just north of Cobá village. Pay close attention to which road you want to avoid a long detour.

Sian Ka'an Biosphere Reserve

Sian Ka'an is Yucatec Maya for "where the sky is born," and it's not hard to see how the original inhabitants arrived at such a poetic name. The unkempt beaches, blue-green sea, bird-filled wetlands and islets, and humble accommodations are manna for bird-watchers, artists, snorkelers, and kayakers. But most visitors come here for the fishing: Sian Ka'an is one of the best fly-fishing spots in the world, with all three "grand slam" catches: bonefish, tarpon, and permit.

The reserve was created in 1986, designated a UNESCO World Heritage Site in 1987, and expanded in 1994. It now encompasses around 1.3 million acres of coastal and mangrove forests and wetlands, and some 113 kilometers (70 miles) of pristine coral reefs just offshore.

A huge variety of **wildlife** thrives in the reserve. There are about 300 species of birds, including toucans, parrots, frigate birds, herons, and egrets. Monkeys, foxes, crocodiles, and boa constrictors also populate the reserve and are spotted by locals and visitors with some regularity. Manatees and jaguars are the reserve's largest animals but also the most reclusive; you need sharp eyes and a great deal of luck to spot either one. More than 20 Maya ruins have been found in the reserve, though most are unexcavated.

Spending a few days in Sian Ka'an is the best way to really appreciate its beauty and pace. Hotels and tour operators there can arrange fishing, bird-watching, and other tours, all with experienced local guides. But if time is short, a number of tour operators in Tulum offer day trips into the reserve as well.

SIGHTS
Muyil Archaeological Zone
The most accessible Maya site within the Sian Ka'an reserve is **Muyil** (Hwy. 307, 25 kilometers/15.5 miles south of Tulum, 8am-5pm daily, US$2.50), on the western edge of the park. Also known as Chunyaxché, it is one of the oldest archaeological sites in the Maya world, dating back to 300 BC and occupied continuously through the conquest. It's believed to have been primarily a seaport, perched on a limestone shelf near the edge of Laguna Muyil; it is connected to the Caribbean via an extant canal system that was constructed by ancient Maya traders.

Only a small portion of the city has been excavated, so it makes for a relatively quick visit. There are six main structures ranging from two-meter-high (6.6-foot) platforms to the impressive **Castillo.** At 17 meters (56 feet), it is one of the tallest structures on the peninsula's Caribbean coast. The Castillo is topped with a unique solid round masonry turret from which the waters of the Caribbean Sea can be seen. Climbing to the top is prohibited.

Once a *sacbé* (raised stone road), a boardwalk-like path now runs through a low swampy forest for about a half kilometer (0.3 mile) from the center of the archaeological site to the edge of the **Laguna Muyil.** Part of this *sacbé* is on ejido property, however, so if you want to access the lagoon from the ruins—you also can get to it by car—there is an additional charge of US$2.50 per person. Along the way, there is a teetering lookout tower with views over Sian Ka'an to the Caribbean.

Once you arrive at the water's edge, it's possible to take a **boat tour** (8am-4pm daily, US$35 pp) that crosses both Muyil and Chunyaxché Lagoons, which are connected by a canal that was carved by the ancient Maya; visitors typically get off the boats and float down the canal with life vests (wear a swimsuit!). It's a pleasant way to enjoy the water, and you'll also get a view of several otherwise inaccessible ruins along the lagoons' edges and through the mangroves, with the final stop being **Xlapak ruins,** a small site thought to have been a trading

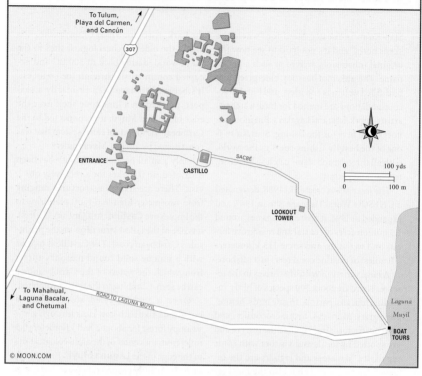

Muyil Archaeological Zone

To Tulum,
Playa del Carmen,
and Cancún

307

ENTRANCE

CASTILLO

SACBÉ

LOOKOUT
TOWER

0   100 yds

0   100 m

To Mahahual,
Laguna Bacalar,
and Chetumal

ROAD TO LAGUNA MUYIL

Laguna
Muyil

BOAT
TOURS

© MOON.COM

post. If arriving by car, look for signs to Muyil Lagoon on Highway 307, just south of the similarly named archaeological site. More thorough tours of this part of Sian Ka'an can be booked in Tulum.

★ Bahía de la Ascensión

Ascension Bay covers about 20 square kilometers (12.4 square miles), and its shallow flats and tangled mangrove islands teem with bonefish, tarpon, and huge permit—some of the biggest ever caught, in fact. It is a fly fisher's dream come true, and it has been attracting anglers from around the world since the mid-1980s. Don't fly-fish? No worries: The spin fishing is also fantastic, while the offshore reef yields plenty of grouper, barracuda, dorado, tuna, sailfish, and marlin.

SPORTS AND RECREATION
Sportfishing

Sportfishing is world-class in and around Sian Ka'an—it's hard to go wrong in the flats and mangrove islands, or with the Caribbean lapping at its shores. All the hotels listed in this section arrange fishing tours, and most specialize in it, using their own boats and guides. If you prefer to go with an independent operator, recommended outfits include **Pesca Maya** (7 kilometers/4.3 miles north of Punta Allen, tel. 998/848-2496, toll-free U.S. tel. 888/894-5642, www.pescamaya.com, 8am-7pm daily); **Palometa Club** (Punta Allen, north of the central plaza, toll-free U.S. tel. 888/824-5420, www.palometaclub.com, 8am-6pm daily); and **Fisherman Lodge** (Punta Allen, south of the central plaza, tel.

Sport and Game Fishing

Cozumel and the Riviera Maya are well known for trolling and deep-sea fishing, while Ascension Bay and the Costa Maya have terrific fly-fishing. Although you can hook into just about any fish at any time of the year, below is information on the peak and extended seasons for a number of top target species. Those fish not listed—tuna, barracuda, yellowtail, snapper, grouper, and bonefish—are prevalent year-round.

SPORTFISHING

Fish	Peak Season	Extended Season	Description
Sailfish	Mar.-June	Jan.-Sept.	Top target species, with a dramatic dorsal fin and a high-flying fighting style.
Blue Marlin	Apr.-Aug.	Mar.-Sept.	Largest Atlantic billfish, up to 500 pounds locally, but much larger elsewhere.
White Marlin	May-July	Mar.-Aug.	Smaller than the blue marlin, but still challenging.
Wahoo	Nov.-Jan.	June-Feb.	Lightning fast, with torpedo-like shape and distinctive blue stripes.
Dorado	May-July	Feb.-Aug.	Hard fighter with shimmery green, gold, and blue coloration; aka dolphin or mahimahi.

FLAT-WATER FISHING

Fish	Peak Season	Extended Season	Description
Tarpon	Mar.-Aug.	Feb.-Oct.	Big hungry tarpon migrate along the coast in summer months.
Snook	July-Aug.	June-Dec.	Popular trophy fish, grows locally up to 30 pounds.
Permit	Mar.-Sept.	year-round	March and April see schools of permit, with some 20-pound individuals.

999/351-5328, www.fishermanlodge.com, 6:30am-10pm daily).

Weeklong fly-fishing trips range US$3,900-4,300 per person, in shared room and shared boat, depending largely on the style and comforts afforded by the lodge. Most packages include airport transfer, daily guided fishing, meals, and admission to the reserve, but it's always a good idea to confirm this before booking. For private room or private boat, expect to pay an additional US$150-215 per day; shorter trips are available, but may incur extra transportation costs to and from the airport.

Fishing day trips can be arranged through most hotels; rates start at around US$480 for a private full-day tour, including lunch. Variations like renting gear, adding people, and half-day options can also be arranged.

Bird-Watching

Sian Ka'an is also an excellent place for bird-watching. Trips to Bird Island and other spots afford a look at various species of water birds, including male frigates showing off their big red balloon-like chests in the winter. Tours often combine bird-watching with snorkeling and walking around one or more bay islands. Hotels in Punta Allen and along the coastal road can arrange tours, as can outfits in Tulum. Prices are typically per boat, so don't be shy about approaching other travelers in town about forming a group.

In Punta Allen, **Punta Allen Coop** (tel. 984/807-1073, toursallen@hotmail.com, 6:30am-2pm daily) is a local cooperative that offers bird-watching tours (US$120-145, 2-3 hours, up to 6 people); look for its two-story wooden shack along the main road near the entrance to town. Other operators to consider include **Community Tours Sian Ka'an** (Calle Osiris Sur near Calle Sol Ote, tel. 984/871-2202, www.siankaantours.org, 7am-7pm daily); and, if your budget permits, **Visit Sian Ka'an** (Sian Ka'an Biosphere Reserve, Carr. Tulum-Punta Allen Km 15.8, cell tel. 984/141-4245, www.visitsiankaan.com), which offers customized private tours.

Kayaking

The tangled mangrove forests, interconnected lagoons, and scenic bays make Sian Ka'an ideal for kayaking. **Community Tours Sian Ka'an** (Calle Osiris Sur near Calle Sol Ote, tel. 984/871-2202, www.siankaantours.org, 7am-7pm daily) offers several kayak excursions, with tours starting at US$75 per person.

FOOD

Punta Allen isn't a foodie's village, but it does have a handful of eateries, all specializing in fresh seafood. A few mini-marts and a *tortille-ria* round things out a bit, especially if you're planning on staying more than a couple of days.

With a gorgeous view of the Caribbean, **Muelle Viejo** (just south of the central plaza, no phone, 11am-9pm Tues.-Sun., US$6-13) serves up fresh seafood dishes and cold beers—perfect for a long, lazy lunch.

Next to the elementary school, **Las Palapas de Juan y Martha** (north of the central plaza, tel. 998/171-9953, 6pm-10pm daily, US$5-12) is a popular dinner spot with an outdoor dining room. Fresh seafood is

served but tacos are the specialty. There's no set menu; instead, the affable owners visit with guests and share what's on offer for the evening.

There are three **mini-marts** in town: on the north end (near the road to the lagoon-side dock), south end (two blocks west of Cuzan Guesthouse), and near the central plaza (one block west). Each sells basic food-stuffs and snacks, though you may have to visit all three to find what you're looking for. If you plan to cook a lot, stock up on supplies in Tulum.

ACCOMMODATIONS

Punta Allen is the only town on the peninsula and has the most options for lodging, food, tours, and other services. Along the long un-paved road leading there is a smattering of lodges and private homes, amid miles and miles of deserted coastline. **Note:** The town of Punta Allen often switches off the electricity grid 2pm-7pm and midnight-11am—and hotels outside of town are entirely off the grid—so air-conditioning and Wi-Fi are not functional unless the establishment has a generator (fans work if the hotel has solar or wind power). If you're staying in a room with kitchen facilities, keep the fridge shut as much as possible to conserve the cold.

Toward Punta Allen

El Ultimo Maya (cell tel. 984/181-8691, www.elultimomaya.com, US$12.50-40 pp tent) is a low-key beach club (US$5 pp) and campsite. There's a simple thatch-roof restaurant serving fresh seafood and beach snacks (US$6-16) and a long beach that's kept clean of seaweed and trash. Campers set up in the sandy parking lot; the cheaper rates are BYO tent and gear; more expensive ones include a tent, a real bed with linens, and breakfast. The bathrooms are clean enough and there's security in the evenings. Best of all is the isolated beach getaway feel…and the stars! It's located two

1: dolphin spotting in Sian Ka'an Biosphere Reserve; **2:** beachfront accommodations at Sol Caribe

kilometers (1.5 miles) south of the Sian Ka'an arch. Cash only.

Eight kilometers (5 miles) north of Punta Allen, **Sol Caribe** (cell tel. 984/139-3839, www.solcaribe-mexico.com, US$175 s/d, US$195-250 *cabaña*, US$100/40 extra per adult/child all-inclusive) offers modern rooms and *cabañas* set on a breezy, palm-laden beach. All feature tropical wood furnishings, terraces with hammocks, 24-hour electricity (fan only), and gorgeous views of the ocean—a true hidden getaway. There's a full-service restaurant on-site.

★ **Mukan Resort** (tel. 998/800-3914, www.mukan.com, US$420-600 s/d all-inclusive) embodies tropical chic with hardwood floors, thatch roofs, sleek furnishings, and fine art. The luxuriousness is only highlighted by staff that anticipate guest needs, such as appearing with cold drinks at the beach or setting up a table for lunch in the shade of a palm tree. Beyond the beach, there's a spacious lounge, a small pool, a rooftop whirlpool tub, and even a cigar bar. The restaurant has a seasonal menu that integrates fresh seafood and local ingredients. Note that except for a daily cocktail hour, the rate does not include alcoholic beverages; those can be added à la carte or as a separate package. The resort is 10 kilometers (6 miles) north of Punta Allen.

Punta Allen

Facing the central plaza, **Posada Sirena** (cell tel. 984/139-1241, www.casasirena.com, US$38-75 s/d) offers simple Robinson Crusoe-style rooms. Most are quite spacious, sleeping 6-8 people, and all have private bathrooms, fully equipped kitchens, and plenty of screened windows to let in the ocean breeze. Area excursions, including fly-fishing, snorkeling, and bird-watching, can be arranged on-site.

The accommodations at **Serenidad Shardon** (road to the lighthouse, cell tel. 984/107-4155, www.shardon.com, US$150 s/d, US$350 cabaña for up to 5 guests, US$500 beach house for up to 8 guests) vary from oceanfront *cabañas* to a large beach house;

all have basic furnishings but are clean and well equipped. You also can camp using your own gear, or rent deluxe tents with real beds, electric lighting, and fans; access to hot showers and a full kitchen is included.

A dedicated fishing lodge, **The Palometa Club** (Punta Allen, north of the central plaza, toll-free U.S. tel. 888/824-5420, www.palometaclub.com) has just six rooms in a two-story structure facing the beach. Each has two double beds, air-conditioning, and a private bathroom. Meals are served family-style, with cocktails and snacks available at the club's outdoor bar, après fishing. The Palometa is designed for serious anglers, with a fly-tying study, one-to-one guiding, and an emphasis on landing permits (*palometa* in Spanish). The all-inclusive seven-night/six-day rate is US$4,250 per person (non-anglers US$2,000/person) in a shared room and boat.

INFORMATION AND SERVICES

Don't expect much in the way of services in Sian Ka'an—if there is something you can't do without, definitely bring it with you. There are **no banking services,** and few establishments accept credit cards. **Wi-Fi** is available at most hotels, though often in the common areas only. Cell phones typically don't work in Sian Ka'an, but there are **public telephones** in town. Punta Allen also has a modest **medical clinic**—look for it on the main road as you enter town. There is **no laundry,** but most hotels will provide the service.

GETTING THERE

Many hotels include airport pickup/drop-off, which is convenient and helps you avoid paying for a week's car rental when you plan on fishing all day. That said, a car is useful if you'd like to do some exploring on your own.

Public Transportation

Public transport to and from Punta Allen is unpredictable at best—build some flexibility into your plans in case of missed (or missing) connections.

A privately run **Tulum-Sian Ka'an shuttle** leaves the iTour Mexico Hotel (Av. Tulum at Av. Cobá, cell tel. 984/115-3875, US$10pp, 1 hour) at 2pm most days. The shuttle drops passengers off at the Sian Ka'an visitors center dock about nine kilometers (5.5 miles) south of the reserve's entrance. There, tour boats that double as **water taxis** (45 min., US$10) are typically waiting to take passengers to Punta Allen. A taxi from Tulum to the visitors center costs around US$30. Return boats leave Punta Allen starting at 5am. The shuttle back to Tulum typically leaves around 7:30am.

Those arriving from the Costa Maya can get to Punta Allen from Carrillo Puerto. State-run **combis** (US$10, 10am and 3pm daily) leave from the market in Carrillo Puerto (a block from the main traffic circle) for a bone-jarring four-hour trip down a private road to the small settlement of Playón. There, **water taxis** (US$2.50 pp, 15 minutes) wait to ferry passengers across the lagoon to Punta Allen. The *combi* back to Carrillo Puerto leaves Playón at 6am.

Car

To get to Punta Allen by car, head south along the coast through (and past) Tulum's Zona Hotelera. About eight kilometers (5 miles) from the Tulum/Zona Hotelera junction is *el arco* (the arch), marking the reserve boundary where you register and pay a US$2 per person per day park fee. From there it's 56 kilometers (35 miles) by dirt road to Punta Allen. The road is much improved from years past, and an ordinary car can make it in 2-3 hours. It can be much more difficult after a heavy rain, however. Be sure to fill the tank in Tulum—there is no gas station along the way or in Punta Allen, though some locals sell gas from their homes.

The Costa Maya

The coastline south of Tulum loops and weaves like the tangled branches of the mangrove trees that blanket much of it. It is a mosaic of savannas, marshes, lagoons, scattered islands, and three huge bays: Bahía de la Ascensión, Bahía del Espiritu Santo, and Bahía de Chetumal. Where it's not covered by mangroves, the shore has sandy beaches and dunes, and just below the turquoise sea is one of the least-impacted sections of the great Mesoamerican Reef. Dozens of Maya archaeological sites have been discovered here, but few excavated, and much remains unknown about pre-Hispanic life here. During the conquest, the snarled coastal forest proved an effective sanctuary for indigenous rebels and refugees fleeing Spanish control, not to mention a haven for pirates, British logwood cutters, and Belizean anglers.

In the 1990s, Quintana Roo officials launched an effort to develop the state's southern coast, which was still extremely isolated despite the breakneck development taking place in and around Cancún. (It has always been a famous fly-fishing area, however.) The first order of business was to construct a huge cruise ship port, which they did in the tiny fishing village of Mahahual. They also needed a catchy name, and came up with the "Costa Maya." The moniker generally applies to the coastal areas south of Tulum, particularly the Sian Ka'an Biosphere Reserve; the towns of Mahahual and Xcalak; Laguna Bacalar; and Chetumal, the state capital and by far the largest city in the area.

It's hard not to be a little cynical about cruise liners coming to such a remote area, whose entire population could fit comfortably on a single ship. The town of Mahahual, nearest the port, is utterly transformed when cruise ships arrive, their passengers moseying about Mahahual, beer bottles in hand, the beaches packed with sun worshippers serenaded by the sound of Jet Skis. Then again,

Mahahual

Map labels:
CALLE ISAAC
MAYA LOST MAYAN KINGDOM
SHOPPING CENTER
MAIN STREET
LAS CASITAS
CRUISE SHIP PIER
AV PASEO DEL PUERTO
CHICLE
CACAO
ZAPOTE
MATZ
PRIVATE ROAD (RESTRICTED USE)
RIO HONDO
OXTANKAH
CALDERITAS
CHETUMAL
KOHUNLICH
LAVANDA
MINISUPER BERE
BACALAR
COSTA MAYA YOGA
THE NATIVE CHOICE
CHACCHOBEN
CHINCHORRO
MOBIUS INTERNET
MAHAHUAL ECOTOURS
CARRETERA CAFETAL MAHAHUAL
← To gas station, Xcalak, Mayan Beach Garden Inn, and Hwy 307
AV MALECON MAHAHUAL
HUACHINANGO
Caribbean Sea
PARGO
SARDINA
RUBIA
LAVANDERÍA 4 HERMANOS
PHARMACY MÉRIDA
CAFÉ COLONIAL
HOSTAL JARDÍN MAHAHUAL
SIERRA
ÑAM ÑAM
BUS TERMINAL
CHERNA
POLICE
MARTILLO
POSADA PACHAMAMA
UNDERTOE MÉXICO
HOTEL CABALLO BLANCO/ DOCTOR DIVE
CENTRO DE SALUD
CORONADO
DIVINO DELICIA ITALIANA
NACIONAL BEACH CLUB AND BUNGALOWS/ AMIGOS DEL MAR
BARRACUDA
MERO
ROBALO
MOJARRA
LIZA
CAZON
NOHOCH KAY
JATUN
PESCARDERÍA SAURI/ CENTRO DE ACOPIO DE LANGOSTA
SULUMAR
ALMEJA
0   500 yds
0   500 m
LAS CABAÑAS DEL DOCTOR
To Maya Luna, Balamku Inn on the Beach, Travel In', and Almaplena Eco Resort and Beach Club
© MOON.COM

it's doubtful the area would have paved roads, power lines, or telephone service if not for the income and demand generated by cruise ships. Driving down the old rutted coastal road to Xcalak (an even smaller town south of Mahahual) used to take a half day or more; today, a two-lane paved road has cut the trip to under an hour. The state government has vowed to control development by limiting hotel size and density, monitoring construction methods, and protecting the mangroves and coral reef. Small, ecofriendly bed-and-breakfasts have thrived, not surprisingly, and more and more independent travelers are drawn to the Costa Maya for its quiet isolation and pristine natural beauty.

Highway 307 from Tulum to Chetumal passes through Carrillo Puerto, the gateway to the Costa Maya. It's a small city that holds little of interest to most travelers except an opportunity to fill up on gas.

MAHAHUAL

Mahahual is a place of two faces: cruise ship days, when the town's one road is packed with day-trippers looking to buy T-shirts and throw back a few beers; and non-cruise ship days, when Mahahual is sleepy and laid-back, and the narrow white-sand beaches are free to walk for miles. Whether you stay here a night or a week, you're likely to see both, which is a good thing. You can be in a major party zone one day, and the next be the only snorkeler in town—all without changing hotels. If you seek long, quiet days every day, though, definitely stay outside of town.

Whether or not there is a cruise ship in town, Mahahual is pretty easy to manage. Most of its hotels and services are located on, or just off, Avenida Mahahual (aka El Malecón), the three-kilometer (1.9-mile) pedestrian walkway that runs through town until it meets up with the coastal road heading south, the Carretera Antigua (literally, Old Highway). Just northwest of town, the tiny residential community of Las Casitas has additional services like an Internet café and a laundry.

The Caste War

On July 18, 1847, a military commander in Valladolid learned of an armed plot to overthrow the government that was being planned by two indigenous men—Miguel Antonio Ay and Cecilio Chí. Ay was arrested and executed. Chí managed to escape punishment and on July 30, 1847, led a small band of armed men into the town of Tepich. Several officials and Euro-Mexican families were killed. The military responded with overwhelming force, burning villages, poisoning wells, and killing scores of people, including many women, children, and elderly. The massacre—and the long-standing oppression of indigenous people at its root—sparked spontaneous uprisings across the peninsula, which quickly developed into a massive, coordinated indigenous rebellion known as the Caste War.

Indigenous troops tore through colonial cities, killing and capturing scores of non-Maya. In some cases, the Maya turned the tables on their former masters, forcing them into slave labor, including building the church in present-day Carrillo Puerto's central plaza. Valladolid was evacuated in 1848 and left abandoned for nearly a year, and by 1849, the peninsula's indigenous people were close to expelling the colonial elite. However, as they were preparing their final assaults on Mérida and Campeche City, the rainy season came early, presenting the Maya soldiers with a bitter choice between victory and (were they to miss the planting season) likely famine. The men turned their backs on a hard-fought and near-certain victory to return to their fields to plant corn.

Mexican troops immediately took advantage of the lull, and the Maya never regained the upper hand. For the next 13 years, captured indigenous soldiers (and increasingly *any* indigenous person) were sold to slave brokers and shipped to Cuba. Many Maya eventually fled into the forests and jungles of southern Quintana Roo. The fighting was rekindled when a wooden cross in the town of Chan Santa Cruz (today, Carrillo Puerto) was said to be channeling the voice of God, urging the Maya to keep fighting. The war ended, however, when troops took control of Chan Santa Cruz in 1901. An official surrender was signed in 1936.

Sights

★ BANCO CHINCHORRO

Chinchorro Bank is by some measurements the largest coral atoll in the Northern Hemisphere and a paradise for divers and snorkelers alike. About 44 kilometers (27 miles) east of Mahahual and 65.4 kilometers (40 miles) northeast of Xcalak, Chinchorro is a marine reserve known for its spectacular coral formations, massive sponges, and abundant sealife…even the largest known population of American crocodiles. Scores of ships have foundered on the shallow reefs through the years, but (contrary to innumerable misreports) the wrecks cannot be dived. Not only are they protected as historical sites, but most are on the eastern side of the atoll, where the surf and currents are too strong for recreational diving. The famous **40 Cannons wreck,** in about three meters (10 feet) of water on the atoll's northwest side, is good for snorkeling but not diving, and thanks to looters

there are far fewer than 40 cannons there. There are small government and fishermen's huts on Cayo Centro, one of the three cays; tourists are permitted to stay overnight, which means spectacular multiday diving and snorkeling opportunities. Reaching Chinchorro requires a 1.5- to 2-hour boat ride, which can be pretty punishing depending on conditions. Groups typically set out around 7am and return to port around 5pm. Dive shops usually require at least five divers or six snorkelers (or a combination of the two) and may not go for days at a time if the weather is bad (summer months are best).

Sports and Recreation

SCUBA DIVING

Mahahual has terrific diving on the coral reef just offshore, with dozens of sites a short boat ride away. It's also one of two jumping-off points for trips to Chinchorro Bank, the largest coral atoll in the Northern Hemisphere.

Lionfish

lionfish mural in Puerto Morelos

The lionfish is a spectacular striped fish with a "mane" of fins and poisonous spines that is changing the underwater landscape of the entire Caribbean. Historically found only in the warm regions of the Pacific and Indian Oceans, lionfish were first sighted in Atlantic waters in 1992 in Biscayne Bay, Florida; it's believed they were released into the wild after a private aquarium was swept into the ocean by Hurricane Andrew. Since then, lionfish have been documented in the Florida Keys, the Bahamas, Cuba, and elsewhere; the first lionfish sighting in the region was in Cozumel in January 2009. Voracious hunters with no natural predators, lionfish can grow to 20 inches long and devour everything from small reef fish to commercial fish like snapper and juvenile grouper. They thrive at depths of just a few feet to more than 500 feet, and their coloring makes them especially well suited for coral environments. Government agencies have taken proactive efforts to help curb the growth of this invasive fish, garnering widespread community support. There are fishing tournaments targeting lionfish, and spear-fishing training for local sport divers; experts are even trying, with some success, to "train" wild sharks and mature grouper to prey on lionfish by introducing them into known hunting grounds. Restaurants are doing their part by creating innovative and tasty dishes from lionfish meat.

The other departure point is Xcalak, south of Mahahual.

Amigos del Mar (Av. Mahahual at Coronado, cell tel. 983/151-6758, www.amigosdelmar.net, 8am-6pm daily) is a friendly shop offering a wide array of dives to local sites (US$70 one tank, US$110 two tanks). It also offers fantastic overnight trips to Banco Chinchorro (US$399 pp, 1 night) that include five dives, meals (including a lobster dinner), drinks, and basic lodging in a stilt house on the water's edge. Snorkelers are welcome, too (US$200 pp). Longer trips to Chinchorro also can be arranged.

Doctor Dive (Yaya Beach Club, Malécon at Calle Coronado, cell tel. 983/834-5619, www.doctordive.com, 8am-6pm daily) offers personalized service for independent travelers. Fun dives are US$65 for one tank, US$95 for two; gear is an extra US$25 per day. Specialty trips, including lionfish hunting and diving unexplored locations, also can be arranged.

SNORKELING

You can rent snorkel gear for around US$10-12 a day from the dive shops or from the kiosks that pop up on cruise ship days. Swim or kayak out to the reef for a do-it-yourself experience, or join a guided tour, where you'll likely see more sealife, plus have extra safety and convenience. Mahahual's dive shops all offer guided snorkel trips for US$40-50 per person, including gear and about 90 minutes in the water.

STAND-UP PADDLING

UnderToe Mexico (Ibiza Sunset Beach Club, Malécon near Calle Coronado, cell tel. 983/154-2293, www.undertoemexico.com, hours vary) offers paddleboarding lessons (US$38.50, 90 minutes) from certified bilingual instructors. Afterward, students enjoy full access to the Ibiza Sunset Beach Club, including two drinks and a snack. SUP yoga—a floating yoga class—also is offered (US$55, 90 minutes).

YOGA

Located in a spacious and bright studio in Las Casitas neighborhood, **Costa Maya Yoga** (Av. Caribe between Calles Bacalar and Kohunlich, cell tel. 983/105-8040, www.costa-maya-yoga.com, hours vary) offers mostly vinyasa, hatha, and restorative yoga classes. Classes run US$15 per person; check the website for the current schedule.

TOURS

The Native Choice (Las Casitas, Av. Paseo del Puerto at Calle Chinchorro, tel. 998/869-4000, www.thenativechoice.com) offers a range of area tours, all led by guides who are extremely knowledgeable about Maya history, culture, and belief systems. Tours include visiting the archaeological sites of Chacchoben, Kohunlich, or Dzibanché (US$55-100 adult, US$45-85 child), a "Mayan Experience Tour," which includes touring Chacchoben ruins and a visit to a home in Chacchoben village (US$75 adult, US$65 child), plus a kayaking and hiking trip on and around Laguna

Bacalar (US$55 adult, US$40 child). The tours are geared toward the cruise ship crowd, but hotel owners warmly recommend the outfit to independent travelers as well.

Mahahual Ecotours (Las Casitas, Calle Caribe s/n, www.mahahualecotours.simdif.com, tel. 983/136-2827) is a tour operator that just gets it. The team of certified guides has a profound knowledge of the area, and a passion for sharing its history and hidden riches, that make for a fascinating outing every time. There's a standard menu of tours, including kayaking, bird-watching, and ruin-hopping, but the operation really specializes in mixing and matching to make custom excursions. The team is out to blow your mind, and there isn't much that can't be arranged.

AMUSEMENT PARKS

For the record, appropriating the Maya pyramids to create a water park for foreign tourists is pretty obnoxious. But in terms of giving families something fun to do, the creators of **Mayá Lost Mayan Kingdom** (Las Casitas, end of Calle Isaac, www.maya-park.com, 8am-5pm Mon.-Sat., US$99/89 adult/child) nailed it. The park includes zip lines, a lazy river, and numerous waterslides (named after Maya gods, of course) ranging from exciting to heart-stopping.

Food
IN TOWN

An open-air eatery and beach club, ★ **Nohoch Kay** (aka Big Fish, Malecón between Calles Liza and Cazón, tel. 983/834-5981, 8am-7pm Mon.-Tues., 8am-10pm Wed.-Sun., US$7-16) serves up some of the best fish tacos in town. Thick pieces of fish—fried or grilled—are served with small tortillas, onion, cilantro, and plenty of lime. On cruise ship days, it gets overrun with clients, but otherwise it's a laid-back place to get a beachfront meal.

A breezy restaurant with hanging shell lamps and a *palapa* roof, **Divino Delicia Italiana** (Calle Huachinango at Calle Coronado, tel. 983/700-2995, 5pm-11pm

Tues.-Sun., US$7-14) serves up freshly made pastas, seafood salads, and wooden tablets loaded with gourmet cheeses and meats. Thin-crust pizzas also are baked in the wood-burning stove, visible from the dining room. An extensive wine list combined with friendly service round out a meal nicely.

★ **Ñam** (Calle Cherna between Malecón and Huachinango, cell tel. 983/131-4417, 3pm-11pm Wed.-Mon., US$3-5) is a hole-in-the-wall eatery serving legit hamburgers as well as tasty empanadas from the owners' native Uruguay. Burgers range from traditional to the "Oink Oink" (half beef, half pork, with caramelized pineapple and barbecue sauce), all served with fries. The empanadas are crispy and flavorful, and all dishes are served on paper-lined baskets at a handful of tables on the sidewalk.

Sulumar (Malecón near Calle Atún, tel. 983/119-2920, 10am-5pm daily, US$4-8) is a great little beachfront restaurant specializing in (what else?) seafood and beach grub. It's best known for its ceviche, and rightly so. Local fishermen come ashore a short distance from here with their daily catch, and Sulumar chefs reportedly get first pick. It's not exactly a locals' place, but certainly far enough south that the clientele is a mix of cruise-shippers and indie travelers. Service is friendly but can be slow.

Café Colonial (Calle Sierra near Malécon, tel. 983/137-3705, 7am-5pm Tues.-Sat., US$3-6) is a good place to grab breakfast. Package deals include a hearty plate of eggs with bread, coffee, and juice for US$6. À la carte items like fruit plates and breakfast sandwiches also are offered. Tables are in a small wood house or on the pedestrian walkway in front.

If you're cooking for yourself, stop by the local fisherman's co-op, **Pescardería Sauri: Centro de Acopio de Langosta** (Calle Huachinango near Calle Almeja, no phone, 7am-7pm daily). At this roadside shack, you can take your pick of lobsters and buy shrimp and fish fillets, all by the kilo.

OUTSIDE OF TOWN

Travel In' (Carr. Antigua Km 5.8, cell tel. 983/110-9496, www.travel-in.com.mx, 5:30pm-9pm Tues.-Sat., US$5-20) is a great little restaurant a few kilometers down the coastal road. Homemade pita bread is baked fresh every day—order it as an appetizer with an assortment of homemade dips. Daily seafood specials vary according to the day's catch. It's open on Mondays from Christmas to Easter.

Even the waves take it easy in Mahahual.

For basic groceries, try **Minisuper Bere** (Las Casitas, Av. Paseo del Puerto near Calle Kohunlich, 8am-11pm daily).

Accommodations

Many of Mahahual's lodgings, especially the ones with beachfront, are outside of the village itself, along the Carretera Antigua that hugs the coast south of town. The rest are in town, either on the Malecón or a stone's throw away.

IN TOWN
Under US$50: Hostal Jardín Mahahual (Calle Sardina near Calle Sierra, tel. 983/834-5722, www.mahahualjardin.co, US$15 pp dorm with a/c, US$64 s/d with a/c) is an appealing hostel with a small interior garden and a friendly staff. The eight-bed dorm has overhead fans, sturdy bunks, thick mattresses, and spotless single-sex bathrooms. Four private rooms are located on the other side of the garden, with whitewashed walls, polished cement floors, and details like throw pillows and original art. Added pluses include a clean common kitchen and complimentary use of bikes.

Set on a grassy lot, **Las Cabañas del Doctor** (Av. Mahahual Km 2, tel. 983/832-2102, www.lascabanasdeldoctor.com, US$5 pp camping, US$45 s/d *cabaña,* US$50 s/d, US$60 s/d with a/c) has a decent range of accommodations—but camping is the reason to stay here. Campers must bring their own gear, but the rate includes an oceanfront tent site, access to cold-water bathrooms, and Wi-Fi.

US$50-100: ★ **Nacional Beach Club and Bungalows** (Malécon near Calle Coronado, tel. 983/834-5719, www.nacionalbeachclub.com, US$65-85 s/d bungalows, US$85-125 s/d with a/c) is a tasteful beachfront hotel with spectacular ocean views and excellent service. Units vary from thatched-roof bungalows with private terraces to spacious hotel rooms with high ceilings and Mexican tile bathrooms. There's a small pool right on the Malécon and a good restaurant on-site. Guests are welcome to use the hotel beach club and its amenities.

Posada Pachamama (Calle Huachinango between Calles Martillo and Coronado, tel. 983/834-5762, www.posadapachamama.com, US$53-67 s/d with a/c) is a small hotel a block from the beach. Rooms are small and sparsely decorated but have updated furnishings and stone-inlaid floors; all have air-conditioning, Wi-Fi, and satellite TV. The higher-priced rooms have small balconies, some with partial beach views. A pleasant patio café is a good place for breakfast.

Over US$100: With direct access to the beach and a rooftop bar, **Hotel Caballo Blanco** (Malecón between Calles Martillo and Coronado, tel. 983/834-5830, www.hotelelcaballoblanco.com, US$110-140 suite with a/c) is a great place to land. If you can turn a blind eye to the old-world village murals and polyester curtains, rooms are quite modern in style. More importantly, they are immensely comfortable with air-conditioning, flat-screen TVs, mini fridges, coffee makers, and Wi-Fi. Most have private balconies too, the more expensive ones overlooking the Caribbean.

OUTSIDE OF TOWN
Under US$100: Owned and operated by friendly Canadian expats, ★ **Balamku Inn on the Beach** (Carr. Antigua Km 5.7, tel. 983/732-1004, www.balamku.com, US$85 s, US$95 d) offers artfully decorated rooms in a handful of *palapa*-roofed buildings. All run on solar power, wind turbines, and a nonpolluting wastewater system. Full breakfast is included, as is use of the hotel's kayaks and a library. Wi-Fi is available in every room.

Maya Luna (Carr. Antigua Km 5.6, tel. 983/836-0905, www.hotelmayaluna.com, US$85 s/d) has four modern bungalows with 24-hour solar/wind power, rainwater showers, and *palapa*-shaded porches. Each has a private rooftop terrace with views of the Caribbean in front and the jungle in back; all have Maya- or ocean-themed murals, too. A hearty and healthy breakfast is included in the rate. Pets are welcome (and will join a cadre of friendly cats and a dog who live on-site).

About 21 kilometers (13 miles) north of Mahahual, **Mayan Beach Garden Inn** (cell tel. 983/130-8658, www.mayanbeachgarden.com, US$75-85 s/d, US$85 s/d with kitchenette, US$25 extra for a/c at night) is a quiet hotel with several rooms and one *cabaña*, all with whitewashed walls and Mexican-style decor, most with ocean views. A hearty breakfast is included in the rate, as are Wi-Fi and the use of kayaks. All-inclusive meal packages are also available. In the high season, there's a three-night minimum.

Over US$100: About 20 minutes south of town, **Almaplena Eco Resort and Beach Club** (Carr. Antigua Km 12.5, cell tel. 983/137-5070, www.almaplenabeachresort.com, US$127-161 s/d) is a small boutique resort with just eight rooms facing a gorgeous and isolated stretch of beach. All have king-size beds, ceiling fans (no air-conditioning), cool stone floors, and tasteful decor. Suites are on the top floor and have private terraces, while standards share a wooden patio with direct access to the beach. All have Wi-Fi, too. Continental breakfast is included, and the on-site restaurant serves fine Mediterranean and Mexican meals.

Information and Services

Cruise ships have brought considerable modernization to this once-isolated fishing village, but services are still somewhat limited.

EMERGENCY SERVICES

The **Centro de Salud** (Calle Coronado between Calles Huachinango and Sardina, no phone, 8am-2:30pm daily, after 2:30pm emergencies only) offers basic health services. For serious health matters, head to Chetumal.

For meds, try **Pharmacy Mérida** (Calle Sardina between Calles Rubia and Sierra, cell tel. 983/132-1845, 7am-11pm Mon.-Fri., 9am-11pm Sat.-Sun.), the best-stocked pharmacy in town.

The **police department** (Calle Huachinango near Calle Martillo, toll-free Mex. tel. 066) is open 24 hours.

MONEY

There is no bank in town, but there are a handful of **ATMs,** all along El Malecón. At the time of research, however, none were affiliated with local banks, so withdrawal charges were hefty. Another option is to go to the gas station outside of town, where there's an **HSBC ATM** (though it often runs out of cash); alternatively, consider bringing enough money to get you through your stay.

MEDIA AND COMMUNICATIONS

The only Internet café is in Las Casitas, where **Mobius Internet** (Calle Chinchorro near Av. Paseo del Puerto, 9am-10pm Mon.-Fri., 9am-2pm and 5pm-10pm Sat.) charges US$1 per hour and offers international telephone service, too (US$0.35-0.45/minute calls to the United States and Europe). Most hotels and some restaurants offer Wi-Fi as well.

LAUNDRY

Lavandería 4 Hermanos (Calle Huachinango near Calle Rubia, 7am-8pm daily) offers same-day laundry service for US$1.50 per kilo (2.2 pounds).

In Las Casitas, try **Lavanda** (Av. Paseo del Puerto at Calle Chetumal, 9am-6pm Mon.-Sat.), which charges US$1.25 per kilo (2.2 pounds).

Getting There and Around

Just south of the grubby roadside town of Limones, a good paved road with signs to Mahahual breaks off Highway 307 and cuts through 58 kilometers (36 miles) of coastal forest and wetlands tangled with mangroves. It's a scenic stretch, whether in a car or on a bus, along which you can occasionally see egrets, herons, and other water birds.

Mahahual proper is very walkable—in fact, the main road that runs through town, El Malecón, is a three-kilometer (1.9-mile) pedestrian walkway. If you're staying outside of town, a car certainly comes in handy, but plenty of people manage without; dive shops and tour operators typically offer hotel pickup, and there are cabs and a local bus.

BUS

Mahahual's bus terminal is a modest affair on Calle Huachinango near Calle Sierra toward the north end of town. Buses to Cancún (US$14, 5 hours) leave at 10:30am and 5:30pm daily, stopping at Carrillo Puerto (US$3.50-8, 2 hours), Tulum (US$8.25, 3 hours), and Playa del Carmen (US$13-19, 4 hours) along the way. To Chetumal (US$6, 2.5 hours) and Bacalar (US$4.50, 1.5 hours), buses depart at 2:30pm and 7:30pm daily. All long-distance buses stop in Limones (US$3, 1 hour). For Xcalak, a second-class bus leaves at 6:30am daily (US$3, 1 hour).

Note: Buses entering Mahahual stop in Las Casitas before arriving at the bus terminal; if you're headed to the beach or any of the hotels, wait to get off until the bus terminal.

CAR AND TAXI

There is a PEMEX gas station (24 hours) on the main road to Mahahual, just east of the turnoff to Xcalak. It occasionally runs out of gas, so definitely fill your tank in Carrillo Puerto or Chetumal on your way here.

Note: There's often a military checkpoint set up just west of the turnoff to Xcalak, where officials conduct searches for illicit drugs and other contraband. As long as you or your passengers don't have anything illegal in the car, the longest you should be delayed is a couple of minutes.

Cabs abound in this town, especially on cruise ship days. Rates are set by zone; in general, rates run around US$1 per kilometer (0.6 mile). If in doubt, ask to see the *tarifario* (official rate chart).

AIRPORT

Mahahual has a small airport just outside of town. Well, it's more like a well-maintained airstrip with a nice shelter. At the time of research, it was only used by private or chartered planes.

XCALAK

The tiny fishing village of Xcalak lies just a short distance from the channel that marks the Mexico-Belize border, and a blessedly long way from anything else. The town started out as a military outpost and didn't get its first real hotel until 1988. Villagers had to wait another decade to get a paved road; before that, the only way in or out of town was by boat or via 55 kilometers (34 miles) of rutted beach tracks. Electrical lines were installed in 2004 but only in the village proper, so many outlying areas (including most of the better hotels) still rely on solar and wind power, as well as generators. The town has no bank, no public phones, and no gas station. That is to say: perfect!

The area doesn't have much beach but makes up for it with world-class fly-fishing, great snorkeling and diving, and a healthy coral reef and lagoon. A small contingent of expats, mostly American and Canadian, have built homes here, some for personal use, others for rent, others as small hotels. Large-scale tourism may be inevitable but still seems a long way off, and Xcalak remains a small and wonderfully laid-back place, perfect for those looking for some honest-to-goodness isolation.

Sights

PARQUE NACIONAL ARRECIFES DE XCALAK

Xcalak Reef National Park was established at the end of 2003, affording protection to the coastal ecosystem as well as Xcalak's nascent tourist economy. The park spans nearly 18,000 hectares (44,479 acres), from the Belize border to well north of town, and includes the reef—and everything else down to 100 meters (328 feet)—as well as the shoreline and numerous inland lagoons.

The main coral reef lies just 90-180 meters (100-200 yards) from shore, and the water is less than 1.5 meters (5 feet) deep almost the whole way out. Many snorkelers prefer the coral heads even closer to shore, which have plenty to see and less swell than the main reef. The shallow waters keep boat traffic to a minimum, and anglers are good about steering clear of snorkelers (you should still stay alert at all times, however).

Divers and snorkelers also can explore the reef at 20 or so official sites and many more unofficial ones. Most are a short distance from town, and shops typically return to port between tanks. **La Poza** is one of the more distinctive dives, drifting through a trench where hundreds, sometimes thousands, of tarpon congregate, varying in size from one-meter (3-foot) "juveniles" to two-meter (7-foot) behemoths. If you have an underwater camera, be sure to bring it.

A fee of US$3.25 per day technically applies to all divers and snorkelers (and kayakers and anglers) in the Parque Nacional Arrecifes de Xcalak; dive shops typically add it to their rates, while most hotels have a stack of wristband permits to sell to guests who want to snorkel right from shore.

Sports and Recreation
SCUBA DIVING AND SNORKELING
XTC Dive Center (north end of town, across bridge, no phone, www.xtcdivecenter.com, 8am-6pm daily) is a highly recommended full-service dive shop offering dives to dozens of sites within Xcalak Reef National Marine Park (US$80 for one tank, US$125 for two tanks). It also specializes in trips to Chinchorro Bank (US$275 for two tanks, US$185 per snorkeler),

including lunch, drinks, and a hike on Cayo Centro, the main cay; overnight trips are also offered. Full gear rental costs US$35 extra. A variety of dive classes also are available; a nice three-meter-deep (9-foot) pool is used for the open-water certification course.

A variety of snorkeling tours are offered by a handful of local tour operators. They cost US$45-75 per person depending on how long and far you go; five-hour trips include jaunts into Chetumal Bay and Bird Island, which can be fascinating, especially in January and February when the birds are most plentiful. Recommended guides include **XTC Dive Center** (north end of town, across bridge, no phone, www.xtcdivecenter.com, 8am-6pm daily) and **Osprey Tours** (no storefront, no phone, www.xcalak-flyfishing.com).

KAYAKING AND STAND-UP PADDLING
XTC Dive Center (north end of town, across bridge, no phone, www.xtcdivecenter.com, 8am-6pm daily, US$35-70 pp) offers 2-5-hour kayaking tours in Xcalak's coastal habitats, including the reef, mangroves, river, and lagoon. If DIY is more your thing, kayak rentals, including an hour of instruction, are available

The Costa Maya is home to some of the world's best fishing.

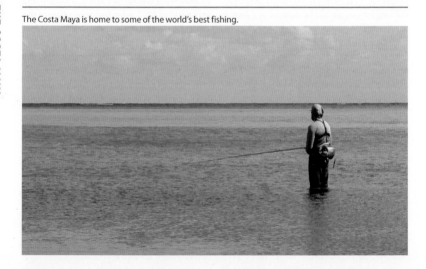

for US$40/60 half/full day. Paddleboard rentals are offered at the same rates.

SPORTFISHING

Xcalak boasts world-class sportfishing, with huge saltwater and brackish flats where hooking into the grand slam of fly-fishing—tarpon, bonefish, and permit—is by no means impossible. Add a snook, and you've got a super slam. Oceanside, tarpon and barracuda abound, in addition to grouper, snapper, and others.

Costa de Cocos (3 kilometers/1.9 miles north of town, no phone, www.costadecocos. com) is the area's oldest fishing resort, with highly experienced guides and numerous magazine write-ups. Two- to seven-night packages (US$2,130-4,405 s, US$1,720-3,395 d) include transportation to and from the Cancún or Chetumal airport, lodging, meals, open bar, fishing license, marine park wristband, and, of course, nonstop fly-fishing. The resort also offers half- and full-day fishing trips (US$175-350), in case you want to fish while in Xcalak without making it a full-on fishing vacation.

Hotel Tierra Maya (2.1 kilometers/1.3 miles north of town, tel. 983/839-8012, www.tierramaya.net) also offers fly-fishing packages for 6-7 nights (US$3,496-4,237 s, US$2,243-2,760 d), though they don't include all the perks—such as airport transportation, open bar, and fishing license fees—that the Costa de Cocos packages do.

With several experienced guides, **Osprey Tours** (no storefront, no phone, www.xcalak-flyfishing.com) is a good option for longtime and beginner fly-fishers. It offers half- and full-day fly-fishing excursions in nearby Chetumal Bay (US$200-300) that include drinks, snacks or lunch, and a guide. Gear is available for rent.

Food

★ **Leaky Palapa** (2 blocks north of the lighthouse, cell tel. 983/165-3223, www. leakypalaparestaurant.com, 5pm-10pm Fri.-Sat. Nov.-May, US$12-27) is an upscale restaurant with boho flair and a menu that reflects the day's catch and market offerings. The food is invariably delicious, with such dishes as homemade ravioli with huitlacoche, lobster, and squash flower cream as well as fresh fish fillet served on a bed of squid ink risotto. Reservations are required and payment is cash or PayPal only.

Restaurant Toby (center of town, across from volleyball court, cell tel. 983/107-5426, 11am-9pm Mon.-Sat., US$7-14) is a popular seafood restaurant serving up, among other tasty dishes, heaping plates of ceviche, coconut shrimp, and fish soup. It's a friendly, low-key place perfect for a beer and a good meal after a day of diving or relaxing on the beach. Wi-Fi is available.

The Maya Grill (Hotel Tierra Maya, 2.1 kilometers/1.3 miles north of town, tel. 983/839-8012, www.tierramaya.net, 6:30am-9pm daily, US$6-14) is a beachfront hotel restaurant with spectacular floor-to-ceiling windows with views of the Caribbean. The menu is solidly Mexican—tacos, quesadillas, enchiladas—with a fair share of seafood, too. Ingredients are fresh and portions are hearty.

The restaurant at Costa de Cocos, **The Reel Inn** (3 kilometers/1.9 miles north of town, no phone, www.costadecocos.com, 7am-8:30pm daily, US$5-26) serves up breakfast classics, burgers, steak, pizza, and all manner of tall tales—though with fishing as good as it is, many just happen to be true. The service is seriously lacking, but the schedule, reservations policy (none required), and full bar make it a reliable option.

If you are cooking for yourself, a **grocery truck** passes through town and down the coastal road several times per week—ask at your hotel for the current schedule. It comes stocked with eggs, yogurt, grains, basic produce, fresh meats, and canned food. You also can buy a broom or two. In town, there are a handful of small **mini-marts** selling basic canned and dried foods. Most are open 9am-9pm daily.

Accommodations

Xcalak's most appealing accommodations are

on the beach road heading north out of town. Few places accept credit cards on-site, but many have payment systems on their websites.

UNDER US$100

Facing the town beach, **Xcalak Caribe Lodge** (center of town, near volleyball court, www.xcalakcaribe.com, cell tel. 983/130-5580, US$35 s, US$60-70 d) is a small hotel with five simple, modern rooms. Three have floor-to-ceiling windows and glass doors for better views of the ocean; these open onto a public sidewalk, however, making them less than private. A breezy rooftop *palapa* serves as the hotel's common space. Snorkeling and fly-fishing tours are offered.

Hotel Tierra Maya (2.1 kilometers/1.3 miles north of town, tel. 983/839-8012, toll-free U.S. tel. 800/216-1902, www.tierramaya.net, US$90-100 s/d, US$150 apartment) is a pleasant hotel with ample rooms decorated with simple furnishings and colorful Mexican rugs. All have private terraces or balconies with views of the Caribbean. Continental breakfast is included in the rate and served in the hotel's excellent beachfront restaurant. Single and double kayaks are available for guest use. Fly-fishing packages are also offered.

US$100-150

It's hard not to feel at home at ★ **Sin Duda** (8 kilometers/5 miles north of town, Can. tel. 306/500-3240, www.sindudavillas.com, US$110 s/d, US$125 studio, US$145 apartment), a gem of a hotel with beautifully decorated rooms and apartments featuring Mexican folk art and breathtaking views. Evening often brings cocktail hour, when guests can join the friendly Canadian hosts for margaritas in the cozy lounge that doubles as a common kitchen and library. Kayaks are available for guests, as are a rooftop solarium and hammocks on the beach. A healthy continental breakfast is included.

Cheerful units with fully equipped kitchenettes make **Casa Paraíso** (2.5 kilometers/1.6 miles north of town, U.S. tel. 404/502-9845, www.casaparaisoxcalak.com, US$130 studio)

a great choice for indie travelers. Add ocean views from private balconies and a wide beach with palm trees, and it's a classic beach vacation. Full breakfast is included in the rate and is served in a pleasant *palapa*-roofed dining area. Kayaks, paddleboards, snorkel gear, and bicycles are available to guests free of charge. Snorkeling and fishing trips also can be arranged, with pickup at the hotel's private dock.

OVER US$150

Playa Sonrisa (6.9 kilometers/4.3 miles north of town, no phone, www.playasonrisa.com, US$160-180 s/d, US$180-250 suite) is a clothing-optional resort on a palm tree-laden stretch of beach. Units are clean and comfortable, though they lack the charm that you'd expect for the rate. What you mostly pay for is the freedom to enjoy the Caribbean in the buff. A continental breakfast is included in the rate, as is Wi-Fi. Geared at naturist couples, the hotel welcomes naturist families from May to October only.

Affiliated with XTC Dive Center, **Flying Cloud** (north end of town, across bridge, no phone, www.xtcdivecenter.com/flyingcloud, US$115-155 s/d, US$145 1-bedroom apt, US$165 suite, US$250 2-bedroom apt) is a five-unit hotel with whitewashed walls, polished cement floors, and spectacular ocean views. Mattresses are thick and bathrooms are spotless. While each unit has different amenities—some have king-size beds, others have kitchenettes—all are comfortable. The top-floor suite has sweeping 360-degree views from its private balcony. Guests enjoy use of the dive shop's pool and sea kayaks.

Information and Services

Xcalak has **no bank, ATM, or currency-exchange office,** and only a few places take credit cards—plan accordingly!

There's a basic **health clinic** (no phone, 8am-noon and 2pm-6pm Mon.-Fri.) two blocks from the soccer field, near the entrance to town.

The **police station** (toll-free Mex. tel. 066) is located behind the lighthouse.

Most hotels have Wi-Fi; in a pinch many hotel owners will let you use their computers to send a quick email. To make an international or domestic call, head to **Telecomm/ Telégrafos** (2 blocks north of the lighthouse, 9am-3pm Mon.-Fri.).

Getting There and Around

Bus service is somewhat erratic in Xcalak. Theoretically, buses bound for Chetumal (US$7, 4-5 hours) via Mahahual (US$3, 1 hour) and Limones (US$5, 2.5 hours) leave twice daily, typically around 5am and 2pm, but it's not unusual for one or both departures to be delayed or canceled. Upon arrival in Xcalak, your hotel may send a car to pick you up; otherwise, a taxi from town is about US$10. A cab from Mahahual runs around US$40.

Most travelers come in a rental car, which certainly simplifies life here. The closest gas station is on the main road to Mahahual, near the turnoff for Xcalak. However, it occasionally runs out of gas, so you should fill up on Highway 307 as well—Carrillo Puerto is a good spot. In a pinch, a few Xcalak families sell gas from barrels in their front yards; ask your hotel owner for help locating them.

If your budget permits, there also is a well-maintained airstrip approximately 2 kilometers (1.2 miles) west of town. Despite rumors that commercial flights will begin using it regularly, at the time of research it was only used sporadically by private or chartered planes.

CHACCHOBEN ARCHAEOLOGICAL ZONE

Chacchoben (8am-5pm daily, US$2.50) got its name from archaeologists who, after uncovering no inscription indicating what the

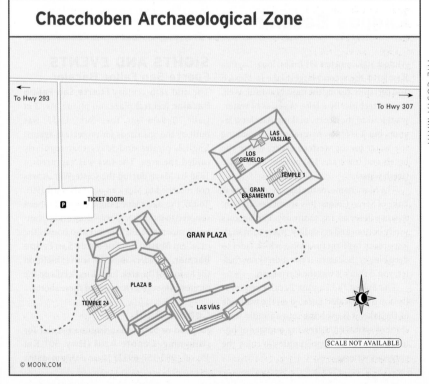

Chacchoben Archaeological Zone

To Hwy 293

To Hwy 307

LAS VASIJAS

LOS GEMELOS

TEMPLE 1

GRAN BASAMENTO

TICKET BOOTH

GRAN PLAZA

PLAZA B

TEMPLE 24

LAS VÍAS

SCALE NOT AVAILABLE

© MOON.COM

city's original residents called it, named it after the Maya village to which the land pertained. The meaning of that name is also lost, even to local villagers, though the accepted translation is Place of Red Corn. The area may have been settled as early as 1000 BC, and most of the building activity probably took place AD 200-700, the Classic period.

Visiting the Ruins

Entering the site, a short path leads first to **Temple 24,** a squat pyramid that is the primary structure of a small, enclosed area called **Plaza B.** Across that plaza—and the larger Gran Plaza beyond it—is a massive raised platform, the **Gran Basamento,** with the site's largest pyramid, **Temple 1,** atop it; this pyramid is believed to have served astronomical and religious purposes. Also on the platform, two smaller structures, dubbed **Las Vasijas** and **Los Gemelos,** were likely used for ceremonial functions. The site has some well-preserved stucco and paint, and for that reason none of the pyramids can be climbed. Though it can get crowded when there's a cruise ship at Mahahual, Chacchoben has an appealingly remote feel, nestled in the forest with towering mahogany and banyan trees, its paths dotted with bromeliads.

Practicalities

Chacchoben is located about 70 kilometers (43 miles) north of Mahahual and 4 kilometers (2.5 miles) west of Limones. By **car,** take Highway 307 and turn west at the sign to Chacchoben ruins and the like-named town, about 3 kilometers (1.9 miles) down a well-paved road. Alternatively, take a **bus** to Limones and then a **cab** (US$5) to the ruins.

Laguna Bacalar

Almost 50 kilometers (31 miles) long, Laguna Bacalar is the second-largest lake in Mexico and certainly among the most beautiful. Well, it's not technically a lake: A series of waterways lead to the ocean, making Bacalar a lagoon, but it is fed by natural springs, making the water on the western shore, where the hotels and town are, 100 percent *agua dulce* (fresh water).

The Maya name for the lagoon translates as Lake of Seven Colors. It is an apt description, as you will see on any sunny day. The lagoon's sandy bottom and crystalline water turn shallow areas a brilliant turquoise, which fades to deep blue in the center. If you didn't know better, you'd think it was the Caribbean.

The hub of the Laguna Bacalar region is the town of Bacalar. Located on the west side of the lake, it is evolving into an indie traveler hot spot with a growing number of hotels, eateries, and opportunities to enjoy the gorgeous waters.

SIGHTS AND EVENTS

Fuerte San Felipe Bacalar

The mid-18th-century **Fuerte San Felipe Bacalar** (central plaza, no phone, Av. 3 at Calle 20, 9am-7pm Tues.-Sun., US$5) was built by the Spaniards for protection against English pirates and Maya that regularly raided the area. The fort was captured in 1858 by Maya during the Caste War. It was not returned to Mexican officials until 1901. Today, the star-shaped stone edifice has been restored to its former glory—drawbridge, cannons, moat, and all. The fort also houses the excellent **Museo del Fuerte de San Felipe Bacalar,** a modern museum with exhibits on the history of the area, including details on the pirates who regularly attacked these shores.

Cenote Azul

As good or better than Laguna Bacalar for swimming, **Cenote Azul** (Hwy. 307 Km 15, tel. 983/157-6932, 10am-5:30pm daily,

Laguna Bacalar

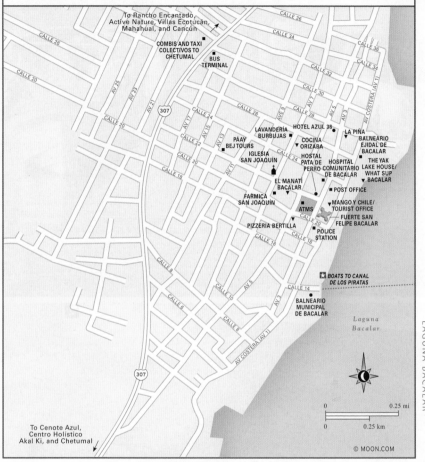

US$1.50) is two kilometers (1.2 miles) south of town. It's the widest cenote in Mexico, some 600 meters (1,969 feet) across at its widest, and 150 meters (492 feet) deep, with crystalline blue water. A rope stretches clear across, so even less-conditioned swimmers can make it to the far side. A large, breezy **restaurant** (tel. 983/834-2038, 9:30am-6pm daily, US$6-16) has the only entrance to the cenote, and charges the admission fee only if you don't order something.

★ Canal de los Piratas

A waterway directly across from the Fuerte San Felipe de Bacalar, the **Canal de los Piratas** is a shallow canal connecting Laguna Bacalar to Laguna Mariscal. Said to have been used by pirates to approach—and attack—the town of Bacalar during the colonial era, the waters are calm and turquoise blue and there are several sandy areas where boats moor while visitors swim, play in the water, and cover themselves in exfoliating mud. Tour

operators do a brisk business shuttling people between Bacalar and the canal, charging US$30 round-trip (up to six people); typically, they sell rides from a kiosk on the main plaza or along the waterfront road.

Fiesta de San Joaquín

In late July/early August, the town of Bacalar celebrates San Joaquín, its patron saint. For nine consecutive days, different neighborhoods host festive celebrations, each trying to outdo the other for the year's best party. Visitors are welcome and should definitely join the fun—expect plenty of food, music, dancing, and performances of all sorts. Kayak and horse races also are popular.

SPORTS AND RECREATION
Tours

A friendly German couple founded **Active Nature** (Hotel Villas Ecotucán, Hwy. 307 Km 27.3, cell tel. 983/120-5742, www. activenaturebacalar.com) after fate and car trouble cut short their planned tour of the Americas and left them in lovely Laguna Bacalar. Tour options include kayaking through mangrove channels, outrigger canoe tours, and sunrise birding walks. Day trips cost US$13-47 per person, including gear, snacks or lunch, and water. Tours begin at Villas Ecotucán, whose guests get a 10 percent discount. Overnight tours can also be arranged.

Asociación de Lancheros (end of Calle 14, tel. 983/835-5505, 8am-5pm daily) is a local co-op offering tours of the lagoon on board a catamaran, pontoon, or sailboat. Tours typically last two hours and cost US$12.50 per person. They include swimming in three nearby cenotes, one of which is ringed by stromatolites (fossilized primitive life forms), as well as a stop at the Canal de los Piratas. From April to June, trips also include a drive-by of

Isla de los Pajaros, a small island that is home to roseate spoonbills, egrets, and grackles. Customized tours also can be arranged.

What SUP Bacalar (The Yak Lake House, Av. Costera between Calles 24 and 26, www. whatsupbacalar.com, no phone) offers a popular stand-up paddleboarding tour of the lagoon twice daily (3 hours, US$22.50 pp). The tour begins with paddling to Cenote Negro, about 400 meters away (0.25 mile), for snorkeling. Afterward, the group heads to the Canal de los Piratas for the swimming and mud baths. The tour includes gear, snacks, breakfast or lunch, and even photos. Beginners welcome.

Páay bej Tours (Posada Casa Madrid, Av. 22 between Calles 11 and 13, tel. 983/154-7580, www.bacalar-tours-paaybej.com) offers guided tours of Maya ruins like Kohunlich, Dzibanché, and Chacchoben (US$45-80 pp, including transport, entrance fees, and boxed lunch), led by a friendly multilingual guide. You can also rent bikes here (US$1/hour, US$8/day).

Swimming

Balneario Ejidal de Bacalar (Av. Costera near Calle 26, no phone, 8am-7pm, US$0.50) is a public swimming area complete with *palapas* for rent (US$3/day), bathrooms, and a restaurant (9am-7pm, US$3-10). There are also kayaks for rent (US$7.50 per hour). Located just 250 meters (0.2 mile) from the central plaza, it's a convenient and inexpensive place to enjoy the water.

Basic but still nice, **Balneario Municipal de Bacalar** (Av. Costera at Calle 14, no phone, 9am-6pm, free) has a large, well-kept grassy area right on the lagoon, a long dock with a ladder for easy entry into the water, and a big *palapa* for shade and snacks (sodas and chips, mostly). Use of bathrooms is US$0.25.

FOOD

★ **El Manatí Bacalar** (Calle 22 between Avs. 5 and 7, tel. 983/834-2021, 8am-9pm Wed.-Mon., US$4-9) is a cavernous café with a gorgeous outdoor patio surrounded by tropical

---

1: boats waiting to take visitors on a tour of Laguna Bacalar; **2:** Fuerte Bacalar, a restored fort that houses an excellent museum trees and flowering plants. Farm-to-table Mexican dishes are the mainstays—think enchiladas, *pozole*, fruit and yogurt dishes, and tortas. A modern art gallery and handicraft shop, both showcasing local artists, entice diners to linger and shop. Live acoustic music is a breakfast treat during the high season.

Next to the fort, ★ **Mango y Chile** (Av. 3 near Calle 22, tel. 983/688-2000, 1pm-9pm Wed.-Mon., US$5-7) serves an entirely vegan menu of burgers, tacos, and salads. Portions are huge and integrate foods like hemp, falafel, and pumpkin seeds. A good variety of coffee drinks, freshly squeezed juices, smoothies, and kombucha round out the menu. Order at the counter and vie for a seat on the patio, which has enviable views over the lagoon.

La Piña (Av. 3 between Calles 26 and 28, no phone, 8am-9pm Thurs.-Tues., US$3-6) is a mom-and-pop restaurant with boho flair. Set in a long, narrow garden with tall trees and a small *palapa*, the menu is classically Mexican with extras like hummus platters and pizza. Good drinks specials—both alcohol- and fruit-based—make this a solid place to while away an afternoon.

Cocina Orizaba (Av. 7 between Calles 24 and 26, tel. 983/834-2069, 8am-3:45pm daily, US$3-10) serves a variety of traditional Mexican dishes in a thatch-roof restaurant a few blocks from the central plaza. The daily *comida corrida* (lunch special) includes an entrée, main dish, and drink.

On the main plaza, the Italian-owned and operated **Pizzeria Bertilla** (Av. 5 between Calles 18 and 20, cell tel. 983/136-8525, 4:30pm-10:30pm Thurs.-Tues., US$6-15) specializes in homemade pasta and pizza, made with top-of-the-line ingredients and toppings. Service can be a bit grumpy, but think of it as part of the experience.

Food stands (US$1.50-3) set up on the central plaza every evening starting at 5pm. You'll find favorites like hot dogs and tacos as well as *marquesitas* (crispy, crepe-like pancakes stuffed with savory or sweet fillings) and *elote* (corn on the cob, served with mayo, chile, and lime). It's a good place for cheap, tasty eats, with the best people-watching in town.

ACCOMMODATIONS
In Town

Backpackers love **The Yak Lake House** (Av. Costera between Calles 24 and 26, tel. 983/834-3175, yakbacalar@gmail.com, US$18-22 pp dorm with a/c, US$85 s/d with a/c), a modern and stylish hostel right on the lake with a hipster vibe and great views. Dorms and private rooms are available and include nighttime air-conditioning and continental breakfast; dorms have individual lockers and reading lights. A long terrace overlooking the lake is perfect for hanging out, and the hostel organizes various free tours and activities; many guests end up extending their stay more than once. Desk service can be oddly surly, however.

★ **Hostal Pata de Perro** (central plaza, Calle 22 between Calles 3 and 5, tel. 983/834-2062, www.patadeperrobacalar.com, US$33 s/d with shared bath and a/c, US$60 suite with kitchen and a/c) is a pleasant surprise, tucked behind a bustling restaurant. A hybrid hotel-hostel, it has five private rooms in the main building that are simple and appealing, with thick mattresses, tropical wood bed frames, and colorful bedding. All share updated bathrooms and a spacious common kitchen, where complimentary coffee and pastries are laid out every morning. For those traveling with kids or in a group, ask about the suites—small apartments, really—which are similar in style to the rooms but have private kitchens.

Hotel Azul 36 (Av. 3 between Calles 26 and 28, tel. 983/834-3165, www.azul36.com. mx, US$65 s/d with a/c) is a small inn that integrates natural building materials—exposed tree trunks, thatch roofs, bamboo fences—with modern furnishings and flair. Rooms have polished cement floors, thick beds on cement frames, and signature blue walls; bathrooms are simple and sleek with washbasin sinks. Units on the 2nd floor have small balconies. Grassy areas run throughout the property and lead to a well-tended pool, complete with wood-frame loungers and handcrafted tables.

Bacalar Bus Schedule

Departures from the **bus terminal** (Hwy. 307 near Calle 30, no phone) are almost all *de paso* (mid-route service), which means there's often a limited availability of seats. Destinations include:

DESTINATION	PRICE	DURATION	SCHEDULE*
Cancún	US$18-21.50	5-6 hours	every 30-60 minutes 12:15am-10:50pm
Chetumal	US$2.50-3.50	50 minutes	every 30-90 minutes 1:20am-11:50pm
Chetumal International Airport	US$7.50	45 minutes	3:50pm
Mahahual	US$5	2 hours	9:45am
Playa del Carmen	US$15-17	4-4.5 hours	take Cancún bus
Tulum	US$11-12	3 hours	take Cancún bus
Xcalak	US$4.50	2.5-3 hours	6:30am and 5:20pm

*Schedules are subject to change.

Outside of Town

Villas Ecotucán (Hwy. 307 Km 27.3, cell tel. 983/120-5743, www.villasecotucan.com, US$68 s/d) has 11 solar-powered, *palapa*-roofed *cabañas,* each spacious and simply decorated and with a veranda to enjoy the view of the lake and surrounding tropical forest. The verdant grounds have hammocks strung throughout, a main building that serves as a restaurant and communal space, and a peaceful dock. A full breakfast and use of kayaks is included. The hotel specializes in guided nature excursions by kayak and on foot.

Rancho Encantado (Hwy. 307 Km 24, tel. 998/884-2071, www.encantado.com, US$106-180 s/d with a/c) has spacious *palapa*-roofed casitas and modern suites, both featuring Mexican tile floors, good beds, and views of either the lush garden or the lagoon; all but one have air-conditioning. The prettiest spot here, however, is a pier that leads to a shady dock strung with hammocks—it's perfect for swimming and relaxing. Guests can receive massages and body treatments in a small kiosk built over the lake; a hot tub is nearby. Breakfast is included.

Set on the shores of Laguna Bacalar, ★ **Centro Holístico Akal Ki** (Hwy 307, Km 12.5, tel. 983/106-1751, www.akalki.com, US$280-US$406 s/d) is a whole-body experience—from the yoga classes and holistic body treatments to organic meals and breathtaking views. Eleven *cabañas* and suites are simple and elegant, with whitewashed walls, tropical wood floors, thick mattresses, and luxurious linens (plus no Wi-Fi or TVs in any of them, so guests can disconnect). Best of all, most units are built over the water—guests fall asleep to the gentle lapping of the lagoon (or jump in, from their private sundeck, first thing in the morning). Guided hikes in the tropical forest, as well as tours of the owners' organic farm, are offered. Breakfast and use of kayaks and bicycles are included.

INFORMATION AND SERVICES

Tourist Information

Bacalar's **tourist office** (Av. 3 between Calles 22 and 24, turismobacalar@hotmail.com, 8am-4pm Mon.-Fri., tel. 983/834-2886) is located across from the hospital; it has loads of brochures and knowledgeable staff members. Also, www.bacalarmosaico.com is a bilingual website with useful information on the area's sights, activities, and businesses.

Emergency Services

Hospital Comunitario de Bacalar (Av. 3 between Calles 22 and 24, tel. 983/834-2969, 24 hours) offers emergency services as well nonurgent medical care; for serious matters, head to Chetumal. For meds, try **Farmacia San Joaquín** (Av. 7 between Calles 20 and 22, no phone, 8am-3pm and 6pm-9pm daily). The **police station** (Calle 20 near Av. 3, toll-free Mex. tel. 066, 24 hours) is located across from the Fuerte San Felipe Bacalar.

Money

There is no bank in town, but there are several ATMs on the west side of the central plaza, including **Banorte and Santander.** If you need other money services, the closest bank is in Chetumal.

Media and Communications

The **post office** (Av. 3 near Calle 24, 8am-4pm Mon.-Fri., 9am-1pm Sat.) is just east of the Fuerte San Felipe Bacalar. For Internet access, most hotels offer complimentary Wi-Fi to guests. The central plaza also has free Wi-Fi.

Laundry

Lavandería Burbujas (Av. 7 between Calles 24 and 26, tel. 983/183-8965, 8am-8pm Mon.-Sat., 9am-1pm Sun.) offers next-day service for US$0.75 per kilo (2.2 pounds).

GETTING THERE AND AROUND

You can easily walk to all the sites of interest in Bacalar, with the exception of Cenote Azul. A taxi there from town costs around US$3; cabs typically wait for passengers around the central plaza and on Avenida 7 in front of Iglesia San Joaquín.

Bus

Bacalar's modest **bus terminal** (Hwy. 307 near Calle 30, tel. 983/833-3163) is on the highway, about a 20-minute walk from the central plaza or a US$1 cab ride. The buses are almost exclusively *de paso* (mid-route) service, which means there's often limited availability of seats—buy your ticket as soon as you know your schedule.

Combi

Combis and *taxi colectivos* (US$2.50, every 30 minutes, 5am-11pm) run between Bacalar and Chetumal daily. You can catch either in front of the bus terminal (Hwy. 307 near Calle 30).

Chetumal

Chetumal is the capital of Quintana Roo and the gateway to Central America. It's not the prettiest of towns, and most travelers just pass through on their way to or from Belize or southern Campeche. However, Chetumal's modern Maya museum is one of the best you'll find in the region (albeit with few original pieces) and is well worth a visit. And if you're dying to see the Guatemalan ruins of Tikal, a shuttle from Chetumal can get you there in eight hours (cutting through Belize) and back again just as fast; a 90-minute boat ride

also will take you to San Pedro, Belize, for a quick overnighter. The area around Chetumal is worth exploring, too, whether the bayside town of Calderitas or the intriguing and little-visited Maya ruins of Kohunlich, Dzibanché, Kinichná, and Oxtankah.

SIGHTS

Museo de la Cultura Maya

One of the best museums in the region, the **Maya Culture Museum** (Av. de los Héroes at Calle Cristóbal Colón, tel. 983/832-6838,

Chetumal

To Main Bus Terminal, Hospital General de Chetumal, Plaza las Americas, Zona Libre, and Hwy 186

AV PRIMO DE VERDAD

AV BELICE

AV 16 DE SEPTIEMBRE

CRISTÓBAL COLÓN

■ FARMACIA SIMILARES

★ TERMINAL SANTA ELENA

■ SECOND-CLASS BUS STATION
■ COMBIS TO CALDERITAS
★ MUSEO DE LA CULTURA MAYA/EDUCAL

AV MAHATMA GANDHI

MONUMENTO ★ AL MESTIZO

■ COMBIS/TAXIS TO BACALAR

Mercado Ignacio Manuel Altamirano

■ CONTINENTAL RENT-A-CAR

EFRAÍN AGUILAR

← To Chetumal Airport and Hwy 186

■ INTERNET CAFÉS

MUSEO DE ★ LA CIUDAD

AV JOSÉ MARÍA MORELOS

AV FRANCISCO I MADERO

AV INDEPENDENCIA

● HOTEL LOS COCOS

HÉROES DE CHAPULTEPEC

AV 5 DE MAYO

LÁZARO CÁRDENAS

■ BANORTE
● URBAN HOTEL 101
■ FARMACIA SIMILARES

AV BENITO JUÁREZ

AV DE LOS HÉROES

■ POST OFFICE

AV MIGUEL HIDALGO

▼ EL TACO LOCO

■ CAFÉ-RESTAURANT LOS MILAGROS

AV REFORMA

CALZ VERACRUZ

CALZ COZUMEL

IGNACIO ZARAGOZA

● FIESTA INN
ALVARO OBREGÓN

▼ LA PANADERÍA TARTALETA

● EUROPCAR

▼ SERGIO'S PIZZA

HOSTELITO ●

HEROICA ESCUELA NAVAL

OTHON P BLANCO

■ LAVANDERÍA DEL CENTRO

AV 16 DE SEPTIEMBRE

HSBC ■

■ CITY TOURIST OFFICE

CARMEN OCHOA DE MERINO

22 DE ENERO

■ PALACIO DE GOBIERNO

MAQUETA PAYO OBISPO ★

Esplanada de la Bandera

BLVD BAHÍA

■ TOURIST INFORMATION BOOTH

ESMERELDA

★ PALACIO LEGISLATIVO

To Las Arracheras de Don José, Calderitas, and Oxtankah Archaeological Zone →

El Malecón

Bahía de Chetumal

0 ── 200 yds
0 ── 200 m

Passenger Ferry to San Pedro and Caye Caulker (Belize)

© MOON.COM

9am-7pm Tues.-Sun., US$2.50 adult, US$1 child) extends over three levels—the upper represents the world of gods, the middle the world of humans, and the lower Xibalba, the underworld. Each floor has impressive, well-designed exhibits describing Maya spiritual beliefs, agricultural practices, astronomy, and more, all in English and Spanish. In fact, the only thing lacking is original artifacts (the replicas, however, are quite good). The exhibition area past the ticket booth usually has good temporary art shows, plus a cinema that hosts free screenings of independent films.

Monumento al Mestizo

Across from the Museo de la Cultura Maya is the **Monumento al Mestizo** (Av. de los Héroes s/n), a striking sculpture symbolizing the creation of a new race—the mestizo—through the union of the shipwrecked Spanish sailor Gonzalo Guerrero and Zazil Há, a Maya woman. Hernán Cortés offered to take Guerrero back to Spain, but Guerrero chose to stay in the Americas, wedding Zazil Há in a Maya marriage ritual. Note that the Maya symbol for the number zero as well as the cycle of life, the snail shell, provides the framework for the entire work of art.

Museo de la Ciudad

The **City Museum** (Calle Héroes de Chapultepec between Avs. Juárez and de los Héroes, tel. 983/832-1350, 9am-5pm Tues.-Sat., 9am-3pm Sun., US$2.50 adult, US$1 child, free Sundays) is small and well organized, and describes the political, economic, and cultural history of Chetumal, spanning the period from its founding in 1898 to the present day. Signage is in Spanish only.

El Malecón

Running six kilometers (3.7 miles) on the Boulevard Bahía, this breezy promenade makes for a fine bayfront stroll. Along it you'll find monuments, plazas, a lighthouse, government buildings, and, hopefully, a cooling breeze. Of particular note are two impressive **murals** found within the **Palacio Legislativo** (end of Av. Reforma, 9am-10pm Mon.-Fri.), a shell-shaped building that houses the state congress. Created by local artist Elio Carmichael, one mural outlines the state's history—from the creation of man to the devastating effects of Hurricane Janet in 1955—while the other depicts the law of the cosmos. Both are located in the reception area and are open to the public.

Maqueta Payo Obispo

Maqueta Payo Obispo (Calle 22 de Enero near Av. Reforma, 9am-2pm Mon.-Fri., free) is a scale model of Chetumal as it looked in the 1930s, with brightly colored clapboard houses, grassy lots, and plenty of palm trees. It's a reproduction of a model made by longtime resident Luis Reinhardt McLiberty. Look for it in a glass-enclosed building across the street from the Palacio Legislativo; glare on sunny days can make it hard to see the exhibit. A small history museum of the city also is on-site; signage is in Spanish only.

ENTERTAINMENT AND SHOPPING

Sunday on El Malecón

Every Sunday after 6pm, locals gather at the **Esplanada de la Bandera** (southern end of Av. de los Héroes) to enjoy city-sponsored events, typically performances by the municipal band or local musicians and singers. The events are free and family friendly, with vendors selling drinks and munchies.

Cinema

If you're hankering to watch the latest Hollywood film, head to **Cinépolis** (Plaza Las Américas, Av. Insurgentes s/n, tel. 983/837-6044, www.cinepolis.com, US$3.50-5), an 11-screen theater where most films are in English with Spanish subtitles.

1: Museo de la Cultura Maya in Chetumal; **2:** the famous masks at Kohunlich ruins; **3:** a Sunday performance in Chetumal

Shopping

Educal (Av. de los Héroes at Calle Cristóbal Colón, tel. 983/129-2832, www.educal.com.mx, 9am-7pm Tues.-Sat., 9am-2pm Sun.) is a good bookstore located inside the Museo de la Cultura Maya.

Mercado Ignacio Manuel Altamirano (Efraín Aguilar between Avs. Belice and de los Héroes, 8am-8pm Mon.-Sat., 8am-3pm Sun.) is a two-story building mostly selling everyday items, from clothing to kitchenware. For travelers, it's a good place to buy a pair of flip-flops, a travel clock, or kitschy souvenirs.

Plaza Las Américas (Av. Insurgentes s/n, 9am-10pm daily) is a classic shopping mall with clothing and shoe boutiques, a megaplex movie theater, and even a Walmart. You'll also find all the typical amenities like ATMs, a food court, and public bathrooms.

The **Zona Libre** (Corozal Duty Free Zone, 9am-7pm daily) is an area just across the Belize border that's jam-packed with stores selling products from around the world, including shoes, clothing, alcohol, and household items. If you're looking for a specialty item, you might find it here. Be sure to bring your passport and Mexico-issued tourist card (which you received upon entry), as you'll need to show them to Mexican immigration officials when leaving and reentering Mexico. It's a painless process as long as you have your papers! Note: The Zona Libre is located just before the Belizean immigration checkpoint, so travelers don't need a Belizean visa or tourist card to visit.

FOOD

A locals' favorite, ★ **El Taco Loco** (Av. Morelos near Av. Zaragoza, tel. 983/129-2090, www.tacoloco.mx, 8am-6pm daily, US$6-8) serves excellent seafood at very accessible prices. It's hard to pick just one item, but you can't really go wrong with dishes like Caribbean ceviche, shrimp cocktail, or octopus tacos. Service is sometimes spotty, and the dining room is decidedly no-frills, but it's all part of the experience.

La Panadería Tartaleta (Av. de los Héroes at Av. Obregón, no phone, 7am-10pm daily, US$2.50-4) is a bustling little bakery serving a sophisticated menu of panini—think smoked salmon, roasted vegetables with goat cheese, and Granny Smith apples with brie. There are also coffee drinks, smoothies, and, of course, beautiful desserts. Be sure to leave room for the chocolate croissants!

Sergio's Pizza (Av. 5 de Mayo at Av. Alvaro Obregón, tel. 983/108-1438, 7am-midnight daily, US$5-14) serves much more than pizza in its dimly lit dining room. The extensive menu covers the gamut of Italian and Mexican dishes—from meat lasagna to *molletes rancheros*. Meals are hearty, making it popular with families.

Located on the Malecón, **Las Arracheras de Don José** (Blvd. Bahía at Calle Josefa Ortiz de Dominguez, tel. 983/832-8895, 5pm-3am daily, US$4-10) serves some of the best tacos in town. Try the *tacos de arrachera* (broiled skirt steak marinated in lemon and spices), which are only improved when paired with a beer.

Café-Restaurant Los Milagros (Calle Ignacio Zaragoza near Av. 5 de Mayo, tel. 983/832-4433, 7am-3pm Mon.-Sat., 7am-1pm Sun., US$3-7) serves up strong coffee drinks and especially good breakfasts. The best seating is outdoors—snag a table where you can, as it can get crowded fast.

ACCOMMODATIONS

Chetumal's status as the state capital and its location on the Belize border make it a busy town, and reservations are recommended, especially on weekdays.

Under US$50

Draped in murals, **Hostelito** (Av. Othón Blanco near Av. de los Héroes, tel. 983/833-3419, US$10 pp dorm with a/c, US$28 s/d with a/c, US$75 suite with kitchen) is an excellent option for budget travelers. The private rooms are where it's at—spacious, clean, and modern—all opening onto a multilevel courtyard with a well-maintained pool, common outdoor kitchen, and hammock lounge. There's one dorm, which is dark and a bit cramped, but the bunks have good mattresses, individual lights, and outlets; air-conditioning is turned on at night. Continental breakfast is included.

Located up a steep set of stairs, **Urban Hotel 101** (Av. de los Héroes near Calle Lázaro Cárdenas, cell tel. 983/752-0735, www.hotelurban101.com, US$35 s/d with a/c) is worth the climb. This new hotel mixes boho charm with clean modern lines, creating a welcoming feel. Rooms have polished cement floors, sleek furnishings, rainfall showerheads, and splashes of color in side chairs and wall art. A nice touch is the windows— long and thin, they let in the sun but keep out the city noise. Continental breakfast is offered daily in a small, quirky lounge.

Over US$50

★ **Fiesta Inn** (Av. Obregón at Av. Independencia, www.fiestainn.com, tel. 983/267-3200, US$88 s/d with a/c, US$115-264 suite) oozes cool with mid-century modern flair. Rooms have gleaming floors and big picture windows with comfortable beds and high-end amenities. There's a spectacular rooftop pool and fitness center with views of the bay; a sushi and sake lounge opens onto it in the evenings. Mornings bring a popular buffet in the main restaurant (US$11/5.50 adult/child), complete with made-to-order omelets and a full line of freshly squeezed juices. Best of all is the service—attentive, personalized, and making you wish you could stay longer.

Hotel Los Cocos (Av. de los Héroes at Calle Héroes de Chapultepec, tel. 983/835-0430, toll-free Mex. tel. 800/719-5840, www.hotelloscocos.com.mx, US$45-55 s/d with a/c) has three categories of rooms, all pleasant and with updated furnishings and modern amenities. The more expensive ones have flat-screen TVs, quiet air-conditioning, and more stylish decor. They all open onto a lush garden, which has a small, inviting pool area. The on-site restaurant, with a spacious outdoor dining area, is great for breakfast and people-watching.

Outside of Chetumal

On the road to the like-named ruins, ★ **Explorean Kohunlich** (off Hwy. 186, tel. 443/310-8137, www.theexplorean.com, US$329-438 s/d all-inclusive) is a luxurious all-inclusive resort with 40 deluxe bungalows set on 30 hectares (74 acres) of tropical forest. Each has gleaming stone floors, high *palapa* ceilings, elegant furnishings, and privacy walls for sunbathing. Larger cabaña suites also have plunge pools. The main building houses a fine restaurant, a full-service spa, and a lap pool that overlooks the jungle (you can see the ruins at Kohunlich from here). The rate includes daily excursions with experienced guides, including rappelling in the jungle, kayaking through a crocodile reserve, or trekking through forgotten forests to little-visited ruins.

INFORMATION AND SERVICES

Tourist Information

Near the waterfront, the **city tourist office** (Av. 5 de Mayo at Carmen Ochoa de Merino, tel. 983/835-0860, 8am-4pm Mon.-Fri.) has a decent selection of brochures and maps. There also are **tourist information booths** in the main bus terminal (Av. Insurgentes at Av. Palermo, 10am-8pm daily) and on El Malecón (near the Palacio Legislativo, Av. Reforma, 8am-3pm Mon.-Fri.).

For online information, check out www.tuchetumal.com, a directory to Chetumal and area sights.

Emergency Services

About two kilometers (1.2 miles) from the center of town, **Hospital General de Chetumal** (Av. Chapultepec between Calles Isla Cancún and Juan José Siordia, tel. 983/835-1920, 24 hours) is the city's main hospital.

For meds, try **Farmacia Similares** (Av. de los Héroes near Calle Plutarco Elias, tel. 983/833-2232, 8am-10pm Mon.-Sat., 9am-9pm Sun.) or its **sister store** (Calle Cristóbal Colón between Avs. Belice and de los Héroes, tel. 983/833-2331, 24 hours Thurs.-Tues.).

Chetumal Bus Schedule

Departures from Chetumal's **main bus terminal** (Av. Insurgentes at Av. Palermo, tel. 983/832-5110) are for first-class service, though some second-class buses stop here as well; tickets for either service can be purchased downtown, in the **second-class bus terminal** (Av. Belice at Av. Cristóbal Colón, no phone). Unless otherwise noted, the schedule is from the main bus terminal:

DESTINATION	PRICE	DURATION	SCHEDULE*
Bacalar	US$2-3.50	50 minutes	every 30-90 minutes 12:30am-11:50pm
Belize City (Belize)	US$10	5 hours	every 60 minutes 11am-5pm (second-class bus terminal only)
Cancún	US$11.50-28	5.5-6 hours	every 30-90 minutes 12:30am-11:59pm
Corozal (Belize)	US$3	1 hour	7am
Flores (Guatemala)	US$35	8-9 hours	8am and 9:30am
Mahahual	US$6-12	2-2.5 hours	8:30am, 8:40am, and 10:30am or take Xcalak bus
Mérida	US$17-22	5.5-6 hours	five departures from 12:30am to 11:30pm
Playa del Carmen	US$10.50-23.50	4.5-5 hours	take any Cancún bus
Tulum	US$8.50-19	3.5-4 hours	take any Cancún bus
Xcalak	US$6.50	3.5-4 hours	5:40am and 4:10pm (second-class bus terminal only)

*Schedules are subject to change.

Buses to the **Zona Libre** (US$1.75, 30 minutes) leave the **Terminal Santa Elena** (Av. Primo de Verdad near Av. Miguel Hidalgo, tel. 983/832-0639) every 20 minutes 6:30am-9pm Monday-Saturday, 7:30am-8:30pm Sunday.

The **police** can be reached by dialing toll-free 066.

Money

HSBC (Av. Othon Blanco between Av. 5 de Mayo and Av. de los Héroes, 9am-4pm Mon.-Fri., 9am-3pm Sat.) is conveniently located downtown. There also is an ATM at the **main bus station** (Av. Insurgentes at Av. Palermo, tel. 983/832-5110).

Media and Communications

The **post office** (Av. Plutarco Elias Calles between Avs. 5 de Mayo and 16 de Septiembre,

8am-4pm Mon.-Fri., 9am-1pm Sat.) is just a block from the main drag. For Internet access, there is a string of **Internet cafés** across from the Mercado Ignacio Manuel Altamirano (Efraín Aguilar between Avs. Belice and de los Héroes); most charge US$0.75 per hour and are open 7:30am-midnight Monday-Friday, 8am-10pm Saturday-Sunday.

Laundry

Lavandería del Centro (Av. Othón Blanco near Av. 5 de Mayo, tel. 983/832-1149, 8am-8pm Mon.-Fri., 9am-2:30pm Sat.) provides next-day laundry service for US$0.75 per kilo (2.2 pounds).

GETTING THERE AND AROUND

Chetumal is a relatively large city, but the parts most travelers are interested in are all within easy walking distance of each other—mostly along Avenida de los Héroes and El Malecón. The exception is the main bus terminal, which is four kilometers (2.5 mi) from the center of town.

Air

The **Chetumal International Airport** (CTM, tel. 983/832-6625) receives only a few flights each day. Airlines serving it include **Interjet** (toll-free Mex. tel. 800/011-2345, toll-free U.S. tel. 866/285-9525, www.interjet. com.mx), **MAYAir** (toll-free Mex. tel. 800/962-9247, toll-free U.S./Can. tel. 844/622-0800, www.mayair.com.mx), and **Volaris** (Mex. tel. 551/102-8000, toll-free U.S. tel. 855/865-2747, www.volaris.com).

Bus

All first-class buses leave from the **main bus terminal** (Av. Insurgentes at Av. Palermo, tel. 983/832-5110), though most second-class buses also stop here on the way into or out of town.

The **second-class bus station** (Avs. Belice and Cristóbal Colón, tel. 983/832-0639) is located just west of the Museo de la Cultura Maya; tickets for first-class buses also can be purchased here if you want to buy your tickets in advance but don't want to make the trek to the main terminal.

Terminal Santa Elena (Av. Primo de Verdad near Av. Miguel Hidalgo, tel. 983/832-0639) has daily bus service to the Zona Libre.

Combi

Combis and *taxis colectivos* (US$2.50, every 30 minutes, 4am-10pm) run between Chetumal and Bacalar daily. You can catch either on Avenida Independencia near Calle Efraín Aguilar. Vehicles leave every 30 minutes or as soon as there are four passengers.

Car

The highways in this area are all paved and well maintained. Car rental agencies in town include **Continental Rent-a-Car** (Av. de los Héroes near Av. Mahatma Gandhi, tel. 983/832-2411, www.continentalcar.com.mx, 8am-8pm daily) and **Europcar** (Av. Obregón at Av. Independencia, tel. 983/833-9959, www.europcar.com, 9am-6pm daily).

Taxi

Taxis can be flagged down easily in downtown Chetumal. Few are metered, so be sure to agree on a price before you set off toward your destination. A cab around downtown and along El Malecón costs around US$2-3.

Water Taxi

Water Jets International (El Muelle Fiscal, Blvd. Bahía s/n, tel. 983/833-3201, Belize tel. 501/226-2194, www.sanpedrowatertaxi.com) provides daily ferry service to San Pedro (US$55, 1.5 hours) and Caye Caulker (US$60, 3 hours) in Belize. Boats leave at 3pm and pass through immigration in San Pedro before continuing to Caye Caulker. The return ferry to Chetumal leaves Caye Caulker at 7am and San Pedro at 8am.

San Pedro Belize Express (El Muelle Fiscal, Blvd. Bahía s/n, Belize tel. 501/223-2225, www.belizewatertaxi.com) offers similar ferry service to Belize (same prices, same destinations as Water Jets), leaving Chetumal at 3:30pm every other day, alternating monthly (i.e., in January, March, May, July, September, and November the ferry operates on even days—the 2nd, 4th, 6th, etc. In February, April, June, August, October, and December, the ferry operates on odd days—the 3rd, 5th, 7th, etc.). The ferry returns from Caye Caulker at 7am and San Pedro at 8:30am.

Around Chetumal

The area around Chetumal has a number of worthwhile attractions, all the better because so few travelers linger here.

CALDERITAS

Located just seven kilometers (4 miles) north of Chetumal, Calderitas is a bayside town known for its **seafood restaurants** (8am-6pm daily, US$4-10)—most along the waterfront across from the main plaza—and its **public beaches.** During the week it's a mellow scene, but on weekends locals descend upon the town for a day of R&R and some revelry, too.

Boat rides can be arranged at many of the bayside establishments to explore **Chetumal Bay** (US$150, up to 8 people) in search of manatees, which were once abundant in these waters, or to visit **Isla Tamalcab** (US$40, up to 8 people), an uninhabited island with white-sand beaches and good snorkeling. It's home to spider monkeys and *tepescuintles* (pacas in English).

If you want to stay overnight, **Yax Há Resort & Explorer** (Av. Yucatán 415, tel. 983/834-4127, US$7.50 pp camping, US$7.50-18 per RV, US$45 s/d with a/c, US$60 s/d with a/c and kitchenette) offers everything from tent and RV sites to bungalows, right on the water. The bungalows, while dated in décor, are quite comfortable. They range from one-room units with air-conditioning, TV, and mini fridges to two-bedroom units with fully equipped kitchens; all have porches overlooking the bay. There's also a pool on-site.

Getting There

Calderitas is a quick bus ride from downtown Chetumal. *Combis* leave from Avenida Cristóbal Colón, behind the Museo de la Cultura Maya, roughly every 30 minutes 6am-9pm daily (US$0.25, 25 minutes). If you have a **car,** head east out of Chetumal on Boulevard Bahía, which becomes the main drag in Calderitas. Alternatively (though less scenic), take Avenida Insurgentes east until you get to the turnoff, and follow the signs from there.

OXTANKAH ARCHAEOLOGICAL ZONE

Oxtankah (8am-5pm daily, US$2.50) is a small archaeological site whose name means "between branches," so called by early archaeologists after the many trees growing amid, and on top of, the structures. Relatively little is known about Oxtankah—including its true name—but it probably arose during the Classic era, between AD 300 and 600, and was dedicated primarily to trade and salt production. Oxtankah's principal structures were constructed in this period, suggesting it was a fairly robust city; at its height, it extended to the shores of Chetumal Bay and included the island of Tamalcab.

Oxtankah was apparently abandoned around AD 600, for unknown reasons. The city was reoccupied by Maya settlers almost a thousand years later, in the 14th or 15th century, during which time a number of structures were expanded or enhanced. It was still occupied, mostly by modest earthen homes, when the first Spanish explorers arrived.

Some researchers have suggested the infamous Spaniard castaway Gonzalo Guerrero lived here; Guerrero was shipwrecked in this area in 1511 and adopted Maya ways, even marrying a chieftain's daughter. Their children are considered the New World's first mestizos, or mixed-race people.

In 1531, conquistador Alonso de Avila attempted to found a colonial city on the site, but he was driven out after two years of bitter conflict with local residents. He did manage to have a Franciscan chapel built, the skeleton of which remains, including an impressive eight-meter (26-foot) arch.

Today, most of the excavated structures in Oxtankah surround two plazas: **Abejas**

Oxtankah Archaeological Zone

FRANCISCAN CHAPEL

P

TICKET BOOTH/ MUSEUM

STRUCTURE IV

PLAZA DE LAS ABEJAS

STRUCTURE I

STRUCTURE X

STRUCTURE III

STRUCTURE IX

PLAZA DE LAS COLUMNAS

STRUCTURE VI

SCALE NOT AVAILABLE

© MOON.COM

(Bees), the city's main ceremonial and elite residential center, and the somewhat smaller **Columnas** (Columns), whose large palace probably served an administrative function. Architecturally, the structures are more closely related to those of the Petén region (present-day Guatemala) than to Yucatecan ones, suggesting a close relationship with the former. There's a small **museum** on-site; signage is in Spanish only.

Getting There

Oxtankah is located seven kilometers (4 miles) north of Calderitas, about one kilometer (0.6 mile) off the bayside road. There's no public transportation to the site; a **cab** from Calderitas costs US$3.50 each way; one from Chetumal will run about US$18 round-trip, including wait time.

KOHUNLICH ARCHAEOLOGICAL ZONE

Swallowed by the jungle over the centuries, **Kohunlich** (8am-5pm daily, US$3.25) was rediscovered in 1912 by American explorer Raymond Merwin, but it was not until the 1960s that excavation of the site began in earnest. Today, the ruins are in harmony with the surrounding vegetation: The site has more than 200 structures, stelae, and uncovered

Kohunlich Archaeological Zone

mounds that have trees growing out of them and moss spreading over their stones—a beautiful sight. Most date to the Late Preclassic (AD 100-200) through the Classic (AD 600-900) periods.

Kohunlich's most famous and compelling structure is the **Temple of the Masks.** Constructed in AD 500, it features six two-meter-tall (6.6-foot) stucco masks, believed to be representations of the Maya sun god, with star-incised eyes, mustaches, and nose plugs. Intriguingly, each is slightly different, leading some to speculate that they also represent successive members of the ruling dynasty; it would not have been unusual for the city's elite to draw an overt connection between themselves and a high god.

Southwest of the Temple of the Masks is **27 Escalones,** the largest and most impressive residential area in Kohunlich. Built on a cliff with a spectacular bird's-eye view of the jungle, it is one of the largest palaces in the Maya world, reached by climbing its namesake 27 steps. As you walk through the site, keep an eye out for *aguadas* (cisterns) that once were part of a complex system of reservoirs.

Getting There

Kohunlich is located about 60 kilometers (37 miles) west of Chetumal. By **car,** take Highway 186 west and turn south (left) at the sign to Kohunlich. An 8.5-kilometer (5.3-mile) paved road leads straight to the site. There is no public transportation to the site.

DZIBANCHÉ AND KINICHNÁ ARCHAEOLOGICAL ZONES

If the crowds at Chichén Itzá and Tulum get you down, these picturesque twin ruins may be the antidote. Dzibanché and its smaller neighbor, Kinichná, see very few visitors—it's not uncommon to have them to yourself, in fact—and feature modest-size temples in varying states of restoration. (A great many structures aren't excavated at all, but even they—abrupt tree-covered mounds—hold a certain mystery and appeal.)

Dzibanché

The larger of the two sites, *Dzibanché* is Yucatec Maya for "Etched in Wood," a name created by archaeologists in reference to a wood lintel inscribed with hieroglyphics that was found in one of the primary temples. A date on the lintel reads AD 618, and the site seems to have flourished between AD 300 and 800. Archaeologists believe this area was occupied by a sprawling, widely dispersed city that covered some 40 square kilometers (25 square miles).

The site has three main plazas, each higher than the next. Dzibanché's namesake lintel is still in the temple atop **Structure VI,** also called the Building of the Lintels, facing one of the plazas. Climbing Structure VI is no longer allowed, but it's just one of several large pyramids here, the rest of which you can clamber up. The largest is **Structure II,** with an ornate temple at its summit where archaeologists found a tomb of a high-ranking leader (judging from the rich offering found

with his remains). The steep stairways and lofty upper temples here are reminiscent of Tikal and other temples in the Petén area of present-day Guatemala, suggesting a strong connection between the two regions.

Kinichná

Kinichná (House of the Sun) has just one structure, but it's a biggie: a massive pyramid whose summit affords a great view of the surrounding countryside. The structure has three distinct levels, each built in a different era over the course of around 400 years. As you climb, it's fascinating to observe how the craftsmanship and artistry changed—generally for the better—over the centuries. At the top is a stucco image of the sun god, hence the site's name. As in Structure II in Dzibanché, archaeologists uncovered a tomb here, this one containing the remains of two people and a cache of fine jade jewelry and figurines.

Practicalities

Dzibanché and Kinichná are open 8am-5pm daily; admission is US$2.75 and valid for both archaeological zones. There is no public transportation to or from the area, and precious little local traffic, so a **car** (or tour van) is essential. To get here, take the turnoff 50 kilometers (31 miles) west of Chetumal on Highway 186, before reaching the town of Francisco Villa; from there it's about 25 kilometers (15 miles) north to the ruins. Along the way, you'll hit the small town of Morocoy; about three kilometers past the town, take a right onto a bumpy road that leads to Dzibanché first, then Kinichná (there's a sign).

Chichén Itzá

For many travelers, Chichén Itzá is the Eiffel

Tower of the Yucatán Peninsula—you can't possibly go home without visiting it.

And for good reason: Chichén Itzá was selected as one of the New Seven Wonders of the World and boasts some of Mexico's most recognizable ancient structures, including its four-sided main pyramid and the Maya world's largest ball court. But that's just the beginning, believe it or not, of things to do in this area. The nearby ruins of Ek' Balam are less crowded than Chichén Itzá and feature an exquisitely preserved stucco frieze. To the north, the coastal town of Río Lagartos is famous for its flamingo reserve and bird-watching tours. Lastly, Valladolid is a lovely but oft-overlooked colonial town, with beautiful

Highlights

Look for ★ to find recommended sights, activities, dining, and lodging.

★ **Chichén Itzá Archaeological Zone:** Voted one of the New Seven Wonders of the World, the Yucatán's most famous ruin is all about hyperbole: the iconic star-aligned pyramid, the gigantic Maya ball court, even the crush of bikini-clad day-trippers from Cancún (page 275).

★ **Iglesia y Ex-Convento San Bernardino de Siena:** Located in a quiet corner of Valladolid, this elegant church has a spacious esplanade and beautiful interior, a small museum, plus a natural cenote inside the convent walls (page 289).

★ **Ek' Balam Archaeological Zone:** A stunning stucco frieze with angel-like figures and a huge "monster mouth" is the highlight of this serene site near Valladolid (page 299).

★ **Cenotes Agua Dulce:** A visit to this set of four cenotes makes for an eerily beautiful afternoon of underground swimming and exploring (page 302).

★ **Flamingo Tours:** The world's largest and pinkest flamingos congregate by the thousands—even tens of thousands—in the mangrove-fringed estuaries near Río Lagartos. Boat tours bring you up close to these most peculiar of birds, plus dozens of other species along the way (page 304).

Chichén Itzá

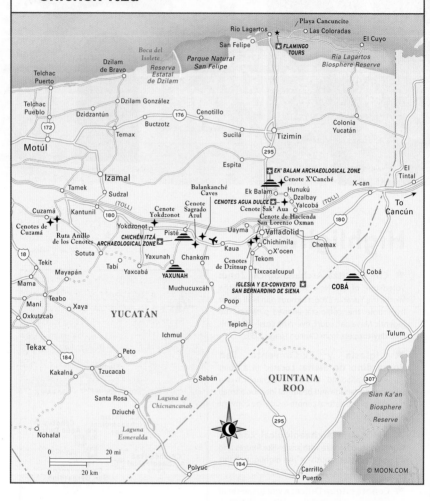

and historic churches, nearby cenotes (even one in town), and plenty of options for lodging and eating. Throughout the area, look for cenotes to explore and admire, or even to take a refreshing dip.

PLANNING YOUR TIME

Chichén Itzá can be visited in a full day; a half day will do if you just want the highlights. There are myriad tours to the site, but having your own car allows you to beat the crowds (hint: arrive early) and to make side trips to

Previous: Chichén Itzá's Nunnery; palm grove; Uayma's remarkable main church.

nearby cenotes and villages. Chichén Itzá also has a worthwhile sound and light show, which you can attend the night before or after you visit the ruins. Ek' Balam is a much smaller site; budget a few hours, including visits to neighboring cenotes. Bird-watching tours at Río Lagartos typically leave in the early morning or late afternoon—consider staying a night there to avoid driving in the dark. Otherwise, Valladolid is a logical base, with interesting sights, good accommodations, and a central location.

Chichén Itzá

Chichén Itzá is one of the finest archaeological sites in Mexico, and in all of Mesoamerica. It is also one of the most visited. Located just two hours from both Cancún and Mérida, the site is lined with vendors hawking their wares and is often inundated by tour groups. That fact should not dissuade independent travelers from visiting—crowded or not, Chichén Itzá is a truly magnificent ruin and a must-see on any archaeology tour of the Yucatán. That said, you can make the most of your visit by arriving right when the gates open, so you can see the big stuff first and be exploring the outer areas by the time vendors have finished setting up their tables and tour buses start to roll in.

ORIENTATION

Chichén Itzá is located in the middle of the Yucatán Peninsula, about 200 kilometers (124 miles) from Cancún and 120 kilometers (74 miles) from Mérida, making it a doable but longish day trip from either. Just two kilometers (1.2 miles) from the ruins sits **Pisté,** a one-road town that's strangely underdeveloped considering its proximity to such an important and heavily visited site. The hotels and restaurants here are unremarkable, and there's not much to do or see in town. There are several higher-end options near and on the road to the ruins. Another option is to stay in Valladolid, just 42 kilometers (26 miles) away—an easy jaunt.

TOP EXPERIENCE

★ CHICHÉN ITZÁ ARCHAEOLOGICAL ZONE

Chichén Itzá (8am-5pm daily, US$12.75 adult, US$3.50 child, US$12-24.25 sound and light show only) is a monumental archaeological site, remarkable for both its size and scope. The ruins include impressive palaces, temples, and altars, as well as the largest-known ball court in the Maya world. One of the most widely recognized (and heavily visited) ruins in the world, it was declared a World Heritage site by UNESCO in 1988 and one of the New Seven Wonders of the World in 2007. In 2012, INAH (Instituto Nacional de Antropología e Historia) even partnered with Google to photograph—by bicycle—the site for Google Street View.

History

What we call Chichén Itzá surely had another name when it was founded. The name means Mouth of the Well of the Itzá, but the Itzá, an illiterate and seminomadic group of uncertain origin, didn't arrive here until the 12th century. Before the Itzá, the area was controlled—or at least greatly influenced—by Toltec migrants who arrived from central Mexico around AD 1000. Most of Chichén's most notable structures, including its famous four-sided pyramid, and images like the reclining *chac-mool,* bear a striking resemblance to structures and images found at

Chichén Itzá Archaeological Zone

Sacred Cenote

SACBÉ

TEMPLE OF THE BEARDED MAN

GREAT BALL COURT

TZOMPANTLI

PLATFORM OF EAGLES AND JAGUARS

PLATFORM OF VENUS

LOWER TEMPLE OF THE JAGUAR

TEMPLE OF TABLES

TEMPLE OF WARRIORS

To Pisté and Hwy 180

P

BUS STOP/ COLECTIVOS TO VALLADOLID

VISITORS CENTER/ MAIN ENTRANCE

EL CASTILLO

GROUP OF A THOUSAND COLUMNS

OSARIO

PALACIO DE LAS COLUMNAS ESCULPIDAS

CASA DEL VENADO

MERCADO

CASA COLORADA

Xtoloc Cenote

ZONA HOTELERA ENTRANCE

THE LODGE AT CHICHÉN ITZÁ/ MAYALAND PLANETARIUM

EL CARACOL

TEMPLE OF RELIEFS

NUNNERY

AKAB DZIB

HACIENDA CHICHÉN / LOS FAISANES BISTRO

VILLAS ARQUEOLÓGICAS CHICHÉN ITZÁ

To Hwy 180, Parque Ecoarqueológico Ik Kil, Grutas de Balankanché, Hotel Oka'an, and Valladolid

0   100 yds
0   100 m

© MOON.COM

Tula, the ancient Toltec capital, in the state of Hidalgo. Before the Toltecs, the area was populated by Maya, evidenced by the Puuc- and Chenes-style design of the earliest structures here, such as the Nunnery and Casa Colorada.

The three major influences—Maya, Toltec, and Itzá—are indisputable, but the exact chronology and circumstances of those groups' interaction (or lack thereof) is one of the most hotly contested issues in Maya archaeology. Part of the difficulty in understanding Chichén Itzá more fully is that its occupants created very few stelae and left few Long Count dates on their monuments. In this way Chichén Itzá is different from virtually every other ancient city in the Yucatán. It's ironic, actually, that Chichén Itzá is the most widely recognized "Maya" ruin considering it was so deeply influenced by non-Maya cultures, and its history and architecture are so atypical of the region.

Chichén Itzá's influence ebbed and flowed over its many centuries of existence and occupation. It first peaked in the mid-9th century, or Late Classic period, when it eclipsed Cobá as the dominant power in the northern Yucatán region. The effects of a widespread collapse of Maya cities to the south (such as Calakmul, Tikal, and Palenque) reached Chichén Itzá in the late 900s, and it too collapsed abruptly. The city rose again under Toltec and later Itzá influence, but went into its final decline after an internal dispute led to the rise of Mayapán, which would come to control much of the Yucatán Peninsula. Chichén Itzá was all but abandoned by the early 1200s, though it remained an important religious pilgrimage site even after the arrival of the Spanish.

El Castillo

The most dramatic structure in Chichén Itzá is **El Castillo** (The Castle), also known as the **Temple of Kukulcán.** At 24 meters (79 feet), it's the tallest structure on the site, and certainly the most recognizable. Dating to around AD 850, El Castillo was built according to strict astronomical guidelines. There are nine levels, which, divided by the central staircase, make for 18 platforms, the number of months in the Maya calendar. Each of the four sides has 91 steps, which, added together along with the platform on top, total 365—one for each day of the year. And there are 52 inset panels on each face of the structure, equal to the number of years in each cycle of the Calendar Round.

On the spring and autumn equinoxes (March 21 and September 22), the afternoon sun lights up a bright zigzag strip on the outside wall of the north staircase as well as the giant serpent heads at the base, giving the appearance of a serpent slithering down the steps. Chichén Itzá is mobbed during those periods, especially by spiritual-minded folks seeking communion with the ancient Maya. The effect also occurs in the days just before and after the equinox, and there are significantly fewer people blocking the view.

Climbing El Castillo used to be a given for any visit to Chichén Itzá, and the views from its top level are breathtaking. However, an elderly tourist died in 2005 after tumbling from near the top of the pyramid to the ground. The accident, combined with longtime warnings from archaeologists that the structure was being irreparably eroded by the hundreds of thousands of visitors who climbed it yearly, prompted officials to close it off. Pyramids at other sites have been restricted as well, and it's become a standard policy at most Maya archaeological zones.

Deep inside El Castillo and accessed by way of a steep, narrow staircase are several chambers; inside one is a red-painted, jade-studded bench in the figure of a jaguar, which may have served as a throne of sorts. You used to be able to climb the stairs to see the chambers and throne—a fascinating, albeit humid and highly claustrophobic affair—but access was closed at the same time climbing the pyramid was prohibited.

El Castillo is among the most scrutinized archaeological structures in all of the Mexico, yet it harbored an incredible secret until very recently. In 2015, archaeologists using specialized probes to study underground electrical properties discovered something startling—there's a massive cenote, around 35 meters (114 feet) across and 20 meters (66 feet) deep, directly underneath the pyramid. The roof of the cenote is still about 5 meters (16 feet) thick, obviously enough to support the pyramid, but like most enclosed cenotes, the roof is eroding from the inside, growing thinner and thinner; eventually it may collapse. Archaeologists believe the Maya deliberately built El Castillo over this cenote, as it was considered a sacred place and a direct link to the underworld. In fact, an underground river connects it to the Sacred Cenote, to the north, as well as another three visible cenotes directly to the south, east, and west—suggesting that the cenote under El Castillo was considered the central, most important, one. Two tunnels from the Osario appear to lead directly to the hidden cenote but were sealed off with huge piles of stone. At the time of research, a team of archaeologists was excavating these passageways in hope of finding an entrance to the cenote.

Great Ball Court

Chichén Itzá's famous **Great Ball Court** is the largest ball court in Mesoamerica by a wide margin. The playing field is 135 meters (443 feet) by 65 meters (213 feet), with two parallel walls 8 meters high (26 feet) and scoring rings in impossibly high perches in the center. The players would've had to hit a 12-pound rubber ball through the rings using only their elbows, wrists, and hips (they wore heavy padding). The game likely lasted for hours; at the game's end, the captain of one team—or even the whole team—was apparently sacrificed, possibly by decapitation. There's disagreement about *which* team got the axe, however. Some say it was the losers—otherwise the game's best players would constantly be wiped out. Some argue that it was the winners, and that being sacrificed would have been the ultimate honor. Of course, it's likely the game varied from city to city and evolved over the many centuries it was played.

Along the walls, reliefs depict the ball game and sacrifices.

On the outside of the ball court, the **Lower Temple of the Jaguar** has incredibly fine relief carvings depicting the Maya creation myth. An upper temple, off-limits to visitors, is decorated with a variety of carvings and remnants of what were likely colorful murals.

The Platforms

As you make your way from the ball court to the Temple of Warriors, you'll pass the gruesome **Tzompantli**, or **Wall of Skulls.** A low T-shaped platform, it is decorated on all sides with row upon row of carved skulls, most with eyes staring out of the large sockets. Among the skulls are images of warriors holding the heads of decapitated victims, skeletons intertwined with snakes, and eagles eating human hearts (a common image in Toltec design, further evidence of their presence here). It is presumed that ceremonies performed on this platform culminated in a sacrificial death for the victim, the head then left on display, perhaps with others already in place. It's estimated that the platform was built AD 1050-1200. Nearby, the **Platform of Venus** and **Platform of Eagles and Jaguars** are smaller square structures, each with low stairways on all four sides, which were likely used for ritualistic music and dancing.

Sacred Cenote

This natural well is 300 meters (984 feet) north of the main structures, along the remains of a *sacbé* (raised stone road) constructed during the Classic period. Almost 60 meters (197 feet) in diameter and 30 meters (98.4 feet) down to the surface of the water, it was a place for sacrifices, mostly to Chaac, the god of rain, who was believed to live in its depths. The cenote has been dredged and scoured by divers numerous times, beginning as early as 1900, and the remains of scores of victims, mostly children and young adults, have been recovered,

1: Chichén Itzá's magnificent main pyramid, El Castillo; **2:** El Caracol, also known as the Observatory

as well as innumerable jade and stone artifacts. (Most are now displayed at the Museo Nacional de Antropología in Mexico City.) On the edge of the cenote is a ruined sweat bath, probably used for purification rituals before sacrificial ceremonies. The name Chichén Itzá (Mouth of the Well of the Itzá) is surely derived from this deeply sacred cenote, and it remained an important Maya pilgrimage site well into the Spanish conquest.

Temple of Warriors and Group of a Thousand Columns

The **Temple of Warriors** is where some of the distinctive reclining *chac-mool* figures are found. However, its name comes from the rectangular monoliths in front, which are carved on all sides with images of warriors. (Some are also prisoners, their hands tied behind their backs.) This temple is also closed to entry, and it can be hard to appreciate the fading images from the rope perimeter. You may be able to get a closer look from the temple's south side, where you can easily make out the figures' expressions and dress (though access is sometimes blocked there as well). The south side is impressive for its facade, too, where a series of well-preserved human and animal figures adorn the lower portion, while above, human faces emerge from serpents' mouths, framed by eagle profiles, with masks of Chaac, the hook-nosed god of rain, on the corners.

The aptly named **Group of a Thousand Columns** is adjacent to the Temple of Warriors. Its perfectly aligned cylindrical columns likely supported a grand roof structure.

Across the plaza, the **Palacio de las Columnas Esculpidas** (Palace of Sculptured Columns) also has cylindrical columns, but with intricate carvings, suggesting this was the ceremonial center of this portion of the complex. Continuing through the trees, you'll reach the **Mercado** (market). The name is purely speculative, though it's easy to imagine a breezy, bustling market here, protected from the sun under a wood and *palapa* roof built atop the structure's remarkably high columns.

Osario, El Caracol, and the Nunnery

From the market, bear left (away from El Castillo, just visible through the trees) until you meet the path leading to the site's southern entrance. You'll pass the **Osario** (ossuary), also known as the Tomb of the High Priest. Like a miniature version of El Castillo, the pyramid at one time had four stairways on each side and a temple at the crest. From the top platform, a vertical passageway leads into a chamber where seven tombs were discovered, along with numerous copper and jade artifacts indicating the deceased were of special importance (hence the temple's name). Continuing on, you'll pass two more large structures, **Casa del Venado** (House of the Deer) and **Casa Colorada** (Red House).

The highlight of this portion of Chichén Itzá is **El Caracol** (The Snail Shell), also known as the Observatory, and perhaps the most graceful structure at Chichén Itzá. A two-tiered circular structure is set atop a broad rectangular platform, with window slits facing south and west, and another aligned according to the path of the moon during the spring equinox. Ancient astronomers used structures like this one to track celestial events and patterns—the orbits of the moon and Venus, and the coming of solar and lunar eclipses, for example—with uncanny accuracy.

Beyond El Caracol is the **Nunnery,** so-named by Spanish explorers who thought it looked like convents back home. Judging from its size, location, and many rooms, the Nunnery was probably an administrative palace. Its exuberant facades show strong Chenes influence, another example of the blending of styles in Chichén Itzá.

Sound and Light Show

A nightly high-tech **sound and light show** (www.nochesdekukulkan.com, US$24.25 Tues.-Sat., US$12 Sun.) tells a broad-stroke history of the Maya that's projected onto the ruins at 7pm in the winter (Oct.-Mar.) and at 8pm in the summer (Apr.-Sept.). The

Chichén Itzá: Sold!

The great Chichén Itzá archaeological zone was actually, until recently, private property. One of the New Seven Wonders of the World, one of Mexico's most popular tourist attractions, one of the most important ancient cities in the Americas, a site still sacred to Maya and New Agers alike—was also a piece of real estate, owned by the Barbachanos, one of Mexico's wealthiest families. But after a long and increasingly bitter dispute over control and ownership of the land, the Mexican government and the Barbachanos agreed on terms—and a price—and the land became property of the Mexican state in 2010.

Chichén Itzá was, of course, indigenous land when Spanish conquistadores arrived. It was later included in Spanish land grants and used for many years for farming and ranching. The ruins were visited by explorers John Stephens and Frederick Catherwood, but the site was largely ignored until American explorer and amateur archaeologist Edward Thompson purchased it in 1894. Thompson, who had excavated other Maya sites, found and removed dozens of artifacts, shipping most to Harvard's Peabody Museum. Thompson nearly lost the land after being accused of stealing Mexican treasures, and eventually sold it to the elder Barbachano in 1944.

Over the years, the Barbachanos created the Mayaland Resort and Hacienda Chichén. They later purchased Uxmal ruins and built hotels there as well. The arrangement was mostly agreeable, with the government and family splitting ticket revenue, and the Barbachanos were adept hoteliers, even hosting a string of celebrity visitors, from European royalty to Saudi sheiks.

The elder Barbachano died in the 1960s, leaving the property to his children and grandchildren. Not long after, the first grumblings were heard: Many Mexicans felt cultural treasures like Chichén Itzá ought not be owned by private families, and local Maya argued it was rightfully theirs. The Mexican government passed a law in 1972 making the ruins (though not the land they sit on) property of the state. Maya vendors stormed the property more than once, demanding greater access for their wares.

By the early 2000s, the Mexican government was exploring the possibility of expropriating the land. The Barbachanos, perhaps sensing the writing on the wall, finally negotiated a sale. The elder Barbachano had once said he'd sell Chichén Itza for US$250 million. In the end, his heirs sold the land for around $220 million pesos, or US$17.6 million. The Mayaland Resort and the Haciendas at Chichén Itzá and Uxmal remain open; there's even a special entrance from Hacienda Chichén directly into the ruins. With over a million visitors to Chichén Itzá alone per year (and increasing), the family that once owned the ruins still has a strong and lucrative stake in its future.

show itself only lasts about 25 minutes but is preceded by a 45-minute self-guided tour of Chichén Itzá's most prominent structures, which are lit up for visitors—a special experience in of itself to wander among the ruins at night.

Admission to the show is separate from the general daytime admission to the ruins; be sure to purchase tickets online, especially during peak seasons. The show often sells out and, if it doesn't, the ticket lines can be daunting.

The program is presented in Spanish, but complimentary iPods with a recorded translations in several languages, including English, are available at the entrance; visitors must leave an ID or a hotel key as a deposit. The iPods also include a narration for the self-guided tour—a nice perk.

Practicalities

The ruins are open 8am-5pm daily. Admission is US$12.75 per adult, US$3.50 per child; if paying by credit card, it's paid in two parts (but at the same window)—one is the state fee (US$9.25), the other federal (US$3.50). If paying in cash, the transactions are combined. Additionally, visitors must pay US$2.25 to enter with a video camera; parking is US$1.50. Note: The daytime admission fee does not include entrance to the sound and light show (www. nochesdekukulkan.com, US$24.25 Tues.-Sat., US$12 Sun.), which can be purchased online.

Guides can be hired at the entrance according to fixed and clearly marked prices: US$45 for a two-hour tour in Spanish, US$50 in English, French, Italian, or German. Prices are per group, which can include up to eight people. Tips are customary and not included in the price. The visitors center has restrooms, an ATM, free luggage storage, a café, a bookstore, a couple of gift shops, and an information center.

MAYALAND PLANETARIUM

The **Planetarium at Mayaland Resort** (Zona Hotelera, Carr. Mérida-Valladolid Km 120, tel. 998/887-2495, www.mayaland. com, US$9) offers half-hour shows about Maya astronomy and scientific advances. The planetarium replicates the shape of Chichén Itzá's famous Caracol structure, just steps away, and itself believed to be an observatory. Typically part of pricey all-day Chichén Itzá package tours from Cancún or Mérida, the show can be seen by independent travelers too; stop by the concierge desk for the schedule and to buy tickets.

GRUTAS DE BALANKANCHÉ

Six kilometers (3.7 miles) east of Chichén Itzá are the **Balankanché Caves** (9am-4pm daily, US$6.85). Explored in 1959 by archaeologist Dr. Wyllys Andrews, the artifacts and ceremonial sites found here gave researchers a better understanding of ancient Maya cosmology, especially as related to *Xibalba* (the underworld). Nowadays, the caves are just a step above a tourist trap—a wide path meandering 500 meters (0.3 mile) down a tunnel set up with urns and other artifacts. Colored lights illuminate the path, but the recorded narration does nothing of the sort—it's so garbled you can hardly understand it, no matter what language it's in.

Entry times are fixed according to language: English at 11am, 1pm, and 3pm; Spanish at 9am, noon, 2pm, and 4pm; French at 10am. A minimum of six visitors are needed for the 45-minute tour to depart. Be sure to wear walking shoes—the path can be slippery in places.

PARQUE ECOARQUEOLÓGICO IK KIL

Three-times host to the Red Bull Cliff Diving World Series, **Parque Ecoarqueológico Ik Kil** (Carr. Mérida-Cancún Km 122, tel. 985/851-0002, www.hotelikkil.com, 9am-5pm daily, US$4.65/2.35 adult/child) is home to the immense, perfectly round **Cenote Sagrado Azul.** Although the cenote is natural, the alterations—supported walls, a set of stairs, a waterfall—make it feel Disney-like. Still, it's a good option if you're traveling with small children and need a spot to cool off. The cenote and restaurant (breakfast US$5-7, lunch buffet US$8) get packed with tour groups 11:30am-2:30pm; try visiting outside those times for a mellower experience. Better yet, stay overnight in one of the comfortable bungalows. The park is located three kilometers (1.9 miles) east of Pisté.

FOOD

Eating options are pretty limited in Pisté but improve somewhat if you have a car and can get to and from the large hotels.

Restaurante Las Mestizas (Calle 15 s/n, tel. 985/851-0069, 7am-10pm daily, US$4-7) is the best sit-down place to eat in Pisté, with an airy, colonial-style interior and tasty, good-sized portions of classic Yucatecan fare, from *panuchos* to *pollo pibil*. Expect a bustling dining room; if there's a wait, it typically moves fast.

La Gran Chaya (Calle 15 s/n, tel. 985/115-2589, 7am-11pm daily, US$2.50-5) is a hole-in-the-wall across from the town church with bright plastic tables and chairs set up in front. Meals range from egg dishes to piping-hot *salbutes*. Be sure to order an *agua* or a *licuado*—frothy cold drinks made with a variety of fresh fruits—to wash it down.

Set in a hacienda-turned-hotel, **Los Faisanes Bistro** (Hacienda Chichén Resort,

Pisté

Zona Hotelera, Carr. Mérida-Valladolid Km 120, tel. 999/920-8407, 7am-10pm daily, US$10-22) is a soothing place to eat, especially after a visit to the ruins. The menu is varied—Yucatecan specialties, pastas, sandwiches—and occasionally, a trio plays regional music. Much of the produce used is grown in the hotel's extensive organic gardens.

ACCOMMODATIONS

A handful of upscale hotels make up the small Zona Hotelera on the east side of Chichén Itzá, complete with its own entrance to the ruins. Nearby, in the town of Pisté, there are also a few budget and midrange options. Be sure to reserve early during the spring and fall equinoxes. All the options below have Wi-Fi available, though often in the reception area only.

Under US$50

The best deal in town, ★ **Posada La Casa de las Lunas** (Calle 15 s/n, tel. 985/851-0289, posada.laslunas@gmail.com, US$35-45 s/d with a/c) has spick-and-span rooms with contemporary décor. Each has thick beds, tile bathrooms, and amenities like flat-screen TVs and silent air-conditioning. All open onto a tidy courtyard with a nice pool. There's off-street parking, too. Look for the entrance just west of the OXXO convenience store.

Pirámide Inn (Calle 15 at Calle 20, tel.

985/851-0115, www.piramideinn.com, US$30 s/d with a/c, US$5 pp camping or in hammock) is a low, sprawling hotel with rooms that have a distinctly 1970s den look, some sporting bubblegum paint jobs and lacquered brick walls; the air conditioners appear to be from the same era. There's also a big pool and lots of green areas. Budget travelers can camp or set up hammocks (BYO gear).

US$50-100

Hotel Chichén Itzá (Calle 15 s/n, tel. 998/887-2495, www.mayaland.com, US$54-79 s/d with a/c) is the one of the nicest hotels in downtown Pisté, featuring rooms with comfortable furnishings, large modern bathrooms, and simple Mexican decor. The less-expensive rooms face the street and can be noisy, while the top-floor ones are larger and overlook the hotel's garden and pool area. The cavernous restaurant (7am-10pm daily) is often packed with tour groups.

Villas Arqueológicas Chichén Itzá (Zona Hotelera, Carr. Mérida-Valladolid Km 120, tel. 985/851-0187, www.villasarqueologicaschichen.com, US$65 s/d with a/c, US$121 suite with a/c) has boxy but nice rooms that are set around a lush courtyard with an L-shaped pool. There's a library/TV room with comfy couches and plenty of books—from romance to archaeology—and there's a decent restaurant too. Very tall guests should note that alcove walls bracket the ends of the beds.

Set in a lush forest, **Hotel Ik Kil** (Parque Ecoarqueológico Ik Kil, Carr. Mérida-Cancún Km 122, tel. 999/437-0148, www.hotelikkil.com, US$54-69 s/d with a/c, US$138 2-bedroom suite with a/c) has 14 modern and ultra-comfortable bungalows. All are spacious with comfy beds and whirlpool tubs. One unit is a two-bedroom suite that's perfect for families. Silent air-conditioning and private porches make them all the better. Guests enjoy unlimited access to the on-site cenote, including after hours.

Over US$100

A hacienda-turned-archaeological-headquarters, ★ **Hacienda Chichén** (Zona Hotelera, Carr. Mérida-Valladolid Km 120, tel. 985/851-0045, www.haciendachichen.com, US$179-199 s/d with a/c, US$215-299 suite with a/c) is now a tranquil hotel with lush grounds. Many of the original cottages were used by the first archaeologists to study Chichén; newer units, though, are charming with tropical wood furnishings and folk art. There's also a gorgeous pool, spa, and dining room. Look for repurposed Maya stone blocks in the main building.

Hotel Oka'an (Carr. Mérida-Cancún Km 122, tel. 985/851-0281, www.hotelokaan.com, US$77-118 s/d with a/c, US$113-132 suite with a/c) beckons with a full spa and mind and body workshops. Rooms are bright and tasteful in a pastel sort of way, with modern bathrooms and balconies. There's an open-air restaurant and infinity pool. Don't miss the view from the *mirador* terrace—El Castillo pops up over the (arduously manicured) tree line. The hotel is 1.5 kilometers (0.9 mile) off the highway.

The Lodge at Chichén Itzá (Zona Hotelera, Carr. Mérida-Valladolid Km 120, tel. 998/887-2495, www.mayaland.com, US$217-265 s/d with a/c, US$269-500 suite with a/c) is on the larger Mayaland resort's grounds: 100 acres of tamed tropical jungle featuring walking trails, a spa, three restaurants, and several pools. Its *palapa*-roofed bungalows are pleasant, with stained glass windows, hardwood furniture, and terraces. While the grounds are set apart, guests may encounter tour groups, somewhat diminishing the charm.

INFORMATION AND SERVICES

There is no tourist office in Pisté. There also isn't a bank, but there are four local ATMs: one inside the OXXO market, two in the

---

1: Restaurante Las Mestizas; 2: the entrance to Hacienda Chichén; 3: The Lodge at Chichén Itzá

Palacio Municipal (across from the church), and the last in Chichén Itzá's visitors center.

Emergency Services

The **police** have an office (tel. 985/851-0365, 24 hrs daily) in the Palacio Municipal, facing the town church; there's usually an officer directing traffic near the plaza. **Centro de Salud Pisté** (Calle 15 s/n, no phone, 7am-1pm and 5pm-7pm Mon.-Fri., 8am-8pm Sat.-Sun.) is one of two clinics in town. For anything serious, head to Mérida or Cancún. **Farmacia Yza** (Calle 15 s/n, no phone, 24 hrs daily), just east of the bus station, is good for meds.

Media and Communications

All of the listed hotels offer free Wi-Fi to guests.

Laundry

Lavandería La Lupita (Calle 10 near Calle 13, 8am-7pm Mon.-Sat.) charges US$1 per kilo (2.2 pounds) to wash and dry clothes; same-day service is available if you drop off your clothes first thing in the morning.

GETTING THERE AND AROUND
Bus

Pisté's small **bus terminal** (Calle 15 s/n, 8am-6pm daily, cash only) is just southeast of the Palacio Municipal, and about 2.5 kilometers (1.5 miles) from the entrance to Chichén Itzá; it's mostly used by second-class buses, which also pick up and drop off passengers at **Parque Ecoarqueológico Ik Kil** and the **Balankanché Caves.** For first-class buses, head to the **ticket office** in the Chichén Itzá gift shop (tel. 985/851-0377, 9am-5pm daily). The visitors center at Chichén Itzá also has **luggage storage** (8am-5:30pm, US$2-5), which makes it easy to catch a bus right after visiting the ruins.

All first-class departures leave from Chichén Itzá only. Second-class departure times listed here are for the terminal in Pisté. Second-class buses coming and going between 8am and 5:30pm stop at both the terminal and the parking lot at the ruins. If you are planning to catch a second-class bus at the ruins, keep in mind that buses headed toward Cancún stop at the ruins slightly after the listed times, while those bound for Mérida pass by slightly earlier. Most bus service to and from Pisté and Chichén Itzá is on Oriente, ADO's second-class line, but the few first-class buses are worth the extra cost. Note that the schedule listed below is subject to change.

- **Cancún:** One first-class bus (US$16.50, 3.5 hours) at 4:30pm; second-class buses (US$8.50, 4-4.5 hours) every 60 minutes 11:30am-5:30pm.

- **Cobá:** For the town and archaeological site, second-class buses (US$4, 2.5 hours) at 1:05pm and 5:05pm.

- **Mérida:** One first-class bus (US$9.50, 2 hours) at 5:30pm; second-class buses (US$5.25, 2.5 hours) every 60 minutes 8:15am-5:15pm.

- **Playa del Carmen:** One first-class bus (US$17.50, 3.5 hours) at 4:30pm; second-class buses (US$8.50, 4 hours) at 1:05pm and 5:05pm.

- **Tulum:** First-class buses (US$12, 2.5 hours) at 8:30am and 4:30pm; second-class departures (US$5.75, 3.5 hours) at 1:05pm and 5:05pm.

- **Valladolid:** First-class buses (US$5.50, 50 minutes) at 8am and 4:30pm; second-class service (US$1.75, 1 hour) every 60 minutes 8:30am-5:30pm.

Colectivos (US$1.75, 1 hour, every 30 minutes 7am-6pm) leave for Valladolid from a small park kitty-corner from the bus terminal and the Chichén Itzá parking lot.

Taxi

There's a **taxi stand** on Pisté's central plaza, toward the west end of town. The fare from there to the ruins is US$2-3; to Parque Ecoarqueológico Ik Kil it's US$4; and to the Balankanché Caves it's US$6. Taxis aren't metered, so be sure to agree on the fare before you get into the cab.

Car

Chichén Itzá lies adjacent to Highway 180, 40 kilometers (25 miles) west of Valladolid, 120 kilometers (75 miles) east of Mérida, and 200 kilometers (124 miles) west of Cancún. For drivers, the quickest way to get there is via the *cuota*, a large, modern freeway extending from Cancún most of the way to Mérida, with a well-marked exit for Chichén Itzá and Pisté. There's a price for speed and convenience, though: The toll from Mérida is US$5, and a whopping US$19 from Cancún. You can also take the old *carretera libre* (free highway) all or part of the way; it's in reasonably good condition but takes much longer, mainly because you pass through numerous small villages and seemingly innumerable *topes* (speed bumps).

Air

Aeropuerto Internacional Chichén Itzá is 16 kilometers (9.9 miles) east of Pisté, near the town of Kaua. Inaugurated in April 2000, it was one of the most modern airports in the country, with an 1,800-meter (5,900-foot) runway capable of receiving 747 jets. Although it initially received dozens of regular and charter flights, its license was suspended in 2001. Today it stands virtually empty, not receiving any flights.

Villages Near Chichén Itzá

Around Chichén Itzá are several small, mostly indigenous villages. They're a short distance on the map, but worlds apart from the buses, hotels, and sheer mass of tourists at the archaeological site. In some villages, travelers can visit off-the-beaten-track ruins, take tours—including visiting local families—and swim in cenotes, even stay the night. Time permitting, a visit to one of these towns can be an excellent complement to the shock and awe of Chichén Itzá.

YOKDZONOT

Located 15 kilometers (9.3 miles) west from Pisté along the *libre*, the village of Yokdzonot has one of the area's loveliest cenotes that's not on a tour bus circuit: **Cenote Yokdzonot** (Calle 20 btwn Calles 27 and 29, tel. 999/149-9315, www.cenoteyokdzonot.weebly.com, 9am-5pm daily, US$3.50 adult, US$2 child under 10). Run by a Maya cooperative of mostly women, the cenote is an open pool 40 meters (131 feet) deep, with trees casting shadows across brilliant teal water, tree roots dangling like ropes down the limestone walls, and mojarra fish glinting in the sunlight. For US$3.25, visitors can zip-line across the cenote or rappel 20 meters (66 feet) down into it. Camping is available on-site for US$15 per person, which includes a four-person tent with bedding. A restaurant (US$4-7) serves all meals.

As a bonus for staying the night (or if you ask nicely after closing time), you can watch bats funnel out at dusk, and March-June, the swallows departing at dawn. The co-op also offers bicycle tours of nearby cenotes (90 minutes, US$4). The highway sign for the cenote is easily missed; go south from the highway on the dirt road just west of the domed cement plaza, aiming for the cell phone tower. Taxis from Pisté charge US$6, or you can take a westbound second-class bus (US$0.75) and walk 300 meters (984 feet) to the cenote.

For more creature comforts, follow the "ecohotel" signs north of the highway to **Yucatán Mayan Retreat** (tel. 985/110-1160, www.yucatanmayanretreat.webs.com, US$10 pp camping with equipment, US$25 s/d with shared bath, US$35 suite with a/c), a forested oasis with a clutch of comfortable *cabañas,* each with flat-screen TV and fridge, a spotless outdoor kitchen, and an aboveground plunge pool. Walk-ins are welcome; stop at the bubblegum-pink house on the road to the hotel for info.

YAXUNAH

The small Maya village of Yaxunah is just 32 kilometers (20 miles) south of Pisté; it has three little-visited sights that make for a worthwhile afternoon of exploring.

Yaxunah ruins (free) is set just beyond the country road leading to its namesake village. Visitors literally drive onto the site—as in pick a pyramid and park your car—and are welcome to explore it on their own or hire a guide from the Yaxunah Centro Cultural. There are no facilities here; instead, surrounded by farmland, there are several small pyramids—including one with rounded walls—lots of platforms, and one large stone mound covered in trees. Yaxunah was first settled around 750-500 BC. Around AD 400-500, its royal family was tortured and murdered, their bodies (11 in all, including several children) thrown haphazardly into a tomb now designated Burial B. The city was conquered by Cobá in AD 600, and its population grew rapidly; most of Yaxunah's primary structures date from that time. Also built was a 100-kilometer (62-mile) *sacbé* (raised road) between the two cities, one of the longest yet discovered. Chichén Itzá conquered Yaxunah around AD 900, but did not occupy it. Yaxunah's population eventually dispersed, and the city was effectively abandoned around AD 1150.

Decorated with a mural depicting the Maya past and present, **Yaxunah Centro Cultural** (one block from central plaza, www.yaxunahcentrocultural.org, 9:30am-7pm daily, US$1.25) houses a small museum with exhibits on the Yaxunah ruins, including a site map, dioramas, pottery fragments, and a re-creation of one of the site's tombs. There also are exhibits on current-day Maya, their culture, and some of their important religious ceremonies. Outside, visitors can explore the botanical garden, which features plants used in everyday Maya life. All signage is in English and Spanish. Occasionally, there are folkloric dance performances; check the website for more information.

Cenote Lol Ha (aka Cenote Yaxunah, one block from central plaza, 10am-5pm daily, US$1.75) is a refreshing swimming hole surrounded by tall shade trees. A sturdy staircase leads to the clear, cool water—a perfect place to cool off. There are picnic tables for BYO snacks and drinks. It's located across from, and managed by, Yaxunah Centro Cultural.

Yaxunah is located 32 kilometers (20 miles) south of Pisté. To get there, head south on Calle 22, passing the village of Popola;

outdoor shower at Yucatán Mayan Retreat

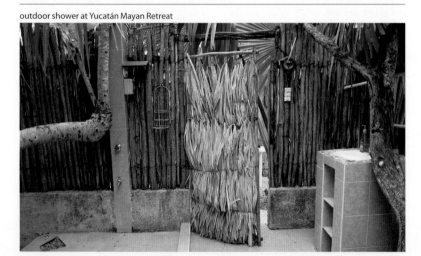

the ruins are 6.5 kilometers (4 miles) past Popola. The namesake town is 1.5 kilometers (0.9 mile) west of there.

MUCHUCUXCÁH

Centro de Turismo Comunitario de Muchucuxcáh, in the town of Muchucuxcáh, offers visitors a hands-on taste of present-day Maya life without feeling overly intrusive. Started and supported by a Mérida-based nonprofit called **El Hombre Sobre La Tierra** (tel. 999/927-0719, http:// elhombresobrelatierra.org), the Centro has eight typical *palapas* (US$35 pp, including meals) in a forest setting; each has hammocks (no beds here), mosquito nets, fans, and clean shared bathrooms. A large swimming pool is a welcome treat after a day of visiting and exploring. Traditional Maya **meals** are prepared using local ingredients and served fresh in a pleasant thatch-roofed dining room. The Centro offers various tours and activities led by local guides, including visiting cenotes and unexcavated ruins, home and village tours, Maya cooking lessons, hammock-weaving classes, and more. The cooperative runs mostly independently, but travelers should contact El Hombre Sobre la Tierra for information and reservations.

Muchucuxcáh is located 35 kilometers (22 miles) south of Pisté. To get to the village, take the *libre* (free highway) east for about 13 kilometers (8 miles), and then take a right onto the turnoff to Chankom. Continue on that road, past two villages, until you arrive at Muchucuxcáh. With only five streets in town, the Centro is impossible to miss. Private transportation to and from Pisté, Valladolid, Mérida, and Cancún can be arranged.

Valladolid

Valladolid draws tourists because of its mellow colonial atmosphere and its central location: 30 minutes from the archaeological zones of Chichén Itzá and Ek' Balam, an hour from the ruins at Cobá, and two hours from Mérida, Cancún, and Tulum. It's an easy bus or car ride to any of these destinations, its restaurants and hotels are reasonably priced, and you have the advantage of staying in a colonial Mexican town. If you're en route to one of the regional sites or simply want to have a small-city experience, consider spending a night here—you're sure to be happily surprised.

HISTORY

The site of several Maya revolts against the Spanish, Valladolid was conquered in 1543 by Francisco de Montejo, cousin of the like-named Spaniard who founded Mérida. It was once the Maya city of Zací. Montejo brutalized its inhabitants and crushed their temples, building large churches and homes in their place. It is perhaps not surprising, then, that the Caste War started in Valladolid, and that the city played an important role in the beginning of the Mexican Revolution. Today, Valladolid is a charming colonial town with a rich history and strong Maya presence.

ORIENTATION

Valladolid is easy to get around. It's laid out in a grid pattern with even-numbered streets running north-south, odd-numbered streets running east-west. The central plaza is bordered by Calles 39, 40, 41, and 42.

SIGHTS
★ Iglesia y Ex-Convento San Bernardino de Siena

Sitting at the end of the Calzada de los Frailes, the **Iglesia y Ex-Convento San Bernardino de Siena** (Calle 41-A, tel. 985/856-2160, 8am-noon and 5pm-8pm daily) is one of Valladolid's most attractive structures. Built by Franciscan missionaries between 1552 and 1560, the church is entered

Valladolid

through a series of arches, and the facade, covered in a checkerboard-like stucco pattern, rises into a squat tower with turrets. Inside, there are original 16th-century frescoes, catacombs, and crypts. Mass is held at 7am and 7pm Monday-Friday; 7am, 8:30am, and 7pm Saturday; and eight times from 7am to 8:30pm on Sunday. An impressive **sound and light show,** depicting the history of Valladolid, is projected onto its façade Tuesday to Sunday at 9pm in Spanish and 9:25pm in English.

Annexed to the church is the **former convent** (9am-7pm daily, US$1.75; free on Sundays). Its rooms radiate from a center courtyard that features a cenote called Sis-Há (Cold Water), which helped the monks be self-reliant. In 2004, an INAH-funded exploration of the cenote resulted in the discovery of 164 muskets, bayonets, spears, and one cannon. The arms were thrown into the cenote between 1847 and 1848; they are believed to have been sent by the British via Jamaica. The arms were used when the monastery served as a fortress during the Caste War. A small exhibit room displays some of these weapons as well as photos and descriptions of the INAH exploration.

Casa de los Venados

If you have even a passing interest in Mexican folk art, **Casa de los Venados** (House of the Deer, Calle 40 between Calles 41 and 43, tel. 985/856-2289, www.casadelosvenados.com, 10am tour daily, US$5) is a must-see. After an award-winning remodel of their 17th-century home, the American owners, John and Dorianne Venator, had so many visitors that they began offering tours of it and their impressive 3,000-piece Mexican folk art collection. The pieces themselves span the Venators' lifelong search and commission of *catrinas,* clay sculptures, wood carvings, paintings, and other decorative objects created by Mexico's most talented artisans; it is the largest privately owned collection outside of a museum. Proceeds benefit a local volunteer-run medical clinic and the Lions Club. Tours are offered in Spanish and English.

Iglesia de San Gervasio

Overlooking the central plaza, the **San Gervasio Church** (Calle 41 at Calle 42, tel. 985/856-3116) has a sober Franciscan style. It was originally built in 1545 but in 1705 was deemed profane and ordered demolished by the local bishop as the result of a political rivalry that involved the storming of the church, the desanctification of its altar, and the death of four politicians. (The incident is now known as *El Crimen de los Alcaldes,* or The Mayors' Crime.) The church was rebuilt a year later, but its orientation changed so that the new altar would not be in the same position as the prior—indeed, the Iglesia de San Gervasio is one of the only colonial-era churches in the Yucatán whose facade faces north instead of west.

Museo San Roque

A long, high-ceilinged room—this used to be a church—the **San Roque Museum** (Calle 41 between Calles 38 and 40, no phone, 8am-8pm Mon.-Fri., 9am-7pm Sat.-Sun., free) needs a serious updating but is still a worthwhile stop, with historical exhibits on Valladolid, many focusing on the Caste War and the beginning of the Mexican Revolution. Signage is in Spanish only.

Museo de Ropa Etnica de México

Museum of Traditional Clothing of Mexico (MUREM, Calle 41 between Calles 38 and 40, tel. 985/856-5832, 10am-6pm daily, US$2.50) is a tiny museum dedicated to Mexico's impressive range of traditional clothing. Mannequins showcase the handcrafted clothing that is still worn in many indigenous communities today. Though signage is in English and Spanish, guided tours are offered and add significantly to a visit. Exhibits change every three to six months.

Palacio Municipal

The 2nd floor of the **city hall** (8am-10pm daily, free) has a large balcony featuring four paintings by local artist Manuel Lizama.

The works depict events in the region's history: pre-Hispanic communities, Valladolid's founding, the Caste War, and the Mexican Revolution. It's not spectacular, but still interesting, and there's a nice view—and great photo ops—of the central plaza from here.

Cenote Zaci

In the middle of town, **Cenote Zaci** (Calle 36 between Calles 37 and 39, tel. 999/930-3760, 8:30am-5:30pm daily, US$1.50 adult, US$0.75 child) is a dark natural pool at the bottom of a huge cavern, with a bank of trees on one side and a path looping down from the entrance above. It's often pooh-poohed as inferior to cenotes at Dzitnup, but it's a perfectly peaceful and attractive spot, and a lot quicker and easier to get to. You may find leaves and pollen floating on the water's surface, but it's still great for swimming. To have the cenote to yourself, go midweek, or better yet right after closing time, entering through the restaurant (you can use its bathroom to change) instead of the main gates.

Cenote de Hacienda San Lorenzo Oxman

About three kilometers (1.8 miles) southwest of town, **Hacienda San Lorenzo Oxman**

(off Calle 54, cell tel. 986/106-5890, 8am-6pm daily, US$3.50 cenote, US$5 cenote and pool) was once a henequen plantation but is now best known for its spectacular cenote. The cenote is around 20 meters (66 feet) from the rim to the water, with tree roots dangling down the sheer walls into the cool turquoise water. There's a stairway to the water's edge, and several spots, including a fun rope swing, where you can leap right in. The hacienda also has a pool and restaurant; late afternoon can get busy with tour groups. A new entrance from Valladolid's southern ring road makes access easy.

Cenotes de Dzitnup

Four kilometers (2.5 miles) west of Valladolid on Highway 180 is the small community of Dzitnup, home to two appealing cenotes. Both make for a unique and refreshing swim, though they are often crowded by tour groups. The cenotes share a ticket kiosk and a large parking lot; there's a discount if you buy tickets for both (US$4 one cenote, US$6 two cenotes). Many small *artesanía* stands sit at the entrance, and you'll be aggressively pursued by children offering to watch your car. Many people ride bikes here, following a paved path that runs parallel to the highway. A cab to the cenotes runs about US$4.

Valladolid's central plaza

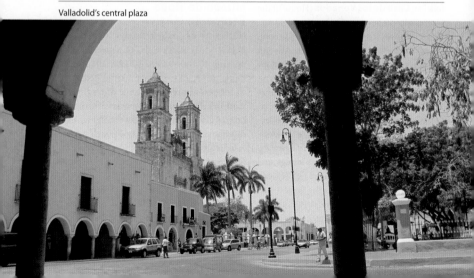

Adopt a Work of Art

Much of Mexico's finest colonial art is not found in a museum or big-city gallery, but rather in the churches, rectories, and nunneries in small towns and out-of-the-way villages. The Yucatán Peninsula is no exception, with a church in virtually every town, some dating to the 17th century or earlier, many boasting surprisingly rich artwork. But such artwork—including gilded altarpieces, gorgeous murals, and ornate stone or tile facades—can be very difficult to preserve, much less restore to its original glory. Enter **Adopte una Obra de Arte** (Adopt a Work of Art, www. adopteunaobradearte.org.mx), a nonprofit organization dedicated to preserving and restoring Mexico's rich colonial and religious art, usually in collaboration with experts from the national anthropology institute, or INAH; it also works to educate residents and visitors about the works' history and significance. The nonprofit's Yucatán chapter opened in 1992 and has restored religious artwork in towns and cities throughout the region. The project makes exploring the region all the more interesting, with stunning art in places you might least expect. Highlights include the following.

VALLADOLID
La Capilla de la Vírgen de la Candelaria: Adopte helped restore this large church's exterior, main altar, pulpit, and numerous small statues and paintings. Much of the interior had been repainted previously but rather poorly; the present condition is thought to closely resemble the original design.

UAYMA
Templo y Ex-convento de Santo Domingo: Located 15 kilometers (9.3 miles) northwest of Valladolid, this 17th-century church was nearly destroyed during the Caste War. It stood roofless and decrepit until 2003, when Adopte began a yearlong restoration. The vibrant color and fantastic flower-adorned facade make this one of the Yucatan's most distinctive churches.

TABI
Iglesia de Tabi: The church in this one-street town, located 50 kilometers (31 miles) southwest of Pisté, has one of the region's finest baroque altarpieces, rescued from near-collapse and beautifully restored by Adopte. Even more remarkable is the *camarín*, a small chamber behind the main altar, completely blanketed in gilded woodwork, murals, and fine paintings.

Although the two are across the street from each other, **Cenote Xkekén** (aka Cenote Dzitnup, no phone, 9am-4pm daily, US$4) is the one often seen on postcards. After a reasonably easy descent (in a few places you'll have to bend over because of a low ceiling; there's a hanging rope to help), you'll come to a circular pond of clear, cool water. It's a pretty, albeit damp, place, with a high dome ceiling that has one small opening at the top letting in a ray of sun and dangling green vines. Often an errant bird can be seen swooping low over the water before heading to the sun and sky through the tiny opening. Stalactites and one large stalagmite adorn the ceiling and cenote floor.

At **Cenote Samula** (no phone, 9am-4pm daily, US$4), tree roots dangle from the cavern roof all the way down to the water. You enter through a narrow tunnel, which opens onto a set of stairs that zigzag down. Fearless kids jump from the stairs into the clear turquoise water below.

Xkopek
Xkopek (Calle 57 at Calle 38, tel. 985/125-0964, xkopek@gmail.com, 9am-5pm Tues.-Sun., US$5) is a family-run beekeeping farm, specializing in the Mayan stingless bee. Bilingual guides lead visitors on fascinating tours of the farm, including stops at man-made and natural hives, information about

the plants that keep the bees happy (and producing), and a historical overview of the importance of bees in the Maya world. The tour also stops at a dry cenote, complete with stalagmites and bats. Tours end with a honey tasting and a no-pressure nudge toward to the gift shop. Tours last around 60-90 minutes, the first starting at 10am. Lodging is also available. The farm is on the edge of town, about a 15-minute walk from the central plaza.

Destilería Mayapán

Along Valladolid's northern ring road, two kilometers (1.2 miles) south of the Cancún toll highway, the artisanal **Mayapán Distillery** (Libremiento Nte. 264, tel. 985/858-0246, www.mayapan.mx, 9am-6pm Mon.-Sat., US$2.50) leads visitors on a brief tour of its agave fields and warehouse-size facility, detailing the traditional steps used to ferment, mash by horse-drawn mill, and distill the agave plant into liquor. They can't call it tequila because it's not made in Jalisco, but your taste buds might not be so finicky. Tours conclude with three different tastings and a not-so-subtle nudge toward the gift shop.

Tours

MexiGo Tours (Calle 43 between Calles 40 and 42, tel. 985/856-0777, www.mexigotours.com, 9am-1pm and 3pm-7pm daily) is highly recommended for its local and regional tours. Popular trips include visits to archaeological sites, cenotes, caves, and outings to spot wildlife like flamingoes, howler monkeys, and even bat-eating snakes. Tours typically include meals and transportation, but not entrance fees. A minimum of three people is required.

Based in the nearby community of X'ocen, **Yucatán Jay Expeditions and Tours** (cell tel. 985/103-4918, 8am-8pm daily) is a co-op specializing in bird-watching tours. (There are 543 species of birds registered in the entire peninsula—a true hot spot for birders).

Tours are led by experienced guides with a passion for their work. Many tours also combine stops in traditional Maya villages and cenotes.

The **tourist office** (Palacio Municipal, Calle 40 at Calle 41, tel. 985/856-2551 ext. 114, 8am-8pm Mon.-Fri., 9am-7pm Sat.-Sun.) leads free walking tours of the city every evening at 7pm. Tours last about an hour; arrive by 6:30pm to secure a spot.

ENTERTAINMENT AND EVENTS

Every afternoon, the city hosts **folkloric dance** and **traditional music performances** in the central plaza (5pm-6:30pm Mon.-Sat., 5pm-8pm Sun.). Food and artisan stands pop up and the park fills with people. On Sundays, **live bands** follow the performances and locals strut their stuff to cumbia and danzón tunes.

In late January-early February, Valladolid celebrates its patron saint, La Vírgen de la Candelaria, with the **Expo-Feria Valladolid**. It's a blowout outdoor festival where you'll see bullfights, rodeos, musical entertainment, and lots of food stands selling local delicacies and heart-stopping goodies. Venues vary; ask at the tourist office or your hotel for details.

Momentos Sagrados Mayas (Sacred Maya Moments, X'ocen, tel. 999/924-4465, US$10) is a popular 90-minute show celebrating the traditional and daily lives of the living Maya people; over 300 people from villages around the Yucatán perform dances, rituals, and scenes from everyday life. The show is presented on an open-air stage in the community of X'ocen, located 14 kilometers (8.5 miles) south of Valladolid. It runs on Sundays at 4pm January-March.

SHOPPING

Calzada de los Frailes, the charming colonial street that connects the Iglesia San Bernardino de Siena with central Valladolid, is dotted with boutique shops selling mostly high-end goods—window-shopping at its best! You'll find traditional *jipi* hat makers, folk art shops, home goods, custom leatherware, and even an artisanal chocolate shop. Most stores are open 10am-8pm daily.

A tranquil courtyard of workshops and shops, the **Mercado Zaci** (Calle 39 between Calles 40 and 42, no phone, 9am-8pm daily) showcases the work of Maya women from Valladolid and nearby villages who make and sell their *huipiles* and hand-stitched blouses on-site. For a wider selection, the **Mercado de Artesanías** (Calle 39 at Calle 44, 8am-8pm Mon.-Sat., 8am-2pm Sun.) has a decent variety of *guayaberas,* embroidered *huipiles,* hammocks, and other popular handicrafts; haggling is par for the course.

If you're interested in high-end Mexican handicrafts and art, **Yalat** (Calle 41 between Calles 40 and 42, tel. 985/856-1969, 8am-10pm daily) is worth a stop. It also sells artisanal products like chocolate, coffee, and honey in its back garden.

A family-owned distillery for over 100 years, **Productos Sosa** (Calle 42 between Calles 47 and 49, tel. 985/856-2142, 10am-2pm and 4pm-7:30pm Mon.-Fri., 10am-2pm Sat.) sells smooth sugarcane liquors infused with ingredients like mint or anise with honey.

FOOD

Yucatecan and Mexican

★ **El Atrio del Mayab** (central plaza, Calle 41 No. 204, tel. 985/856-2394, 7am-11:30pm daily, US$6-10) serves a wide range of traditional Yucatecan dishes in a leafy garden setting complete with gurgling fountain and picturesque views of Iglesia San Gervasio. Meals are flavorful and artfully presented; they're complemented by an extensive list of cocktails and artisanal beers. Service is tops.

Yerbabuena del Sisal (Calle 54-A at Calle 49, tel. 985/856-1406, www.yerbabuenadelsisal.com, 7:30am-9pm Tues.-Sun., US$4-6) is a whimsical place offering fresh Mexican dishes with a good variety of vegetarian options. Entrees range from *tortas* (Mexican-style sandwiches) and *chilaquiles* (a tortilla-and-egg dish) to veggie burgers and curry lentils. Seating is in a patio garden.

★ **La Palapita de los Tamales** (Calle 42 at Calle 33, tel. 985/856-2895, 8am-10pm Mon.-Sat., US$2-4) is a great little restaurant selling Yucatecan-style tamales. Tamales are steamed over an open fire at the entrance while diners come and go. Among the most popular are the *chachawa* (chicken and egg tamale served in a tomato sauce), *espelón* (pork, beans, and egg tamale wrapped in

Huevos rancheros are a classic Mexican breakfast dish.

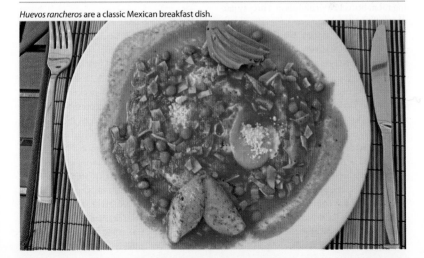

a banana leaf), and *colados* (strained corn dough tamales).

Low lighting and an open-air dining room at **Taberna de los Frailes** (Calle 49 at Calle 41A, tel. 985/856-0689, www.tabernadelosfrailes.com, 1pm-11pm daily, US$8-20) set an elegant backdrop for a menu of creative Yucatecan mainstays and seafood dishes. Its upscale bar has sofa seating and a terrace area shaded by a canopy of passion fruit vines. Look for it across from the San Bernardino de Siena church.

El Bazar Municipal (central plaza, Calle 39 at Calle 40, 6am-10pm, US$1.50-3) is a local food court with a dozen or so inexpensive eateries selling mostly Yucatecan specialties. Hours vary, but all are open for breakfast and lunch. Order something off the menu, like *huevos rancheros* or *salbutes*, to be sure it's freshly made.

Other Specialties

Café del Profesor Pitágoras (Calle 37 btwn Calles 40 and 42, tel. 985/856-4448, 8am-9pm daily, US$4-6) is an artsy café specializing in organic and vegetarian meals, including falafel plates, pasta dishes, salads, and sandwiches made with artisanal breads. All manner of coffee drinks and freshly squeezed juices are served too. Seating is in a cozy dining room bedecked in murals or a breezy garden with shade trees.

Next to the bus station, **Squimz** (Calle 39 near Calle 46, tel. 985/856-4156, www.squimz.com.mx, 7am-11pm daily, US$3-7) is well worth a stop even if you're not on your way out of town. Big breakfasts and sandwiches are the specialties, though the coffee drinks and to-die-for milk shakes shouldn't be overlooked. Those with a sweet tooth should try the homemade flan.

Bohemia is alive and well at **Casa Conato Cultural** (Calle 40 between Calles 45 and 47, tel. 985/856-2586, 5pm-1am daily, US$4-7), where religious iconography, murals, and images of Frida Kahlo cover the walls of the spacious garden dining patio. Yucatecan-influenced dishes, big salads, and pasta dishes

have creative flourishes, while the dessert crepes are almost too pretty to eat. Live music and late hours make this a popular place for drinks.

Meaning "three will do," **Tresvanbien** (Calzada de los Frailes near Calle 48, tel. 984/114-9966, 10am-9pm daily, US$4.50-7) is an Argentinian eatery specializing in empanadas, turnovers filled with savory ingredients—from spinach with béchamel to seasoned ground beef—and baked till golden. (They are smallish so, yes, "three will do" if you're hungry.) The setting is boho meets shabby-chic, with a breezy garden complete with hanging chairs and communal tables.

Cafeína Food Company (Calzada de los Frailes near Calle 48, tel. 985/856-2654, 7am-2am daily, US$4.50-15) serves up thin-crust pizza, burgers, salads, and chicken wings in a pub-like setting. Try the Yuc-Mex pizza with homemade sausage, cheese, avocado, and *pico de gallo*—it packs an unexpected punch. Drink specials, from beer to milk shakes, are offered.

ACCOMMODATIONS

Valladolid offers a good selection of simple and midrange hotels. Most are convenient to the central plaza. All have free Wi-Fi and most provide parking.

Under US$50

★ **Xkopek** (Calle 57 at Calle 38, tel. 985/125-0964, xkopek@gmail.com, US$5-8 pp camping including gear, US$13/20 bungalow with shared bathroom, US$15/23 s/d, US$18/25 s/d with a/c), a stingless beekeeping farm, offers excellent budget accommodations on its extensive property. Options include well-maintained tents with real mattresses and linens, traditional thatch-roofed bungalows, and simple modern rooms with private bathrooms. All have access to spick-and-span shared bathrooms and a fully equipped common kitchen. Bike rentals are available.

Hostel Candelaria (Parque la Candelaria, Calle 35 near Calle 44, tel. 985/856-2267, www.hostelvalladolidyucatan.com, US$12.50

dorm, US$15 dorm with a/c, US$63 s/d with shared bathroom with a/c, US$66 s/d with a/c) has cramped dorms and several small, artsy private rooms. What units lack in space is made up for by a sprawling back garden, an al fresco kitchen, and hammocks with personal reading lights. There's a TV lounge and plenty of lockers too. Breakfast is included.

Casa Hipil (Calle 42 between Calles 33 and 35, tel. 985/856-0832, http://casahipil. wixsite.com/hotelcasahipil, US$40-47 s/d with a/c, US$74 suite with a/c) is a pleasant little hotel with spacious rooms featuring gorgeous stone and tile work; all have patios facing a courtyard. There's also a well-stocked communal kitchen, a small plunge pool, and a garden with fruit trees. The hotel's name derives from a type of traditional embroidery, of which there are some incredible examples on display.

La Aurora (Calle 42 between Calles 35 and 37, tel. 985/856-1219, www.hotellaaurora.com, US$30/38 s/d with a/c) is a charming place with rooms opening onto a sunny courtyard with a pool. Units are basic but comfortable with good beds, modern bathrooms, and flat-screen TVs. Original tile floors, bromeliads, and ironwork lanterns help create a colonial ambience. For a treat, head to the roof, where there are two soaking pools and views of the city.

US$50-100

Casa Quetzal (Calle 51 between Calles 50 and 52, tel. 985/856-4796, www.casa-quetzal. com, US$60-66 s/d with a/c, US$67-80 suite with a/c) is a charming, well-run bed-and-breakfast. Large, attractive, high-ceilinged rooms surround a pretty garden and pool, while a lounge featuring Oaxacan folk art lends a homey feel. Continental breakfast is included. The hotel is somewhat removed from the central plaza, but the walk there—along the iconic Calzada de los Frailes—is a pleasure in itself.

Casa San Roque (Calle 41 between Calles 38 and 40, tel. 985/856-2642, www. casasanroquevalladolid.com, US$79 s/d with a/c) is a six-room colonial-style hotel. Rooms are modern with gleaming tile floors, heavy wood furnishings, and splashes of color; bathrooms are sleek and spotless. There's a pleasant outdoor sitting area where breakfast is served and there's a refreshing pool too—a welcome sight after a day of sightseeing. It's just one block from the central plaza.

The combined hotels of **Casa Tía Micha** and **Casa Marlene** (Calle 39 between Calles 38 and 40, 985/856-0499, www.casatiamicha. com, US$85-100 s/d with a/c, US$90-115 suite with a/c) are quite comfortable, but the feel is very colonial meets grandma—think stately wood doors and antique furniture alongside porcelain knickknacks and rocking chairs. There's a refreshing pool plus a tranquil fruit tree garden, with an old *pozo* (well), where full breakfast is served.

Over US$100

★ **Hotel Posada San Juan** (Parque San Juan, Calle 40 at Calle 49, tel. 985/856-0129, www.posadasanjuan.com, US$122 s/d with a/c) is a meticulously renovated 19th-century mansion with eight elegant but homey rooms. All have high-end furnishings, folk art, and custom-designed tile floors. Bathrooms bring the outside in with skylights, exposed stone walls, rainfall showerheads, and tropical plants. Full breakfast is served on the wide veranda with views of the garden and pool. Service is genuinely friendly.

Casa Hamaca Guesthouse (Parque San Juan, Calle 49 at Calle 40, tel. 985/856-5287, www.casahamaca.com, US$94-150 s/d with a/c) faces a quiet church plaza. The guesthouse is spacious and bright with a lush garden and small pool that only add to the tranquility. Its eight rooms vary in size and décor though all have Maya-inspired murals. There's an open-air restaurant (7am-10pm daily) where a hearty complimentary breakfast is served. Rewarding volunteer opportunities also can be arranged.

Hotel Zenti'k Project (Calle 30 between Calles 27 and 29, tel. 985/104-9171, www.hotelzentik.com, US$125 s/d with a/c) is a fantastic (and fantastical) hotel with

Valladolid Bus Schedule

Departures from Valladolid's **bus station** (Calle 39 at Calle 46, tel. 985/856-3448) include:

DESTINATION	PRICE	DURATION	SCHEDULE*
Cancún	US$8-13	2.25 hrs	12 departures 12:25am-9:55pm
Chichén Itzá (Pisté)	US$6	50 mins	9:50am, 10:50am, 3:30pm
Chiquilá (Isla Holbox)	US$10	2.5 hrs	9:50pm
Cobá	US$2.50	1 hr	8:30am, 9:30am, 2:45pm
Ek' Balam	US$4.50	1 hr	8:30am
Izamal	US$3.50	2.5 hrs	12:50pm
Mérida	US$10-12	2.25 hrs	31 departures 3:05am-10:05pm
Playa del Carmen	US$11-13	2.5-3 hrs	11 departures 8am-10:40pm
Tizimín	US$1.50	1 hr	every 30-75 mins
Tulum	US$6-8	1.5 hrs	8 departures 8am-10:40pm

*Schedules are subject to change.

wow-inducing features at every turn. It has an underground saltwater pool, built into a cenote-like cavern, plus an aboveground pool and a private spa. Murals, sculptures, and other artwork abound, including surreal paintings splashed across some guest room walls. Rooms are spacious and comfortable, and the restaurant (7:30am-10:30pm daily, US$5-15) serves inventive and delicious meals.

INFORMATION AND SERVICES
Tourist Information
Area knowledge is hit or miss at Valladolid's **tourist office** (Palacio Municipal, Calle 40 at Calle 41, tel. 985/856-2551, 8am-7pm Mon.-Fri., 9am-7pm Sat.-Sun.). At the very least, free daily **walking tours,** led by licensed bilingual guides, leave here every evening at 7pm; tips are appreciated.

Valladolid English Library (Parque San Juan, Calle 49 at Calle 40, tel. 985/111-7688, 9am-1pm Mon.-Sat. and 5:30-7:30pm Mon. and Thurs.) is a lending library with over 2,500 books. There's everything from children's fiction to "how-to" reads. The library often hosts an interesting speaker series on topics as varied as public safety and Maya medicine.

Emergency Services
Hospital General de Valladolid (Av. Chan Yokdzonot, tel. 985/856-2883, 24 hours) is located 4.5 kilometers (2.8 miles) south of the *cuota* highway. For meds, head to **Farmacia Yza** (Calle 41 near Calle 40, tel. 985/856-4018, 24 hrs).

The **police** (Parque Bacalar, Calle 41 s/n, tel. 985/856-2100, ext. 113, 24 hrs) can be reached toll-free at 060.

Money
Near the central plaza, **HSBC** (Calle 41 between Calles 42 and 44, 9am-5pm Mon.-Fri., 9am-3pm Sat.) and **Banamex** (Calle 41 between Calles 42 and 44, 9am-4pm Mon.-Fri.) have ATMs.

Media and Communications
A tiny **post office** (Calle 40 between Calles 39 and 41, 8am-4:30pm Mon.-Fri., 8am-1pm Sat.) sits on the central plaza.

All of the listed hotels have Wi-Fi. There's also free Wi-Fi in the central plaza; the signal is strongest in front of the Palacio Municipal (look for the cadre of teens on their phones).

Laundry

Lava Más (Calle 40 btwn Calles 35 and 37, tel. 985/115-4356, 7am-8pm Mon.-Sat., 8am-4pm Sun.) charges US$0.60 per kilo (2.2 pounds), with a three-kilo minimum.

GETTING THERE AND AROUND

Bus

Valladolid's **bus terminal** (Calle 39 at Calle 46, tel. 985/856-3448) is an easy walk from the central plaza, or if you have a lot of bags, a cheap taxi ride.

Taxi

Taxis are relatively easy to flag down, especially around the central plaza, and typically cost US$1.50-2 around town.

Colectivos (shared vans and taxis) to Pisté and Chichén Itzá (US$1.75, 1 hour, every 30 minutes, 7am-9pm daily) depart from Calle 39 near the ADO bus terminal, and those for Mérida (US$9, 2.5 hours) leave from the terminal. Shared taxis for Cancún (US$10, 2.5 hours), Cobá (US$7.50, 1hr), and Tulum (US$10, 1.5 hrs) congregate at Calle 38 between Calles 39 and 41 from 3am to 10pm daily.

Car

If you arrive from the toll highway (*cuota*), you'll enter town via Calle 42 (and return on Calle 40). It's a sobering US$15.25 from Cancún, US$8.75 from Mérida (Kantunil), and US$3.75 to Chichén Itzá (Pisté). In the center, eastbound Calle 41 and westbound Calle 39 access the free highway (*libre*).

Bicycle

For bike rentals, including tandems, head to **MexiGo Tours** (Calle 43 between Calles 40 and 42, tel. 985/856-0777, www.mexigotours. com, 9am-1pm and 3pm-7pm daily, US$1.25-2.75 per hour, US$7.50-19 per day).

Ek' Balam

Ek' Balam, Maya for "black jaguar," is a unique and fascinating archaeological site whose significance has only recently been revealed and appreciated. Serious restoration of Ek' Balam didn't begin until the mid-1990s, and it was then that an incredibly well-preserved stucco frieze was discovered, hidden under an innocuous stone facade near the top of the site's main pyramid. The discovery rocketed Ek' Balam into preeminence, first among Maya scholars and more slowly among travelers in the Yucatán, once the frieze was excavated and opened to the public. Much remains a mystery about Ek' Balam, but archaeologists believe it was founded around 300 BC and became an important commercial center, its influence peaking in AD 700-1100.

Ek' Balam sees a fraction of the tourists that visit other Maya sites, despite its proximity to Valladolid, Cancún, and Mérida.

The site is small enough that even an hour is enough to appreciate its treasures; even better, it's a tranquil place that doesn't get besieged by mammoth tour groups.

ORIENTATION

Ek' Balam is located 30 kilometers (19 miles) north of Valladolid, off of Highway 295. **Ek' Balam village** is two kilometers (1.2 miles) west, with one excellent option for an overnight stay and one decent restaurant.

★ EK' BALAM ARCHAEOLOGICAL ZONE

Entering **Ek' Balam** (8am-5pm daily, US$10.25), you'll pass through a low, thick wall and an elegant corbeled arch. Walls are rare in Maya cities and were most commonly used for defense, as in the cases of Becán and

Ek' Balam Archaeological Zone

© MOON.COM

Tulum. Ek' Balam's walls would not have slowed marauding rivals, however, and so they most likely served to enforce social divisions, with some areas off-limits (but not out of view) to all but the elite. They may also have been decorative—the city possessed great aesthetic flair, as the entry arch and the famous stucco frieze demonstrate.

Acrópolis and El Trono

The highlight of Ek' Balam is an artful and remarkably pristine stucco frieze known as

El Trono (The Throne), located under a protective *palapa* roof two-thirds of the way up Ek' Balam's main pyramid, the **Acrópolis.** A steep stairway leads up the center of the pyramid, and a platform to the left of the stairs provides visitors a close-up view of El Trono.

About 85 percent of El Trono is the original stucco. Often structures like this would have been painted blue or red, but not so here. In fact, shortly after it was built, El Trono was sealed behind a stone wall 50-60 centimeters (19-24 inches) thick. It remained there untouched until the 1990s, when restoration workers accidentally—and fortuitously—dislodged one of the protective stones, revealing the hidden chamber beneath.

The tall, winged figures immediately catch your eye, as they appear so much like angels. In fact, they are high priests. Notice that one is deformed—his left arm is longer than the right and has only four fingers. The Maya considered birth defects to be a sign of divinity, and the priest depicted here may have risen to his position precisely because of his deformation.

Directly over the door is a seated figure (unfortunately, the head is missing). This represents Ukit Kan Le'k Tok', one of Ek' Balam's former rulers, described in inscriptions as the "king of kings," and the person for whom El Trono was built and dedicated. A tomb was discovered in the chamber behind the frieze, containing thousands of jade, gold, obsidian, and ceramic artifacts left as offerings to this powerful leader. The small face at the king-figure's navel represents a rival whom he defeated in war.

Viewed as a whole, the frieze is unmistakably a Chenes-style monster mouth: a huge stylized mask in which the doorway represents the gaping mouth of a high god. The pointed upper and lower teeth are easy to spot, as are the spiral eyes. Monster mouths are never mundane, but this one is especially elaborate. Notice how two beautifully crafted figures straddle the lower eyelids while hoisting the upper lids with their shoulders. At least five more figures, plus lattice patterns and other designs, adorn the rest of the mask.

Before heading down, climb the rest of the way to the top of the Acrópolis for a panoramic vista. At 32 meters (105 feet) high and 158 meters (515 feet) wide, the Acrópolis is bigger than Chichén Itzá's main pyramid, and in fact is one of the largest Maya pyramids ever built, a detail that's often overlooked amid the excitement surrounding El Trono. The scene from atop is memorable; with the exception of the odd telephone and radio tower, and the site's visitors center, the view

of the broad Yucatecan landscape is probably not all that different from the one Maya priests and kings enjoyed from this very same vantage point more than a thousand years ago.

South Plaza

Descending the pyramid, you can see that Ek' Balam is a fairly small site, with two midsize plazas (north and south), a ball court in the middle, and its main structures crowded together.

On the south side of the **south plaza** stands La Rodonda, or the **Oval Palace**. A squat midsize structure, the Oval Palace has an eclectic array of overlapping lines and curves, stairs, and terraces. It underwent numerous iterations, as did virtually all Maya temples, but the result here was especially eclectic. Archaeologists suspect the Oval Palace was used for astronomical observations, and the discovery of several richly adorned tombs suggest it had a ceremonial purpose as well.

Flanking La Redonda are Las Gemelas, or **The Twin Sisters,** known as Structure 17. As the plaque indicates, these identical structures are perhaps the best example of Ek' Balam's particular architectural style. Having perfected the use of stucco, Ek' Balam's builders did not concern themselves with precise masonry, as the stones would be covered in a thick stucco cap. However, stucco proved much less resilient to erosion, and centuries later the structures here appear shabbier than even much older ones, such as those in Campeche's Río Bec region, where stucco was less common and stone blocks were more carefully cut and fitted. Recent excavations have focused on these two buildings, where intriguing freehand marks and paintings—perhaps akin to graffiti today—have been discovered.

Practicalities

Guides can be hired at the entrance to the ruins (US$30, 1-1.5 hours, available in Spanish or English). Additionally, there's a US$2.25 fee to enter with a video camera; parking is free.

CENOTE X'CANCHÉ

Cenote X'Canché (cell tel. 985/100-9915, www.ekbalam.com.mx, 8am-5pm daily, US$2.50) is a community-run ecotourism project, and a great add-on to a visit to Ek' Balam. From the ruins' parking lot, follow the signs to a wide path that winds 1.5 kilometers (0.9 mile) through low, dense forest to the cenote, which is 14 meters (46 feet) deep and nearly circular, with sheer walls and tree roots descending picturesquely to cool, clean water. A wooden staircase leads to the water's edge, great for swimming. For an adrenaline rush, consider rappelling from the cenote edge or zip-lining across it instead (US$5-25).

The path from the parking lot to the cenote is a pleasant shaded walk, though many visitors rent bikes (US$3.50 per 3 hours) or take advantage of the tricycle taxis (US$6 pp round-trip). Facilities include restrooms, shower and changing areas, a restaurant, and *palapa*-shaded hammocks. For those wanting to stay overnight, there are simple **cabins** (US$30 s/d) and **campsites** (US$6 pp, BYO gear).

CENOTE SAK' AUA

Cenote Sak' Aua (tel. 985/125-5944, 9am-5pm daily, US$4.50) is a rewarding post-ruins visit if you have a car. It is 15 kilometers (9 miles) east of Ek' Balam, via a back road from Ek' Balam to Highway 180 through the Maya villages of Hunukú and Dzalbay; impossibly large signage marks the way. You'll pass men on bikes loaded down with wood, women balancing jugs of water on their heads, and skinny dogs running after your car. Once at the cenote, a 350-meter (0.2 mile) trail leads to the entrance—a hole in the ground with a rickety staircase. As your eyes adjust, you'll see an island with leafy trees in a perfectly round cavern—a doughnut hole—surrounded by crystal-clear teal water. Openings in the cavern roof let in light and long tree roots. The water itself is refreshing and cool, home to small catfish and turtles, and the occasional swallow swoops down to skim the surface of the water. It's an eerily gorgeous site with few visitors; midweek, you're likely to have it to yourself. Facilities include changing rooms and a questionable toilet.

★ CENOTES AGUA DULCE

Cenotes Agua Dulce (tel. 985/856-2200, 8:30am-5pm daily, US$4.50-6 per cenote, US$14 all cenotes) is a set of four stunning cenotes: **Agua Dulce, Palomitas, Las Cavernas,** and **El Oasis.** The first two are classic cenotes—deep underground pools of crystalline turquoise water surrounded by stalagmites and stalactites. They're reached by long staircases leading several dozen meters down into the earth. The second two are for exploring—one is dry (making it a cavern, not a cenote), the other is too shallow to swim in. They're worth a visit if you can avoid the tour groups, which typically stop here on Mondays and Fridays. There's a restaurant on-site serving buffet lunch (US$8), and there are changing areas and bathrooms. Life vests are included. The site is just north of the village of Yalcobá, about 20 kilometers (12 miles) from Ek' Balam and 24 kilometers (14.5 miles) northeast of Valladolid.

FOOD AND ACCOMMODATIONS

In Ek' Balam village, **Dolce Vacanza** (tel. 999/913-9670, noon-6pm Tues.-Sun., US$5-7) serves solid Italian food, including fresh handmade ravioli, fettuccini, and other pasta. Meals are served in a large, tasteful dining room overlooking an unruly garden.

★ **Genesis Eco-Oasis** (cell tel. 985/101-0277, www.genesisretreat.com, US$45 s/d with shared bathroom and a/c, US$65-75 s/d, US$79 s/d/t/q) has artful rooms set on a leafy property in Ek' Balam village, all created from repurposed materials. Each faces a biofiltered pool in a jungle garden. Continental breakfast is included; full organic breakfasts and dinners are also offered. The hardworking

---

1: Cenote Sak' Aua; 2: Ek' Balam's frieze, known as El Trono; 3: the lush grounds at Genesis Eco-Oasis

Canadian owner offers tours of the village and artisan workshops. Note that several friendly pooches lounge about the property.

Close by the ruins, **Cenote X'Canché** (cell tel. 985/100-9815, www.ekbalam.com.mx, US$6 pp tent, US$30 s/d) rents three well-built and solar-powered *palapa cabañas* near the cenote, each with queen bed and a hammock (plus mosquito nets). The windows have good screens, and there's hot water and fans. There also are campsites (US$6 pp, BYO gear). A three-course lunch or dinner at the on-site restaurant costs US$8; breakfast is US$7.

GETTING THERE AND AROUND
Car
From Valladolid, drive north on Highway 295 toward Tizimín for about 17 kilometers (10.5 miles), past the town of Temozón, to a well-marked right-hand turn to Ek' Balam. From there, drive another 11 kilometers (6.8 miles) to an intersection; turn left to reach the village, or continue straight to reach the archaeological site.

Taxi
Colectivo (shared) taxis from Valladolid to the village of Ek' Balam leave from a stop on Calle 44 between Calles 35 and 37 (US$2); mornings have the most frequent departures. Otherwise, a private taxi costs about US$15 for up to four people. If you're planning on visiting the ruins only, you can often negotiate with the driver to wait there for a couple of hours and bring you back for around US$25.

Río Lagartos and San Felipe

A little more than 100 kilometers (62 miles) north of Valladolid, the Reserva de la Bíosfera de Ría Lagartos (Biosphere Reserve of Ría Lagartos) is justly famous for the huge colonies of flamingos that nest and feed there. Designated a biosphere reserve in 1999, it covers over 63,000 hectares (155,700 acres); beyond flamingos, the reserve is home to 395 bird species. Río Lagartos is the nearest town to the reserve. Most tour operators offering excursions into the reserve are based here; travelers also will find small inns and basic restaurants. San Felipe is just west of Río Lagartos and makes for a pleasant afternoon visit. If you have a car, consider staying in Río Lagartos and driving to San Felipe for a post-tour meal.

RÍO LAGARTOS
Every year tens of thousands of pink and cerise *Phoenicopterus ruber ruber* flamingos come to Río Lagartos to feed and nest in the salt flats at the end of the long coastal lagoon, or *ría,* extending east of town. It's also a favorite haunt of plovers, white egrets, herons, cormorants, hawks, and pelicans (not to mention bird-watchers).

Río Lagartos itself is an isolated community that wouldn't really merit a visit were it not for the flamingo and bird-watching tours. The population is a mix of longtime local families and an ever-fluctuating supply of itinerant workers, many from as far away as Chiapas and Veracruz. Most come to work at the nearby Las Coloradas salt factory; salt has been harvested along the Gulf coast since pre-Hispanic times, and remains one of the region's most important exports.

Sights

TOP EXPERIENCE

★ **FLAMINGO TOURS**
It's possible to see flamingos in Río Lagartos year-round, but the highest concentration is present April-September. Spring and summer are brooding season, and visitors are not

allowed to approach the nesting area lest parent flamingos (skittish by nature) accidentally knock their lone eggs out of the nests; you can still visit the feeding area, however. In the fall and winter, you'll likely see juvenile flamingos beginning to color. Flamingos are gray or white when they hatch and gradually grow pink from beta carotene in their diet, mostly from algae and brine shrimp. At three months, the black feathers along their wings begin to grow.

Tours are offered 6am-5pm daily, but early morning is the best time to go. It takes almost 45 minutes to get to the flamingo sites, and leaving early lets you see more birds along the way. The water is also calmer in the morning. Binoculars aren't absolutely necessary but are nice to have; bring your own or ask to borrow a pair.

Río Lagartos Adventures (Ría Maya Restaurant, Calle 19 at Calle 14, cell tel. 986/100-8390, www.riolagartosnaturetours. com) is the most experienced and recommended tour operator, with English-speaking guides and well-equipped boats. Trips last three hours and include short stops at a spot called Las Salinas, where you can take a mineral-rich mud bath, and at the beach opposite town, where you wash it all off (US$139 for up to 6 people). Visitors wanting more time can book a four-hour tour that goes slower and deeper into the mangroves, perfect for photographers and birders (US$169 for up to 6 people). Evening boat tours to spot crocodiles in the reserve also can be arranged (US$110 for up to 6 people). Tours do not include US$2.50 admission per person to enter the reserve.

Another option is to take a flamingo tour with the local cooperative (cell tel. 986/107-3082). It's effectively the same boat trip in two hours (US$60-80 for up to 6 people). The differences are that the boats tend to be older and less comfortable; also, guides typically aren't bilingual. Crocodile tours and fishing trips also can be arranged. Look for the co-op's kiosk on the waterfront, just south of Hotel Villa de Pescadores.

BALNEARIO CHIQUILÁ

On the eastern end of town, **Balneario Chiquilá** (free) is a freshwater swimming hole just steps from the estuary. It's a popular spot for locals—on any given day, you'll find kids splashing and cannonballing into the refreshing clear water. Small palapas provide shade and a place to chill out. Nearby, there's a lookout tower with views of the estuary. There's also an **open-air restaurant** (8am-7pm daily, US$4-8) serving fresh fish plates and classic Mexican dishes. On the far end of the parking lot, look for the wooden boardwalk leading through a mangrove forest to two springs surrounded by lush vegetation; swimming is not permitted at the springs.

PLAYA CANCUNCITO

If you're aching for beach time, Playa Cancuncito provides an easy fix. A windswept beach with tawny sand and calm teal waters, it's a perfect place for beachcombing or just sitting back with a paperback novel. Be sure to bring your own snacks and plenty of water—there's nothing here but surf and sand. If you have a car, follow the road signs to the town of Las Coloradas; you'll hit Cancuncito immediately after you've crossed the bridge (and before you arrive at Las Coloradas). You also can hire a boat to take you from Río Lagartos (US$20 for up to 6 people); ask at your hotel or at the local cooperative (cell tel. 986/107-3082) about arranging the boat trip.

Food

El Perico Marinero (waterfront near Calle 19, tel. 998/103-5042, www.elpericomarinero. com, 7am-10pm daily, US$8-17) has a large and accessible menu, making it a good choice for travelers and groups of all stripes. Seafood is the specialty, of course; everything is fresh and tasty though the service can be uneven. Especially nice are the ocean views from the 2nd-floor dining area.

La Mojarrita Río Lagartos (waterfront at Calle 17, tel. 998/103-5042, 9am-7pm daily, US$5-14) is a small, no-frills eatery that serves super-fresh seafood, from perfectly cooked octopus to crispy fried fish. Family owned and operated, it has friendly service and nice views of the waterfront.

Accommodations

Hotel Punta Ponto (waterfront at Calle 19, tel. 986/862-0509, www. hotelpuntapontoreserva.com, US$37-65 s/d with a/c) is a family-run hotel with small, simple rooms with mini fridges. All are on the 2nd story of the owner's home and open onto a wide veranda with sweeping views of the estuary. There are plenty of outdoor chairs and tables—perfect for relaxing after a day of bird-watching. Breakfast is included in the rate.

Hotel Villa de Pescadores (waterfront at Calle 14, tel. 986/106-9579, www. hotelvilladepescadores.com, US$54-63 s/d with a/c) is a longtime traveler favorite with spectacular views of the estuary from its 12 rooms. Each is clean and spacious with a private balcony. Be sure to head to the roof to get a bird's-eye view of the town and its surroundings waters—sunset is particularly pretty. There's also a good restaurant on-site.

Hotel Río Lagartos (Calle 14 btwn Calles 17 and 19, tel. 986/112-9014, www. hotelriolagartos.mx, US$41-91 s/d with a/c, US$82-133 suite with a/c) is a large modern hotel with tidy rooms, many with outstanding views of the waterfront and estuary. There's a small pool, a restaurant, and tables and palapas on the rooftop, perfect for viewing the sunset. The hotel offers some great online specials.

Information and Services

There is **no tourist office** in Río Lagartos, but the folks at Río Lagartos Adventures are knowledgeable and happy to help. There is **no bank or ATM** either—bring enough cash to cover your time here. For medical attention, head to Valladolid. All of the listed hotels have Wi-Fi.

Getting There and Around

Noreste (Calle 19 btwn Calles 8 and 10) offers second-class bus service to and from Río Lagartos. Departures for San Felipe (US$1, 15 minutes) continue to Tizimín (US$2.25, 1.5 hours, 10 departures, 5:30am-5:15pm); four buses continue to Mérida (US$12.50, 4.5 hours, 5:30am, 6:30am, 11am, and 3:30pm), or you can connect in Tizimín. Note that the last bus to Tizimín usually arrives too late for riders to catch the last connecting bus to Mérida.

Río Lagartos is at the end of Highway 295, about 100 kilometers (62 miles) north of Valladolid by car. From the free or toll highways, follow signs toward Tizimín, but skip the city center by taking the western bypass road just before town (follow the Mérida/Highway 176 signs). Continue on the bypass road for 12 kilometers (7.5 miles) until it rejoins the Río Lagartos/Highway 295 route.

SAN FELIPE

While Río Lagartos is somewhat downtrodden, San Felipe has well-maintained streets and sidewalks, brightly painted houses, and a clean, attractive waterfront promenade. It makes for a nice side trip from Río Lagartos to experience life in a typical fishing village.

If you need a bit more action than people-watching, San Felipe has excellent sportfishing, especially for flat-water targets like tarpon, snook, bonefish, and permit. **Yucatán Fly Fishing Adventures** (toll-free U.S. tel. 800/552-2729, www.yucatanflyfishing.com) offers recommended day trips as well as multiday tours.

Another reason to stop here is ★ **El Popular Vaselina** (Calle 9 at Calle 12, tel. 986/862-2083, 8:30am-6:30pm Mon.-Fri., 8:30am-7:30pm Sat.-Sun., US$5-8), a huge thatch-roofed restaurant known throughout the peninsula for its excellent fresh seafood. Don't miss the ceviche—it's usually an appetizer, but the serving is big enough to make a meal (and then some). Fronting San Felipe's pleasant promenade, the tables have

---

1: Río Lagartos, overlooking a massive estuary and national park; **2:** El Popular Vaselina restaurant, a San Felipe institution; **3:** flamingos in flight; **4:** San Felipe's sleepy main avenue

nice views of the water. Service is friendly and prompt.

Information and Services

San Felipe has no bank, ATM, or tourist office. A small **medical clinic** is on Calle 15 at Calle 10-A, but is open limited hours only.

Getting There and Around

Noreste provides second-class bus service to and from San Felipe. The terminal is on the main street entering town, but may be closed if there's no imminent arrival or departure. Check Río Lagartos's routes for departure times; buses stop in San Felipe about 15 minutes later en route to Tizimín (US$2.50, 1.25 hour) or Mérida (US$11.50, 4 hours).

If you're driving, the well-signed turnoff to San Felipe is a few kilometers (less than 2 miles) before entering Río Lagartos.

TIZIMÍN

There's no real reason to stop in Tizimín, a busy, nondescript town, unless you're switching buses or staying the night on your way to or from Río Lagartos.

Food and Accommodations

Hotel 49 (Calle 49 btwn Calles 46 and 48, tel. 986/863-2136, www.hotel49.com, US$28-36 s/d with a/c) is a solid option, with tile-floored rooms that are surprisingly modern and clean; cable TV, Wi-Fi, and a tidy little café make it even better. There's lots of secure parking and the bus station is just a couple of blocks away.

Pizza Messina's (central park, Calle 53 at Calle 50, tel. 986/863-6940, www.messinaspizza.com, 11am-midnight Sun.-Thurs., 11am-1am Fri.-Sat., US$3.75-8) is a longtime locals' favorite serving tasty pizza pies, cold and hot subs, and pasta dishes. In the evening, take your eats to a bench outside to admire the dramatically lit Iglesia de los Santos Reyes.

Getting There and Around

Tizimín's shiny **ADO/Oriente terminal** (Calle 46 btwn Calles 45 and 47, tel. 986/863-2424) makes for a pleasant and comfortable stopover. Departures include:

• Cancún: US$9, 3 hours, 1:15pm

• Mérida: US$5, 4 hours, 5:30am and 4pm

• Valladolid: US$1.50, 1 hour, every 60-90 mins, 4:30am-8:15pm

The **Noreste terminal** (Calle 47 btwn Calles 46 and 48, tel. 986/863-2034) is around the corner and has second-class service to:

• Cancún: US$9, 3.25 hours, 5:30am and 6:45am

• Mérida: US$5, 4 hours, 6:30am, 11am, and 3:30pm

• Río Lagartos and San Felipe: US$2.25-2.50, 1.25-1.5 hours, 12 departures, 4:30am-7:50pm

For faster and more frequent service to Mérida, shared air-conditioned vans called *colectivos* (US$7, 2 hours) depart approximately every 75 minutes—or when full—5:30am-2:30pm from the corner of Calles 47 and 46.

Mérida, the Puuc Route, and Campeche

If there's a heart of the Yucatán Peninsula, surely it's Mérida and its rich surroundings.

Mérida is one of Mexico's finest colonial cities, with spectacular museums and galleries, daily performances and cultural events, and a genuinely warm and welcoming population. On Sundays, the city center (and many surrounding blocks) are closed to traffic and open to families, street performances, and food carts. Outside of Mérida is Izamal, another lovely colonial town, known for its historic church and the mustard-yellow hue of many of its homes and buildings. Also reachable in a day are the coastal towns of Progreso, a nice beach get-away, and Celestún, where you can tour a nearby flamingo reserve. South of Mérida is the utterly amazing Puuc Route, home to must-see

Highlights

Look for ★ to find recommended sights, activities, dining, and lodging.

★ **Domingo en Mérida:** Every Sunday, locals and tourists alike throng to Mérida's main plaza to munch on street food, watch dance performances, and share in the pleasure of simply being there, while a long stretch of Paseo de Montejo is closed to traffic (page 321).

★ **Convento de San Antonio de Padua:** Izamal's famous church-convent is awesome for its size—only the Vatican has a bigger church atrium—but troubling for having been built atop one of the Maya's most sacred sites; some of the pilfered stones are still visible in the convent's thick walls (page 354).

★ **Uxmal Archaeological Zone:** From the soaring Pyramid of the Magician to the stately Governor's Palace, Uxmal is one of the most remarkable of all Maya ruins. Plan on spending more than a day—Uxmal has a nighttime light show and a slew of caves, villages, and smaller ruins nearby (page 361).

★ **Cenotes de Cuzamá:** It's hard to say what's more fun—clattering along colonial-era rails on a horse-drawn trolley through abandoned henequen fields, or climbing down a rickety ladder through a crack in the earth to swim in the cool iridescent waters of ancient cenotes (page 382).

★ **Campeche's City Walls:** Built three centuries ago to ward off marauding pirates, the massive stone walls and imposing bastions that encircle Campeche City's colonial center have been converted into picturesque elevated walkways and first-rate museums (page 393).

★ **Calakmul Archaeological Zone and Reserve:** Deep in a nature reserve, Calakmul is home to toucans, monkeys, and even pumas and jaguars, if you're lucky enough to spot them. The ancient Maya city here covers 70 square kilometers (27 square miles) and has 6,000 structures, including one of the largest pyramids the Maya ever built (page 411).

Maya ruins like Uxmal and Kabah, plus small villages, gaping caves, and otherworldly cenotes. Farther still is the oft-overlooked state of Campeche; its capital, Campeche City, rivals Mérida with its colorful city center and historical attractions. The city was plagued by pirate attacks, and walls and forts built for defense have been put to use as museums and galleries. Meanwhile, southern Campeche boasts incredible (and little-visited) Maya ruins, including Calakmul, located deep in a nature reserve teeming with wildlife.

PLANNING YOUR TIME

This chapter covers a lot of ground—the more time you can budget here, the better! Merida is well worth 3-4 full days, and is especially lively on Sundays. Plan on a day trip to the Gulf coast beaches at Progreso and another jaunt (possibly overnight) to Izamal and its surroundings. The Puuc Route also brims with attractions; there are daylong tours from Mérida, but you can easily fill 2-3 full days visiting Maya ruins, colonial villages, and unique caves and cenotes. West of Mérida, the flamingo reserve at Celestún is best visited in the early morning or early evening. South from there is the state of Campeche—budget two days for Campeche City, a colonial gem with nearby ruins and haciendas, and another 2-3 days for the majestic archaeological sites and nature reserves in the Río Bec region. Bus service is limited outside the cities; having your own car is highly recommended.

Uxmal's Pyramid of the Magician is distinctive for its oval-shaped base.

Previous: Oxkutzcab's market; entering the Convento de San Antonio de Padua in Izamal; Cenote Kankirixché.

Mérida, the Puuc Route, and Campeche

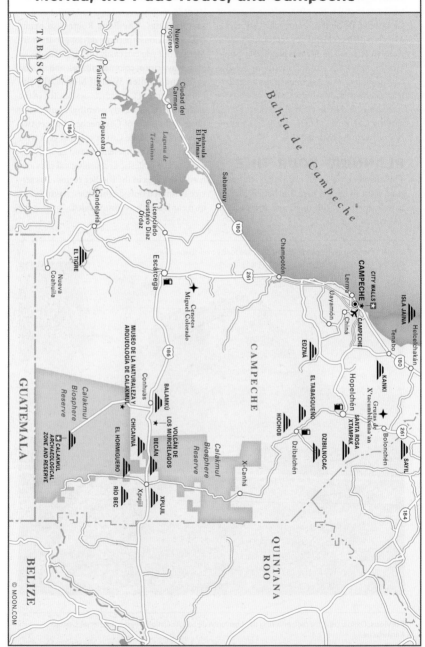

TABASCO

Nuevo Progreso

Palizada

Ciudad del Carmen

Península El Palmar

Laguna de Términos

Bahía de Campeche

El Aguacatal

Candelaria

Sabancuy

Licenciado Gustavo Díaz Ordaz

Nueva Coahuila

EL TIGRE

Escalcega

Cenotes Miguel Colorado

Champotón

Lerma

CAMPECHE

CAMPECHE

CITY WALLS

ISLA JAINA

Uayamón

Chiná

Tenabo

Helelchakán

KANKI

Grutas de X'tacumbilxunu'an

EDZNÁ

CAMPECHE

Hopelchén

Bolonchén

SAVIL

GUATEMALA

Calakmul Biosphere Reserve

MUSEO DE LA NATURALEZA Y ARQUEOLOGÍA DE CALAKMUL

Conhuas

BALAMKÚ

CALAKMUL ARCHAEOLOGICAL ZONE AND RESERVE

EL HORMIGUERO

CHICANNÁ

VOLCÁN DE LOS MURCIÉLAGOS

BECÁN

RÍO BEC

Xpuijil

XPUJIL

Calakmul Biosphere Reserve

X-Canhá

EL TABASQUEÑO

HOCHOB

Dzibalchén

SANTA ROSA XTAMPAK

DZIBILNOCAC

BELIZE

QUINTANA ROO

© MOON.COM

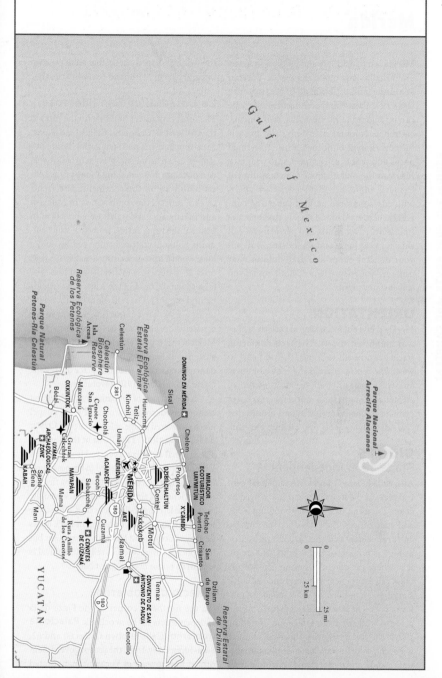

Gulf of Mexico

Parque Nacional
Arrecife Alacranes

Reserva Ecológica
de los Petenes

Parque Natural
Petenes-Ria Celestún

Celestún
Biosphere
Reserve

Isla
Arena

Celestún

Reserva Ecológica
Estatal El Palmar

Hunucmá

Kinchil

Tetiz

Chocholá

Chochola

Umán

DOMINGO EN MÉRIDA

Sisal

Chelem

Progreso

Chuburná

Conkal

MIRADOR
ECOTURISTICO
UAYMITÚN

DZIBILCHALTÚN

MÉRIDA

ACANCEH

X'CAMBO

Telchac
Puerto

Telchac
Pueblo

San
Crisanto

Dzilam
de Bravo

Reserva Estatal
de Dzilam

Motul

Temax

AKÉ

T'HO KOB

Izamal

CENOTES
DE CUZAMÁ

Ruta Anillo
de los Cenotes

Cuzamá

Tecoh

Sabacché

Mama

CONVENTO DE SAN
ANTONIO DE PADUA

Cenotillo

Bécal

OXKINTOK

Maxcanú

Calcehtok

UXMAL
ARCHAEOLOGICAL
ZONE

Grutas
Calcehtok

Cenote
San Ignacio

MAYAPÁN

KABAH

Santa
Elena

Maní

YUCATÁN

281

180

180
D

0   25 km

0   25 mi

Mérida

Mérida bursts with art and culture, in a way unrivaled by any other city on the Yucatán Peninsula (and by few in all of Mexico). The city's rich artistic and architectural heritage can be enjoyed in its museums, monuments, churches, colonial mansions, and beautiful government buildings, while tree-lined parks and plazas offer a peek into ordinary Mexican life. But it's the city's commitment to music and dance that really sets it apart, with city-sponsored performances and concerts held every day and weekly street parties that feature live bands and performers—all this, all year long, and all for free. Pull out your dancing shoes and grab hold of your camera—you're sure to need both even if you stay just one night.

ORIENTATION

Mérida is laid out in a neat grid pattern of one-way numbered streets. The even-numbered streets run north to south, the odd east to west. The central plaza is the center of town, and you can easily walk to most downtown attractions, shops, and marketplaces. Buses provide frequent service in and around the city and outlying areas, and cabs are plentiful.

SIGHTS

Plaza de la Independencia

Also called Plaza Grande, Mérida's leafy central plaza is the heart of town. It is ringed by colonial-era and 19th-century buildings—city and state offices, the cathedral, the Olimpo cultural center, and the MACAY museum, as well as numerous restaurants and shops. It is where the core of Domingo en Mérida takes place, complete with food and artesanía stands and a number of ballet folklórico performances. The plaza itself is also just a perfect place to while away an afternoon, watching guayabera-clad men having their shoes shined, women in colorful huipiles tending small sidewalk stands, and teens texting each other from the white S-shaped chairs that were once an integral part of Méridiano courtship rituals.

La Catedral de San Ildefonso

The most prominent building on the plaza is the cathedral (Calle 60 at Calle 61, no phone, 6am-1pm and 4:30pm-8pm daily). Built with stones taken from Maya structures, it was completed in 1598, making it one of the oldest buildings on the continent. The architecture reflects the combination of Moorish and Renaissance styles that were prevalent in Spain at the time. Inside, immense stone columns hold up a latticed stone ceiling, and a huge wood Christ measuring 8 meters (26 feet) on a 12-meter cross (39 feet)—said to be the largest wood Christ in the Americas—stands behind the altar. Overall, the exterior and interior are stark in comparison to some of the ornately adorned churches in other parts of Mexico; this is partly owing to the traditional austerity of Franciscan design, and partly to damage and looting that took place during the Caste War and the 1910 Revolution.

On the left side of the cathedral, a small but elaborately decorated iron and glass chapel houses a revered image of Jesus called El Cristo de las Ampollas (The Christ of the Blisters). The original crucifix was carved from a tree in Ichmul that had been engulfed in flames but remained undamaged; later a devastating fire destroyed Ichmul's church but only blackened the statue and left blister-like welts on it. The statue was moved to Mérida's cathedral in 1645; it was destroyed during the Mexican Revolution but its replica is still revered. A religious festival is held in its honor every September.

Palacio de Gobierno

On the northeast corner of the Plaza de la Independencia is the neoclassic Palacio de Gobierno (Calle 61 btwn Calles 60 and 62, 8am-10pm daily, free), the seat of government offices for the state of Yucatán. Inaugurated

Mérida

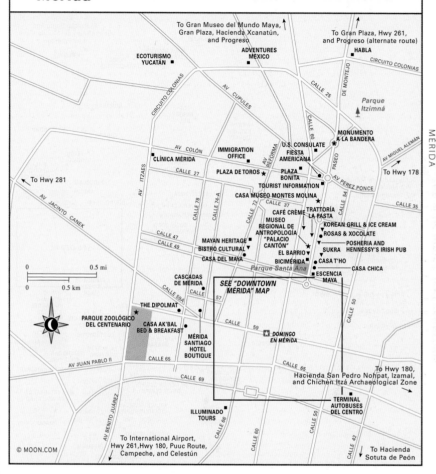

To Gran Museo del Mundo Maya,
Gran Plaza, Hacienda Xcanatún,
and Progreso

To Gran Plaza, Hwy 261,
and Progreso (alternate route)

ECOTURISMO
YUCATÁN ■

ADVENTURES
MEXICO ■

HABLA ■

CIRCUITO COLONIAS

CIRCUITO COLONIAS

AV CUPULES

AV DE MONTEJO

CALLE 25

Parque
▲ Itzimná

AV COLÓN

IMMIGRATION
OFFICE ■

CLÍNICA MÉRIDA ■

CALLE 27

PLAZA DE TOROS ★

AV ITZAES

AV REFORMA

CALLE 60

U.S. CONSULATE ■
FIESTA
AMERICANA ■

PLAZA
BONITA ■

TOURIST INFORMATION ■

MONUMENTO
★ A LA BANDERA

PASEO DE MONTEJO

AV MIGUEL ALEMÁN

AV PEREZ PONCE

To Hwy 178

To Hwy 281

AV JACINTO CANEK

CALLE 78

CALLE 74-A

CALLE 72

CASA MUSEO MONTES MOLINA ■

CALLE 37

CAFÉ CRÈME ■
MUSEO
REGIONAL DE
ANTROPOLOGÍA
"PALACIO
CANTÓN" ★

MAYAN HERITAGE ■
BISTRO CULTURAL ▼

CASA DEL MAYA ■

CALLE 47

CALLE 49

TRATTORÍA
LA PASTA ▼

CALLE 54

CALLE 35

KOREAN GRILL & ICE CREAM ●
ROSAS & XOCOLATE ●

EL BARRIO ▼

BICIMÉRIDA ■
★ CASA T'HO

POSHERIA AND
SUKRA HENNESSY'S IRISH PUB ●

CASA CHICA

Parque Santa Ana

ESCENCIA
■ MAYA

0   0.5 mi

0   0.5 km

CASCADAS
DE MÉRIDA ■

SEE "DOWNTOWN
MÉRIDA" MAP

CALLE 59A

CALLE

CALLE
57

THE DIPOLMAT ■

PARQUE ZOOLÓGICO
DEL CENTENARIO ★

CASA AK'BAL
BED & BREAKFAST ■

MÉRIDA
SANTIAGO
HOTEL
BOUTIQUE ■

CALLE 65

AV JUAN PABLO II

CALLE 69

CALLE ★ 59

■ DOMINGO
EN MÉRIDA

CALLE 50

CALLE 65

To Hwy 180,
Hacienda San Pedro Nohpat, Izamal,
and Chichén Itzá Archaeological Zone →

AV BENITO JUAREZ

ILLUMINADO
TOURS ■

CALLE 66

TERMINAL
AUTOBUSES
DEL CENTRO ■

CALLE 60

CALLE 50

CALLE 42

© MOON.COM

To International Airport,
Hwy 261, Hwy 180, Puuc Route,
Campeche, and Celestún

To Hacienda
Sotuta de Peón

---

in 1892, it contains several impressive abstract murals by the famous Mérida-born artist Fernando Castro Pacheco. Created between 1971 and 1974 and showcased along the staircase and in the upper galleries, these works depict the history of the region, from the ancient Maya to modern-day Mexico. Restoration of these works was completed in 2004 under the supervision of Pacheco himself by four professional restoration artists from the Centro de Restauración de Bellas Artes in Mexico City.

On the west side of the Plaza de la Independencia is the **Palacio Municipal** (Calle 62 btwn Calles 61 and 62), which serves as Mérida's city hall. Dating to 1735, this architectural beauty is two stories of arch upon arch with a four-sided clock tower. It boasts the oldest coat of arms of the city of Mérida—look for it at the bottom of the main staircase.

Museo Casa Montejo

Facing the southern edge of the central plaza is the **Casa Montejo** (Calle 63

Downtown Mérida

© MOON.COM

Sign Language

In colonial times, Mérida's street signs had both words and pictures.

As you navigate the numbered streets of Mérida, you'll soon begin noticing whimsical street signs—carved pictures of animals, household items, and people—adorning street corners. These signs pay homage to Mérida's past when, because of the high illiteracy rate, the city hung painted wooden signs of familiar figures so that every inhabitant could find an address. Typically, these signs directly related to establishments or sights nearby: a pair of nuns to signal a convent, a violin to indicate an instrument maker, a bull to direct people to the Plaza de Toros (bullring). Look around and you'll not only get a flavor of where things were in Mérida's past, but also where they might still be today.

btwn Calles 60 and 62, tel. 999/923-0633, www.casasdeculturabanamex.com/museo casamontejo, 10am-7pm Tues.-Sat., 10am-2pm Sun., free), built between 1543 and 1549 by Maya slaves. Initially, the portico was the only decoration on the facade; note the intricate carvings of Spaniards with their feet firmly planted on the heads of Maya—a lasting reminder of Spanish tyranny. Originally a soldiers' barracks, it became the home of Francisco de Montejo "El Adelantado" (The Older) and was eventually bequeathed to Francisco de Montejo "El Mozo" (The Younger). Thirteen generations of Montejos lived in the house until it was sold to Simón Peón y Peón in 1839. Peón's descendants subsequently lived in the house until it was sold to Banamex in 1980.

The bank now takes up the back wing of the mansion, but in 2010 the sections opening onto the enormous interior courtyard opened as a museum. Inside are several rooms, decorated in Victorian style. Highlights include a 1678 painting of the (third) reconstruction of the Santiago de Guatemala Cathedral as well as a grand dining room with wood-paneled doors and walls, the ceiling painted in a way that gives the illusion of being outdoors. Beyond these rooms, there's a gallery with rotating exhibits, and interactive computer stations that utilize talking deer and stiff-looking conquistadors to narrate history lessons.

Interpretive signage is in both English and Spanish. Free guided tours in Spanish also are offered Tuesday-Saturday at 11am, 1pm, and 5pm, Sunday at 11am and 1pm only. The air-conditioning inside the entire museum hovers around subzero, and the bathrooms are well maintained if you need a pit stop while sightseeing.

Museo Regional de Antropología "Palacio Cantón"

Museum of Anthropology "Canton Palace" (Paseo de Montejo at Calle 43, tel. 999/923-0557, www.palaciocanton.inah.gob.mx, 8am-5pm Tues.-Sun., US$3) houses the finest collections of Maya artifacts in the Yucatán Peninsula, spanning from the Preclassic era to the present day. Only the Museo Nacional de Antropología in Mexico City is better, though there's no shortage of wow-power in Mérida: The collection ranges from ornately painted ceramic jars to massive funerary urns, from delicate jewelry and ritual items made of jade, obsidian, and seashells to imposing stone monoliths covered in hieroglyphics. There are also detailed descriptions of the Maya calendar and advancements in astronomy, architecture, and agriculture, all in Spanish and English.

The museum itself is housed in one of Mérida's ornate mansions, most of which were built during the henequen boom in the early 20th century. Designed by Italian architect Enrico Deserti—the same architect who built the Teatro Peón Contreras—it was originally the home of a governor of Yucatán, General Francisco Cantón Rosado. It served as the official state residence from 1948 to 1960, and eventually, in 1977, the mansion became the city's Museo Regional de Antropología.

Museo Macay

Museo Fernando García Ponce-Macay (Pasaje Revolución btwn Calles 58 and 60, tel. 999/928-3236, www.macay.org, 10am-6pm Wed.-Mon., free) is a first-class modern art museum boasting an impressive collection of Yucatecan art, including paintings by its namesake Fernando García Ponce, Gabriel Ramírez Aznar, and Fernando Castro Pacheco (who painted the arresting murals in the Palacio de Gobierno).

The museum occupies the beautiful 16th-century **Palacio Arzobispal** (Palace of the Archbishop), which is next to the cathedral; the passageway between the two is administered by the Museo Macay and often features large-scale outdoor exhibits. Construction on the sprawling building began in 1573 under the direction of Fray Diego de Landa. Completed in the 1600s, it was the residence of several of Yucatán's bishops. The building was connected to the cathedral via two chapels—Rosario and San José—until the early 20th century, when the pedestrian walkway now known as the **Pasaje Revolución** was created in their place. The Palace of the Archbishop served several purposes after it was separated physically from the cathedral—military post, cultural center, government offices—until it was transformed into the Museo Macay in 1993. There is a second entrance on Calle 60 near Calle 63.

Gran Museo del Mundo Maya

Worth the 12-kilometer (7.5-mile) trek from the center, **Gran Museo del Mundo Maya** (Calle 60 Nte. near Calle 55, tel. 999/341-0435, www.granmuseodelmundomaya.com.mx, 8am-5pm Wed.-Mon., US$7.50) is an attractive modern museum with easy-to-digest displays on ancient Maya civilization, modern Maya culture, and even prehistoric times. The layout is roomy and engaging, with plenty of videos and multimedia intermixed with traditional displays. Serious Maya buffs may be somewhat underwhelmed, but it's an accessible and informative intro for everyone else. Taxis charge about US$3 from the center, or take a Siglo XXI bus (US$0.40, 25 minutes) from the corner of Calles 58 and 59.

Museo de la Ciudad de Mérida

The **Museo de la Ciudad de Mérida** (Parque Eulogio Rosado, Calle 56 btwn Calles 65 and 65-A, tel. 999/924-4264, 9am-6pm Tues.-Fri., 9am-2pm Sat.-Sun., free) does Mérida's rich history justice, with interesting and artful exhibits spanning from pre-Hispanic to contemporary times, all well translated and of manageable depth. There's even some sly humor: One display suggests the word Yucatán may have come from the Maya term *Yuk ak katan,* or "I don't understand your language." The museum is itself a work of art, with soaring passageways and stunning tile floors, belying the fact that it was formerly the central post office. Be sure to visit the art galleries on the 2nd and 3rd floors, displaying the work of local artists.

Museo de Arte Popular de Yucatán

Housed in a restored *casona* (large colonial home), the **Museo de Arte Popular de Yucatán** (Casa Molina, Calle 50A btwn Calles 57 and 59, tel. 999/928-5263, 10am-5pm Tues.-Sat., 10am-3pm Sun., free) boasts a gorgeous collection of Mexican folk art created by master artisans. An entire room is dedicated to Yucatecan *artesanía*, though you'll find a magnificent range of ceramics, textiles, cardboard, and wood items from throughout the country. The modest gift shop sells beautiful works of folk art too.

Other Museums

Inaugurated in 2018, **Palacio de la Música** (Calle 58 btwn Calles 57 and 59, 10am-4pm Tues.-Sun., free) is a behemoth building, a huge slab of concrete plopped down in the middle of the historic center. Inside is a concert hall and a state-of-the-art museum that traces the evolution of the region's music from precolonial times to the present. Listening stations, touch screens, even digital record players engage visitors throughout. Tours are offered at 9am, 11am, and 2pm.

    Museo de la Canción Yucateca (Calle 57 at Calle 48, tel. 999/923-7224, www.museodelacancionyucateca.com, 9am-5pm Tues.-Fri., 9am-3pm Sat.-Sun., US$1, free Sun.) examines the development of the region's music, paying homage to Yucatán's most famous composers, singers, and musicians. Signage is in Spanish only; English translations are available at the front desk.

    Pinacoteca del Estado Juan Gamboa Guzmán (Calle 59 btwn Calles 58 and 60, tel. 999/924-5233, 9am-5pm Tues.-Sat., 10am-5pm Sun., US$2) is located in an annex to the restored Jesuit church, known as the Tercera Orden. It houses mostly religious works of art from the colonial period, though it also has a handful of paintings by the famous Yucatecan artist Juan Gamboa Guzmán and bronze statutes by Enrique Gottidiener, an influential Mexican artist who lived and died in Mérida.

    A stately mansion popular for weddings, **Casa Museo Montes Molina** (Paseo de Montejo btwn Calles 33 and 35, tel. 999/925-5999, www.laquintamm.com, 9am-5pm Mon.-Fri., 9am-1pm Sat., US$5) is a unique experience in that it's still intermittently lived in by the octogenarian descendant of sisal hacienda owners. It's a working household, not a static relic, and visitors can ogle the French-influenced architecture and Tiffany stained glass doors upstairs as well as the servants' quarters downstairs. The 40-minute tours are given in English at 9am, 11am, and 3pm Monday-Friday, and 9am and 11am Saturday; in Spanish, tours are at 10am, noon, 2pm, and 4pm Monday-Friday, and 10am and noon Saturday.

Parque Zoológico del Centenario

Referred to as *"El Centenario,"* the **city zoo** (Av. Itzáes at Calle 59, www.merida.gob.mx/centenario, 8am-5pm Tues.-Sun., free) is a popular spot for families, especially on weekends. It has kiddie rides (including a train that loops around the park), playgrounds, and loads of concession stands. The zoo also has a decent selection of animals, but the cramped quarters can be upsetting for some. On Sunday, magicians, clowns, puppets, and theater groups come out to entertain the kids.

SPORTS AND RECREATION
Bullfights

If you're interested in what makes bullfighting so popular in Mexico, catch a *corrida* (literally, a running) at the **Plaza de Toros Mérida** (Calle 72 at Calle 33, US$15-50). Unless you want to work on your tan, opt for the premium *sombra* (shade) seats—the extra charge is worth every bead of sweat you save. Tickets are sold online (www.boletea.com.mx) or same day at the box office—the cost depends on the experience of the bullfighter and the seat. Look for posters advertising the next *corrida* around the Plaza de la Independencia.

ENTERTAINMENT AND EVENTS

As one of Mexico's colonial shining stars, Mérida is the region's cultural supernova. With free nightly performances, theaters, art galleries, cinemas, and a planetarium, there is something for everyone. For up-to-date information on monthly events, check out the free tourism magazines and brochures; the most helpful include *Yucatán Today, Explore Yucatán,* and the *Cartelera Cultural* (www.merida.gob.mx/turismo/contenido/cultura/eventos.htm).

TOP EXPERIENCE

★ Domingo en Mérida

Sunday is a wonderful day in Mérida. Everyone puts on their Sunday best and comes to the city center, where the streets are closed to traffic. *Artesanía* vendors set up stalls, and pushcarts do a lively business selling *tortas* (sandwiches), *elote* (corn on the cob), drinks, and sweets. Be sure to catch one of the many free performances throughout the day. The most popular is folkloric dancing presented in front of the Palacio Municipal (1pm), often featuring the city's remarkably skilled youth dance troupe. Another worthwhile event is the **Bici-Ruta** (www.merida.gob.mx/biciruta, 8am-12:30pm), a 5-kilometer (3.1-mile) route, including a section of Paseo de Montejo, where the road is closed to make room for bicycling; it's popular with local families, but visitors can easily rent bikes (US$1.50/hour) and join in—look for the bike rental stand in front of the Palacio Municipal or go to

Bicimérida (Paseo de Montejo at Calle 45, tel. 999/287-3538, 8am-10pm Mon.- Sat., 7am-5pm Sun.).

Nightlife

Opened in 1918, **La Negrita** (Calle 62 at Calle 49, tel. 999/121-0411, noon-10pm daily) is a one-time dive bar that has been relaunched as a cool-cat hot spot. The look is old-school Yucatán meets hipster Mérida. And the drinks are the same: Tecate meets artisanal mezcal, moonshine meets microbrews. *Botanas* (appetizers) come with each round of drinks, plus there's live music daily.

Malahat Speakeasy & Mixology (Parque Santa Lucia, Calle 55 at Calle 60, tel. 999/923 1979, 7:30pm-3am Wed.-Sun.) is a tiny and uber-cool speakeasy—just a few tables and a short bar—and really hard to find (look for the door near the dumpster); ask at Apoala, its sister restaurant in the same park, if you're stumped. Mixologists climb a steel ladder to access a high wall of liquor bottles, and their creations are out of this world. DJs spin up a nice vibe.

Hermana República (Calle 64 btwn Calles 55 and 57, tel. 999/924-8911, noon-11pm Mon.-Thurs., noon-midnight Fri.-Sat., noon-6pm Sun.) is a labyrinthine brewpub set in a dramatic—and crumbling—colonial home lacking a roof (but gaining a fabulous night sky). Patito, a local artisanal brew, is what's served; typically, there are eight beers on tap, from pilsner to dry stout. Traditional Yucatecan eats are offered.

Over three dozen artisanal mezcals fill the shelves at **Fundación La Mezcalería** (Calle 56 btwn Calles 53 and 55, tel. 999/102-0033, 8pm-3am Wed.-Sun.), where a 20-something crowd sips cocktails and throws back shots in an artsy lounge peppered with vintage sofas, mismatched tables, and modular plastic chairs. Folks start moving to the DJ around 10:30pm.

A wall of masks and another of skulls are just two of the many striking decorations in **Cara Negra** (Calle 62 btwn 51 and 53, no phone, www.caranegra.mx, 7pm-3am

Mérida's Weekly Cultural Events

SUNDAY (DOMINGO EN MÉRIDA)

- **Bici-Ruta:** 5 kilometers (3.1 miles) of streets in the historic center are open to bicyclists and pedestrians only (8am-12:30pm); rent bicycles in front of the Palacio Municipal and along Paseo de Montejo (US$1.50/hour)
- **Plaza de la Independencia:** handicrafts market and outdoor food stands (9am-9pm)
- **Parque Santa Lucía:** live music and dancing (11am-3pm)
- **Palacio Municipal:** regional dance performance (1pm)
- **Paseo de Montejo (at Calle 35):** outdoor art market (9am-1pm)

MONDAY

- **Palacio Municipal:** regional dance performance (9pm)

TUESDAY

- **Parque Santiago:** live big-band music and dancing (8:30pm)

WEDNESDAY

- **Casa de Montejo:** a sound and light show illuminates the façade of this historic building,

Wed.-Sat.), a popular downtown bar. There's a shamanistic theme in the décor, while the music tends toward electronica and the cocktails are tasty and strong; overall, the ambience is cool and modern, and DJs get folks dancing most nights.

Live rock and reggae play at **Mayan Pub** (Calle 62 btwn Calles 55 and 57, tel. 999/923-1271, 7pm-3am Wed.-Sun.), a boho restaurant-bar set in a renovated colonial home. Stick to beers and head to the leafy garden for the best seats in the house.

Hennessy's Irish Pub (Paseo de Montejo btwn Calles 41 and 43, tel. 999/923-8993, www.hennessysirishpub.mx, noon-midnight daily) is set in a grand colonial mansion plastered with memorabilia from the Emerald Isle. It's a friendly place to meet locals (and not just expats) over darts, billiards, or a sturdy helping of bangers and mash. Live music and telecast sporting events entertain throughout

the week. Guinness is served in cans only, unfortunately.

Tropical drinks, chill music, and leafy ferns give the bar-eatery **Casa Chica** (Paseo de Montejo btwn Calles 45 and 47, tel. 999/918-5969, 6pm-2am daily) a vibe that's part Miami, part Cayman Islands, while high ceilings give a sense of airy space. More bar than restaurant, the menu still has several items worth sampling.

Music and Dance

Music is heard all over Mérida, and dancing is a way of life. Informal and free concerts and other entertainment are regularly presented for Mérida's residents and visitors at parks and plazas throughout the city. Sunday features traditional music and dance performances in the center of town from early morning to late evening. In fact, all the regularly scheduled events throughout the week involve music highlighting its distinctive features and the relationship between the conquistadors and Maya; a regional dance performance follows (8pm, subtitles in English)

- **Cementerio General:** guided tour of the grave sites of the famous people buried in Mérida's main cemetery (8pm)

THURSDAY

- **Parque Santa Lucía:** regional dance, music, and spoken-word performances (9pm)

FRIDAY

- **Catedral de San Ildefonso:** 3-D sound and light show describing the construction of the cathedral, accompanied by a live performance by the city chorus (9pm)

SATURDAY

- **Catedral de San Ildefonso:** reenactment of ancient Maya ball game (8pm)

- **Paseo de Montejo at Calle 47:** Noche Mexicana—food stalls, handicrafts booths, live music, and dance performances (8pm-11pm)

- **Bici-Ruta:** 5 kilometers (3.1 miles) of streets in the historic center are open to bicyclists and pedestrians only (6pm-10pm, first Saturday of the month only); rent bicycles in front of the Palacio Municipal and along Paseo de Montejo (US$1.50/hour)

and dancing in some way, whether to watch or to join in.

Built during Mérida's henequen boom, the ornate **Teatro José Peón Contreras** (Calle 60 at Calle 57, tel. 999/923-7354, 9am-9pm daily, US$8-20) mostly hosts music concerts and dance performances, including those by the resident **Orquesta Sinfónica de Yucatán** (www.sinfonicadeyucatan.com.mx) September-December. For a listing of events, stop by the box office or check at the tourist information center next door. During the day when there aren't rehearsals, you can take a look around the theater if the staff isn't busy cleaning it.

Museo de la Canción Yucateca (Calle 57 at Calle 48, tel. 999/923-7224, www.museodelacancionyucateca.com) hosts concerts the first and last Wednesday of every month; performances start at 8:30pm and highlight Yucatecan classics. Tickets typically cost around US$3.

Theater

Teatro Armando Manzanero (Calle 62 btwn Calles 59 and 61, tel. 999/924-9990, 10am-10pm daily) is an art deco venue housing a main theater and two smaller ones. It's an artsy place with top-notch programming year-round—productions vary from modern dance performances to international film festivals.

Teatro Daniel Ayala Pérez (Calle 60 btwn Calles 59 and 61, tel. 999/928-6863, 10am-10pm daily) is a cavernous theater used mainly for dramatic performances. Ticket prices range US$5-10.

Cultural Centers

Housed in an award-winning building, **Centro Cultural de Mérida Olimpo** (Calle 61 at Calle 62, tel. 999/942-0000, ext. 80130, 10am-8pm Tues.-Sat., 10am-3pm Sun.) is chock-full of programming every month, hosting everything from indie films to music concerts. There's also a planetarium, research library, and galleries with temporary exhibits—check the bulletin board at the entrance for listings.

Mérida English Library (Calle 53 btwn Calles 66 and 68, tel. 999/924-8401, www.meridaenglishlibrary.com, 10am-1pm Mon.-Sat. plus 6:30pm-9:30pm Mon. and 4pm-8pm Wed.) definitely has a huge selection of English-language books to borrow or buy, but it also serves as an important cultural center for English speakers with weekly programs and get-togethers, including a lecture series, open mic nights, and house and garden tours. A bulletin board also has postings of tours, short- and long-term housing, and items for sale.

Cinema

If you're hankering for a Hollywood fix, **Cinemex Rex** (Parque Santiago, Calle 57 btwn Calles 70 and 72, tel. 999/928-5980, www.cinemex.com, US$1.50) screens U.S. and Mexican films in its two theaters.

Teatro Armando Manzanero (Calle 62 btwn Calles 59 and 61, tel. 999/924-9990, 10am-10pm daily) occasionally screens alternative films and hosts film festivals.

Festivals and Events

Mérida Fest is monthlong festival held every January to commemorate the city's founding on January 6, 1542. It's kicked off in the Plaza Grande with hundreds of *trova* musicians serenading the city, fireworks lighting up the sky, and mass in the cathedral. Throughout the month, hundreds of artists keep the celebration going with dance, music, drama, film, and spoken word performances. Most are free and held in Mérida's historic buildings and parks. For a list of scheduled events, stop by one of the tourist offices.

From March to November, the annual **Festival de Aves Toh** (Toh Bird Festival, tel. 999/988-4437, www.festivalavesyucatan.com) offers myriad bird-related activities: birdwatching tours, photo contests, conferences, workshops, and more. The festival culminates in a weekend-long "Maratón del las Aves Xoc Ch'ich," when participants gather in teams to observe and count as many of the 465 bird species registered in the state as possible (543 species are registered in the entire peninsula). It's a well-attended event and one that welcomes amateurs and experts alike. It's a great way to see the state of Yucatán and, of course, to learn about its birds.

La Noche Blanca (8pm-2am, free) is a citywide celebration of the arts, when galleries, concert halls, museums, and theaters open their doors late into the night. Held in May and December, more than 50 organizations typically participate. The city provides complimentary shuttle service to all the locales, and also sponsors concerts and dance performances in city parks and public buildings.

Another arts explosion, **Otoño Cultural** lasts for a month during September and October, with dance, *trova*, theater, and literary events that are mostly free. Stop by one of the tourist offices for a schedule of events.

Paseo de las Ánimas, or Procession of the Souls, is the culmination of Mérida's weeklong Day of the Dead festivities, when families remember and welcome back the spirits of their loved ones. The procession itself is a two-mile walk in the evening, beginning at the city cemetery and ending at Parque de San Juan; altars, skeleton face painters, and food stands line the road. Thousands of people join in, often in traditional dress and with faces painted and carrying candles—it's a remarkable sight. It's typically held on October 31.

Festival de Danza Oc' Ohtic is a dance festival featuring top modern dance companies from around the world. The festival typically takes place during the first two weeks of December and often creates such a buzz that shows have long lines; arrive early to get a good seat. Ticket prices range around US$5-15.

1: Museo Regional de Antropología "Palacio Cantón"; **2:** La Catedral de San Ildefonso; **3:** Domingo en Mérida, showcasing traditional dance performances throughout the day

SHOPPING

From rambling family-run stores to high-end boutiques, Mérida attracts the treasures of the region. Look for hammocks, *guayaberas*, *huipiles*, panama hats, one-of-a-kind T-shirts, designer shoes, and more.

Markets

Mercado Lucas de Gálvez (Calle 67 btwn Calles 56 and 58, 6am-7pm daily)—better known as the **Mercado Municipal**—is a city block-wide building bustling with movement. The 1st floor—with its myriad colors and layers of scents—is the center of the action: rows of neatly stacked fruits and vegetables, flowers of all sorts, animal parts (you'll see heads, hooves, stomachs, and more), mountains of herbs and spices, incense and religious icons, children's toys, rows of women's shoes, stand upon stand of gold jewelry—just about anything you're looking for (and aren't) is here. The 2nd floor is quieter and focused on *artesanía: guayaberas,* handwoven hammocks, sandals, and *huipiles* from the Yucatán, plus folk art from other parts of the country. And if you get hungry and have a strong stomach, there are dozens of restaurants serving cheap local fare on both floors.

Artesanías Bazar García Rejón (Calle 60 at Calle 65, 9am-7pm Mon.-Sat., 9am-5pm Sun.) is devoted entirely to local handicrafts. There's a good selection of sandals, clothing, hammocks, and more. Remember to bargain—most items have been marked up in anticipation of the custom.

A boho **open-air market** (Calle 60 btwn Calles 57 and 59, sunset-11pm Fri.-Sat.) is often set up on weekend evenings alongside Parque Maternidad. Handmade jewelry, batik, feather art, and clothing from Chiapas are the top sellers.

Each Sunday, an **Artesanía Bazaar** is held at Parque Santa Lucía (11am-3pm) as part of the weekly city-sponsored Domingo en Mérida. Booths wind through the park and are packed with all sorts of tchotchkes, local crafts, and tempting *antojitos*. Live Yucatecan music is featured in the early afternoon.

Artesanía

Casa de las Artesanías del Estado de Yucatán (Calle 63 btwn Calles 64 and 66, tel. 999/928-6676, www.artesanias.yucatan. gob.mx, 8:30am-9pm Mon.-Sat., 10am-5pm Sun.) is one of the best shops at which to purchase regional folk art—the selection is wide and well made and the prices are fair. Some kitsch has crept into the inventory; once you hit the coconut monkeys, head to the register.

Artesanaria (Calle 60 at Calle 55, tel. 999/163-2924, 10am-11pm Tues.-Sun.) is a small shop chock-full of quality folk art from around the country; everything from home goods to jewelry is sold. Prices speak to the high quality found here.

La Poblana (Calle 65 btwn Calles 58 and 60, tel. 999/928-6093, www. hamacaslapoblana.com, 9am-6pm Mon.-Fri.) is a mom-and-pop shop specializing in hammocks. It offers a huge variety of sizes and materials, from budget to high-end. International shipping is available.

Posheria (Paseo de Montejo btwn Calles 41 and 43, tel. 999/221-8756, 9am-9pm daily) specializes in *pox* (pronounced pohsh), a traditional liquor made from sugarcane and corn. Originally used in religious ceremonies among the Maya populations in Chiapas, it quickly grew to be a social drink in and beyond those communities. This shop sells a variety of artisanal *pox;* tastings are offered. Chiapanecan coffee and handicrafts are sold too.

Clothing and Shoes

Although you'll find traditional clothing in Mérida's markets, there are several shops with excellent—and updated—takes on the same offerings.

Kukul Bout'ik (Calle 55 btwn Calles 60 and 62, tel. 999/923-2240, www.kukulboutik. com, 11am-9pm daily) specializes in luxury clothing and home goods that celebrate Mexican indigenous artistry. You'll find traditional *huipiles* and handwoven bags sitting side by side with Tzotzil-stitched boat shoes and whimsical pillowcases made from the sansevieria plant.

Similarly, **Amerindio** (Calle 55 btwn Calles 60 and 62, tel. 999/923-0945, 11am-9pm Mon.-Sat., 11am-7pm Sun.) sells products using designs inspired by the indigenous art but with a focus on menswear. You'll find everything from guayaberas and panama hats to wallets and shoes for men of all sizes.

If you're on the search for the perfect *huipil* or *terno*, try **Escencia Maya** (Parque Santa Ana, Calle 47 btwn Calles 58 and 60, tel. 999/923-0040, 8am-10pm Mon.-Fri., 8am-11pm Sat.) and **Camisería Canul** (Calle 62 btwn Calles 57 and 59, tel. 999/923-0157, 9am-8pm Mon.-Sat.).

For a fine guayabera (traditional men's shirt), head to **Fábrica de Guayaberas Jack** (Calle 59 btwn Calles 60 and 62, tel. 999/928-6002, 10am-8:30pm Mon.-Sat., 10am-3:30pm Sun.) and **Canul Jr.** (Calle 59 btwn Calles 60 and 62, tel. 999/923-1811, 9am-8pm Mon.-Sat., 10am-1pm Sun.). Custom-made guayaberas are made in about a week for off-the-rack prices.

For hipster, limited-edition T-shirts, **Tejon Rojo** (Calle 53 btwn Calles 60 and 62, 999/923-2935, www.tejonrojo.com, noon-9pm Mon.-Sat., noon-6pm Sun.) is where it's at. Owner and artist Annie Farias designs and hand stitches them all, using Mexican pop art as inspiration. Mugs, hats, and bags are also sold. It's a great choice for mementos and special gifts.

Tags Alpargatas (Calle 58 at Calle 49, tel. 999/901-1917, 10am-9pm Mon.-Fri., noon-11pm Sat., 9am-1pm Sun.) specializes in stylish espadrilles and boots, all handmade by local artisans, using unique designs that celebrate all things Mexico: monarch butterfly migrations, indigenous art, Day of the Dead, and more. Shoes are fair trade but also accessibly priced (US$13-18). Custom sizes are made, too.

Traditional panama or *jipi* hats are sold at **Fábrica de Guayaberas Jack** (Calle 59 btwn Calles 60 and 62, tel. 999/928-6002, 10am-8:30pm Mon.-Sat., 10am-3:30pm Sun.) and **Casa de las Artesanías del Estado de Yucatán** (Calle 63 btwn Calles 64 and 66, tel. 999/928-6676, www.artesanias.yucatan.gob. mx, 8:30am-9pm Mon.-Sat., 10am-5pm Sun.). Not cheap, *finos* (the supplest) can run as high as US$90.

Bookstores

Next to the Palacio Municipal, **Dante Olimpo** (Calle 61 near Calle 62, tel. 999/928-2611, www.libreriadante.com.mx, 8am-10:30pm daily) has an excellent selection of reading material in English. It has a sister store downtown: **Dante 59** (Calle 59 btwn Calles 60 and 62, tel. 999/928-3674, 8am-9:30pm Mon.-Sat., 10am-6pm Sun.).

Shopping Centers

Set in what was once an elegant mansion, **Casa T'ho** (Paseo de Montejo btwn Calle 45 and 47, tel. 999/923-2350, www.casatho.com, 10am-10pm daily) is now home to nine stylish boutiques selling everything from couture clothing to clever knickknacks, most created by Mexican designers. Shoppers seamlessly move from room to room, entering different shops through each doorway.

Coqui Coqui Oficios Artesanos (Calle 55 btwn Calles 62 and 64, tel. 999/923-5905, www.coquicoqui.com, 11am-7pm daily) is a collection of boutiques selling high-end clothing, accessories, and homewares. The setting is reason enough to stop by—an elegant *casona* (large colonial home) with gurgling fountains and fine art throughout. There's also an open-air **café** (US$3-5) specializing in caffeinated drinks and sweets.

Gran Plaza (Calle 50 Diagonal 460, tel. 999/944-7658, www.granplaza.com.mx, 10am-9pm daily) is the city's largest and fanciest mall, with dozens of upper-end stores and a multiplex movie theater.

FOOD

Mérida has a rich selection of restaurants, from great hole-in-the-wall joints to award-winning restaurants. Yucatecan and Mexican cuisine predominates, but there are several good alternatives around town.

Yucatecan and Mexican

Tall wooden doors frame a columned colonial courtyard at **La Chaya Maya** (Calle 55 btwn Calles 60 and 62, tel. 999/928-2295, www. lachayamaya.com, 7am-11pm daily, US$5-15), where every dish is beautifully presented, from *papadzules* to *crepas tres mosqueteros yucatecos* (Yucatecan crepes). While you wait for your meal, watch handmade tortillas being made in the courtyard. A like-named **sister restaurant** (Calle 62 at Calle 57, same hours and prices) is equally tasty though the modern décor is not as pleasing to the eye.

On Parque Santa Lucía, ★ **Apaola** (Calle 60 at Calle 55, tel. 999/923-1979, www.apoala. mx, 1pm-midnight Mon.-Sat., 2pm-10pm Sun., US$12-30) serves up a fierce fusion of Oaxacan, Yucatecan, and other traditional Mexican dishes. The presentation is gourmet all the way, with flourishes of flavor and unexpected artistic flair; creative cocktails pair well with meals. Best of all, there's plenty of outdoor seating—perfect on a Thursday evening when the city sponsors free music and dance performances at the park. Reservations highly recommended.

La Piñuela (Hotel Merida, Calle 60 btwn Calles 55 and 57, tel. 999/429-5386, www. pinuela.mx, 7am-midnight, US$6-19) is an attractive hotel restaurant with an upscale menu and presentation, yet a pleasantly low-key ambiance. Daytime favorites include chilaquiles and enchiladas served in a pool of *mole*; at night try the octopus *chicharron* or short ribs over risotto. Prices are reasonable, but service can be somewhat uneven.

A popular chain, **Los Trompos** (Calle 60 at Calle 59, tel. 999/926-4654, www.lostrompos. com.mx, 7:30am-1am Sun.-Thurs., 7am-2am Fri.-Sat., US$2-14) draws the meat- and cheese-loving crowds with tasty fast-food items like pizza *pastoreña* (with pineapple and spit-grilled pork) and *poc-chuc* tacos, though there's a pricier full menu as well. The decor is upscale coffee shop, with exposed stone walls and historical photos of Mérida.

Parque Santa Ana (Calle 60 at Calle 47) and **Parque Santiago** (Calle 59 at Calle 72)

also have reliable *cocinas económicas* (mom-and-pop eateries) serving Yucatecan fare. Most meals run around $2-4 and come quick and hot. Order a cold beer or a pitcher of lemonade to wash it down. The spots are typically open 9am-9pm daily.

Italian and Mediterranean

★ **Oliva Enoteca** (Calle 47 and Calle 54, tel. 999/923-3081, www.olivamerida.com, 1pm-5pm and 7pm-midnight Mon.-Sat., US$12-30) is a small upscale Italian restaurant serving gorgeous antipasto plates, homemade pastas, and to-die-for entrées. If you like seafood, start your meal with fried baby squid with fresh green beans and pecorino cheese—it's perfection on a plate. A second, larger restaurant, **Oliva Kitchen** (Calle 56 at Calle 49, tel. 999/923-2248, 7pm-11pm Mon.-Sat., US$10-25), gives its little sister a run for her money.

Illuminati Pizza (Calle 64 at Calle 55, tel. 999/461-0264, 5pm-11:30pm Mon.-Sat., US$3-11) has terrific pizza and so much more. The pies come in all sorts of creative varieties, like *chilaquiles* pizza and buffalo chicken and blue cheese pizza, all perfectly baked. But don't miss side dishes like garlic bread, mac and cheese, and the oh-so-good "French Nachos." There's good service, and a lovely owner too.

Pita (Calle 55 btwn Calle 58 and 60, tel. 999/923-1592, 8am-10pm Tues.-Sat., 8am-4pm Sun.-Mon., US$5-14) is a small restaurant specializing in delicious Lebanese-Israeli fare—falafel plates, tabbouleh, hummus, shawarma, and pita wraps. Classic Mexican breakfasts also are served each morning. Service is quick and friendly. Head to the back patio for a table with a breeze.

With sidewalk tables along the tree-lined Paseo de Montejo, **Trattoría La Pasta** (Paseo de Montejo btwn Calles 39 and 41, tel. 999/157-8986, www.trattorialapasta.com, 12:30pm-5pm and 7:30pm-1am Mon.-Fri., 7:30pm-2am Sat., US$6-16) is a convivial and casual spot for delectable homemade pastas, salads, and Tuscan-style pizza. (The owner-chef hails from Pisa, and credits his grandmother for most of the recipes.) There's a good selection of wine and beer and a few rich desserts like mango panna cotta.

Other Specialties

★ **Mercado 60** (Calle 60 btwn Calles 51 and 53, www.mercado60.com, 6pm-late daily) is a trendy gourmet food court spanning the spectrum of foods from sushi to ribs. It's a huge open-air hall with vine-covered walls and twinkling lights; diners sit at long communal tables or pay a little extra for private seating and waiter service. As the night progresses, meals are replaced by cocktails and artisanal beers. Live salsa bands often get people moving.

Bistro Cultural (Calle 66 btwn Calles 41 and 43, tel. 999/923-2013, 8:30am-5:30pm daily, US$4-7) serves French cuisine in an artsy bohemian space and on a shady patio. The menu changes daily but includes items like crepes, quiche, tartelettes, and colorful salads; many of the vegetables used are harvested from the restaurant's own organic gardens. Save room—there's often an enticing lineup of French pastries too.

Korean Grill & Ice Cream (Paseo de Montejo btwn Calles 37 and 39, tel. 999/291-7250, noon-10pm daily, US$6-12) is known for its unique dishes and top-notch service, making it a fine choice for dinner (and dessert, of course). Korean barbecue purists may quibble with some flavors and the lack of in-table grills, but the overall experience is great. If in doubt, order ramen.

Micaela Mar y Leña (Calle 47 at Calle 52, tel. 999/518-1702, 1pm-midnight Mon.-Sat., noon-6pm Sun., US$16-24) is all about delicious, creative seafood combined with bright, engaging decor. Together they make this a very enjoyable place for a nice dinner out. Meals begin with a cup of shrimp broth followed by main dishes like whole grilled fish and wood-fired octopus. Service is attentive but not hovering.

Fresh seafood is the draw at **Marlín Azul** (Calle 62 btwn Calles 57 and 59, tel. 999/224-3052, 8am-4:30pm Mon.-Thurs., 9am-4:30pm Fri.-Sat., US$5-8), a locals' favorite with a long counter and a few tables. Street noise and loud music may battle for dominance, but the excellent ceviches, shrimp fajitas, and fish fillets stuffed with shrimp and octopus have kept this place buzzing for almost 30 years.

Cafés

Homemade baked goods greet you at ★ **El Barrio** (Calle 45 at Calle 58, tel. 999/197-4745, 8am-2pm daily and 6pm-10pm Thurs.-Sat., US$4.50-6.50), a cozy café specializing in breakfast and brunch, usually prepared with organic and seasonal foods. Dishes are artfully presented, often with colorful herbs and edible flowers. There are lots of vegetarian and gluten-free options. Service can be slow (admire the remarkable murals while you wait).

Sukra (Paseo de Montejo btwn Calles 43 and 44, tel. 999/923-4453, 9am-6pm Tues.-Sat., 9am-2pm Sun., US$4-7) is a popular café with outdoor seating on swanky Paseo de Montejo. Menu items vary from omelets and taco plates to sandwiches and big salads; the coffee and pastries also are worth a stop. On Sundays, live music fills the air starting at 10am.

Linger in the garden patio of French-run **Café Crème** (Calle 41 at Calle 60, tel. 999/278-5073, 8:30am-5:30pm Mon.-Fri., 8:30am-2pm Sat., US$3.75-5) with exquisite quiches, cheese plates, pâtés, and strong espresso, plus complimentary chocolates for dessert. Arrive early: Pastries and croissants typically sell out by 11am.

Manifesto (Calle 59 btwn Calles 66 and 68, www.manifesto.mx, 8am-9pm Mon.-Fri., 8am-8pm Sat., US$2-4). The name is a reference to the café's strict standards for making a great cup of coffee: only the best beans, hand-roasted, freshly ground, and brewed with quality water. It certainly works—the coffee is amazing and the welcoming shop is a perfect place to enjoy a cup.

Sweets

Ki Xocolatl (Parque Santa Lucía, Calle 55 btwn Calles 60 and 62, tel. 999/920-5869,

9am-11pm Mon.-Sat., 9am-6pm Sun.) specializes in artisanal chocolates made from 100 percent Mexican ingredients: cacao from Chiapas and Tabasco, vanilla from Veracruz, and sugarcane from Yucatán, among others. Chocolate can be purchased by the piece, kilo, or in artful packaging—any which way, it's addicting. **Pola** (Calle 55 btwn Calles 62 and 64, tel. 999/330-3441, www.polagelato.com, noon-10pm daily, US$1.25-3) scoops up delicious, creamy, homemade gelato; flavors change daily but often include chai, peanut butter cup, bitter orange, and yes, chocolate. An artsy lounge makes it easy to linger (and tempting to order a second cone). **El Retorno** (Calle 62 btwn Calles 59 and 61, tel. 999/928-5634, www.panificadoraelretorno.com, 6am-9pm daily, US$0.40-2.50) is one of Mérida's most reliable bakery chains, with a shop half a block from the Plaza Grande. You'll find traditional cookies, cakes, and breads of many tastes and shapes.

Markets

Mercado Municipal (Calle 67 btwn Calles 56 and 58, 8am-8pm daily) is a rambling two-story market offering every fruit, vegetable, and meat sold in the region. Upstairs, there are about a dozen cheap eateries—not the cleanest, but the bustling shoppers and yelling vendors are definitely an experience; *comidas corridas* (two-course meals with a drink) cost just US$2-5.

Mercado Santos Degollado (Parque Santiago, Calle 57 btwn Calles 70 and 72, 6am-2pm daily) is a popular neighborhood market filled with myriad fruit and veggie stands, *tortillerías,* shoe repair shops, and flower sellers. Stay for a meal—the handful of small restaurants are known citywide for their excellent seafood tacos and *tortas* (US$2-6).

1: gourmet breakfast board greeting guests at The Diplomat; **2:** lunchtime platter at La Chaya Maya restaurant; **3:** Mérida's huge Mercado Municipal; **4:** Hotel La Piazzetta

ACCOMMODATIONS

Mérida has a profusion of charming inns and bed-and-breakfasts, suited to all tastes and budgets. Many are in restored *casonas* (large colonial home) or colonial-era buildings, giving visitors a taste of a Mérida long ago. Most listed here have fewer than 10 rooms, so it's best to call ahead or reserve online. All have Wi-Fi.

Under US$50

Nómadas (Calle 62 at Calle 51, tel. 999/924-5223, www.nomadastravel.com, US$9.50-10.50 dorm, US$31 s/d, US$35 s/d with a/c) offers a variety of comfortable dorms with bunks that have individual lights, fans, and lockers. Private rooms are basic and clean. Continental breakfast is included, and there's a common kitchen and a pool. Salsa dancing and Yucatecan cooking lessons are offered—a fun way to meet other travelers. Reserve early; it's often fully booked.

★ **Hostal Catedral** (Calle 61 btwn Calles 58 and 60, tel. 999/429-4678, US$8.25-9.25 dorm) couldn't be more centrally located unless you camp in the central plaza. A friendly, well-operated hostel, it has clean beds, huge bathrooms, individual lockers, and blissfully powerful air-conditioning (nighttime only). The breakfast spread is huge, and guests are treated to a glass of cool fresh juice on arrival. There's a large kitchen and dining area, but not much common space otherwise.

Hostel Zócalo (Calle 63 btwn Calles 60 and 62, tel. 999/930-9562, www.hostalzocalo.com, US$9 dorm, US$22-25 s/d with shared bath, US$28 s/d) is a rambling place with private rooms tucked in among the dorms, and lots of common areas throughout. The six-bed dorms—one just for women—have good, firm mattresses, and some of the private rooms have picture-perfect views over the main plaza. A buffet breakfast is included in the rate.

Hotel La Piazzetta (Calle 50 btwn Calles 57 and 59, tel. 999/923-3909, www.hotellapiazzettamerida.com, US$40-55 s/d with a/c) has 10 rooms with shabby-chic flair

Haciendas Turned Hotels

After lying abandoned for decades or even centuries, the Yucatán Peninsula's old henequen haciendas are returning to—and sometimes surpassing—their former colonial glory. Many have been restored as unique and super-deluxe hotels, making great use of the thick walls, high ceilings, and lush grounds. They're not cheap, but the setting and service are unforgettable. Here are a few of the best near Mérida.

Once a sisal-producing hacienda, **La Hacienda Xcanatún** (Carr. Mérida-Progreso Km 12, toll-free Mex. tel. 800/202-2566, www.xcanatun.com, US$285-360 s/d with a/c) boasts 18 beautifully restored suites opening onto gorgeous tropical gardens. Rooms have hand-carved furnishings, Mexican and Asian antiques, and original oil paintings. Most enjoy private sitting areas and whirlpool tubs too. There's also a full-service spa, two pools, and a gourmet restaurant on-site.

Hacienda San José Pachul (Carr. Tetiz-Kinchil Km 41, tel. 999/125-5230, www.haciendasanjosepachul.com, US$130-150 s/d with a/c) has two gorgeous guest rooms—one modern with floor-to-ceiling windows and a private garden, the other a colonial-style affair with 5.5-meter (18-foot) ceilings and a private sitting room. Both have king-size beds, luxurious linens, a music system, flat-screen TVs, and Wi-Fi. There's a gourmet restaurant and pool on-site. The hacienda is 36 kilometers (22 miles) east of Mérida, toward Celestún. Reservations can be made through www.AirBnB.com.

Hacienda Temozón (Hwy. 261 Km 182, tel. 999/923-8089, www.marriott.com, US$340-480 s/d with a/c) has 28 elegant rooms and suites. Each has 5-7-meter (16.4-23-foot) ceilings, gleaming tile floors, luxurious amenities, and modern furnishings; suites have open-air bathtubs. Outside, the manicured grounds feature walking trails, a pool, and a tennis court. There also are three on-site cenotes. The original machinery used to process henequen sits at the entrance to the full-service spa—a nice touch.

Hacienda Santa Rosa (off Hwy. 180, tel. 999/923-1923, www.marriott.com, US$340-480 s/d with a/c) is as classy as Temozón though on a smaller scale: 11 luxurious rooms, beautifully maintained but smallish grounds, a pool with shade trees, and an outdoor spa. The main attractions here are privacy and personalized service. You won't find the bells and whistles of other haciendas, but you'll enjoy a restful and ultra-comfortable stay.

A 400-year-old estate, **Hacienda San Pedro Nohpat** (off Hwy. 180, tel. 999/988-0542, www.haciendaholidays.com, US$95-125 s/d with a/c) has three suites, each decorated in a mishmash of styles. All have modern amenities like quiet air conditioners, satellite TV, and mini fridges. The grounds are well kept and include a pool, hot tub, and several lounge areas. A full breakfast is included in the rate. The estate is located just one kilometer (0.6 mile) from Mérida's city limits.

and lots of natural light. All have pillow-top beds—you've come to sleep, after all—and a couple have Juliet balconies with views of Parque Mejorada. Rates include a big breakfast at the hotel's trendy restaurant, which makes for a great start to the day. There's a rooftop lounge too.

Guest rooms at **Casa Ak'Bal Bed and Breakfast** (Calle 78 btwn Calles 59 and 61, tel. 999/287-4688, www.casaakbal.com, US$36-44 s/d with a/c) surround an inviting pool and patio area, forming a quiet oasis that you may be reluctant to leave. Rooms vary in size and feature striking floral decorations

and cozy hand-stitched blankets and pillows. A simple, tasty breakfast is included. The hosts are friendly and informative.

US$50-100

Once a convent, **Hotel Luz en Yucatán** (Calle 55 btwn Calles 58 and 60, tel. 999/924-0035, www.luzenyucatan.com, US$49-75 s/d with a/c, US$79-85 s/d with kitchen and a/c) has a variety of rooms. Some are a bit dark, but others—especially the studios and one-bedrooms—have lots of natural light and are a great value too, with kitchens and private patios. All have whimsical decor plus modern amenities. A small pool, a garden, and free parking seal the deal.

Casa Ana (Calle 52 btwn Calles 51 and 53, tel. 999/924-0005, www.casaana.com, US$50 s/d with a/c) is a low-key place with five airy rooms, all simply decorated. All face a lush garden with a small pool, *palapa* lounge, and a pleasant dining area where breakfast is served. The namesake owner is a wealth of information and a gracious host. It's a good option if you don't mind the longish walk to the Plaza Grande.

Hotel del Peregrino (Calle 51 btwn Calles 54 and 56, tel. 999/924-3007, www. hoteldelperegrino.com, US$70 s/d with a/c) occupies a gorgeous colonial home with high ceilings and original tile floors. Rooms are comfortable and simple with wood furnishings and smart TVs. Continental-plus breakfast—fruit, yogurt, pastries, pancakes—is served on the central patio, and there's a fully equipped open-air kitchen for guest use. Best of all, there's a rooftop terrace with city views and a whirpool tub.

Hotel Marionetas (Calle 49 btwn Calles 62 and 64, tel. 999/928-3377, www. hotelmarionetas.com, US$63-76 s/d with a/c, US$105 suite with a/c) is named after the building's former tenant—a puppet company. The spacious rooms are modern and welcoming, each with gorgeous tile floors and a signature piece like an ornate wood-framed mirror or a wrought-iron vanity. There's a sunny courtyard and small pool plus a pleasant on-site restaurant where tasty meals are served.

Oozing colonial charm, ★ **Hotel Julamis** (Calle 53 at Calle 54, tel. 999/924-1818, www. hoteljulamis.com, US$59-85 s/d with a/c, US$85 suite with a/c and kitchenette, US$99 two-bdrm house with a/c) is in an updated 200-year-old house with tile floors, intricate murals, and bursts of bougainvillea. A verdant courtyard is the setting for a gourmet breakfast prepared by the owner, an accomplished chef. A terrace with whirpool tub, lounge beds, and a guest-only bar gazes out over the city.

Hotel Medio Mundo (Calle 55 btwn Calles 64 and 66, tel. 999/924-5472, www. hotelmediomundo.com,US$76-80 s/d with a/c) is a hacienda-style guesthouse with high blue-painted walls and two courtyards—one with a lush garden and fountain, the other with a small swimming pool and shaded tables. Ten spacious rooms offer deep beds, spotless bathrooms, and very spare decor, save the original tile floors. A hearty continental breakfast is included and served at the on-site vegan restaurant.

Cascadas de Mérida (Calle 57 btwn Calles 74-A and 76, tel. 999/923-8484, www. cascadasdemerida.com, US$95-100 s/d with a/c) is named after the *cascadas* (waterfalls) built into the perimeter walls; the sound of gurgling water is relaxing and drowns out the city. The four rooms have exposed stone walls, skylights, and attractive Mexican furnishings; each has a glass-walled shower. Outside there's a large pool surrounded by hammocks and leafy plants. A bountiful breakfast, served family-style, is included.

Virtually every inch of wall space at **Los Arcos Bed & Breakfast** (Calle 66 btwn Calles 49 and 53, tel. 999/928-0214, www. losarcosmerida.com, US$85-95 s/d with a/c) is filled with artwork. Add houseplants, a small swimming pool, and some dogs, and you've got this unique, eclectic guesthouse. The rooms—there are only two—are comfy, with high ceilings, spacious bathrooms, cable TV, and CD players. A big breakfast is included. No children under 17 are allowed.

US$100-150

Casa del Maya (Calle 66 btwn Calles 45 and 47, tel. 999/366-9469, www.casadelmaya. com, US$105-110 s/d with a/c) offers a perfect combination of comfort and service. The six spacious rooms have pillow-top mattresses, luxurious linens, and handcrafted furniture. There's a lap pool surrounded by a leafy garden and lounge areas. A gourmet breakfast, complete with to-die-for cinnamon rolls, is served under a large *palapa*. Reservations for tours, restaurants, and spa services are happily made.

Hotel Casa Lucía (Parque Santa Lucía, Calle 60 btwn Calles 53 and 55, tel. 999/928-0740, www.casalucia.com.mx, US$78-108 s/d with a/c, US$125 suite with a/c) is an elegant hotel built in a 19th-century mansion. Rooms are spacious with deep beds, high-thread-count linens, and marble bathrooms; exposed wood beams, oil paintings, and antique furnishings are nice touches. There's a pool and *palapa* lounge too—a fine place to cool off after a day of sightseeing.

Villa Verde (Calle 56 btwn Calles 53 and 55, tel. 999/290-7759, www.villaverdemerida. com, US$145 s/d with a/c) is a gorgeously renovated colonial mansion with five spacious rooms. Each has original mosaic tile floors, six-meter-high (20-foot) ceilings, and modern art. Outside there's a waterfall pool, lounge areas, and a terrace where gourmet breakfast is served. The owners, Robert and Michael, are genuinely welcoming; their friendly pets lounge around the property, making it feel like home.

Over US$150

★ **The Diplomat** (Calle 78 btwn Calles 59 and 59-A, cell tel. 999/117-2972, www. thediplomatmerida.com, US$195-235 s/d with a/c) welcomes its guests like VIPs: poolside drinks, snacks, a chat with the affable owners. Stylish rooms are equally embracing with deep beds, luxe linens, soaring ceilings, fresh flowers, and details like personalized notes and artisanal chocolate. A breezy courtyard with hammocks doubles as the lounge/dining area; an honor bar and gourmet breakfast with pour-your-own coffee seal the deal.

Mérida Santiago Hotel Boutique (Calle 74A btwn Calles 57 and 59A, tel. 999/285-4447, www.hotelmeridasantiago. com, US$225-240 s/d with a/c) is a small boutique hotel with six spacious rooms. All have high ceilings, gorgeous tile floors, and upscale amenities; colorful *artesanía* and coffee-table books make them homey. Experienced chefs whip up delicious breakfasts every morning and are on call for other meals. A cocktail

hour by the pool, often with the gracious owners, is a nightly highlight.

Koox Casa de las Palomas (Calle 64 at Calle 49, tel. 999/291-1334, www.kooxhotels. com, US$152-169 s/d with a/c) is a boutique hotel set in a gorgeously remodeled *casona*. Rooms are spacious with king-size beds, exposed stone walls, and traditional tile floors; units on the ground floor have luxurious outdoor showers (one has a tub). A shady pool in the central courtyard adds to the charm. Adults only.

Casa Lecanda (Calle 47 btwn Calles 54 and 56, tel. 999/928-0112, www.casalecanda. com, US$245-290 s/d with a/c, US$330 suite with a/c) is a serene place with seven rooms. Three are in a 19th-century house with three-meter-high (10-foot) ceilings, the rest are garden suites in a newer addition. All have touches of Victorian-era décor; luxurious linens and amenities make it easy to relax. A small pool, gurgling fountains, and breezy archways round out the experience.

Fashioned from two *casonas*, rooms at **Rosas & Xocolate** (Paseo de Montejo at Calle 41, tel. 999/924-2992, www.rosasandxocolate. com, US$245-275 s/d with a/c, US$695 suite with a/c) feature luxurious fabrics, fluffy comforters, and cedar cabinetry; all have magnificent open-air bathtubs and double-paned windows to reduce street noise. There's also a full spa, small pool, and good-sized gym. Full breakfast is included and served in the property's fusion cuisine restaurant.

INFORMATION AND SERVICES
Tourist Information

When you get to Mérida, pick up a copy of *Yucatán Today* (www.yucatantoday.com) or *Explore Yucatán* (www.revistaexplore.com), two truly helpful tourist magazines. Published monthly and distributed free at hotels, shops, and tourist offices, the magazines have maps, suggested itineraries, short articles, and lists of upcoming events. While focusing on Mérida, both also cover Progreso, the Puuc Route, Izamal, Chichén Itzá, and Valladolid.

The city and state tourism boards—**Información Turística del Ayuntamiento** and **Departamento de Turismo del Estado de Yucatán,** respectively—both offer a wide selection of maps, brochures, and usually someone who speaks English. In general, however, the staff at the city office can give tailored answers to specific questions and offer information not found in the brochures; it also has a free city walking tour every morning at 9:30am. The two offices are located two blocks apart: the city tourism board is next to the Teatro José Peón Contreras (Calle 60 btwn Calles 55 and 57, tel. 999/924-9290, www.merida.gob.mx, 8am-8pm daily), and the state tourism board is just inside the Palacio de Gobierno (central plaza, Calle 61 at Calle 60, tel. 999/923-1827, www.yucatan.travel, 8am-9pm Mon.-Sat., 8am-8pm Sun.).

Other convenient city tourist offices are located in the Palacio Municipal (central plaza, Calle 62 btwn Calles 61 and 63, tel. 999/942-0000, ext. 80119, 8am-8pm daily), a sidewalk kiosk on Paseo de Montejo (at Av. Colón, 8am-8pm daily), and at a booth in the arrivals *(llegadas)* area of the CAME first-class bus terminal (Calle 69 btwn Calles 68 and 70, 8am-8pm Mon.-Sat., 8am-2pm Sun.).

Emergency Services

Considered the best hospital in town, **Clínica de Mérida** (Av. Itzáes 242, Col. García Ginerés, tel. 999/924-1800, www.clinicademerida.com.mx) is a state-of-the-art facility with 24-hour emergency service. For meds, head to the well-stocked **Yza Farmacia** (central plaza, Calle 63 btwn Calles 60 and 62, tel. 999/924-9510, 24 hours), which delivers. The **police station** (Calle 57 btwn Calles 52 and 54, tel. 999/942-0060, toll-free Mex. tel. 066) is open 24 hours.

Money

You'll have no problem accessing your money in Mérida. Virtually every bank in town—and there are a lot of them—has a 24-hour ATM that happily accepts foreign debit cards. Many convenience stores also have cash machines.

Most banks will exchange U.S. dollars and euros, and a few will change other currencies. You can also try changing cash at a *casa de cambio* (currency-exchange office) or at the front desk of any upscale hotel, but the rates are rarely good.

Most of the banks and ATMs are on or near the Plaza de la Independencia and along Calle 59. Convenient options include **Banamex** (Casa de Montejo, Calle 63 btwn Calles 60 and 62, 9am-4pm Mon.-Fri., 10am-2pm Sat.) and **HSBC** (Calle 59 btwn Calles 68 and 70, 9am-5pm Mon.-Fri.).

Media and Communications

The **post office** is located on Calle 53 between Calles 52 and 54 (8am-2pm Mon.-Fri.). Internet cafés can be a bit sparse, though there are several **side-by-side cybercafes** near Parque Santiago (Calle 59 btwn Calles 72 and 74), all of them charging around US$0.75 per hour and open 8:30am-10:30pm Monday-Saturday. Most city parks have free Wi-Fi. The central plaza even has outlets beside many of the benches so you can recharge your phone or tablet while feeding the pigeons—look for the *Centro de Carga* (charging center) signs.

Laundry and Storage

Lavandería La Fe (Calle 64 at Calle 55, tel. 999/924-4531, 8am-6pm Mon.-Fri., 8am-3pm Sat.) charges US$4 for the first three kilos (6.6 pounds) and US$1-2 each additional kilo. Drop off your clothes early for same-day service; pickup and delivery is available for US$5.

Most hotels have free luggage storage for guests, even those checking out. If yours doesn't, **Guarda Plus** (Calle 70 btwn Calles 69 and 71, 6am-9:30pm daily) is across from the CAME bus station and stores bags for US$0.50-1.25 per hour per bag, depending on the size. There is no daily rate, unfortunately.

Language and Instruction

One of the most popular language schools in Mérida, **Habla** (Calle 26 btwn Calles 19 and 21, tel. 999/948-1872, www.habla.org) tailors classes to individual students—their interests, learning style, and Spanish-language abilities. Classes are led by educators with deep expertise in teaching Spanish, who typically integrate Mexican cultural themes into courses. Homestays are encouraged and facilitated.

Centro Idiomas del Sureste (CIS, Calle 52 btwn Calles 49 and 51, tel. 999/923-0954, www.cisyucatan.com.mx) offers all levels of Spanish instruction, with class sizes varying from one to eight students. Courses last at least one week and start every Monday. Students also can get intensive language training that's focused on an area of interest—CIS is a favorite with Maya scholars because of it. Homestays and area excursions are integral parts of the program.

Los Dos (Calle 68 btwn Calles 65 and 67, no phone, www.los-dos.com) is a popular cooking school based in a gorgeous colonial home. Offering fun and informative classes, the most popular is the Taste of Yucatán course (US$200 pp, minimum 6 people, 8:30am-4pm Tues. and Thurs.). It starts with a light breakfast and an introduction to Yucatecan cuisine, and then it's off to the market to buy fresh vegetables, proteins, corn dough—everything you'll need for the class. Back in the kitchen, you'll prepare a midday snack and then the real cooking begins—*cochinita pibil, pollo pibil,* tamales, *panuchos,* and other Yucatecan classics. The class ends with a grand white-tablecloth meal featuring your creations. Private courses also can be arranged. Reservations required.

GETTING THERE
Air

Manuel Crescencio Rejón International Airport (MID, Av. Itzáes/Hwy. 180, tel. 999/940-6090) is located seven kilometers (4.3 miles) southwest of the town center. The airport has several car rental agencies and a 24-hour ATM.

The following airlines serve Mérida's International Airport:

• **Aeroméxico** (airport tel. 999/946-1530, toll-free Mex. tel. 800/237-6639, www.aeromexico.com)

• **Interjet** (toll-free Mex. tel. 800/011-2345, toll-free U.S. tel. 866/285-9525, www.interjet.com.mx)

• **MAYAir** (toll-free Mex. tel. 800/962-9247, toll-free U.S. tel. 844/622-0800, www.mayair.com.mx)

• **United Airlines** (toll-free Mex. tel. 800/900-5000, toll-free U.S. tel. 800/864-8331, www.united.com)

• **Viva Aerobus** (tel. 818/215-0150, toll-free U.S. tel. 888/935-9848, www.vivaaerobus.com)

• **Volaris** (tel. 551/102-8000, toll-free U.S. tel. 855/865-2747, www.volaris.mx)

Bus

Mérida has several bus stations. The first-class station is known by the acronym **CAME** (pronounced KAH-meh, Calle 69 btwn Calles 68 and 70, tel. 999/920-4444, www.ado.com.mx) and has ADO, ADO-GL, OCC, and ADO Platino service. Most of your bus travel, especially long distance, will be from here. There's another first-class bus station in Plaza Bonita, known as **Fiesta Americana** (Av. Colón at Calle 60, tel. 999/924-8391) because of its location behind the same-named hotel. Service is limited but includes nonstop service to Cancún International Airport, Cancún, and Playa del Carmen.

Buses from the **second-class bus terminal** (Calle 69 btwn Calles 68 and 70, tel. 999/924-8391), around the corner from CAME, serve many of the same destinations but make more stops at small towns along the way. Buses tend to be dumpier, the trips longer, and the price marginally lower—better to stick with first-class service whenever possible. That said, the Sunday Puuc Route Tour bus leaves from here as do buses to Chiquilá, for those headed to Isla Holbox.

Terminal Noreste (Calle 67 btwn Calles 50 and 52, Noreste tel. 999/924-6355, Oriente tel. 999/928-6230, Líneas Unidas tel. 999/924-7865) is the base for regional bus lines. Most

Driving Distances from Downtown Mérida

LOCATION	DISTANCE	LOCATION	DISTANCE
Airport	7 km (4 mi)	Izamal	72 km (44 mi)
Calakmul	480 km (298 mi)	Mahahual	389 km (241 mi)
Campeche City	253 km (158 mi)	Palenque	555 km (346 mi)
Cancún	320 km (199 mi)	Playa del Carmen	288 km (178 mi)
Celestún	86 km (52 mi)	Progreso	33 km (20 mi)
Chetumal	416 km (258 mi)	Río Lagartos	263 km (165 mi)
Chichén Itzá	120 km (75 mi)	Tulum	274 km (171 mi)
Cobá	232 km (145 mi)	Uxmal	80 km (50 mi)
Dzibilchaltún	16 km (10 mi)	Valladolid	160 km (100 mi)
Ek' Balam	179 km (111 mi)	Xpujil	476 km (295 mi)

tourists using this terminal are headed to Río Lagartos to see the flamingos, or to Cuzamá to visit the cenotes; other destinations include Mayapán, Maní, and Izamal.

Terminal Auto-Progreso (Calle 62 btwn Calles 65 and 67, tel. 999/924-8991, www.autoprogreso.com) primarily serves Progreso (US$1, 55 minutes), with departures every 10-15 minutes 5am-10pm.

Terminal Autobuses del Centro (Calle 65 btwn Calles 46 and 48, tel. 999/923-9940) provides service to Aké archaeological zone (US$1.50, 1 hour) at 5:30am, 8:40am, 4pm, and 7pm.

Car

Good highways approach Mérida from all directions. Once in the city, be prepared for one-way streets, and avoid arriving on Sunday, when a large area in the center of town is closed to vehicles. If you don't know the city, it can be a real headache to drive to your hotel, because many are downtown. If you're **arriving via Highway 180,** note that it becomes Calle 65 and hits the busy Mercado Municipal area at Calle 56—it's less congested if you bypass this area by jogging right on Calle 52 and then left onto Calle 61 to reach the center.

The *periférico* is a wide, paved traffic loop that circumscribes the city, making it possible to bypass the congested downtown streets if you're headed from Chichén Itzá to Celestún, for example.

Parking is restricted in the center, with yellow-and-red curbs marking prohibited areas, though this is relaxed between 9pm and 7am Monday-Saturday and all day Sunday. Street parking is easier to find the farther you go from the Plaza de la Independencia. There are several public parking lots in the center; most charge US$0.75-1 per hour. Be sure to check the opening time if you park overnight and need to leave early in the morning.

Highway 180 is a modern toll highway (*carretera cuota*) that runs from Mérida to Cancún and Playa del Carmen. It begins 16 kilometers (9.9 miles) east of Mérida at Kantunil; from Mérida take Highway 180 toward Valladolid. Tolls are steep—US$5 to Chichén Itzá, US$8.75 to Valladolid, US$24 to Playa del Carmen, and US$24 to Cancún—but the road is in great condition, with rest stops, gas stations, and clearly marked exits; it's also nearly empty because most bus and trucking companies choose to take the *libre* (free road), which runs parallel to the highway. Although the *libre* is slower and teeming with speed bumps, it takes drivers through small villages and past fields of henequen and corn—sights worth seeing if you're not in a rush.

Mérida Bus Schedule

The first-class bus station CAME (Calle 69 btwn. Calles 68 and 70, tel. 999/924-0830, www.ado.com.mx) serves most major destinations, including:

DESTINATION	PRICE	DURATION	SCHEDULE*
Campeche	US$13-17	2.5-3 hrs	53 departures
Cancún	US$20-32	4-5 hrs	58 departures
Cancún airport	US$25-37	3.5-4 hrs	5:15am, 8:30am, noon, and 10:55pm from Fiesta Americana terminal
Chetumal	US$16-23	5.5 hrs	7:30am, 1pm, 3:30pm, 6pm, and 11pm
Chichén Itzá (Pisté)	US$8-9	2 hrs	6:30am, 7:15am, 8:15am, and 9:15am or take 2nd-class bus
Chiquilá (Isla Holbox)	US$21-22	5-5.5 hrs	6:45am and 7:15am
Mexico City	US$50-85	20-22 hrs	8 departures
Palenque	US$25-36	8-8.5 hrs	8:30am, 8:40pm, 10pm, and 11:45pm
Playa del Carmen	US$15-30	4-6 hrs	25 departures
Tulum	US$10-18	4-4.5 hrs	6:30am, 10:40am, 12:40pm, 5:40pm, and 8:15pm
Valladolid	US$7-12	2.5-3 hrs	30 departures

The second-class bus terminal (Calle 69 btwn. Calles 68 and 70, tel. 999/924-8391) serves nearer destinations, including:

DESTINATION	PRICE	DURATION	SCHEDULE*
Chichén Itzá (Pisté)	US$5	2 hrs	hourly
Chiquilá (Isla Holbox)	US$11.25-14	6-8 hrs	7:45am, 10:15am, 10:30pm
Puuc Route	US$14	8-8.5 hrs	8am Sunday (round-trip)
Santa Elena	US$3.50	1.5 hrs	5 departures
Ticul	US$3	1.5 hrs	hourly
Uxmal	US$3.50	1.5 hrs	5 departures
Valladolid	US$7	3 hrs	hourly

Terminal Noreste (Calle 67 btwn. Calles 50 and 52, Noreste tel. 999/928-6230, Oriente tel. 999/924-6355, Líneas Unidas tel. 999/924-7865) has several small bus lines serving regional destinations, including:

DESTINATION	PRICE	DURATION	SCHEDULE*
Celestún	US$3	2.5 hrs	13 departures
Cuzamá (combi)	US$1.50	1 hr	every 30-45 mins
Izamal	US$1.50	1.5 hrs	hourly
Maní	US$3.15	2.5 hrs	13 departures
Mayapán Ruins	US$3.15	1.5 hrs	8:30am and 4pm
Río Lagartos & San Felipe	US$8.50-8.75	3.5-4 hrs	5:30pm
Tizimín	US$6	2.5-4 hrs	6am and 4:45pm

*Schedules are subject to change.

GETTING AROUND

The best way to see Mérida is on foot. Granted, some of the sidewalks are narrow and the traffic can be heavy, but the city is a pleasure to wander. Look for street names, which are usually found high up on building corners.

To and From the Airport

Taxis charge a fixed US$10 from the airport to town, while the reverse trip costs approximately US$6—agree on a price beforehand. There is no airport bus per se, but vans marked UMAN leave every 10 minutes from Parque San Juan (Calle 69 btwn Calles 62 and 64) and pass the airport entrance road (US$0.40, 25 minutes). Be sure to ask the driver to let you off at *el aeropuerto;* it's a 500-meter (0.3-mile) walk from the stop to the terminal. From the airport, you can walk to Avenida Itzáes and catch an UMAN van to Parque San Juan—there is a bus stop just to your right when you reach the main road. Or wait for a 79-Aviación bus (US$0.40, 30 minutes) in front of the Budget car rental office just outside the terminal—they pass less frequently (every 15-20 minutes), but you don't have to walk so far. Bus No. 79 goes to Parque San Juan as well, passing the first- and second-class bus terminals along the way. Note that the UMAN vans don't have much room for luggage—if you are loaded down, you may be turned away by the driver; consider springing for a cab from the get-go.

Bus

The most useful city buses are the ones that go between downtown and points along Paseo de Montejo. Downtown, catch an "Itzamná" bus on Calle 59 between Calles 56 and 58 (US$0.40). You can take the same bus all along Paseo de Montejo in either direction. Mérida's bus routes also are published online: https://merida.transpublico.com.

Taxi

Cabs can be hailed on the street or at taxi stands at most neighborhood parks. For late-night service, most hotels, restaurants, bars, and nightclubs can call one for you upon request. Many taxis aren't metered, so establish your fare in advance; expect to pay US$2-3 in the downtown area, and US$4-5 as far as the *periférico*, while a ride to the airport runs around US$10. If you happen to get into a cab with a *taximetro* (meter), the minimum fare is US$1.

Bike

Bicimérida (Paseo de Montejo at Calle 45, tel. 999/287-3538, 8am-10pm daily) rents bikes for US$1.50 per hour or US$2.50 per two hours. Most bikes have baskets and come with locks upon request (no helmets though).

Car

Mérida has a slew of car rental agencies, and rental rates fluctuate with the season—expect a spike during Christmas and other holidays—and how many days you're renting. Non-holiday base rates average US$55 per day for a basic car, including tax and insurance. Remember, you'll get better rates online, even last minute, than you will by simply walking into a rental agency.

Several international companies have offices downtown, along Paseo de Montejo and the airport. Recommended local agencies include **Easy Way Rent a Car** (Calle 60 btwn Calles 55 and 57, tel. 999/930-9500, toll-free U.S./Can. tel. 877/640-3279, www.easywayrentacar.com, 7am-10pm daily) and **Veloz** (Calle 60 btwn Calles 55 and 57, tel. 999/928-0373, toll-free Mex. tel. 800/712-1375, www.velozrentacar.mx, 8am-8pm daily).

Tours

There is a *lot* to see and do in and around Mérida: Maya ruins, colonial churches, cenotes, caves, bird-watching, rappelling, and more. Guided tours are a practical way—and in a few cases, the only way—to see and do it all. But don't feel bound by set trips: Small tour companies often customize outings to fit travelers' particular interests and stamina. You just have to ask.

CITY TOURS

Bus tours of the city are a good way to get your bearings, and to get a sense of which places in Mérida you'd like to return to (and which not). There are two bus operators that provide a good lay of the land.

Camión Carnavalito (Parque Santa Lucía, Calle 55 between Calles 60 and 62, tel. 999/927-6119, www.carnavalitocitytour.com.mx, US$6 adult, US$3.50 child) offers a two-hour city tour on a colorful open-air school bus; the route includes the historic center and outlying neighborhoods. Tours leave at 10am, 1pm, 4pm, and 7pm Monday-Saturday, and 1pm and 3pm Sunday. Guides speak English and Spanish.

Turibus (tel. 999/946-2424, www.turibus.com.mx, 9am-9pm daily, US$6 adult, US$2.50 child under 13) operates a fleet of apple-red double-decker buses that have hop-on, hop-off service along three preset routes; stops include the central plaza, Museum of Anthropology, Itzimná church and park, Monumento a la Bandera, and more. Buses pass any given stop approximately every 55 minutes; tickets can be purchased on board. Multilingual recorded explanations of the various historic buildings and points of interest are played along the way.

Mérida's narrow streets were originally designed for *calesas* (horse-drawn buggies), and you can still ride one through the historic center where mansions with carved facades, stone gargoyles, and wrought-iron fences still stand. Sunday is the best day to hire a *calesa,* as many streets are closed to vehicular traffic and the rest are relatively quiet. You can hire a *calesa* at the Plaza de la Independencia anytime between 8am and midnight. Tours last 30-90 minutes and range US$20-40. Be sure to agree upon a price before sitting down for the ride.

The **city tourist office** (Palacio Municipal, Calle 62 btwn Calles 61 and 63, tel. 999/942-0000) offers a free walking tour Monday-Saturday at 9:30am in English and Spanish. The tour lasts 1.5 hours and focuses on the buildings around the Plaza de la Independencia. Arrive at the office by 9:15am to join the tour.

REGIONAL TOURS

Tour options vary widely, from large tour buses hitting must-see destinations like Chichén Itzá, Uxmal, and Celestún, to personalized outings to little-visited places, or exploring specific themes, like Maya culture or local wildlife. Prices vary as well, from US$50 for day trips to weeklong expeditions running US$2,000 or more. No matter your preference, be sure to ask about extra costs, like admission to the ruins and whether trips include guide service or simply transportation.

Ecoturismo Yucatán (Calle 3 btwn Calles 32-A and 34, tel. 999/920-2772, www.ecoyuc.com) offers excellent outdoors tours to flamingo sanctuaries and cenotes as well as to haciendas and archaeological sites; many excursions involve biking and kayaking too. The agency is known for customized 7- to 15-day tours that range as far as Calakmul in southern Campeche and Akumal on the Caribbean coast. **Mayan Heritage** (Calle 79 btwn Calles 64 and 64-A, tel. 999/924-8283, www.mayanheritage.com.mx) offers similar organized and custom excursions.

Iluminado Tours (Calle 66 No. 588 btwn Calles 73 and 75, tel. 999/924-3176, www.iluminado-tours.com) specializes in multiday tours that emphasize Maya spirituality and personal enlightenment. Tours are based on guided visits to ruins and integrate lectures, meditation, and even yoga. Iluminado is run by a Canadian expat in association with local experts, including a former director of Chichén Itzá.

Adventures Mexico (Calle Pedregales de Tanlum 374, tel. 999/925-1700, www.adventures-mexico.com) offers classes and guided tours of all sorts and lengths, garnering virtually universal rave reviews. In Merida, the Street Food Walking Tour and Taste of Yucatán cooking class (which includes a visit to the market) are especially popular, and a great way to spend a day in town. Further afield, check out their tours of the Puuc Route, cenotes, and more. Rates aren't cheap, but you can count on a quality excursion.

Celestún

Celestún is a fishing village on the northwest shoulder of the Yucatán Peninsula; it sits on the mainland side of a 22-kilometer-long (13.6-mile) inlet-estuary known as the Ría Celestún, which is located in the Celestún Biosphere Reserve. The shallow, salty waters are an ideal breeding and feeding area for *Phoenicopterus ruber ruber,* the largest and pinkest of the world's five flamingo species and Celestún's primary attraction. The reserve (which is home to myriad other bird species as well) has helped to make this inlet one of Mexico's best bird-watching areas and is known by bird enthusiasts worldwide.

Though tourism is growing, Celestún's coastal waters teem with fish and octopus, and catching them is still the main industry of locals here. The town has about 7,000 permanent residents, but 10,000 fishermen ply the coast from here to Río Lagartos during octopus season (August-December). Celestún is also an important salt-extraction area, producing 21,000 tons of salt every year. In fact, salt production has been a vital industry since AD 600, and fishing goes back even further, of course.

If you're not a hard-core bird-watcher, a trip to the flamingo reserve is about the only reason to come to Celestún, and the town is just close enough to Mérida (96 kilometers/60 miles) to make day trips possible. Numerous operators offer tours here from Mérida, or you can do it yourself relatively easily by bus—either way, it's a pretty long day. If you have some time and a car, staying a night or even two lets you visit the reserve pressure-free, check out some additional area tours, and have some beach time.

RESERVA ECOLÓGICA DE LOS PETENES

The **Flamingo Reserve (Petenes Ecological Reserve)** is one of just a few breeding areas in the Northern Hemisphere for the American flamingo. It is home to the species' largest colony—up to 35,000 flamingos in the December-February mating season. Hundreds of other birds and waterfowl nest in the wetlands and mangrove forests; about 300 of the 509 identified bird species in the Yucatán Peninsula can be spied here. It's not unusual to see a blue heron or an anhinga perched on a tree stump with wings outstretched, drying in the sun.

One reason for the diversity of birdlife is the diversity of habitat, which includes mangrove forests, coastal dunes, savannas, low deciduous forest, hummocks (small islands of mangroves in the wetlands), seashore, and, of course, the Celestún estuaries.

TOP EXPERIENCE

Flamingo Tours

A standard flamingo tour unfolds in three parts: a visit to the flamingo feeding grounds, followed by a short ride through the mangroves, and then a stop to swim in an *ojo de agua* (a freshwater spring). Because the sites are relatively far apart, you spend quite a lot of time motoring from one place to the next. In a 90-minute trip, you'll spend 20-30 minutes observing flamingos, and somewhat less at the other spots. It doesn't sound like much, but the boat ride itself is pleasant enough, and most people find the stops sufficient. If you want more time with the flamingos—especially if the flock is at its height—private guides are the most flexible. With either the state guide service or the fishermen's cooperative, you'll have to get everyone in the boat (and the guide) to agree to adjust the schedule.

Parador Turístico Celestún (tel. 999/942-1900, 8am-5pm daily) is the rather inelegant name for the pier and visitors center where the state-sponsored guide service is based. It is three kilometers (1.9 miles) from Celestún, on the west side of the highway bridge spanning the *ría*. From there, you can book a complete tour (US$75, 1 hour, up to 6 people); there's also an additional US$3.50 per person park fee. The people at the ticket counter won't necessarily offer to put small groups together, but you can do so yourself by simply asking around; arrive around 10am (that's the 8am bus from Mérida) for the best chance at forming a group. Guide service is available in Spanish and English.

Celestún's **fishermen's cooperative** (no phone, 8am-4pm daily) also offers flamingo tours, leaving from the beach at the end of Calle 11. Trips from here are basically the same, though longer, as you first have to motor down the coast to the entrance of the estuary. Tours cost US$100 (2 hours, up to 9 people). If you end up waiting more than an hour for a group to form, captains often will take smaller groups at a reduced cost.

Another cooperative, **Parador Ecoturístico Manglares de Dzinitún** (tel. 999/645-4310, dzinitun@gmail.com, 7:30am-4pm), offers a more active two-hour tour (US$35 pp) where you walk a short distance through a mangrove canal on a wooden boardwalk and then canoe or kayak out to see the flamingos (you can paddle your own kayak, but guides row the canoe). Boats drop off at a different location, and you're met with bicycles to use for an easy ride back to your starting point.

FOOD

On the inland side of the main drag, **Restaurante Chivirico** (Calle 12 at Calle 11, tel. 988/916-2001, noon-8pm daily, US$5-9) is a locals' favorite for super-fresh seafood and is well worth the sacrifice in ocean view. The specialty is fish fillet stuffed with shrimp, but the crab ceviche is tough to beat.

La Palapa (Calle 12 btwn Calles 11 and 13, tel. 988/916-2063, 11:30am-6pm daily, US$7-12) is the most popular beachfront restaurant in Celestún, serving tasty seafood plus various chicken and beef dishes, all beneath a soaring *palapa* roof. Tour groups often eat here, but the dining area is large enough to give everyone space.

On the central plaza, **El Lobo** (Calle 10 at Calle 13, tel. 988/916-2071, 8am-11am and 7pm-midnight Tues.-Sun., US$3-7) serves up classic comfort food for breakfast—big plates of pancakes, eggs, fruit, and granola—and switches to pizza and burgers at night. For a change of pace, try the pizza with banana slices and pineapple.

The **Mercado Municipal** (central plaza,

Celeste Vida Guest House

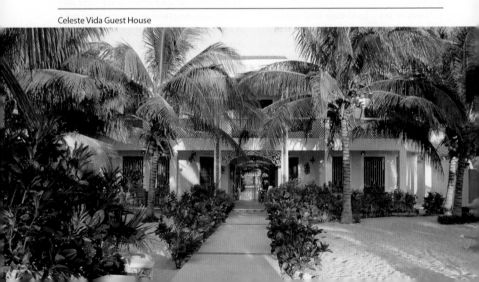

7am-6pm daily) has a decent selection of fruits, veggies, bread, and other foodstuffs. There are also several cheap taco stands near the entrance.

ACCOMMODATIONS
Under US$50

Hotel Gutiérrez (Calle 12 at Calle 13, tel. 988/916-2648, US$35-42 s/d with a/c) is a basic family-run hotel with good beds (all full-sized) and upgraded bathrooms. Wi-Fi is available, but spotty, in the rooms. Outside, the beach is kept clean and the staff is accommodating. There's also a nice little restaurant on-site—perfect for a leisurely breakfast with a view.

US$50-100

One kilometer (0.6 mile) north of town, ★ **Celeste Vida Guest House** (Calle 12 s/n, tel. 988/916-2536, www.hotelcelestevida. com, US$95 studio, US$130 apartment) has three cheery fan-cooled units (two studios and an apartment) with kitchenettes. There's a huge guest kitchen and barbecue grill for socializing as well as beachfront *palapas*. Kayaks, paddleboards, and bikes are available too. The affable Canadian owners are an excellent source of information. There's a two-night minimum.

On the north end of town, **Castillito Kin-Nah** (Calle 12 near Calle 2, tel. 988/916-2627, www.castillito-kin-nah.com, US$85-95 with a/c) is a small hotel with spick-and-span rooms that have details like coffee makers, satellite TV, and even bedside books. There's a good-sized pool—a treat in these parts—with lots of lounge beds and a well-tended beach just beyond. Bikes are available for rent.

Over US$100

Eleven kilometers (6.8 miles) from town, **Hotel Xixim** (Antigua Carr. a Sisal Km 10, tel. 988/916-2100, www.hotelxixim.com, US$282-346 s/d, US$430 master suite) features 32 *palapa*-roofed bungalows nestled in a cluster of coastal dunes. All have beachy décor with luxe amenities (though no air-conditioning)

and patios with ocean views. Two pools and, of course, the beach—scenic, unmanicured, and loaded with seashells—are a short walk away. There's also a yoga studio and a fusion restaurant.

INFORMATION AND SERVICES

Centro de Salud Celestún (Calle 5 btwn Calles 8 and 10, tel. 985/916-2046, 7am-noon and 1pm-4pm Mon.-Fri.) is a basic health clinic. While emergency service is provided, serious injuries should be treated in Mérida. For medications, try **Farmacia Celestún** (central plaza, tel. 988/916-2106, 8am-11pm daily). The **police** (central plaza, tel. 988/957-0200, 24 hours) are stationed in the Palacio Municipal (city hall).

Celestún has no banks, but there's a 24-hour ATM outside the **Palacio Municipal** and a second inside **Super Willy's** (7am-10pm daily); both are on the central plaza. For internet, try **Cyberline** (central plaza, 10am-2pm and 5pm-9pm daily, US$0.75 per hour).

GETTING THERE AND AROUND
Bus

Buses to Celestún leave from Mérida's Terminal Noreste almost hourly from 5am-8pm daily (US$3, 2 hours). Assuming you're coming for the flamingo tours, the driver usually stops at the *Parador Turístico* before going the rest of the way into town. In Celestún, the small bus terminal (tel. 988/916-2067) is at the southeast corner of the central park. There are buses to Mérida (US$3, 2 hours, hourly 5am-8pm).

Car

From Mérida, take Avenida Aviación past the airport and toward the town of Umán. In Umán, you'll come to a tangled four-way intersection in the center of town, typically packed with cars, bicycle taxis, pedestrians, and an overworked traffic cop. Bear right at two consecutive forks—at the church and then at the market—and then turn right again onto Calle 25, just a few blocks later. There are street signs for Celestún, but they're easy to miss. Calle 25 leads out of town toward Kinchil, then connects to Highway 281 toward the coast.

Triciclos and Mototaxis

You can walk just about anywhere in Celestún, although when it's hot you may prefer to take a *triciclo,* or bicycle taxi. A ride in town costs around US$1, or for US$1.50 you can get a ride to the *Parador Turístico.* With baggage, your best bet is a *mototaxi* (US$2).

Progreso

Set on the Gulf of Mexico, Progreso is Mérida's closest access to the sea, an easy 33-kilometer (20.5-mile) drive from the city on Highway 261. Méridanos—as many as 150,000 during July and August weekends—flock here in summer to escape the city's intense heat and sticky humidity. Cruise ships also land here 3-4 times a week, disgorging several thousand passengers each. With tourists in town, Progreso comes to life; the restaurants are all open, the shops are bustling, and the beaches are filled with families enjoying the surf and sea. It's no Riviera Maya, but it does the trick if you're burning up in Mérida.

The city was founded in 1856 and rose to prominence in the halcyon days of the henequen industry; henequen barons built grand estates east of town, and huge ships were a regular feature of the town waterfront. (Progreso's wharf was "only" two kilometers [1.2 miles] long then—less than a third its current length—but already an engineering marvel.) With the collapse of the henequen industry, Progreso's glimmer faded significantly; the port remained active, but the town took on a dumpy industrial aspect that persisted for decades.

Progreso has made a number of renovations in an attempt to brighten its image and entice day-trippers and cruise ship passengers to spend more time in town. The effort has paid off, especially along the waterfront, which has an attractive walkway and clean beach. It has also developed into a popular destination for Canadian snowbirds. One thing the town can't fix, however, is the frequent and sometimes powerful coastal wind, which buffets the entire northern coast and sometimes makes sunbathing a bit like being in a sandblaster. It's not all bad though: You can always take kiteboarding lessons to harvest the winds.

SIGHTS

Playa Central

Travelers arriving from the Caribbean side of the peninsula will find the Gulf coast rather underwhelming. The sand is coarser, and the water doesn't have the brilliant shades of blue that make the Quintana Roo coast justly famous. But the beach at Progreso is still fairly broad and clean and will do just fine, especially when the mercury rises inland. The water stays shallow a long way out and is relatively calm, although expect some chop during the stormy season (June-October) and know that the wind never really dies down. The beach is dotted with *palapa*-roofed sun shelters; across the street is a line of restaurants and cafés.

Street vendors rent **beach chairs with umbrellas** (US$8/day) on the beachfront road near Calle 76. There also are **bathrooms** (US$0.50), **showers** (US$0.75), and **changing areas** (US$0.50) here.

El Muelle

At the turn of the 20th century, Progreso's two-kilometer-long (1.2-mile) pier was the longest stone wharf in the world. It had to be—the Yucatán Peninsula sits on a long limestone shelf that drops ever so gradually into

Progreso

Map labels:
- Gulf of Mexico
- EL MUELLE ★
- CRUISE SHIP TERMINAL
- Playa Central
- Malecón
- CRABSTER
- CALLE 19
- TOURIST INFORMATION
- BEACH RENTALS/ RESTROOM
- HOTEL & SUITES DOMANI
- Parque de la Paz
- CALLE 21
- To La Antigua
- CALLE 23
- LAVANDERÍA GLORIA
- CALLE 25
- TOURIST OFFICE EL FARO ★
- MERCADO MUNICIPAL
- MARIA'S NICHTE-HA
- AUTO-PROGRESO TERMINAL
- BANAMEX
- FARMACIA YZA
- PLAZA DEL MAR/ ADO
- CALLE 27
- COMBIS TO CHICXULUB PUERTO, UAYMITÚN, AND DZILAM DE BRAVO
- VANS TO MÉRIDA
- EL TACONAZO
- HOTEL SAN MIGUEL
- CALLE 29
- BANORTE
- CALLE 31
- Plaza Central
- POST OFFICE
- CALLE 33
- CENTRO MÉDICO AMERICANO
- CALLE 86, CALLE 84, CALLE 82, CALLE 80, CALLE 78, CALLE 76, CALLE 74, CALLE 72, CALLE 70, CALLE 68, CALLE 66, CALLE 64, CALLE 62
- CALLE 35
- CALLE 37
- CALLE 39
- 261
- To Hwy 261, Casa de Piedra, Dzibalchaltún Archaeological Zone, and Mérida
- To Uaymitún Reserve, Xcambó Archaeological Zone, Telchac Puerto, San Crisanto, and Dzilam de Bravo
- SCALE NOT AVAILABLE
- © MOON.COM

the Gulf, making this and most of its bays extremely shallow. In fact, some scientists conjecture that at one time Yucatán, Cuba, and Florida were all one long extension of land.

Despite the length of Progreso's pier, it sat in only six meters (19.7 feet) of water, which proved insufficient for larger container ships. The activity on the pier declined greatly after a second pier was built in 1968 in the Yucalpetén harbor, six kilometers (3.7 miles) west of town. Progreso's pier continued to receive ships—mostly cruise ships and those that came to pick up exports such as honey, cement, fish, salt, and steel. In an effort to accommodate them and to attract more, the pier

was lengthened and now extends an amazing seven kilometers (4.3 miles) into the Gulf. A fleet of trucks and buses ferry cruise shippers and cargo back and forth. The public used to be able to walk to the end of the pier, but it's no longer allowed due to heightened security measures.

El Faro

Built between 1885 and 1891 on the site of an earlier lighthouse, today's 40-meter (131-foot) *faro* (lighthouse) was originally lit with kerosene. It was converted to electricity in 1923; a 1,000-watt lightbulb and a backup generator ensure there's always light to lead sailors through the shallow Gulf waters into Progreso. It's not officially open to tourists, but lighthouse buffs may be able to finagle a visit by asking for permission at the tourist office.

Parque Nacional Arrecife Alacranes

A United Nations-designated biosphere reserve, **Parque Nacional Arrecife Alacranes** is made up of five islands (Desterrada, Desertora, Pájaros, Pérez, Chica) located 125 kilometers (78 miles) north of Progreso in the Gulf of Mexico. Covering nearly 300 square kilometers (116 square miles)—the islands themselves make up only a fraction of its size—the reserve is a haven for a variety of marine animals, many at risk of extinction. Unfortunately, there are no organized tours to the park—lack of interest combined with the high cost of fuel make trips too expensive to be profitable. If you're interested in a private tour, contact the Comisión Nacional de Áreas Naturales Protegidas (CONANP), the national park's office in Mérida (Calle 18 at Av. Pérez Ponce, tel. 999/938-0709), which can recommend reputable tour operators.

SPORTS AND RECREATION

Personal watercraft, kayaks, and beach gear can be rented from small kiosks on the beach, including in front of **El Viejo y El Mar restaurant** (Calle 19 at Calle 78). The equipment is available roughly 10am-4:30pm daily; ask in the restaurant if you don't find anyone on the beach.

Yuckite (tel. 999/279-0255, www.yuckite. com) offers kiteboarding classes (US$50/hour private, US$45/hour group) as well as magnificent stand-up paddling tours (US$15-23 pp, plus US$10 for guide) to some of the region's most beautiful mangroves and lagoons.

SHOPPING

For Mexican folk art and crafts, check out the open-air *artesanía* market on the boardwalk whenever there's a cruise ship in town, typically Monday and Wednesday.

FOOD
Restaurants

★ **La Antigua** (Calle 21 near Calle 60, tel. 969/103-6169, 7:30am-11:30pm daily, US$4-14) is set in a gorgeously renovated *casona*—high ceilings, colorful tile floors, wood-beam ceilings, a huge wraparound veranda... the works. Traditional Mexican and seafood are the specialties, but breakfast brings expat faves like pancakes and bagels with lox. For kids, there's a nice pool and an indoor play area. For grown-ups, there's live jazz Thursday to Saturday (9pm-11pm) and Sunday (2pm-4pm).

Mid-century meets colonial Mexico at **Crabster** (Calle 19 btwn Calles 74 and 76, tel. 969/103-6522, 8am-8pm daily, US$7-16), with a gorgeous tiled back wall and huge windows overlooking the ocean and beachfront walkway. Dishes are fresh and inventive, from snail carpaccio to charred octopus, plus classics like ceviche and crab cake burgers. Prices are a smidge inflated and service can suffer when busy, but it's popular for good reason.

For cheap nighttime eats, head to **El Taconazo** (Calle 80 near central park, tel. 969/935-6405, 7pm-midnight daily, US$2-4), a hole-in-the-wall serving great tacos *al pastor*.

Casa de Piedra (Hacienda Xcanatún, Carr. Mérida-Progreso Km 12, www. xcanatun.com, tel. 999/930-2140, 8am-11am daily, 1pm-10pm Mon.-Wed., 1pm-11pm Thurs.-Sat., 1pm-8pm Sun., US$16-25) serves an exquisite fusion of Caribbean and Yucatecan dishes in a beautifully renovated hacienda. Just minutes from Progreso, diners enjoy meals in an elegant dining room or on the breezy patio. It's a great choice if you're looking for something upscale. Reservations are recommended on weekends.

Groceries

The **Mercado Municipal** (Calle 80 btwn Calles 25 and 27, 7am-3pm daily, food stalls open until 8pm) is where locals shop for their

---

1: a view of the *faro* (lighthouse) in Progreso; **2:** fresh fruit at Progreso's colorful market

daily needs, from fruits, veggies, and fresh meats to clothes, toiletries, and other personal items. There are a handful of eateries offering cheap meals and snacks.

ACCOMMODATIONS

Progreso has a limited selection of decent accommodations. Finding a reasonable room can be hard in July and August as well as during Semana Santa—be sure to make reservations. All hotels listed here have Wi-Fi.

Hotel San Miguel (Calle 78 btwn Calle 29 and 31, tel. 969/935-1357, sanmiguelhotel@hotmail.com, US$28 s/d with a/c) offers clean and simple rooms near the central plaza. Those on the 1st floor have high ceilings; those on the 2nd can only be reached by climbing a steep flight of stairs. Each is updated with mini fridge and cable TV. Best of all, it's just a few blocks from the beach.

Located in a quiet neighborhood near the pier, ★ **Maria's Nichte-Ha** (Calle 27 btwn Calles 86 and 88, tel. 969/103-6233, US$38 s/d with a/c, US$43 suite with a/c) is a homey hotel with two stories of spacious and bright rooms, most with bamboo furnishings and colorful tilework. All open onto a courtyard with a pool and hammock area. There's a well-equipped common kitchen and a lounge filled with knickknacks from other eras. It's popular with snowbirds.

Ocean-view suites at **Hotel & Suites Domani** (Calle 19 btwn Calles 72 and 74, tel. 969/935-0707, www.hoteldomanisuites.com, US$32-48 s/d with a/c, US$39-55 suite with a/c) have kitchenettes and are worth the extra cost at this popular and well-priced hotel. Beds are a bit hard, the pool is unheated, and weekends can bring boisterous guests. But the friendly attentive service, super-clean facilities, and terrific beachfront location carry the day for most.

INFORMATION AND SERVICES
Tourist Information
The **tourist office** (Calle 80 at Calle 25, tel. 969/103-0161, turismo@ayuntamiento deprogreso.gob.mx, 8am-8pm Mon.-Fri., 9am-1pm Sat.) provides friendly and capable assistance from its bustling office in the Casa de Cultura. When there are cruise ships in port, a staffer mans an **information kiosk** (Calle 80 at the beach, no phone, 9am-1pm) on the boardwalk.

Emergency Services
Centro Médico Americano (Calle 33 btwn Calles 80 and 82, tel. 969/935-0951) is the best hospital in Progreso, with a 24-hour emergency room. For meds, head to **Farmacia Yza** (Calle 78 at Calle 29, tel. 969/935-0684, 24 hours). The **police station** (tel. 969/935-0026, 24 hours) is located just west of Progreso in the town of Yucalpetén.

Money
A block apart, **Banamex** (Calle 80 btwn Calles 27 and 29, 9am-4pm Mon.-Sat.) and **Banorte** (Calle 80 at Calle 31, 8:30am-4pm Mon.-Fri.) have reliable ATMs and exchange foreign cash.

Media and Communications
Send snail mail at Progreso's **post office** (Calle 31 btwn Calles 78 and 80, 8am-4pm Mon.-Fri., 9am-noon Sat.), just east of Parque Independencia. Wi-Fi is available in all the hotels listed.

Laundry
Lavandería Gloria (Calle 76 btwn Calles 25 and 27, cell tel. 999/552-8871, 8:30am-9pm Mon.-Sat.) charges US$0.70-1 per kilo (2.2 pounds) for next-day service, US$1.25 per kilo for same-day service. There's a three-kilo (6.6-pound) minimum.

GETTING THERE AND AROUND
Bus
From Mérida, buses leave the **Auto-Progreso** terminal on Calle 62 between Calles 65 and 67 every 10-15 minutes 4am-10pm (US$1, 50 minutes). They arrive at the Progreso **bus station** (Calle 29 btwn Calles 80 and 82,

Dzibilchaltún Archaeological Zone

SUB-STRUCTURE 38 GROUP
VISITORS CENTER
MUSEO DEL PUEBLO MAYA
STRUCTURE 57
PLATFORM OF THE KNIVES
SACBÉ
STRUCTURE 45
THE CHAPEL
Cenote Xlacah
STRUCTURE 41
Central Plaza
STRUCTURE 42
STRUCTURE 44
RESIDENTIAL COMPLEX
TEMPLE OF THE SEVEN DOLLS
0   100 yds
0   100 m
© MOON.COM

tel. 999/900-4796, www.autoprogreso.com), a few blocks from the center of town. The return schedule is every 15 minutes 6am-10pm. Auto-Progreso also organizes **day trips**, including flamingo spotting (US$25) and visits to ruins like X'cambo (US$25) and Uxmal (US$49). Entrance fees and bilingual guide are included. Though geared at cruise ship visitors, tours are open to all. Email in advance (or stop by the night before) to see if you can join an existing trip.

Vans (US$1) also shuttle between Mérida and Progreso, leaving Mérida every 15 minutes or so from a small station at Calle 60 between Calles 65 and 67; in Progreso, the station is on Calle 80 between Calles 29 and 31, with the last departure to Mérida at 8pm.

For destinations east or west of Progreso, go to the corner of Calles 82 and 29, where there's a parking lot for **combis** (minivans) and old **buses** headed to towns like Chicxulub Puerto and Uaymitún. *Combis* leave about every 10-15 minutes and cost US$0.75 (6:15am-8:45pm daily). To reach Dzilam de Bravo (US$2.25, 2.5 hours) and towns along the coastal route, a bus leaves at 7:30am and 2:30pm. Alternatively, travelers can puddle jump from town to town, transferring *combis* or buses until reaching their destination.

There's no first-class ADO service to or from Progreso, but you can buy advance tickets for departures from Mérida at the local office of **ADO** (Plaza del Mar mall, Calle 27 btwn Calles 76 and 78, tel. 969/935-2433, 9am-9pm Mon.-Fri., 10am-6pm Sat.-Sun.).

Car

From downtown Mérida, drive north on either Paseo de Montejo or Calle 60. The two streets eventually merge and become Highway 261, which leads directly to Progreso. To go east or west of Progreso by car, head south from town on Highway 261 until you hit the turnoffs.

DZIBILCHALTÚN ARCHAEOLOGICAL ZONE

A short detour off the highway between Mérida and Progreso is the Maya ruin of **Dzibilchaltún** (Hwy. 261 Km 15, 8am-5pm daily, US$7.75, parking US$1). Recognized as the oldest continuously used Maya ceremonial and administrative center on the peninsula, Dzibilchaltún (dzee-beel-chawl-TOON) was inhabited from as early as 1000 BC clear up to the arrival of the Spanish. The **Temple of the Seven Dolls** is the only known Maya temple with windows, and its orientation suggests it was used for astronomical observations—during the fall and spring equinoxes, the sun rises directly through the temple doors. The temple is named for a set of small clay figures that were found inside during its excavation. The ruins of a 16th-century church, built by the Spanish, also sit on the site.

The seven dolls and other artifacts are displayed in the site's **Museo del Pueblo Maya** (8am-3:30pm Tues.-Sun.). It focuses on the history of Dzibilchaltún as well as the area's cultural and economic development; signage is in Spanish and English. A 350-meter-long (1,148-foot) **ecological path** (8am-3:30pm Tues.-Sun.) links the museum to the ruins. Along the way, trees and plants are labeled, and small *palapa*-roofed billboards have information on local flora and fauna.

Don't forget a swimsuit so you can cool off in the blue waters of its **Cenote Xlakáh** (8am-3:30pm Tues.-Sun.), an open pool speckled with lily pads and a popular weekend spot for locals.

Getting There and Around

Dzibilchaltún is located 16 kilometers (10 miles) north of Mérida. If driving, follow Highway 261 north toward Progreso for 12 kilometers (7.4 miles), where a road sign indicates the exit for the ruins. Follow this road east for about 4 kilometers (2.5 miles), past a village and directly to Dzibilchaltún. If taking public transportation from Mérida, vans (US$0.85, 30 minutes) leave frequently from the *combi* stop near Parque Maternidad on Calle 58 between Calles 57 and 59.

East of Progreso

The coastal area east of Progreso has seen increasing development in the past few years in the form of upmarket homes and condominiums, many owned by Canadian expats and rented online. A handful of sleepy towns also dot the landscape, all tuned into life on the sea. The beaches are less visited than those at Progreso, though steady winds make them popular with kitesurfers. There's a modest archaeological site, a small flamingo reserve, and mangrove tours, but blissfully little else.

GETTING THERE AND AROUND

Having your own **car** is by far the easiest and surest way to visit this quiet coastline. From Mérida, take Highway 261 north toward the coast; as you approach Progreso, follow signs east toward Telchac Puerto and Dzilam de Bravo. From Izamal or Valladolid, zigzag through small inland villages until you hit Highway 176 north to Dzilam de Bravo.

To travel by public transportation, the easiest option is to take a **bus** from Progreso to Dzilam de Bravo at 7:30am or 2:30pm

(US$2.25), which stops in every town along the coastal route (just let the driver know where you'd like to be dropped off). The same bus returns to Progreso from Dzilam de Bravo's main plaza at noon and 4pm. Alternatively, *combis* (minivans) run from Progreso to Chicxulub Puerto and Uaymitún every 10-15 minutes from 6:15am to 8:45pm daily (US$0.75). From either place, travelers must transfer *combis,* town to town, until reaching their destination. All *combis* and buses serving this coastline leave from a parking lot in Progreso (Calle 82 at Calle 29).

RESERVA UAYMITÚN

About 16 kilometers (10 miles) east of Progreso, the coastal road wanders behind a long string of upscale houses and past fishing villages to the small town of Uaymitún (why-mih-TOON), home of the **Mirador Ecoturístico Uaymitún** (Uaymitún Ecotouristic Viewpoint, Carr. Chicxulub-Telchac Puerto Km 15, tel. 999/942-1900, 8am-5pm daily, free). Well worth a stop, it's a high wooden platform overlooking a

East of Progreso

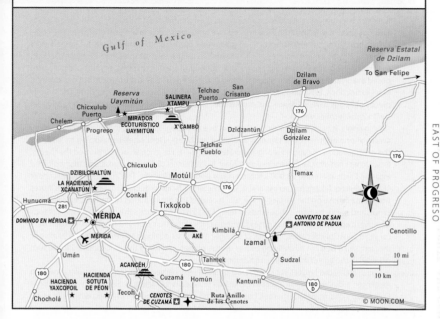

protected part of the extensive marshland that runs just inland along much of the Gulf coast. Thousands of flamingos typically come here to feed, and with binoculars you can get a decent look at these beautiful, peculiar birds in their natural habitat. If you're lucky, some may come closer to the platform. November-March is the best time to see flamingos, but there are a variety of bird species that can be seen year-round from the *mirador*. Binoculars can be rented at the information booth for US$1.

Tip: Another spot to see flamingos is along the road to X'Cambó ruins; the road cuts across the marshland, where the birds often feed.

SALINERA XTAMPU

Just off the coastal highway, **Salinera Xtampu** (Hwy 27 at turnoff to X'Cambó Ruins, cell tel. 991/102-4772, 24 hrs daily, free) is a traditional Maya salt farm, producing salt as it has been done for thousands of years on this coast. Visitors are free to walk among the

pink salt flats, taking photos of the mounds of salt that rise like small icebergs from the ground. More rewarding is to request a tour with the owner, Don Raul Inés, to learn more about the process (tips appreciated). If you opt to walk about the site on your own, consider buying a snack and a bottle of water (or a bag of salt!) from the family, who live on-site.

X'CAMBÓ ARCHAEOLOGICAL ZONE

Six kilometers (3.7 miles) inland from Telchac Puerto, on the road to Tixkokob, are the Maya ruins of **X'Cambó** (Carr. Dzemul-X'Cambó Km 14, 8am-5pm daily, US$3.50). Sometimes referred to as Xtampu, the name means either Place of the Crabs or Place of the Crocodiles. X'Cambó was inhabited as early as 150 BC and was a major salt and salted-fish distribution center for the Maya cities of Izamal, Chichén Itzá, and Uxmal. It enjoyed the wealth that came from these commodities—the 600 skeletons that were unearthed during its

Chicxulub Crater

In 1978, a scientist using magnetic scanning and gravitational maps to scout for oil-drilling sites for Mexico's state-owned oil company noticed two huge arcs—one in the Gulf of Mexico, the other on the northern Yucatán Peninsula—that together appeared to form a circle. He immediately suspected it was a meteor crater, but was unable to secure core samples from PEMEX to back up the claim. A short time later, but unaware of the Gulf of Mexico findings, several scientists proposed a radical theory—that a meteor impact had caused the well-documented but unexplained mass extinctions, including of the dinosaurs, around 65 million years ago; they cited numerous pieces of suggestive evidence, but lacked the "smoking gun": a crater big enough to suggest such a cataclysmic event.

Amazingly, it wasn't until 1990, and thanks to a newspaper reporter, that the parties became aware of one another. Core samples and other analyses—from satellite mapping to studying the configuration of cenotes along the crater's edge—have since all but confirmed the theory. Researchers believe the meteorite was at least 10 kilometers (6.2 miles) across, and that it plowed into the Earth at around 72,000 kilometers per hour (44,740 mph). The impact gouged a crater 180 kilometers (112 miles) across and 2.5 kilometers (1.6 miles) deep, generating temperatures three times those on the surface of the sun. It caused the entire planet to tremble, volcanoes to erupt, and mega-tsunamis thousands of feet high to ricochet across the oceans. Millions of tons of pulverized rock and noxious gases formed a thick cloud that plunged the Earth into darkness for years, possibly decades. The lack of sunlight and other ecologic trauma led to the demise of more than 70 percent of all living things on the planet, including the dinosaurs, which in turn ushered in the age of mammals and humankind.

The crater—the largest yet discovered on Earth—is named after the closest settlement to its center: a dusty northern Yucatán Peninsula town called Chicxulub. Say what you will about Chicxulub's charm, or lack thereof, but it bears the unique distinction of being where life as we know it began.

excavation showed no signs of disease and had jewel-encrusted teeth, an indication of status. Archaeologists also discovered ceramics from distant Maya cities in Belize and Guatemala.

Today, the site is somewhat underwhelming, with various low-lying structures surrounding two plazas. None have surface ornamentation, though the tallest—the Pyramid of the Cross—affords a distant view of the coast. The site also has a small Catholic chapel, which was built on an even smaller Maya structure using stones from the site. It was erected where the Virgin Mary is said to have appeared to local villagers; a festival in her honor is held here every May 30.

TELCHAC PUERTO

The largest of the villages along this coastline is Telchac Puerto, about 40 kilometers (25 miles) east of Progreso. Not particularly charming, it has a handful of restaurants as well as an all-inclusive resort, an anomaly in these parts.

Food and Accommodations

Come hungry to **El Angelito** (Calle 23 btwn Calles 2 and 4, cell tel. 999/135-0696, 10am-9pm Mon.-Sat., US$4-9); this friendly, out-of-the-way eatery may be small but the portions are giant. Seafood is the specialty, ranging from whole fried fish to grilled octopus to huge platefuls of ceviche, most served with sides of rice, fries, and thick slices of avocado.

Near the town pier, **Los Tiburones** (Calle 20 btwn Calles 19 and 21, tel. 991/917-4000, 8am-7pm daily, US$4-8) serves fresh seafood dishes—from ceviches to *pulpo en su tinta*—all at reasonable prices. Meals come with a generous selection of appetizers too. Traditional Mexican breakfasts are also a hit (be sure to order a glass of freshly squeezed OJ).

Hotel Reef Yucatán (Hwy 27 Km 35.6, tel. 999/917-5000, www.reefyucatan.com, US$88/156 s/d with a/c) is a basic all-inclusive resort. Rooms are simple—a place to sleep, not much more. The food is one-note too—Mexican—which can wear thin for guests staying more than a weekend. The beach and pools, however, are where it's at: well tended, clean, and with lots of lounge areas. Tennis courts, a mini-golf course, and a kids' club are pluses.

SAN CRISANTO

Nine kilometers (5.6 miles) east of Telchac Puerto, San Crisanto is a small fishing village lined with swaying coconut trees. It has a nice beach, good overnight options to the west, and rewarding mangrove tours to the east.

Manglares de San Crisanto

Centro Integración Turística (CIST, tel. 991/105-3710, www.sancrisanto.org, 9am-5pm daily) offers paddling tours of the nearby mangroves. Outings are on tiny boats—they max out at three or four adults—that guides move through the water with long wooden poles. During daytime tours (US$3, 1.5 hours), visitors are treated to myriad bird sightings and a stop for swimming in a freshwater spring. Evening tours (US$6, 2.5 hours) focus on finding crocodiles, including even holding a baby one. To book a tour, stop by CIST's visitors center, on the eastern end of town; look for the huge palapa-roofed building just south of the main road. **Note:** CIST also manages Cabañas Kanab-Nah and Balneario Zac-Ha, listed below.

Food and Accommodations

On the main road, there are a couple of **mom-and-pop eateries** (US$3-7) open weekends only. If staying overnight, stock up on food in Progreso.

Sitting on a gorgeous beach just west of town, ★ **Cabañas Kanab-Nah** (Carr. Costera s/n, tel. 991/105-3710, ejido_sancrisanto@hotmail.com, US$45 one-bdrm and two-bdrm bungalows) has five simple palapa-roof bungalows with sand floors. All have separate sleeping areas and private bathrooms, a screened-in living room, and mini fridges. Cement floors in the bedrooms help guests sleep sand-free. The one-bedroom bungalow also has a kitchenette. The beach itself is windswept and filled with shells.

Nearby, **Balneario Zac-Ha** (Carr. Costera s/n, tel. 991/105-3710, ejido_sancrisanto@hotmail.com, 8am-5pm daily, US$2.50 pp admission, US$5 pp camping) is a gorgeous beach thick with palm trees. Locals come to spend the day enjoying the sand and surf but travelers with camping gear come to spend a few days and nights, set up in tents under big palapas and starry skies. There are decent bathrooms but, unfortunately, no cooking facilities.

DZILAM DE BRAVO

At the end of the line is the quiet fishing town of Dzilam de Bravo, where legend has it that the pirate Jean Lafitte is buried. The real draws, though, are the miles of pristine coastline and mangrove forests east of town, teeming with birds and wildlife and dotted with lonely beaches and freshwater upwellings that make for a refreshing swim.

In Dzilam de Bravo, **Sayachuleb** (Calle 9 btwn Calles 2 and 2-A, tel. 999/141-2532, www.dzilamdebravoyucatanecoturismo.blogspot.mx, 8am-4pm daily) is a local fishermen's cooperative that offers 2-5-hour tours into the reserves by motorboat or kayak, visiting various bocas, tangled waterways, and isolated beaches; fishing, bird-watching, and even camping can be incorporated into most trips. Excursions are limited to eight people (US$45-125 per motorboat, US$15-20 pp by kayak). The co-op also runs a good **on-site restaurant** (11am-5pm daily, US$5-7), serving fresh seafood dishes under a breezy oceanfront palapa. It's located on the eastern edge of town, next to the lighthouse.

Reserva Estatal de Dzilam and Parque Natural San Felipe

Extending east of Dzilam de Bravo nearly

to the town of San Felipe are two state nature preserves: the modest **Dzilam State Reserve** (www.sds.yucatan.gob.mx) and the much larger **San Felipe Natural Park** (tel. 999/930-3380). Together they cover nearly a thousand square kilometers (386 square miles) of pristine beaches, coastal wetlands, mangrove forests, and a narrow *tierra firme* (dry land) buffer. The reserves are home to four types of protected mangroves—red, black, white, and *botoncillo*—and numerous bird and animal species, from pelicans to crocodiles to spider monkeys. The area is also notable for its freshwater upwellings known as *bocas* (literally, mouths); some are ensconced in mangroves, others bubble up right in the middle of the ocean, making for unique ecosystems and in some cases refreshing swimming holes. The largest and most famous—Xbuya Ha—spews an impressive 3,500 liters (925 gallons) of freshwater per minute.

Izamal

Nestled between Mérida and Chichén Itzá, Izamal is an old colonial city with a beautiful and famous convent, friendly residents, and a fascinating history. Most tourists arrive here on a tour bus, visit the convent and the city center for an hour or so, and then motor off again. But Izamal is a great place for independent travelers to stay a night or two, soaking in the atmosphere and rich history of this classic Yucatecan town.

The first thing you notice about Izamal is the color: Virtually all the buildings and facades in Izamal are painted a rich mustard yellow, as is the convent. And Izamal has not one but two large, tree-filled plazas—Parque Zamná and Parque 5 de Mayo—which form the heart of the city. It is a very walkable city, and part of the pleasure of Izamal is simply wandering about its narrow streets, discovering picturesque facades, stone churches, artistic workshops, and even Maya pyramids.

HISTORY

Pope John Paul II visited Izamal in August 1993, instantly transforming the city and its cathedral into places of high Catholic importance. But it has been an important religious site since the time of the ancient Maya—it was one of three major pilgrimage sites in pre-Columbian Yucatán, along with Chichén Itzá and San Gervasio on Isla Cozumel. Spanish priests and colonizers recognized the area's importance and lost little time constructing a magnificent convent and church atop one of the largest existing Maya pyramids, even using the same stones as building materials. Fray Diego de Landa, who would later gain notoriety for burning dozens of Maya codices, oversaw the church.

SIGHTS
★ Convento de San Antonio de Padua

The most imposing structure in this small town is the mustard-colored **Convento de San Antonio de Padua** (Parque 5 de Mayo, 6am-8pm daily, free). Completed in 1562 under the direction of Fray Diego de Landa, the convent was built upon—and used many of the stones of—what was once the immense Maya temple Pap Hol Chac. If you look closely, you'll even see some Maya glyphs in the church walls themselves. A 7,806-square-meter (84,023-square-foot) grassy atrium enclosed by 75 arches sits at the front of this beautiful complex. It's the largest open-air atrium in the Americas and, many claim, the second-largest in the world (the largest being at St. Peter's in the Vatican). Another pays homage to Nuestra Señora de Izamal, the Yucatán's religious patroness. A nearby sanctuary is home to a statue of her, which is said to have performed several miracles, and religious followers from around the Yucatán

Izamal

To Police

CALLE 25

CALLE 30

CALLE 28

KINICH KAKMÓ

CALLE 28B

CALLE 26

CALLE 26A

KINICH

CALLE 27

To Lavandería Maguis

CALLE 29

CALLE 28

CALLE 26A

CALLE 26

KABUL

CALLE 31A

CALLE 34

POSADA ZAMNÁ

Parque Zamná

CAFÉ LOS ARCOS

ITZAMATUL

CENTRO CULTURAL Y ARTESANAL IZAMAL

FARMACIA YZA

To Cenotillo

IZAMAL BIKES AND CRAFTS

CALESAS

BANORTE

CALLE 31

TOURIST OFFICE

To Parque de los Cañones, Kimbilá, and Aké

COMBIS TO MÉRIDA

Parque 5 de Mayo

MUSEO COMUNITARIO ITZMAL KAUIL

CALLE 28

EL CONEJO

POST OFFICE

CALLE 30A

CONVENTO DE SAN ANTONIO DE PADUA

TERMINAL ORIENTE

CALLE 31-A

To Mérida and Kimbilá

HOTEL SAN MIGUEL ARCÁNGEL/ HECHO A MANO

Mercado Municipal

CALLE 33

EL TORO RESTAURANTE

SUPER WILLY'S/ ATM

POST OFFICE

HOTEL RINCONADA DEL CONVENTO

CALLE 34

To Macan Ché B&B and Hacienda Hotel Santo Domingo

CALLE 35

HABUK

HOSPITAL

CALLE 37

CALLE 24

SCALE NOT AVAILABLE

AVENIDA ZAMNA

© MOON.COM

CALLE 32

CALLE 30

CALLE 28

CALLE 26

To Hwy 180

Cenotes Off the Beaten Path

Avid swimmers and admirers of cenotes may want to check out some of these less-visited sites.

- Often declared one of the loveliest cenotes on the peninsula, the semi-open **Cenote Kankirixché** (9am-6pm daily, US$1.50) contains turquoise water striped with ropy tree roots, stalagmites, and stalactites. It's located between the towns of Abala and Mukuyché, 60 kilometers (37 miles) south of Mérida, just 8 kilometers (5 miles) east of Highway 261.

- **Cenote X-Batun** and **Cenote Dzonbacal,** also known as **Cenotes San Antonio Mulix** (tel. 999/132-8026, 9:30am-6pm daily, US$3) for a nearby hacienda, are contrasting sister cenotes. X-Batun is a long, sunny pool at the foot of a vine-draped cliff, while Dzonbacal is ensconced in a tree-covered cavern and reached by steep stairs. The cenotes are near Umán, 50 kilometers (31 miles) south of Merida.

Cenote Kankirixché is an unexpectedly beautiful place to cool off.

- About 48 kilometers (30 miles) east of Izamal, the village of **Cenotillo** (Little Cenote) boasts almost 150 cenotes nearby; popular ones include Kaipech, Xayín, and Yook Chac (9am-6pm daily). Stop by the Palacio Municipal to inquire about finding a local guide.

- In the small town and former henequen estate of **Sabacché,** a local cooperative maintains two cenotes, a restaurant, and *cabaña* and tent lodging, and also rents out bicycles and snorkeling equipment. Of the two cenotes, the semi-open **Calcuch** (8am-5pm daily, US$1.50) is the lovelier, with a dramatic circular stairway that descends 14 meters (46 feet). The town is located between Cuzamá and San Isidro Ochil.

- Stalactites bristle from the roof of the illuminated **Cenote San Ignacio** (tel. 999/278-6294, www.cenotesanignacio.com, 10am-6pm daily, 8pm-midnight Mon.-Sat., US$4.50 day, US$11 night), a smaller cenote with a restaurant and children's wading pools and a playground,. Visitors can splash and snorkel in its six-meter-deep (19.7-foot) waters day or night—a rare treat. It's located in Chocholá, south of Mérida along Highway 180 to Campeche.

often make pilgrimages to see her; you may see some of them climbing the steps of the convent on their knees. There's also a small **museum** (9am-8pm daily, US$0.25) commemorating Pope John Paul II's visit.

Archaeological Zones

Kinich Kakmó (aka Kinich Kak Moo, Calle 28 btwn Calles 25 and 27, 8am-5pm daily, free) is one of numerous Maya ruins in Izamal proper. While the others are relatively modest, Kinich Kakmó is a whopping 195 meters (640 feet) long, 173 meters (568 feet) wide, and 34 meters (112 feet) high, making it the

largest pyramid in the state of Yucatán, and the third- to fifth-largest in Mexico, depending on how you define "large." Built between AD 250 and 600, the pyramid was dedicated to the sun god, or Fire Macaw, and was the principal structure of a massive plaza that extended over much of present-day Izamal. It was once a deeply important site for Maya shamans and worshippers, just as Izamal's Convento de San Antonio de Padua has become for Mexican Catholics today. Kinich Kakmó is not as fully restored as pyramids like El Castillo in Chichén Itzá, but it is still worth a climb, especially for the views of the city and surroundings. On a clear day, you can even see Chichén Itzá, 50 kilometers (31 miles) to the east.

Other smaller pyramids that can be visited include **Itzamatul** (Calle 26 at Calle 31, 8am-5pm daily, free), which affords a fine view of the city and Kinich Kakmó; **El Conejo** (Calle 22 btwn Calles 31 and 33, 8am-5pm daily, free); and **Habuk** (Calle 28 btwn Calles 35 and 37, 8am-5pm daily, free).

Museums

Located in a renovated 16th-century home, the **Centro Cultural y Artesanal Izamal** (Parque 5 de Mayo, Calle 31 btwn Calles 30 and 32, tel. 988/954-1012, www.centroculturalizamal.org.mx, 9am-8pm Mon.-Sat., 10am-5pm Sun., US$1.25) is a spectacular museum of Mexican folk art. Works displayed were created by the country's grand master artisans and include pieces in clay, wood, paper, and handwoven fabrics. There's an entire room dedicated to Yucatecan *artesanía* too. A **gift shop** (open til 11pm daily) sells beautiful—if pricey—crafts from the region; sales directly benefit the indigenous cooperative that creates them. Wandering around the property, you'll also find an exhibit on the henequen haciendas, a

small café, and the Maya ruin of Kabul, which dates to the 6th century (closed at the time of research).

Museo del Convento de San Antonio de Padua (Parque 5 de Mayo, 9am-8pm daily, US$0.25) is a small museum inside the convent that commemorates Pope John Paul II's 1993 visit to Izamal. Though it's not terribly engaging, there are lots of photos and some interesting information.

Museo Comunitario Itzmal Kauil (Calle 30 s/n, tel. 995/940-0032, 9am-1pm and 4pm-5pm daily, free) has modest displays on Izamal's ancient, colonial, and modern-day history. Displays are all in Spanish.

Artisan Workshops

There are several artisan workshops where passersby can stop in, watch how a particular piece of folk art is made, and, of course, buy something straight from the artist. Wandering around town, you'll see signs for tin workers, hammock weavers, woodworkers, and jewelry makers. Most of the workshops are run out of people's homes, so opening hours are pretty casual; don't be shy about knocking if the shop appears closed—at worst, you'll be told when to come back later. Free city maps listing the location of many of the workshops are

The Yucatán's best handicrafts and folk art are made by experienced *artesanas* (artisans).

distributed at the tourist office and the Centro Cultural y Artesanal Izamal.

Sound and Light Show

Three evenings per week, Izamal hosts a **sound and light show** (8pm Thurs.-Sat., US$6) entitled "Senderos de Luz" (Paths of Light), which travels down Calle 31 from Parque de los Cañones (Calle 31 at Calle 40) to Parque 5 de Mayo (Calle 31 at Calle 30) with the grand finale at the Convento de San Antonio de Padua (Parque 5 de Mayo). The show is a series of high-quality projections with audio that tells the story of the Maya and Izamal. The streetside show is free; US$6 is charged for those entering the convent grounds to watch the end.

SHOPPING

Hecho a Mano (Calle 31-A btwn Calles 30 and 30-A, tel. 988/954-0109, 9am-2:30pm daily, 4pm-8pm Fri.-Sat.) is a small folk-art boutique specializing in museum-quality items (and prices to match). If you're looking for a special gift or simply like window-shopping, you'll enjoy a stop here.

Izamal Bikes and Crafts (Parque 5 de Mayo, Calle 31 btwn Calles 30 and 32, tel. 999/101-0409, 9am-8pm Tues.-Sat., 9am-5pm Sun.-Mon.) sells beautiful regional clothing, colorful bags and purses, and handcrafted jewelry. It's a good place for mementos and small gifts too.

If you're in the market for local folk art, head to one of the many **artisan workshops** around town, where you can buy items that you watched being made; free city maps listing workshop locations are distributed at the tourist office and the Centro Cultural y Artesanal Izamal. Another option is browsing the *artesanía* tables set up in Parque 5 de Mayo. Most days, vendors set up display tables in the park 10am-4pm.

The nearby town of Kimbilá is the place to go for fine *guayaberas* and *huipiles* at wholesale prices; in fact, many regional shop owners stock up there. For a good selection, head to the town's central plaza, where there are several well-stocked mom-and-pop shops. From Izamal, head west on Calle 31 for about 10 kilometers (6.2 miles); in the village of Citilcum, turn left onto Calle 20 and continue for 2 kilometers (1.2 miles) until you hit Kimbilá's central plaza.

FOOD

An upscale place, ★ **Kinich** (Calle 27 btwn Calles 28 and 30, tel. 988/954-0489, 11am-7pm daily, US$6-12) is a breezy *palapa*-roofed restaurant known for its quality regional dishes, including excellent *poc-chuc* (marinated grilled pork). And if you've never seen tortillas being made, check out the tiny *palapa* in back, where you'll find women at a small fire, patting and cooking tortillas for your meal.

Café Los Arcos (Parque Zamná, Calle 28 near Calle 31-A, tel. 988/954-0662, 10am-11pm, US$3-6) offers a change of pace from *típico* with hamburgers, sandwiches, salads, and sweet treats. Streetside tables make for great people-watching while you eat.

Across from the Mercado, **El Toro Restaurante** (Calle 33 btwn Calles 30 and 32, tel. 988/954-1169, 8am-11pm daily, US$5-7) serves decent regional fare in a pleasant dining room—try the *salbutes, papadzules,* or quesadillas.

Mercado Municipal (facing Parque 5 de Mayo) sells fresh produce, dairy, and meats. Shops are open 6am-2pm daily, and some stay open as late as 8pm Monday-Saturday.

ACCOMMODATIONS

Lodging is somewhat limited in Izamal. Many visitors arrive on large tour buses and stay just long enough to visit the convent and climb the pyramid at Kinich Kakmó. Staying a night or two gives travelers the freedom to wander the quiet streets, stop in artisan workshops, and enjoy the lifestyle of this slow-paced town. All the options listed have Wi-Fi.

Cheap and central, **Posada Zamná** (Calle 33 btwn Calle 31 and 31-A, tel. 988/954-0758, US$20 s/d with a/c) may blind you with its startlingly white walls and floor tiling, but once your eyes adjust you'll find basic hotel rooms with firm beds, spotless bathrooms (though no toilet seats), flat-screen TVs, and quiet air-conditioning. There's a nice seating area, and Parque Zamná is just outside.

Facing Parque 5 de Mayo, **Hotel San Miguel Arcángel** (Calle 31-A btwn Calles 30 and 30-A, tel. 988/954-0109, www.sanmiguelhotel.com.mx, US$38-41 s/d with a/c) is a good option if you don't mind the sound of traffic in the morning or bird cacophony in the evening. Rooms have high ceilings and tile floors; some have balconies overlooking the park and convent. Continental breakfast is included and served in the small courtyard.

★ **Macan Ché Bed & Breakfast** (Calle 22 btwn Calles 33 and 35, tel. 988/954-0287, www.macanche.com, US$48 s/d, US$58-70 s/d with a/c, US$140 house with a/c) comprises bungalows and suites, many with decorative themes, nestled in a tropical garden. There's a small stone-bottom pool as well as a *palapa* lounge where breakfast is served. For longer stays, ask about the on-site houses. The only downside? A longish walk to town.

Hotel Rinconada del Convento (Calle 33 btwn Calles 28 and 30, tel. 999/357-9006, www.hotelizamal.com, US$50-58 s/d with a/c) is a rambling remodeled home facing the convent. There are 11 comfortable, somewhat sterile rooms with sleek décor; some have partial views of the convent. The highlight here is the common space—a beautiful terraced garden, a well-maintained lap pool, and a tile-roofed patio overlooking it all.

Near the town limits, **Hacienda Hotel Santo Domingo** (Calle 18 near Calle 33, cell tel. 988/967-6136, www.izamalhotel.com, US$75-95 s/d with a/c, US$130-135 suite with a/c) offers units in what once were the living quarters and stables of this former henequen hacienda. Far from rustic, each is updated with luxe amenities and king-size beds, and some have features like open-air showers. The grounds are lush and include a well-tended

pool and restaurant, where guests enjoy hearty breakfasts.

INFORMATION AND SERVICES
Tourist Information
The **tourist office** (Parque 5 de Mayo, tel. 988/954-0009, 8am-8pm Mon.-Sat., 9am-2pm Sun.) is in the Palacio Municipal. There are plenty of brochures and maps; some staffers speak English.

Emergency Services
Izamal's public **hospital** (Calle 24 btwn Calles 35 and 37, tel. 988/954-0241) has a 24-hour emergency room. The telephone is answered only 8am-8pm; after hours, go directly to the clinic. **Farmacia Yza** (Calle 28 at Calle 31, tel. 988/954-0600, 24 hours) faces the east side of Parque Zamná. The **tourist police** in Izamal may be the friendliest in the Yucatán Peninsula, and sometimes flag down travelers simply to offer assistance (no tip expected). One or more officers are usually stationed at intersections around the center. The **municipal police** are located at the former train station, the *ex-estación de tren* (Calle 30 at Calle 19, tel. 988/954-0505, toll-free Mex. tel. 066, 24 hours).

Money
There's no bank in town, though **Banorte** (Calle 28 at Calle 31) has a 24-hour ATM, and there's another cash machine inside **Super Willy's** (Calle 33 btwn Calles 30 and 32, 7am-10:30pm daily).

Media and Communications
The **post office** (8am-1pm Mon.-Sat.) is on Calle 30-A, inside the Palacio del Gobierno. Parque Zamná and Parque 5 de Mayo have free **Wi-Fi,** as do all of the listed hotels.

Laundry
Lavandería Maguis (Calle 23 near Calle 42, tel. 988/103-0778, 8am-8pm Thurs.-Tues.) charges US$0.60 per kilo (2.2 pounds), with a three-kilo (6.6-pound) minimum.

GETTING THERE AND AROUND

Izamal is served by first- and second-class buses, though having a car will allow you to visit outlying areas such as Kimbilá. The town itself is quite easy to navigate on foot: The bus terminal, major sights, and a handful of hotels and restaurants are all within easy walking distance of each other.

Bus

Izamal has two bus terminals located two blocks apart: **Terminal de Autobuses Centro** (Calle 33 btwn Calles 30 and 32, tel. 988/667-6615) and **Terminal Oriente** (Calle 32 at Calle 31-A, tel. 988/954-0107). Both have second-class bus service only and have similar routes.

- Cancún: US$9-10, 5 hours, 15 departures, 12:15am-10:50
- Mérida: US$1.50-2, 1.5 hours, 31 departures, 12:30am-8pm
- Tizimín (Terminal Oriente only): US$4.75, 2.5 hours, 7:30am and 6:10pm
- Valladolid: US$3.50-3.75, 2 hours, take any Cancún bus

There also is *combi* (van) service to Mérida (US$1.75, 1.5 hours) every 30 minutes from 4am to 6pm daily. *Combis* line up just north of the Terminal Oriente on Calle 31.

Car

The *cuota* (toll road) has well-marked turnoffs to Izamal at Kilometer 68, coming from either Cancún or Mérida. Arriving on the *libre* (free road), follow the signs to head north at Kantunil. For a more scenic route from Mérida, follow Calle 65 out of town and across the *periférico*. Using rural roads, you'll pass through the town of Tixcocob, and can make side jaunts to the Aké ruins and Hacienda San José Cholul.

Bicycle

Izamal Bikes and Crafts (Parque 5 de Mayo, Calle 31 btwn Calles 30 and 32, tel. 999/101-0409, 9am-8pm Tues.-Sat., 9am-5pm Sun.-Mon.) rents retro bikes in a variety of sizes (US$2 per hour).

Tours

All day long there's a queue of *calesas* parked along the long northern wall of the convent offering **horse-carriage tours.** Ostensibly for tourists—a scenic 30-60-minute tour around town runs US$7.50-15, depending on its duration—these tiny horse-pulled buggies also do an active business carrying local families from place to place.

HACIENDA AND RUINS AKÉ

A visit to the Maya ruins of **Aké** (8am-5pm daily, US$1.25) makes for a good excursion from Izamal. Believed to have been occupied from the Late Preclassic until the Postclassic period, Aké reached its height of influence sometime between AD 600 and 1200; it was abandoned around 1450. The city was the nucleus of many *sacbés* (raised roads), including one 32 kilometers (20 miles) long that connected it to Izamal. However, at some point a wall was built around the site, suggesting that alliances must have soured. The village was also the backdrop for a fierce battle in 1528 between the Maya and Francisco de Montejo "El Mozo" (The Younger).

Entering the site, two restored structures sit on a large open plaza. Structure 1, also known as the Estructura de las Pilastras (Structure of the Pillars), is the more striking of the two. A rectangular platform 104 meters (341 feet) long, 36.5 meters (120 feet) wide, and 8.5 meters (28 feet) high, its stairs are actually large blocks of stone—some up to 1.8 meters (6 feet) long. But its most unusual feature is a phalanx of 35 stacked-square columns (approximately 4.6 meters/15 feet high) that must have supported an enormous roof. Between Structure 1 and the entrance is the site's tallest building, Structure 2, which can be climbed from the plaza side for treetop views of the surrounding area.

Next door, the **Hacienda de San Lorenzo de Aké** (tel. 999/126-4199, www.ruinasdeake.com, US$10, tour by appointment) is a 19th-century mansion and henequen production facility that still makes sisal twine. Ninety-minute tours feature a short film (in English or Spanish) about the hacienda and visits to the *desfibradora* (henequen mill) and the *cordelería* (rope factory), where workers spin bales of fiber into twine. A blazing-yellow chapel lords above the hacienda from what looks like a hill, but upon closer inspection is Maya stonework.

To get here from Izamal, take Highway 180 west to the signed turnoff at Kilometer 41 and continue north 11 kilometers (6.8 miles). The site also is accessible from the Izamal-Tixkokob road, though it's not signed well. By public transportation it's easiest from Mérida; second-class buses (US$1.50, 1 hour) leave from the **Terminal Autobuses del Centro** (Calle 65 btwn Calles 46 and 48, tel. 999/923-9962) at 10:45am and 7:35pm. To return, catch a taxi or *colectivo* to Tixkokob, where there are frequent *colectivos* to and from Mérida.

The Puuc Route

You can easily spend two full days (or more) in the region south of Mérida, with its rich concentration of Maya ruins, caves, and appealing towns. The Puuc ruins are the main attraction, of course, from the stunning size and accomplishment of Uxmal to the fantastic artistry of smaller sites like Labná and Kabah. The route also includes the Loltún caves, a great introduction to the Yucatán's vast underground world.

GETTING THERE AND AROUND

Bus

On Sunday only, an Oriente bus headed for the Puuc Route leaves Mérida's second-class bus terminal at 8am and spends 30 minutes apiece at Sayil, Labná, and Xlapak, 40 minutes at Kabah, and two hours at Uxmal, before returning to Mérida around 5pm (US$14); entrance fees, food, drinks, and guide service are not included. Merida tour agencies are another option if you don't want to rent a car.

There are daily buses to Uxmal (US$3.50, 1.5 hours, 4 departures, 6am-5pm) that leave from Mérida's second-class bus terminal; there's also service to the nearby towns of Ticul and Santa Elena. Returning to Mérida, you can flag down a second-class bus on the highway at the Uxmal turnoff, but they only pass every hour or so.

Car

If you're driving, Highway 261 leads to the Puuc Route. From Mérida, the drive to Uxmal takes about one hour; from Campeche City allow two hours.

TOP EXPERIENCE

★ UXMAL ARCHAEOLOGICAL ZONE

The massive scale, elegant structures, and intricate decoration of **Uxmal** (8am-5pm daily, US$11.75 ruins, US$5 sound and light show) make it one of the most memorable Maya ruins in the Yucatán, and a perennial favorite for casual visitors and Maya buffs alike. It was the greatest of the Maya cities in the Puuc region, and contains some of the best—and best-preserved—examples of Puuc-style architecture. And though Uxmal is located just 80 kilometers (50 miles) from Mérida, it doesn't get the crush of visitors (or vendors) that sites like Chichén Itzá and Tulum do, making a visit here all the more enjoyable.

History

Some believe Uxmal was founded by Maya from Guatemala's Petén region in the 6th century. Others contend it dates back even further, perhaps to the Preclassic period. Unlike

The Puuc Route

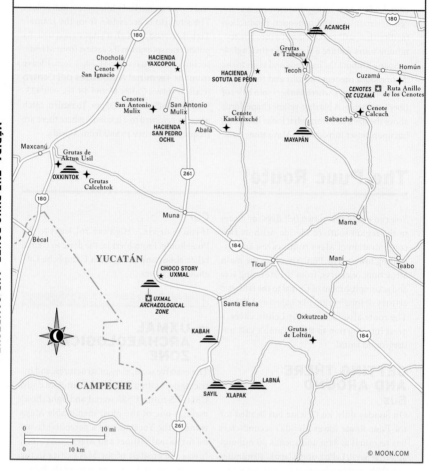

most of northern Yucatán, the Puuc region has good soils, allowing for greater population density than other areas. Uxmal emerged as the dominant city-state between AD 850 and 900, when the Pyramid of the Magician, the Great Pyramid, and the Nunnery were built, and is believed to have been the hub of a district of about 160 square kilometers (62 square miles) encompassing many sites, including the lesser sites in the area: Kabah, Sayil, Labná, and Xlapak. However, in the mid-10th century Uxmal was abruptly abandoned, probably

after being defeated by armies from Chichén Itzá and as part of a pan-Maya collapse around that time. During the Postclassic era, the Xiu clan based in the nearby town of Maní spuriously claimed to be descended from Uxmal's rulers and occupied the ruins. All that said, however, relatively few stelae have been found at Uxmal, so less is known about the ruling dynasties here than at other major sites.

The Maya word *uxmal* (oosh-MAHL) means "thrice built." The name notwithstanding, it is believed that Uxmal was built five

Uxmal Archaeological Zone

NORTH
GROUP

STELA
PLATFORM

CEMETERY
GROUP

NUNNERY
QUADRANGLE

To Entrance

PYRAMID OF
THE MAGICIAN

QUADRANGLE
OF THE BIRDS

BALL COURT

HOUSE OF
THE TURTLES

CHENES
BUILDING

GOVERNOR'S
PALACE

LA PICOTA

JAGUAR
THRONE

DOVECOTE

GREAT
PYRAMID

HOUSE OF THE
OLD WOMAN

WALL

WALL

WALL

0   100 yds

0   100 m

© MOON.COM

times, each time over top of the last. Puuc architecture is one of the major achievements of Mesoamerica; its hallmarks include unadorned lower levels, heavily decorated upper friezes, boot-shaped vault stones, thin squares of limestone veneer, and rows of pseudocolumns. The constant threat of drought also inspired the Maya to adorn their structures with hundreds of stone masks and carvings representing the rain god, Chaac, easily identified by his prominent hooked nose. Unlike most Maya centers in Yucatán, Uxmal was not built around a cenote (there are none in this arid part of the peninsula). Rainwater was collected in *aguadas* (natural holes in the ground) as well as in manufactured *chultúnes* (cisterns) built into the ground, sometimes right inside a house or under a patio.

Pyramid of the Magician

Passing through the visitors center and up a gently sloping pathway, the first structure you reach is Uxmal's tallest and among its most distinctive. The Pyramid of the Magician stands 38 meters (125 feet) high and has a unique elliptical base, rather than the square or rectangular base of most pyramids. The softly curved edges, combined with its impressive height and girth, lend the temple a striking elegance. You will approach the Pyramid of the Magician from the back, but the other (west) side is by far the most ornate. There, a staircase rises at an imposing 60-degree angle, lined by the hooked-nose masks representing Chaac, the rain god. Three-quarters of the way up, a huge monster-mouth facade—borrowed from Chenes-style construction from present-day Campeche—surrounds a temple door. At the top is a two-story rectangular temple, with crosshatch panels beside the doors. You'll have to take our word for it, though, as tourists are no longer allowed to climb the pyramid, to prevent undue erosion as well as accidents.

You'll also often see guides standing in front of the Pyramid of the Magician and clapping their hands once—the sound can be heard bouncing off the surrounding structures, with a bird-like reverberation. It's a curious and impressive architectural feat, and one that elicits images of speeches being made to Maya crowds long ago.

Before leaving, take note of the small but attractive plaza on the Pyramid of the Magician's west side. It's known as the **Quadrangle of the Birds,** so named for the birds carved into the upper frieze of the small building opposite the Pyramid of the Magician. And there are more than just birds, including Puuc-style decorative columns, faux thatching (or perhaps, bird feathers), and crescent-moon edging, all in remarkably good condition.

Nunnery Quadrangle

The Nunnery Quadrangle is the huge courtyard directly west of the Pyramid of the Magician. Covering an area 60 by 45 meters (197 by 148 feet), the (almost) square is bounded on each side by long buildings. The buildings contain numerous small rooms, and reminded the first Spanish explorers of nunneries in Spain, hence the name. The buildings evidently were built in a single concentrated effort at the end of the 9th century, shortly before the city's collapse.

The combination of a plain lower level topped by an ornate frieze—a staple of Puuc architecture—can be seen in all four buildings of the Nunnery Quadrangle. The **west building** has the most ornate frieze. Notice the stacked Chaac masks at either end and, working toward the center, geometric spirals that represent clouds (note that the Maya glyph for *cloud* has a similar design). Interspersed are panels with lattice patterns, also typical of Puuc design; here they are especially fine, embedded with flowers. The niche over the center door contains the figure of the God of the Underworld (God N, to archaeologists), with the body of a turtle, sitting under a canopy of feathers. The designers of Uxmal were obsessed with the male phallus, and figures at the ends of the facade are disrobed, with rather prodigious members that appear scarred or tattooed (ouch!). A large phallus also once stood in the center of the Nunnery Quadrangle, but it has since disappeared. Finally, notice the two long, feathered snakes that weave (and interweave) the length of the frieze. From the mouth of one emerges a human face, a way of emphasizing the divine origin of Uxmal's leaders.

The **north building** is the largest and highest of the four, affording great views of the entire site from its broad platform. The frieze contains exquisite Chaac masks, with finely curved incisor teeth and distinct upper and lower eyelids.

To many observers, the **east building** is the most refined in its design and execution. Simple latticework is broken by triangular forms over the doors. On closer look, you can see the forms are in fact an inverted stack of two-headed feathered serpents. Above them are shields depicting owls, which the Maya associated with warfare and sacrifice.

The **south building** has a vaulted arch, giving access to and from the quadrangle. High on its sloped walls, look for red handprints, left from the original construction. Notice, too, the carvings of thatched huts, or *na*, over each of the doors. In fact, you can see such images in numerous temples in this region, and beyond. The precise meaning of the huts is unclear—they may have represented the newborn universe, as in some Maya creation myths—but like the handprints in the archway, they lend a powerful humanity to these ancient ruins, not least because the very same *na* remain a fixture of Maya communities today.

Governor's Palace

An archway leads out of the Nunnery Quadrangle across a grassy esplanade and past Uxmal's modest **ball court.** Bearing left, you'll climb a large platform to the Governor's Palace. At the top of the steps, pause a moment to appreciate the scope of this complex, considered by some to be the height of Puuc architecture. The platform you just climbed is artificial—it was built by hand out of piled stone, and measures a mind-boggling 187 meters (613.5 feet) long, 170 meters (558 feet) wide, and 8-10 meters (26-33 feet) high. On top of it are a number of structures, the most notable being the Governor's Palace, which measures 98 meters (321.5 feet) long and 12 meters (39 feet) wide (and it's built on still another 7-meter/23-foot-high platform). The upper frieze has lattice patterns, feathered serpents, and over 100 Chaac masks; in all, it took some 15,000 individual stone pieces to create it. Over the center door was the face—now gone—of a god, probably Lord Chaac, surrounded by a feather headdress, featuring Chaac masks. Two arrow-shaped corbel arches originally allowed passage from one side to the other, but were later plugged, perhaps to create more rooms or to stabilize the structure. The high-vaulted interior rooms are musty and unpleasant, but do walk around the north end, where, at the corners, near the ground, some excellent carved pieces can be examined close-up.

On the small platform in front of the palace, a throne in the shape of a two-headed **jaguar** was uncovered by John Stephens in 1841, and remains today. Such thrones were a common symbol of Maya authority—a similar one was found in Palenque and a single-headed one deep inside El Castillo at Chichén Itzá. Stephens tried to take the artifact with him but, lucky for us, found it "too heavy to carry away." He evidently never thought to look beneath it—there, archaeologists found a cache of nearly a thousand extremely fine jade, obsidian, and ceramic items.

Also on this platform is the **House of the Turtles,** a simple but elegant structure measuring 11 by 30 meters (36 by 98 feet). The lower half is very plain, but the upper part is decorated with a frieze of columns, topped by a cornice adorned by a series of turtles. The Maya associated turtles and other wetland creatures with rain and fertility, and this structure, like so much else in Uxmal, was probably used for ceremonies to bring rain. Inside is a sunny courtyard, and from the north side is a fine view of the ball court, with

the Nunnery Quadrangle and the Pyramid of the Magician beyond.

The Great Pyramid

Behind the Governor's Palace is the Great Pyramid, a more typical Maya pyramid, standing 30 meters (98 feet) on a series of terraces. You can see that it predates the Governor's Palace, as the latter's platform partially overlaps the pyramid's northeast corner. At the top—you can still climb this one—a small temple contains an impressively large but partially buried Chaac mask. The temple's exterior is adorned with latticework and, most notably, panels depicting macaws.

Dovecote

Beside the Great Pyramid is the part of Uxmal known as the Dovecote. The name derives from the patchwork of niches in the roof comb of the complex's most prominent feature, a high wall separating two of the three large plazas identified here. In addition to its ornate roof comb, the wall contains a beautiful vaulted arch and several vaulted rooms on its lower level. Its facade once had large figures molded from stucco; they've long since been destroyed or removed, but several protruding stone struts remain.

Sound and Light Show

Every evening at 7pm in the winter (Oct.-Apr.) and at 8pm in the summer (May-Sept.) there's a sound and light show overlooking the Nunnery Quadrangle. Different structures are lit up as an accompaniment to the Maya lore that is played over loudspeakers (Spanish only). The program itself is a bit slow but it's worth checking out, if only to be at this remarkable archaeological site at night, with the looming ancient stone structures and the occasional flash of lightning in the distance. You can't help but cast your mind back to ancient times, to imagine living in this mysterious city

on a warm night gazing at the stars, the same ones we see today.

Practicalities

The ruins and museum are open 8am-5pm daily; the sound and light show takes place at 7pm in the winter (Oct.-Apr.) and at 8pm in the summer (May-Sept.). Admission to the ruins is US$11.75; tickets to the sound and light show cost an additional US$5. Parking is US$1.50 per car; use of a video camera is US$2.25.

Guides to the ruins charge fixed prices and can be hired at the entrance. Tours last around 90 minutes and cost US$40 in Spanish or US$44 for English, Italian, French, or German (8 people maximum on any tour).

In addition to the museum and gift shops, the visitors center has an ATM, restaurant, snack bar, and postal drop box.

Food and Accommodations

Two large upper-end hotels (each with a restaurant) are near the entrance of Uxmal. Smaller and more affordable lodging and food can be had in the nearby towns of Santa Elena, Ticul, and Oxkutzcab.

Hacienda Uxmal (Carr. Mérida-Campeche Km 78, toll-free Mex. tel. 800/719-5465, toll-free U.S. tel. 877/240-5864, www.mayaland.com, US$108-151 s/d with a/c, US$369-503 suite with a/c) was the residence of the archaeologists that first excavated Uxmal. Today, it is a colonial-style hotel with manicured grounds, a restaurant, and a nice pool. Rooms are classically Yucatecan, with Talavera tile floors, marble bathrooms, heavy carved furniture, and ironwork beds. Past guests include Queen Elizabeth, the Shah of Iran, and Jackie O.

Directly across from the ruins is **The Lodge at Uxmal** (Carr. Mérida-Campeche Km 78, toll-free Mex. tel. 800/719-5465, toll-free U.S. tel. 877/240-5864, www.mayaland.com, US$217-550 s/d with a/c). It's a comfortable boutique hotel with a great location, but nightly rates are simply overpriced for the goods. Check the website for discounts or

---

1: Uxmal's Great Pyramid; **2:** Nunnery Quadrangle archway and the Governor's Palace hope there's a tour group at Hacienda Uxmal, when independent travelers get free upgrades to this location.

Just steps from Uxmal's entrance, **Coole Chepa Chi** (The Lodge at Uxmal, tel. 997/976-2030, 7am-10pm daily, US$12-25) is an open-air restaurant perfect for a post-ruins or pre-sound-and-light-show meal. The kitchen serves up a decent variety of dishes—from Mexican to Italian to sandwiches and salads. If you're really hungry, opt for the Yucatecan buffet (US$25).

CHOCO STORY UXMAL

Across from Uxmal, **Choco Story Uxmal** (Hwy. 261 Km 78, tel. 999/289-9914, www.choco-storymexico.com, 9am-7:30pm daily, US$7 adult, US$3.50 child 6-12) pulls back the curtain on chocolate, its role in Maya culture, and its development in the world market. It's set in a series of thatch-roofed huts and organized by historical periods. Visitors are treated to a Maya ritual offering to the rain god, Chaac, as well as a chocolate-making demonstration. (There's also a small animal rescue with jaguars and spider monkeys.) Signage is in English and Spanish. A small café sells panino sandwiches and—surprise!—chocolate, though not as many decadent treats as one might hope.

KABAH ARCHAEOLOGICAL ZONE

Kabah (8am-5pm daily, US$2.50) is located 22 kilometers (13.7 miles) southeast of Uxmal, on the other side of the small town of Santa Elena. Kabah's major temples were constructed in AD 850-900, though the area was probably first settled as far back as 300 BC-AD 250. The site spans many square kilometers, though only the ceremonial center has been cleared and restored. The highway cuts right through the ancient city, so there are ruins on either side. The main points of interest are on the east side of the road, where the ticket booth is located.

Codz Poop

From the entrance, walk parallel to the road to the southernmost structure. A short but very steep staircase leads to a raised platform and to Codz Poop, Kabah's most ornate building and one of the most arresting structures on the Puuc Route. Dedicated to the rain god, Chaac, and measuring nearly 45 meters (148 feet) long and 6 meters (19.7 feet) high, the temple's entire west facade is covered in some 250 Chaac masks, with the typical googly eyes and long hooked nose. Even the steps into the doorways are modified Chaac noses. Looking closely, you can see how each mask is made of the same set of pieces, and can imagine a Maya manufacturing line, with carvers churning out scores of eyelids, pupils, and teeth, and others assembling the masks on the temple.

The rear side of Codz Poop is nearly as impressive, with huge stucco figures set against a latticework frieze. Be sure to peek at the side panels of the main door, where impressive bas-reliefs depict battle scenes.

Palacio and Temple of the Columns

A path from Codz Poop leads to the raised platform where the Palacio (Palace) stands. A broken set of stairs goes to the top, though climbing it is not allowed. The Palacio displays more typical Puuc architecture, with ornate friezes atop unadorned lower facades.

Around the northern edge of the Palacio, a path leads through the trees to the mildly interesting Temple of the Columns. The name says it all, as the facade is covered in attached decorative columns. Two *chultúnes* that used to collect and store water flank the path just as you reach the temple—be careful not to tumble in! Pottery, *metates* (grinding stones), and hearths from a kitchen used to prepare food for the city's rulers were recently discovered here.

Kabah Archaeological Zone

To Santa Elena,
✚ *UXMAL ARCHAEOLOGICAL ZONE,*
and Mérida

SACBÉ

GREAT PYRAMID

ARCH OF KABAH

To Temple of
the Columns

TICKETS AND
RESTROOMS

P

PALACIO

0   50 yds

0   50 m

CODZ POOP

261

To Sayil Archaeological Zone,
Grutas de Loltún, and Campeche

© MOON.COM

Arch of Kabah and Great Pyramid

On the other side of the road (past the parking lot), a path leads 200 meters (656 feet) to the impressive Arch of Kabah. The six-meter-high (19.7-foot) arch dates to AD 670-770 and marked one end of a grand *sacbé*, or raised stone road, that extended 30 kilometers (19 miles) from Kabah to Uxmal and is still traceable today. For the first 15 kilometers (9.3 miles), from Kabah to the settlement of Nohpat, the road runs perfectly straight, before veering slightly to reach Uxmal. North of the path leading to the arch is the Great Pyramid, the largest structure in Kabah. Yet to be excavated and off-limits to climbing, it remains an impressively huge mound covered in grass and trees.

SAYIL ARCHAEOLOGICAL ZONE

Sayil (8am-5pm daily, US$2.50) is even more spread out than Kabah, but the long, leafy paths between monuments are part of the pleasure of visiting this site. Archaeologists believe the area was settled as early as the 2nd or 3rd century AD, though virtually all of its major structures were built in the short period between the end of the 8th century and middle of the 10th. Sayil's population most likely peaked at around 10,000 people, with another 7,000 living in outlying areas.

Sayil is located just seven kilometers (4.3 miles) from Kabah; coming from Kabah on Highway 261, look for the well-marked left-hand turnoff.

Gran Palacio

The path from the parking and ticket area leads past several deeply decayed stelae to the Great Palace, also called Palacio Norte. The structure contains more than 90 rooms and may have housed up to 350 people. Although the palace appears to be three stories, in fact each level is supported by a core of piled stone, as opposed to the story below it—an example of how Maya architects were accomplished illusionists. Visitors aren't allowed to climb to the upper levels, but you can still appreciate the craftsmanship of the palace's 2nd-floor frieze; most notable are curious "Diving Gods" over the doorways, their upturned legs easily discerned. Tulum and Cobá have similar figures, which may represent the God of Maize (God E, to archaeologists). The corners have imposing Chaac masks, and decorative columns help unify the nearly 60-meter-long (197-foot) building.

El Mirador

A path leads south from the palace to El Mirador (The Lookout), a small temple. Built atop a crumbling pyramid, the structure has five rooms and a high-reaching roof comb. Though substantially collapsed, the structure is still impressive for its height and the complexity of its comb.

Sayil Archaeological Zone

To Kabah Archaeological Zone, Santa Elena, and ✈UXMAL ARCHAEOLOGICAL ZONE

TICKETS AND RESTROOMS
STELA 4
STELA 3
P
CHULTÚN
GRAN PALACIO
To Labná Archaeological Zone and Grutas de Loltún

TEMPLE OF THE HIEROGLYPHIC JAMBS
EL MIRADOR
YUM KEEP

0   200 yds
0   200 m

PALACIO SUR
BALL COURT

© MOON.COM

Yum Keep

Continuing another 50 meters (164 feet) past El Mirador, the path leads to Yum Keep, or the Stela of the Phallus. Kabah's spiritual leaders, like those of Uxmal and other cities, were obsessed with the phallus. Here, a rather poorly executed stone panel depicts an ancient Dirk Diggler, his face and hands still partly visible, and an enormous penis hanging to his knees.

Other Structures

Sayil's remaining structures aren't terribly impressive, but the walk there, with sunlight filtering through the foliage overhead, is rewarding. To see them, follow the path that forks off the main one between the Palacio and El Mirador. First, you'll come upon the

Temple of the Hieroglyphic Jambs, which is not nearly as interesting as its name might suggest. The structure is literally buried in the forest floor, with only the roof and a small portion of the carved doorways visible. The path continues 500 meters (0.3 mile) to the much-decayed Palacio Sur, with columns, broken Chaac masks, and other figures discernable on the southern frieze. Beside the complex is Sayil's ball court, also in significant disrepair.

XLAPAK ARCHAEOLOGICAL ZONE

Xlapak (8am-5pm daily, free) is the smallest of the Puuc Route ruins, a Late Classic site that may have originally been part of nearby Labná. Because it has just one restored building, organized tours and independent travelers often skip Xlapak to have more time at the larger sites. That said, Xlapak's lone structure is an attractive one, with ornate facades on both sides and some very well-preserved Chaac masks. The path through the site is well maintained and shady too—a good place to spot birds and other wildlife.

LABNÁ ARCHAEOLOGICAL ZONE

Labná (8am-5pm daily, US$2.50) is a favorite of the four smaller Puuc ruins. Rising to prominence in the Classic period, Labná likely had a peak population of 3,000-plus residents, judging from the numerous *chultúnes* (underground water cisterns) found at the site—more than 60 at last count. Like so many Classic period cities, the apex of its development—around AD 600-750—was followed in short order by abrupt collapse and abandonment in the 9th century.

El Palacio

Labná's impressive main palace is the first structure you come to after passing through the ticket area. It underwent at least 12 different constructions and has 67 rooms distributed over two main levels and seven patios. The palace stretches 135 meters (443 feet)

and stands on an even larger artificial platform. The west end (left, as you face it) likely housed Labná's ruling family, while the east side contained *metates* (stones used for grinding corn) and was therefore most likely used by their servants.

Take time to appreciate the palace's fantastic frieze. Many familiar elements are especially embellished here: The noses and eyes of the Chaac masks are turned upward as if peering into the sky, and the latticework is more complex than simple X-patterns seen elsewhere. On one corner, right of the central stairs, a human face can be seen emerging from the mouth of a feathered snake. It seems to have been a late modification: Notice how the hooked nose of the prior mask was turned around to make room for the snake's gaping mouth. Some argue the presence of the plumed snake—shown here "giving birth" to the man emerging from

Labná Archaeological Zone

its mouth—suggests strong influence from central Mexico, where the Quetzalcoatl (aka Kukulcán, the feathered snake) was widely worshipped.

Arch of Labná

From the Palacio, a *sacbé* (raised road) leads across a plaza of high flowing grass to the south side of the site and its most famous structure, the Arch of Labná. It's an exquisitely constructed portal vault, with a smooth elliptical ceiling, forming a spacious three-by-six-meter (10-by-20-foot) passageway—one of the largest and finest arches known in the Maya world. In its heyday, the arch most likely served as an elegant passageway between residential and administrative structures, both reserved for Labná's elite. Both sides of the arch are decorated, one with deep-relief spirals and checkerboard patterns (associated with clouds and rain) and the other with two *na,* or thatched Maya huts. The doors of the huts were used as niches, probably to display important figures, and red and blue paint is still visible there. Remarkably, only the arch's stairs and the roof comb required significant restoration. The rest has stood, as is, for over a thousand years.

El Mirador

Opposite the arch, a squat temple sits at the peak of a high, steep pile of rocks. Atop the temple, an impressive roof comb soars even higher. This is El Mirador, the building that explorer John Lloyd Stephens called "the most curious and extraordinary structure" he'd seen in his travels through the Maya world. Stone struts suggest the roof comb was once adorned with a complex array of stucco figures, including a huge statue over the center door. Stephens reported only "scattered arms and legs" remained at his visit, more than a century and a half ago; today only the legs of a single figure remain.

GRUTAS DE LOLTÚN

Seven kilometers (4.3 miles) southwest of Oxkutzcab, the **Loltún caves** are the largest known caves in Yucatán. This vast underground network served ancient people as a source of water and pottery clay—ceramics and carved reliefs dating from 1600 BC have been discovered here. It eventually developed into an important pilgrimage and ceremonial space for Maya (caves typically represented fertility and the entrance to Xibalba, the underworld). Researchers working in Loltún also uncovered bones belonging to mastodons and

Labná's arch is one of the best-preserved arches in the Maya world.

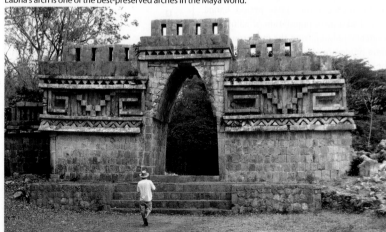

other extinct mammals that date to 9000 BC. While some argue that early hunters dragged these animals to the caves, it has yet to be proven. For now, stone tools dating to 5000-3000 BC mark the earliest sign of humans in Loltún.

Visiting the Caves

A route through the caverns is illuminated with colored lights, which are turned on as groups descend into the site. Loltún means "stone flower" in Maya, and you'll see many carvings of small flowers. One of the more intriguing sights is dozens of handprints on the cavern walls, either in silhouette or negative outline, whose meaning remains a mystery. Early Maya also placed stone cisterns (*chultúnes*) under the dripping stalactites to catch "virgin water," important in ceremonies honoring Chaac, the rain god. The most important archaeological find here is the relief dubbed The Warrior, which is carved on a rock face just outside the Nahkab entrance to Loltún. Strangely, it appears to follow the Izapan style of Kaminaljuyú, the enormous Preclassic city near Guatemala City. Toward the end of the hour-long tour, you come to an opening in the roof of an enormous two-story-high cavern. The sun pours into the room, creating shafts of golden light. The gnarled trunk of a towering tree grows from the floor of the cave, reaching hundreds of feet up through the sunny opening, and flocks of birds twitter and flit in and around the leafy vines that dangle freely into the immense chamber from above.

Practicalities

Wear good walking shoes in the caves. For the most part it's an easy one-kilometer (0.6-mile) walk; however, it's dark and damp, and in a few places the paths between chambers are steep, rocky, and slippery.

For safety reasons, you may only enter the cave with a guide. Tours are at 9:30am, 11am, 12:30pm, 2pm, 3pm, and 4pm, and last about 80 minutes. Admission is US$6.25 and parking US$1; budget another US$2 per person for a tip. Tours are in English or Spanish—let the ticket seller know which language you prefer so you're paired with the right guide.

From Oxkutzcab, it's best to take a taxi (US$6) and agree on a return pickup time, as there's not much traffic back from the site. You also can take a *combi* (US$1) from the market to Loltún, though the return times are unpredictable.

TICUL

Northeast of Santa Elena, the town of Ticul is a pottery and shoemaking center. If you're on a tight budget, Ticul is a good place to base yourself if you think you'll want more than one day along the Puuc Route. You'll avoid the long trip back to Mérida after the first day of ruins and can get an early start the next day. Note that many businesses close 2pm-5pm.

Sights

Ticul's elaborate, high-domed 18th-century church, **Templo de San Antonio de Padua** (Calle 25A btwn Calles 24 and 26), has a beautiful stained glass window over an arched doorway framed by simple columns. Other than those flourishes, the structure possesses the unadorned austerity typical of so many Franciscan churches in this region. Next to it is a Franciscan monastery built 200 years earlier. Both are on the central plaza—impossible to miss.

Galería de Arte Juanita Canché de Manzanero (central plaza, tel. 997/972-0701, times vary) is a modest gallery with temporary art exhibits and occasional music or dance performances. Opening hours depend mostly on the offerings—look for the schedule on the front door. It is named for the mother of famed Mexican crooner Armando Manzanero, who wrote and performed hundreds of songs, including "Somos Novios" and "Voy a Apagar la Luz." Manzanero was born in Mérida, but his mother is a native of Ticul.

Shopping

The hills and riverbeds around Ticul have famous red clay, and the town has long

Ticul

been known for its pottery. By far, the most highly regarded studio here is **Arte Maya de Ticul** (Calle 23 btwn Calles 46 and 46-A, tel. 997/133-1633, www.artemaya.net, 8am-8pm daily), on the highway toward Muna. The family-run studio was founded by the late Wilbert González and now operates as an art school and pottery store. The shop specializes in high-quality reproductions of classic Maya art, using laboriously prepared clay and all-natural paint made from local soils and minerals. The artists typically model their work from photographs of pieces found during archaeological excavations—the finished products are by no means cheap, but they are remarkable in their faithfulness to the originals. Short tours (in Spanish) are given on request, and if someone is working, you are usually welcome to watch.

Food

Facing the central plaza, **La Carmelita** (Calle 23 at Calle 26, tel. 997/972-0515, 9:30am-6pm Tues.-Thurs., US$3-5) is a mom-and-pop restaurant serving good no-frills Yucatecan dishes to a loyal clientele. The fish plates and shrimp cocktails are particularly popular, and with good reason—they're fresh and tasty, a rarity this far from the coast.

Pizzería La Gondola (Calle 23 at Calle 26-A, tel. 997/972-0112, 8am-1pm and 5:30pm-midnight daily, US$4-8) may have somewhat reluctant service, but the pizza and pasta dishes are well prepared and make for a good alternative to Mexican food.

Ticul's *mercado* (Calle 21 btwn Calles 28 and 30, 6am-2pm and 5:30pm-9pm daily) has fresh fruits, vegetables, and cheap lunch stands.

Accommodations

Hotel San Antonio (Calle 25-A at Calle 26, tel. 997/972-1893, hotelsan-antonioticul@hotmail.com, US$14 s with a/c, US$17-25 d with a/c, US$28-33 suite with a/c) is basic but comfortable enough for a night or two. Rooms are located in two separate buildings. All have cable TV and in-room phones. Suites are larger and have updated amenities; standards are bare-bones but have Juliet balconies. Parking is available.

Hotel Plaza (Calle 23 btwn Calles 26 and 26-A, tel. 997/972-0484, www.hotelplazayucatan.com, US$21 s with a/c, US$28 d with a/c), has simple, stark rooms that open onto a breezy interior courtyard with 70s-style decor. Beds are decent and bathrooms are clean. Secure parking is available, though it's a few blocks away.

Information and Services

For a 24-hour pharmacy, head to the well-stocked **YZA Farmacia** (Calle 23 at Calle 28, tel. 997/972-1080). The **police station** (tel. 997/972-0210, 24 hours) is on the central plaza.

Also on the central plaza, **Banamex** (Calle 26 btwn Calles 23 and 24, 9am-4pm Mon.-Fri.) and **HSBC** (Calle 23 at Calle 24-A, 9am-5pm Mon.-Fri.) have 24-hour ATMs; Banamex exchanges dollars and euros too. The **post office** (Calle 23 at Calle 26, 8am-4pm Mon.-Fri., 8am-noon Sat.) is near the entrance to the Palacio Municipal.

Getting There and Around

Ticul's **bus terminal** (tel. 997/972-0162) and *colectivo* **terminal** sit across the street from each other on Calle 24 behind the central plaza. A number of smaller terminals nearby have *colectivo* service to nearby towns.

There's second-class bus service to Mérida (US$5.75, 1.5 hours, hourly 4am-1am), though *colectivos* (US$2.50, 1.5 hours, 4am-8pm) are cheaper and typically leave every 30 minutes or as soon as they're full (whichever comes first). Tickets for both have numbered seats.

Colectivos to nearby villages use separate terminals, including to Santa Elena (US$0.75, 20 minutes, board on Calle 30 btwn Calles 25 and 25-A), Muna (US$1, 15 minutes, board on Calle 23 btwn Calles 26-A and 28), and Oxkutzcab (US$1, 30 minutes, board on Calle 25-A btwn Calles 24 and 26). *Colectivos* leave whenever they fill up, typically every 15-30 minutes, roughly 6am-8pm.

You also can get from town to town quite affordably by taxi, and that is recommended at night when *colectivo* service is reduced or nil. A taxi from Ticul to Santa Elena, for example, costs US$4.

SANTA ELENA

This peaceful community lies smack-dab in the middle of the Puuc Route, just 16 kilometers (9.9 miles) southeast of Uxmal and seven kilometers (4.3 miles) north of Kabah, the first of the smaller sites. It's a pleasant and convenient base for exploring the entire region, with three fine lodging options, a couple of good restaurants, and an impressive church.

Sights

Long before reaching Santa Elena, the town's imposing **Iglesia de San Mateo** (10am-1pm and 4pm-8pm daily) rises like a misplaced airplane hangar on a distant hilltop. (Some say it was built atop a Maya ruin—not at all uncommon—but you can see from the town's central plaza that it's simply a rocky hill.) A huge, pinkish stone box standing 35 meters (115 feet) high, 50 meters (164 feet) long, and 20 meters (66 feet) wide, the church has almost no exterior adornment. The cavernous nave is also austere, with thick white walls and wood pews. The exceptions are the ornate wooden altar and large wooden *retablos* (hand-carved religious scenes depicted in ornate boxes) along the walls. Be sure to ask the church attendant (he's usually hanging out in the nave) to let you up to the roof, reached via a rickety spiral staircase. Near the top is the organ platform (sans organ) with a dizzying view down into the nave. The roof affords an awesome vista of the surrounding countryside.

A small **museum** (9am-5pm daily, US$0.25) alongside the church has detailed and somewhat disturbing displays of the mummified remains of four children who died in the church floor in the 1800s and were buried in the church floor (a common practice) and uncovered during renovations in 1980. Twelve bodies were discovered; five were reburied, three were taken by authorities and never returned, and four are displayed in glass cases here. The tiny corpses may have been children of German transplants, brought during the French occupation, who died (or were killed) during the Caste War. The museum also has a replica Maya tomb under glass in the floor of the same room. It shows a skeleton and common burial items such as a stone axe and ceramic dishes, thought to be needed in the next world. Photos, a painted Maya doorway, a few pre-Hispanic and colonial items, and henequen-related information round out the displays. Tours in English and Spanish are offered.

Food

In the evening, visitors inevitably migrate to ★ **The Pickled Onion** (Hwy. 261 at Ticul road, cell tel. 997/111-7922, www. thepickledonionyucatan.com, 7:30am-8:30pm daily, US$4-7), a labor of love by a hospitable English-Canadian expat. Enjoy Yucatecan faves like melt-in-your-mouth *poc-chuc;* try the juicy meatballs with almonds, raisins, and mint; or order a box lunch to take ruin-hopping—a great idea, as there are so few places to eat along the Puuc Route.

On the main road to the ruins, **Restaurant El Chac-Mool** (Calle 18 No. 211-B, tel. 997/978-5117, 9am-10pm daily, US$4-7) serves basic Yucatecan specialties, sandwiches, and a smattering of vegetarian options. The food is unremarkable—sometimes reheated, sometimes freshly made—but it's reliable. Service is friendly but sluggish.

Accommodations

★ **The Pickled Onion** (Hwy. 261 at Ticul road, cell tel. 997/111-7922, www. thepickledonionyucatan.com, US$50-70 s/d) has eight freestanding *palapa*-roofed units with outdoor sitting areas, mosaic-tiled bathrooms, mini fridges, coffee makers, and well-screened windows. There's a refreshing pool and an outdoor hammock lounge for relaxing after a day of ruin-hopping. A hearty continental breakfast is served on a leafy patio reserved for guests only, while the on-site restaurant is popular with visitors from beyond the hotel walls.

The Flycatcher Inn (southern end of town, off Hwy. 261, tel. 997/978-5350, www. flycatcherinn.com, US$80-96 s/d with a/c) is a tranquil bed-and-breakfast set on several hectares of lush tropical forest. Guest rooms have cheerful Mexican folk art, handmade ironwork furniture, and sunny patios. There's also a pool and a small Maya ruin dating to AD 1000. See it, along with myriad trees, butterflies, and birds, along a short nature trail. Children age six and over only.

Set on seven hectares (17 acres) of low forest, **La Nueva Altia** (Hwy. 261 Km 159, cell tel. 998/106-6822, www.nuevaaltia.com, US$76 s/d) has twelve two-story bungalows. Units are simple but comfortable with white-washed walls, good beds, and large terraces. There's a tiny pool and an open-air dining area where breakfast is served. There's a large screened-in *palapa* too, used for yoga, meditation, and other classes and workshops.

Information and Services

There is almost nothing in the way of traveler services in this town; it's still very much a small Yucatecan village despite the popularity of the area. **The Pickled Onion** (Hwy. 261 at Ticul road, cell tel. 997/111-7922, 7:30am-8:30pm daily) has Wi-Fi available for free to its patrons as do the other listed hotels. The nearest **ATMs** are at the Uxmal ruins and in Ticul.

Getting There and Around

Like almost everywhere on the Puuc Route, Santa Elena is easiest to reach and negotiate if you have a car. That said, many people do visit by bus and do just fine. Second-class buses between Campeche and Mérida pass in both directions on Highway 261, a block from the Flycatcher Inn and right in front of The Pickled Onion, Sacbe Boutique Inn, and La Nueva Altia.

Buses to Campeche (US$7, 3 hours) and Mérida (US$3.50, 1.5 hours) pass through Santa Elena approximately every two to three hours, 6am-8pm. Lodgings have the most current schedules. Buses to Mérida can drop you off at Uxmal, a 20-minute trip (US$1).

All the Santa Elena hotels listed are along Highway 261, on the southern outskirts of town. Headed south from Uxmal, do not enter Santa Elena proper; instead, continue on the highway 1-2 kilometers (0.6-1.2 miles) and look for the hotel signs. From Ticul, cut through town to the highway—the Flycatcher Inn is directly across the road, The Pickled Onion is at the junction, and La Nueva Altia is to the left about a kilometer (0.6 mile) away. The nearest **gas stations** are in Ticul and Muna, though you can buy small amounts of gas from private homes in Santa Elena; ask at your hotel for one close by.

OXKUTZCAB

Oxkutzcab is conveniently located near the Loltún caves and the Puuc Route. It's a small village that is surrounded by extremely fertile land. Known as *La Huerta de Yucatán* (The Orchard of Yucatán), you'll see orange groves alongside high, healthy fields of corn, bananas, and coconut palms as you arrive. Nearby, there's also a huge citrus processing plant that employs many area residents.

Sights and Events

Oxkutzcab's **central plaza** is bordered by a large Franciscan church, the **Templo y Ex-Convento de San Francisco,** and an attractive arched building that holds municipal offices. The plaza itself has concrete benches, a gazebo, and lots of shade trees.

Facing the town church, **Mercado 20 de Noviembre** (6am-3pm daily, food stalls open 6am-9pm Mon.-Fri. and 6am-3pm Sat.-Sun.) is worth exploring. A long, colorful **mural** mirrors the scene just below it, with indigenous women sitting in front of huge piles of fruit and packing boxes stacked in every free

breakfast time at The Pickled Onion, just outside Santa Elena

Fray Diego de Landa

Just north of Oxkutzcab, the town of Maní has a quiet, peaceful atmosphere that belies a wrenching history. It was here, in 1562, that Friar Diego de Landa conducted a now-infamous *auto de fé*, in which he burned at least two dozen irreplaceable Maya codices and thousands of painted vases and other items, because he deemed them works of the devil. He accused numerous Maya religious leaders and laypeople of idolatry, and ordered them tortured, publicly humiliated, and imprisoned. The act was outrageous, even by Spanish colonial standards, and Landa was shipped back to Spain to face the Council of the Indies, the colonial authority, for conducting an illegal inquisition. He was eventually absolved—a panel of inspectors found he had broken no laws—but not before Landa came to regret his act, at least somewhat. Confined to a convent awaiting judgment, he set about writing down all he could remember about the Maya.

Countless Maya codices were destroyed in front of Maní's church.

It was no minor undertaking: Landa spoke Yucatec Maya fluently and had lived, traveled, and preached throughout the Yucatán for 13 years before his expulsion. In all, Landa spent close to a decade completing *An Account of the Things of Yucatán*. He returned to Mérida in 1571 as the newly appointed Bishop of Yucatán, and died there in 1579. Landa's manuscript was largely forgotten until being rediscovered in 1863. Among other things, the manuscript contains a crude alphabet (or more precisely, a syllabary), which has proved invaluable to the modern-day decoding of the Maya hieroglyphics. Ironically, the very man who destroyed so much of the Maya's written history also provided the key for future researchers to unlock what remained.

space. Most memorable is the incredible assortment of citrus fruits, including oranges, limes, grapefruit, bright pink *pitayas,* and tiny yellow *nanzim.* The best market days are Tuesday, Thursday, and Sunday.

Leonardo Paz is the accomplished painter, muralist, and Oxkutzcab native son who created the mural in the market as well as several smaller works around town. In the plaza, look on the back side of the gazebo to see paintings depicting the Caste War and the infamous *auto de fé,* when in 1562 Franciscan priest Fray Diego de Landa burned scores of irreplaceable Maya codices and sculptures.

Oxkutzcab's two-week **Orange Festival** is celebrated in late October or early November and is renowned throughout Yucatán. Definitely stop by if you are in the area, and be sure to make a hotel reservation

if you want to stay overnight during the festivities.

Food and Accommodations

Restaurante Labná (Calle 55 at Calle 44, tel. 997/975-0103, 7am-4pm Mon.-Sat., US$3-6) serves regional food in a simple, brightly decorated dining area. Menu items include Yucatecan-style chicken and pork plus Mexican standards such as quesadillas and grilled beef.

For more options, head to the **Mercado 20 de Noviembre** (6am-9pm Mon.-Fri., 6am-3pm Sat.-Sun., US$2-4), where several simple eateries serve Yucatecan specialties and fresh juices.

Hotel Puuc (Calle 55 at Calle 44, tel. 997/975-0103, www.oxkutzcab-hotelpuuc. com, US$17-22 s/d with fan, US$20-26 s/d with a/c, US$27 suite, US$31 suite with a/c) offers more than four dozen rooms, all spacious and squeaky clean, with modern amenities; suites even have king-size beds, mini fridges, and smart TVs. Set on a huge lot, there's plenty of parking and a large shaded pool. The friendly staff also is a good resource for area sights.

Information and Services

For meds, **Farmacia Yza** (Calle 51 at Calle 52, tel. 997/975-1600, 24 hrs daily) is behind the market. For cash, **Banamex** (Calle 50 btwn Calles 51 and 53, 9am-4pm Mon.-Fri.), on the central plaza, has an ATM and exchanges foreign currencies.

Getting There and Around

Oxkutzcab's **main bus terminal** (tel. 997/975-0308, Calle 51 at Calle 56) has second-class bus service to Mérida (US$3, 2 hours, hourly 5:30am-11pm), with stops along the way in Umán, Muna, and Ticul.

You can catch *colectivos* to Ticul (US$1.25, 30 minutes) every 10-15 minutes 6am-8:30pm daily, from the corner of Calles 51 and 54.

To get to the Loltún caves, flag down a *combi* outside Hotel Puuc (US$1) or take a taxi (US$6).

NORTHWEST OF THE PUUC ROUTE

Hacienda Yaxcopoil

Hacienda Yaxcopoil (Hwy. 261 Km 220, tel. 999/900-1193, www.yaxcopoil.com, 8am-6pm Mon.-Sat., 9am-3pm Sun., US$5) was one of dozens of huge henequen estates that dotted the Yucatán Peninsula. Built in the 17th century, Yaxcopoil (yawsh-ko-po-EEL) grew to encompass 11,000 hectares (27,181 acres), reaching its zenith during World War I, when rope made from the thorny, fibrous henequen plant was in great demand. A visit to the hacienda today leaves a bit to be desired—consistent guide service or written descriptions, mostly—but you can stroll through the grand old rooms, where antique furniture, old photos, and original tile floors give a sense of

the life the *patrones* (landowners) enjoyed. You can even spend the night in the simple guesthouse (US$135 s/d/t/q with a/c), including breakfast and dinner. But don't leave without visiting the machine room out back, which you may have to ask to be unlocked. There, huge machinery once used to extract fiber from the henequen leaves and bind it into bales still stands. The high brick chimney is from the days of steam power (notice the narrow tubes running underfoot), while the massive diesel engine was added in 1913 and used until the hacienda stopped production in 1984.

Admission to Yaxcopoil is a bit much considering how little formal information there is, but if you speak any Spanish, definitely chat up whoever is there—many staffers' parents or grandparents worked the hacienda, and most have interesting stories to share. The history of henequen production—the grandeur of the estates, the cruel exploitation of indigenous workers, the political and economic influence wielded by hacienda owners—is as fascinating as it is little understood.

Hacienda San Pedro Ochil

Best visited for a meal before or after a day trip from Mérida, the terrace restaurant at 17th-century **Hacienda San Pedro Ochil** (Hwy. 261 Km 176.5, tel. 999/924-7465, www.haciendaochil.com, 10am-6pm daily, US$7-14) serves traditional Yucatecan dishes, including an excellent *cochinita pibil* (marinated pork). You can wander the decaying old hacienda grounds, including the machine shop and smokestack, and even take a ride on the tracks that were once used to cart sisal. There's a cenote too, but there's no swimming allowed in it; instead there are two small pools for a dip. There's also a museum with rotating exhibits. There's a US$2 admission if you want to poke around or swim without eating.

Muna

This small town is home to many of the people who work at or around the Uxmal archaeological site. For travelers, there's not much reason to stop, and now that the highway loops around it, many people don't make it into town. But Muna does have a 17th-century Franciscan church—**Templo de la Virgen de la Asunción**—that's notable for its facade, which is adorned with lacy belfries that glow a mellow gold in the late afternoon. People are friendly, and the shady plaza has a number of fruit stands. This is also a good place to fill your gas tank (the **Pemex gas station** is on the central plaza).

Oxkintok Archaeological Zone
Though seldom visited, **Oxkintok** (8am-5pm daily, US$2.75) is a large, well-maintained site that's both scenic and archaeologically significant, with palaces, temples, and plazas scattered amid trees and high grass. Though not awe-inspiring like other sites, it's the sort of place that makes spending an extra day or two on the Puuc Route so rewarding, especially combined with a visit to the nearby Calcehtok caves.

Oxkintok (Three Stone Suns) is notable for having a very early Long Count date, found on a stone lintel, corresponding to the year AD 475; evidence suggests the site was occupied as early as the 3rd century BC. It was a powerful, and at times dominant, commercial center during much of the Classic period, before experiencing a rapid and mysterious decline in the 9th century—the latest dated inscription is from AD 859.

Oxkintok's most famous feature, however, is a small structure known as **Tzat tun tzat,** or El Laberinto (The Labyrinth). Located behind the cluster of structures to your right as you enter the site, and unique in Maya construction, Tzat tun tzat has more than a dozen chambers interwoven over three levels and connected by narrow tunnels, stairways, gates, and vaulted passages. Archaeologists are unsure of the building's exact significance, though it seems likely to have been related to myths of journeying from Earth to the lower and upper worlds, and may have been used as a tomb or for symbolic rituals. Unfortunately, visitors are no longer permitted to enter the

structure, so you have to forge your own theories from outside.

To the left of the entrance is a larger cluster of structures called **Ah Canul,** where a number of columns, incised with human forms, can be seen in various states of disrepair. The figures represent gods, warriors, and local elite, and may have been a precursor to warrior columns found in sites like Chichén Itzá and Mayapán.

Oxkintok has undergone sporadic exploration and investigation, including visits by Stephens and Catherwood in 1842 and later by pioneering Mayanist Tatiana Proskouriakoff (who studied the warrior columns). More recent research has focused on the remains of the site's surprisingly extensive urban center, covering as much as eight square kilometers (3 square miles). Tombs have been found in a number of the structures, though many artifacts have been lost to looters.

To reach Oxkintok by car, follow the signs eastbound from Highway 180, or westbound on Highway 184. There's no regular public transport there, though you may be able to get a cab or motorcycle taxi from the towns of Maxcanú or Calcehtok. Consider combining a visit here with a tour of the Aktun Usil and Calcehtok Caves.

Grutas Aktun Usil
Located two kilometers (1.2 miles) south of Oxkintok ruins is the remarkable and little-visited **Aktun Usil Caves.** According to INAH (Mexico's National Institute of Anthropology and History), it was an ancient Maya ritual site, where calendars related to agricultural and societal cycles were created as early as AD 750. Today, visitors can tour its three main chambers with a guide. The first features a 12-meter-high (39-foot) ceiling with an impressive display of Maya hieroglyphs and cave paintings of turtles and frogs honoring Chaac, the god of rain. The second room has mammoth stalagmites and stalactites, *chultúnes* (natural stone cisterns used to collect water), rock carvings, and even stone masks wedged into crevices. The final

chamber is the smallest but, in some ways, the most human—several handprints, in silhouette, can be easily seen on the ceiling above, and fragments of bones, pottery, and stone phalluses are strewn on the cave floor below.

Aktun Usil is still considered sacred to the local Maya. Though visitors could access the cave on their own—it's relatively easy to clamber in, and there's natural light through several openings above—they must enter with a local guide. This ensures that certain customs are properly followed, such as asking the cave "permission" to enter and passing copal incense over visitors to purify them before entering. Tours typically cost US$30-55 (1-1.5 hours for up to 4 people). Victor Chim (cell tel. 997/113-3910) is a recommended bilingual local guide with extensive knowledge of the cave and the surrounding ruins; most official Oxkintok guides also can lead tours to the site.

Grutas de Calcehtok

Calcehtok Caves (aka Grutas de X'pukil, off Hwy. 184, tel. 999/262-7292, 8am-5pm daily) are part of the Yucatán's second-largest cave system (only Loltún is larger) and certainly among the most adventurous to visit. Up to four kilometers (2.5 miles) of the cave can be explored, during which you squeeze through narrow gaps, teeter along slippery pathways, and crawl and clamber through muddy passageways. Along the way are huge chambers— one with a 30-meter-high (99-foot) domed ceiling—filled with stalactites and stalagmites, and tiny rooms where archaeologists have found human bones, tools, and other remains of pre-Hispanic Maya ceremonies. There also are leftover shelters built by Maya who hid in these caves during the Caste War. Calcehtok's caves are definitely less commercialized than others—you don't need any technical experience, but be prepared to get dirty.

Guides typically wait for visitors at the crest of a short path leading from the parking lot toward the cave entrance. (If no one is there, it means they are with other visitors, and you can either wait or come back later. *Never* enter this or any other cave without a guide.) Various tours are available, ranging from one hour to several, depending on how deep into the cave you want to go. Prices vary accordingly but start at US$5 per hour per person (up to 4 people). Before going in, agree with the guide how long the tour will last and how far into the cave you will get. If you have a flashlight, bring it as a backup. Sneakers or hiking boots are best, although Tevas should be fine. Some visitors also wear dust masks to avoid possible infection from fungus on bat guano.

To get here, follow the signs on Highway 184 until you reach a turnoff that leads to a small parking lot.

RUTA DE LOS CONVENTOS

Located along Highway 18, the Ruta de los Conventos is a route dotted with interesting sights and notable colonial convents in small towns; all are easily reached by car and make for interesting stops between Mérida and the Puuc Route. Oxkutzcab and Ticul are the best towns to spend the night if you can't pack it all in on a day trip. Driving from the *periférico* in Mérida, follow signs for Kanasín. **Note:** Most churches are closed 1pm-4pm daily.

Acancéh Archaeological Zone

Meaning "the moan of the deer" in Maya, the ruins of **Acancéh** (8am-5pm daily, US$2.25) consist of two main areas: a large pyramid with a secondary temple in the center of the namesake town, and a second, somewhat smaller structure called **El Palacio de Estucos** (Palace of the Stuccos) a few blocks away. In reality, the majority of the remains of this ancient city are scattered throughout town; most are on private property—in backyards, under houses, and so on—and it is either impossible or impractical to excavate them. Still, archaeologists believe the area was settled as early as 300 BC but didn't reach its peak until AD 400-600. Curiously, Acancéh's structures show strong influences from Petén (northern Guatemala) as well as Teotihuacán in central Mexico, both quite distant.

As you drive through town, the **pyramid** is impossible to miss, facing a large dirt lot (Acancéh's central plaza, actually). A small kiosk at the corner serves as the ticket booth, and a guide may accompany you up the pyramid (no fee, but a small tip is appreciated). At the top, under a protective tin roof, are a series of large stucco masks; unfortunately, the actual faces are missing or significantly deteriorated. They surely depicted Maya gods, but archaeologists have been unable to identify most of them.

If you're driving, the guide will lead you to the **Palacio de los Estucos** on his bike. A large, complex palace, it has a blend of architectural styles, including, for example, both curved and squared corners. On the uppermost level is a long frieze of impressive stucco designs (hence the structure's name) in the shapes of birds, a ram, and a man-jaguar, among others. Be sure to look for the lintel of one of the top-level doorways, which is made of a deeply grooved *metate*, used for grinding corn. Too worn down for its original purpose, it was reused in the construction here. Not only resourceful, it lends a certain human touch to the structure.

★ Cenotes de Cuzamá

A tour of the **Cenotes de Cuzamá** (aka Chunkanán cenotes, no phone, 8am-4pm daily, US$20/trolley, up to 4 people) is a favorite outing from Mérida. When the henequen plantations were functioning, the harvest was stacked on *trukes*, small trolleys that were pulled by horses over long networks of lightweight rails. Here, local residents have put their trolleys back to use, outfitting the carts to hold four passengers and offering horse-drawn tours to three beautiful cenotes along the rail line. The trip to the cenotes is half the fun—there is only one set of rails and an unspoken etiquette as to which driver has to pull over, which entails unloading the passengers and hoisting the cart off the tracks before the other trolley clatters past. With a few starts and stops, you make it to the cenotes. The first, **Cenote Chacsinicche,** is the largest

and easiest to get into, with concrete stairs leading to a cavernous pool. The second two, **Cenotes Chan-Ucil** and **Bolonchoojol,** are more challenging—at both you have to negotiate a slippery ladder from the cavern roof down to the water. Wear Tevas or sneakers. The effort is worth it, however, for the sublime experience of swimming in the crystalline water with sunbeams and tree roots angling down through the roof. The whole trip is 18 kilometers (11 miles) round-trip and takes about three hours with a half-hour stop at each cenote. *Tábanos* (horseflies) are the only annoyance, buzzing around the horse and cart. They have a nasty bite, so be careful not to let one land on you.

In Cuzamá, **Sac Nicté** (tel. 999/923-7598, www.sacnictemx.blogspot.com, US$67 up to 4 people) is a compound of three Maya-style *palapa*-roofed *cabañas* that together have a kitchen, dining area, hot-water bathroom, and space for four hammocks, plus a pool. There are no beds. Authentic Maya meals can be delivered "fresh and smoky" to your door, and several guided tours—including a moonlight visit to the cenotes—can be arranged.

The entrance to the cenotes is in the village of Chunkanán, just over three kilometers (1.9 miles) from the larger town of Cuzamá. To get there by public transport, catch a Cuzamá-bound *colectivo* outside Mérida's Terminal Noreste (US$1.50, 1 hour, every 30-45 minutes 8am-8pm, last return bus at 7:15pm), then hop a *triciclo,* or bicycle taxi, to the cenotes (US$2 each way). **Note:** There are several competing cenote tours along the road with vendors trying to flag you down. To be sure you're at the right one, look for the big parking lot on the right-hand side of the road with *trukes* in sight. If confused, simply ask for the names the cenotes you'll visit to be sure you're at the right place.

Ruta Anillo de los Cenotes

Three kilometers (1.8 miles) west of Cuzamá is the **Ruta Anillo de los Cenotes** (Ring of the Cenotes Route, 8am-5pm daily, US$1.50-2 per cenote), a collection of ten cenotes found in and around the town of Homún. Little visited, they are a strikingly beautiful group, running the gamut from open-air sinkholes with turquoise water to crystal-clear pools deep inside caves. All are well signed and easy to find: three are located within town (Tza Ujun Kat, Santa Rosa, and San Antonio), and the rest sit side-by-side along a small unpaved road in the forest (Yaxchabaltun, 3 Oches, Santa María, Canunchen, Holcosom, Balmin, and Bal-Min). If you're driving your own car, follow the signs from the main road. Alternatively, hire a *mototaxi* (Calle 21 btwn Calles 10 and 12, tel. 999/905-9551, US$13-15, up to four people) to guide you to each cenote. Tours typically include your choice of five cenotes and last from three to six hours. Look for the *mototaxi* stand just off the main road, on the east side of town.

Grutas de Tzabnah

Located just outside of the village of Tecoh, the **Tzabnah caves** (9am-5pm daily, US$5) make for a worthwhile underground adventure if getting muddy and being in tight spaces isn't problematic for you. A 1.5-hour guided tour leads past ten crystalline underground cenotes, climbing steep sections and wriggling through small passages complete with limestone formations, stalagmites, and the occasional bat. The payoff is a 50-meter (164-foot) crawl to the last and largest cenote, which has beams of sunlight entering from two holes in the roof and makes for a refreshing swim. Guides can be found at the entrance to the cave. Headlamps and helmets are included in the cost; some guides also provide kneepads.

Hacienda Sotuta de Péon

A visit to the 19th-century **Hacienda Sotuta de Péon** (off Hwy. 184, tel. 999/941-6441, www.haciendaviva.com, tours 10am and 1pm daily, US$27.50) is a popular day trip from Mérida. The 2.5-hour tour of a working henequen plantation allows visitors to see the process from start to finish. Bilingual guides give an excellent crash course in the economic and social history of the region. Mule-drawn trolleys take visitors through the fields of "green gold," and there's a splendid and dramatically lit cenote cavern and large pool for swimming. There's also a good restaurant and luxurious *cabañas* if you want to spend the night (US$222-312 s/d with a/c). Though catering to groups, its proximity to town is a bonus.

By car, the hacienda is about 45 minutes from Mérida, leaving the city via Calle 42

Shafts of sunlight illuminate the clear water and craggy interior of a cenote in Cuzamá.

Mayapán Archaeological Zone

To Mérida

To Puuc Route

184

TICKETS AND RESTROOMS

STRUCTURE Q-62

TEMPLO DEL PESCADOR

TEMPLO DE LOS NICHOS PINTADOS

TEMPLO DE LOS GUERREROS

TEMPLO DE VENUS

OBSERVATORY

CASTILLO DE KUKULCÁN

CHAAC COMPLEX

WALL

0   50 yds
0   50 m

© MOON.COM

Sur, or 50 minutes via Highway 184 by way of Tecoh; both routes are well signed. If you don't have a car, the hacienda offers a US$53 per person package that includes admission and round-trip transportation.

Mayapán Archaeological Zone

Located about 65 kilometers (40 miles) northeast of Uxmal, **Mayapán** (8am-5pm daily, US$2.25) is thought by some to have been one of the most important cities in the pre-Hispanic Maya world, although you'd never know from the trickle of visitors the site gets nowadays. Mayapán is not on many tour itineraries, and independent travelers tend to skip it going to or from the "main" Puuc sites farther south. While not as grand as Uxmal or

Chichén Itzá, it rarely disappoints the people who do stop. Mayapán is a compact, immaculately maintained site with two primary pyramids, an observatory, a cenote, and excellent fresco paintings and stucco masks. It was founded around AD 1000 after the powerful Cocom dynasty left Chichén Itzá to establish the region's capital here. (Chichén Itzá was subsequently abandoned except as a place for religious worship and pilgrimages.) Mayapán dominated northern Yucatán until almost the mid-15th century, when it was abruptly abandoned, perhaps because of an internal revolt. The first indigenous people met by the Spanish newcomers still called themselves *maya uinic* (Maya men) in reference to their former capital, and it is from there that modern use of the word *Maya* emerged. Unfortunately, there are few explanatory plaques on-site.

Second-class buses from Mérida's Terminal Noreste pass the ruins' entrance in both directions (US$2.50, 1.5 hours, hourly 5:30am-8pm); take the bus headed to the town of Telchaquillo and let the driver know you'd like to get off at Mayapán ruins (not Mayapán town, which is in an entirely different place!).

Maní

The town of Maní is best known as the site of Fray Diego de Landa's egregious 1562 *auto de fé*, an inquisition that destroyed many of the most precious objects of Maya culture. Prior to that, it was the nucleus of the powerful Xiu dynasty, whose leader converted to Christianity and allied himself with the Spanish. Today, the buildings across from the church reveal some of the carved Maya stones repurposed and incorporated into their facades.

Built on the site of a Maya temple using many of the former building's stones, the beautiful 1549 **Ex-Convento de San Miguel**

Arcángel (9am-noon and 4pm-7pm Wed.-Sun.) is one of the oldest monasteries in the Yucatán. The church contains an intricate three-tiered *retablo* surrounded by frescoes, including one of Michael, the town's patron saint, vanquishing the devil, and another of the stigmata of St. Francis of Assisi. The grassy area in front of the church was where Fray de Landa's infamous burning of Maya codices and precious items took place.

★ **Restaurante El Príncipe Tutul-Xiu** (Calle 26 btwn Calles 25 and 27, tel. 997/978-4257, 11am-7pm daily, US$5-8) has a devoted following from around Yucatán that keeps it busy, especially on weekends. A series of connected *palapas* with basketry lighting and a profusion of Maya-themed stone decor are the backdrop for the tender and delectable *pocchuc* that keeps customers coming. Servings are ample and come with *cebollas asadas* (grilled onions), *frijol colado* (spicy black bean sauce), and handmade tortillas.

Colectivos to Oxkutzcab (US$0.50, 15 minutes) depart from the corner of Calles 26 and 25, and there are hourly local buses to Merida (US$3, 2 hours).

The Chenes Region

The Maya of the Chenes region (today, central Campeche) chose a decidedly hostile location to found their cities. Hot and dry conditions, common throughout the Yucatán Peninsula, are especially persistent here. Worse, the water table is quite low—whereas other Maya relied on cenotes to provide fresh water, residents here had to venture deep into caves in search of water. (In fact, the word *chen* is Yucatec Maya for "well," and modern-day communities like Hopelchén and Bolonchén are named, in part, for the well around which they were originally founded.) Yet the Chenes Maya thrived, not only founding numerous magnificent cities, but devising innovative ways to collect and store water. They also created an ornate architectural style that quickly

spread across the peninsula; Chenes "monster mouth" facades, which turn the exterior wall of a building into the fantastic face of a deity, are among the most recognizable features in Maya archaeological sites.

Chenes sites are no easier to visit today than they were to live in millennia ago, located deep in the forest and as hot and dry as ever. They may be too far off the beaten path for average visitors, but for ruin hounds the isolation is divine.

EDZNÁ ARCHAEOLOGICAL ZONE

Edzná (8am-5pm daily, US$3) is the nearest major archaeological site to Campeche City, and makes for an excellent day trip. Tour

Edzná Archaeological Zone

To Entrance

CENTRAL
CEREMONIAL
GROUP

PLATFORM OF
THE KNIVES

GRAN ACRÓPOLIS

SACBE

NOHOCH-NÁ

PUUC
PATIO

NORTHWEST
TEMPLE

Gran Plaza

TEMPLE OF
FIVE STORIES

HOUSE OF
THE MOON

SOUTHWEST
TEMPLE

BALL COURT

STRUCTURE
419-2

TEMPLE OF
THE RELIEF
STAIRWAYS

TEMPLE OF
THE MASKS

SMALL
ACROPOLIS

0   50 yds

0   50 m

© MOON.COM

operators in Campeche offer van service to Edzná, with or without a guide, which can be convenient if your time is short or you don't want to risk missing the bus home. Guides at the site charge around US$20 for 1.5-hour tours of the ruins in either Spanish or English.

History

Nestled in a fertile valley between low mountains, the area is thought to have been settled by small farmers as early as 600 BC, and its earliest lasting structures built around 300 BC. It eventually grew into a large city and regional power, supporting a population in the tens of thousands. Edzná's regional influence is illustrated by the variety of architectural styles and influences found there, including Petén, Chenes, and Río Bec styles, as well as some of the earliest-known examples of Puuc architecture. Edzná is also notable for its network of water canals, measuring 22 kilometers (13.7 miles) in all, which helped control flooding, irrigate fields, and drain fields. Archaeologists have also found some 70 *chultúnes* (underground reservoirs) used to collect and store water for Edzná's burgeoning population. Several scenes in Mel Gibson's 2006 release *Apocalypto* were filmed at Edzná, the actual temples serving as backdrop for models built by the crew.

Edzná entered its peak period around AD 600 and prospered until around AD 900, when it went into a rapid decline, as did many other Maya cities at that time. But Edzná managed to avoid total collapse—probably thanks to its consistently rich agricultural resources—and remained an important population center as late as AD 1450, when it was finally abandoned. Early researchers postulated that Edzná meant "House of Grimaces" and was a reference to a series of masks that decorated the comb of the Temple of Five Stories. Now archaeologists believe the name means "Home of the Itzás," a reference to settlers who emigrated from central Mexico well after the Maya collapse of the 9th and 10th centuries and reoccupied many of the fallen cities. If so, the city's original name has been lost to history.

Gran Plaza

Coming from the entrance, a path deposits you on the northwest corner of a huge grassy courtyard known as the Gran Plaza. To your left is the **Platform of the Knives,** on top of which are the much-decayed remains of several fine residences, most likely used by Edzná's elite. The platform's name comes from a small offering of flint knives found by archaeologists in one of the structures. To your right is the narrow end of another platform, this one called **Nohoch-Ná** (Big House) that extends an impressive 125 meters (410 feet) along the Gran Plaza's western edge. Atop are bases for what were once four long halls, probably used for administrative functions like collecting tributes or mediating conflicts. High stairs run the entire length and most likely doubled as bleachers for events and ceremonies held in the Gran Plaza itself. Visitors often stand at the top of this structure and clap their hands once—the sound can be heard throughout the site, like thunder, bouncing off the walls of structures.

It's an impressive architectural feat, and one that elicits images of speeches made to ancient Maya crowds in the plaza below.

Gran Acrópolis

On the east side of the Gran Plaza, a wide bank of stairs leads up to the Gran Acrópolis, an artificial platform 160 meters (525 feet) wide and 7.5 meters (25 feet) high. It was the center of ceremonial life at Edzná, and contains the site's most significant structure, the 31-meter (102-foot) **Temple of Five Stories.** Though visible above the vegetation from a great distance, the imposing pyramid can no longer be climbed; the restriction is mostly to prevent further erosion of the stairs but also for the safety of visitors. The temple underwent at least five distinct construction periods, each one adding to the last. The temple's first four levels were probably used by priests as living quarters; a shrine and altar are on the highest level, with a roof comb (a decorative element built to make the pyramid appear even higher) rising over that. At one time, this comb was covered with ornate stucco masks and carvings, and the rest of the building's stones were coated with smooth stucco and painted brilliant colors.

Flanking the Temple of Five Stories are several smaller structures, including the **Northwest Temple, Southwest Temple,** and the **House of the Moon,** with its steep stairs leading to vestiges of rooms on the top platform. Like the chambers in the main temple, rooms in and around the smaller structures also probably served as residences for priests.

Ball Court

Dividing the two areas is the Ball Court, with a north-south pitch, and ramps and scoring rings (barely visible here) on the east and west sides. This orientation, common in Maya ball courts, emphasized the religious significance attached to the game, casting it as sunrise versus sunset, light versus dark, good versus evil. Royalty would have likely watched the game from rooms on top of the two ramps, while commoners would have crowded around the ends, if they were allowed to watch at all.

Small Acropolis

South of the Gran Plaza is the Small Acropolis, which includes not only some of Edzná's oldest structures, but also some of its newest. Archaeologists believe the Small Acropolis served as the ceremonial center until the Classic era, when it was overshadowed by the building of the Gran Acrópolis and the Temple of Five Stories. Centuries later, after Edzná's sudden collapse and slow recovery, its new residents once again began construction projects in this area of the city. The **Temple of the Relief Stairways,** built in the Late Classic or Early Postclassic era, is the largest such structure. Its name comes from the curious use of *stelae* (carved monoliths) left over from Edzná's glory days to build the new temple's staircase; this may have been a deliberate insult to the fallen kings, but a simpler explanation is that the newcomers were illiterate and short on stones.

At the south edge of the Small Acropolis, the **Temple of the Masks** contains Edzná's best-preserved stucco decorations. The carved stone masks at the temple's east and west ends represent the sun god's face in its dawn (young) and dusk (old) incarnations, respectively. The faces have scarifications on the cheeks, large ear ornaments, and teeth filed to a point—all characteristics of the Maya nobility. Traces of the original red paint remain.

Getting There

If you're driving from Campeche, take Highway 180 east to Chencoyil and then go east on Highway 261 to Cayal, where you turn right and continue to the Edzná site (the signage is very good). The 60-kilometer (37-mile) drive takes about one hour. If you don't have a car, *colectivos* (vans, US$2, 50 min) make the trip to the site, leaving Campeche hourly 7am-4pm from Calle Tamaulipas, one block south of Baluarte San Pedro. *Colectivos* stop at the entrance and return to Campeche hourly 9am-3:30pm. Be sure to leave town early in order to have plenty of time to see the ruins and make the last bus back.

EL TABASQUEÑO ARCHAEOLOGICAL ZONE

Dating to the Classic period, **El Tabasqueño** (aka Xtabás, 8am-5pm daily, free) reached its peak between AD 750 and 900. It is a small site, with the excavated structures facing a rectangular plaza. The most notable is the one-story Structure 1, often called the **Temple Palace;** the facade has an impressive monster-mouth doorway, the corners of which are flanked by two rows of eight Chaac masks, a classic Chenes feature. The rest of the structure consists of eight rooms, a temple, and a central staircase. To the southwest stands a 3.5-meter (11.5-foot) **tower.**

The site is down a well-signed two-kilometer (1.2-mile) gravel road that begins from Highway 269 a few kilometers south of Pakchén.

HOCHOB ARCHAEOLOGICAL ZONE

Meaning "Place of the Corn Cobs," **Hochob** (8am-5pm daily, US$2.25) sits on a 30-meter-high (98-foot) rise, the top of which was flattened to build part of the city. It consists of three plazas, though only one has been significantly excavated. Fortunately, it is in that plaza that the most stunning of the site's buildings is found: Structure 1, or the **Main Palace.** Consisting of just three rooms, it has a wildly ornate facade with open-mouth serpents and masks, all representative of Itzamná, the creator deity. The doorway is a classic monster-mouth mask, with fangs, piercing eyes, and enormous earflaps. It is flanked by cascades of Chaac masks, hooked nose and all, on the corners. **Structure 5,** on the same plaza, has two temples, the eastern one sporting the remains of a roof comb. As you walk through the site, notice the *chultúnes* (natural stone cisterns) that were used to collect water in ancient times.

To arrive, take Highway 269 south past Dzibalchén to the town of Chencoh, where a 3.5-kilometer (2.2-mile) paved road leads to the site. There's no sign going southbound; turn right at the Pemex station.

DZIBILNOCAC ARCHAEOLOGICAL ZONE

Unlike the other Chenes sites, **Dzibilnocac** (8am-5pm daily, free) sits in a flat, wide-open space. With a name meaning "Painted Vault" or "Great Painted Turtle," the first evidence of human occupation dates to 500-50 BC, though it reached its height between AD 300 and 900. It is a fairly large site measuring 1.32 square kilometers (0.8 square mile), with several groups of structures consisting of pyramids, administrative buildings, and dwellings. Most of the site is unexcavated, however, so only a small portion can be visited. In that area, the most impressive building is Structure A1, the **Palace-Temple,** a raised platform with three Río Bec-style towers, each set on rounded bases. Only one tower, however, is significantly well preserved; it is covered in intricate monster masks with representations of Chaac on the corners.

Dzibilnocac is located 400 meters (0.2 mile) east of the town of Iturbide, 18 kilometers (11 miles) north of Highway 269. There's second-class bus service from Campeche City via Hopelchén (3 hours, US$5.50); be sure to leave Campeche early so you have time to get back (there are no hotels in Iturbide).

SANTA ROSA XTAMPAK ARCHAEOLOGICAL ZONE

Like many Maya cities in the Yucatán Peninsula, **Santa Rosa Xtampak** (8am-5pm daily, US$2.25) reached its heyday around AD 600-850, and archaeologists believe that this old city was once the heart of the Chenes empire. It had more than 60 *chultúnes* (underground water reservoirs), suggesting a population of more than 10,000 people. Its main structure, the **Palace,** is one of the most architecturally complex buildings in the Maya world, with three floors, 11 staircases, and 44 rooms. The site has scores of structures, though only a half dozen or so have been extricated from the thick trees and brush. Opposite the palace is a **residential structure** with a beautiful monster-mouth entrance, a classic feature of Chenes sites. Farther down the path, the huge **Cuartel** hulks, in semi-collapse, amid the trees.

John Stephens visited Xtampak in 1842, but major excavation didn't begin until the mid-1990s, and continues today. For that reason, much of the palace is off-limits, as are other structures, but if you're there when workers are present, it offers a unique opportunity to see the difficult and dirty process of archaeology in action.

Santa Rosa Xtampak lies 45 kilometers (28 miles) down a paved road off Highway 261. If this is a stopover between Campeche and Mérida—or even a side trip from the Puuc Route—start early. Driving from Campeche, take Highway 261 past Hopelchén to the marked turnoff just north of town.

HOPELCHÉN

Maya for "Place of the Five Wells," Hopelchén is notable as the municipal seat for the Chenes region and as the main market town for the large population of Mennonites living in the area. The plaza is often filled with Mennonites in their distinctive garb, the men in matching black bib overalls and straw cowboy hats and the women in pioneer frocks and bonnets.

Sights

Otherwise unadorned, the 1667 **Iglesia San Antonio de Padua** (main plaza) boasts an intricately carved and painted baroque altar—one of the oldest in the Yucatán Peninsula—that's lined with gold and silver and segmented by corkscrew columns.

Just outside of town, the **Toh Cok Archaeological Zone** (aka Tacob Archaeological Zone, 8am-5pm daily, free) is a small Late Classic site that peaked about AD 600-750. It contains approximately 40 structures spread throughout some five hectares (12 acres), though only a few have been restored. Even so, the ones on view are worth a look for the Puuc-style columns, vaulted rooms, and the newly restored frieze of the rain god Chaac. The chatty caretaker loves to show off his beloved ruins; he can guide you to a *chultún* (subterranean cistern) on the other side of the road, and show you the jumble of carved stones that have yet to be reassembled. Signed as Tacob, the ruins are along Highway 261, 3.5 kilometers (2.2 miles) northwest of Hopelchén. Yellow-and-white school buses putter between the ruins and the town plaza every half hour 8am-6pm and charge US$0.50. Walking also is an easy, and pleasant, option.

Food and Accommodations

Hotel Jaguar (Av Manuel Crescencio near Calle 11, tel. 996/102-3458, US$15/20 s/d with a/c) is a welcome sight in this tiny town, where you might not expect to find such a pleasant place to crash. Two floors of clean and tidy air-conditioned rooms open onto a walkway and garden, with colorful paintings on the opposite wall. Service is friendly and the price unbeatable.

Restaurant Los Arcos (Calle 23 s/n, cell tel. 996/100-8782, 7am-3pm daily, US$3-5) is a simple eatery serving gut-busting meat-and-vegetable platters that are a hit with the local Mennonites. Look for it next to the like-named hotel on the main plaza.

Information and Services

There's a small **tourism office** (Calle 23 s/n, hours vary) in the Casa de Cultura one block north of the main plaza, and a **Bancomer** (Calle 20 s/n, 8:30am-4pm Mon.-Fri.) with a 24-hour ATM, just off the plaza itself.

Getting There

The town's **bus terminal** (Calle 16 btwn Calles 17 and 19), at the Mercado Municipal, has second-class service to Mérida (US$6, 3 hours, 6 departures, 5am-6:30pm) and Campeche (US$3.50, 1.5 hours, 11 departures, 4:30am-5:30pm). Faster *colectivos* (vans) to Campeche (US$3.50, 1.25 hours) leave every 30 minutes from beside the church.

GRUTAS DE X'TACUMBILXUNA'AN

Meaning "Hidden Lady," the **X'tacumbilxuna'an caves** (9am-5pm daily, US$5) are named after a Maya legend that recalls how Earth hid its daughter, Water, underground to prevent her from being found by her lover, Man. John L. Stephens and Frederick Catherwood were the first westerners to see the cave system, in 1841; it was made famous by the latter's lithograph, which shows locals hauling pails of water up a long ladder to the surface. Today, a portion of the cave has been outfitted for visitors, with steps, level walkways, and some slippery spots (be sure to wear sturdy shoes); snazzy lighting highlights some of the spectacular stalagmites and stalactites along the way, and guides narrate points of interest. Outside, a forested trail leads to an opening high above the cave floor, where visitors can peer down for a thrill. At the time of research, an electrical storm had blown out the cave's lighting system, changing the tour from well-lit to headlamp-lit and significantly reducing the visibility. The timeline for repairs had not yet been established.

Getting There

The Grutas de X'tacumbilxuna'an are located three kilometers (1.9 miles) north of the town of Bolonchén de Rejón, off Highway 261. If you're busing it, take a second-class bus from Hopelchén to Mérida (US$1, 30 minutes to turnoff) and ask to be dropped off at the turnoff to the cave; the entrance is about half a kilometer (0.3 mile) from the highway.

KANKI ARCHAEOLOGICAL ZONE

Kanki (8am-5pm daily, free) is a modest but decently excavated site located in a hilly area of northern Campeche state and

Isla Jaina Archaeological Zone

About 96 kilometers (59 miles) north of Campeche City is the swampy offshore island of Jaina. Meaning "House in the Water," this island site holds the largest-known Maya burial ground on the Yucatán Peninsula; more than 1,000 interments have been found on it. According to the archaeologist Sylvanus Morley, who discovered the site in 1943, Jaina was used by the Maya elite—probably Puuc nobility—beginning in AD 652. Bodies were carried in long, colorful processions to this island and were interred in burial jars in crouched positions, their skin often stained red—a symbol of eternal life—and bodies wrapped in either a straw mat or white cloth. Some were found with a jade stone in their mouths. Plates with food, jewelry, weapons, tools, and other precious items were placed on the heads of the dead to accompany them to the afterlife. Small figurines (10-25 centimeters/4-10 inches tall) also were buried, resting on the deceased's folded arms. These finely crafted ceramic sculptures now are considered masterpieces of Mesoamerican art. They portray the buried in ritual costumes, like those of warriors and ball players, and are frozen in ritual positions, including as captives being tortured. These tiny sculptures also often doubled as rattles, with clay balls rolling around the hollow interiors.

The island is off-limits to all but INAH-approved researchers, but it contains two structure groups that have been extensively restored: **Zacpool** on the southeastern side of the island, and **Zayasol** on the northwestern side. They are each composed of pyramids, temple platforms, and dwellings—all made of limestone clay covered in stone. Interestingly, to build these structures the Maya raised the low elevation of the island by building platforms made of *sascab* (limestone material), brought from the mainland in canoes.

The next best thing to visiting the island is checking out the small but spectacular collection of Isla Jaina figurines and burial art at the **Museo Arqueológico Maya del Camino Real** (8am-5pm daily, US$2). Located on the central plaza in the town of Hecelchakán, this modest museum also has a fine set of Maya stelae and columns in the garden. Hecelchakán is located about 70 kilometers (43 miles) north of Campeche on Highway 180 toward Mérida.

surrounded by farmland. Its builders took advantage of the hills to construct interconnected structures and patios over different levels. The site's primary structure, designated **Structure 1,** is a two-level palace surrounded by 10 courtyards. The structure most likely served ceremonial and administrative purposes, and perhaps as a residence for royalty. Kanki's architecture is mainly Puuc, with corbelled vaults, long passages with multiple doorways, and buildings that feature plain lower sections and highly decorative upper friezes and roof combs. Much of Kanki's decorative features have collapsed, thanks to time and vegetation, but remnants of Chaac masks and other designs can be spotted. Kanki was first settled around AD 500, reached its peak around AD 600 to 650, declined, and was eventually abandoned around AD 900. The site's original name is unknown; Kanki is Yucatec Maya for "Place of Chultunes," a reference to the numerous stone water basins (*chultúnes*) found there.

Getting There

To arrive, take Highway 180 to the town of Tenabo. At the exit, go east, following the signs to the ruins for about 15 kilometers (9.3 miles). You'll be traveling on a country road, passing corn and squash fields along the way. The last 1.5 kilometers (0.9 mile) is on a well-maintained dirt road.

Campeche City

Campeche City is a gorgeous, historically rich city with a meticulously restored center, fascinating sights, and a UNESCO World Heritage designation to boot. Long considered a lesser version of Mérida, Campeche City has truly come into its own, with much-improved lodging and eating options and a warm, tourist-friendly atmosphere. The city's unique network of walls, bastions, and forts—built centuries ago to ward off pirates—have been cleverly repurposed as museums. And the compact city center is ideal for exploring, with its colorful facades, historic churches, cobblestone streets (some pedestrian only), and a leafy central plaza that's frequently used for free performances and events.

HISTORY

Campeche is a Spanish corruption of "Ah Kim Pech," the name of the Maya town that occupied the same spot. Ah Kim Pech was an important indigenous commercial center, serving as a gateway between the Yucatán Peninsula and central Mexico. Spanish explorers first arrived here by ship in 1517; recognizing the town's strategic location, they immediately set out to control it themselves. The Maya were not pleased, and dealt the would-be conquerors one demoralizing defeat after another. It wasn't until October 4, 1540, that Spanish soldiers led by Francisco de Montejo finally conquered Ah Kim Pech and founded the city of Campeche. Before long, the city was once again a major port and trade center, though for Spanish galleons instead of Maya canoes. Among other exports was *palo de Campeche* (Campeche wood), a tropical wood used to make fabric dyes—highly valued in Europe and elsewhere.

The Spanish had their favor returned, however, in the form of marauding pirates. Many were supported by Spain's archenemies, England and France, and were attracted by the easy pickings at Campeche's ports and busy shipping lanes. For nearly 200 years—until Campeche's defensive walls were finally completed—the people of Campeche endured nearly constant harassment and assault from ne'er-do-wells and scalawags. The city was destroyed on several occasions, including February 9, 1663, when pirates killed scores of men, women, and children in the worst massacre in the city's history. Another infamous assault was led by Laurent Graff, also known as Lorencillo, who attacked Campeche with an army of 700 men on July 6, 1685. They didn't stop with just sacking the city; they also took dozens of prisoners and demanded the city leaders pay an exorbitant ransom. After two months of occupation, the city hadn't paid—it didn't have the money—and so the pirates planned a mass execution. After the first round of killings, a city representative talked the pirates out of the plan, and even out of the city.

The ordeal prompted the Spanish crown to build fortifications, which would eventually bring relative peace and protection to Campeche. A solid stone and mortar wall was built around the city, eight meters (26 feet) high and three meters (10 feet) thick. There were gates on each of the four sides; two of them—Puerta del Mar (Sea Gate) and Puerta de la Tierra (Land Gate)—are still used. Nine *baluartes* (bastions) were erected in strategic locations. Part of the wall extended into the sea and was outfitted with a huge gate, which was opened to let merchants in, but could be quickly closed against any pirates in close pursuit. Although isolated attacks continued until 1717, the walls served their purpose, bringing the reign of pirate terror to an end.

SIGHTS

Bright pastel facades and cobblestoned streets make Campeche's city center one of the most beautiful in the whole peninsula.

Campeche City

To Parador Gastrónomico de Cocteleros, Baseball Stadium, and Hwy 180

SEE "DOWNTOWN CAMPECHE CITY" MAP

Gulf of

Mexico

FUERTE DE SAN JOSÉ EL ALTO/MUSEO DE ARMAS Y BARCOS

AV CUAHTEMOC

To Edzná, Chenes Region, and Hwy 261

TERMINAL ANTIGUA (SECOND CLASS BUS STATION)

AV HÉROES DE NACOZARI

INTERNATIONAL AIRPORT

To Balneario Playa Bonita, Hwy 180, and Champotón

To Hacienda Uayamón and Edzna

BATERÍA DE SAN LUIS

FUERTE DE SAN MIGUEL/ MUSEO ARQUEOLÓGICO DE CAMPECHE

To Hwy 180D, Champotón, and Escárcega

TERMINAL NUEVA (FIRST CLASS BUS STATION)

0   0.25 mi
0   0.25 km

© MOON.COM

TOP EXPERIENCE

★ The City Walls

Campeche's imposing walls, bastions, and forts lend a wonderful old-world ambience to the city. Most contain museums, and exploring them is a great way to spend an afternoon, or a whole day. Five of the seven bastions surrounding the city center can be visited, as can two forts on the city's edges. The city and Instituto Nacional de Antropología e Historia (INAH, National Institute of Anthropology and History) are in ongoing discussions about the feasibility of reconstructing more sections.

Built in 1690, **Baluarte de la Soledad** (Calle 8 at Calle 57, 8:30am-5pm Tues.-Sun., US$2.25) is the largest of the city's bastions and home to a small but very worthwhile museum. The **Museo de la Arquitectura Maya** has a superb collection of stelae and other artifacts from the Río Bec, Chenes, and Puuc regions, accompanied by explanations in both Spanish and English. With just four rooms, it offers a primer on Maya writing, sculpture, and architectural styles without being overwhelming. The shining star, however, is a room holding a spectacular jade funerary mask and several other ceremonial items found in a royal tomb at Calakmul ruins. Dating to AD 640, the tomb lay undisturbed for over 1,300 years until archaeologists discovered it. Outside, a ramp leads to the top of the wall and a bird's-eye view of the central plaza.

At the corner of Calle 55 and Calle 8, don't overlook the detailed **bronze model of the walled city** by artist Pablo Rafael López Artasánchez; it depicts what Campeche looked like when it was encircled by walls. Residents of the historic center often stroll by and point out the location of their houses.

Puerta de Tierra (Calle 59 at Calle 18, 8am-9pm Mon.-Fri., 9am-9pm Sat.-Sun., US$0.75) was one of two heavily fortified gates into the city; today it is the only original section of the city's wall in existence. The entrance fee allows you to climb onto the eight-meter (26-foot) wall, where a narrow causeway makes for a memorable stroll to **Baluarte San Juan** (Calle 63 at Calle 18) on one end and **Baluarte San Francisco** (Calle 57 at Calle 18) on the other. From above, you'll get a (low-flying) bird's-eye view of the city center, including gorgeous facades with only ruins and overgrown lots behind them. Ring the big bronze bell at the end of your walk to have the exit door opened. Baluarte San Francisco also has a tiny **exhibit** (9am-4pm, free) on some of the region's most famous pirates.

The Puerta de la Tierra also has a **pirate show** (8pm Thurs.-Sun., US$3 adult, US$1.50 child). An hour long, it retells Campeche's violent past with flashing lights, blasting speakers, some firecrackers, and a couple live sword fights atop the wall. It's kind of corny but lots of fun for kids. Audio translation is available for an additional US$2.

The first of the nine bastions to be built, **Baluarte San Carlos** (Calle 8 btwn Calles 63 and 65, 8am-8pm daily, free) now houses the **Museo de la Ciudad** (City Museum). An anemic museum focusing on Campeche's pirate history, the exhibits are limited to three rooms with somewhat empty display cases. The basement, which once served as a dungeon, has two creepy pirate mannequins, chained to the walls. The highlight is actually on the roof, where visitors can stroll about, check out the cannons, and take good photos of town.

Built in the early 1700s, **Baluarte San Pedro** (Calle 16 at Calle 51) has had several incarnations—a stronghold, barracks, INAH research center, arts and crafts market, and a folk art museum. At the time of research, it stood empty, waiting for its next role. As you walk by, look at the coat of arms above the door, which features the two keys of heaven and the papal crown, the symbol of Saint Peter.

Baluarte Santiago (Calle 49-C at Calle 8, 8am-9pm Mon.-Fri., 9am-9pm Sat.-Sun., US$0.75) was completed in 1704, nearly a century after the first fort was built. It was torn down in the early 1900s to make room for government offices, but was reconstructed at the same location in 1955, bearing little resemblance to the original building. Today, this tiny fort houses the **Jardín Botánico**

Campeche City's Sculptures

While exploring the main plazas and walkways of Campeche City's historic center, you're sure to encounter life-size bronze sculptures of everyday Campechanos. They are the work of acclaimed sculptor Antonio Miguel Horn, who also has exhibited in New York, Philadelphia, and elsewhere. There are five sculptures in all, each depicting a character from a classic Campechano song by Zoila Quijano McGregor: a fisherman, an old woman, a street vendor, a bread maker, and *el pregonero* (the town crier). Simple yet resonant, the pieces were commissioned in 2010, during Mexico's bicentennial celebrations, as a reminder of simpler lives and yesteryear's pursuits amid the hubbub of today's modern world.

Xmuch'haltun, a botanical garden boasting more than 200 varieties of native plant species.

Outlying Forts

If you go to only one sight, make it **Fuerte de San Miguel** and its **Museo Arqueológico de Campeche** (Av. Escárcega s/n, 8:30am-5:30pm Tues.-Sun., US$2.75), about 2.5 kilometers (1.6 miles) south of the center. Built at the end of the 18th century, the fort sits atop a large hill and includes a moat, drawbridge, and a breathtaking view of the Gulf. The museum here is the real highlight though, housing a truly fantastic collection of Maya artifacts from around the state, including several pieces from the ruins at Isla Jaina, two spectacular jade funeral masks found at Calakmul, and urns decorated with tapirs, monkeys, and turtles from Río Bec. Signage is in Spanish; look for the cardboard information sheets in each exhibit hall for English translations. If using public transportation, take a Playa Bonita/Lerma bus from in front of the post office (US$0.35). The bus will drop you off at the turnoff to the fort, which is about another 500 meters (0.3 mile) up a steep hill. A taxi from the center of town costs around US$3.50.

Below the Fuerte de San Miguel is the **Batería de San Luis** (Avenida Resurgimiento s/n, 8am-6pm daily, free), a small fortification that has been repurposed into naval offices. The lobby has an exhibit on Capitán Pedro Sainz de Baranda y Borreiro, a naval commander and native son who became the governor of Yucatán in 1835.

On the other side of town, the **Fuerte de San José El Alto** (Av. Francisco Morazán s/n, 9:30am-6pm Tues.-Sun., free) is a well-renovated fort complete with cannons, thick walls, and a spectacular view of the Gulf of Mexico. It also houses the **Museo de Armas y Barcos,** a one-room maritime museum where you'll find model ships and a few colonial-era artifacts. Signage is in Spanish only. To get here, take a San José El Alto bus from the *mercado* (US$0.35). A taxi costs US$3.50.

Parque Principal

The **Parque Principal** (Calle 10 at Calle 55), or central plaza, is a pleasant, shady spot to rest your feet, and a good place to begin and end a tour of Campeche's many sights. Better yet, on Saturday and Sunday the streets around the central plaza are blocked to traffic and fill up with food carts and small vendors, and local families come out to chat and stroll about. In the evening, one or two *lotería* (Mexican bingo) games start up (6pm-11pm, US$0.05/card)—tourists are welcome—and the municipal band gives a classic oompah concert in the central kiosk, blaring forth on trumpets, clarinets, tubas, and cymbals with the energy of a great orchestra. In addition, at 8pm every evening (except Monday), a spectacular **sound and light show** is projected onto the former Palacio Municipal (city hall); it celebrates Campeche's history and Maya beginnings in a magnificent display of lights, colors, imagery, and music.

El Palacio Centro Cultural

Named after the gorgeously renovated building it occupies—the former Palacio Municipal (city hall)—**El Palacio Centro Cultural** (central park, Calle 8 btwn Calles 55 and 57, tel. 981/811-0366, 10am-7pm Tues.-Sun., free) is more a city museum than a cultural center. Three extensive exhibit halls describe different parts of the city's early history: its fortifications, commerce, and boats. Beyond the well-maintained antiquities and bilingual signage are hands-on multimedia exhibits, engaging movies (Spanish only), and even a simulation of an Atlantic boat crossing (visitors step onto a replica of a galleon—take hold of your seat, you'll hit stormy weather and be chased by pirates). This is a fascinating, educational, and must-see stop. Guided visits leave hourly 10:30am-1:30pm and 4pm-6pm.

Churches

On the east side of the plaza, **Catedral de Nuestra Señora de la Purísima Concepción** (Calle 55 btwn Calles 8 and 10, 7am-9pm daily) is the city's cathedral and one of the oldest churches on the Yucatán Peninsula. Construction was ordered by Francisco de Montejo in 1540, eventually reaching completion in 1760. However, it wasn't until 1895 that the church was proclaimed the town's cathedral by Pope Léon XIII. Architecturally, the building is notable as having one of the only baroque facades in the Yucatán Peninsula; its towers also remain among the highest structures in the city.

Built by the Jesuits in 1756, the **Ex-Templo de San José** (Calle 10 at Calle 63, 10am-8pm Mon.-Sat., 10am-6pm Sun.) is a beautiful structure, decorated with an impressive blue-and-yellow tile facade. Inside, the striking colonial architecture makes for good photo ops. The history of the building is as varied as that of the city of Campeche: It has gone from being a church to a lighthouse (check out the weather vane) to a library to a warehouse to—today—the temporary home of **Bazar Artesanal,** a folk art market whose building is being remodeled.

Templo de San Francisquito (Calle 12 at Calle 59, 8am-7pm daily) was built by

Downtown Campeche City

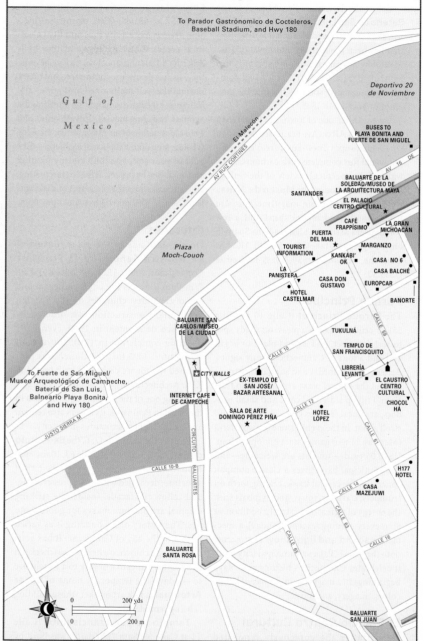

To Parador Gastrónomico de Cocteleros,
Baseball Stadium, and Hwy 180

Gulf of

Mexico

Deportivo 20
de Noviembre

El Malecón

AV RUIZ CORTINES

AV 16 DE

BUSES TO
PLAYA BONITA AND
FUERTE DE SAN MIGUEL

BALUARTE DE LA
SOLEDAD/MUSEO DE
LA ARQUITECTURA MAYA

SANTANDER

EL PALACIO
CENTRO CULTURAL

*Plaza
Moch-Couoh*

CAFÉ
FRAPPÍSIMO

LA GRAN
MICHOACÁN

PUERTA
DEL MAR

MARGANZO

TOURIST
INFORMATION

KANKABI'
OK

CASA NO 6

LA
PANISTERA

CASA DON
GUSTAVO

CASA BALCHÉ

EUROPCAR

HOTEL
CASTELMAR

BANORTE

CALLE 10

BALUARTE SAN
CARLOS/MUSEO
DE LA CIUDAD

TUKULNÁ

TEMPLO DE
SAN FRANCISQUITO

CALLE 59

To Fuerte de San Miguel/
Museo Arqueológico de Campeche,
Batería de San Luis,
Balneario Playa Bonita,
and Hwy 180

CITY WALLS

LIBRERÍA
LEVANTE

EL CAUSTRO
CENTRO
CULTURAL

EX-TEMPLO DE
SAN JOSÉ/
BAZAR ARTESANAL

CHOCOL
HÁ

INTERNET CAFÉ
DE CAMPECHE

CALLE 12

SALA DE ARTE
DOMINGO PÉREZ PIÑA

HOTEL
LÓPEZ

CALLE 61

JUSTO SIERRA M

CIRCUITO BALUARTES

CALLE 10-B

H177
HOTEL

CALLE 14

CASA
MAZEJUWI

CALLE 63

BALUARTE
SANTA ROSA

CALLE 65

CALLE 16

0   200 yds

0   200 m

BALUARTE
SAN JUAN

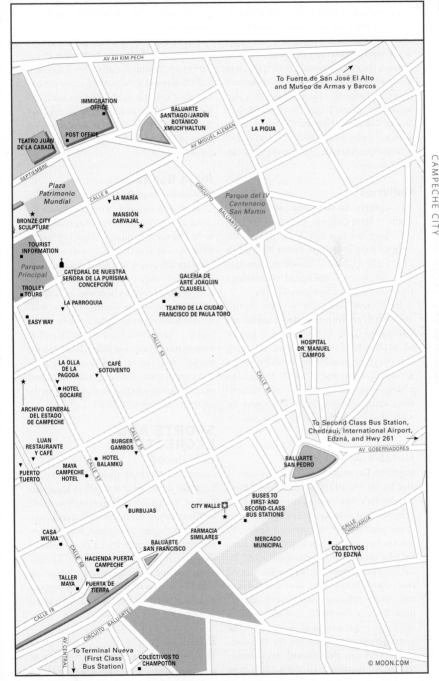

AV AH KIM-PECH

To Fuerte de San José El Alto
and Museo de Armas y Barcos

IMMIGRATION
OFFICE

POST OFFICE

BALUARTE
SANTIAGO/JARDÍN
BOTÁNICO
XMUCH'HALTUN

LA PIGUA

TEATRO JUAN
DE LA CABADA

SEPTIEMBRE

AV MIGUEL ALEMÁN

CIRCUITO BALUARTES

Plaza
Patrimonio
Mundial

CALLE 8

LA MARÍA

MANSIÓN
CARVAJAL

Parque del IV
Centenario
San Martín

BRONZE CITY
SCULPTURE

TOURIST
INFORMATION

Parque
Principal

CATEDRAL DE NUESTRA
SEÑORA DE LA PURÍSIMA
CONCEPCIÓN

GALERÍA DE
ARTE JOAQUIN
CLAUSELL

TROLLEY
TOURS

LA PARROQUIA

TEATRO DE LA CIUDAD
FRANCISCO DE PAULA TORO

EASY WAY

CALLE 59

HOSPITAL
DR. MANUEL
CAMPOS

LA OLLA
DE LA
PAGODA

CAFÉ
SOTOVENTO

HOTEL
SOCAIRE

CALLE 51

ARCHIVO GENERAL
DEL ESTADO
DE CAMPECHE

To Second Class Bus Station,
Chedraui, International Airport,
Edzná, and Hwy 261

LUAN
RESTAURANTE
Y CAFÉ

BURGER
GAMBOS

CALLE 55

AV. GOBERNADORES

MAYA
CAMPECHE
HOTEL

HOTEL
BALAMKÚ

CALLE 57

PUERTO
TUERTO

BALUARTE
SAN PEDRO

BURBUJAS

CITY WALLS

BUSES TO
FIRST- AND
SECOND-CLASS
BUS STATIONS

CASA
WILMA

CALLE 18

CALLE 59

FARMACIA
SIMILARES

BALUARTE
SAN FRANCISCO

MERCADO
MUNICIPAL

CALLE CHIHUAHUA

COLECTIVOS
TO EDZNÁ

HACIENDA PUERTA
CAMPECHE

TALLER
MAYA

PUERTA DE
TIERRA

CALLE 18

CIRCUITO BALUARTES

AV CENTRAL

To Terminal Nueva
(First Class
Bus Station)

COLECTIVOS TO
CHAMPOTÓN

© MOON.COM

the Franciscan Order in the mid-17th century to replace the church and cloister that had been destroyed by successive pirate invasions—and to protect against future ones. As a result, the exterior is stark with thick stone walls, while the interior is graced by intricate baroque altarpieces that are covered in phytomorphic reliefs. Today, the cloister houses the **El Claustro Centro Cultural** (Calle 12 btwn Calles 59 and 61, tel. 981/816-2957, 8:30am-9pm Mon.-Fri.), one of the city's cultural centers.

Galleries

The **Galería de Arte Joaquín Clausell** (Calle 12 btwn Calles 51 and 53, tel. 981/811-3653, 9am-3pm and 4pm-8pm, free) and the **Sala de Arte Domingo Pérez Piña** (Calle 12 at Calle 65, tel. 981/816-6056, 8am-8pm Tues.-Sat., free) are small galleries featuring a rotation of artwork by regional artists.

Peek into the state archive building, **Archivo General del Estado de Campeche** (Calle 12 btwn Calles 57 and 59, tel. 981/816-0939, 8am-3pm Mon.-Fri., free), to see its latest art or historical exhibit. Shows are usually compiled by INAH or ICC, the national and state history and cultural institutes, and can be quite good. Don't miss the video that relates the history of the state in both Spanish and English.

Notable Architecture

Mansión Carvajal (Calle 10 btwn Calles 51 and 53, tel. 981/811-3384, 8am-3pm Mon.-Fri., free) is a 19th-century mansion that has been restored to its original elegance. Built at the beginning of the 1800s, it originally was the home of the wealthy Carvajal family, who owned the Uayamón hacienda. By the late 1900s, however, it had been converted twice—once into a hotel, later into a dance hall. Today, it houses state government offices. Open to the public, it is well worth a quick visit to get a sense of the opulence the upper classes enjoyed during the 19th century. Check out the Moorish-style architecture, art nouveau staircase with Carrera marble steps, Tuscan columns, and iron balustrade.

Steps from the central plaza, a very mini Vegas-style **water fountain** (Plaza Patrimonio Mundial, Calle 8 btwn Calles 55 and 53) is timed to "dance" to classical beats and multicolored lights. Performances are every night at 7pm and 9pm (20 minutes, free). Buy a *paleta* (Popsicle) from a local vendor, scout out a spot on a park bench, and enjoy the show.

Playa Bonita

Balneario Playa Bonita (8am-5pm daily, US$0.10) is a pleasant swimming beach located about 13 kilometers (8 mi) south of town. The tawny sand is hard-packed but the water is calm and there are loads of shells. The tiny admission fee includes use of well-maintained *palapas*, bathrooms, and showers. Lounge chairs also can be rented for US$0.25 per day. A couple of on-site restaurants (US$4-9) serve guests beachside. To arrive by public transportation, take a Playa Bonita/Lerma bus from in front of the post office (US$0.35); the bus will drop you off at the entrance. Taxis cost around US$6. If driving, take the coastal road south, just past the town of Lerma to the entrance; parking is US$0.50.

SPORTS AND RECREATION

El Malecón

Campeche's **Malecón** (boardwalk) stretches for three kilometers (1.9 miles) along the Gulf of Mexico. It's a pleasant walkway with well-maintained pavement, monuments, and benches, although during rush hours the avenue that runs alongside of it can get packed with cars. It's especially popular in the early mornings and evenings, when it's bustling with dog-walkers, in-line skaters, joggers, and couples out for a brisk stroll. Join along or, better yet, rent a bike to explore it.

Baseball

The **Piratas de Campeche** (www.piratasdecampeche.mx) are one of 16 teams that make up Mexico's professional baseball league, the Liga Mexicana de Béisbol. You can catch a game on the north side of town at the **Estadio Nelson Barrera Romellón** (Filiberto Qui Farfán No. 2, Col. Camino Real, US$3-8) April-August.

ENTERTAINMENT AND EVENTS

One of the best resources for free cultural events is the monthly *Cartelera Cultural* (www.culturacampeche.com), a guide available at the state tourist office, El Claustro Centro Cultural, and other locations around town.

Weekends and Evenings in the Parque Principal

Every weekend, the city streets around the central plaza are closed to cars, restaurants place their tables outdoors, food and trinket vendors set up stalls, and bingo games get going around the kiosk for US$0.05 per game.

Most evenings, a spectacular **sound and light show** (central plaza, 8pm Tues.-Sun., free) is projected onto the facade of the former Palacio Municipal (city hall). Called *Celebramos Campeche* (Celebrate Campeche), it's a brilliant multimedia presentation of the state's origins and riches, beginning with the ancient Maya and the state's remarkable biodiversity, continuing with the Spanish conquest and life in the New World, and ending with today's popular celebrations like Day of the Dead and Carnaval. It is a breathtaking show—arrive early for a good seat.

Nightlife

Campeche is not known for its nightlife. In the colonial center, most people either have drinks at the outdoor cafés and bars on Calle 59 or go for a stroll around the central plaza. If you feel like dancing or are looking for a change of scenery, head south on the Malecón, where you'll find a handful of discos and bars about one kilometer (0.6 mile) from the center of town.

Theater

Teatro de la Ciudad Francisco de Paula Toro (Calle 12 btwn Calles 51 and 53, tel. 981/811-3653, US$5-30) was commissioned by the commander in chief of Campeche, Don Francisco de Paula Toro, a Cuban immigrant who eventually became the governor of Yucatán. It was built during the middle of a cholera epidemic, against the wishes of the clergy, who wanted the funds to be funneled to the church instead. Nevertheless, the theater was inaugurated in September 1834, and it quickly became the center of cultural activity in Campeche. Today, the theater remains an important part of city life, hosting dance, dramatic, and musical performances throughout the year. It's open only when there is a scheduled event; stop by or call to see if there is anything showing while you're in town.

Teatro Juan de la Cabada (Av. 16 de Septiembre at Calle 53, tel. 981/811-0008, noon-8pm daily, US$5-30) is the city's modern theater space; it offers a wide range of dramatic, dance, and musical programming.

Cultural Centers

A restored mansion, **Centro Cultural Casa No. 6** (central plaza, Calle 57 btwn Calles 8 and 10, tel. 981/816-1782, 8am-9pm Mon.-Fri., 9am-9pm Sat.-Sun., US$1) showcases how the Campechano upper crust lived in the 19th century; rooms transport visitors back with period furnishings and art. There's also an artsy gift shop off the back courtyard.

El Claustro Centro Cultural (Calle 12 btwn Calles 59 and 61, tel. 981/816-2957, elclaustro@culturacampeche.com, 8:30am-9pm Mon.-Fri.) organizes numerous arts and cultural events throughout the year; check out the bulletin boards at the entrance for the schedule. Notably, it's located inside the former cloister of the Templo de San Francisquito.

Festivals and Events

Held every February, **Carnaval** is Campeche's blowout party of the year. Typically occurring over two weeks, it features musical

performances, dances, the crowning of the king and queen, costume parties, even a "funerary" parade along the Malecón where an effigy of a pirate is burned and thrown into the Gulf of Mexico. If you plan to be in town during the festivities, definitely make hotel reservations well in advance.

Every July, Campeche hosts the **Festival de Jazz.** Lasting approximately two weeks, it attracts musicians from all over the world. Stop by the state tourism office for details on scheduled events and concerts.

Festival Internacional del Centro Histórico de Campeche is a major festival when musicians, dance troupes, and artists perform or exhibit their work in and around the city. Each year, organizers select one Mexican state and one foreign country to be the focus of the programming. Most of the events take place in the central plaza, including the kickoff concert. It lasts the entire month of December; festivalgoers also enjoy the added bonus of the street-side stands selling local handicrafts and eats.

SHOPPING

Memento shopping in Campeche is a limited sport. Most shops are geared toward local needs, so you'll find lots of paper stores, teen clothing boutiques, and shoe shops. Stores geared toward tourists often specialize in kitsch, with T-shirts, ashtrays, and key chains galore.

Located inside the gorgeous Ex-Templo de San José, the **Bazar Artesanal** (Calle 10 at Calle 63, 10am-8pm Mon.-Sat., 10am-6pm Sun.) is the city's folk art market. Artisans sell their work directly to customers at individual stands; light haggling is welcome.

Tukulná (Calle 10 btwn Calles 59 and 61, tel. 981/816-9088, 8am-8pm daily) is a state-run shop specializing in Campechano handicrafts created by local artisans. There's everything from handmade clothing to

rocking chairs. In the back, there's also a re-creation of a Maya home and a *jipi* hat cave, complete with awkward-looking mannequins.

For *guayaberas, huipiles,* and other traditional wear, head to **Casa Wilma** (Calle 59 btwn Calles 16 and 18, tel. 981/816-4326, www.casawilma.com, 9am-9pm daily). A mom-and-pop boutique, it sells high-quality handmade clothing, mostly in linen and cotton. There's also a small but good selection of shoes, hats, and handbags, most incorporating local designs and styles.

Taller Maya (Calle 59 btwn Calles 16 and 18, tel. 981/811-5703, www.tallermaya.org, 9am-9pm Mon.-Sat., 9am-5pm Sun.) is a nonprofit selling items created through a collaboration between Maya artisans and contemporary Mexican designers. You'll find linens with Maya designs, artisanal soaps made with organic honey, modern jewelry made with colorful beans, and more. Prices are high but reflect living wages paid to all the artists.

Librería Levante (Calle 12 btwn Calles 59 and 61, tel. 981/816-5473, 9am-8pm Mon.-Fri., 9am-5pm Sat., 10am-3pm Sun.) carries a few English-language titles, including travel guidebooks, books on the Maya, and children's books. Decent regional maps are also sold.

FOOD

Campeche has a smattering of cozy cafés and classy Mexican and international restaurants. Not sure what you feel like eating? Take a stroll down Calle 59, a pedestrian-only street with a wide variety of restaurants and cafés, most with outdoor seating.

Campechano and Mexican

A half block from the central plaza, **La María** (Calle 8 near Calle 53, tel. 981/816-3618, 2pm-9pm Wed.-Mon., US$5-10) specializes in *típico* Campechano served with artistic flair like texture and color coming into play (a streak of green sauce here, a curled plantain chip there). The dining room is simple—wood tables and *papel picado,* mostly—and service

1: entrance to Fuerte de San Miguel, one of Campeche's outlying forts; 2: touring town by trolley; 3: Campeche's cathedral overlooking its pleasant main plaza is prompt and polite. Daily specials are worth asking about.

La Olla de la Pagoda (Calle 57 btwn Calles 12 and 14, tel. 981/816-2570, noon-5pm Mon.-Sat., US$4-7) is a locals' favorite, serving simple but delicious meals at rock-bottom prices. It's open for lunch only, serving *comida corrida*: traditional Mexican lunch specials that include soup, main dish, and dessert. You can also order off the menu, from grilled fish to *chili relleno*.

A restaurant-bar on Campeche's pedestrian street, **Puerto Tuerto** (Calle 59 btwn Calles 12 and 14, tel. 981/811-0015, 6:30pm-midnight Mon.-Wed., 6:30pm-3am Thurs.-Sat., US$5-12) has a lively atmosphere and great people-watching. The menu has a variety of international dishes—pastas, salads, sandwiches—but the tacos are tops here: fresh corn tortillas, steak, seafood, and chicken fillings plus loads of toppings.

Open 24 hours, the diner-style **La Parroquia** (Calle 55 btwn Calles 10 and 12, tel. 981/816-2530, US$4-12) is always bustling. You'll find good Campechano dishes, traditional Mexican meals, and a TV tuned to soap operas or soccer games. The daily lunch special (US$4.50) includes a main dish, rice and beans, dessert, and a large drink.

Seafood

Considered one of the best restaurants in town, ★ **La Pigua** (Av. Miguel Alemán btwn Calles 49-A and 49-B, tel. 981/811-3365, www.lapigua.com.mx, noon-6pm Sun.-Tues., noon-10pm Wed.-Sat., US$9-15) is an upscale and popular lunchtime spot for professionals and couples. The food is pricey but excellent—coconut shrimp with apple chutney is the specialty—and the service is first-rate. Reservations are recommended, especially on weekends.

Marganzo (Calle 8 btwn Calles 57 and 59, tel. 981/811-3899, 7am-11pm daily, US$7-16) screams tourist trap—the staff sports name tags and traditional dress—but it's hard to beat for tasty food and prices. Seafood is the specialty—*pampano relleno de mariscos*

(whitefish filled with seafood) is a favorite among regulars—but the *pollo pibil* and other meat dishes don't disappoint. Servings are large and come with a tableful of complimentary appetizers.

For fresh seafood right on the water, head to the **Parador Gastrónomico de Cocteleros** (Malecón at Calle Adriano Chino Wong, 11am-7pm daily, US$5-11). A locals' scene, this string of *palapa*-roofed restaurants all pretty much specialize in the same dishes: shrimp cocktail, oyster empanadas, grilled and fried fish, and ceviche. On weekends afternoons, most feature live music. They are located four kilometers (2.5 miles) north of the colonial center.

Cafés

Checkerboard floors, old wood tables, and porcelain dishes give ★ **Luan Restaurante y Café** (Calle 59 at Calle 14, tel. 981/811-5205, 8am-3pm Mon.-Sat., 9am-3pm Sun., US$4-6) a shabby-chic feel. Diners come here for comfort food in the form of big breakfasts: egg plates, oatmeal bowls, Nutella pancakes, and *chilaquiles*. Don't miss the huge mugs of coffee and freshly squeezed juices.

Café Frappísimo (Calle 8 btwn Calles 55 and 57, tel. 981/811-0145, 8:30am-11pm Sun.-Thurs., 8:30am-midnight Fri.-Sat., US$1.50-4) is an air-conditioned café where young professionals ooh and aah over the espresso drinks, baguette sandwiches, and pastries. It's located next to El Palacio Centro Cultural, with a view of its interior courtyard.

Burger Gambos (Calle 55 btwn Calles 14 and 16, cell tel. 981/122-2686, 8am-3pm Mon.-Sat., US$1-3) offers an extensive menu of cheap and tasty burgers—the most basic *hamburguesa* comes with ham, cheese, cabbage, tomato, and onion (US$1). From there, diners can work their way up to specialty burgers with toppings like grilled pineapple, fried bananas, beans, and guacamole. Hot dogs, chicken burgers, and veggie sandwiches round out the menu. Fries are a must.

Café Sotovento (Calle 55 btwn Calles 12 and 14, tel. 981/811-2130, 7am-11pm daily,

US$4-9) is an artsy café—paintings, posters, and masks fill the walls—with a good breakfast and sandwich menu. The coffee drinks also are recommended and include a choice of brewing methods: drip, French press, even siphon. Service, unfortunately, can be painfully slow.

Sweets

★ **La Panistera** (Calle 8 near Calle 61, cell tel. 981/100-4097, 8:30am-9pm Mon.-Sat., US$0.75-3 baked goods, US$2-4 meals) tempts passersby with the smells of freshly baked artisanal breads and sweet things. Step in and the sight is irresistible: artful displays of chocolate croissants, lemon tarts, cinnamon buns, brioche, country bread, pesto focaccia, and more. Creative sandwiches and salads also offered. A handful of tables make it easy to linger.

Chocol Há (Calle 59 btwn Calles 12 and 14, tel. 981/811-7893, 8am-10:30pm Mon.-Sat., US$1.50-4) delights with a menu of both sweet and savory crepes, tamales, and fabulous chocolate drinks made with chili, vanilla, mint, and other tasty ingredients. A grassy back patio has soft lighting, and there's Wi-Fi throughout.

Just west of the central plaza, **La Gran Michoacán** (Calle 8 btwn Calles 57 and 59, 8am-10pm daily, US$1-3) offers a good variety of refreshing treats—homemade Popsicles, ice cream, and fruit juices.

Markets

For the freshest fruits and vegetables, head to the **Mercado Municipal** (Circuito Baluartes Este at Calle 57, 6am-7pm daily), which is located just outside of the colonial center's walls. This also is a good spot for cheap eats, with a string of eateries selling local dishes (US$2-3).

ACCOMMODATIONS

Campeche's city center has vastly improved its hotel offerings in the past few years. Where before bright exteriors gave way to poorly maintained interiors, today you'll often find modern hotels and upgraded colonial-style inns.

Under US$50

Casa Balché (Calle 57 near Calle 10, tel. 981/811-0087, US$12 dorm, US$38-45 s/d) is as upscale as a hostel can be. Common areas have spectacular views of the plaza, exposed stone walls, trendy furniture. Dorms themselves are bright and airy, with three bunk beds apiece; all have thick mattresses, individual reading lights, high-quality linens, and handcrafted throw pillows. There's also a well-equipped common kitchen. Breakfast, however, is not included.

Maya Campeche Hotel (Calle 57 btwn Calles 14 and 16, tel. 981/816-8053, www.mayacampechehotel.com, US$27/33 s/d with a/c) offers cozy rooms in the heart of the city; all have high ceilings, stenciled walls, and ironwork furnishings. Some are a bit dark—reminiscent of large closets, actually—but quiet air-conditioning, flat-screen TVs, and spotless bathrooms make that easy to overlook. A rooftop lounge makes a great place to watch the sunset over the city.

Hotel Balamkú (Calle 57 btwn Calles 14 and 16, tel. 981/811-6488, balamkuhotelcafe@gmail.com, US$33-50 s/d with a/c) is a six-room hotel set in a remodeled colonial home. Rooms are compact and clean with whitewashed walls and handwoven bedspreads and throw pillows; all have flat screen TVs. A small interior courtyard with colorful tile floors and plenty of seating doubles as a dining area. Full breakfast is included.

The contemporary **H177 Hotel** (Calle 14 btwn Calles 59 and 61, tel. 981/816-4463, www.h177hotel.com, US$35/40 s/d with a/c, US$48 suite with a/c) has minimalist rooms with stone accent walls that boast flat-screen TVs, rainfall showerheads, and good beds with duvets and comfy pillows. Rooftop suites open onto a spacious terrace for lounging. There's also a plunge pool in the center courtyard.

US$50-100

★ **Casa Mazejuwi** (Calle 14 btwn Calles 61 and 63, tel. 981/122-4033, www.mazejuwi.com, US$73-87 s/d with a/c) is one of those truly delightful hotels, a labor of love for its charming owners. Spacious rooms and common areas have a Middle Eastern theme, with low beds and sofas, warm colors, and ornate woodwork. Thoughtful details abound, like complimentary water and baskets of amenities (toothbrushes, makeup remover, etc.), and the owners are founts of info and good cheer.

Hotel Socaire (Calle 57 btwn Calles 12 and 14, tel. 981/811-2130, www.hotelsocaire.com.mx, US$76-99 s/d with a/c, US$99 suite with a/c) is a beautifully restored colonial hotel. Rooms, though simple in decor, have original tile floors, high ceilings, and exposed stone walls. Beds are thick and linens are luxurious; bathrooms are modern and the air-conditioning is quiet. Some suites have private whirlpool tubs. Common areas include outdoor lounges, a pool, and an artsy café.

Hotel López (Calle 12 btwn Calles 61 and 63, tel. 981/816-3344, www.hotellopezcampeche.com.mx, US$48/54 s/d with a/c) has modern, somewhat sparse rooms, but the quiet air-conditioning, good beds, and soft linens make up for any design shortcomings. Most rooms have balconies, some with gorgeous city views. There's a small pool and free parking too. If you're after comfort and value, this is a fine choice.

Built in 1880, **Hotel Castelmar** (Calle 61 near Calle 8, tel. 981/811-1204, www.castelmarhotel.com, US$47-52 s/d with a/c, US$68 suite with a/c), charms with its original tile floors, double-high ceilings, and dramatic wall hangings of oversized rosaries and bells. Rooms are a bit dark but still comfortable. There are heavy wooden rocking chairs in the lobby, a lovely lap pool, and lots of places to lounge under the wood-beamed arcades. Breakfast is available in the courtyard.

Over US$100

Casa Don Gustavo (Calle 59 btwn Calles 8 and 10, tel. 981/816-8090, www.casadongustavo.com, US$180 s/d with a/c, US$212-223 suite with a/c) has 10 luxurious suites in a restored 18th-century home. All have original French-style furniture, wooden ceiling beams, and crystal chandeliers, plus modern bathrooms with bidets. Two balcony rooms overlook the pedestrian-only street. Outdoor spaces include a small swimming pool, lush garden, and rooftop whirlpool tub with cathedral views. Continental breakfast is included.

★ **Hacienda Puerta Campeche** (Calle 59 at Calle 18, tel. 981/816-7508, www.marriott.com, US$299 s/d with a/c, US$379-439 suite with a/c) is a boutique hotel carved out of several adjoining 17th-century houses. Rooms are luxurious with 18-foot ceilings, large marble bathrooms, and artful decor. There's also a gourmet restaurant and rooftop lounge. The swimming pool is the crown jewel though, weaving through several enclosed rooms, complete with doorways and painted walls.

Outside of Town

Hacienda Uayamón (Carr. China-Edzná Km 20, tel. 981/813-0530, www.marriott.com, US$299-379 suite with a/c) has 12 freestanding units with elegant furnishings, private terraces, and luxe amenities. The grounds feature several buildings that have been left in a state of semi-disrepair; the pool, for instance, is ensconced within the two remaining walls of the once-elegant ballroom. The gourmet restaurant looks out over former henequen fields; reservations are required for nonguests. It's located 20 kilometers (12.4 miles) from Campeche City.

INFORMATION AND SERVICES
Tourist Information

The **city tourist office** (Calle 55 btwn Calles 8 and 10, tel. 981/811-3989, 8am-9pm Mon.-Fri., 9am-9pm Sat.-Sun.) sits in the kiosk in the central plaza. It has plenty of maps and brochures that often prove more helpful than the staffers. If it's busy, head to its **second office** (Calle 8 btwn Calles 59 and 61, no phone, same hours) in a small stand-alone building, just two blocks away.

The state also has informative, and very useful, tourism and cultural events websites: www.campeche.travel and www. culturacampeche.com.

Emergency Services

Campeche City's main hospital is the **Hospital Dr. Manuel Campos** (Calle 49 at Calle 14, tel. 981/811-1709, 24 hours). For prescriptions, bustling **Farmacia Similares** (Circuito Baluartes at Calle 55, tel. 981/816-1787, 24 hours) has good prices. To reach the **police**, dial 066 from any phone.

Money

There are lots of banks in the city center that have ATMs, though only a few also have currency-exchange services. Convenient ones with both include **Banorte** (central plaza, Calle 57 at Calle 10, 8:30am-4pm Mon.-Sat.) and **Santander** (Av 16 de Septiembre at Calle 59, 9am-4pm Mon.-Fri., 10am-2pm Sat.).

Media and Communications

The **post office** (Av. 16 de Septiembre at Calle 53, 8am-4pm Mon.-Fri., 8am-noon Sat.) is in the Palacio Federal. For web access, head to **Internet Café de Campeche** (Calle 65 btwn Calles 10 and 12, 7am-9:30pm Mon.-Thurs., 7am-9pm Fri., Sat., 8am-2pm Sat., US$0.50/hour); all the listed hotels also have Wi-Fi.

There are three big newspapers covering Campeche: *Tribuna de Campeche* (www.tribunacampeche.com), *Novedades Campeche* (www.novedadesdecampeche. com.mx), and *El Sur de Campeche* (www. elsur.mx). All are available in hardcopy at newsstands around the state.

Laundry

Burbujas (Calle 57 btwn Calles 12 and 14, tel. 981/811-6900, 8am-8pm Mon.-Sat., US$0.65 per kilo [2.2 pounds]) offers same-day service if you drop off your laundry early. There's a four-kilo minimum.

GETTING THERE

Campeche City is on the Gulf coast, 190 kilometers (118 miles) southwest of Mérida, and is a natural stopover on your way to (or from) the states of Chiapas or Tabasco.

Air

Campeche International Airport (CPE, Av. López Portillo s/n, tel. 981/823-4059) lies about two kilometers (1.2 miles) northeast of town. Frequent "China" buses (US$0.35) from the *mercado* drop off at the roundabout in front of the airport entrance; it's a five-minute walk to the terminal. Taxis from town cost US$8; from the airport, taxis charge a flat US$20.

Campeche City only has service to/from Mexico City on **Aeroméxico** (toll-free Mex. tel. 800/237-6639, www.aeromexico.com) and **Interjet** (toll-free Mex. tel. 800/011-2345, toll-free U.S. tel. 866/285-9525, www.interjet.com. mx).

Bus

Campeche's **first-class ADO station** (Av. Central at Av. Casa de Justicia, tel. 981/811-9910, toll-free Mex. tel. 800/702-8000, www. ado.com.mx), known as *la terminal nueva* (the new terminal), is located on the outskirts of town. Advance tickets also can be purchased at the local office of **ADO** (Malecón at Calle Dársena, no phone, 9am-7pm daily) in the Galerias Campeche, a modern shopping mall near the Reducto de San José El Alto fort.

Campeche also has a **second-class station** (Av. Gobernadores at Calle Chile, tel. 981/816-3445), known as *la terminal antigua* (the old terminal) or the "ex-ADO." It's located a few blocks from the colonial center.

For the **Edzná** archaeological site, *colectivos* (vans, US$2, 50 min) leave hourly 7am-4pm from Calle Tamaulipas, one block south of Baluarte San Pedro. Buses drop off at the entrance and return to Campeche hourly 9am-3:30pm.

Campeche Bus Schedule

Campeche's **first-class bus station** (tel. 981/811-9910, www.ado.com.mx) is located on Avenida Central at Avenida Casa de Justicia—a bit too far to walk with bags, but under 10 minutes in a taxi (US$3). Many buses here are *de paso* (mid-route), which means they have limited space and may depart up to 15 minutes early or late. Tickets on *de paso* buses can only be purchased same-day, so get to the terminal at least a half hour early to be sure to snag a seat:

DESTINATION	PRICE	DURATION	SCHEDULE*
Cancún	US$38-45	7-8 hrs	8 departures, 6am-11:55pm
Chetumal	US$27	6.5 hrs	2pm
Mérida	US$13-17	2.5-3 hrs	52 departures, 2:30am-11:55pm
Mexico City	US$87-105	18-20 hrs	6 departures, 12:15am-11pm
Palenque	US$25	5.5-6 hrs	5 departures, 12:30am-11:10pm
Xpujil	US$19	4.5 hrs	2pm

Campeche's **second-class bus station** (Av. Gobernadores at Calle Chile, tel. 981/816-3445) is several long, noisy blocks beyond the city walls; it's also known as the "ex-ADO" terminal:

DESTINATION	PRICE	DURATION	SCHEDULE*
Dzibalchén	US$5.50	3 hrs	hourly (5am-6:30pm)
Hopelchén	US$3.50	1.5 hrs	take Dzibalché bus
Santa Elena	US$7.50	3 hrs	6am, 9:15am, noon, 2:30pm, and 5pm
Uxmal	US$7	2.5 hrs	take Santa Elena bus
Xpujil	US$12	5.5 hrs	5:15am, 8:15am, 6:30pm, and 10pm

*Schedules are subject to change.

Car

Two good highways link Campeche City and Mérida. Highway 180 is known as the *vía corta* (the short route) and goes north from Campeche through Hecelchakán, Bécal, and Umán. Highway 261 is known as the *vía larga* (the long route) because it veers east through Hopelchén and then north through Santa Elena and the Puuc region. Their monikers notwithstanding, driving time is about the same (2-2.5 hours). If you're driving to Uxmal and the Puuc region (and aren't planning to stop at Edzná), take Highway 180 to Hecelchakán and cut across to Highway 261.

With fewer towns to pass through, you'll save about 45 minutes.

From Campeche south to Champotón, you can take Highway 180-Cuota (toll road) or Highway 180-Libre (free road). The former is a wide, fast highway and costs US$3.60; the latter goes nearer the ocean (but not always right alongside it) and passes through several small towns with their ubiquitous speed bumps. At Champotón, you can continue on Highway 180 to Ciudad del Carmen and on to Tabasco state, or take Highway 261 farther south to Escárcega, where you turn right for Palenque and the highlands of Chiapas or left for Calakmul and, eventually, the Caribbean coast.

GETTING AROUND

Campeche's city center is small and very easy to navigate on foot, but unless you have a bike or rental car, you will need a taxi or local bus to get to and from the bus terminals, airport, and some of the outlying sights.

Bus

To get to the **first-class ADO bus station,** take a "Circuito Miguel Hidalgo" or "S.E.P./Av. Central" bus or minivan (US$0.35, every 10-15 minutes) from the corner of Calle 18 at Calle 53, in front of the market; the trip takes about 20 minutes. For the **second-class terminal,** catch the "Terminal Sur" bus at the same stop. To get to either **Playa Bonita** or **Fuerte de San Miguel,** take a "Lerma/Playa Bonita" bus (US$0.35, every 30 minutes) from the corner of Calle 55 at Circuito Baluartes (on the market side) or the post office (Av. 16 de Septiembre at Calle 53); for the latter destination, ask the driver to let you off at *la subida* San Miguel (the climb to San Miguel), about 2.5 kilometers (1.6 miles) south of town. From there, it's a tough 0.5-kilometer (0.3-mile) climb to the fort. To get to the **Fuerte de San José El Alto,** take a "San José El Alto" bus from the market (US$0.35, every 30 minutes); it'll drop you off a block from the entrance.

Taxi

Cabs are relatively easy to flag down around town, and there are taxi stands next to the cathedral, near the market, and in front of both bus terminals. Your hotel should also be able to call one for you; if not, try **Radio Taxi Gaviotas** (tel. 981/815-3036). Fares around town are US$2-3 during the day, US$4-5 after

11pm (or if you call them). A cab to the airport will run about US$8. Be sure to confirm the price before getting in.

Car

Europcar (Calle 10 near Calle 59, tel. 981/811-0277, www.europcar.com, 8am-6pm daily) and **Easy Way** (Calle 57 btwn Calles 10 and 12, tel. 981/135-9186, www.campechecarrental.com, 9am-9pm daily) are located in the center. Compact cars with automatic transmission start around US$50 per day. A handful of additional car rental agencies are located at the airport.

Bicycle

Bikes can be a fun way to see the Malecón and the outlying sights. **Kankabi' Ok** (Calle 59 btwn Calles 8 and 10, tel. 981/811-2792, www.kankabiok.com.mx, 9am-1pm and 5pm-9pm Mon.-Sat.) rents well-maintained bicycles by the hour (US$1.50).

Tours

Trolley tours of Campeche's city center, historic neighborhoods, and its outlying forts are offered by **Tranvía de la Ciudad** (Calle 8 btwn Calles 55 and 53, tel. 981/816-4711, 9am-3pm and 5pm-8pm daily, US$5-8). Tours are bilingual and last 60-100 minutes, depending on the route. Look for the trolleys in the central plaza.

Requiring a minimum of two people, **Kankabi' Ok** (Calle 59 btwn Calles 8 and 10, tel. 981/811-2792, www.kankabiok.com.mx, 9am-1pm and 5pm-9pm Mon.-Sat.) organizes guided tours or just transportation to area sights, from half-day jaunts to Edzná to (very) long day excursions to the Río Bec region and Calakmul. Kayaking tours in nearby mangrove forests and bike tours of Campeche City are also offered.

South of Campeche City

The coast south of Campeche City is rarely visited by foreign travelers—it's mostly a local affair dotted with fishing villages. From Campeche City, the route south via Escárcega is the fastest way to reach Calakmul and the Río Bec region.

CHAMPOTÓN

Seafood lovers get a faraway look in their eyes when talking about Champotón, a seaside town between Campeche and Escárcega that's renowned for its *coctelerías* (seafood cocktail restaurants). Situated along the mouth of the Río Champotón, its bay was the site of an infamous 1517 battle where Spaniard Francisco Hernández de Córdova was routed by Maya leader Moch Couoh, giving rise to the name Bahia de la Mala Pelea (Bay of the Bad Fight).

Food and Accommodations

On the coastal road through town, **Pelícanos** (Av. Carlos Sansores Pérez btwn Calles 11 and 13, tel. 982/828-1418, www.restaurantpelicanos.blogspot.mx,

7:30am-7pm daily, US$5-10) serves up superfresh seafood dishes. Don't underestimate the size of the free appetizers—you needn't order any of your own. Air-conditioning and tablecloths are pluses.

Most folks come to town just to eat at the *coctelerías,* restaurants specializing in shrimp and other spicy seafood cocktails. If you're driving, the best place to go is just north of town, where there are a row of waterfront *palapas* (8am-8pm daily). The *cocteles* start at US$4, and you can swim along the sandy shoreline.

Just a couple blocks from the bus station, **Hotel Aaktun Kay** (Calle 30 btwn Calle 28-B and Av. Revolución, tel. 982/828-1800, US$25/33 s/d with a/c) is a modern hotel with rooms opening onto a courtyard with a well-maintained pool. Each room has good beds, flat-screen TVs, Wi-Fi, and, almost best of all, an ample terrace overlooking the bay.

Information and Services

ATMs can be found inside the ADO bus terminal and at **Banamex** (Calle 29, off the

Ceviche is a classic dish in Champotón.

main plaza, 9am-4pm Mon.-Fri.), which also changes money.

Getting There

On the main road, first- and second-class buses service the **ADO terminal** (Av. Revolución at Calle 32, tel. 982/828-0003). Daily first-class departures include:

- Campeche: US$5-6, 1 hour, 13 departures, 3:30am-10:55pm (second-class every 30 minutes, US$2)
- Mérida: US$13-17, 3.5-4 hours, 12 departures, 3:30am-10:55pm
- Xpujil: US$16, 3.5 hours, 3:05pm (second-class 6:20am, 9:35am, and 11:25pm, US$9.50)

Across the street, *colectivos* (public minivans) travel to and from Campeche City every 10-15 minutes 5am-10pm daily (US$1.75).

By car, Highway 180-Cuota is a toll road running from Champotón to Campeche (US$3.60). Alternatively, drivers can take Highway 180-Libre, a free road that runs north and south from town, along the Campechano coast (but not always right alongside it); it passes through several small towns and over countless speed bumps.

CENOTES MIGUEL COLORADO

If you're driving, the ecotourism project of **Cenotes Miguel Colorado** (cell tel. 981/186-5893, 7am-6pm daily, US$10) makes a worthy detour between Champotón and Escárcega. Located in the small *ejido* of Miguel Colorado, the main attraction here is **Cenote Agua Azul,** an open pool buffered by tall limestone cliffs and thick forest. The admission fee includes two blood-pumping zip line rides, each 244 meters (800 feet) across and 85 meters (279 feet) above the water, and kayaking through and swimming in the cenote's deep blue waters. The water is clearest in the winter when the trees shed their leaves, letting more light through.

An undulating trail winds around Cenote Agua Azul to **Cenote Los Patos,** where migratory birds gather in the mornings, including noisy Canada geese in December. Throughout the forest canopy, it's easy to see (and hear) the resident spider and howler monkeys. Wildlife-watchers should arrange a guided visit at dusk, when thousands of bats swarm and ascend in a vortex from a crater named **K41** (US$2.50 pp).

Food is available on-site, made by local women (US$3-5).

Getting There

The town and project are well signed from Highway 261. Go 10 kilometers (6.2 miles) east on a road with sneaky potholes, then left another 3 kilometers (1.9 miles) from the "cenote" sign in town.

ESCÁRCEGA

Escárcega is a dreary town at the junction of Highways 186 and 261. For tourists it is mainly a gas stop as they head east to the archaeological sites in the Río Bec area (154 kilometers/95 miles) or north to Campeche City (150 kilometers/93 miles), or a place to change buses.

Food and Accommodations

Global Express Hotel Escárcega (Carr. Escárcega-Villahermosa Km 152, tel. 982/824-0424, www.globalescarcega. mx, US$50-75 s/d with a/c) is your best bet in town. Units are contemporary in style and have updated amenities like quiet air-conditioning, flat-screen TVs, and Wi-Fi. Service is good and there's a small pool too. It's located at the entrance to town, next to the PEMEX station, which makes it easy to spot but a bit noisy.

Hotel Escárcega (Av. Justo Sierra Méndez 87, tel. 982/824-0187, hotelescarcega@hotmail. com, US$13 s/d, US$23 s/d with a/c) is short on personality—basic rooms, cleanish bathrooms, threadbare linens—but it'll do for a night if you're tight on cash. The rooms near reception are in the best condition.

For eats, there are a number of small family-run restaurants near the main bus station (Highway 261 and Av. Justo Sierra Méndez).

Information and Services

Near the second-class bus terminal, **Bancomer** (Calle 27 s/n, 9am-4pm Mon.-Fri.) has an ATM; there's another ATM in the ADO bus terminal.

Getting There

The **ADO bus terminal** (Hwy. 261 at Av. Justo Sierra Méndez, tel. 982/824-0144) is located on the north side of town, on the road to Campeche City. Always arrive a half hour early—service here is *de paso* (mid-route), which means seats are limited and buses may come 15 minutes early or late.

Daily departures include:

• Cancún: US$28-42, 9-10 hours, 6 departures, 12:25am-11:40pm

• Campeche: US$11-12, 2-2.25 hours, 6 departures, 12:15am-5:10pm

• Chetumal: US$15-18, 3.5-4 hours, 8 departures, 12:25am-9:20pm

• Mérida: US$23-24, 5 hours, 5 departures, 12:15am-5:10pm

• Palenque: US$11-16, 3-4 hours, 5 departures, 1:25am-1:15pm

• Xpujil: US$8-11, 2-2.25 hours, 5 departures, 8:50am-11:40pm

The **second-class bus terminal** (Av. Justo Sierra Méndez at Calle 31, tel. 982/824-0498) also offers routes headed to Xpujil and Chetumal that drop off at the Calakmul turnoff (US$4, 1 hour) or the hotels just west of Xpujil (US$7, 2 hours); departures are at 8am, 11:30am, 1:40pm, 5:30pm, 11pm, and 1am.

Note: The gas stations here are the last eastbound until Xpujil.

Río Bec Region

Campeche's Río Bec region is located in the southern part of the state, cut lengthwise by Highway 186. It's flanked by the tiny towns of Xpujil and Escárcega, and filled with the remarkable—and remarkably untouristed—Río Bec archaeological sites. The earliest occupation of the Río Bec area occurred between 1000 and 300 BC, though the height of construction was much later, between AD 550 and 830. At the end of the 9th century, however, Maya cities across the region suddenly collapsed, and their populations dispersed. By the time of the Spanish conquest, the once-glorious cities were almost completely abandoned. The Río Bec sites were rediscovered early in the 20th century by chicle tappers and are still being explored and excavated today. Indeed, this area has been the source of many of the most noteworthy archaeological discoveries of the last few decades.

Today, you'll find the massive Calakmul ruins, the mother of Río Bec sites, and possibly of the Maya world. The site boasts the largest Maya pyramid, the largest number of stelae of any Maya ruin, and possibly the greatest number of total structures (they are still being mapped and counted). If that weren't enough reason to visit, Calakmul is located deep in a nature reserve, and it's common to spot monkeys and tropical birds in the thick tree cover.

Farther along Highway 186 are several smaller sites that, while lacking the sheer size and scale of Calakmul, are no less compelling. Balamkú is near the turnoff to Calakmul; Chicanná, Becán, and Xpujil are closer to the village of Xpujil (the only town of any size in the area); and El Hormiguero is down a dirt road that's passable by most cars outside of the rainy season. The Río Bec archaeological zone is spread out over a wide area and accessible by 4WD or high-clearance vehicle only; guided tours are the best way to access and explore the sites.

Calakmul Archaeological Zone

To Entrance

ACRÓPOLIS
CHII'K NAAB

CASA DEL
6 AHAU

RESIDENTIAL
GROUP

STRUCTURE
XIII

STRUCTURE
VII

STRUCTURE
VIII

STRUCTURE
IX

TEMPLE
(STRUCTURE
XIV)

BALL
COURT

Gran
Plaza

STRUCTURE
IV

STRUCTURE
X

TEMPLE
(STRUCTURE VI)

GRAN
ACRÓPOLIS

STRUCTURE XV

STRUCTURE XX

TEMPLE
(STRUCTURE V)

EAST GROUP

TEMPLE
(STRUCTURE III)

0   200 yds

0   200 m

GREAT PYRAMID
(STRUCTURE II)

PYRAMID
(STRUCTURE I)

© MOON.COM

Most sites share the distinctive Río Bec architectural style, with its meticulous stonework and high steeple-like towers. There's no doubt that this area is the next Puuc Route, but for now you can have these stunning sites practically to yourself.

TOP EXPERIENCE

★ CALAKMUL ARCHAEOLOGICAL ZONE AND RESERVE

A UNESCO World Heritage Site, **Calakmul** (8am-5pm daily, US$3.50) may be the remains of one of the largest city-states in Maya history, home to as many as 60,000 people—and thousands more under its sphere of influence—and the seat of immense military, cultural, and economic power. Calakmul boasts the largest Maya pyramid yet discovered, looming nearly 60 meters (197 feet) above the forest floor. A whopping 6,750 structures have been mapped, and thousands more remain covered in thick brush and forest. Nine jade funeral masks and some 120 stelae have been found here, more than at any other Maya site. Another measure of Calakmul's influence can be found in the stelae of other Maya cities, in which Calakmul appears more often than any other.

History

Calakmul was originally called Kaan (Kingdom of the Serpent Head). The Maya name *Calakmul* (Two Adjacent Mounds) was coined by a Maya-speaking botanist and explorer who spotted the site's two most prominent pyramids from an airplane while surveying for chicle in 1931. However, the site went unexplored for over 50 years, even as archaeologists discovered numerous references in the inscriptions of Palenque, Tikal, and other cities to a powerful but as-yet-unknown kingdom. The first major excavation of Calakmul began in 1985, and the importance of the long-lost city quickly emerged.

It's clear that the city was enormous, with more than 6,000 structures spread over 70 square kilometers (27 square miles). Around 60,000 people lived here at the city's peak, one of the largest Maya cities ever. It was also a very old city, first settled in the 6th century BC, with many of its major structures erected by AD 250. The size of Calakmul's structures is attributable, in part, to the Maya custom of adding new temples and layers over and atop existing structures to mark significant dates or political changes. Over the centuries, they added up to create some of the Maya world's largest pyramids.

Calakmul emerged as a major power in the Classic era; the greatest number of stelae found here are dated between AD 431 and 790. The city used its military and economic power to forge many strategic alliances (usually skewed to Calakmul's advantage), and waged fierce battle with those kingdoms with whom it couldn't come to terms. Calakmul attacked Palenque in AD 599 and 611, and then Tikal in 657, under the leadership of king Yukom the Great. That ruler's son, known as Jaguar Paw, attacked Tikal again in 695 but was defeated, and his capture is glorified in inscriptions at Tikal. After that ignominious loss, Calakmul went into steady decline, a precursor to the widespread collapse of Classic-era Maya cities over the next two centuries.

Visiting the Ruins

Calakmul is deep within the **Calakmul Biosphere Reserve,** a dense protected forest teeming with animal life. Look for howler and spider monkeys, toucans, parrots, and other assorted birds and rodents as you wander the site, as well as on the winding 60-kilometer (37-mile) road from the highway to the entrance. The reserve also is home to five of Mexico's six wildcat species, including jaguars and pumas, and every so often visitors are treated to a glimpse of one. (Be aware that mosquitoes can be voracious during the rainy season, or after any heavy rain; wear long clothes and bring heavy-duty insect repellent.)

The best time to see wildlife is early morning or late afternoon, when monkeys and birds are most active. The exception is the big cats, which are most active just before dawn. (Then again, we spotted a puma—our one and only—trotting down the road at 5pm!) The fact is, spotting animals is mostly a matter of luck. Even if you don't see many (or any at all), the jungle is impressive, especially viewed from atop one of the pyramids.

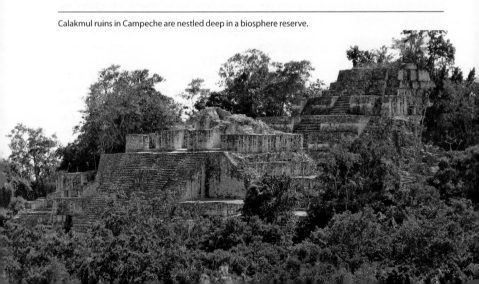

Calakmul ruins in Campeche are nestled deep in a biosphere reserve.

The ruins are just 35 kilometers (22 miles) from Guatemala, and on a clear day you can spot El Mirador ruins, just across the border.

Excellent **guided tours** of the ruins can be arranged through **Ka'an Expeditions** (Av. Calakmul s/n, tel. 983/871-6000, www.kaanexpeditions.com, noon-8pm Tues.-Sun.) and **Visit Calakmul** (Av. Calakmul s/n, tel. 981/171-7783, www.visitcalakmul.com, 9am-6pm Mon.-Fri., 9am-1pm Sat.), both based in Xpujil.

From the entrance, a path leads about a kilometer (0.6 mile) through the forest before splitting into long, medium, and short routes. The long route loops past two smaller complexes and begins in earnest in the Gran Acrópolis. The short route leads directly to the Gran Plaza, which has the largest and most impressive structures. The following route was adapted from a self-guided tour prepared by Diane Lalonde of Río Bec Dreams hotel.

Acrópolis Chii'k Naab (North Group)

Following the Ruta Larga (long route) path, you'll pass a right-hand turnoff for the **Acrópolis Chii'k Naab.** A conglomeration of 68 mapped buildings within a 2.4-hectare (6-acre) boundary, this grouping has been a hot topic ever since archaeologists discovered a series of substructures under its largest building, **Structure I.** In 2004, they uncovered a three-tiered and vividly painted sub-pyramid, believed to have been built between 600 and 700 BC, that was covered in pristine murals. Besides their excellent state of preservation, what makes these frescoes so important to Mayanists is that they depict the lives of the common people, not the nobles, gods, or spiritual representations that comprise the subject matter of all other known Maya murals. The tableaus have been pored over by academics eager to learn more about people's daily lives in that period, including what kind of food they ate and the clothes they wore. At the time of research, the structure was not yet open to the public.

Gran Acrópolis

Continue on the path to another turnoff, this one to the **Residential Group,** aka **Casa del 6 Ahau,** an elegant complex of rooms most likely used by one of Calakmul's elite extended families. The rooms' walls have niches and holes, which were surely used to hold wooden doors, curtain rods, or beams supporting the thatched roof. Rooms vary in size, some facing a central patio, others reached by narrow corridors, and it's easy to imagine a nuanced domestic scene unfolding here, with royal leaders coming and going, and children playing in the patio watched by elder grandparents sitting in their doorways. The kingly name "6 Ahau" was inscribed on a vault here, though nothing more of that ruler is known.

The path leads over a small rise to the **Gran Acrópolis. Structure XX** will be on your right, with its small maze of rooms and columns. Continuing counterclockwise (keeping the structures to your right), you'll pass **Structures XVI, XVII,** and **XV,** all with huge deteriorating stelae at their bases. The next one, **Structure X,** has somewhat better-preserved stelae, including **Stela 75,** which purportedly marks the birth of Yukom the Great, Calakmul's most accomplished leader, in AD 600. The stairway of Structure X is crumbling, but an older stairway—preserved beneath the outer one, a consequence of the Maya habit of draping new structures upon existing ones—has been exposed and is easily climbed.

Continue across the acropolis's center through Calakmul's modest **Ball Court,** which was built from stones gathered from an older building that was destroyed. At the north end of the Ball Court is a remarkably well-preserved stela depicting a ballplayer. An inscription on the stela suggests the ball court was constructed in AD 751.

At the north end of the Gran Acrópolis is **Structure XIII.** Impressive in its own right, Structure XIII is also notable for being one of the best places to get a photograph of **Structure II** (the big one). Getting to the top is a little tricky: Climb the stairs and go to the

The Maya Collapse

Something went terribly wrong for the Maya between the years AD 800 and 900. Hundreds of Classic Maya cities were abandoned, monarchies disappeared, and the population fell by millions, mainly due to death and plummeting birth rates. The collapse was widespread but was most dramatic in the Southern Lowlands, a swath of tropical forest stretching from the Gulf of Mexico to Honduras and including once-glorious cities such as Palenque, Tikal, and Copán.

Archaeologists first suspected a collapse after noticing a sudden drop-off in inscriptions; it has been confirmed through excavations of peasant dwellings from before and after the 9th century. There are many theories for the collapse, varying from climate change and epidemic diseases to foreign invasion and peasant revolt. In his carefully argued book *The Fall of the Ancient Maya* (Thames and Hudson, 2002), archaeologist and professor of anthropology at Pennsylvania State University David Webster suggests it was a series of conditions, rather than a single event, that led to the collapse.

To a certain degree, it was the very success of Maya cities during the Classic era that set the stage for their demise. Webster points to a population boom just before the collapse, which would have left agricultural lands dangerously depleted just as demand spiked. Classic-era farming techniques were ill-suited to meet the challenge; in particular, the lack of draft animals kept productivity low, meaning Maya farmers could not generate large surpluses of corn and other food. (Even if they could, storage was difficult given the hot, humid climate.) The lack of animals also limited how far away farmers could cultivate land and still be able to transport their crops to the city center; as a result, available land was overused. As Webster puts it, "too many farmers [growing] too many crops on too much of the landscape left the Classic Maya world acutely vulnerable to an environmental catastrophe, such as drought or crop disease."

Certain kingdoms reached their tipping point before others (prompting some to launch 11th-hour military campaigns against weakened rivals), but few escaped the wave of malnutrition, disease, lower birth rates, and outright starvation that seems to have swept across the Maya world in the 9th century. Kings and nobility would have faced increasing unrest and insurrection—after

far left. There, you can clamber up the end of a broken wall, and then another, to reach the third level. Go back to the center and cut through one of the doorways, where a narrow ledge zigzags to the top.

Gran Plaza

Descend Structure XIII and bear left to **Structure XIV,** a rare "two-sided" temple with stairways on either side of the structure. It dates to the Late Classic era and has stelae marking the year of the temple's construction, AD 740. Climb up and over Structure XIV—or take the path around—and continue beneath the trees to the **Gran Plaza.** As in the Gran Acrópolis, make a counterclockwise loop through this large plaza, keeping the buildings to your right.

The first one you pass is **Structure VI,** a large pyramid-like temple with two reasonably well-preserved stelae at its summit; some of the original red paint is still visible. The structure's precise orientation suggests it was used for astronomical purposes, primarily observations of the sun; it is aligned with Structure IV, on the opposite side of the plaza, allowing Maya astronomers to mark the yearly equinoxes and solstices.

Continuing on, you'll encounter **Structure V,** a small square temple surrounded by well-preserved stelae. Dates on the stelae are from the 7th century, and the glyphs and images commemorate accomplishments of Yukom the Great and his father, Scroll-Serpent.

And then there's the big one: **Structure II,** also known as the **Great Pyramid.** It forms the southern edge of the Gran Plaza, rising 53 meters (174 feet) over a hefty two-hectare (5-acre) footprint. It's the largest Maya pyramid yet discovered, and the highest in the Yucatán

Decapitated figures at Maya sites often symbolize death or calamity.

all, their legitimacy was based on their ability to induce the gods to bestow rain, fertility, and prosperity—further destabilizing the social structure and food supply.

The collapse was not universal, of course, and the fall of lowland powers gave other city-states an opportunity to expand and gain influence. But the Maya world was dramatically and permanently changed by it; the grand cities built by the Classic-era Maya were abandoned to the jungle, most never to be reoccupied, and, as Webster notes, "Cortés and his little army almost starved in 1525 while crossing a wilderness that had supported millions of people seven centuries earlier."

Peninsula. Unlike sites such as Chichén Itzá, where the most impressive structures were built relatively late, Structure II dates to the very beginning of Calakmul's rise to power, in the Preclassic period. The huge stoic masks flanking the central staircase were covered by subsequent additions, and were discovered only recently. Structure II has proved a treasure trove of Maya artifacts: Several exquisite jade funeral masks have been found in elaborate tombs housed in temples at the top of the structure. (A total of nine such masks have been found in Calakmul, more than any other site; three are on display in Campeche City at the Museo Arqueológico de Campeche and the Museo de la Arquitectura Maya, while the rest are in the Museo Nacional de Antropología in Mexico City.) More recently, archaeologists discovered a perfectly preserved temple deep within Structure II's core

with a large stucco frieze. The temple is still being excavated and is off-limits to the public, but in time visitors may be allowed to view this inner sanctum via a short tunnel about halfway up the main stairway. Climbing Structure II is a must for most visitors, though it's no easy task—use the right-hand staircase, as it's in the best condition.

Continuing around the Gran Plaza, **Structure IV** is the oldest building in the group, and one of the oldest in the city. Its core sections—others were added in later years—date to between 300 BC and AD 250. **Structure VII** completes the loop around the plaza; it was here that one of Calakmul's most recognizable jade masks was found. Climb Structure VII for one last look, over the treetops, of Structure II in all its glory.

From the Gran Plaza, a path cuts between Structures IV and VII and back to the entrance and parking lot. For those who can't get enough, two more structures await your exploration: **Structure I,** another huge pyramid, is visible from Structure II, though it remains almost completely ensconced in dark green vegetation. To get there, look for a path on the east side of Structure II. From Structure I, another path leads to **Structure III,** a Petén-style structure and the principal temple in the East Group, the oldest part of the city. Structure III is unique for apparently having never been altered; two jade masks were found in tombs here. From the East Group, a path leads back to the Gran Plaza.

Museo de Naturaleza y Arqueología de Calakmul

A good complement to the Calakmul experience is a stop at the solar-powered **Museo de Naturaleza y Arqueología de Calakmul** (7am-3pm daily, US$1). Located 20 kilometers (12.4 miles) from the highway turnoff, it contains four spacious exhibition rooms dedicated to the geology, biodiversity, and archaeology of the area. Some interpretive materials are in English. Randomly, admission also includes a ride on a 60-meter-high (197-foot) zip line behind the building. Welcome amenities here include a snack bar and bathrooms that are a million times nicer than those at the ruins.

Food and Accommodations

The Calakmul area has little in the way of lodging and dining options. Those available, however, span the budget spectrum, which makes staying near the ruins possible for everyone.

Seven kilometers (4.3 miles) down the road to Calakmul, **Campamento Yaax'che** (tel. 983/101-1921, US$5 pp, US$16 pp including gear) is one of the few honest-to-goodness campgrounds in the region. Campsites are scattered in a pleasant wooded area, and tents have all the necessary equipment (including airbeds). There are compost toilets and barrels

of water for bathing. There's also a **simple eatery** (US$3-5). Tours of the reserve and ruins are offered by experienced guides.

In the village of Conhuas, **Garra de Jaguar** (tel. 982/105-1981, US$40 s/d) has a clutch of Maya-style bungalows with white-washed walls and painted cement floors. They are sparsely decorated (the towel art is basically it) but clean and comfortable. There's a restaurant on-site, which is convenient for breakfast and dinner.

At the turnoff to Calakmul ruins, **Hotel Puerta Calakmul** (turnoff at Carr. Escárcega-Chetumal Km 98, tel. 998/884-3378, www.puertacalakmul.com.mx, US$150 s/d) has 15 spacious cabins in a wooded area near the highway (read: You'll hear late-night trucks and early-morning songbirds). The cabins are comfortable but not luxe (and a bit pricey for the goods): firm beds, murals, painted cement floors, and terraces. There's a restaurant (US$8-22) and a small pool on-site. Continental breakfast is included.

Getting There

Calakmul is a solid two-hour drive from Xpujil. From the turnoff on Highway 186, it's 60 kilometers (37 miles) down a paved but narrow and winding road to the museum and archaeological zone. Drive carefully and be ready to stop or pull over for other cars, animals, and (most commonly) large families of dim-witted oscillated turkeys in the road. And get your wallet out: There's a US$2.50 per person toll to use the road, which is on *ejido* land; another US$4 charge to enter the biosphere reserve at Kilometer 20; and a US$3.50 ruins entrance fee. Cabs also can be hired from Xpujil (US$75 up to 4 people); be sure they have the necessary permits to enter the biosphere reserve. If not, they will only be able to take you as far as the entrance to the reserve, where you'll have to hire another taxi to take you to the site (US$50 up to 4 people).

Note: Visitors are not permitted to enter the biosphere reserve after 2:30pm.

BALAMKÚ ARCHAEOLOGICAL ZONE

For years, archaeologists and the area's few tourists paid scant attention to little old **Balamkú** (8am-5pm daily, US$2.25), preferring instead to focus on Calakmul, Becán, and the grander sites of this region. But in 1990 archaeologists uncovered an incredibly well-preserved 20-meter (66-foot) **stucco frieze** inside a ruined pyramid here, and Balamkú instantly became a must-see on the southern Campeche Maya route. Relatively little has been excavated here, so there's not much to see beyond the frieze.

History

Balamkú (House of the Jaguar) shows signs of occupation as early as 300 BC. It reached its peak in the Early Classic era (AD 300-600) before collapsing, along with so many other Maya cities, toward the end of the first millennium. The frieze was built around AD 550-650 and is located in one of three bases that make up **Structure I**, in the site's central group. The frieze had been deliberately covered, probably in the course of enlarging the pyramid.

The Frieze

Balamkú's **frieze** depicts a rich scene of gods, animals, and men quite different from those appearing at surrounding sites. Some 20 meters (66 feet) long and in remarkably good condition, including a great deal of original color, the frieze has four frames. At the center of each is an animal—a toad and two crocodiles are discernible, the fourth has decomposed. Toads and crocodiles (both amphibious) represented fertility to the Maya, especially in this arid region. Above the animal figures—in the case of the toad, emerging from its gaping upturned mouth—are kings, sitting cross-legged on jaguar-skin cushions and surrounded by lilies, another sign of fertility. The implication is that the king, too, is endowed with powers of rebirth and prosperity, and will deliver them to his subjects. The

Balamkú Archaeological Zone

STRUCTURE I

FRIEZE

CENTRAL GROUP

SCALE NOT AVAILABLE

SOUTHERN GROUP

To Entrance

© MOON.COM

frames are separated by jaguars with reptile heads. Two are bound like prisoners, and were likely meant to evoke war, ritual sacrifice, and the middle world between life and death.

The cardinal directions figure prominently in Maya mythology, and Maya artisans had to develop ways of portraying the four directions in two-dimensional forms. In Balamkú's frieze, the bottom of each frame has a mask portraying Cauac, the snaggle-toothed Earth Monster. The end masks are in profile and represent north and south. The center masks both face forward; however, the one beneath the toad is pictured with a serpent devouring a bird, a symbol for west. Epigraphers, who decipher ancient writing, believe such devices would have been readily understood by most Maya observers, even illiterate commoners, and visitors from far-off cities and kingdoms.

The chamber where the frieze was found

has been carefully reconstructed to protect the fragile stucco and preserve the appearance of the surrounding structure and plaza—from the outside you can hardly tell anything is there. It is accessible through a side door. If it's locked, ask the attendant at the entrance to open the door for a peek inside.

Getting There

Balamkú is located just off Highway 186, about five kilometers (3.1 miles) west of the turnoff to Calakmul.

CHICANNÁ ARCHAEOLOGICAL ZONE

The name **Chicanná** (8am-5pm daily, US$2.75), meaning "House of the Serpent Mouth," is a reference to the site's most impressive feature: huge stone jaws framing the doorway of the main palace. The ornate design, commonly called a "monster mouth," is a classic feature of Chenes-style architecture, and Chicanná's is one of the best around. But the site also contains elements of Río Bec architecture, another example of the mixing of styles common in this region.

If you visit Chicanná in the afternoon, keep your eyes peeled for families of keel-billed toucans and the similar-looking collared aracari—a real treat. In the trees, look for rodents and small mammals, including the gray fox.

History

Despite its ominous name, archaeologists believe Chicanná was a retreat used by the elite of Becán, which is just two kilometers (1.2 miles) west and connected by an ancient roadway. Dating to the Late Preclassic period, it reached its apogee between AD 500 and 700. By AD 1100, however, it had been abandoned.

Structures XX and XI

From the entrance, you'll first pass **Structure XX,** a small but exquisitely designed **temple-residence.** Its main doorway is framed by a monster mouth, and gives way to a foyer-type room and, farther in, a twin staircase leading to the upper level. The upper facade

also has a monster-mouth doorway and, to either side, columns of masks representing Chaac, the hook-nosed god of rain. The elegance of this structure and others, plus details like the small rosettes on the 1st floor (with little human faces in the middle!) are a primary reason Chicanná is thought to have been a royal retreat. Continuing along the path, you'll pass a turnoff to **Structure XI,** the oldest in the group, dating to AD 300, before reaching Chicanná's Central Plaza.

Central Plaza

The first building you reach in the Central Plaza is **Structure I,** whose two tall, steeply pitched towers are typical of Río Bec style. Opposite is **Structure II,** with its spectacular monster-mouth facade framing the doorway. The two spiral features above the door are the eyes; similar spirals to each side are the ears, and the teeth are quite obvious, above the door and protruding from the patio like a snake with a mean underbite. A section of red glyphs can be seen to the right of the door. Left of the main entrance, a smaller door is topped with a stone decoration in the form of a *na,* the traditional thatched hut used by ancient Maya and still common today. The exact meaning of the image here (and seen at Uxmal, Labná, and other ruins) is unclear, though a thatched hut—with a three-stone hearth inside it—represents the beginning of the universe in some Maya creation myths.

Completing the Central Plaza are **Structures III** and **IV,** both multiroom buildings, while newly excavated **Structure VI,** with a dramatic windowed roof comb and red paint visible on its back side, stands a short distance southeast of the plaza. Look for a footpath between Structures II and IV leading there.

Getting There

Chicanná is located 8.8 kilometers (5.5 miles) west of Xpujil on Highway 186. The site is just 500 meters (0.3 mile) from the highway turnoff.

Chicanná Archaeological Zone

To Xpujil and Chetumal →

To Escárcega ←

186

TICKETS AND RESTROOMS

TEMPLE-RESIDENCE

CHULTÚN

STRUCTURE III

CENTRAL PLAZA

STRUCTURE II

STRUCTURE I   STRUCTURE IV

STRUCTURE XI

STRUCTURE VI

SCALE NOT AVAILABLE

© MOON.COM

BECÁN ARCHAEOLOGICAL ZONE

East of Chicanná on Highway 186 is the turn-off to **Becán** (8am-5pm daily, US$3). The largest of the Río Bec sites after Calakmul. Becán is a fascinating site, especially if you enjoy climbing and clambering around.

History

The area around Becán was settled as early as 600 BC but did not rise to greatness until more than 1,000 years later, in part because it dwelled under the ever-present shadow of Calakmul. When Calakmul went into decline at the turn of the 8th century, Becán quickly emerged as one of the most important commercial and political centers of the Río Bec region. The sheer size of its pyramids and other structures suggests it commanded a labor force of many thousands.

The Moat

The name *Becán* means "ravine formed by water," no doubt a reference to the huge dry **moat** that forms a half moon around the site.

Measuring an impressive 15 meters (49 feet) wide and 4 meters (13 feet) deep, the moat was most likely used for defense, and is one of very few such structures found in Mesoamerica.

Central Plaza

A pathway from the ticket booth leads through the trees, across the moat, and to the back side of **Structure IV**, which has a profusion of decorative elements and openings. As tempting as it will be to clamber up it, there is much better access from the other side, at the end of your visit. Instead, continue through Becán's unique **corbelled alley**—a long covered passageway that functioned as a public street. It contains small niches that likely held images of deities, and where passersby might have paused to make small offerings.

Emerging onto the **Central Plaza,** the massive pyramids, **Structures VIII** and **IX,** loom to your right in the northeast corner of the plaza. Both can be climbed, and afford spectacular views of the countryside. Structure IX, at 30 meters (98 feet) high, is the tallest structure at Becán; at the top is a

Becán Archaeological Zone

Dry Moat

West Plaza

RESIDENCES
(STRUCTURE X)

PYRAMID
(STRUCTURE IX)

Central
Plaza

BALL
COURT

STUCCO
MASK

STRUCTURE VI

PYRAMID
(STRUCTURE VIII)

RESIDENCE
(STRUCTURE IV)

STRUCTURE II

East
Plaza

STRUCTURE III

PALACE
(STRUCTURE I)

ENTRANCE

TICKETS
AND
RESTROOMS

To Chicanná
and Escárcega

0   100 yds

0   100 m

© MOON.COM

To Xpujil and Chetumal

platform with a huge mask on one end and a shield-image on the other.

At the west end of the Central Plaza is **Structure X.** Though not as imposing as the two pyramids, many visitors find this one the site's most fascinating. Walking around the back, or west, side, you'll see that the structure contains several large central chambers (12 in all) and innumerable smaller rooms, spread over several levels and connected by way of winding staircases and passageways; there's even a hidden 2nd-floor patio on the south end. While many Maya structures gained complexity as new rooms and levels were added, Structure X's elegant design suggests it was planned from the start. The rooms are clearly residences, and some archaeologists speculate Structure X was a dormitory of sorts, possibly for Becán's religious leaders.

Be sure not to miss the beautiful and extremely well-preserved stucco mask on Structure X's southern exterior wall. Only recently uncovered, the mask may depict the sun god Kinichná. It has much of its original red paint and is protected by a pane of glass and a tarp, the latter of which visitors must lift to get a peek at the mask. The **Ball Court** lies adjacent to the southern end of Structure X.

East Plaza

A short path leads through trees along the edge of the site to the **East Plaza.** The long, imposing palace you see is **Structure I.** Its twin towers are much decayed, but still have remains of the impossibly steep staircases typical of the Río Bec style. The stairs on the southeast side are the least perilous. Below, two levels of vaulted rooms are clearly more luxurious than the austere cells in Structure X; it's not hard to imagine Becán's elite occupying these grand, roomy chambers.

Structure I's back wall forms one side of the East Plaza. On the opposite side is **Structure IV,** the same building you encountered entering the site, albeit from the other side. Structure IV's staircase is well preserved, and a rope makes it even more climbable. At the top, look for narrow doorways on either side of the platform leading to spiral staircases down to musty rooms and passages in the structure's interior.

Back on the East Plaza, a staircase at the northeast corner (between Structures III and IV) leads down to the path you take to exit the site.

Getting There

Becán is located five kilometers (3.1 miles)

one of Becán's massive pyramids, Structure VIII

east of Chicanná and seven kilometers (4.3 miles) west of Xpujil. The turnoff is well marked, and an access road of several hundred meters brings you to the entrance area.

XPUJIL ARCHAEOLOGICAL ZONE

Xpujil (8am-5pm daily, US$2.75) is a small but well-preserved site. It dates to 400 BC, though it reached its height between AD 500 and 750. Structure I, built in classic Río Bec style, is the most famous of the few structures that have been excavated here. It has three towers—a central one flanked by two smaller ones—unusual in that most temples in the region only have two. There are also several false staircases. On the back of the central tower, check out what's left of two huge, stylized masks. Notably, Structure I also has 12 rooms that are oriented toward the cardinal points; the building itself is aligned with Structure VIII at the Becán ruins, 10 kilometers (6.2 miles) away. The remaining buildings, Structures II, III, and IV, are believed to have been aristocratic residences.

Getting There

The well-marked Xpujil ruins are located on the western edge of the like-named town, right next to the highway.

EL HORMIGUERO ARCHAEOLOGICAL ZONE

Spanish for "The Anthill," El Hormiguero (8am-5pm daily, free) reached its height between AD 730 and 830. It is a site that few people visit, mostly because of the difficulty in reaching it, especially if it has rained. Although only a few structures have been excavated, those that have been uncovered are dramatic (and worth the trip!). It is most notable for Structure II, a 50-meter-long (164-foot) building in the Southern Group with two tall towers flanking an enormous monster-mouth doorway. From there, a path leads visitors directly to the Central Group, where Structure V—and its imposing monster-mouth entrance—looms. There is no signage,

unfortunately, but with so many unexcavated mounds, the site really fires the imagination. In the late afternoon, listen and look for howler monkeys foraging in the trees high overhead.

Getting There

Located 22 kilometers (13.7 miles) south of Xpujil town, Hormiguero was, until recently, almost impossible to access without a heavy-duty 4WD vehicle and a lot of time. The road has improved significantly, and though it is still no autobahn, just about any car can jostle through as long as you go slowly; the last 1.5 km (0.9 mi) is a single-lane dirt road, which can be especially rough after it has rained. Expect to startle the caretaker—he rarely sees visitors.

RÍO BEC ARCHAEOLOGICAL ZONE

The namesake site of this region is made up of 70 scattered groups (2,000 mapped mounds) and is currently being excavated. The architecture follows the region's dominant style, with high, steep towers and tight-fitting stonework. A lack of a central plaza and no evidence of a larger settlement suggest that Río Bec was a getaway of sorts for the elite. It is believed that each group of structures functioned like a colonial-era hacienda, occupied by a privileged family and a small staff.

Getting There

Unfortunately, Río Bec is quite difficult to visit. The access road is rutted and so overgrown that 4WD or high-clearance vehicles are needed; after rain, it can be impassable. The best way to visit it is on a guided tour, which can be arranged locally.

VOLCÁN DE LOS MURCIÉLAGOS

Between Kilometers 105 and 106 on Highway 186, there is a small turnoff on the north side, just big enough to pull your car off the road. From there, walk a couple of hundred meters through the trees and up a small hill to a huge sinkhole, at the bottom of which is a narrow cave opening. About 30 minutes before dusk every night, an estimated three million small black bats emerge from this cave in an endless whirling rush. Known locally as the *volcán de los murciélagos* (volcano of the bats), it is an incredible spectacle and like no other. At the height, you can feel the wind from their collective wings and winding upward flight—a few may even crash into you or stop for a rest on your pant leg. (No worries—they're harmless to humans, feeding mostly on insects.)

If driving near the cave at dusk, heed the yellow bat signs on the highway and slow down so you don't hit them. Better yet, pull over and watch the bats darkening the sky.

XPUJIL TOWN AND AROUND

A small, dusty village with one traffic light, Xpujil is the only place in the Río Bec region with basic services for tourists. Not a particularly pleasant town, it's a convenient place to stay if you don't have a car. If you do have a rental, it's worth staying outside of town and coming in for some meals and to fill your gas tank.

Tours

Ka'an Expeditions (Av. Calakmul s/n, tel. 983/871-6000, www.kaanexpeditions.com, noon-8pm Tues.-Sun., US$43-75) offers fantastic tours of the Río Bec region's archaeological sites, highlighting Maya history and culture. Other excursions include hikes through the Calakmul Biosphere Reserve to view its mind-boggling variety of flora and fauna. Adventurous multiday camping trips also can be arranged. Guides are bilingual certified naturalists.

Visit Calakmul (Av. Calakmul s/n, tel. 981/171-7783, www.visitcalakmul.com, 9am-6pm Mon.-Fri., 9am-1pm Sat.) is an arm of Pronatura, Mexico's largest environmental conservation NGO. More than a tour agency, the organization provides information on area sites and connects visitors with ecotourism projects in nearby villages. Activities include guided tours to Maya ruins, caving in Cristóbal Colón, trekking and mountain biking through the low forests near El Hormiguero, and visiting artisanal workshops in the village of 20 de Noviembre. Listings of recommended private guides and accommodations (including camping) are provided. The office also can help visitors create multiday tour packages. English is spoken. It's located on the eastern edge of town, before the gas station.

Food

The restaurant selection in and around Xpujil is slowly improving, with a handful of good sit-down restaurants and many mom-and-pop stands. Many hotels have on-site restaurants or kitchenettes for light cooking.

IN TOWN

Sazón Veracruzano (Av. Calakmul 92, no phone, 7am-11pm Mon.-Sat., US$3-5) is a pleasant restaurant across from Xpujil ruins. The menu is classic Mexican—tacos, fajitas, quesadillas—with a handful of salads, sandwiches, and pastas; there's a kids' menu too. The dining experience is upscale for these parts, with tablecloths and handpainted plates. Eat on the breezy porch for a bit of people-watching.

La Pizzeta (Calle Chicanná at Av. Calakmul, tel. 983/871-6034, 4pm-11pm daily, US$2-4) is often bursting at the seams with travelers craving a change of pace. Double cheeseburgers and thin-crust pizza come fast and piping hot. Try to nab a table streetside for the breeze. It's located just half block from the main drag, near the town's only stoplight.

La Tejita (Restaurante Génesis, Av. Calakmul s/n, tel. 983/127-9937, 24 hrs daily, US$1.50-3) is the only eatery in town that never closes (the owners live on-site). Come here for *sopes* and *guaraches,* thick tortillas topped or filled with meat, chicken, or veggie combos. It's located on the west end of town.

For one-stop grocery shopping, head to **Abarrotes Willy's** (Av. Calakmul s/n, 8am-10pm daily) near the bus station.

OUTSIDE OF TOWN

Río Bec Dreams (Carr. Escárcega-Chetumal Km 141, cell tel. 983/126-3526, www.riobecdreams.com, 7:30am-9pm daily, US$7-12) has an international menu with an unexpected variety of dishes: hummus with pita bread, Niçoise salad, chicken curry, and salmon with hollandaise sauce. Dishes are hearty and presented with flair. Box lunches also are available with advance notice, and are highly recommended for long days at the ruins.

Accommodations

Xpujil town has some basic, affordable hotels, but the area's best lodging options are a few kilometers west of town, along Highway 186. If you're planning to visit Calakmul, consider spending at least one night near the site.

IN TOWN

Hotel Maya Balam (Calle Xpujil near Av. Calakmul, tel. 983/835-7527, maya_balam_hotel@hotmail.com, US$7.50 dorm, US$27/38 s/d with a/c) is the best option in town. A modern building in a residential neighborhood (read: early-morning rooster crows), it has three floors of spacious rooms, all with good beds and hot-water bathrooms. There's a separate dorm building with five basic rooms, each with two twin beds and shared spick-and-span bathrooms. The on-site restaurant is decent.

Next to the bus station, **Hotel Victoria** (Av. Calakmul s/n, tel. 982/435-9343, US$17/19 s/d with a/c) is a basic hotel with a few frills—air-conditioning, Wi-Fi, satellite TV—that make for a fine night's stay. Ask for a room toward to the back to minimize the sound of idling buses and trucks passing at night.

OUTSIDE OF TOWN

Sitting on 20 hectares (50 acres) of low forest in Valentín Goméz Farías, ★ **Casa Ka'an** (Camino a Laguna Carolina Km 1, tel. 983/871-6000, www.casakaan.com, US$60-130 s/d with a/c) is like an oasis: six little houses shaded by fruit trees, each modern in function and style, with full kitchen and private porch. Amenities include Wi-Fi, a minibar, luxe linens, even food baskets. Each morning, a chef prepares breakfast en suite, complete with fresh coffee and juice. Bike rentals are available.

In the village of Bécan, **Hotel Otoch Beek** (Calle Niños Héroes, tel. 983/135-1043, US$30-35 s/d with a/c) comprises four standalone units on a leafy lot, each with one or two spacious private rooms. All have hot-water bathrooms, flat-screen TVs, and small terraces where continental breakfast is served. Owned by a father-daughter team, service is friendly and accommodating. Look for it next to the soccer field.

Río Bec Dreams (Carr. Escárcega-Chetumal Km 141, cell tel. 983/126-3526, www.riobecdreams.com, US$55 s/d jungalow, US$64-69 s/d cabin) has just seven units: lovely "jungalows"—bungalows in the jungle—and spacious *palapa*-roofed cabins. All have comfy beds and private bathrooms plus details like high-thread-count linens, hand-painted sinks, and coffee machines. Well-lit paths connect the units to a plunge pool and a great on-site restaurant. Wi-Fi is available. The hotel is along the highway 12 kilometers (7.4 miles) west of Xpujil.

Information and Services

Visit Calakmul (Av. Calakmul s/n, tel. 981/171-7783, www.visitcalakmul.com, 9am-6pm Mon.-Fri., 9am-1pm Sat.) provides in-depth information on area sites, including recommendations for private guides. Look for the bright yellow building on the eastern edge of town, right before the gas station. English is spoken.

Xpujil Hospital Integral (Av. Siluituc btwn Calles Balamkú and Balakbal, tel. 983/871-6209) is a basic clinic with 24-hour emergency service. For meds, try **Farmacia del Centro** (Av. Calakmul, tel. 983/871-6285, 24 hours) next to Abarrotes Willy's.

License, Please

There are numerous military and police checkpoints in southern Campeche, especially east of Xpujil near the border with Quintana Roo. You also may encounter them on the Carretera Fronteriza outside Palenque, and on coastal roads in the Costa Maya. Checkpoints are typically announced by orange pylons placed down the center lane and large signs flanked by uniformed soldiers or officers. Drug smugglers and illegal immigrants are the main targets, and most tourists are waved through. The etiquette is to roll through slowly, coming to a full stop only if the soldier or officer signals you to do so. If you are stopped, you may be asked for your passport, driver's license, or vehicle registration, and the trunk of your car may be searched, as may the contents of your bags (though this is fairly rare). Friendly cooperation—and not having anything illegal—is the best way to get through these checkpoints as quickly as possible.

For cash, there's a **24-hour ATM** (Av. Halaltún btwn Calles Balakbal and Becán) outside of the Palacio Municipal (city hall), and another inside **Abarrotes Willy's** (Av. Calakmul s/n, 8am-10pm daily).

Getting There and Around

Having a rental car is all but essential to enjoy the ruins here. Without one, you'll either spend a lot of time waiting for rides or a lot of money on taxi service, or both. Hitching is possible to and from Calakmul but not a sure thing.

BUS

The **first- and second-class bus station** (tel. 983/871-6511) is on the main drag near the only traffic light in town. Daily departures include:

- Bacalar (US$8, 1.5 hours, 1:05am)
- Campeche (US$12-20, 4.5 hours, 5 departures, 4am-4:25pm)
- Cancún (US$23, 7-8 hours, 6 departures, 1am-11:45pm)
- Chetumal (US$5-9, 2 hours, 7 departures, 2am-11:45pm)
- Escárcega (US$7, 2 hours, 14 departures, 12:20am-10:25pm)
- Palenque (US$20, 6-7 hours, 2:40am)
- Playa del Carmen (US$20, 6-7 hours, 6 departures, 1am-11:45pm)
- Tulum (US$17, 4-5 hours, 6 departures, 1am-11:45pm)

Colectivos to Chetumal (US$7, 1.5 hours, every 15-30 minutes 7am-10am) and Campeche (US$11, 4 hours, 3am) leave from Abarrotes Willy's, kitty-corner from the bus terminal.

CAR

Explora Car Rental (cell tel. 983/120-8263, www.exploracarrental.com) is a convenient for people traveling by bus who want the convenience of exploring the Río Bec region by car. The fleet ranges from hatchbacks to minivans; all come fully insured. Rates begin at US$48 per day.

There are three **gas stations** to choose from—two as you head east from town and one just to the west.

TAXI

If you don't have a car, your best bet is to take a cab to the ruins. You can either call one from the **main taxi cooperative** (983/871-6101) or stop by the taxi stand next to the town's one traffic light. Round-trip transportation for up to four people (including wait time) costs US$75 to Calakmul and Balamkú; US$75 to Kohunlich and Dzibanché; US$50 to Río Bec; US$25 Chicanná and Becán; and US$25 to Hormiguero.

Palenque

True, Palenque and the state of Chiapas are not technically part of the Yucatán Peninsula (in fact, they don't even share a border). But the two regions' history and culture are so deeply intertwined, it's impossible to truly understand one without knowledge of the other.

The main connection is Maya, of course, from pre-Hispanic times to the present. Much of what archaeologists know about the ancient Maya throughout Mesoamerica stems from work conducted at Palenque, from early advances in deciphering Maya writing to the discovery of the tomb of Lord Pakal. Palenque is also, quite simply, a masterpiece of Maya construction, a must-see for its elegant structures and artful inscriptions.

Highlights

Look for ★ to find recommended sights, activities, dining, and lodging.

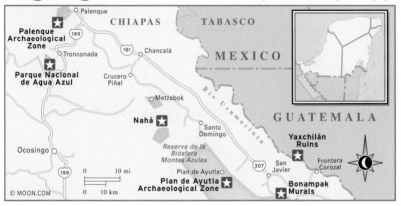

★ **Palenque Archaeological Zone:** One of the most important Maya sites, Palenque also happens to be among the most beautiful, with graceful structures and well-preserved carvings and hieroglyphics. And unlike many other ruins, it has a terrific museum (page 429).

★ **Parque Nacional de Agua Azul:** Pictures don't do justice to this remarkable natural phenomenon: Luminescent blue water tumbles over a series of powerful waterfalls and gathers in calm clear pools, perfect for swimming. It's a great day trip from Palenque, but plan on going midweek—this place definitely draws a crowd (page 447).

★ **Nahá:** Deep in the rainforest, this Lacandón Maya village isn't easy to reach, but it's all the more rewarding when you do. Visitors sleep in cabins, explore pristine lakes and forest trails, and experience ancient Maya ceremonies, all in a welcoming but unadulterated atmosphere (page 449).

★ **Plan de Ayutla Archaeological Zone:** Climb to the tops of twin pyramids to discover wondrous semi-excavated temples, some with high, peaked ceilings, others with ancient glyphs painted on their walls. Best of all, there's not a soul in sight (page 453).

★ **Bonampak Murals:** Inside a temple halfway up Bonampak's main staircase are some of the finest and best-preserved Maya murals yet discovered. In brilliant colors they tell of the ascension of a boy king, jungle warfare, and ritual bloodletting (page 458).

★ **Yaxchilán Ruins:** Perched on a leafy riverbank, Yaxchilán exudes a regal bearing, as if waiting assuredly for its glory days to return. When you're not admiring the gorgeous carvings and complex layout, keep an eye out for huge crocodiles sunning themselves on the banks and howler monkeys swinging in the trees (page 463).

Palenque

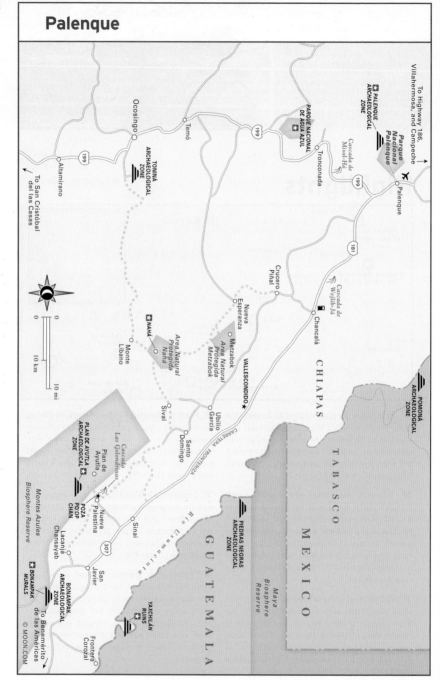

To Highway 186, Villahermosa, and Campeche

PALENQUE ARCHAEOLOGICAL ZONE

Parque Nacional Palenque

Palenque

PARQUE NACIONAL DE AGUA AZUL

Troncoonada

Cascada de Misol-Ha

Ocosingo

Temó

199

199

181

TONINÁ ARCHAEOLOGICAL ZONE

199

Altamirano

To San Cristóbal del las Casas

Crucero Piñal

Cascada de Wejlib-la

Chancalá

Nueva Esperanza

Metzabok

Area Natural Protegida Metzabok

NAHÁ

Area Natural Protegida Nahá

Monte Libano

VALLESCONDIDO ★

CHIAPAS

POMONÁ ARCHAEOLOGICAL ZONE

Sival

Ubilio Garcia

Santo Domingo

CARRETERA FRONTERIZA

TABASCO

M E X I C O

PLAN DE AYUTLA ARCHAEOLOGICAL ZONE

Cascada Las Golondrinas

Plan de Ayutla

POZA PO'OP CHAN

Nueva Palestina

Sinai

307

Lacanjá Chansayab

Montes Azules Biosphere Reserve

BONAMPAK ARCHAEOLOGICAL ZONE

BONAMPAK MURALS

San Javier

To Benemérito de las Américas

Río Usumacinta

PIEDRAS NEGRAS ARCHAEOLOGICAL ZONE

Maya Biosphere Reserve

YAXCHILÁN RUINS

Frontera Corozal

G U A T E M A L A

0   10 km

0   10 mi

© MOON.COM

Palenque and the Yucatán are bound by modern Maya society as well. The Lacandón Maya of central Chiapas are direct descendants of Yucatec Maya who fled into the rainforest to escape Spanish conquest. Today they continue to speak Yucatec Maya, even as they've adapted to a vastly different environment and circumstances. And like the Yucatán, Palenque's marquee attraction is just the beginning of what a visitor can see and do there. Popular day trips include visiting additional (and striking) ruins like Yaxchilán and Bonampak, and a series of scenic waterfalls along the peculiarly turquoise Tulijá River; longer excursions include visiting remote Lacandón villages, nestled deep in the rainforest.

PLANNING YOUR TIME

It's worth budgeting a full day to visit the archaeological site at Palenque; although it isn't terribly big, it's a place many enjoying lingering over, and the on-site museum is highly recommended. The popular day trips from town—visiting Yaxchilán and Bonampak, or the waterfalls—each require a full day; a trip to the remote Lacandón villages requires at least two days and a night, preferably more. If time is short, there's a much more accessible Lacandón community near Bonampak ruins, but it is also significantly more commercialized.

Palenque Archaeological Zone and Town

The town of Santo Domingo de Palenque, usually just called Palenque, is eight kilometers (5 miles) from the Palenque archaeological zone. The town itself is rather grubby and nondescript, but it bulges at the seams with tourists here to visit the ruins. Avenida Juárez, the main drag, is where you'll find the bus terminal, tour agencies, and other services, plus a number of no-frills hotels. Many travelers find the leafy neighborhood of La Cañada and the hotels along the road to the ruins to be more pleasant spots to spend the night, though they cost a bit more. There's a small central plaza at one end of Avenida Juárez, and a large sculpture of a Maya warrior's head (and the turnoff to the ruins) at the other.

TOP EXPERIENCE

★ PALENQUE ARCHAEOLOGICAL ZONE

Palenque (8am-5pm daily, US$3.50) is a must-see on any itinerary of Maya ruins. It is a relatively small site—by no means as large as Chichén Itzá or Tikal—but considered by many to be the *Mona Lisa* of Maya ruins, with a particularly graceful design and construction. Its setting, on a lush green shelf at the edge of the Sierra de Chiapas forest, perfectly complements its elegant design and ornate carvings. And unlike many archaeological sites, Palenque's museum is terrific, with a small but exquisite collection of stone, ceramic, and stucco artifacts accompanied by well-written explanations.

Previous: Palenque's Temple of the Inscriptions; mural at Bonampak archaeological site; crocodile sunning itself along the Río Usumacinta.

Palenque Archaeological Zone

To Museum, Gift Shops, and Palenque Town

P

TICKETS AND RESTROOMS

TEMPLE OF THE SKULL

TOMB OF THE RED QUEEN

TEMPLE OF THE INSCRIPTIONS

TEMPLE OF THE JAGUAR

FUNERARY CORRIDOR

HOUSE OF ENTHRONEMENT

PATIO OF THE WARRIORS

THE PALACE

PATIO OF THE CAPTIVES

TEMPLE OF THE SUN

TEMPLE XIV

CROSSES GROUP

TEMPLE OF THE CROSS

TEMPLE OF THE FOLIATED CROSS

TEMPLE II

TEMPLE OF THE COUNT

NORTH GROUP

BALL COURT

Río

Otolum

RESTROOMS

Queen's Bath

To Bats Group, Museum, and Exit

0   60 yds
0   60 m

© MOON.COM

History

The word *Palenque,* Spanish for "fortification," is a rough translation of the Ch'ol Maya term *Otolum* (Strong Houses); that's how local residents described the mysterious stone ruins to Spanish explorers at the time of the conquest. The ancient city's true original name was Lakam Ha, or Big Water, surely a reference to the many springs and streams found in the area. It was the capital of a city-state known as B'aak (Bone Kingdom).

Scholars have been able to decipher enough Maya glyphs to construct a reasonable genealogy of the Palenque kings, from the rule of Chaacal I (AD 501) to the demise of Kuk (AD 783). But it was the period from AD 615 to 702, during the glorious reigns of Pakal the Great and his eldest son, Kan Balam, that Palenque grew from a minor city to an important economic and political center.

Palenque's most distinguished leader, Pakal the Great (properly called K'inich Janaab' Pakal, or Great Sun Shield, but also referred to as Lord Pakal or Pakal II) was born in AD 603 and ascended to the throne in AD 615, when he was just 12 years old. Pakal lived to be 81 years old—remarkable for that time—and during his long rule expanded Palenque's influence throughout the western Maya lowlands. He built the Temple of the Inscriptions to house his own elaborate tomb, and commissioned many of the most notable structures and artworks in the palace.

Pakal was succeeded by his eldest son, Kan Balam (Serpent Jaguar, also written as Chan Balam), who was noteworthy for having six digits on his hands and feet. (To maintain the royal bloodline, Maya rulers often took relatives as wives, eventually leading to birth defects. Pakal himself had a clubfoot, and some archaeologists believe his mother and father were siblings.) Kan Balam reigned for 18 years and built the Temples of the Cross, Foliated Cross, and Sun to prove the preordination of his rule.

When Kan Balam died in AD 702, his younger brother, Kan Xul, took the reins of power. His rule was Palenque's apogee in terms of population—over 50,000 by some estimates—and political power, controlling a region that extended nearly from the Sierra Madre to the Gulf of Mexico. But the glory was not to last; in AD 711, Palenque attacked its longtime rival, Toniná, but was unexpectedly defeated by the much smaller kingdom. Palenque's king was captured and killed—described in victorious carvings and texts in Toniná—leaving Palenque in disarray, with

Palenque's Palace

no supreme ruler for over a decade. A new king named K'inich Akal Mo' Nab'—presumably a descendant of the Pakal dynasty, but it's uncertain—emerged in AD 722, and was succeeded by his son and grandson. Several new structures were commissioned under their reigns, and Palenque appeared to be on the rise once again. However, the historical record abruptly ends in AD 799, after which the city underwent a rapid and lasting decline, part of a widespread Maya collapse during that period.

The first detailed account of Palenque by Europeans was made by a Spanish army captain, Antonio del Río, who passed through in March 1785. (Two centuries earlier, Hernán Cortés came within a few dozen kilometers of the ruins but apparently never knew they were there.) Del Río drew maps and plans and eventually received a royal order to excavate the site for a year. But the Spaniard's "excavation" was amateur and brutish and led to the destruction of a number of structures. Captain del Río also broadcast wild and fantastic assumptions about the beginnings of the Maya. It wasn't long before Europeans envisioned Palenque as the lost city of Atlantis or a sister civilization to the ancient Egyptians. A true picture of Palenque didn't emerge until the mid-1800s, when the American diplomat John L. Stephens and English artist Frederick Catherwood visited the site and wrote and drew realistic and detailed accounts of what they saw.

Temples XII and XIII

Through the entrance you follow a short road and ascend a few steps to Palenque's main plaza. The first two temples on your right are Temples XII and XIII, known as **Funerary Corridor** for their deathly ornamentation and content.

Temple XII is also known as the **Temple of the Skull,** so named for the stucco relief of a rabbit skull, visible at the base of one of the pillars on the upper temple and probably representing a god of the underworld. (Unfortunately, you can't climb the stairs

to get a better look.) In the 1990s, archaeologists uncovered a passageway leading from that same upper patio to a sarcophagus deep in the structure's interior, just as was famously discovered in the site's Temple of the Inscriptions. Inside the tomb were the remains of a leader, as yet unidentified, plus several other bodies, most likely the leader's servants. Alas, the passage and tomb are also off-limits to visitors.

Temple XIII contains a crypt discovered in 1994. Dubbed the **Tomb of the Red Queen,** the three-room chamber has a large stone sarcophagus in which archaeologists discovered the remains of a woman. The woman had been interred with a jade mask, a rich collection of jade jewelry, pearls, obsidian knives, and bone needles, and was covered in cinnabar powder, a prized red pigment—hence the evocative name. The woman's identity hasn't been determined, thanks to the lack of inscriptions of any kind. Because of its similarities to the tomb of Pakal the Great, archaeologists originally suspected the remains were of his mother; however, DNA tests found no commonalities between the skeletons. It is now believed the remains are of Pakal's wife, Tz'ak-bu Ajaw. The remains of the Red Queen were removed and reinterred in a different location to better preserve them. Visitors can see the tomb and sarcophagus (which is itself painted red) through a passageway near the bottom of the stairs. This is not the original entryway, however: It was created to study—and now showcase—the inner tomb. The original entry has not yet been discovered.

Temple of the Inscriptions

Just beyond Temple XIII is the **Temple of the Inscriptions,** a 24-meter-high (79-foot) pyramid and Palenque's most famous structure. Its name derives from the magnificent glyph-covered tablets found in the spacious temple at its summit, which tell the ancestral history of the Palenque rulers. It was toward the rear of that lofty gallery that Mexican archaeologist Alberto Ruz L'Huillier first uncovered, in 1949, a secret stairway cleverly hidden under

Maya Funerary Rites

From ancient times to today, across cultures and continents, funeral rites have played an important role in virtually all human societies. The Maya were (and are) no exception, with elaborate practices and beliefs associated with death, laying the dead to rest, and what occurs in the afterlife. Although modern religion has extinguished many traditional practices, especially related to death and burial, vestiges still remain in Maya communities of today.

Ancient Maya believed that most people who died had to travel through a dark and perilous underworld known as Xibalba. Those who died in battle, by sacrifice or suicide, or as infants were spared the trip, but everyone else needed supplies: Bodies were often buried with corn in their mouths (for nourishment), with a jade or other precious stone in their mouth (for currency), and with objects like whistles or figurines (for guidance or protection); a body might also be buried with a personal tool or possession, possibly to help identify the deceased in the afterlife. Early Maya tended to bury their dead in a fetal position or inside large urns; later, it was more common to extend the body with the head facing north or west.

Common people were usually buried in graves dug right into the floor of their homes. (In fact, looking for human remains beneath a structure is one way archaeologists determine if it was a residence or not.) Royalty were afforded far more elaborate rites, including the construction of massive vaults and pyramids in their honor. The tombs of royalty were often filled with precious items, including jade masks, fine pottery, elaborate tools and weapons, beads, jewelry, and platters of food and drink. In some cases, the nobleperson's attendants were sacrificed and buried at their sides. Remains have also been found in cenotes (sacrificial victims, most likely) and in caves (where ritual burials may have taken place).

Of course, failing to follow such rites can be a sign of social unrest. Archaeologists have discovered tombs filled with a jumble of bodies, sometimes decapitated or mutilated—these may be unfortunate royalty, killed by rivals or in peasant uprisings, whose haphazard burial would have been a deliberate insult.

Today, many Maya follow primarily Catholic (or evangelical Christian) mores, including burial in graveyards, overseen by church leaders. Yet certain traditional practices remain, including sacrificing animals, ritual cleansings, and the role of shamans, harkening back to pre-Hispanic times.

a stone slab. The stairs were intentionally jammed with rubble and debris, clearly to prevent access to whatever lay beneath.

It took Ruz three years to excavate the stairway, which descended in several sections all the way to ground level. At the foot of the stairs, Ruz found another sealed passage, in front of which were clay dishes filled with red pigment, jade earplugs, beads, a large oblong pearl, and the skeletons of six sacrificial victims. A final large stone door was removed, and on June 15, 1952, Ruz made what many consider to be the greatest discovery of Maya archaeology: the untouched crypt of K'inich Janaab' Pakal, or Pakal the Great.

The centerpiece of the chamber is the massive sarcophagus, hewn from a single stone and topped by a flat four-meter-long (13-foot), five-ton slab of stone. The slab is beautifully carved with the figure of Pakal in death, surrounded by monsters, serpents, sun and shell signs, and many more glyphs that recount death and its passage. The walls of the chamber are decorated with various gods, from which scientists have deduced a tremendous amount about the Palencanos's theology.

Working slowly to preserve everything in its pristine state, Ruz didn't open the lid of the sarcophagus for six months. It then took a week of difficult work in the stifling, dust-choked room to finally lift the five-ton slab. On November 28, 1952, the scientists had their first peek inside. In the large rectangular sarcophagus they found another, body-shaped sarcophagus, within which was Pakal's skeleton, with precious jewelry and special accoutrements to accompany him on his journey into the next world. A jade mosaic mask covered the face, under which his teeth had been painted red. (The mask was exhibited at the Museo Nacional de Antropología in Mexico City until December 24, 1985, when it was stolen along with several other precious historical artifacts. The mask was recovered in an abandoned house in Acapulco in 1989, mostly undamaged.)

The excavation of the Temple of the Inscriptions forced a revision of archaeologists' conception and understanding of the ancient Maya. It was long believed that the pyramids had served a single function: to provide a platform for ceremonial temples and rituals to be closer to the heavens. But the discovery of Pakal's tomb revealed that pyramids were used as tombs for revered leaders as well, and numerous other such temple-crypts have since been discovered.

The Temple of the Inscriptions and the passageway to Pakal's tomb have been closed for several years, as erosion caused by hundreds of thousands of visitors became increasingly severe. A true-to-life reproduction of the tomb can be seen at the site museum.

The Palace

Palenque's **Palace** is one of the Maya world's most compelling and impressive complexes. Built atop a platform 10 meters (33 feet) high and covering an area larger than a city block, it is composed of 13 vaulted "houses," four enclosed patios, and three spacious underground arcades. It was built in phases over the course of nearly four centuries, and served as both residential quarters for the city's elite and as an exclusive administrative and ceremonial center. The iconic **tower** is unique in Maya architecture—only a handful of minor tower-like structures even compare—and archaeologists have speculated that it was built to provide a ceremonial observation point of the winter solstice (December 22), when the sun appears to drop directly into the Temple of the Inscriptions. It may also have been used to make astronomical calculations, an important part of Maya religious rites, or was simply a watchtower. Unfortunately, the top of the tower had collapsed by the time it was rediscovered, so the structure's original height and appearance—and therefore function—could only be guessed from the pattern of rubble.

Two sunken patios on the palace's northern half are each dedicated to a different purpose. The **Patio of the Captives,** in the northeast corner, contains large stone panels depicting important prisoners captured in war; notice how each has his hand on the opposite shoulder, a common gesture of submission. In the northwest corner, the smaller **Patio of the Warrior Chiefs** is believed to have served as a meeting place for military leaders. Pillars facing into this patio have remnants of stucco moldings depicting figures in elaborate militaristic regalia.

The southern half of the palace is more residential and ceremonial in nature, with enclosed rooms and small, tidy patios. In the southwest corner, two holes marked with notched stones probably served as toilets, and are connected to a surprisingly sophisticated drainage and plumbing system built beneath the stone floors. It still works too—after heavy rain, maintenance workers sweep standing water into the holes to drain it out. Also look for a narrow flight of stairs leading down into a maze of underground rooms that likely served as royal sleeping quarters.

Dividing the southwest and southeast sections is the palace's most notable temple, the **House of Enthronement.** It was here that Palenque's supreme *ahau* (high lords or kings) were officially throned, likely in elaborate ceremonies attended by a small cadre of religious, military, and political leaders. On the western exterior wall is the **Oval Tablet,** which depicts the city's best-known ruler, Pakal the Great, receiving the insignias of power from his mother in AD 615. Also look for paintings of flowers on the same wall—they're originals.

Even the Palace's exterior facades are fascinating, and easy to miss while exploring the labyrinthine interior. The **West Gallery,** atop a long bank of stairs facing the main plaza, has six stout pillars, four of which are still decorated with large stucco reliefs. A plaque at one end describes what's depicted there, including a man holding a serpent and dancing with a woman dressed in a traditional *huipil,* and an incarnation of Chaac, the god of rain, decapitating captives. The **East Gallery** has similarly elaborate relief carvings, including several circular frames that probably contained images of assorted gods (but which were destroyed or looted long ago). A vaulted archway leads back into the Patio of the Captives.

Crosses Group

Across a small stream from the Temple of the Inscriptions and the Palace, the **Crosses Group,** also known as the Grupo Sur (South Group), rises from a bluff. The group contains three temples, all built during the reign of Kan Balam, the son and heir of Pakal the Great.

The largest and most prominent structure in the group is the **Temple of the Cross,** standing atop a nine-level pyramid-like base and crowned by a grand roof comb. Inside the upper structure—you are not permitted to climb the stairs—is a shrine where archaeologists discovered a remarkable relief carving relating the ascension of Kan Balam to the throne and his place among a long line of rulers. In the carving, Kan Balam is pictured with his father, Pakal the Great, on either side of an ornate "world tree," a stylized cross symbolizing a sacred ceiba tree, which in Maya cosmology joins the corporal world to the mythic upper and lower realms. Pakal is dressed in funerary clothes, suggesting he has already died, and indeed the text describes Kan Balam visiting his deceased father to receive the accoutrements of power. The two figures are flanked by extensive hieroglyphic text telling of ancestors, gods, and former rulers, meant to legitimize Kan Balam's claim to power. Side panels depict Kan Balam wearing the full paraphernalia of royalty after his accession, as well as a wizened figure archaeologists classify as God-L, a lord of the underworld, shown smoking a cigar and wearing an owl-feather headdress. Archaeologists also discovered a major tomb at the base of the

Temple of the Cross, containing the headless body of an official, perhaps the governor of a neighboring city, and hundreds of pieces of jade. They also found a collection of extremely fine ceramic figurines and incense burners, many of which are on display in the museum.

On the Crosses Group's east side, a winding path leads up a steep incline to the **Temple of the Foliated Cross.** The structure is much deteriorated, but notable for the large keyhole-shaped niches in the corners of its upper facade. And like the Temple of the Sun, the enclosed gallery contains a terrific relief carving depicting Kan Balam assuming kingly power and duties from his deceased father, this time in the form of a bloodletting tool. The cross between them—hence the temple's name—is adorned with corn leaves, symbolizing life and the birth of mankind, as well as a striking forward-facing deity representing rebirth.

The **Temple of the Sun** is the smallest of the three temples, but in many ways the best preserved. Built atop a modest platform on the grouping's west side—climbing is prohibited here as well—its pillars, facade, and roof comb have elaborate stucco decoration. Although you can't see it from below, the temple contains yet another relief carving depicting Kan Balam and Pakal the Great at the former's enthronement. Instead of a cross between them, however, there is a disk-like shield, held up by two kneeling deities and representing the sun and warfare.

The Ball Court and North Group

A large grassy plaza on the palace's north side is flanked by several structures. Closest to the Palace is Palenque's **Ball Court,** notable for its I-shaped playing area and believed to have doubled as a site for ritual sacrifices. Perpendicular to the Ball Court is the **North Group,** made up of five temples, most quite deteriorated. **Temple II** is the best preserved, a sturdy stone structure crowning a terraced platform; at the foot of the stairs is a well-preserved stucco molding depicting Tláloc, a deity most likely introduced to the Maya

by emissaries from the great central Mexican city of Teotihuacán. Finally, the **Temple of the Count** is a similarly stout structure atop a supporting pyramid, so-named for Jean-Frédéric Waldeck, an eccentric French count who lived there in the early 1830s and whose embellished drawings and wild speculations fostered lasting misconceptions of the Maya, especially regarding an alleged connection to ancient Egypt.

A well-marked path leads from the Palace, past the Ball Court, and down a steep hillside to the main road. Along the way you'll pass the **Bats Group,** a maze of low foundations that most likely served as elite residential quarters, and the **Queen's Bath,** a scenic waterfall and pool; bathing is no longer permitted, however. This is a good way to exit the ruins (assuming you came by *combi*), as the path emerges from the trees not far from Palenque's museum.

Museum

After you see the ruins, be sure to leave time to visit Palenque's **museum** (no phone, 9am-4:30pm Tues.-Sun.), which contains a truly incredible collection of stucco and stone artifacts found at Palenque, including ornate incense burners and perfectly preserved relief carvings and hieroglyphic panels, with excellent explanations in both Spanish and English. It's not a huge museum—an hour should suffice—but absolutely worth visiting, and for many people a highlight of their visit to Palenque. An exhibit called "The Tomb of Pakal" includes a life-size reproduction of the sarcophagus and elaborately carved lid, installed in an exact replica of the crypt made of Plexiglas so you can see through to appreciate its unique design. (It's more effective than it sounds.) Professionally produced videos and wall displays describe the tomb's discovery and explain the symbols and imagery found within. The exhibit space is relatively tight so entrance is limited to every 30 minutes—first

1: Palenque's tower; 2: Maya glyphs; 3: souvenirs sitting in front of the Palace

come, first served—to prevent overcrowding. Typically, there's no line but if you see a tour group arrive, make a run for it.

Admission to the museum is included with admission to the ruins—be sure to hang on to your ticket! **Note:** Although the ruins are open daily, the museum is closed on Monday.

Practicalities

The archaeological site is open 8am-5pm daily (US$3.50, last entry at 4:30pm). The museum is open 9am-4:30pm Tuesday-Sunday only. Official guides can be hired at the entrance to the ruins and at the ticket stand; rates run US$45 for a two-hour tour in English or in Spanish, or you can test your luck with one of the freelance guides hanging out near the entrance, who charge US$20-25 for a somewhat shorter tour, and who typically speak Spanish only.

Palenque is technically part of a national park, and there's a park-service gate a kilometer (0.6 mile) or so before reaching the ruins; daily admission is US$1.75 per person. There is parking at the ruins, although on busy days drivers end up parking well down the access road.

It is possible to enter the archaeological site at a smaller gate just past the museum, but from there it's a steep uphill walk to the main structures. A better idea, if you're arriving by *combi,* is to enter at the main gate and exit through the lower one, from where it's just a short walk to the museum.

ALUXES ECOPARQUE PALENQUE

Aluxes Ecoparque Palenque (Carr. Ruínas Km 2.6, tel. 916/688-0026, www. ecoparquepalenque.com, 9am-5pm daily, US$7.50 adult, US$3.75 child) is a conservation park located partway between Palenque town and the ruins. Paths lead through several acres of protected rainforest and past enclosures of rescued animals, some endangered and most saved from illegal trafficking. The ecopark helps support the foundation's animal rehabilitation program—creatures are returned to the wild whenever possible—so there's a chance to see jaguars, alligators, howler monkeys, and countless tropical birds. Early mornings and late afternoons are when the animals are most active; set aside about two hours to explore the park in depth. Guided nighttime tours are also offered.

SHOPPING

Two **gift shops** (8am-5pm Tues.-Sun.) next to Palenque's museum have reasonably good selections of books and locally produced *artesanía*. Otherwise, shops line the main streets of Palenque selling postcards, T-shirts, and arts and crafts—good if you're running short on time or are looking for something a little kitschy.

FOOD

Palenque has a large but not particularly inspiring selection of restaurants. With a few exceptions, you'll typically find standard Mexican dishes at moderate prices.

In Town

★ **Café Jade** (La Cañada, Calle Merle Green at Calle 5 Pte. Nte., tel. 916/345-4815, 7am-11pm daily, US$3-9) is a modern indoor/outdoor café in the leafy La Cañada neighborhood. Dishes vary from traditional Mexican and Maya dishes to pasta and burgers; the breakfast menu is especially extensive. There's a great selection of coffee drinks and smoothies too. It's a place equally popular with backpackers and ladies who lunch.

Las Tinajas (Calle 20 de Noviembre at Calle Abasolo, tel. 916/345-4970, 7am-10:30pm daily, US$5-7) serves heaping portions of Mexican fare, though there also is a good variety of pasta dishes, sandwiches, and salads. *Jarras* (pitchers) of fruit drinks are a good deal for the very, very thirsty.

Tropi Tacos (Av. Benito Juárez near Calle Aldama, tel. 916/345-0204, 7am-1am daily, US$3-5) is a two-story eatery specializing in street tacos. Pick among standard à la carte fillings—steak, chicken, *al pastor*—or ask for an *ordén* of five of the same. All come with

a trio of salsas—*pico de gallo* (mild), *salsa verde* (medium), and *tomate con chile* (hot). Vegetarian options are available. For the best breeze, get a booth upstairs.

El Huachinago Feliz (La Cañada, Calle Merle Green at Calle Hidalgo, tel. 916/129-8231, 9am-11pm daily, US$5-10) is a popular open-air restaurant serving tasty seafood dishes in the La Cañada neighborhood. For a sure thing, try the fish baked in banana leaves. Meals are served in a verdant, quiet setting.

Near the Ruins

Arguably Palenque's finest restaurant and certainly one of its most distinctive, ★ **Restaurante Bajlum** (Carr. Ruínas Km 2.8, tel. 916/107-8518, 2pm-11pm daily, US$8-13) serves Maya-inspired meals, many straight from the owners' family cookbook. Look for meats like deer and rabbit, prepared with locally sourced herbs and veggies. The owners can often be found in the dining room, explaining the fascinating history and provenance of their dishes. Cash only.

Don Mucho (El Panchán, Carr. Ruínas Km 4.5, tel. 916/112-8338, 7am-1am Tues.-Thurs., 7am-3am Fri.-Sat., 7am-midnight Sun.-Mon., US$4-10) is a popular spot in the jungle neighborhood of El Panchán. Homemade pastas, wood-oven pizzas, and *comida típica* fill happy bellies here. There's live music and fire dancers starting at 8pm on weeknights, 9:30pm on weekends, which keeps the place hopping well into the night.

Seafood is the specialty at **Don Camaron** (Carr. Ruínas Km 1.4, tel. 916/345-3705, noon-9pm daily, US$7-9), a small and welcoming restaurant on the road to the ruins. You'll find shrimp skewers, shrimp and octopus cocktail, crab soup, and more—all super tasty and served in ample portions. Service is friendly and the prices very reasonable.

A short walk from Palenque's site museum, **Mayabell** (Carr. Ruínas Km 6, tel. 916/341-6977, www.mayabell.mx, 7am-11pm daily, US$4-9) is a convenient spot for a meal after a visit to the ruins. Order at the counter from

Palenque Town

a menu that ranges from sandwiches and pastas to enchiladas and steak; there are plenty of vegetarian options too. Live music starts every night at 8pm.

ACCOMMODATIONS

Hotels in Palenque town tend to be barebones, adequate for a night or two but not especially charming. The advantage is having easy access to the bus terminal and tour agencies, plus banks, Internet, and restaurants. In the northwest corner of town, a neighborhood called **La Cañada** has better lodging options in a more serene setting, but is somewhat removed from the conveniences in town. There are also several pleasant mid- and high-end resorts on the road to the ruins, and a neighborhood called **El Panchán,** nestled in the forest, with (mostly) basic accommodations and a distinctly bohemian air. Getting back and forth to town can be somewhat inconvenient if you don't have a car, especially at night after *combi* service ends; then again, the laid-back atmosphere may convince you there's not much reason to go into town anyway.

In Town
UNDER US$35
Hotel Canek (Av. 20 de Noviembre near Calle Abasolo, tel. 916/345-0150, www. hotelcanek.com, US$30 s with a/c, US$33 d with a/c) offers big, clean rooms with hot-water bathrooms, cable TV, and Wi-Fi. A rooftop *palapa* with hammocks and chairs makes for a breezy common space and has arguably the best view in town. Service is friendly if a bit sluggish.

Posada Kin (Calle Abasolo near Calle 5 de Mayo, tel. 916/345-1714, posadakin@hotmail. com, US$26 s/d with a/c) is a large, reliable hotel for travelers on a budget. Rooms are simple and perfectly comfortable, if not terribly memorable, and come with continental breakfast. The staff is friendly and accommodating, and the location puts you nearby shops, restaurants, and more.

Yaxkin Hostel (La Cañada, Calle Merle Green at Calle 5 Pte. Nte., tel. 916/345-0102, www.yaxkinhostels.com, US$8 dorm, US$14 s/d with shared bath, US$35 s/d with a/c) is hit or miss: Rooms are either pleasant and airy or like cement boxes; the kitchen is poorly equipped but there's a great café; Wi-Fi is available but only in reception. Service, too, runs lukewarm. It's good if you're on a tight budget, but be sure to look around before committing.

US$35-50
★ **Casa 5 Bed & Breakfast** (Emilio Rabasa 45, tel. 916/142-0862, casacincopalenque@ gmail.com, US$37 s/d with a/c) is a stylish and comfortable B&B, located in a mostly residential area but well worth the extra few blocks of walking to the center. Spacious guest rooms have pedestal beds and basin sinks, and the artwork throughout the hotel is striking. Fresh continental breakfast is included, and shuttles to and from the ruins stop nearby.

Hotel Xibalba (La Cañada, Calle Merle Green 9, tel. 612/175-0860, www.hotelxibalba. com, US$40-43 s/d with a/c) has airy and well-maintained rooms in the Cañada neighborhood, all with modern amenities. Rooms in the main building are spacious and simple; units in the annex, with its replica Maya entryway, are smaller and have a certain coziness and isolation some prefer. The upper floors in both buildings get better light and are worth requesting. There's a decent café.

Maya Rue Hotel (Calle Aldama near Av. Benito Juárez, tel. 916/345-0743, www. hotelmayaruepalenque.com, US$31-35 s/d with a/c) is a walk-up hotel in the center of town. Rooms have an urban-industrial feel—lots of cement, whitewashed walls, and black-and-white photos—but are comfortable at heart, each with a good bed, hot-water bathroom, flat-screen TV, and good Wi-Fi. Third-floor rooms have high ceilings and nice views of the surrounding hills.

1: fire dancers providing nightly entertainment in the neighborhood of El Panchán; **2:** cozy screened cabin at Cabañas Kin Balam

OVER US$50

Hotel Maya Tulipanes (La Cañada, Calle Merle Green 6, tel. 916/345-0201, toll-free Mex. tel. 800/714-4710, www.hmtexpress. com, US$67 s/d with a/c) is a large hotel in La Cañada. The rooms are a bit plain-Jane but perfectly comfortable, with good beds and clean bathrooms. There's also a small pool and restaurant. Tour groups often stay here, but it doesn't seem to affect the service independent guests receive, other than the hustle and bustle at breakfast.

Hotel Chablis (La Cañada, Calle Merle Green 7, tel. 916/345-0870, www.hotelchablis. com, US$82 s/d with a/c) has 51 rooms with a dash of style and nice amenities like quiet air-conditioning and flat-screen TVs. There's even a small pool with a whirlpool tub, as well as a restaurant. The hotel caters to independent travelers, which may be important to some. It's a fine choice, budget permitting.

Near the Ruins
UNDER US$35

★ **Margarita and Ed Cabañas** (El Panchán, Carr. Ruínas Km 4.5, tel. 916/348-6990, www.margaritaandedcabanas.blogspot. com, US$15 s/d *cabañas*, US$16-21 s/d, US$29 s/d with a/c) is perfect for travelers who like jungle settings but want creature comforts. Three brick buildings with wide verandas house the rooms; units are spotless, with gleaming tile floors, upgraded bathrooms, firm beds, and reliable fans or air-conditioning. Flower-pattern bedspreads and buy-by-the-dozen paintings add some character. A couple of rustic *cabañas* with private hot-water bathrooms also are available near the property's entrance; each accommodates 2-4 people.

Jungle Palace (El Panchán, Carr. Ruínas Km 4.5, tel. 916/345-1111, US$7.50/10 s/d with shared bath, US$13/15 s/d) offers basic cabins in the middle of El Panchán. Units are hit or miss: Some have gleaming tile floors, decent beds and porches, while others have makeshift window screens, saggy beds, and chipping walls. Try for a 2nd-floor unit with

a balcony—generally, these are in the best condition.

El Jaguar (El Panchán, Carr. Ruínas Km 4.5, tel. 916/119-2829, US$2 pp camping) is the only place to camp in El Panchán. If you have your own gear, head here. Be sure to wear your flips-flops in the shared bathrooms—they're in need of a serious scrubbing.

US$35-50

Across the highway from El Panchán, **Cabañas Kin Balam** (Carr. Ruínas Km 4.5, tel. 916/345-1826, www.kin-balam.com, US$13-16 dorm, US$33 s/d with shared bath, US$43-57 s/d) has several stand-alone cabins that open onto a well-tended pool. Each has a thatch roof, big windows with mosquito screens, and firm beds. Bathrooms, whether en suite or shared, are clean and have hot water. Though not in the thick of the jungle, the cleared grounds offer spectacular stargazing.

Mayabell (Carr. Ruínas Km 6, tel. 916/341-6977, www.mayabell.mx, US$4 pp camping, US$1.50 hammock rental with US$7.50 deposit, US$18 s/d with shared bath, US$41 s/d, US$55 s/d with a/c) is a great option for budget and midrange travelers. A string of open-air *palapas* shelter tents and hammocks while *cabañas* are surprisingly pleasant, with low, comfortable beds and shady patios. There's also large swimming pool and an affordable restaurant with live music nightly.

OVER US$50

★ **Boutique Hotel Quinta Chanabnal** (Carr. Ruínas Km 2.2, tel. 916/345-5320, www. quintachanabnal.com, US$150-280 suite with a/c, US$350 master suite with a/c) has eight luxe suites with high ceilings, high-end furnishings, and amenities like in-room safes and minibars. The lush grounds feature impressive replicas of Maya temples and reliefs, and a mosaic-tiled pool is a treat. Adding to the experience are the sounds and sights of the rainforest: bromeliads, howler monkeys, and green parrots. Continental breakfast is included.

Piedra de Agua (Carr. Ruínas Km 2.5, tel. 916/345-0842, www.palenque.piedradeagua. com, US$89 s/d) has elegant rooms with tropical wood furnishings, colorful folk art, and mosaic tile floors. Each has a spacious patio with a *palapa* roof and an outdoor tub. There's no air-conditioning though—a deal breaker for some, especially considering the rate (it also makes for a slightly musty smell). The leafy grounds include a lap pool, spa, and a welcoming lounge near reception.

Chan-Kah Resort Village (Carr. Ruínas Km 3, tel. 916/345-1134, www.chan-kah.com. mx, US$72 s/d with a/c, US$215 master suite with a/c) has several spacious casitas in a manicured jungle setting. They're somewhat dated in style but have large bathrooms, shaded patios, and updated amenities. The resort's huge stone-bottom pool is a hit with kids; a second, smaller pool exudes the natural peacefulness of the surroundings. There's also a decent restaurant-bar on-site.

INFORMATION AND SERVICES
Tourist Information
The **state tourist office** (Av. Juárez at Abasolo, no phone, www.turismochiapas. gob.mx, 9am-8pm Mon.-Sat., 9am-1pm Sun.) hands out decent maps and can answer basic questions. The **city tourism office** (9am-2pm and 6pm-9pm Mon.-Fri.) has a tiny kiosk on the central plaza; service is hit or miss.

Emergency Services
Hospital General Palenque (Av. Juárez s/n, tel. 916/345-5090, 24 hours) is one block east of the bus station. For meds, try **Farmacia del Ahorro** (Av. Juárez at Calle Abasolo, tel. 916/345-5014, 7am-10pm daily). The **police station** (Av. Independencia near Hidalgo, tel. 916/345-0405, toll-free Mex. tel. 066, 24 hours) is in the Palacio Municipal.

Money
Located on Avenida Juárez, **Bancomer** (8:30am-4pm Mon.-Fri.) and **Banamex** (9am-4pm Mon.-Fri.) have 24-hour ATMs. There's also a Santander ATM in the bus station (Carr. 199 at Av. Juárez).

Media and Communications
The **post office** (Av. Independencia at Calle Bravo) is open 8am-8:30pm Monday-Friday and 8am-noon Saturday. Almost all of the hotels have Wi-Fi. In a pinch, **Don Mucho** (El Panchán, Carr. Ruínas Km 4.5, tel. 916/112-8338, 7am-1am Tues.-Thurs., 7am-3am Fri.-Sat., 7am-midnight Sun.-Mon.) offers Wi-Fi for US$1.50 per hour.

Laundry and Storage
Lavandería CK Dora (5 Av. Nte. near Calle Abasolo, tel. 916/345-0915, 8am-8:30pm Mon.-Sat., 8am-2pm Sun.) charges US$0.60 per kilo (2.2 pounds) for next-day service.

There's **luggage storage** at the bus station (Hwy. 199 at Av. Juárez, tel. 916/345-1344, 7am-11pm daily) for US$0.40-1 per bag per hour.

GETTING THERE
Air
Palenque International Airport (PQM, Hwy. 199 Km 24.5, tel. 916/345-1692) is a tiny affair located about five kilometers (3.1 miles) north of town. At the time of research, **Interjet** (toll-free Mex. tel. 800/011-2345, toll-free U.S. tel. 866/285-9525, www.interjet.com. mx) was the only airline with regularly scheduled flights into the airport; it flies twice a week from Mexico City.

Bus
The **ADO bus terminal** (Hwy. 199 at Av. Juárez, tel. 916/345-1344) is located at the entrance to town, across from the Maya Head monument. Destinations include:

- Campeche City: US$25, 5.5-6 hours, 2am, 4:30am, 8am, 8:45pm, 10pm, and 11:30pm
- Cancún: US$36-57, 12.5-13 hours, 3:45am, 6pm, 9:10pm, 9:45pm, and 11:50pm
- Mérida: US$32-36, 8-9 hours, 1:15am, 4:40am, 8am, 8:45pm, and 11:30pm

Side Trip: Comalcalco

SCALE NOT AVAILABLE

© MOON.COM

Like Chiapas, the state of Tabasco is not technically part of the Yucatán Peninsula, but can make a quick and rewarding detour if you've got the time. An hour north of the state capital, Villahermosa, are the Maya ruins of Comalcalco, notable for being constructed of adobe-like brick instead of stone. Comalcalco also is the heart of chocolate country—visiting a working plantation to learn how cacao is grown and processed makes for a worthwhile day trip.

Comalcalco archaeological zone (8am-4pm daily, US$3) is located in a lush agricultural

- Mexico City: US$45, 14-15 hours, 6:30pm
- Villahermosa: US$7-12, 2.5 hours, 10 departures, 3:45am-11pm
- Villahermosa Airport: US$16.50, 2-2.5 hours, 5 departures, 7am-8:30pm

Combi

Autotransporte Chamoan (Av. Miguel Hidalgo btwn Calles 4 and Allende, cell tel. 916/348-4684) provides *combi* service to destinations in the Río Usumacinta valley, including Nueva Palestina (US$2.75, 2 hours); Lacanjá Chansayab (US$7, 2.5 hours); Crucero Bonampak (US$4.75, 2.5 hours), where you can catch another *combi* to Bonampak ruins; and finally to Frontera Corozal (US$7.25, 3 hours), where you can catch boats to

Yaxchilán ruins. *Combis* leave hourly from Palenque (4am-5pm daily) and Frontera Corozal (4am-4pm).

Car

Dollar Rent-a-Car (Palenque International Airport, Hwy. 199 Km 24.5, cell tel. 916/112-3811, toll-free Mex. tel. 800/365-1111, www.dollarmexico.com.mx, 7:30am-1pm and 3pm-8pm Mon.-Sat., 7:30am-4pm Sun.) is the only car rental agency in Palenque. (Otherwise, the nearest rental agency is in Villahermosa, 150 kilometers [93 miles] away.) To save yourself a trip to the airport, call in advance to have your rental delivered to your hotel. A couple of tips: Stick to driving during daylight hours; security has improved immensely in this area, but setting a short distance from a like-named town. The site's earliest structures date to around AD 250 and consist of large mounds made from dirt mixed with crushed oyster shells for strength and cohesion. Around AD 500-700, distinctive bricks were developed as an alternative to stone, which is rare and difficult to quarry in Tabasco's swampy environment. The bricks were made of a mixture of dirt and crushed oyster shells and then fired in kilns; they were then used to cover and expand the earlier packed-dirt temples, and in some cases were incised with designs, including animals, humans, glyphs, and patterns.

Temple 1, the immense structure on the left as you enter, has the best remaining example of the stucco high relief that once covered most of the structures. Look for the animal figures along the pyramid's southeast corner as well as a molded skull about halfway up the main stairway. Opposite Temple 1, the **Great Acropolis** is 80 meters (262 feet) long and has a stucco mask of Kinich Ahau, the sun god. To the right, walk up a hill to the **palace,** which reveals a panoramic view of the countryside, including unexcavated mounds and a chocolate plantation in the distance.

A small but very interesting **museum** has several artifacts as well as a few human skeletons found by workers while excavating the site.

A few blocks from the town's central plaza, **Hacienda La Luz** (Calle Leandro Rovirosa Wade s/n, tel. 999/337-1122, www.haciendalaluz.mx, US$5) offers an interesting hour-long "chocotour" of its cacao plantation. Visitors stroll through the orchard and then visit the factory where the cacao seeds are processed and turned into chocolate candies. Tours are offered at 9am, 11am, 1pm, and 3pm Tuesday-Sunday. There's also a small museum with antique machinery once used to process cacao seeds and, of course, a gift shop selling chocolate products made on-site. Chocolate-making workshops are also offered.

PRACTICALITIES

Near the ADO bus station in Villahermosa, **Autotransportes Comalli Plus** (Calle Reforma at Calle Bravo, tel. 933/334-0582) provides *combi* (van) service to and from Comalcalco (every 30-60 minutes, 4:30am-9pm daily, US$4.50).

To get to the ruins from the center of town, take any bus headed north on Carretera Comalcalco-Paraíso (US$0.35, 10 minutes). From the highway drop-off, it's about a 10-minute walk to the entrance of the ruins. A cab from town costs about US$2.

the occasional robbery does occur, almost always after dark. Also, fill your gas tank whenever you can, as gas stations are few and far between. In a pinch, look for roadside gasoline stands, which typically sell gas in semitransparent jugs of 5, 10, or 20 liters.

GETTING AROUND

Palenque town is easy to navigate on foot. To get to the ruins or accommodations outside of town, though, you'll either have to take a *colectivo* or a taxi.

Colectivo

Local shuttle companies provide *colectivo* service to and from the ruins (US$1.25, every 10-15 minutes, 6am-6pm daily). You can board at their terminals in town, at the Maya Head monument, or anywhere along the road to the ruins. Be aware that if you buy your ticket at the terminal, the cashier may try to sell you a round-trip ticket. Don't bother—this saves no money and no time; instead, it means you'll have to wait for a *colectivo* from that specific company when you're ready to leave.

Taxi

A taxi between town and El Panchán or the ruins costs around US$5. Within the town limit (the *periférico*), a cab ride is US$2.75; to the airport, plan on US$7.50. After dark, taxis add a surcharge of US$0.75, regardless of the destination.

Travel Agencies

Lots of travel agencies want your business in this town. Prices vary according to the level of service. The least expensive typically include transport only—no guides or entrance fees. For more, the tour may include entrance fees, guide service, and even meals. Definitely ask what's included before booking. The most popular trips are to Misol-Há and Agua Azul (US$16-18 pp, noon-6:30pm); to Bonampak and Yaxchilán ruins (US$88-125 pp, 6am-7pm); and two-day excursions to Bonampak, Yaxchilán, and the Lacandón forest (US$150-200 pp, including meals and lodging). You can also do a combination trip, such as a morning tour of Palenque ruins followed by an afternoon at Misol-Há and Agua Azul (US$18 pp, 8am-6pm).

Tour operators also offer convenient "drop-off" tours so you don't have to backtrack to Palenque. These include spending the morning at Misol-Há and Agua Azul, then continuing to San Cristóbal de las Casas (US$24 pp); or, if you're headed to Guatemala, spending the day visiting Bonampak and Yaxchilán, spending the night near the border, and the next morning taking a 30-minute boat ride to Betel, Guatemala, where a shuttle takes you to Flores (US$155 pp, including all transport, meals, and lodging).

In town, **Kim Tours** (across from the bus station, Av. Juárez s/n, tel. 916/345-0336, 9am-6pm Mon.-Fri.) and **Kichan Bajlun** (Av. Juárez btwn Calles Aldama and Abasolo, tel. 916/345-2452, www.kichanbajlum.com, 7am-9pm daily) are reliable agencies. In El Panchán, **El Mono Blanco del Panchán** (El Panchán, Carr. Ruínas Km 4.5, tel. 916/100-3654, 7am-9pm daily) has a travel agency that books the same tours, at the same prices, as those offered in town. Look for it near the entrance to the neighborhood.

Along the Río Tulijá

There's no mistaking the Río Tulijá, a ribbon of luminescent turquoise water wending through farmland and dense tropical forest, visible from parts of Highway 199 between Palenque and Ocosingo. Known to local Maya as Yaks-Ha (Blue Water), the river was described by Chiapanecan poet Elva Macías as "a peacock dragging its watery tail," and you'd be forgiven if at first glance you thought it was the result of contamination or a mineral dissolved in the water. In fact, the water is not only clean but perfectly transparent, and the unusual color is the result of sunlight reflecting off the limestone riverbed. (For that reason, the effect isn't visible all year; during rainy season—roughly August-January—sediment washes into the river and turns the water a turbid brown.)

ORIENTATION

There are two especially impressive sights along the Río Tulijá: **Misol-Há** (a high, beautiful waterfall) and **Agua Azul** (a series of powerful waterfalls). Both are reached by way of access roads (2-4 kilometers/1.2-2.5 miles long) that are well marked on Highway 199. Tour operators in Palenque offer popular and affordable tours to the falls, typically spending 30-60 minutes at Misol-Há and 2-3 hours at Agua Azul before returning to Palenque. You also can visit them independently, preferably by car, as there's little public transport along the access roads.

CASCADA DE MISOL-HÁ

Maya for "waterfall," **Misol-Há** (Hwy. 199 Km 18, tel. 555/151-3377, www.misol-ha.com, 7am-6pm daily, US$1 admission, US$0.50 toll) is definitely that, and a beautiful one, falling some 30 meters (98 feet) from an overhanging semicircular cliff down into a broad, shimmering pool. The water doesn't appear blue here—the pool is too deep—but it's a gorgeous sight nonetheless, and fantastic for swimming, especially on hot afternoons. (Unfortunately, most tours stop here in the morning, before you've had a chance to get hot and sweaty!) There's a fairly deep cave on the far side, but getting there is the most memorable part—by way of a slippery path along the base of the cliff and behind the falls, buffeted by mist from the falling water. Occasionally, an additional admission (US$0.50) to enter the cave is charged, though it includes a flashlight.

Food and Accommodations

Misol-Há has a dozen wood *cabañas* (US$17-32 s/d, US$34-40 cabin with kitchenette) built in a stand of thick trees within earshot of the crashing waterfall. Surprisingly well outfitted, all have hot-water bathrooms, fans, and one or two queen beds; larger units have separate bedrooms, fully equipped kitchenettes, and dining areas. Best of all, you have the falls all to yourself in the early morning and late afternoon. The admission fee, but not the toll, is included in the rate.

A modern welcome center includes a large **restaurant** (7am-10pm daily, US$4-9), bathrooms, Wi-Fi, and parking. From there, it's just 50 meters (164 feet) to the falls.

Getting There

The turnoff to Misol-Há is about 21 kilometers (13 miles) south of Palenque, and the welcome center and falls are about 2 kilometers (1.2 miles) from the highway turnoff. To get here by *combi* from Palenque, **Transporte Volcán** (Av. Juárez at Calle 5a Pte. Sur A, no phone) provides service to and from the turnoff every 20 minutes 4am-6pm daily (US$2, 30 minutes). From the turnoff, it's about a 20-minute walk to the falls. All visitors, whether arriving by vehicle or foot, must pay a US$0.50 toll to use the road to the falls.

★ PARQUE NACIONAL DE AGUA AZUL

The churning cascades and serene pools of **Agua Azul National Park** (Hwy. 199 Km 58, 7am-6pm daily, US$2) are reason enough to visit, but the blue-teal color of the water is what makes it especially impressive. The Tulijá is quite powerful here (having been joined upstream by another river, the Río Shumuljá) and tumbles down several kilometers of stair-stepped limestone, variously splintering and rejoining, and forming hundreds of waterfalls in the process. Between the falls—which range from just a few feet to several stories high—are pools of water where the water's teal hue can be appreciated. Several of the largest pools have been shored up to allow swimming and wading, and various *miradores* (vista points) afford fine views of the falls from above and below.

A wide paved path leads from the parking area up alongside the falls, with smaller trails leading to the observation points and designated swimming areas. There also are restroom and changing areas (US$0.75) available. Unfortunately, there are also myriad stalls crammed along the pathway, hawking food, T-shirts, *artesanía*, souvenirs, and more. The first several hundred meters have the most shops—and also the largest falls and most accessible pools, not coincidentally. However, even on busy days (it's a madhouse during Christmas and Semana Santa), the park's upper section remains much quieter and less crowded, and a number of scenic pools are great for cooling off. The upper section starts about a kilometer (0.6 mile) from the entrance, where the path turns to dirt. Even farther, about an hour's hike, is El Cañon (The Canyon), where the valley narrows and a number of additional falls are located.

Be cautious when swimming or wading in Agua Azul, as the current is deceptively strong in many places, even those that look placid. Drownings have occurred, and there are relatively few signs warning of the danger.

Food and Accommodations

There are several **mom-and-pop restaurants** (7am-7pm daily, US$3-8) along the path leading visitors past the different waterfalls and swimming areas. They sell basic

Mexican eats—quesadillas, empanadas, tacos, and so on—and freshly made juices.

Cabañas Yax Ha (aka Cabañas Cascadas de Agua Azul, tel. 916/118-1297, US$38 s/d) has eight modern cabins on a well-tended jungle lot, with sturdy wood-plank walls, cement floors, and lots of natural light. Each has two double beds with thick mattresses and unexpected niceties like flat-screen TVs and Wi-Fi. Breakfast is included for a nominal fee. Best of all, you can enjoy the waterfalls after hours, with no tourists or vendors around.

If you have your own gear, there are 20 **campsites** (US$3.25 pp) alongside the river, near the parking lot as you enter the site. Most of the sites have cement floors and a *palapa* cover. Shared bathrooms are a bit grim, but will do for a night or two (wear flip-flops). For availability, ask at nearby Cabañas Los Almendros.

Getting There

Agua Azul is located off Highway 199, about 60 kilometers (37 miles) south of Palenque. The entrance is about 4 kilometers (2.5 miles) down a windy road from a well-marked turnoff on the highway. To get here by *combi* from Palenque, **Transporte Volcán** (Av. Juárez at Calle 5a Pte. Sur A, no phone) provides service to and from the turnoff every 20 minutes 4am-6pm daily (US$2.25, 1-1.5 hours). Taxis (US$1) are often waiting at the turnoff to ferry passengers who arrive by *combi*; otherwise, it's an hour's walk down, and an even longer walk back up. **Note:** There are two tolls to use the road, each US$1 per vehicle.

Villages along the Carretera Fronteriza

The Carretera Fronteriza (Border Highway) runs from Palenque southeast along the Río Usumacinta and the Guatemalan border to the town of Frontera Corozal; from there it loops down and west again, eventually reaching the city of Comitán in central Chiapas.

The first section, between Palenque and Frontera Corozal, is covered here, including a variety of villages, detours, and roadside attractions, roughly in the order you'd encounter them driving from Palenque. Some make for a quick stop, others an extended side trip; some have food and lodging, others do not.

A number of agencies in Palenque offer transportation through this region, hitting the major destinations, and are recommended for their convenience and reasonable prices. Alternatively, *colectivos* ply the Carretera Fronteriza throughout the day, and a rental car is very handy for places off the main road, as bus service to those areas can be very slow and unpredictable.

CASCADA WEJLIB-JÁ

Ch'ol Maya for "falling water," **Wejlib-Já** (tel. 916/596-0303, 8am-6pm daily, US$1.25) is a large waterfall and swimming area that's popular among locals and a reasonably worthwhile stop for travelers looking for a place to cool off. From the parking area, a path follows the riverbank past several swimming holes and waterside picnic tables. (There's also a simple eatery near the entrance.) It's a short distance farther to the falls, a thick rope of water lumbering through a limestone notch and crashing into a large pool 20 meters (66 feet) below. There's a zip line (US$2.50) across it, and a path winds around to the bottom where you can swim as well. The falls are most powerful in September and October, at the end of the rainy season, but the water is clearer during the dry months.

Getting There

A huge sign marks the turnoff to Wejlib-Já, about 30 kilometers (19 miles) from Palenque.

From there, it's 500 meters (0.3 mile) by dirt road to the entrance.

VALLESCONDIDO

More a roadside business than a village, ★ **Finca Vallescondido** (Carr. Fronteriza del Sur Km 61, cell tel. 916/100-0399, www. fincavallescondido.com) is arguably the best lodging and food between Palenque and Frontera Corozal. A fresh, well-prepared buffet breakfast (7am-10am daily, US$6.50 pp) includes eggs, beans, coffee and juice, fresh fruit, and handmade tortillas. It's served in an open-air dining area beneath a thick forest canopy. It can get crowded—tour groups often eat here on the way to Bonampak and Yaxchilán—but it's a great stop nonetheless. Lunch and dinner is served upon request.

Vallescondido's *cabañas* (US$97-102 s/d) are on the opposite side of the highway, near the owners' house. Fourteen units share several one-story buildings with long, wide porches. Each has high sloped ceilings and oversized windows; bathrooms are tucked behind attractive stone walls. A beautiful creek runs through the property and makes for a popular spot for guests to cool off. Full breakfast is included in the rate.

Getting There

Vallescondido is located between Chancalá and the turnoff to Nueva Palestina. There are huge road signs as you approach, making it easy to spot.

★ NAHÁ

The remote Lacandón village of Nahá is situated beside a beautiful lake and surrounded by hills covered in a lush rainforest. About 70 Lacandón Maya families live here, surviving in much the same way their predecessors did generations ago, mostly by fishing and small-scale farming. Tourists are a fairly new development here, and are received with cordial reserve befitting this resourceful and reclusive indigenous group. As the Lacandón village of Lacanjá Chansayab, near the Bonampak ruins, grows exceedingly touristy, a small

but steady number of travelers are making the far more difficult trip to Nahá (and the even smaller and less-visited sister village of Metzabok) in search of more "authentic" Lacandón culture and community.

Sights

Nahá is a good place to observe and learn about Lacandón culture and lifestyle, while Metzabok has somewhat richer outdoor opportunities. A highlight for many visitors is a 30-minute ritual ceremony with **Don Antonio** (tel. 555/150-5953, US$10 pp, advance notice required), a revered nonagenarian spiritual leader and successor to the great now-deceased Lacandón shaman Chan K'in Viejo. The village also has a modest **museum** (open by appointment, US$1) with photos and artifacts explaining Lacandón history, beliefs, and practices. Signage is in Spanish, with some English translations.

Centro Ecoturístico Nahá Canan K'ax (tel. 555/150-5953, www.nahaecoturismo.com, US$10-12.50 pp, up to 4 people) offers various nature outings. Excursions include a short (2 kilometers/1.2 miles) **nature trail** that leads from the village to Laguna Nahá. There it's possible to **canoe** on the lake, whose reed-filled shallows and curving tree-shaded banks offer fine bird-watching. There's also a **waterfall** within walking distance, and numerous opportunities to see and learn more about the rich rainforest flora, such as medicinal plants.

Food and Accommodations

★ **Hotel Naha Ecolodge** (tel. 555/150-5953, www.nahaecoturismo.com, US$15 s/d with shared bath, US$42 s/d) is a sight for sore eyes after the long, mostly dirt-road journey to this remote Lacandón village. Four thatched cabins are warmly appointed, with firm beds, colorful Lacandón-themed decor, and either shared or private bathrooms. Meals are made with local organic products and served in a screened communal dining area. Local guides are available for fascinating activities and tours of the area.

Centro Ecoturístico Nahá Canan K'ax (tel. 555/150-5953, www.nahaecoturismo.com, US$5 pp camping, US$15-23 s/d with shared bath, US$38-43 s/d) offers simple but surprisingly comfortable thatch-roofed cabins on a grassy plot. Each has one or two decent beds (including a few king-size ones), mosquito nets, colorful linens, and 24-hour electricity. There are hooks for hammocks too. There also is space for camping, provided you bring your own gear.

A small *comedor* (US$4.50-6) serves traditional Lacandón and Mexican meals alongside a gurgling creek.

Getting There

COMBI

Transportes Pajchiltic (Calle 3 Sur Ote. near Calle 5 Pte. Sur, US$4.50, 4 hours) provides daily *combi* (public van) service from Palenque to Nahá with departures at 9am and 11am. On the return, there's only one *combi* from Nahá at 4am. Be sure to buy your ticket in advance and arrive early to claim a seat; *combis* fill up fast. Also keep in mind that departure and arrival times are estimates at best, and some *combis* are canceled altogether without notice—plan accordingly.

CAR

Driving to Nahá on your own is a difficult but not impossible task, and affords more flexibility to come and go. A truck is definitely preferable, but it's doable in a midsize rental car as long as the road is dry. Whatever you're driving, be sure your tank is full and you have a spare tire, and leave early to have plenty of daylight.

Nahá is about 100 kilometers (62 miles) from Palenque. To get there, head east on Carretera Fronteriza del Sur for 44 kilometers (27 miles) to the town of La Reforma. Turn right and continue another 14 kilometers (8.7 miles) to an intersection known as Crucero Piñal, where a sign directs you to the right again. The road is paved to there and for another 3.5 kilometers (2 miles) beyond, before turning to gravel and eventually dirt. In the village of Piedrón (3.5 kilometers/2 miles after the pavement ends), continue straight to the fork; from there the road is easy to follow but increasingly rough, passing through small settlements and the town of Nueva Esperanza. Forty kilometers (25 miles) from La Reforma is a well-marked turnoff to Metzabok (6 kilometers/3.7 miles); it's another 18 rutted kilometers (11 miles) to reach Nahá. Budget at least three hours for the trip.

METZABOK

Metzabok is a quiet Lacandón community of just 20 families, who live in simple wood homes in a region of numerous lakes and waterways. The community is situated on the edge of **Laguna Tzibana,** whose name means "painted house" in Lacandón Maya, and is most likely a reference to prehistoric paintings visible along the lake's edge. (The word *Metzabok* comes from the god of the Maya ball game, though it's unclear why the name was used here.) Laguna Tzibana is connected by a natural canal to Laguna Metzabok, a much larger lake and the source of several of the rainforest's streams and rivers. The entire region is protected as part of a federal nature reserve, and is home to a rich array of plants, birds, and mammals.

Metzabok's residents are less accustomed to outsiders and generally more reserved than Nahá's, making it harder (but not impossible) to experience Lacandón life and culture. By the same token, the surrounding rainforest and waterways are even more pristine, and excursions longer and more varied.

There are no public telephones, Internet, or other services in Metzabok, and cabins and meal service are available with advance notice only. The tourism contact person is **Enrique Valenzuela** at the Palenque office of the **Comisión Nacional de Áreas Naturales Protegidas** (CONANP, Calle 5 Pte. Sur near Av. 4 Sur Pte., tel. 916/345-0967,

---

1: Cascada de Misol-Há; 2: frothy waterfalls and turquoise pools at Parque Nacional de Agua Azul; 3: pictograms in Metzabok; 4: simple family-style dining, the norm in Lacanjá Chansayab

metzabok_05@yahoo.com.mx, 9am-6pm Mon.-Fri.), which oversees the reserve and tourism there.

Sights

Because it's surrounded by water, it's no surprise that the best way to enjoy Metzabok's sights is by boat. Local men and boys give paddling tours, whose length and price depends on what you want to see and how many people are in the group. **Basic tours** (US$20-40, 1.5-3 hours) typically begin by paddling across Laguna Tzibana to a set of red *pinturas rupestras* (prehistoric pictograms) on a sheer stone wall right on the edge of the lake. Though streaked and faded, various designs are discernible, including handprints, deities, birds, and monkeys. Nearby, a small **cave** has a clutch of ceremonial artifacts, including incense holders, urns, and even a human skull, though it's unclear how old they are.

A short paddle from the paintings is an **unexcavated archaeological site,** also near the water's edge; very little is known about the history or origins of the site, though it's quite extensive, including numerous mounds and foundations and at least one large pyramid-like structure. The thick forest cover makes it difficult to appreciate, but clambering over and around the tree cover also adds to the appeal and mystery of this ancient site.

Looming over Laguna Tzibana is a high, round **butte;** tours often include climbing a winding trail to the top, where a *mirador* (vista point) offers all-embracing views of the lagoons and verdant forest beyond.

Longer excursions (US$50-70, 5 hours) include all of the above, plus paddling into **Laguna Metzabok,** where there is another set of prehistoric paintings (in multiple colors), a large cave, and additional opportunities for short walks in the forest.

Food and Accommodations

Near the entrance of town, several small thatched-roof *cabañas* (tel. 916/345-0967, US$35 s/d) are available for rent, each with two queen beds, hammock hooks, and private bathroom. They're reasonably comfortable, though far from luxurious—don't be startled by insects or even the occasional mouse, as the units are shuttered between visitors, sometimes for long periods of time. Advance notice is required to be sure the key is available and the cabins tidied up.

There are no restaurants in town, but **home-cooked meals** (US$3-6) can be prepared by a local family or community member. As with the cabins, advance notice is required to allow time to buy necessary supplies.

Getting There
COMBI

There is no reliable *combi* service to Metzabok. *Combis* to Nahá from Palenque typically drop off passengers at the turnoff (US$3), which is about six hilly kilometers (3.7 miles) from town; if there are enough people headed to Metzabok, though, the driver will take a detour to town. To return to Palenque, travelers need to be at the Metzabok turnoff at 3am to catch the *combi* from Nahá—not a good plan, especially in the middle of the night. A better option is to take an inbound *combi* to Nahá (two *combis* pass the turnoff between noon and 2pm) and spend some time there before catching a bus back to Palenque. That way, if the bus is late or canceled, you're in town instead of at a lonely crossroads.

CAR

Metzabok is some 80 kilometers (50 miles) from Palenque, half by dirt road. To get there, head east on Carretera Fronteriza del Sur for 44 kilometers (27 miles) to the town of La Reforma. Turn right and continue another 14 kilometers (8.7 miles) to an intersection known as Crucero Piñal, where a sign directs you to the right again. The road is paved to there and for another 3.5 kilometers (2 miles) beyond, before turning to gravel and eventually dirt. In the village of Piedrón (3.5 kilometers/2 miles after the pavement ends), continue straight to the fork; from there the road is easy to follow but increasingly rough, passing through small settlements and the town of Nueva Esperanza. Forty kilometers (25 miles) from La Reforma is a well-marked turnoff to Metzabok (6 kilometers/3.7 miles). Budget at least two hours for the trip.

NUEVA PALESTINA

Wide, dusty streets and an unusually large central square make this Tzeltal Maya village seem even sleepier than it already is. The best reason to make a detour to Nueva Palestina, located 11 kilometers (6.8 miles) south of the main highway by paved road, is to visit Plan de Ayutla archaeological zone, a fascinating and little-visited site that researchers believe may be the remains of a long-sought Classic-era city. Other local sights, including a large natural swimming hole and a frothing waterfall, wouldn't really merit a special trip themselves, but can be nice places to cool off after visiting the ruins.

Nueva Palestina has limited services. You'll find a handful of shops, including mini-marts, a pharmacy, and an Internet café, around the main square and on the wide avenues leading into and away from town.

Sights
POZA PO'OP CHAN

As if the English connotation weren't concerning enough, Po'op Chan is Tzeltal Maya for "Serpent in the Water"—not the most enticing name for a swimming hole! Nevertheless, this large aqua-blue poza (pool) makes for a pleasant and cooling swim, and at 70 meters (230 feet) across is even big enough to navigate by kayak. A platform at the downstream end of the pool makes getting in easy, and there are several tables along the bank for having a picnic lunch.

Poza Po'op Chan is located in the rear of Campamento Poza Po'op Chan (tel. 967/678-3909, infosendasur@prodigy.net.mx, 8:30am-6pm daily), which charges US$1 admission and rents inflatable kayaks for US$2 per hour. A trail connects Poza Po'op Chan and Cascada Las Golondrinas, a mild and pleasant walk of about three kilometers (1.9 miles).

CASCADA LAS GOLONDRINAS (CH'EN ULICH)

This sloping, multipart falls gets its name, Cascada Las Golondrinas, or Swallows Falls (8:30am-6pm daily, US$1), from a cave behind the main curtain of water that's a favorite nesting area for the loud, energetic birds. A low wooden footbridge extends across the river at the foot of the main cascade, making for a cool and misty vista point. Several small pools are popular for swimming and wading. At the entrance are several palapa umbrellas with small tables beneath them, plus bathrooms and a modest eatery.

The turnoff to the falls is about two kilometers (1.2 miles) north of Nueva Palestina (before entering town, if you're coming from the highway); from there it's another kilometer (0.6 mile) down a dirt road to the parking area and entrance. You can also walk to the falls on a trail from Campamento Poza Po'op Chan (tel. 967/678-3909, infosendasur@prodigy.net.mx), about three kilometers (1.9 miles) each way.

★ PLAN DE AYUTLA ARCHAEOLOGICAL ZONE

For all the attention paid to must-see archaeological sites like Palenque and Yaxchilán, the ruins of Plan de Ayutla rank among the most fascinating and memorable in the region. Seven kilometers (4.3 miles) outside Nueva Palestina and way off the beaten path, the ruins consist of twin pyramids ensconced in trees and vegetation and crowned by a complex of remarkably well-preserved structures that are a thrill to explore and clamber about. What's more, there is growing evidence that these are the remains of the ancient Maya city of Sak Tz'i', whose location has been one of the enduring archaeological mysteries of the Río Usumacinta and Lacandón region.

For decades, archaeologists have known of Sak Tz'i' (Tzeltal Maya for "White Dog") from inscriptions at Piedras Negras and Bonampak but could never find the city's location or remains. The city seems to have played the role of ancient swing voter (or "catalyzing agent" in archaeological parlance)—never a major player itself, yet capable of tipping the balance of power among the dominant cities through strategic alliances. This role is suggested in part by military defeats at the hands of various rivals, including Piedras Negras in AD 628, Yaxchilán and Bonampak in AD 726—possibly the battle portrayed in Bonampak's famous murals—and Toniná even later. But Sak Tz'i' may have had the last laugh: As the major powers collapsed one by one around the turn of the 9th century, Sak Tz'i' held on until at least AD 864, making it one of the last significant Maya cities to fall.

The buildings atop the pyramid on the left (as you enter the site) are larger and more elaborate, including several multiroom "palace structures" with original stucco and paint still visible, and two temples with stunning 10-meter (33-foot) vaulted ceilings. Together they form a grand multilevel complex that probably served as **residential quarters** for the city's elite, and today makes for fun exploring. The structures on the other pyramid are smaller—probably related to administrative functions—but no less impressive. In particular, a small but artful building dubbed **Temple of the Inscription** has faint hieroglyphic text on two sides, while a nearby structure has a distinctive temple-within-a-temple design, similar to structures found at Palenque.

Several plazas occupy the space between the acropolises and contain various structures. One, designated Structure 39, is a **ball court**—at 65 meters (213 feet) long, it's the largest ball court in the region, even bigger than the ones at Palenque and Toniná. Archaeologists have also uncovered an **ancient theater,** complete with bleacher-style seating, and, most remarkably, what appears to be a **royal bath,** complete with drainage and water basins. Baths are extremely rare in Mesoamerican archaeology—in Mexico, only three others have been identified (two of those are also in Chiapas, at Palenque and Toniná, while the third is at Teotihuacán, near Mexico City). There's clearly much more to be learned and excavated at Plan de Ayutla; the city covered around 24 hectares (60 acres) and contains more than 70 structures.

To get to the ruins, continue on the main road past Nueva Palestina for 4.25 kilometers (2.6 miles), looking for a smaller unmarked road just before a bridge and curve. Turn left there and go another 3 kilometers (1.9 miles) to where the road makes a curious S-curve beneath a stand of trees—there are no signs, but you can't miss the twin pyramids looming on either side of the road. The archaeological site is technically on private property, and you may be asked to pay an admission fee of US$2.25 per person.

Food and Accommodations

Campamento Poza Po'op Chan (tel. 967/678-3909, www.sendasur.com.mx, camping US$2.50 pp) has large wooden platforms with *palapa* roofs where guests can pitch a tent or hang a hammock, with a gurgling stream nearby. There are shared tables and grills, and passable toilets and showers. A handful of cabins were closed and unmaintained at last check.

The *campamento* receives mostly groups, which typically bring their own food supplies; otherwise, there are several simple eateries in town.

Getting There

The turnoff to Nueva Palestina is at Kilometer 107, right where a major military checkpoint is located. From there, it's 11 kilometers (6.8 miles) into town, all paved.

Autotransporte Chamoan (in Palenque, Av. Miguel Hidalgo btwn Calles 4 and Allende, cell tel. 916/348-4684) provides daily *combi* service from Palenque to Nuevo Palestina (US$2.75, 2 hours) at 11:30am and 12:30pm. To return, *combis* leave the small terminal facing the main square at 4am and 5am. A taxi from the central plaza to

Campamento Poza Po'op Chan (or returning from the *campamento* to town) is US$2.50. Or take a taxi to the highway turnoff (US$4), where you can flag down a *combi* headed in either direction.

LACANJÁ CHANSAYAB

For many years, the Lacandón village of Lacanjá Chansayab was a true off-the-beaten-path destination—an adventuresome jaunt into the *selva Lacandona* (Lacandón jungle) that was occasionally added to still-nascent tours of Yaxchilán and Bonampak. How things have changed. Today, Lacanjá Chansayab more closely resembles a summer camp than it does an indigenous village, with virtually every family engaged in tourism, mainly in the form of *campamentos* (rustic lodging) and cookie-cutter tours along well-worn forest trails. Competition seems to have quickly overpowered most sense of community spirit among local residents. A visit here can still be rewarding—the rainforest remains impressive, and nighttime is quiet and reflective—but it's not the sublime eco-cultural encounter many expect.

Sights and Activities

Every *campamento* offers **guided walks,** or *caminatas*, through the rainforest to nearby sights, typically lasting 3-4 hours and costing US$15-28 (up to 10 people). Popular excursions include **Ruínas Lacanjá,** a minimally excavated archaeological site ensconced in lush rainforest, with a small main temple with traces of the original red paint still visible and several inscribed panels and stelae; and **Cascadas Las Golondrinas** (aka Cascadas Ya Toch Kusam), a scenic waterfall comprising four different cascades pouring over a 30-meter-wide (90 feet) cliff. The latter is easy enough to reach on your own, following a 2.5-kilometer (1.5-mile) trail accessed through Parador Sak Nok' (US$2 pp).

For a more challenging walk, **Sendero Río Cedro** (Cedar River Trail) connects Lacanjá Chansayab to the Lacandón village of Nueva Palestina, a 6-8-hour hike that ranges from cornfields to pristine rainforest of the Montes Azules Biosphere Reserve, passes waterfalls and massive ceiba trees, and heads across numerous waterways, including the namesake Río Cedro. **Camping** is possible at Campamento Río Cedro, a small Lacandón settlement about two hours from Nueva Palestina, where local guides lead short side trips into the forest and to nearby lagoons. The trail splits and fades in numerous places, making a private guide all but essential. Ask for guides and prices at one of the lodges.

Class II to Class IV **rafting trips** (US$38-55 pp) down the Río Lacanjá also are offered by **Campamento Río Lacanjá** (tel. 967/631-7498, toll-free Mex. tel. 800/397-5072, www.ecochiapas.com/campamento-rio-lacanja) and **Campamento Topche** (tel. 967/678-3909, www.sendasur.com.mx). Most trips include a two-hour hike back to town, with stops at Lacanjá ruins and Cascadas Las Golondrinas.

Food

All the *campamentos* have small **restaurants** (7am-9pm daily), which are open to guests and nonguests alike. Standard Mexican meals are served at moderate prices (US$4-6), typically in open-air dining rooms.

Accommodations

★ **Campamento Río Lacanjá** (tel. 967/631-7498, toll-free Mex. tel. 800/397-5072, www.ecochiapas.com/campamento-rio-lacanja, US$35 s/d with shared bath, US$52 s/d) is the most atmospheric of the *campamentos*. The complex includes 13 simple wood cabins with small porches and hammocks, built in a shady grove alongside a small river. Spotless bathrooms and hot-water showers are in a central building. To get here, turn left at the village center and continue to the end of the road.

Campamento Topche (tel. 967/678-3909, www.sendasur.com.mx, US$37 s/d with shared bath, US$65 s/d), 0.5 kilometer (0.3 mile) west of the main intersection, is run by the amiable Chankin Paniagua family. The shared-bath units have cement floors and plywood walls that don't quite meet the ceiling. Much more appealing are the private units with terra cotta tile floors and high, sloped *palapa* ceilings; some sit alongside the river. Wi-Fi (US$2/hour) is available in common areas.

Campamento Ya'aj Che (tel. 967/678-3909, www.sendasur.com.mx, campamento_yaajche@hotmail.com, US$9 pp with shared bath, US$30 s/d), just south of the main intersection, has simple wood cabins with corrugated metal roofs and shared bathrooms located within earshot of a gurgling stream. Boxy private units are more comfortable, with private bathrooms and tile floors, but lack the outdoorsy ambience.

Information and Services
There's **Wi-Fi** (US$2/hour) at **Campamento Topche** (tel. 967/678-3909, www.sendasur. com.mx). The village also has a very basic **medical clinic,** but for medical issues of any severity head to Palenque or Villahermosa.

Getting There
The well-marked turnoff to Lacanjá Chansayab is at the roadside town of San Javier, about 130 kilometers (81 miles) from Palenque. Bear right there, and again at a second intersection about a kilometer (0.6 mile) later. Continue for 8 kilometers (5 miles) to the village center.

Autotransporte Chamoan (in Palenque, Av. Miguel Hidalgo btwn Calles 4 and Allende, cell tel. 916/348-4684) provides daily *combi* service from Palenque to Lacanjá Chansayab (US$7, 2.5 hours) on vans headed to Frontera Corozal—at least they're *supposed* to drive passengers all the way into the village, provided you inform the driver in advance. If for some reason you are dropped in San Javier on the highway, a taxi to the village costs US$3.

FRONTERA COROZAL
This quiet community along the banks of the Río Usumacinta is the jumping-off point for visiting the Yaxchilán archaeological site, a terrific Maya ruin located about 25 kilometers (15.5 miles) downriver. It's also a convenient border crossing into Guatemala, just across the river, and you may be asked to show your passport (and pay a small fee) at a checkpoint at the entrance of town, even if you intend to remain in Mexico. The town itself is quite new, founded in 1976 by Ch'ol Maya émigrés from northern Chiapas, along with a small number of Lacandón and

Many *cabañas* in Lacanjá Chansayab are built alongside the river.

Tzeltal families. Relations are far from perfect, but locals take pride in their town's multicultural origins.

Sights

Museo Comunitario Frontera Corozal (9am-5pm daily, US$1.50) is a well-organized one-room museum, with exhibits on the history of the community, local flora and fauna, and archaeological discoveries, including the museum's pièces de résistance: two three-meter (10-foot), three-ton stelae found in the surrounding forest, carefully restored and installed here. Signage is in Spanish only.

Food

Restaurante Imperio Maya (no phone, 7:30am-3pm daily, US$4-6) serves up simple but reliable Mexican food in a spacious, *palapa*-roofed dining room. It typically offers a *comida corrida* (lunch special) that includes soup, main dish, and drink for US$5. Look for it on the main street, next to the Yaxchilán ticket booth.

Escudo Jaguar (tel. 919/153-5637, www. sendasur.com.mx) and **Centro Turístico Nueva Alianza** (cell tel. 919/209-2456, www. hotelnuevaalianza.com) both have open-air **restaurants** (7am-8pm daily, US$4-8) serving decent regional fare in large *palapa*-covered dining areas. They cater to tour groups and thus can get pretty busy, especially at lunch.

Accommodations

Escudo Jaguar (tel. 919/153-5637, www. sendasur.com.mx, US$7.50 pp camping, US$29 s/d with shared bath, US$34 s/d) is a tour group favorite with several thatch-roofed *cabañas* on a manicured riverfront lot. All have ceiling fans, mosquito nets, and 24-hour electricity. Smaller units share clean single-sex bathrooms; larger ones have en suite bathrooms and patios with hammocks. Camping is available on a flat, grassy area (BYO gear), plus there's a decent pool. Wi-Fi (US$1.25/ hour) is available at the restaurant.

Hotel Nueva Alianza (cell tel. 919/209-2456, US$15 s/d with shared bath, US$30 s/d) has pleasant thatch-roof cabins set on a verdant lot. All have tile bathrooms and porches strung with hammocks. Units with shared bathrooms also share walls that don't quite reach the ceiling (prepare to hear—and be heard by—your neighbors). These have mosquito netting, cement floors, and a lightbulb. They're simple but a decent value. Complimentary Wi-Fi is available in the common areas.

Information and Services

There is no bank or ATM in town, and only Hotel Nueva Alianza accepts credit cards; plan on bringing enough cash to get you through your stay. **Escudo Jaguar** (tel. 919/153-5637, www.sendasur.com.mx) offers Wi-Fi to hotel guests and diners for US$1.25 per hour; all others can usually plead their case (or just buy a soda to qualify for diner status).

The **immigration office** (no phone, 8am-6pm daily) is on the main drag, across from the Yaxchilán ticket booth.

Getting There and Around
COMBI
From Palenque, **Autotransporte Chamoan** (Av. Miguel Hidalgo btwn Calles 4 and Allende, cell tel. 916/348-4684) provides *combi* service to Frontera Corozal (US$7.25, 3 hours) hourly 4am-5pm daily. The bus stops in front of the Yaxchilán ruins ticket booth, a short distance from the river dock, where you can catch a boat to the ruins. The same *combis* return to Palenque hourly 4am-4pm daily. If arriving by car, prepare to pay a US$1 toll to enter town.

CAR
From Palenque, follow the Carretera Fronteriza for 162 kilometers (100 miles) to Crucero Corozal, a well-marked turnoff. From there, it's another 22 kilometers (13.7 miles) to town. Once there, all vehicles must pay a US$1.50 toll. Be sure to keep your ticket handy for your departure; if you don't have one, you'll be charged a second toll.

The road between Palenque and Frontera Corozal was once unsafe due to frequent armed robberies. The situation has improved immensely, however, and the 185-kilometer (115-mile) stretch is now considered safe. Nevertheless, for the sake of caution, driving during daylight hours only is recommended.

BOAT

The **boat cooperative** (Guatemala tel. 502/5369-6769) that goes to Yaxchilán archaeological zone also provides one-way transportation to **Betel, Guatemala** (US$23 for 1-3 people, US$27 for 4, 40 minutes), where **buses to Flores** (US$10, 4.5 hours), near the archaeological site of Tikal, depart several times per day. Remember to stop at Mexican **immigration** (no phone, 8am-6pm daily) to hand in your tourist permit (or obtain it, if arriving from Guatemala); the office is across the street from the Yaxchilán ticket booth, on the main drag. Guatemalan immigration is in Betel.

Bonampak Archaeological Zone

Bonampak (8am-5pm daily, US$3.50) is a modest site overall, but home to some of the best ancient Maya murals ever discovered. The famous murals adorn the interior walls of a small temple built innocuously on the staircase of the city's main acropolis; painted in brilliant teal, red, and other colors, they depict sacrifices, ritual bloodletting, and violent battle scenes. The images shattered previous assumptions about the Maya, who had been portrayed by many researchers as a peace-loving civilization, in sharp contrast to Central Mexican indigenous groups and, of course, the Spanish colonizers.

HISTORY

Located in a fertile valley, the ruins are near a small tributary of the Río Lacanjá, with protective hills to one side. The earliest evidence of human occupation at Bonampak are ceramics dated to AD 100; the city reached its apogee in the Late Classic era (AD 600-800). Bonampak had a close and surprisingly amicable relationship with the nearby city of Yaxchilán, just 20 kilometers (12.4 miles) to the southeast. Bonampak's most notable leader, Chaan-Muan, was married to the sister of Yaxchilán's great king Shield Jaguar. The brothers-in-law joined forces in a war against a third city in the 7th century, possibly Sak Tz'i', known today as Plan de Ayutla. The battle is commemorated in part of Bonampak's famous murals and lintels. Relatively little else is known about the city, however.

Much more ink, however, has been dedicated to the scandal that arose around the site's discovery in the 1946. In February, two Americans—Charles "Carlos" Frey, a World War II conscientious objector, and John Bourne, the heir to the Singer sewing machine fortune—were led to the ruins by a Lacandón named Chan Bor in exchange for a phonograph. They spent several days studying the site but evidently missed the murals. A few months later, Chan Bor led a different team to the ruins, this one headed by photographer-archaeologist Giles Healy, who documented the murals and made international headlines for the find. Frey spent years trying to convince the world he was the true discoverer of the site, to no avail. In 1949, he was part of an ill-advised expedition organized by the Mexican Fine Arts Institute, during which he drowned in the Río Lacanjá, reportedly trying to save a fellow team member after their canoe capsized.

★ BONAMPAK MURALS

Bonampak's murals are housed in **Templo de las Pinturas** (Temple of the Paintings), which stands on a low level of the **Acrópolis,**

Bonampak Archaeological Zone

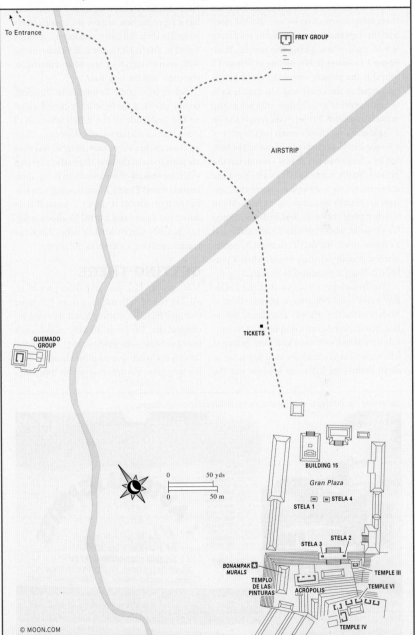

To Entrance

FREY GROUP

AIRSTRIP

QUEMADO GROUP

TICKETS

BUILDING 15

Gran Plaza

STELA 4

STELA 1

0   50 yds

0   50 m

STELA 2

STELA 3

TEMPLE III

BONAMPAK MURALS

TEMPLO DE LAS PINTURAS

ACRÓPOLIS

TEMPLE VI

TEMPLE IV

© MOON.COM

a large stepped structure that backs onto a jungle-covered hill. In front of the Acrópolis is a plaza with low buildings around the other three sides. Researchers believe that the story told through the murals should be read from left to right when facing the temple, from Room 1 to Room 3: The setting of **Room 1**'s mural is the palace, where the child-heir is presented to the court and 336 days later is the focal point of a celebration with actors and musicians. **Room 2** is set in the jungle and on a flight of stairs. These murals tell the story of a jungle battle, probably in honor of the heir, led by Chaan-Muan. This is considered the greatest battle scene in Maya art. Next the scene moves to a staircase, where the captives are ritually tortured while Chaan-Muan watches from above. In **Room 3,** the setting is a pyramid, where costumed lords dance and a captive awaits his death. To the side, noble-women ritually let their blood, while a pot-bellied dwarf is presented to the court.

Anthropologists believe that the child-heir never ruled Bonampak, because there is evidence that the site was abandoned before the murals were even completed. The murals have faded with time and were damaged when the first researchers used kerosene to clean them—the kerosene brought out the colors but weakened the paints' adhesion and hastened the flaking and decay. The Museo Nacional de Antropología, in Mexico City, has a reproduction of how the murals likely looked in their full glory, and lesser copies are found in Tuxtla Gutiérrez and Villahermosa. Still, even though they are old and damaged, you can't beat the originals.

Before leaving the Templo de las Pinturas, be sure to look at the beautifully carved scenes on the underside of the lintels (the slab of stone that forms the top of a doorway). Their location makes them easy to miss, but they are truly some of the best Maya relief carvings you'll see outside of a museum. In Bonampak, **Lintel I** shows Chaan-Muan holding a captive by the hair; **Lintel II** shows Itzanaaj B'alam doing the same; and **Lintel III** shows a figure, possibly Chaan-Muan's father, Knot Eye Jaguar, spearing a victim in the chest.

GETTING THERE

Most people visit Bonampak as part of an all-day round-trip package from Palenque that also includes visiting Yaxchilán archaeological site. The "tour" usually includes just transportation—no guide service, though the drivers are often quite knowledgeable. This is a very practical option, even for those who

---

Combis are a good way to visit Bonampak, Yaxchilán, and nearby villages.

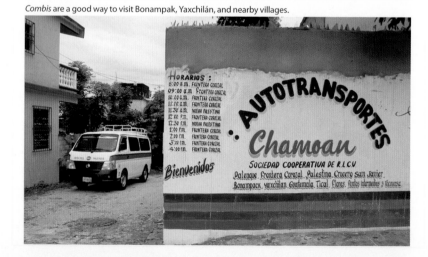

eschew packages of any sort, because visiting both ruins in a day requires keeping a tight schedule, which is impossible if you're traveling by *combi*.

A rental car is quicker, but you still get pinched for things that are included in the tour price (not to mention gas and the rental itself): Independent travelers must pay a toll (US$1.50) at the highway turnoff to use the road approaching Bonampak. From there, a local cooperative controls the 10-kilometer (6.2-mile) access road to the ruins and charges US$5 per person (3 or more passengers) or US$12.50 per shuttle (fewer than 3 passengers) for round-trip shuttle service to the ruins. Anyone not arriving by tour must take a shuttle, whether arriving by public transportation or car, though small discounts are available for students and seniors. Your best shot at sharing a ride is to be at the shuttle stop between 1pm and 3pm, when tour groups from Yaxchilán are arriving.

Combi

From Palenque, *combis* operated by **Autotransporte Chamoan** (Av. Miguel Hidalgo btwn Calles 4 and Allende, cell tel. 916/348-4684) leave for Frontera Corozal hourly 4am-5pm daily; be sure to ask the driver to drop you at Crucero Bonampak (Bonampak turnoff, US$4.75, 2.5 hours), which is a kilometer (0.6 mile) off the main road and not an automatic stop. From there, you must take a local van (US$5 pp, 3 or more passengers; US$12.50 fewer than 3 passengers) to the ruins.

Car

About 130 kilometers (81 miles) southeast of Palenque in the town of San Javier are large signs and a prominent intersection marking the turnoff to Bonampak. Turn right and go a short distance farther to a second intersection, known as Crucero Bonampak (Bonampak turnoff); a US$1.50 toll must be paid here. It's another 10 kilometers (6.2 miles) to the ruins, but private cars aren't allowed past; instead you must park and take a local shuttle round-trip (US$5 pp, 3 or more passengers; US$12.50 fewer than 3 passengers). There's a parking lot (free, at least) from where the shuttle departs.

Yaxchilán Archaeological Zone

Yaxchilán (8am-5pm daily, US$3.50) lies on the Río Usumacinta, Mexico's largest river and the border between Mexico and Guatemala. Archaeologists have found at least 35 stelae, 60 carved lintels, 21 altars, and 5 stairways covered with hieroglyphs here—a treasure trove for epigraphers. Yaxchilán's rulers were obsessed with venerating their dynasty as well as legitimizing their rule, and endowed a major monument-carving operation to achieve these goals. In fact, it was Yaxchilán's hieroglyphs that provided much of the raw material that led to the deciphering of the Maya writing system. **Note:** Tickets should be purchased at the ticket booth on the main drag in Frontera Corozal. While there is a ticket counter at the ruins themselves, it's often unmanned. Visitors arriving without a ticket risk not being allowed into the site.

HISTORY

Yaxchilán was a powerful city-state during the Classic era, ruled by the Jaguar dynasty, which traced its roots to AD 320 and a ruler named Yat B'alam (Jaguar Penis). The earliest recorded date at the site is from AD 435, and the first major monuments appeared early in the 6th century.

Yaxchilán's greatest ruler was Izamnaaj B'alam, or Shield Jaguar, who was born in AD 647 and ruled for more than six decades (AD 681-742), a remarkable feat for a man whose life expectancy would have

Yaxchilán Archaeological Zone

To Pier

RESTROOMS

Río Usumacinta

STRUCTURE 44

EL LABERINTO

Main Plaza

SMALL ACROPOLIS

TEMPLE (STRUCTURE 23)

STELA 1

HIEROGLYPHIC STAIRCASE

GRAND STAIRCASE

STRUCTURE 21

GREAT ACROPOLIS

TEMPLE (STRUCTURE 33)

STRUCTURE 20

STELA 3

SOUTH ACROPOLIS

STRUCTURE 40

0   50 yds

0   50 m

© MOON.COM

been less than 40 years. He undertook numerous construction projects, including the construction of Structure 23 on the main plaza. Dedicated to his wife, Lady Xoc, it is the only Maya temple known to have been built specifically in honor of a woman. (Palenque's Temple XIII, in which archaeologists excavated the so-called Tomb of the Red Queen, may be another, but that is not confirmed.) But the construction and dedication of Structure 23 may have had more to do with politics than enlightenment; Shield Jaguar took a second wife late in life and named the son from that union, Bird Jaguar, heir to the throne. Structure 23, which shows Lady Xoc conducting various noble rituals, may have been a way of appeasing her powerful family.

Curiously, Bird Jaguar was not crowned until AD 752, a full 10 years after his father's death. Archaeologists interpret this as a sign of tepid political support for the young monarch; as further evidence, they point to Bird Jaguar's obsessive self-aggrandizement once he finally did assume the throne, as if he were desperate to legitimize his position. Bird Jaguar built numerous buildings, most notably Structure 33, and seems to have commissioned a stelae or relief carving to commemorate his every accomplishment, including military victories, bloodletting ceremonies, the sacrifice of important captives, and even winning a ball game match. Bird Jaguar was the beginning of the end for the Jaguar dynasty, which lasted until about AD 800. Its last ruler, Ta-Skull, Bird Jaguar's grandson, is credited with just two small, rather poorly constructed temples (Structures 3 and 64), which contain the latest known date inscription at Yaxchilán, AD 808, commemorating a military victory. Yaxchilán gradually depopulated and by AD 900 had been returned to the jungle.

★ YAXCHILÁN RUINS

A steep path leads up from the boat pier to Yaxchilán's on-site ticket booth, which is often unmanned. (Be sure to buy your ticket in Frontera Corozal or risk not being allowed in. Look for the ticket booth in Frontera Corozal on the main street as you approach the river.) Entering the site, a wide path leads to the Gran Plaza, with the Great Acropolis a long, steep flight of stairs above. Instead of following this path, consider taking the small path that cuts to your right up the hill to the **Small Acropolis.** It's a steep climb, but once there the rest of your visit is downhill. The most important structure in this complex is **Structure 44,** which was built by Shield Jaguar in celebration of his military successes.

Continue on the path to reach the **Great Acropolis** from the back side. It's a pleasant walk, and you may spot howler monkeys in the trees along the way. Around front, you'll be at the top of a long flight of stone stairs and in front of one of Yaxchilán's most notable structures, **Structure 33,** with its intricate facade and soaring roof comb. Built by Bird Jaguar to celebrate himself—who else?—it includes incredibly fine lintels (the slab of stone that forms the top of a doorway) and panels depicting the ruler's accomplishments, including summoning his deceased ancestors in the midst of a ball game.

Descending the stairs, you'll reach the **Gran Plaza,** a long rectangular plaza built alongside the riverbank, framed by numerous structures and dotted with large stelae. **Structure 20** and **Structure 21** are to the right of the staircase as you reach the bottom; built by Shield Jaguar and Bird Jaguar, respectively, both have lintels portraying rituals related to the birth of heirs. On the other side of the staircase, **Structure 23** is the famous temple built by Shield Jaguar and dedicated to Lady Xoc. This is where archaeologists discovered exquisitely carved panels portraying the noblewoman performing rituals, including drawing a thorny twine through her tongue.

At the west end of the Gran Plaza is a complex called **El Laberinto** (The Labyrinth), so named for its maze of vaulted passageways and chambers; it likely served as residential quarters. The main path leads back through the trees to the boat landing.

GETTING THERE

Yaxchilán is located 25 kilometers (15.5 miles) down the Río Usumacinta from the town of Frontera Corozal, and can only be reached by *lancha* (a long, colorful, canoe-like boat with a sun cover and powerful outboard motor). The 45- to 60-minute ride leaves from a pier at the end of the main road, where a number of cooperatives and private outfits compete for arriving tourists. The first boats leave Frontera Corozal at 7am, the last at 3pm. Be sure to buy your admission ticket to the ruins at the booth as you approach the pier.

The boat trip is definitely part of the fun of visiting this remote site, zipping down the river in a long, colorful *lancha* with Guatemala on one side and Mexico on the other, with the chance to see birds, howler monkeys, and beefy crocodiles sunning themselves on the riverbank. Round-trip prices are fairly uniform and depend on the size of your group: US$40 for 1-3 passengers, US$53 for 4, US$73 for 5-7, and US$90 for 8-10. The price includes two hours at the site; you can stay longer, but you'll have to tip the boatman (even better, throw in a Coke and something to eat as well). **Tip:** If you're looking to share a boat, wait in front of the Yaxchilán ticket booth in Frontera Corozal. Tour groups typically arrive between 8am and 9am—ask the guide if you can join for the ride.

Background

The Landscape

The history of the Yucatán Peninsula is deeply intertwined with the region's unique geology and ecology. From the ancient Maya to modern-day tourism, the land and its resources have shaped the course of Yucatecan events. And the Yucatán, in turn, has helped shape the course of Mexican history, from being the stage upon which the early Spanish conquest was conducted to helping rescue a moribund Mexican economy in the 1980s. An understanding of the Yucatán Peninsula's land, ecology, culture, and politics is vital to understanding the region today.

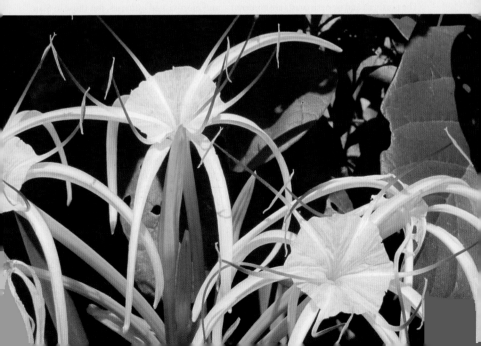

GEOGRAPHY

The Yucatán Peninsula spans some 113,000 square kilometers (70,215 square miles) in southeastern Mexico, and is made up of three states: Yucatán, Campeche, and Quintana Roo. It has more than 1,600 kilometers (994 miles) of shoreline, with the Caribbean Sea to the east and the Gulf of Mexico to the north and west. To the southwest are the Mexican states of Tabasco and Chiapas, and directly south are the countries of Belize and Guatemala.

Geologically, the Yucatán Peninsula is a flat shelf of limestone, a porous rock that acts like a huge sponge. Rainfall is absorbed into the ground and delivered to natural stone-lined sinks and underground rivers. The result is that the Yucatán has virtually no surface water, neither rivers nor lakes. It also has very few hills. The geology changes as you move south, and the first sizable river—the Río Hondo—forms a natural boundary between Belize and Mexico.

The Coast

The northern and western coasts are bordered by the emerald waters of the Gulf of Mexico. Just inland, the land is dotted with lagoons, sandbars, and swamps. The east coast is edged by the turquoise Caribbean, and the glorious islands of Isla Cozumel, Isla Mujeres, and Isla Contoy lie just offshore. Along the coast runs the Mesoamerican Reef, the second-longest coral reef in the world.

Cenotes

Over the course of millennia, water that seeped below the Yucatán's porous limestone shelf eroded a vast network of underground rivers and caves. When a cave's ceiling wears thin, it may eventually cave in, exposing the water below. The Maya called such sinkholes *dzo'not,* which Spanish explorers recorded as *cenotes.* Most cenotes are extremely deep, and interconnected by way of underground channels. A cenote's surface may be near ground level, but more often it is much farther down, as much as 90 meters (295 feet) below ground level. In those cases, the Maya gathered water by carving stairs into the slick limestone walls or by hanging long ladders into abysmal hollows that led to underground lakes.

Estuaries

The Yucatán's countless estuaries, or *rías,* play host to hundreds of bird species; a boat ride into one of them will give you an opportunity to see American flamingos, a variety of wintering ducks from North America, blue-winged teals, northern shovelers, and lesser scaups. You'll also see a variety of wading birds feeding in the shallow waters, including numerous types of herons, snowy egrets, and, in the summer, white ibis. There are 14 species of birds endemic to the Yucatán Peninsula, including the ocellated turkey, Yucatán whippoorwill, Yucatán flycatcher, orange oriole, black catbird, and the yellow-lored parrot. Río Lagartos and Celestún are the best-known and most-visited estuaries, but those in Sian Ka'an Biosphere Reserve, Isla Holbox, and Xcalak are also vibrant and accessible.

CLIMATE

The weather in the Yucatán falls into a rainy season (May-October) and a dry season (November-April). Travelers to the region in the dry season will experience warm days, occasional brief storms called *nortes,* and plenty of tourists. In the rainy season, expect spectacular storms and hot, muggy days. The region is infamous for its heat and humidity in May and June, which hovers around 90°F *and* 90 percent humidity.

Hurricane season runs July-November, with most activity occurring mid-August to mid-October. Cloudy conditions and scattered showers are common during this period, occasionally developing into tropical storms.

Previous: blooms dotting the Yucatán region's forests.

Hurricanes are still relatively rare, but their effects are wide-reaching—even if a storm isn't predicted to hit the Yucatán, it may send plenty of heavy rain and surf in its direction. If a hurricane *is* bearing down, don't try to tough it out; cut short your trip or head inland immediately.

ENVIRONMENTAL ISSUES

Hurricanes

Evidence that global warming may cause an increase in the number and/or intensity of Atlantic hurricanes has serious implications for the Yucatán Peninsula, already known to be within Hurricane Alley. The region has weathered countless storms, but something was different about Hurricanes Wilma (2005) and Dean (2007)—both storms broke records for intensity and caused major structural damage, but they also reshaped the shoreline in a way not seen before. Cancún's beaches were especially hard hit, the sand stripped away in many places to expose the hardened limestone beneath. Elsewhere, unusually thick deposits of sand on the coral reef and inland mangroves wiped out large portions of both important ecosystems.

Overdevelopment

Runaway construction along the Riviera Maya has a host of interconnected environmental impacts, some well known, others poorly understood (and surely many that have yet to be identified). An obvious impact is the destruction of mangrove swamps, which extend along much of the coast a short distance inland from the beach. Well known for supporting wildlife, mangroves also help buffer the effects of hurricane-related surge and currents and are an important source of nutrients for coral and other sealife, as water from the wetlands drains into the ocean. Although protected by federal law, mangroves have been a primary victim of massive development projects.

Mangroves are emblematic of a more general characteristic of the Riviera Maya: highly porous earth and a weblike underground watershed. Contamination is extremely difficult to clean up or even contain, as it spreads quickly in multiple directions via underground currents, including into the ocean. This is damaging not only to the environment but also to local communities—and the resorts themselves—which draw drinking water from the same system.

And those local communities are growing even faster than the resorts—by some estimates, resorts require an average of five employees for every guest room. Multiply that by the number of resorts operating and being built, and it's no surprise that the region's population is booming. In that sense, development is doubly dangerous: increasing the risk of contamination while simultaneously spurring demand for the very resource it most threatens.

Deforestation

Among the top concerns of environmentalists in Mexico is deforestation, which has accelerated with Mexico's burgeoning population. Slash-and-burn farming is still widely practiced in remote areas, with or without regulation. In an effort to protect the land, environmentalists are searching for alternative sources of income for locals. One is to train them to become guides by teaching them about the flora and fauna of the region as well as how to speak English. While not solving the problem, it does place an economic value on the forest itself and provides an incentive for preserving it.

Another focus is the plight of the palm tree. The palm is an important part of the cultural and practical lifestyle of the indigenous people of the Yucatán. The fan-like chit palm (*thrinax radiate*) and ghostly Mexican silver palm (*coccothrinax readii*) have been used for millennia for everything from thatch roofing to constructing lobster traps. However, both palms are increasingly threatened; they grow best on coastal areas, right where development is more intense. NGOs like Amigos de Sian Ka'an and the World Wildlife Fund have worked to better understand the palms' growth patterns and to develop sustainable management plans. Other forest-friendly projects include establishing nature reserves, forming partnerships with local Maya communities, and developing ecotourism projects.

Plants and Animals

Many of the Yucatán Peninsula's coastal areas are home to mangroves, bamboo, and swamp cypresses. Ferns, vines, and flowers creep from tree to tree and create a dense growth. The southern part of the peninsula, with its classic tropical rainforest, hosts tall mahoganies, *campeche zapote*, and *kapok*—all covered in wild jungle vines. On topmost limbs, orchids and air ferns reach for the sun.

Many animals found nowhere else in Mexico inhabit the Yucatán Peninsula's expansive flatlands and thick jungle forests. Spotting them can be difficult, though with patience and a skilled guide, not impossible.

TREES

A wide variety of palm trees and their relatives grow on the peninsula—tall, short, fruited, and even oil-producing varieties. Though similar, palms have distinct characteristics:

• Queen palms are often used for landscaping and bear a sweet fruit.

• Thatch palms are called *chit* by Maya, who use the fronds extensively for roof thatch.

• Coconut palms—the ones often seen on the beach—produce oil, food, drink, and shelter and are valued by locals as a nutritious food source and cash crop.

• Royal palms are tall with smooth trunks.

• Henequen is a cousin to the palm tree; from its fiber come twine, rope, matting, and other products. Because of its abundance, new uses for it are constantly sought.

Fruit Trees

The region is known for its sweet and sour oranges, limes, and grapefruit. Avocado is abundant, and the papaya tree is practically a weed. The *mamey* grows full and tall (15-20 meters/49-65 feet), providing not only welcome shade but also an avocado-shaped fruit, brown on the outside with a vivid, salmon-pink flesh that tastes like a sweet yam. The *guaya* is another unusual fruit tree and a member of the lychee nut family. This rangy evergreen thrives on sea air and is commonly seen along the coast. Its small, green, leathery pods grow in clumps like grapes and contain a sweet, yellowish, jellylike flesh—tasty! The calabash tree provides gourds used for containers by Maya.

Other Trees

The ceiba (also called *kapok*) is a sacred tree for the Maya. Considered the link between the underworld, the material world, and the heavens, this huge tree is revered and left undisturbed—even if it sprouts in the middle of a fertile cornfield.

When visiting in the summer, you can't miss the beautiful *framboyanes* (royal poinciana). When in bloom, its wide-spreading branches become covered in clusters of brilliant orange-red flowers. These trees often line sidewalks and plazas, and when clustered together present a dazzling show.

FLOWERS

While wandering through jungle regions, you'll see numerous flowering plants. Here in their natural environment, these plants thrive in a way unknown to windowsills at home: Crotons exhibit wild colors, pothos grow 30-centimeter (11.8-inch) leaves, the philodendron splits every leaf in gargantuan glory, and common morning glory creeps and climbs effortlessly over bushes and trees. You'll also be introduced to lesser-known residents of this semitropical world: the exotic white and red ginger, plumeria (sometimes called frangipani) with its wonderful fragrance and myriad colors, and hibiscus and bougainvillea, which bloom in an array of bright hues.

Orchids

Orchids can be found on the highest limbs of the tallest trees, especially in the state of Quintana Roo. Of the 71 species reported in the Yucatán Peninsula, 80 percent are epiphytic, attached to host trees and deriving moisture and nutrients from the air and rain. Orchids grow in myriad sizes and shapes: tiny buttons spanning the length of a half-meter-long (two-foot) branch, large-petaled blossoms with ruffled edges, or intense tiger-striped miniatures.

MAMMALS
Nine-Banded Armadillos

The size of a small dog and sporting a thick coat of armor, this peculiar creature gets its name from the nine bands (or external "joints") that circle its midsection and give the little tank some flexibility. The armadillo's keen sense of smell can detect insects and grubs—its primary food source—up to 15 centimeters (6 inches) underground, and its sharp claws make digging for them easy. An armadillo also digs underground burrows, into which it may carry a full bushel of grass to make its nest, where it will sleep through the hot day and emerge at night. Unlike armadillos that roll up into a tight ball when threatened, this species will race to its burrow, arch its back, and wedge in so that it cannot be pulled out. The Yucatán Peninsula is a favored habitat for its scant rainfall; too much rain floods the burrow and can drown young armadillos.

Giant Anteaters

A cousin of the armadillo, this extraordinary animal measures two meters (6.6 feet) from the tip of its tubular snout to the end of its bushy tail. Its coarse coat is colored shades of brown-gray; the hindquarters are darker in tone, while a contrasting wedge-shaped pattern of black and white decorates the throat and shoulders. Characterized by an elongated head, long tubular mouth, and extended tongue (but no teeth), it can weigh up to 39 kilograms (86 pounds). The anteater walks on the knuckles of its paws, allowing its claws to remain tucked under while it looks for food.

Giant anteaters are found in forests and swampy areas in Mexico and throughout Central and South America. It is mainly diurnal in areas where there are few people but nocturnal in densely populated places. Its razor-sharp claws allow it to rip open the leathery mud walls of termite and ant nests, the contents of which are a main food source. After opening the nest, the anteater rapidly flicks its viscous tongue in and out of its small mouth opening. Few ants escape.

Tapirs

The Central American tapir, or the Baird's tapir, is the largest land mammal in Mexico, with adults averaging two meters (6.6 feet) in length and weighing from 150 kilograms (330 pounds) to a whopping 400 kilograms (880 pounds). The nose and upper lip extend into a short but very mobile proboscis. Baird's tapirs are mostly black or gray, save distinctive cream-colored patches on their faces. Tapirs usually live near streams or rivers, which they use for daily bathing and as an escape from predators, especially jaguars and humans. If attacked, the tapir lowers its head and blindly crashes off through the forest; they've been known to collide with trees and knock themselves out in their chaotic attempt to flee. Tapirs are solitary and require large tracts of land for their nighttime foraging; this makes them especially vulnerable to habitat fragmentation. In Mexico, there are around a thousand wild tapirs found in only four states—Campeche, Quintana Roo, Chiapas, and Oaxaca.

Peccaries

Next to deer, peccaries are the most widely hunted game on the Yucatán Peninsula. Two species of peccaries are found here: the collared javelina peccary and the white-lipped peccary. The feisty collared javelina stands 50 centimeters (20 inches) at the shoulder and can be one meter (3.3 feet) long, weighing as much as 30 kilograms (66 pounds). It is black and white with a narrow, semicircular collar of white hair on the shoulders. The name *javelina* (which means "spear" in Spanish) comes from the two tusks that protrude from its mouth. A related species, the white-lipped peccary, is reddish brown to black and has an area of white around its mouth. Larger than the javelina, it can grow to 105 centimeters (41 inches) long, and is found deep in tropical rainforests living in herds of 100 or more. Peccaries often are compared to the wild pigs found in Europe, but in fact they belong to entirely different families.

Felines

Seven species of cats are found in North America, four in the tropics. One of them—the jaguar—is heavy chested with sturdy, muscled forelegs. It has small, rounded ears and its tail is relatively short. Its color varies from tan and white to pure black. The male can weigh 65-115 kilograms (143-254 pounds), females 45-85 kilograms (99-187 pounds). The largest of the cats on the peninsula, the jaguar is about the same size as a leopard. Other cats found here are the ocelot and puma. In tropical forests of the past, the large cats were the only predators capable of controlling the populations of hoofed game such as deer, peccaries, and tapirs. If hunting is poor and times are tough, the jaguar will go into rivers and scoop up fish with its large paws. The river is also one of the jaguar's favorite spots for hunting tapirs, when the latter come to drink.

Monkeys

The jungles of Mexico are home to three species of monkeys: spider, howler, and black howler. Intelligent and endearing, these creatures are prime targets for the pet trade. They have been so hunted, in fact, that today all three are in danger of extinction. Experts estimate that for every monkey sold, three die during transportation and distribution. In an effort to protect these creatures, the Mexican government has prohibited their capture or trade. Tropical monkeys are most active at sunrise and sundown. If you go to Muyil, Cobá, or Punta Laguna Spider Monkey Reserve, keep your ears perked and your eyes peeled. You may see—or at least hear—a few monkeys. If possible, consider waking early or staying late to increase your chances of spotting a few. Other places to see spider and howler monkeys are Calakmul and Yaxchilán archaeological sites.

SEALIFE
Coral Reefs

The spectacular coral reefs that grace the peninsula's east coast are made up of millions of tiny carnivorous organisms called polyps. Individual polyps can be less than a centimeter (0.4 inch) long or up to 15 centimeters (6 inches) in diameter. Related to the jellyfish and sea anemone, coral polyps capture prey with tiny tentacles that deliver a deadly sting.

Reef-building polyps have limestone exoskeletons, which they create by extracting calcium from the seawater. Reefs are formed as generation after generation of polyps attach themselves to each other. Different species attach in different ways, resulting in the many shapes and sizes of ocean reefs: delicate lace, trees with reaching branches, pleated mushrooms, stovepipes, petaled flowers, fans, domes, heads of cabbage, and stalks of broccoli. Though made up of individual polyps, coral structures function like a single organism, sharing nutrients through a central gastrovascular system. Even in ideal conditions, most coral grows no more than five centimeters (two inches) per year.

Reefs are divided into three types: barrier, atoll, and fringing. A barrier reef runs parallel to the coast, with long stretches separated by narrow channels. The Mesoamerican Reef extends 250 kilometers (155 miles) from the tip of Isla Mujeres to Sapodilla Cay in the Gulf of Honduras—only the Great Barrier Reef in Australia is longer. An atoll typically forms around the crater of a submerged volcano. The polyps begin building their colonies along the lip of the crater, forming a circular coral island with a lagoon in the center. The Chinchorro Bank, off the southern coast of Quintana Roo, is the largest coral atoll in the Northern Hemisphere, measuring 48 kilometers long and 14 kilometers wide (30 miles by 9 miles). A fringing reef is coral living on a shallow shelf that extends outward from shore into the sea.

Fish

The Yucatán's barrier reef is home to myriad fish species, including parrot fish, candy bass, moray eels, spotted scorpion fish, turquoise angelfish, fairy basslets, flame fish, and gargantuan manta rays. Several species of shark also thrive in the waters off Quintana Roo, though they're not considered a serious threat to swimmers and divers. Sport fish—sailfish, marlin, and bluefin tuna—also inhabit the outer Caribbean waters.

Inland, anglers will find hard-fighting bonefish and pompano in the area's lagoons, and snorkelers and divers will find several species of blind fish in the crystal-clear waters of cenotes. These fish live out their existence in dark underground rivers and lakes and have no use for eyes.

Sea Turtles

Tens of thousands of sea turtles of various species once nested on the coastal beaches of Quintana Roo. As the coast became populated, turtles were severely overhunted for their eggs, meat, and shells, and their numbers began to fall. Hotel and resort developments have hastened the decline, as there are fewer and fewer patches of untrammeled sand in which turtles can dig nests and lay their eggs. The Mexican government and various ecological organizations are trying hard to save the dwindling turtle population. Turtle eggs are dug up and reburied in sand on safe beaches; or, when the hatchlings break through their shells, they are brought to a beach and allowed to rush toward the sea in hopes of imprinting a sense of belonging there so that they will later return to the spot. In some cases the hatchlings are scooped up and placed in tanks to grow larger before being released into the open sea. The government is also enforcing tough penalties for people who take turtle eggs or capture, kill, or sell these creatures once they hatch.

Manatees

The manatee—sometimes called the sea cow—is a gentle, inquisitive giant. Manatees are closely related to dugongs, and more distantly to elephants, aardvarks, and hyraxes. Newborns weigh 30-35 kilograms (66-77 pounds), while adults can weigh nearly 1,600 kilograms (3,500 pounds) and measure four meters (13 feet) in length. Shaped like an Idaho potato, manatees have coarse pinkish-gray skin, tiny sunken eyes, a flattened tail, flipper-like forelimbs (including toenails), and prehensile lips covered in sensitive whiskers. The manatee is the only aquatic mammal that's completely vegetarian, eating an astounding 10 percent of its body weight every day in aquatic grass and vegetation; it's unique among all mammals for constantly growing new teeth to replace those worn down by its voracious feeding.

Large numbers of them once roamed the shallow inlets, bays, and estuaries of the Caribbean; their images are frequently seen in the art of the ancient Maya, who hunted them for food. Today, though posing no threat to humans or other animals, and ecologically important for their ability to clear waterways of oxygen-choking vegetation, manatees are endangered in the Yucatán and elsewhere. The population has been reduced by the encroachment of people in their habitats along

The Yucatán's Biosphere Reserves

Mexico is one of the most biodiverse places on the planet—in league with places like Brazil, Congo, and Indonesia. It boasts deserts, rainforests, mountains, coral reefs, and over 200,000 species of plants and animals, half of which exist nowhere else. Mexico has set aside nearly 10 percent of its national territory as protected areas of various kinds. These include biosphere reserves—a United Nations-certified designation—that have at least 10,000 hectares (24,771 acres) of protected habitat and a pristine core with no human disturbance or settlements. Mexico has a whopping 40 biosphere reserves—only the United States, Russia, and Spain have more. Six are in the Yucatán Peninsula (described below), and there are another eight in Chiapas, including two near Palenque.

Flamingos are found along the Yucatán's northern coast.

Sian Ka'an: Yucatec Maya for "Birthplace of the Sky," Sian Ka'an covers more than a half million hectares (1.2 million acres) of coastal forest, wetlands, and shallow bays and is home to turtles, dolphins, and innumerable birds. Tours are available from Tulum, including visiting Maya sites within the reserve.

Ría Lagartos: Accessible from the Gulf coast town of Río Lagartos, the like-named *ría* (estuary) is best known as a flamingo reserve, but is also home to hundreds of bird species (many rare or endemic) plus turtles and other reptiles.

Ría Celestún: Another well-known flamingo reserve, Ría Celestún is rich with birds, reptiles, and wetland and coastal vegetation of all kinds. Tours are available from the town of Celestún; it also is a popular day trip from Mérida.

Calakmul: Located in southern Campeche, this reserve spans 723,000 hectares (1.8 million acres) of tropical rainforest and teems with animals such as spider monkeys, howler monkeys, jaguars, and toucans. The reserve's namesake is the massive Maya ruin at its heart, home to some of the largest known pyramids in Mesoamerica. It's accessible from Campeche's Río Bec region.

Banco Chinchorro: One of the largest coral atolls in the world, Chinchorro Bank is 30 kilometers (19 miles) off the Costa Maya. Notoriously treacherous for colonial-era ships, today it's a diving and snorkeling paradise, with rich coral and marine life. Tours are available from Mahahual or Xcalak.

Arrecifes Alacranes: Over a hundred kilometers (62 miles) out to sea from the Gulf coast town of Progreso, the circular coral atoll known as Arrecifes Alacranes (Scorpion Reef) is Yucatán state's only major coral reef. Birds populate the small sandy islands, and there's a century-old lighthouse. No regular tours are available, however.

the riverways and shorelines. Ever-growing numbers of motorboats also inflict deadly gashes on these surface-feeding creatures. Nowadays it is very rare to spot one; the most sightings are reported in Punta Allen and Bahía de la Ascensión.

BIRDS

Because a major part of the Yucatán Peninsula is still undeveloped and covered with trees and brush, it isn't surprising to find exotic, rarely seen birds across the landscape. The Mexican government is beginning to realize the great value in this and is making efforts to protect nesting grounds. In addition to the growing number of nature reserves, some of the best bird-watching locales are the archaeological zones. At dawn and dusk, when most of the visitors are absent, the trees that surround the ancient structures come alive with birdsong. Of all the ruins, Cobá—with its marsh-rimmed lakes, nearby cornfields, and relatively tall, humid forest—is a particularly good site for bird-watching. One of the more impressive birds to look for here is the keel-billed toucan, often seen perched high on a bare limb in the early hours of the morning. Others include *chachalacas* (held in reverence by the Maya), screeching parrots, and, occasionally, the ocellated turkey.

Flamingos

The wetlands along the Yucatán's northern coast are shallow and murky and bordered in many places by thick mangrove forests. The water content is unusually high in salt and other minerals—the ancient Maya gathered salt here, and several salt factories still operate. A formidable habitat for most creatures, it's ideal for *phoenicopterus ruber ruber*—the American flamingo, the largest and pinkest of the world's five flamingo species. Nearly 30,000 of the peculiar birds nest here, feeding on algae and other tiny organisms that thrive in the salty water. Flamingos are actually born white, but they turn pink from the carotene in the algae they eat.

For years, flamingos only nested around Río Lagartos, near the peninsula's northeastern tip. But in 1988, Hurricane Gilbert destroyed their nesting grounds—not to mention the town of Río Lagartos—and forced the birds to relocate. They are now found all along the north coast, including at three major feeding and reproduction grounds: Río Lagartos, Celestún, and Uaymitún. Though in smaller numbers, they also can be found on Isla Holbox.

The best way to observe flamingos is on a boat tour at sunrise, when the birds are most active, turning their heads upside down and dragging their beaks along the bottom of the shallow water to suck in the mud that contains their food. (In the morning, you should see dozens of other birds too, such as storks, herons, and kingfishers.) If you go in the spring, you may see the male flamingos performing their strange mating dance—craning their necks, clucking loudly, and generally strutting their stuff.

Although flamingos live in the region year-round, you'll see the highest numbers at Río Lagartos from April to September and at Celestún from December to February. Uaymitún has a pretty steady population but has no boat tours—instead you observe the birds through binoculars from a raised platform. No matter when you go, make as little noise as possible and ask your guide to keep his distance. Flamingos are nervous and easily spooked into flying away en masse. While the exodus is an impressive sight, it may cause the birds to abandon the site altogether.

Quetzals

Though the ancient Maya made abundant use of the dazzling quetzal feathers for ceremonial costumes and headdresses, they hunted other fowl for food; nevertheless, the quetzal is the only known bird from the pre-Columbian era and is now almost extinct. Today, it is still found (though rarely) in the high cloud forests of Chiapas and Central America, where it thrives on the constant moisture.

REPTILES

Although reptiles thrive in Yucatán's warm, sunny environment, humans are their worst enemy. In the past, some species were greatly reduced in number—hunted for their unusual skin. Although hunting them is now illegal, black marketers still take their toll on the species.

Caimans

The caiman is a member of the crocodilian order. Its habits and appearance are similar to those of crocodiles, with the main difference being in its underskin: The caiman's skin is reinforced with bony plates on the belly, making it useless for the leather market. (Alligators and crocodiles, with smooth belly skin and sides, have been hunted almost to extinction in some parts of the world because of the value of their skin.)

Several species of caiman frequent the brackish inlet waters near the estuaries of Río Lagartos (literally, River of Lizards); though seen less frequently, they also inhabit mangroves on the Caribbean coast. A large caiman can be 2.5 meters (8.2 feet) long and very dark gray-green and broad-snouted with eyelids that look swollen and wrinkled. Some caiman species have eyelids that look like a pair of blunt horns. They are quicker than alligators and have longer, sharper teeth. Skilled hunters, caiman are quick in water and on land and will attack a person if cornered. The best advice is to give caimans a wide berth if spotted.

Iguanas

This group of American lizards—Iguanidae family—includes various large plant-eaters seen frequently in the region. Iguanas grow to be one meter (3.3 feet) long and have a blunt head and long, flat tail. Bands of black and gray circle their bodies, and a serrated column reaches down the middle of their backs almost to the tail. The young iguana is bright emerald green and often supplements its diet by eating insects and larvae.

The lizard's forelimbs hold the front half of its body up off the ground while its two back limbs are kept relaxed and splayed alongside its hindquarters. When the iguana is frightened, however, its hind legs do everything they're supposed to, and the iguana crashes quickly (though clumsily) into the brush searching for its burrow and safety. This reptile is not aggressive—it mostly enjoys basking in the bright sunshine—but if cornered it will bite and use its tail in self-defense.

From centuries past, recorded references attest to the iguana's medicinal value, which partly explains the active trade in live iguana. Iguana stew is believed to cure or relieve various human ailments.

Other Lizards

You'll see a great variety of other lizards on the peninsula; some are brightly striped in various shades of green and yellow, while others are earth-toned and blend in with the gray and beige limestone that dots the landscape. Skinny as wisps of thread running on hind legs, or chunky and waddling with armor-like skin, the range is endless and fascinating.

Be sure to look for the black anole, which changes colors to match its environment, either when danger is imminent or as subterfuge to fool the insects on which it feeds. At mating time, the male anole puffs out its bright-red throat-fan so that all female lizards will see it.

Coral Snakes

Two species of coral snakes, which are related to the cobra, are found in the southern part of the Yucatán Peninsula. They have prominent rings around their bodies in the same sequence of red, black, yellow, or white and grow to 1-1.5 meters (3.3-4.9 feet). Their bodies are slender, with no pronounced distinction between the head and neck.

Coral snakes spend the day in mossy clumps under rocks or logs, emerging only at night. Though the bite of a coral snake can kill within 24 hours, chances of the average tourist being bitten by a coral (or any other) snake are slim.

Tropical Rattlesnakes

The tropical rattlesnake (*cascabel* in Spanish) is the deadliest and most treacherous species of rattler. It differs slightly from other species by having vividly contrasting neckbands. It grows 2-2.5 meters (6.6-8.2 feet) long and is found mainly in the higher and drier areas of the tropics. Contrary to popular myth, this serpent doesn't always rattle a warning of its impending strike.

INSECTS AND ARACHNIDS

Air-breathing invertebrates are unavoidable in any tropical locale. Some are annoying (gnats and no-see-ums), some are dangerous (black widows, bird spiders, and scorpions), and others can cause pain when they bite (red ants), but many are beautiful (butterflies and moths), and *all* are fascinating.

Butterflies and Moths

The Yucatán has an incredible abundance of beautiful moths and butterflies, some 40,000 species in all. Hikers might see the magnificent blue morpho, orange-barred sulphur, copperhead, cloudless sulphur, malachite, admiral, calico, ruddy daggerwing, tropical buckeye, and emperor. The famous monarch is also a visitor during its annual migration from the northeastern United States. It usually makes a stopover on the Yucatán's Caribbean coast on its way south to the Central American mountains where it spends the winter. The huge black witch moth—males can have a wingspan of seven inches and are sometimes mistaken for bats—is called *mariposa de la muerte* ("butterfly of death" in Spanish) or *ma ha na* (Yucatec Maya for "enter the home"), stemming from a common belief that if the moth enters the home of a sick person, that person will soon die.

Spiders and Scorpions

The Yucatán has some scary-looking spiders and scorpions (*arañas* and *alacranes*), but none is particularly dangerous. The Yucatán rust rump tarantula is surely the most striking, a hairy medium-size tarantula with long legs and a distinctive orange or rust-colored rear. Like most tarantulas, it is nocturnal and fairly timid, with females spending much of their time in burrows in the ground, and males roaming around incessantly looking for them. Its bite is harmless, but that doesn't mean you should handle one: When threatened, tarantulas can shake off a cloud of tiny hairs, which are highly irritating if inhaled.

The Yucatán's long black scorpions—up to 10 centimeters (4 inches)—have a painful, nonlethal sting that can cause swelling, and for some people shortness of breath. Like tarantulas, scorpions avoid humans and are therefore rare to see; that said, it's always a good idea to shake out shoes and beach towels before using them, just in case.

Bees

The Yucatán's most famous bee—of numerous species found here—is the aptly named Yucatán bee, also known as the Maya bee. The small stingless insect produces a particularly sweet honey that was prized by the ancient Maya, and was one of the most widely traded commodities in the Maya world. (Some researchers say the Descending God figure at Tulum and other archaeological sites is the god of bees.) The ancient Maya were expert beekeepers, a tradition that lives on today, albeit much reduced thanks in part to the availability of cheap standard honey. Yucatán honey (harvested using more modern methods) is still sold in Mexico and abroad, mostly online and in organic and specialty stores.

History

ACROSS THE BERING LAND BRIDGE

People and animals from Asia crossed the Bering land bridge into North America in the Pleistocene epoch about 50,000 years ago, when sea levels were much lower. As early as 10,000 BC, ice age humans hunted woolly mammoth and other large animals roaming the cool, moist landscape of central Mexico. The earliest traces of humans in the Yucatán Peninsula are obsidian spear points and stone tools dating to 9,000 BC. The Loltún caves in the state of Yucatán contained a cache of mammoth bones, which are thought to have been dragged there by a roving band of hunters. As the region dried out and large game disappeared in the ensuing millennia, tools of a more settled way of life appeared, such as grinding stones for preparing seeds and plant fibers.

ANCIENT CIVILIZATION

Between 7,000 and 2,000 BC, society evolved from hunting and gathering to farming; corn, squash, and beans were independently cultivated in widely separated areas in Mexico. Archaeologists believe that the earliest people who we can call Maya, or proto-Maya, inhabited the Pacific coast of Chiapas and Guatemala. These tribes lived in villages that held more than 1,000 inhabitants apiece; beautiful painted and incised ceramic jars for food storage have been found from this region and time period. After 1,000 BC this way of life spread south to the highlands site of Kaminaljuyú (now part of Guatemala City) and, through the next millennium, to the rest of the Maya world. Meanwhile, in what are now the Mexican states of Veracruz and Tabasco, another culture, the Olmecs, was developing what is now considered Mesoamerica's first civilization. Its influence was felt throughout Mexico and Central America. Archaeologists believe that before the Olmecs disappeared around 300 BC, they contributed two crucial cultural advances to the Maya: the Long Count calendar and the hieroglyphic writing system.

LATE PRECLASSIC PERIOD

During the Late Preclassic era (300 BC-AD 250), the Pacific coastal plain saw the rise of a Maya culture in Izapa near Tapachula, Chiapas. The Izapans worshipped gods that were precursors of the Classic Maya pantheon and commemorated religious and historical events in bas-relief carvings that emphasized costume and finery.

During the same period, the northern Guatemalan highlands were booming with construction; this was the heyday of Kaminaljuyú, which grew to enormous size, with more than 120 temple-mounds and numerous stelae. The earliest calendar inscription that researchers are able to read comes from a monument found at El Baúl to the southwest of Kaminaljuyú; it has been translated as AD 36.

In the Petén jungle region just north of the highlands, the dominant culture was the Chicanel, whose hallmarks are elaborate temple-pyramids lined with enormous stucco god-masks (as in Kohunlich). The Petén sites of Nakbé and El Mirador are the most spectacular Chicanel cities yet found. El Mirador contains a 70-meter-tall (230-foot) temple-pyramid complex that is the tallest ancient structure in Mesoamerica. Despite the obvious prosperity of this region, there is almost no evidence of Long Count dates or writing systems in either the Petén jungle or the Yucatán Peninsula just to the north.

EARLY CLASSIC PERIOD

The great efflorescence of the southern Maya world stopped at the end of the Early Classic period (AD 250-600). Kaminaljuyú

Early Civilizations and Maya Timeline

- **Paleoindian:** before 7000 BC
- **Archaic:** 7000-2500 BC
- **Early Preclassic:** 2500-1000 BC
- **Middle Preclassic:** 1000-400 BC
- **Late Preclassic:** 400 BC-AD 250
- **Early Classic:** AD 250-600
- **Late Classic:** AD 600-800
- **Terminal Classic:** AD 800-1000
- **Early Postclassic:** AD 1000-1250
- **Late Postclassic:** AD 1250-1519

and other cities were abandoned; researchers believe that the area was invaded by Teotihuacano warriors extending the reach of their Valley of Mexico-based empire. On the Yucatán Peninsula, there is evidence of Teotihuacano occupation at the Río Bec site of Becán and at Acanceh near Mérida. You can see Teotihuacano-style costumes and gods in carvings at the great Petén city of Tikal and at Copán in Honduras. By AD 600, the Teotihuacano empire had collapsed, and the stage was set for the Classic Maya eras.

LATE CLASSIC PERIOD

The Maya heartland of the Late Classic period (AD 600-900) extended from Copán in Honduras through Tikal in Guatemala and ended at Palenque in Chiapas. The development of these city-states, which also included Yaxchilán and Bonampak, almost always followed the same pattern. Early in this era, a new and vigorous breed of rulers founded a series of dynasties bent on deifying themselves and their ancestors. All the arts and sciences of the Maya world, from architecture to astronomy, were focused on this goal. The Long Count calendar and the hieroglyphic writing system were the most crucial tools in this effort, as the rulers needed to recount the stories of their dynasties and of their own glorious careers.

During the Late Classic era, painting, sculpture, and carving reached their climax; objects such as Lord Pakal's sarcophagus lid from Palenque are now recognized as among the finest pieces of world art. Royal monuments stood at the center of large and bustling cities. In 2017, researchers used airborne lasers to reveal tens of thousands of previously unknown structures at Tikal and other northern Guatemalan sites; most are stone platforms for small dwellings, suggesting a much larger and denser population throughout the Maya world than previously thought—perhaps as high as 15 million people, three times higher than long-held estimates. The study also revealed huge raised causeways, most likely a sign of vigorous intercity trade. Each Classic city-state reached its apogee at a different time; the southern cities peaked first, with the northern Puuc region cities following close behind.

By AD 925, nearly all of the city-states had collapsed and were left in a state of near-abandonment. The Classic Maya decline is one of the great enigmas of Mesoamerican archaeology. There are myriad theories—disease, invasion, peasant revolt—but many researchers now believe the collapse was caused by a combination of factors, including overpopulation, environmental degradation, and a series of devastating droughts. With the abandonment of the cities, the cultural advances disappeared as well. The last Long Count date was recorded in AD 909, and many religious customs and beliefs were never seen again.

EARLY POSTCLASSIC PERIOD

After the Puuc region was abandoned—almost certainly because of a foreign invasion—the center of Maya power moved east to Chichén. During this Early Postclassic era (AD 925-1200), the Toltec influence took hold, marking the end of the most artistic era and the birth of a new militaristic society built around a blend of ceremonialism, civic and social organization, and conquest. Chichén was the great power of northern Yucatán. Competing city-states either submitted to its warriors or, like the Puuc cities and Cobá, were destroyed.

LATE POSTCLASSIC PERIOD

After Chichén's fall in AD 1224—probably due to an invasion—a heretofore lowly tribe calling themselves the Itzá became the Late Postclassic (AD 1200-1530) masters of Yucatecan power politics. Kukulcán II of Chichén founded Mayapán in AD 1263-1283. After his death and the abandonment of Chichén, an aggressive Itzá lineage named the Cocom seized power and used Mayapán as a base to take over northern Yucatán. They succeeded through wars using Tabascan mercenaries and intermarrying with other powerful lineages. Foreign lineage heads were forced to live in Mayapán where they could easily be controlled. At its height, the city covered 6.5 square kilometers (4 square miles) within a defensive wall that contained more than 15,000 inhabitants. Architecturally, Mayapán leaves much to be desired; the city plan was haphazard, and its greatest monument was a sloppy, smaller copy of Chichén's Pyramid of Kukulcán.

The Cocom ruled for 250 years until AD 1441-1461, when an upstart Uxmal-based lineage named the Xiu rebelled and slaughtered the Cocom. Mayapán was abandoned and Yucatán's city-states were weakened in a series of bloody intramural wars that left them hopelessly divided when the conquistadors arrived. By the time of that conquest, culture was once again being imported from outside the Maya world. Putún Maya, seafaring traders, brought new styles of art and religious beliefs back from their trips to central Mexico. Their influence can be seen in the Mixtec-style frescoes at Tulum on the Quintana Roo coast.

SPANISH ARRIVAL AND CONQUEST

After Columbus's arrival in the New World, other adventurers traveling the same seas soon found the Yucatán Peninsula. In 1519, 34-year-old Hernán Cortés set out from Cuba—against the wishes of the Spanish governor—with 11 ships, 120 sailors, and 550 soldiers to search for slaves, a lucrative business. His search began on the Yucatán coast but eventually encompassed most of present-day Mexico. However, it took many decades and many lives for Spanish conquistadors to quell the Maya's resistance and cunning, despite a major advantage in military technology, including horses, gunpowder, and metal swords and armor. Francisco de Montejo, who took part in Cortés's earlier expedition into central Mexico, spent 1528-1535 trying to conquer the Yucatán, first from the east at Tulum and later from the west near Campeche and Tabasco, but was driven out each time. Montejo's son, also named Francisco de Montejo "El Mozo" (The Younger), took up the effort and eventually founded the city of Mérida in 1542 and Campeche in 1546. From those strongholds, the Spanish conquest slowly spread across the peninsula.

Economic and religious oppression were central to the conquest, too. The Xiu indigenous group proved an important ally to the Spanish after its leader converted to Christianity. And in 1562, a friar named Diego de Landa, upon learning his converts still practiced certain Maya ceremonies, became enraged and ordered the torture and imprisonment of numerous Maya spiritual leaders. He also gathered all the religious artifacts and Maya texts—which he said contained "superstitions and the devil's lies"—and had them burned. It was a staggering loss—at least 27 codices—and one that Landa later seemed to regret and attempted to reconcile by writing a detailed record of Maya customs, mathematics, and writing.

The Caste War

By the 1840s, the brutalized and subjugated Maya organized a revolt against Euro-Mexican colonizers. Called the Caste War, this savage war saw Maya taking revenge on every white man, woman, and child by means of murder and rape. European survivors made their way to the last Spanish strongholds of Mérida and Campeche. The governments of the two cities appealed for help to Spain, France, and the United States. No one answered the call. It was soon apparent that the remaining two cities would be wiped out.

But just as Mérida's leaders were preparing to evacuate the city, the Maya abruptly picked up their weapons and left. The reason was an unusually early appearance of flying ants, a sign of coming rain and to the Maya an all-important signal to begin planting corn. Despite the suffering visited upon them over three centuries of Spanish conquest, the Maya warriors, who were also farmers, simply could not risk missing the planting season. They turned their backs on certain victory and returned to their villages to tend their fields.

The unexpected reprieve allowed time for thousands of troops to arrive from Cuba, Mexico City, and the United States, and the vengeance was merciless. Maya were killed indiscriminately. Some were taken prisoner and sold to Cuba as slaves; others left their villages and hid in the jungles—in some cases, for decades. Between 1846 and 1850, the population of the Yucatán Peninsula was reduced from 500,000 to 300,000. Quintana Roo along the Caribbean coast was considered a dangerous no-man's-land for almost another 100 years.

Growing Maya Power

Many Maya Indians escaped slaughter during the Caste War by fleeing to the isolated coastal forests of present-day Quintana Roo. A large number regrouped under the cult of the "Talking Cross"—an actual wooden cross that, with the help of a priest and a ventriloquist, spoke to the beleaguered indigenous fighters, urging them to continue fighting. Followers called themselves *Cruzob* (People of the Cross) and made a stronghold in the town of Chan Santa Cruz, today Carrillo Puerto. Research (and common sense) suggests the Maya knew full well that a human voice was responsible for the "talking," but that many believed it was inspired by God.

From their base close to the border with British Honduras (now Belize), the leaders of Chan Santa Cruz began selling timber to the British and were given weapons in return. Simultaneously (roughly 1855-1857), internal strife weakened relations between Campeche and Mérida, and their mutual defense as well. Maya leaders took advantage of the conflict and attacked Fort Bacalar, eventually gaining control of the entire southern Caribbean coast.

Up until that time, indigenous soldiers simply killed the people they captured, but starting in 1858 they took lessons from the colonials and began to keep whites for slave labor. Women were put to work doing household chores and some became concubines, while men were forced to work the fields and build new constructions. (The main church in Carrillo Puerto was built largely by white slaves.)

For the next 40 years, the Maya people and soldiers based in and around Chan Santa Cruz kept the east coast of the Yucatán for themselves, and a shaky truce with the Mexican government endured. The native people were economically independent, self-governing, and, with no roads in or out of the region, almost totally isolated. They were not at war as long as everyone left them alone.

The Last Stand

Only when President Porfirio Díaz took power in 1877 did the Mexican federal government begin to think seriously about the Yucatán Peninsula. Through the years, Quintana Roo's isolation and the strength of the Maya in their treacherous jungle had foiled repeated efforts by Mexican soldiers to capture the region. The army's expeditions were infrequent, but it rankled Díaz that a relatively small and modestly armed Maya force had been able to keep the Mexican army at bay for so long. An assault in 1901, under the command of General Ignacio Bravo, broke the government's losing streak. The general captured a village, laid railroad tracks, and built a walled fort. Supplies arriving by rail kept the fort stocked, but the indigenous defenders responded by holding the fort under siege for an entire year. Reinforcements finally came from the capital and the Maya were forced to retreat, first from the fort and then from many of their villages and strongholds. A period of brutal Mexican occupation followed, lasting until 1915, yet Maya partisans still didn't give up. They conducted guerrilla raids from the tangled coastal forest until the Mexican army, frustrated and demoralized, pulled out and returned Quintana Roo to the Maya.

Beginning in 1917 and lasting to 1920, however, influenza and smallpox swept through the Maya-held territories, killing hundreds of thousands of Maya. In 1920, with the last of their army severely diminished and foreign gum-tappers creeping into former Maya territories, indigenous leaders entered into a negotiated settlement with the Mexican federal government. The final treaties were signed in 1936, erasing the last vestiges of Maya national sovereignty in the region.

LAND REFORMS

Beginning in 1875, international demand for twine and rope made from henequen, a type of agave cactus that thrives in northern Yucatán, brought prosperity to Mérida, the state capital. Beautiful mansions were built by entrepreneurs who lived the good life, sending their children to school in Europe and cruising with their wives to New Orleans in search of new luxuries and entertainment. Port towns were developed on the Gulf coast, and a two-kilometer (1.2-mile) wharf

in Progreso was built to accommodate the large ships that came for sisal (hemp from the henequen plant).

The only thing that didn't change was the lifestyle of indigenous people, who provided most of the labor on colonial haciendas. Henequen plants have incredibly hard, sharp spines and at certain times emit a horrendous stench. Maya workers labored long, hard hours, living in constant debt to the hacienda store.

Prosperity helped bring the Yucatán to the attention of the world. But in 1908, an American journalist named John Kenneth Turner stirred things up when he documented the difficult lives of the indigenous plantation workers and the accompanying opulence enjoyed by the owners. The report set a series of reforms into motion. Carrillo Puerto, the first socialist governor of Mérida, helped native workers set up a labor union, educational center, and political club that served to organize and focus resistance to the powerful hacienda system. Carrillo made numerous agrarian reforms, including decreeing that abandoned haciendas could be appropriated by the government. With his power and popularity growing, conservatives saw only one way to stop him: In 1923, Carrillo Puerto was assassinated.

By then, though, the Mexican Revolution had been won and reforms were being made throughout the country, including redistribution of land and mandatory education. Mexico entered its golden years, a 40-year period of sustained and substantial growth dubbed the Mexican Miracle, all the more miraculous because it took place in defiance of the worldwide Great Depression. In the late 1930s, President Lázaro Cárdenas undertook a massive nationalization program, claiming the major electricity, oil, and other companies for the state, and created state-run companies like PEMEX, the oil conglomerate still in existence today. In the Yucatán, Cárdenas usurped large parts of hacienda lands—as much as half of the Yucatán's total arable land, by some accounts, most dedicated to the growing of henequen—and redistributed it to poor farmers.

THE PRI YEARS

The economic prosperity allowed the ruling Institutional Revolutionary Party (PRI) to consolidate power, and before long it held every major office in the federal government, and most state governments as well. The Mexican Miracle had not ameliorated all social inequalities—and in fact had exacerbated some—but the PRI grew increasingly intolerant of dissent. Deeply corrupt, the party—and by extension the state—resorted to brutal and increasingly blatant repression to silence detractors. The most notorious example was the gunning down of scores of student demonstrators—some say up to 250—by security forces in 1968 in Mexico City's Tlatelolco Plaza. The massacre took place at night; by morning the plaza was cleared of bodies and scrubbed of blood, and the government simply denied that it ever happened.

The oil crisis that struck the United States in the early 1970s was at first a boon for Mexico, whose coffers were filled with money from pricey oil exports. But a failure to diversify the economy left Mexico vulnerable; as oil prices stabilized, the peso began to devalue. It had fallen as much as 500 percent by 1982, prompting then-president López Portillo to nationalize Mexico's banks. Foreign investment quickly dried up, and the 1980s were dubbed La Década Perdida (The Lost Decade) for Mexico and much of Latin America, a time of severe economic stagnation and crisis. In September 1985, a magnitude-8.1 earthquake struck Mexico City, killing 9,000 people and leaving 100,000 more homeless. It seemed Mexico had hit its nadir.

Yet it was during this same period that Cancún began to take off as a major vacation destination, drawing tourism and much-needed foreign dollars into the Mexican economy. The crises were not over—the implementation of the North American Free Trade Agreement (NAFTA) in 1994 was met simultaneously by a massive devaluation of the peso and an armed uprising by a peasant army called the Zapatistas in the state of Chiapas—but Mexico's economy regained some of its footing. A series of electoral reforms implemented in the late 1980s and through the 1990s paved the way for the historic 2000 presidential election, in which an opposition candidate—former Coca-Cola executive Vicente Fox of the right-of-center Partido de Acción Nacional (PAN)—defeated the PRI, ending the latter's 70-year reign of power. Fox was succeeded in 2006 by another PAN member, Felipe Calderón Hinojosa, in an election in which the PRI finished a distant third.

President Calderón campaigned on a promise to expand Mexico's job market and encourage foreign investment, including for new tourism projects in the Yucatán and elsewhere. But it was another pledge—to break up the drug trade and the cartels that controlled it—that consumed his entire presidency and plunged parts of Mexico into a spasm of violence unlike any since the revolution.

THE DRUG WAR

"The Drug War," as it is generally called, has its roots in the insatiable demand for drugs in the United States. Mexican drug cartels gained strength as operations in Colombia and the Caribbean were choked off in the 1990s; drug production in Mexico itself has also grown, especially methamphetamines. Mexican cartels traditionally operated within strictly defined territories—such as the Gulf cartel, the Sinaloa cartel, the Juárez cartel—and did so largely with impunity, thanks to corruption in the police and PRI-controlled local governments. The arrangement, though illicit, kept violence to a minimum as cartels kept to themselves and politicians and police turned a blind eye.

In 2006, encouraged by the United States, President Calderón dispatched the Mexican military to various northern cities to break up the cartels and their distribution networks. They achieved some initial success, but the broader effect was to disrupt the longtime balance of power. As control of routes and territories wavered, violence between rival cartels erupted with shocking speed and ferocity, with frequent shoot-outs and a gruesome cycle of attacks and reprisals. The official death toll is a staggering 60,000 people, though some estimates put it at double that. The vast majority of victims were gang-affiliated, though at least 2,000 police, soldiers, journalists, politicians, and even children were killed. It's notable that virtually all the weapons used in the drug war were smuggled into Mexico from the United States.

Drug violence fell in 2012 with the election of PRI presidential candidate Enrique Peña Nieto, who scaled back the aggressive military-guided approach used by his predecessor. Violence continued falling for five years, and cities like Ciudad Juarez and Chihuahua seemed to reawaken. At the same time, Mexican and U.S. agents scored several high-profile arrests of top drug cartel figures, including Joaquin "El Chapo" Guzmán Loera, who was extradited to the United States in 2017 and convicted on all counts against him in 2019. These arrests, however, fractured Mexico's cartels, leading to bloody leadership battles; violence surged again, spilling into previously tranquil places like Cancún and the Rivera Maya. Tourists remain largely unaffected, though—the vast majority of violence is between cartel members, mostly in non-touristed neighborhoods.

MEXICO TODAY

The election of Donald Trump to the U.S. presidency thrust Mexico back into the spotlight for many Americans. Trump riled up crowds by calling Mexicans dangerous criminals, deriding NAFTA, and claiming repeatedly that Mexico would pay for a border wall. Mexico's response was measured but categorical: it certainly would not pay for a wall, and it held fast in NAFTA negotiations—the new agreement (dubbed USMCA) contained only minor changes.

The region continues apace on a US$1 billion infrastructure overhaul, including new roads, bridges, and bus and ferry terminals. One part of the project—a circular train route through the Yucatán Peninsula, known as the Maya Train—has attracted controversy. Supporters, including Mexico's new leftist president Andrés Manuel López Obrador, say the Maya Train will bring vital economic development to the region's poor rural areas. Opponents warn of corruption and potential for massive environmental damage, with some plans showing train tracks cutting through protected forest reserves.

Government and Economy

GOVERNMENT

Mexico enjoys a constitutional democracy modeled after that of the United States, including a president (who serves one six-year term), a two-house legislature, and a judiciary branch. For 66 years (until the year 2000), Mexico was controlled by one party, the so-called moderate Partido Revolucionario Institucional (PRI). A few cities and states elected candidates from the main opposition parties—the conservative Partido de Acción Nacional (PAN) and leftist Partido de la Revolución Democrática (PRD)—but the presidency and most of the important government positions were passed from one hand-picked PRI candidate to the next, amid rampant electoral fraud.

That changed in 2000, when PAN candidate Vicente Fox, a businessman and former Coca-Cola executive from Guanajuato, won the presidency, promising electoral reforms, a stronger private sector, and closer relations with the United States. He knew U.S. president-elect George W. Bush personally, having worked with him on border issues during Bush's term as governor of Texas. Progress was being made until the terrorist attacks of September 11, 2001, pushed Mexico far down on the U.S. administration's priority list. The reforms Fox seemed poised to achieve were largely incomplete by the time his term ended.

Fox was succeeded by fellow PAN candidate Felipe Calderón Hinojosa. The 2006 election was bitterly contested, and ultimately decided by a margin of just 0.5 percent. The opposition candidate was the former mayor of Mexico City, left-wing candidate Andrés Manuel López Obrador, making the first of his three presidential bids. Supporters were convinced López Obrador had been robbed; they blocked major thoroughfares for weeks and fistfights broke out in the legislative chamber during Calderón's inauguration.

Calderón was confronted with a number of thorny problems upon inauguration, but none greater than the sudden escalation of violence that has come to be known as the Mexican Drug War. Calderón dispatched the Mexican military to staunch growing gang- and drug-related crime in cities like Tijuana and Juárez, but rather than ending the violence, the move sparked an all-out war between cartels, police, and the military.

In 2012, PRI candidate Enrique Peña Nieto was elected president, promising a shift away from military solutions and a focus instead on drug abuse, unemployment, and local corruption. Violence did diminish during Peña Nieto's early years, but he could never shed the image of being an experienced lightweight. He was roundly criticized for a too-tepid response to the kidnapping and murder of 43 student-teachers in the state of Guerrero in September 2014.

After two unsuccessful runs for president, leftist populist Andrés Manuel López Obrador (aka AMLO) finally won Mexico's top position in 2018, in a landslide. The result seemed especially significant given the rise of right-wing strongmen in places like Brazil and elsewhere; AMLO, by contrast, proposed selling off Mexico's presidential planes and limos, and traveling in his VW Jetta. AMLO has promised major changes to Mexico's social programs, from doubling pensions for Mexico's elderly to improving employment in rural areas. He proposed a "strategy for peace" for the drug war that includes demilitarization, amnesty for low-level workers in the drug trade, and combating drug abuse by addressing poverty and unemployment. Critics argue that AMLO cannot possibly pay for all the social programs he has proposed; he has six years in the top position to prove them wrong.

ECONOMY
Oil

Oil is a leading industry on the Yucatán Peninsula and throughout the Gulf coast, from Campeche to the Texas border. Mexico has long been one of the largest oil producers in the Western Hemisphere and the world, and for years it was a net exporter of crude oil and natural gas to the United States and elsewhere. However, declining crude oil production in the Gulf of Mexico, a lack of refining capacity in Mexico, and the rapid expansion of U.S. natural gas production (and high Mexican demand for natural gas) has turned the relationship on its head. Mexico still exports crude oil to the United States, but is one of the main importers of American refined products like gasoline. Mexico also imports natural gas and liquefied natural gas from the United States, spurring plans for cross-border pipelines. Cities in the Yucatán Peninsula have long benefited from Mexico's strong energy sector, but the effects of the worldwide decline in oil prices, coupled with a shifting relationship with the United States, may spell changes for the future.

Fishing

Yucatecan fisheries also are abundant along the Gulf coast. At one time fishing was not much more than a family business, but today fleets of large purse seiners with their adjacent processing plants can be seen on the Gulf of Mexico. With the renewed interest in preserving fishing grounds for the future, the industry could continue to thrive for many years.

Tourism

Until the 1970s, Quintana Roo's economy amounted to very little. For a few years the chicle boom brought a flurry of activity up and down the state (it was shipped from the harbor of Isla Cozumel). Native and hardwood trees have always been in demand; coconuts and fishing were the only other natural resources that added to the economy, but neither on a large scale.

With the development of an offshore sandbar—Cancún—into a multimillion-dollar resort town, tourism became the region's number one moneymaker. The development of the Riviera Maya (extending from Cancún to Tulum)—and now, the Costa Maya (south of Sian Ka'an to the border of Belize)—only guaranteed the continued success of the economy. New roads now give access to previously unknown beaches and Maya structures. Extra attention is going to archaeological zones ignored for hundreds of years, and all but the smallest now have restrooms, ticket offices, and gift shops.

People and Culture

DEMOGRAPHICS

Today, 75-80 percent of the Mexican population is estimated to be mestizo (a combination of the indigenous and Spanish-Caucasian races). Only 10-15 percent are considered to be indigenous peoples. For comparison, as recently as 1870, the indigenous made up more than 50 percent of the population. While there are important native communities throughout Mexico, the majority of the country's indigenous peoples live in the Yucatán Peninsula, Oaxaca, and Chiapas.

RELIGION

The vast majority of Mexicans are Roman Catholic, especially in the generally conservative Yucatán Peninsula. However, a vigorous evangelical movement gains more and more converts every year.

LANGUAGE

The farther away you are from a city in the Yucatán—and in Mexico in general—the less Spanish you'll hear and the more dialects of indigenous languages you'll encounter. The government estimates that of the 10 million indigenous people in the country, about 25 percent do not speak Spanish. Of the original 125 native languages, 70 are still spoken, 20 of which are classified as Maya languages, including Tzeltal, Tzotzil, Chol, and Yucatec.

Although education was made compulsory for children in 1917, this law was not enforced in the Yucatán Peninsula until recently. Today, schools throughout the peninsula use Spanish-language books, even though many children do not speak the language. In some of the rural schools, bilingual teachers are recruited to help children make the transition.

ART

Mexico has an incredibly rich colonial and folk-art tradition. While not considered art to the people who make and use it, traditional indigenous clothing is beautiful, and

Regional Holidays and Celebrations

- Jan. 1: **New Year's Day**

- Jan. 6: **Día de los Reyes Magos:** Three Kings Day—Christmas gifts exchanged

- Feb. 2: **Virgen de la Candelaria:** Religious candlelight processions light up several towns

- Feb./Mar.: **Carnaval:** Seven-day celebration before Ash Wednesday; celebrated big on Isla Cozumel

- Mar. 21: **Birthday of Benito Juárez:** President of Mexico for five terms; born in 1806

- Mar. 21: **Vernal Equinox in Chichén Itzá:** A phenomenon of light and shadow displays a serpent slithering down the steps of El Castillo

- Apr. 19: **Festival de San Telmo:** Culmination of a two-week festival celebrating the patron saint of fishermen; celebrated on Isla Holbox

- May 1: **Día del Trabajador:** Labor Day

- May 3: **Day of the Holy Cross:** Dance of the Pigs' Head performed in the town of El Cedral on Isla Cozumel

- May 5: **Cinco de Mayo:** Commemoration of the Mexican army's 1862 defeat of the French at the Battle of Puebla

- Sept. 16: **Independence Day:** Celebrated on the night of the 15th

- Sept. 27-Oct. 14: **El Señor de las Ampollas:** Religious celebration in Mérida

- Sept. 29: **Fiesta de San Miguel Arcángel:** Celebration of Isla Cozumel's patron saint

- Oct. 12: **Día de la Raza:** Indigenous Peoples Day; celebrated instead of Columbus Day

- Oct. 18-28: **El Cristo de Sitilpech:** Religious celebration in Izamal; the peak is on the 25th

- Nov. 1-2: **All Souls' Day and Day of the Dead:** Church ceremonies and graveside celebrations in honor of the deceased

- Nov. 20: **Día de la Revolución:** Celebration of the beginning of the Mexican Revolution in 1910

- Dec. 8: **Feast of the Immaculate Conception:** Religious celebrations in Izamal and Celestún

- Dec. 12: **Virgen de Guadalupe:** Religious celebration in honor of Mexico's patron saint

- Dec. 25: **Christmas:** Celebrated on the night of the 24th

travelers and collectors are increasingly able to buy it in local shops and markets. Prices for these items can be high, for the simple fact that they are hand-woven and can literally take months to complete. Mérida is an especially good place to purchase pottery, carving, and textiles from around the Yucatán and beyond.

HOLIDAYS AND FESTIVALS

Mexicans take celebrations and holidays seriously—of their country, their saints, and their families. You'll be hard-pressed to find a two-week period when something or someone isn't being celebrated. On major holidays—Christmas, New Year's Eve, and Easter—be prepared for crowds at the beaches and ruins. Be sure to book your hotel and buy your airline and bus tickets well in advance; during holidays, the travel industry is saturated with Mexican travelers.

In addition to officially recognized holidays, villages and cities hold numerous festivals and celebrations: for patron saints, birthdays of officials, a good crop, a birth of a child. You name it, it's probably celebrated. Festivals typically take place in and around the central plaza of a town with dancing, live music, colorful decorations, and fireworks. Food booths are set up around the plaza and typically sell tamales (both sweet and meat), *buñuelos* (sweet rolls), tacos, *churros* (fried dough dusted with sugar), *carne asada* (barbecued meat), and plenty of regional drinks.

Papel Picado

Mexicans are famous for their celebrations—whether it's to honor a patron saint or to celebrate a neighbor's birthday, partying is part of the culture. Typically, fiestas feature live music, lots of food, fireworks, and brightly colored decorations, often including *papel picado* (literally, diced paper).

Papel picado is tissue paper cut or stamped with a design that reflects the occasion in some way: a manger scene at Christmas, church bells for a wedding, skeletons in swooping hats for Day of the Dead. Once cut, row upon row of *papel picado* is strung across city streets, in front of churches, or in people's backyards. It typically stays up until wind or rain leaves just a thin cord and a few bits of torn paper as a reminder of the celebration that was.

Essentials

Getting There

For centuries, getting to the Yucatán Peninsula required a major sea voyage to one of the few ports on the Gulf of Mexico, only to be followed by harrowing and uncertain land treks limited to mule trains and narrow paths through the tangled jungle. Today, the peninsula is easily accessible. Visitors from all over the world arrive every day via modern airports, a network of good highways, excellent bus service, or by cruise ship.

AIR

The main international airports on the Yucatán Peninsula are in Cancún and Mérida. The **Cancún** airport is by far the busiest, with dozens of daily domestic and international flights. There are smaller airports in **Cozumel, Chetumal, Campeche City,** and **Palenque.** In addition, there are small airports in **Playa del Carmen, Mahahual,** and **Isla Holbox** for private planes and air taxis.

Most travelers use the Cancún airport—it's well located for those vacationing in the Caribbean as well as for those traveling inland. Fares typically are cheaper to Cancún than to any other airport in the region.

Travelers who are planning to spend their entire time inland often choose to fly to Mérida instead—the city itself is an important destination, and it's close to many of the area's key sights and archaeological ruins.

Similarly, many travelers who only will be visiting Isla Cozumel fly directly there—it's often more expensive than landing in Cancún but avoids the time and hassle of traveling from the mainland to the island (more time to dive and to enjoy the island!).

There also are airports in Chetumal, Campeche City, and Palenque, which are typically used for domestic travel. However, for travelers planning to spend most of their time in the Costa Maya, Campeche, or Chiapas, they may be more convenient.

Departure Tax

There is a departure tax to fly out of any Mexican airport—the cost varies depending on the location (US$48 at the Cancún International Airport, US$18 at the Cozumel International Airport). Most airlines incorporate the tax into their tickets, but it's worth setting aside some cash just in case.

BUS

The Yucatán's main interstate bus hubs are Mérida and Cancún, with service to and from Mexico City, Veracruz, Oaxaca, and other major destinations in the country. There also are buses between Chetumal and cities in Belize and Guatemala. Tour operators in Palenque offer van service to various cities in Guatemala, including Flores, Quetzaltenango, and Antigua.

CAR

Foreigners driving into Mexico are required to show a valid driver's license, title, registration, and proof of insurance for their vehicle. Mexican authorities do not recognize foreign-issued insurance; Mexican vehicle insurance is available at most border towns 24 hours a day, and several companies also sell policies over the Internet. Do not cross the border with your car until you have obtained the proper papers.

CRUISE SHIP

Increasing numbers of cruise ships stop along Mexico's Caribbean coast every year, some carrying as many as 5,000 people. Many sail out of Miami and Fort Lauderdale, stopping at Key West before continuing to Punta Venado (Riviera Maya), Isla Cozumel, Mahahual, and Progreso.

Prices are competitive, and ships vary in services, amenities, activities, and entertainment. Pools, restaurants, nightclubs, and cinemas are commonplace. Fitness centers and shops also make ship life convenient. To hone in on the type of cruise you'd like to go on, research options on the Internet, in the travel section of your local newspaper, and by contacting your travel agent.

If your budget is tight, consider traveling standby. Ships want to sail full and are willing to cut their prices—sometimes up to 50 percent—to do so. Airfare usually is not included. **Note:** Once you're on the standby list, you typically will have no choice of cabin location or size.

Previous: horse-drawn carriages called *calesas,* a pleasant way to tour a city's downtown area.

Navigating the Cancún Airport

Some travelers find Cancún's airport somewhat daunting to navigate. The key is to not get drawn into any of the many sales pitches you'll encounter. Leaving the plane, simply follow the crowd, queueing first for immigration, then retrieving your luggage, then queueing again for customs, where you're asked to press a button: Green means go, red means stop and have your bags searched. Once through customs, you'll enter a large, busy foyer packed with vendor booths, salespeople, and tourist office folks ranging from peppy to pushy, virtually all of whom you can ignore or politely rebuff with a *"no, gracias."* If you're renting a car, look for the booth of the company you've reserved with and let the attendant know you've arrived; he or she will direct you to a shuttle to take you to the rental center. If you need a taxi, look for one of three "Yellow Transfers" booths, the official airport taxi service. To catch a bus, walk out of the terminal—ignoring the hagglers and taxi drivers clustered in front—and look for the large ADO buses parked a few steps to your right; you can buy your ticket at the mobile desk set up there. If your resort has arranged transport for you, look for a driver outside the terminal with your name or the name of the resort on a sign. None of the options requires much walking, so you don't really need a porter; if you do use one, a couple of dollars per bag is the customary tip.

NEIGHBORING COUNTRIES

Cancún is an important international hub, not only for tourists from North America and Europe but also for regional flights to Central America and the Caribbean. In southern Quintana Roo, Chetumal is the gateway to Belize, and there's a direct bus to Flores, Guatemala (i.e., the town neighboring Tikal Archaeological Zone). Most travel to Guatemala, however, is through Chiapas, from the towns of Palenque and San Cristóbal de las Casas. Most travelers do not need prearranged visas to enter either country, but they may have to pay an entrance fee at the airport or border.

Cancún has long been a major gateway to Cuba, especially for Americans circumventing U.S. travel restrictions to the island. In 2014, the Obama administration made it much easier for Americans to travel to Cuba legally and directly, but many of those changes were rescinded by President Trump just three years later. For many Americans, Cancún remains a convenient and necessary portal to Cuba.

Getting Around

AIR

Although budget airlines like Interjet are starting to appear on the Mexican airline scene, flying domestically is still relatively expensive, and the Yucatán is no exception. Once you factor in the check-in process, security, and baggage claim, there are very few flights within the region that make sense travel-wise, unless your time is incredibly tight. And if that is the case, you may as well see what you can do by car or bus and start planning a return trip.

BUS

Mexico's bus and public transportation system is one of the best in Latin America, if not the Western Hemisphere. In the Yucatán Peninsula, ADO and its affiliate bus lines practically have a monopoly, but that has not made bus travel any less efficient or less affordable. Dozens of buses cover every major route many times per day, and even smaller towns have frequent and reliable service.

Buses come in three main categories:

First Class: Known as *primera clase* or sometimes *ejecutivo*, first class is the most common and the one travelers use most often. Buses have reclining seats and TVs where movies are played on long trips. First-class buses make some intermediate stops but only in large towns. The main first-class lines in the Yucatán are ADO and OCC (primarily serving Chiapas).

Deluxe Class: Usually called *lujo* (luxury), deluxe class is a step up; trips often are slightly faster because they're typically nonstop. The main deluxe line is ADO-GL, which costs 10-25 percent more than regular ADO. ADO-GL buses have nicer seats and better televisions (and even more recent movies). Sometimes there are even free bottles of water in a cooler at the back. Even nicer are ADO-Platino buses, which often charge twice as much as regular ADO. Platino offers cushy, extra-wide seats (only three across instead of four), headphones, and sometimes a light meal like a sandwich and soda.

Second Class: *Segunda clase,* or second class, is significantly slower and less comfortable than first class, and it's not all that much cheaper. Whenever possible, pay the dollar or two extra for first class. Second-class buses are handy in that you can flag them down anywhere on the roadside, but that is also precisely the reason they're so slow. In smaller towns, second class may be the only service available, and it's fine for shorter trips. The main second-class lines in the Yucatán are Mayab, Oriente, Noreste, and ATS.

For overnight trips, definitely take first-class or deluxe. Not only will you be much more comfortable, second-class buses are sometimes targeted by roadside thieves because they drive on secondary roads and stop frequently.

Wherever bus service is thin, you can count on there being frequent **colectivos** or **combis**—vans or minibuses—that cover local routes. They can be flagged down anywhere along the road.

FERRY

Ferries are used to get to and from the region's most visited islands, including Isla Mujeres (reached from Cancún), Isla Cozumel (reached from Playa del Carmen), and Isla Holbox (reached from Chiquilá). Service is safe, reliable, frequent, and affordable.

CAR

As great as Mexico's bus system is, a car is the best way to tour the Yucatán Peninsula. Most of the sights—ruins, deserted beaches, haciendas, caves, cenotes, wildlife—are well outside of the region's cities, down long access roads, or on the way from one town to the next. Having a car also saves you the time and effort of walking or the cost of cabbing to all those "missing links"; it also allows you to enjoy the sights for as much or as little time as you choose.

If you're here for a short time—a week or less—and want to sightsee, definitely get a car for the simple reason that you'll have the option of seeing and doing twice as much. If renting for your entire vacation isn't feasible moneywise, consider getting a car for just a couple of days to explore a bit: Chichén Itzá and other nearby archaeological zones, DIY cenotes, the Puuc Route and the Río Bec archaeological zones, and the less-accessible parts of Quintana Roo like the Sian Ka'an Biosphere Reserve and the Costa Maya. You also may want a car for a day in Cozumel to check out the island. Cars aren't necessary to visit Cancún, Isla Mujeres, or Playa del Carmen.

Car Rental

The best rates (and best vehicles) are typically found online with the major international rental chains like Hertz, Thrifty, Budget, and Avis. That said, there are local agencies in cities like Cancún, Cozumel, and Mérida, and they occasionally have good deals.

- It's best to book on the car rental company's own website rather than a travel website. The prices are virtually the same, and

Taxi Scam

Beware of any taxi driver who tries to convince you that the hotel you're going to is closed, roach infested, flooded, burned down, has no running water, was destroyed by a hurricane (add your disaster of choice). As sincere as the driver might seem, he is more often than not retaliating against hotels that refuse to pay a finder's fee. Taxi drivers can earn significant commissions— as much as US$10 per person *per night*—for bringing guests to certain establishments. Some hotels refuse to pay the fee, and taxi drivers, in turn, try to take their clients to "cooperative" hotels instead. Don't fall for it. You may have to be firm, but insist that your driver take you to the hotel of your choice. Your best option is to call ahead for a room reservation, which also serves to confirm that the hotel actually is open and operational.

if there are any problems, the rental office can't blame it on the other website.

- Ask your credit card company if your card provides free collision (liability) insurance on rental cars abroad (most do). Unlike ordinary insurance, if you have an accident, you'll have to pay for repairs upfront and then file for reimbursement. The coverage is usually better, though, with zero deductible and coverage even on dirt roads. Remember you have to actually use the card to pay for the rental in order to get the benefit!

- Car rental agencies make most of their money off the insurance, not the vehicle. That's why they push so hard for you to buy coverage. They'll warn you that with credit card insurance you'll have to pay 100 percent of any damages upfront; this is true, but it will be reimbursed when you file a claim back home. They may require you to authorize a larger "hold" on your card, as much as US$5,000, for potential damages. This is no big deal—it's not an actual charge—but that amount will be unavailable for other purchases. Consider bringing

two or more credit cards, especially if your credit limit is low.

- Third-party insurance is required by law, and rental agencies are technically required to provide it. However, rental agencies typically say third-party coverage is free for anyone who also purchases collision insurance. But if you decline their collision insurance (because you get it through your credit card), there's a charge for third-party coverage. Credit cards typically do not offer third-party coverage, so you end up having to pay it. It's less expensive than collision insurance, but still a bummer to pay.

Before driving off, the attendant will review the car for existing damage—be an active part of it and don't be shy about pointing out every nick, scratch, ding, and crack. If the care has hubcaps, be sure all the tires have them. Other things to confirm before driving off include:

- There is a spare tire (preferably a full-size, not temporary, one) and a working jack and tire iron.

- All doors lock and unlock, including the trunk.

- The headlights, brake lights, and turn signals work.

- All the windows roll up and down properly.

- The proper—and current—car registration is in the car. In some cases, your car rental contract serves as the registration.

- The amount of gas in the tank—you'll have to return it with the same amount.

- There is a 24-hour telephone number for the rental agency in case of an emergency.

Highways and Road Conditions

Driving in the Yucatán isn't as nerve-wracking as you might think. The highways are in excellent condition, and even secondary roads are well maintained. There are a few dirt and sand roads—mostly along the Costa Maya and in the Sian Ka'an Biosphere Reserve, to some of the lesser-visited archaeological sites in Campeche, and in the

Driving Distances (Kilometers)

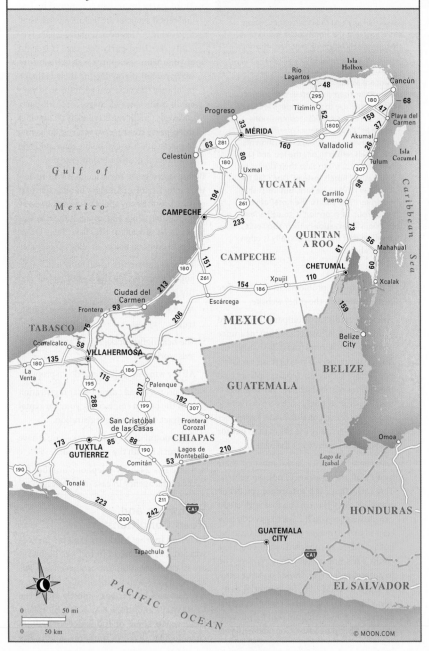

© MOON.COM

Driving in the Yucatán

Having a car can make exploring the Yucatán Peninsula quicker and easier, and there are many places you can only reach with your own wheels. Here are some tips to make your driving experience a bit smoother:

Off the highways, the biggest hazards are *topes* (speed bumps). They are common on all roads and highways, save the toll roads. They vary in size, but many are big and burly, and hitting them at even a slow speed can do a number on you, your passengers, and your car. As soon as you see a sign announcing an upcoming town or village, be ready to slow down.

Narrow one-way streets are common in many cities in the Yucatán. Fortunately, the **stop signs** in those areas usually have smaller plaques (beneath the big red one) indicating direction and right of way. A **black rectangle** means you have the right of way, a **red one** means you don't.

If you break down or run out of gas on a main road during daylight hours, stay with your car. **Los Ángeles Verdes** (The Green Angels, toll-free Mex. tel. 078 or 800/903-9200), a government-sponsored tow-truck and repair service, cruise many of these roads on the lookout for drivers in trouble 8am-6pm daily. They carry a CB radio, gas, and small parts, and are prepared to fix tires. If you have a cell phone—or happen to be near a pay phone—call your car rental agency first; the Ángeles Verdes are a great backup.

Lacandón region of Chiapas. If anything, frequent—and sometimes unexpected—*topes* (speed bumps) in small towns are the biggest driving hazard.

The main highways in the region are Highway 307, which runs the length of Mexico's Caribbean coast; Highway 180, the thoroughfare that links Cancún, Mérida, and Campeche City; Highway 186, which crosses the southern portion of the Yucatán Peninsula and leads travelers to Campeche's Río Bec region and Comalcalco in Tabasco; and Highways 195, 190, and 200, which crisscross the state of Chiapas.

In the entire region, there are only two toll roads, both sections of Highway 180: between Mérida and Cancún (a whopping US$24—US$15.25 from Cancún to Valladolid, US$3.75 from Valladolid to Pisté, and US$5 from Pisté to Mérida) and between Campeche City and Champotón (US$3.60). Far from cheap, these toll roads can save you a significant amount of driving time, and are safer for driving at night. Secondary roads are free and pass through picturesque countryside and indigenous villages; they are slower and have more obstacles like pedestrians, bicycles, and speed bumps, but can be a rewarding way to

go. **Note:** Be sure to keep your toll booth receipts! In the event of an accident, they serve as proof of insurance against any claims of damage to the toll road.

Driving Scams

Most travelers have heard horror stories about Mexican police and worry about being taken for all their money or trundled off to jail without reason. While it is true that there is corruption among the police, they don't target tourists; foreigners are, after all, the economic lifeblood of the region—the police don't want to scare them away.

As long as you are a careful and defensive driver, it is very unlikely you'll have any interaction with the police. Most travelers who are pulled over actually have done something wrong—speeding, running a stop sign, turning on red. In those situations, remain calm and polite. If you have an explanation, definitely give it; it is not uncommon to discuss a given situation with an officer. Who knows, you may even convince him you're right—it's happened to us!

Of greater concern are gas station attendants. Full service is the norm here—you pull up, tell the person how much you want, and the attendant does the rest. A common scam is for one attendant to distract you with questions about wiper fluid or gas additives while another starts the pump at 50 or 100 pesos. Before you answer any questions, be sure the attendant resets, or "zeroes," the pump before starting to pump.

HITCHHIKING

Hitchhiking is not recommended for either men or women. That said, it sometimes can be hard to know what is a private vehicle and what is a *colectivo* (shared van). If there's no bus terminal nearby, your best bet is to look for locals who are waiting for public transportation and see which vans they take. If you have no choice but to hitch a ride, opt for a pickup truck, where you can sit in the back.

TOURS

Local tour operators offer a vast range of organized trips. You pay extra, of course, but all arrangements and reservations are made for you, from guides and transportation to hotels and meals. Special-interest trips also are common—archaeological tours, hacienda and convent routes, bird-watching and dive trips. Ask around and surf the Internet—you'll find a world of organized adventure.

Visas and Officialdom

PASSPORTS

Gone are the days you could zip down to Mexico with just your driver's license and birth certificate. All nationalities must have a valid passport to enter Mexico by air, land, or sea.

VISAS AND TOURIST CARDS

Citizens of most countries, including the United States, Canada, and members of the EU, do not need to obtain a visa to enter Mexico. All foreigners, however, are issued a white tourist card when they enter, with the number of days that they are permitted to stay in the country written at the bottom, typically 30-60 days. If you plan to stay for more than a month, politely ask the official to give you the amount of time you need; the maximum stay is 180 days.

Hold onto your tourist card! It must be returned to immigration officials when you leave Mexico. If you lose it, you'll be fined and may not be permitted to leave the country (much less the immigration office) until you pay.

To extend your stay up to 180 days, head to the nearest immigration office a week *before* your tourist card expires. Be sure to bring it along with your passport. There, you'll fill out several forms, go to a bank to pay the processing fee (US$25 approximately), make photocopies of all the paperwork (including your passport, entry stamp, tourist card, and credit card), and then return to the office to get the extension. For every extra 30 days requested, foreigners must prove that they have US$1,000 available, either in cash or by showing a current credit card. The process can take anywhere from a couple of hours to a week, depending on the office.

Immigration Offices

- **Campeche:** Av. 16 de Septiembre at Calle 53, tel. 981/816-0369, 9am-1pm Monday-Friday
- **Cancún:** Av. Nader at Av. Uxmal, tel. 998/881-3560, 9am-1pm Monday-Friday
- **Chetumal:** Av. México s/n, tel. 983/834-5046, 9am-1pm Monday-Friday
- **Cozumel:** Av. 15 at Calle 5 Sur, tel. 987/872-0071, 9am-1pm Monday-Friday; there are immigration agents at the airport too (7am-9pm daily)

- **Isla Mujeres:** Av. Rueda Medina near Av. Morelos, tel. 998/877-0189, 9am-4pm daily
- **Mérida:** Av. Colón between Calles 8 and 10, Col. García Ginerés, tel. 999/925-5009, 9am-1pm Monday-Friday
- **Playa del Carmen:** Plaza Antigua, Av. 10 s/n, 2nd Fl., tel. 984/873-1884, 9am-1pm Monday-Friday
- **Progreso:** Calle 80 at Calle 39, tel. 969/935-0022, 9am-1pm Monday-Friday
- **Valladolid:** Hwy 295 Km 2.5, tel. 985/856-2075, 9am-1pm Monday-Friday

CUSTOMS

Plants and fresh foods are not allowed into Mexico, and there are special limits on alcohol, tobacco, and electronic products. Archaeological artifacts, certain antiques, and colonial art cannot be exported from Mexico without special permission.

Above all, do not attempt to bring marijuana or any other narcotic into or out of Mexico. Jail is one place your trusty guidebook won't come in handy.

Returning home, you will be required to declare all items you bought in Mexico. Citizens of the United States are allowed to reenter with US$800 worth of purchases duty-free; the figure for other travelers varies by country.

CONSULATES

The consulates in Cancún and Mérida handle passport issues (replacing a lost one, adding pages, etc.) and can help their citizens if they are in a serious or emergency situation, including hospitalization, assault, arrest, lawsuits, or death. They usually do not help resolve common disputes—with tour operators or hotels, for example.

In Cancún, the **Casa Consular** (Blvd. Kukulcán Km. 13, tel. 998/840-6082, www.casaconsular.org, 9am-3pm Mon.-Fri.) helps international travelers connect with their consular representatives. The office also offers advice to those travelers needing to contact Mexican authorities with everything from immigration issues to theft reports. English is spoken.

Foreign consulates and consular agencies in the region include:

AUSTRALIA
Cancún: Av. Nader 28, 3rd Fl., tel. 998/898-1900, ext. 213, asis.consul.australia@gmail.com, by appointment only

CANADA
Cancún: Centro Empresarial, Blvd. Kukulcán Km. 12, tel. 998/883-3360, www.canada.org.mx, 9am-1pm Monday-Friday
Playa del Carmen: Plaza Paraíso Caribe, Av. 10 btwn Calles 3 and 5, tel. 984/803-2411, www.canada.org.mx, 9am-1pm Monday-Friday

CUBA
Cancún: Pecari 17, tel. 998/884-3423, www.consuladocuba.com, 9am-1:30pm Monday-Friday

UNITED KINGDOM
Cancún: Torre La Europea, Blvd. Kukulcán Km. 13, 24-hr tel. 551/670-3200, www.ukinmexico.fco.gov.uk, 8am-1pm Monday-Friday

UNITED STATES
Cancún: Torre La Europea, Blvd. Kukulcán Km. 13, tel. 998/883-0272, https://mx.usembassy.gov/embassy-consulates/merida/consular-agencies, 8:30am-1pm Monday-Friday, appointment required for some services
Cozumel (emergencies only): tel. 999/942-5700, conagentcozumel@state.gov, by appointment only
Mérida: Calle 60 btwn Calles 29 and 31, tel. 999/942-5700, https://mx.usembassy.gov/embassy-consulates/merida, 7:30am-4:30pm Monday-Friday, appointment required for some services
Playa del Carmen: Plaza Progreso, Carretera Puerto Juarez-Chetumal btwn Calles 27 and 29, tel. 984/873-0303, https://mx.usembassy.gov/embassy-consulates/

UNDERAGE TRAVELERS

In the United States, anyone under 18 traveling internationally without *both* parents or legal guardians must present a signed, notarized letter from the parent(s) or guardian(s) granting the minor permission to leave the country. This requirement is aimed at preventing international abductions, but it causes frequent and major disruptions for vacationers.

Conduct and Customs

CLOTHING

Perhaps the single most abused social custom in Mexico is the use of shorts. Mexicans rarely wear them outside the home or off the beach, while many foreign travelers seem to have packed nothing but shorts. There is a bit more flexibility in beach areas, but it's worth getting in the habit of wearing long pants or skirts whenever going to dinner, attending performances, and especially when entering churches and government offices, where shorts and tank tops are considered inappropriate (and, in some cases, disrespectful).

Topless and nude sunbathing are not customary on Mexican beaches, and are rarely practiced in Cancún and other areas frequented by Americans and Canadians. However, on beaches popular with Europeans, especially Playa del Carmen and Tulum, it is more commonplace. Wherever you are, take a look around to help decide whether baring some or all is appropriate.

PHOTOGRAPHING LOCALS

No one enjoys having a stranger take his or her picture for no good reason, and Mexicans—indigenous or otherwise—are no different. The best policy is simply not to take these photographs unless you've first asked the person's permission and he or she has agreed. **Tip:** If the potential subject of your photo is a vendor, buy something and *then* ask if you can take a photo—you're more likely to get a positive response.

GREETINGS

Even a small amount of Spanish can go a long way in showing respect and consideration for people you encounter. Make a point of learning basic greetings like *buenos días* (good morning) and *buenas tardes* (good afternoon) and using them in passing, or as preface to a conversation; it is considered somewhat impolite to launch into a discussion without greeting the other person first.

Travel Tips

ACCOMMODATIONS

Lodging in the Yucatán Peninsula truly runs the gamut: campgrounds, hostels, small hotels, bed-and-breakfasts, boutique hotels, large modern hotels, and all-inclusive resorts. There are a handful of fishing lodges in places like Sian Ka'an Biosphere Reserve, and a number of large ex-haciendas that have been converted into deluxe hotels, primarily in Yucatán and Campeche states.

Taxes on your hotel bill, referred to generally as IVA (value-added tax; pronounced *EE-va* in Spanish), are usually 12 percent but can be as high as 17-22 percent. Be sure to ask if the rate you're quoted includes taxes (*¿Incluye impuestos?*); in many cases, especially at smaller hotels, the taxes are charged only if you pay by credit card.

You may be required to make a deposit in order to reserve a room, especially in popular areas during high season. However, in Mexico credit cards cannot be charged without a physical signature, so occasionally, smaller hotels won't accept them for deposits. Many hotels utilize PayPal or a similar service; those that do not will give you the name of their bank and account number, and you must transfer the money or stop by a branch and make the deposit in person. In either case, be sure to get a receipt, and notify the hotel after making the deposit.

Cancellation policies tend to be rather unforgiving, especially during high season; you may be required to give a month or more advance notice to receive even a partial refund. Trip insurance is a good idea if your plans are less than concrete.

WHAT TO PACK

Essentials for the Yucatán include sunscreen, sunglasses, and a billed hat. If you wear contacts or glasses, bring a replacement set. A good pair of shoes—or at least Teva-style sandals—is vital for exploring Maya ruins safely, and insect repellent definitely can come in handy. If you lose or forget something, Cancún, Cozumel, Playa del Carmen, Tulum, Chetumal, Mérida, and Campeche all have huge supermarkets, including Walmart.

ACCESS FOR TRAVELERS WITH DISABILITIES

Mexico has made many improvements for the blind and people in wheelchairs—many large stores and tourist centers have ramps or elevators. A growing number of hotels also have rooms designed for guests with disabilities, and museums occasionally create exhibits with, for example, replicas of Maya artifacts or folk art that visually impaired travelers can hold and touch. That said, Mexico is still a hard place to navigate if you have a disability. Smaller towns are the most problematic, as

their sidewalks can be narrow, and even some main streets are not paved. Definitely ask for help—for what Mexico lacks in infrastructure, its people often make up for in graciousness.

TRAVELING WITH CHILDREN

The Yucatán Peninsula is a great place to take kids, whether youngsters or teenagers. The variety of activities and relative ease of transportation help keep everyone happy and engaged. Cancún and the Riviera Maya are especially family friendly, with several different ecoparks and water parks, miles of beaches, and (if all else fails) plenty of malls with movie theaters, arcades, bowling, mini-golf, aquariums, and more. Perhaps best of all, Mexico is a country where family is paramount, so kids—even fussy ones—are welcome just about everywhere.

WOMEN TRAVELING ALONE

Solo women should expect a certain amount of unwanted attention, mostly in the form of whistles and catcalls. It typically happens as they walk down the street and sometimes comes from the most unlikely sources— we saw a man dressed as a clown turn mid-balloon animal to whistle at a woman walking by. Two or more women walking together attract much less unwanted attention, and a woman and man walking together will get none at all (at least of this sort—street vendors are a different story). While annoying and often unnerving, this sort of attention is almost always completely benign, and ignoring it is definitely the best response. Making eye contact or snapping a smart retort only will inspire more attention. Occasionally men will hustle alongside a woman and try to strike up a conversation—if you don't want to engage, a brief *"no, gracias"* should make that clear. To minimize unwanted attention, avoid revealing clothing, such as tight jeans, low-cut shirts, or bikini tops, as street wear. Carrying a notebook—or creating the appearance of working—also helps.

SENIOR TRAVELERS

Seniors should feel very welcome and safe visiting the Yucatán. Mexico is a country that affords great respect to *personas de la tercera edad* (literally, "people of the third age"), and especially in the tradition-minded Yucatán Peninsula. But as anywhere, older travelers should take certain precautions. The Yucatán, particularly Mérida and inland areas, is known to be extremely hot and humid, especially May-July. Seniors should take extra care to stay cool and hydrated. Exploring the Maya ruins also can be hot, not to mention exhausting. Bring water and snacks, especially to smaller sites where they may not be commonly sold. Travelers with balance or mobility concerns should think twice about climbing any of the pyramids or other structures. They can be deceptively treacherous, with steps that are steep, uneven, and slick.

Cancún, Playa del Carmen, and Mérida have state-of-the-art hospitals, staffed by skilled doctors, nurses, and technicians, many of whom speak English. Most prescription medications are available in Mexico, often at discount prices. However, pharmacists are woefully under-trained, and you should always double-check the active ingredients and dosage of any pills you buy here.

GAY AND LESBIAN TRAVELERS

While openly gay women are still rare in Mexico, gay men are increasingly visible in large cities and certain tourist areas. Mérida has a fairly large gay community, of which a number of expat hotel and guesthouse owners are a prominent part. Cancún and Playa del Carmen both have a visible gay presence and a number of gay-friendly venues. Nevertheless, many locals—even in large cities—are not accustomed to open displays of homosexuality and may react openly and negatively. Many hotel attendants also simply don't understand that two travel companions of the same gender may prefer one bed—in some cases they will outright refuse to grant the request. Some couples find it easier to book a room with two queen-size beds and just sleep in one.

TRAVELING WITH IMPORTANT DOCUMENTS

Scan and/or make copies of your passport and tourist card. Whether you're traveling solo or with others, leave a copy of each with someone you trust at home. Store another copy online (i.e., in your email account or on the cloud), and if you have a travel companion, give a copy to him or her. Be sure to carry a *copy* of your passport and tourist card in your purse or wallet and leave the originals in the hotel safe or locked in your bag; they're a lot more likely to be lost or stolen on the street than taken by hotel staff. When you move from place to place, carry your passport and important documents in a travel pouch, always under your clothing. Write down your credit card and ATM numbers and the 24-hour service numbers and keep those in a safe place.

Health and Safety

SUNBURN

Common sense is the most important factor in avoiding sunburn. Use waterproof and sweatproof sunscreen with a high SPF. Reapply regularly—even the most heavy-duty waterproof sunscreen washes off faster than it claims to on the bottle (or gets rubbed off when you use your towel to dry off). Be extra careful to protect parts of your body that aren't normally exposed to the sun—a good way to cover every inch is to apply sunscreen *before* you get dressed—and give your skin a break from direct sun every few hours. Remember that redness from a sunburn takes several hours to appear—that is, you can be sunburned long before you *look* sunburned.

If you get sunburned, treat it like any other burn by running cool water over it for as long and as often as you can. Do not expose your skin to more sun. Re-burning the skin can result in painful blisters that can easily become infected. There are a number of products designed to relieve sunburns, most with aloe extracts. Finally, be sure to drink plenty of water to keep your skin hydrated.

HEAT EXHAUSTION AND HEAT STROKE

The symptoms of heat exhaustion are cool, moist skin, profuse sweating, headache, fatigue, and drowsiness. It is associated with dehydration and commonly happens during or after a strenuous day in the sun, such as while visiting ruins. You should get out of the sun, remove any tight or restrictive clothing, and sip a sports drink such as Gatorade. Cool compresses and raising your feet and legs help too.

Heat exhaustion is not the same as heat stroke, and is distinguished by a high body temperature, a rapid pulse, and sometimes delirium or even unconsciousness. It is an extremely serious, potentially fatal condition, and victims should be taken to the hospital immediately. In the meantime, wrap the victim in wet sheets, massage the arms and legs to increase circulation, and do not administer large amounts of liquids. Never give liquids if the victim is unconscious.

DIARRHEA

Diarrhea is not an illness in itself, but your body's attempt to get rid of something bad in a hurry; that something can be any one of a number of strains of bacteria, parasites, or amoebae that are often passed from contaminated water. No fun, it is usually accompanied by cramping, dehydration, fever, and, of course, frequent trips to the bathroom.

If you get diarrhea, it should pass in a day or two. Anti-diarrheals such as Lomotil and Imodium A-D will plug you up but don't cure you—use them only if you can't be near a

bathroom. The malaise you feel from diarrhea typically is from dehydration, not the actual infection, so be sure to drink plenty of fluids—a sports drink such as Gatorade is best. If it's especially bad, ask at your hotel for the nearest *laboratorio* (laboratory or clinic), where a stool sample can be analyzed for around US$5 to determine if you have a parasitic infection or a virus. If it's a common infection, the lab technician will tell you what medicine to take. Be aware that medicines for stomach infection are seriously potent, killing not only the bad stuff but the good stuff as well; they'll cure you but leave you vulnerable to another infection. Avoid alcohol and spicy foods for several days afterward.

A few tips for avoiding diarrhea include:

- Only drink bottled water. Avoid using tap water even for brushing your teeth.

- Avoid raw fruits or vegetables that you haven't disinfected and cut yourself. Lettuce is particularly dangerous because water is easily trapped in the leaves. Also, as tasty as they look, avoid the bags of sliced fruit sold from street carts.

- Order your meat dishes well done, even if it's an upscale restaurant. If you've been to a market, you'll see that meat is handled very differently here.

INSECTS

Insects are not of particular concern in the Yucatán, certainly not as they are in other parts of the tropics. Mosquitoes are common, but are not known to carry malaria. Dengue fever, also transmitted by mosquitoes, is present but still rare. The Zika virus is a concern, of course: Since 2016, Mexico has had 400 confirmed cases. The Yucatán, however, has benefited from robust anti-mosquito measures already in place, thanks to dengue and chikungunya outbreaks in years past. Just as those diseases have been fairly well contained, regional health and tourism officials believe Zika does not pose a major threat to locals or visitors. Needless to say, be sure to review the latest information before traveling, and take sensible precautions, like wearing repellent and long pants and sleeves.

Finally, some remote beaches, like Isla Holbox and the Costa Maya, may have sand flies or horseflies, but they have been all but eliminated in the more touristed areas. Certain destinations are more likely to be buggy, such as forested archaeological zones and coastal bird-watching areas, and travelers should bring and use insect repellent there, if only for extra comfort.

VACCINATIONS

Vaccines are recommended for anyone traveling to the Yucatán Peninsula. Be aware that some vaccines require several months to be effective, so plan ahead. The Centers for Disease Control (CDC) recommend all travelers be vaccinated against flu, typhoid, and hepatitis A, the last of those being spread through contaminated food and water. A hepatitis B vaccine is recommended for anyone at risk of exposure to bodily fluids, such as sexual contact, tattooing, or needle sharing. (Combination hepatitis A and B vaccines are widely available.) Likewise, a rabies vaccine is recommended for travelers whose plans put them at high risk of animal bites, such as hiking or caving in remote areas.

Malaria, dengue, and Zika, all spread by mosquitos, are also present but transmission is not common in most tourist areas. Some medications can help prevent malaria infection, but there is no vaccine for these diseases. The best prevention is to be vigilant against mosquito bites, including slathering on insect repellant (except children under 2 months) and using long sleeves and pants. Mosquitos bite day and night, but especially around sunrise and sunset. The CDC recommends

pregnant women not travel to this region due to the risk of Zika.

CRIME

The Yucatán Peninsula is generally quite safe, and few travelers report problems with crime of any kind. There has been an uptick of violent crime in the Riviera Maya since 2017, and the U.S. State Department issued an advisory to travelers to "exercise increased caution." However, the incidents are almost certainly related to drug cartel rivalries, with particular people targeted, as opposed to random muggings and assault. While certainly shocking, this sort of violence rarely impacts tourists, assuming you steer well clear of drug activity. Drug possession has always been prosecuted vigorously here, especially involving foreigners, and the cartel-related violence is another reason to avoid drugs while in Mexico. (Your country's embassy can do very little to help in these situations, by the way.)

Sexual assault and rape have been reported by women at nightclubs, sometimes after having been slipped a "date rape drug." While the clubs are raucous and sexually charged by definition, women should be especially alert to the people around them and wary of accepting drinks from strangers.

In all areas, commonsense precautions are always recommended, such as taking a taxi at night instead of walking (especially if you've been drinking) and avoiding flashing your money and valuables or leaving them unattended on the beach or elsewhere. Utilize the safety deposit box in your hotel room, if one is available; if not, consider locking your valuables in your luggage. If you rent a car, get one with a trunk so your bags will not be visible through the window.

Information and Services

MONEY

Currency and Exchange Rates

Mexico's official currency is the peso, divided into 100 centavos. It is typically designated with the symbol $, but you may also see MN$ (*moneda nacional,* or national currency). We've listed virtually all prices in their U.S. dollar equivalent, but occasionally use M$ to indicate the price is in Mexican pesos.

U.S. dollars and EU euros are accepted in a few highly touristed locations like the Zona Hotelera in Cancún and the shopping districts of Cozumel and Playa del Carmen. However, you'll want and need pesos everywhere else, as most shopkeepers appreciate visitors paying in the local currency. **Note:** Foreign bills only are accepted because coins can't be changed to pesos.

At the time of research, US$1 was equal to M$20, CAN$1 was approximately M$15, and €1 was equal to M$22.

ATMs

Almost every town in the Yucatán Peninsula has an ATM, and they are without question the easiest, fastest, and best way to manage your money. Be aware that you may be charged a transaction fee by the ATM (US$2-3 typically) as well as your home bank (as much as US$10). It's worth asking your bank if it partners with a Mexican bank, and whether transaction fees are lower if you use that bank's cash machines. Also, be sure to use ATMs that are affiliated with a recognizable bank, to avoid exorbitant service charges. Finally, if your card is rejected or the ATM seems to be malfunctioning, switch to another machine or, if possible, another bank rather than making repeated withdrawal attempts; the ATM may confiscate your card as an anti-fraud measure.

Travelers Checks

With the spread of ATMs, travelers checks have stopped being convenient for most travel, especially in a country as developed as Mexico. If you do bring them, you will have to exchange them at a bank or a *casa de cambio* (exchange booth).

Credit Cards

Visa and MasterCard are accepted at all large hotels and many medium and small ones, as well as upscale restaurants, main bus terminals, travel agencies, and many shops throughout Mexico. American Express is accepted much less frequently. Some merchants tack on a 3-10 percent surcharge for any credit card purchase—ask before you pay. And many credit card companies, but not all, charge a foreign transaction fee; it pays to check in advance which of your cards has the lowest fees.

Cash

It's a good idea to bring a small amount of U.S. cash, on the off chance that your ATM or credit cards suddenly stop working; a US$200 reserve should be more than enough for a two-week visit. Stow it away with your other important documents, to be used only if necessary. Credit cards are widely accepted; the only exceptions are Isla Holbox, Tulum (especially along the beach road), and the Río Bec region, where many businesses accept cash only.

Tax

A 12 percent value-added tax (IVA, *EE-va* in Spanish) applies to hotel rates, restaurant and bar tabs, and gift purchases. When checking in or making reservations at a hotel, ask if tax has already been added. In some cases, the tax is 17 percent.

Bargaining

Bargaining is common and expected in street and artisans' markets, but try not to be too aggressive. Some tourists derive immense and almost irrational pride from haggling over every last cent, and then turn around and spend several times that amount on beer or snacks. The fact is, most bargaining comes down to the difference of a few dollars or even less, and earning those extra dollars is a much bigger deal for most artisans than spending them is to most tourists.

Tipping

While tipping is always a choice, it is a key supplement to many workers' paychecks. In fact, for some—like baggers at the grocery store—the tip is the *only* pay they receive. And while dollars and euros are appreciated, pesos are preferred. **Note:** Foreign coins can't be changed to pesos, and thus are useless to workers. Average gratuities in the region include:

- Archaeological zone guides: 10-15 percent if you're satisfied with the service; for informal guides (typically boys who show you around the site), US$2-3 is customary.

- Gas station attendants: around US$0.50-1 if your windshield has been cleaned, tires have been filled, or the oil and water have been checked; no tip is expected for simply pumping gas.

- Grocery store baggers: US$0.25-0.50.

- Housekeepers: US$3-4 per day; either left daily or as a lump sum at the end of your stay.

- Porters: about US$2 per bag.

- Taxi drivers: Tipping is not customary.

- Tour guides: 10-15 percent; don't forget the driver—US$2-3 is typical.

- Waiters: 10-15 percent; make sure the gratuity is not already included in the bill.

COMMUNICATIONS AND MEDIA
Postal Service

Mailing letters and postcards from Mexico is neither cheap nor necessarily reliable. Delivery times vary greatly, and letters get "lost" somewhat more than postcards. Letters (under 20 grams) and postcards cost around US$0.85 to the United States and Canada, US$0.95 to Europe and South America, and US$1 to the rest of the world. Visit the **Correos de México** website (www.correosdemexico. gob.mx) for pricing on larger packages and other services.

Telephone

It is very likely you can continue to use your personal cell phone in Mexico for calls, text, and Internet, though the cost ranges from zero to outrageous. Most smartphones are functional in Mexico, and most carriers offer international roaming of some sort, whether standard or as an add-on. Just be sure to check the price for your particular plan. (And of course many phones allow for Wi-Fi calling.) If you have an **unlocked GSM cell phone,** you can also purchase a local SIM card for around US$10, including US$5 credit, for use during your trip. Calls can be expensive, but text messaging is relatively cheap, including internationally.

Public telephones are becoming increasingly obsolete in Mexico. If you find one that's working, you'll need a *tarjeta Ladatel*—a plastic phone card, the size and stiffness of a credit card, bearing a chip—to get phone service. The cards are sold at mini-marts and supermarkets in 50-, 100-, and 200-peso denominations. Insert the card into any public pay phone, and the amount on the card will be displayed on the screen. Rates and dialing instructions (in Spanish and English) are inside the phone cabin. At the time of research, rates were roughly US$0.15 per call to a local landline, US$0.08 per minute to a local cell phone, and US$0.30 per minute for calls to the United States and Canada.

Internet cafés typically offer inexpensive **Web-based phone service.** Rates tend to be significantly lower than those of public telephones, and you don't have to worry about your card running out.

Useful Telephone Numbers

TRAVELER ASSISTANCE
- Emergencies: 060 or 066
- Ángeles Verdes (Green Angels): 078 or 800/903-9200
- Directory Assistance: 044

LONG-DISTANCE DIRECT DIALING
- Domestic long-distance: 01 + area code + number
- International long-distance (United States only): 001 + area code + number
- International long-distance (rest of the world): 00 + country code + area code + number

LONG-DISTANCE COLLECT CALLS
- Domestic long-distance operator: 02
- International long-distance operator (English-speaking): 09

Beware of phones offering "free" collect or credit card calls; far from being free, their rates are outrageous.

Internet Access

Wireless Internet (Wi-Fi) is widely available, usually for free, at hotels, restaurants, coffee shops, and even in the central plazas of many towns and cities. Some first-class buses often offer Wi-Fi as well, though the connection can be spotty.

Internet cafés are sprinkled throughout the region. Most charge around US$1 per hour, though prices can be much higher in heavily touristed areas.

Newspapers

The most popular daily newspapers in the Yucatán Peninsula are *Milenio Novedades* (https://sipse.com/milenio), *Novedades Quintana Roo* (www.sipse.com/novedades), *MILED* (http://miledqroo.com.mx), *¡Por Esto!* (www.poresto.net), *El Diario de Yucatán* (www.yucatan.com.mx), *Tribuna de Campeche* (www.tribunacampeche. com), *Novedades Campeche* (www.

novedadesdecampeche.com.mx), and *El Sur de Campeche* (www.elsur.mx). The main national newspapers are also readily available, including *Reforma* (www.reforma.com), *La Prensa* (www.la-prensa.com.mx), and *La Jornada* (www.jornada.unam.mx). For local news in English, check out *The Yucatan Times* (www.theyucatantimes.com).

Radio and Television

Most large hotels and a number of midsize and small ones have cable or satellite TV, which usually includes CNN (though sometimes in Spanish only), MTV, and other U.S. channels. AM and FM radio options are surprisingly bland—you're more likely to find a good *rock en español* station in California than you are in the Yucatán.

MAPS AND TOURIST INFORMATION

Maps

A husband-and-wife team creates **MapChick maps** (www.cancunmap.com), exhaustively detailed maps of Cancún, Playa del Carmen, the Riviera Maya, Isla Cozumel, Isla Mujeres,

Cell Phone Calls

MEXICAN LANDLINE TO MEXICAN CELL PHONE:

· Within the same area code: 044 + 3-digit area code + 7-digit phone number

· Different area code: 045 + 3-digit area code + 7-digit phone number

MEXICAN CELL PHONE TO MEXICAN CELL PHONE:

· Within the same area code: 7-digit number only

· Different area code: 3-digit area code + 7-digit number

INTERNATIONAL LANDLINE/CELL PHONE TO A MEXICAN CELL PHONE:

· From U.S. or Canada: 011 + 52 + 1 + 3-digit area code + 7-digit number

· From other countries: international access code + 52 + 1 + 3-digit area code + 7-digit number

and inland archaeological zones. They're as much guidebooks as maps, with virtually every building and business identified, many with short personal reviews, plus useful information like taxi rates, driving distances, ferry schedules, and more. Maps cost around US$15 and often come with a couple of smaller secondary maps; they're sold on the MapChick website as well as on Amazon.com.

In Mérida, **Dante** (Calle 61 near Calle 62, tel. 999/928-2611, 8am-10:30pm daily) produces reliable maps of the entire Yucatán Peninsula; it also operates a chain of excellent bookstores.

Most local tourist offices distribute maps to tourists free of charge, though quality varies considerably. Car rental agencies often have maps, and many hotels create maps for their guests of nearby restaurants and sights.

Tourist Offices

Most cities in the region have a tourist information office or kiosk. Some are staffed with friendly and knowledgeable people and have a good sense of what tourists are looking for. At others, you'll seriously wonder how the staffers were hired. It is certainly worth stopping in if you have a question—you may well get it answered, but don't be surprised if you don't.

Photography and Video

Digital cameras are as ubiquitous in Mexico as they are everywhere else, but chips can be prohibitively expensive; bring a spare one in case your primary chip gets lost or damaged. If your chip's capacity is relatively small, plan on uploading your photos to your tablet or the cloud.

Video is another great way to capture the color and movement of the region. Be aware that archaeological sites charge an additional fee to bring in a video camera; tripods often are prohibited.

WEIGHTS AND MEASURES
Measurements

Mexico uses the metric system, so distances are in kilometers, weights are in kilograms, gasoline is sold by the liter, and temperatures are given in Celsius.

Time Zone

The entire Yucatán Peninsula and Chiapas used to be on Central Standard Time (along with Mexico City and much of central Mexico), with a region-wide shift in fall and spring for daylight savings. However, beginning in 2015, the state of Quintana Roo (which includes the entire Riviera Maya and Costa Maya) shifted to Eastern Standard Time October-April only. Put another way, while the rest of the Yucatán and the Central Time Zone "fall back" in October, Quintana Roo stays on daylight savings time, making it one hour ahead of its neighbors (and thus the same as the Eastern Time Zone). In April, the Central Time Zone "catches up" and the entire region is on the same hour again. The change is meant to give the Riviera Maya a longer-feeling day during the winter months and make travel from the U.S. East Coast easier. It can make travel to and from the Yucatecan interior a bit confusing, however; be sure to double-check your flight and bus times to avoid missed connections.

Electricity

Mexico uses the 60-cycle, 110-volt AC current common in the United States. Bring a surge protector if you plan to plug in a laptop.

Resources

Spanish Glossary

The form of Spanish spoken in the Yucatán Peninsula is quite clear and understandable, and far less clipped or colloquial than in other countries. That's good news for anyone new to the language and hoping to use their trip to learn more.

abarrotería: small grocery store

alcalde: mayor or municipal judge

alfarería: pottery

alfarero, alfarera: potter

amigo, amiga: friend

andador: walkway or strolling path

antojitos: Mexican snacks, such as huaraches, flautas, and quesadillas

artesanías: handicrafts, as distinguished from *artesano, artesana,* the person who makes handicrafts

audiencia: one of the royal executive-judicial panels sent to rule areas of Latin America during the 16th century

ayuntamiento: either the town council or the building where it meets

bienes raices: literally "good roots," but popularly, real estate

boleto: ticket, boarding pass

bucear, buzo: to scuba dive, scuba diver

caballero: gentleman

cabecera: head town of a municipal district, or headquarters in general

cabrón: a bastard; sometimes used affectionately

cacique: chief or boss

calesa: early 1800s-style horse-drawn carriage; also called *calandria*

camionera central: central bus station; alternatively, *terminal camionera*

campesino: country person; farm worker

canasta: basket

cárcel: jail

casa de huéspedes: guesthouse, often operated in a family home

caudillo: dictator or political chief

charro, charra: cowboy, cowgirl

churrigueresque: Spanish baroque architectural style incorporated into many Mexican colonial churches, named after José Churriguera (1665-1725)

cofradía: Catholic fraternal service association, either male or female, mainly in charge of financing and organizing religious festivals

colectivo: a shared public taxi or minibus that picks up and drops off passengers along a designated route; alternatively, *combi*

colegio: preparatory school

colonia: city neighborhood or subdivision; similar to *fraccionamiento* or *barrio*

combi: a shared public minibus; alternatively, *colectivo*

comedor: small restaurant

correo: post office

criollo: person of all-Spanish descent born in the New World

cuadra: city block

Cuaresma: Lent

cuota: literally "toll," commonly refers to a toll highway

curandero, curandera: indigenous medicine man or woman

dama: lady

Domingo de Ramos: Palm Sunday

Don, Doña: title of respect, generally used for an older man or woman

ejido: a constitutional, government-sponsored form of community, with shared land ownership and cooperative decision making

encomienda: colonial award of tribute from a designated indigenous district

farmacia: pharmacy or drugstore

finca: farm

fraccionamiento: city sector or subdivision; similar to *colonia* or *barrio*

gasolinera: gasoline station

gringo: term referring to North American Caucasians, sometimes derogatorily, sometimes not

grito: impassioned cry; *El Grito* commonly refers to Mexican Independence Day celebrations, from Hidalgo's *Grito de Dolores*

hacienda: large landed estate; also the government treasury

impuestos, I.V.A. (pronounced EE-va): taxes, value-added tax

indígena: indigenous person; commonly, but incorrectly, an Indian (*indio*)

jardín: garden or small park

jejenes: "no-see-um" biting gnats

judiciales: the federal or state police, best known to motorists for their highway checkpoint inspections; alternatively, *federales*

lancha: small motorboat; alternatively, *panga*

larga distancia: long-distance telephone service, or the *caseta* (booth) where it's provided

licenciado: academic degree (abbr. Lic.) approximately equivalent to a bachelor's degree

lonchería: small lunch counter, usually serving juices, sandwiches, and *antojitos* (Mexican snacks)

machismo; macho: exaggerated sense of maleness; person who holds such a sense of himself

mescal: alcoholic beverage distilled from the fermented hearts of maguey (century plant)

mestizo: person of mixed European/indigenous descent

milpa: native farm plot, usually of corn, squash, and/or beans

mordida: slang for bribe; literally, "little bite"

palapa: thatched-roof structure, often open-air

panga: small motorboat; alternatively, *lancha*

parque central: town plaza or central square; alternatively, *zócalo*

PEMEX: government gasoline station; acronym for "Petróleos Mexicanos," Mexico's national oil corporation

peninsulares: the Spanish-born ruling colonial elite

petate: a mat, traditionally woven of palm leaf

plan: political manifesto, usually by a leader or group consolidating or seeking power

plaza: shopping mall

policía: municipal police; alternatively, *preventativa*

Porfiriato: the 34-year (1876-1910) ruling period of president-dictator Porfirio Díaz

pozole: popular stew of hominy in broth, usually topped by shredded pork, cabbage, and diced onion

presidencia municipal: the headquarters, like a U.S. city or county hall, of a Mexican *municipio*, a county-like local governmental unit

propina: tip, as at a restaurant or hotel; alternatively, *servicio*

pueblo: town or people

puta: whore

quinta: a villa or country house

retorno: highway turnaround

Semana Santa: literally Holy Week, the week before Easter, a popular travel period for Mexicans

temporada: season, as in *temporada alta/baja* (high/low season)

tenate: soft, pliable basket, without handle, woven of palm leaf

terminal camionera: central bus station; alternatively, *camionera central*

vecinidad: neighborhood; alternatively, *barrio*

zócalo: town plaza or central square; alternatively, *parque central*

ABBREVIATIONS

Av.: *avenida* (avenue)

Blvd.: *bulevar* (boulevard)

Calz.: *calzada* (thoroughfare, main road)

Carr.: *carretera* (highway)

Col.: *colonia* (subdivision)

Nte.: *norte* (north)
Ote.: *oriente* (east)

Pte.: *poniente* (west)
s/n: *sin número* (no street number)

Yucatec Maya Glossary

The Maya language family includes 30 distinct languages, together spoken by nearly six million people in Mexico, Guatemala, and Belize. Yucatec Maya is spoken by around 800,000 people and is the most commonly spoken Maya language in the Yucatán Peninsula (and second overall, after K'iche in Guatemala). Most ancient glyphs were written in early forms of Yucatec Maya or another Maya language, Ch'ol.

MAYA GODS AND CEREMONIES

Acanum: protective deity of hunters
Ahau Can: serpent lord and highest priest
Ahau Chamehes: deity of medicine
Ah Cantzicnal: aquatic deity
Ah Chuy Kak: god of violent death and sacrifice
Ahcit Dzamalcum: protective god of fishermen
Ah Cup Cacap: god of the underworld who denies air
Ah Itzám: the water witch
Ah kines: priests that consult the oracles and preside over ceremonies and sacrifices
Ahpua: god of fishing
Ah Puch: god of death
Ak'Al: sacred marsh where water abounds
Bacaboob: supporters of the sky and guardians of the cardinal points, who form a single god, Ah Cantzicnal Becabs
Bolontiku: the nine lords of the night
Chaac: god of rain and agriculture
Chac Bolay Can: butcher serpent living in the underworld
Chaces: priests' assistants in agricultural and other ceremonies
Cihuateteo: women who become goddesses through death in childbirth
Cit Chac Coh: god of war
Hetzmek: ceremony when the child is first carried astride the hip

Hobnil Bacab: bee god, protector of beekeepers
Holcanes: warriors charged with obtaining slaves for sacrifice
Hunab Ku: giver of life, builder of the universe, and father of Itzámna
Ik: god of the wind
Itzámna: lord of the skies, creator of the beginning, god of time
Ixchel: goddess of birth, fertility, and medicine; credited with inventing spinning
Ixtab: goddess of the cord and of suicide by hanging
Kinich: face of the sun
Kukulcán: quetzal-serpent, plumed serpent
Metnal: the underworld, place of the dead
Nacom: warrior chief
Noh Ek: Venus
Pakat: god of violent death
Zec: spirit lords of beehives

FOOD AND DRINK

alche: inebriating drink, sweetened with honey and used for ceremonies and offerings
ic: chili
itz: sweet potato
kabaxbuul: heaviest meal of the day, eaten at dusk and containing cooked black beans
kah: pinole flour
kayem: ground maize
macal: a root
muxubbak: tamale
on: avocado
op: plum
p'ac: tomatoes
put: papaya
tzamna: black bean
uah: tortillas
za: maize drink

ANIMALS

acehpek: dog used for deer hunting
ah maax cal: prattling monkey
ah maycuy: chestnut deer
ah sac dziu: white thrush
ah xixteel ul: rugged land conch
bil: hairless dog reared for food
cutz: wild turkey
cutzha: duck
hoh: crow
icim: owl
jaleb: hairless dog
keh: deer
kitam: wild boar
muan: evil bird related to death
que: parrot
thul: rabbit
tzo: domestic turkey
utiu: coyote

MUSIC AND FESTIVALS

ah paxboob: musicians
bexelac: turtle shell used as percussion instrument
chohom: dance performed in ceremonies related to fishing
chul: flute
hom: trumpet
kayab: percussion instrument fashioned from turtle shell
Oc na: festival where old idols of a temple are broken and replaced with new ones
okot uil: dance performed during the Pocan ceremony
Pacum chac: festival in honor of the war gods
tunkul: drum
zacatan: drum made from a hollowed tree trunk; one opening is covered with hide

ELEMENTS OF TIME

baktun: 144,000-day Maya calendar
chumuc akab: midnight
chumuc kin: midday
emelkin: sunset
haab: solar calendar of 360 days plus five extra days of misfortune, which complete the final month
kaz akab: dusk

kin: the sun, the day, the unity of time
potakab: time before dawn
yalhalcab: dawn

NUMBERS

hun: one
ca: two
ox: three
can: four
ho: five
uac: six
uuc: seven
uacax: eight
bolon: nine
iahun: ten
buluc: eleven
iahca: twelve
oxlahum: thirteen
canlahum: fourteen
holahun: fifteen
uaclahun: sixteen
uuclahun: seventeen
uacaclahun: eighteen
bolontahun: nineteen
hunkal: twenty

PLANTS AND TREES

ha: cacao seed
kan ak: plant that produces a yellow dye
ki: sisal
kiixpaxhkum: chayote
kikche: tree trunk that is used to make canoes
kuche: red cedar tree
k'uxub: annatto tree
piim: fiber of the cotton tree
taman: cotton plant
tauch: black zapote tree
tazon te: moss

MISCELLANEOUS WORDS

ah kay kin bak: meat-seller
chaltun: water cistern
cha te: black vegetable dye
chi te: eugenia, plant for dyeing
ch'oh: indigo
ek: dye
hadzab: wooden swords

halach uinic: leader
mayacimil: smallpox epidemic
palapa: traditional Maya structure constructed without nails or tools
pic: underskirt
ploms: rich people

suyen: square blanket
xanab: sandals
xicul: sleeveless jacket decorated with feathers
xul: stake with a pointed, fire-hardened tip
yuntun: slings

Spanish Phrasebook

Whether you speak a little or a lot, using your Spanish will surely make your vacation a lot more fun. You'll soon see that Mexicans truly appreciate your efforts and your willingness to speak their language.

Spanish commonly uses 30 letters—the familiar English 26, plus four straightforward additions: ch, ll, ñ, and rr.

PRONUNCIATION

Once you learn them, Spanish pronunciation rules—in contrast to English and other languages—generally don't change. Spanish vowels generally sound softer than in English.

Vowels

a like ah, as in "hah": *agua* AH-gooah (water), *pan* PAHN (bread), and *casa* CAH-sah (house)

e like eh, as in "hem": *mesa* MEH-sah (table), *tela* TEH-lah (cloth), and *de* DEH (of, from)

i like ee, as in "need": *diez* dee-EHZ (ten), *comida* ko-MEE-dah (meal), and *fin* FEEN (end)

o like oh, as in "go": *peso* PEH-soh (weight), *ocho* OH-choh (eight), and *poco* POH-koh (a bit)

u like oo, as in "cool": *uno* OO-noh (one), *cuarto* KOOAHR-toh (room), and *usted* oos-TEHD (you); when it follows a "q" the **u** is silent: *quiero* ki-EH-ro (I want); when it follows an "h" or has an umlaut, it's pronounced like "w": *huevo* WEH-vo (egg)

Consonants

b, d, f, k, l, m, n, p, q, s, t, v, w, x, y, z, ch pronounced almost as in English; **h** is silent

c like k, as in "keep": *cuarto* KOOAR-toh (room), *Tepic* tay-PEEK (capital of Nayarit state); when it precedes "e" or "i," pronounce **c** like s, as in "sit": *cerveza* sehr-VEH-sah (beer), *encima* ehn-SEE-mah (atop)

g like g, as in "gift" when it precedes "a," "o," "u," or a consonant: *gato* GAH-toh (cat), *hago* AH-goh (I do, make); otherwise, pronounce **g** like h, as in "hat": *giro* HEE-roh (money order), *gente* HEN-tay (people)

j like h, as in "has": *Jueves* HOOEH-vehs (Thursday), *mejor* meh-HOR (better)

ll like y, as in "yes": *toalla* toh-AH-yah (towel), *ellos* EH-yohs (they, them)

ñ like ny, as in "canyon": *año* AH-nyo (year), *señor* SEH-nyor (mister, sir)

r is lightly trilled: *pero* PEH-roh (but), *tres* TREHS (three), *cuatro* KOOAH-troh (four)

rr like a Spanish r, but with much more emphasis and trill: *burro* (donkey), *carretera* (highway), *ferrocarril* (railroad)

Note: The single exception to the above is the pronunciation of **y** when it's being used as the Spanish word for "and," as in *Eva y Leo.* In such case, pronounce it like the English ee, as in "keep": Eva "ee" Leo (Eva and Leo).

Accent

The rule for accent, the relative stress given to syllables within a given word, is straightforward. If a word ends in a vowel, an "n," or an "s," accent the next-to-last syllable; if not, accent the last syllable.

Pronounce *gracias* GRAH-seeahs (thank you), *orden* OHR-dehn (order), and *carretera* kah-reh-

TEH-rah (highway) with the stress on the next-to-last syllable.

Otherwise, accent the last syllable: *venir* vay-NEER (to come), *ferrocarril* feh-roh-cah-REEL (railroad), and *edad* eh-DAHD (age).

Exceptions to the accent rule are always marked with an accent sign: (á, é, í, ó, or ú), such as *teléfono* teh-LEH-foh-noh (telephone), *jabón* hah-BON (soap), and *rápido* RAH-pee-doh (rapid).

BASIC AND COURTEOUS EXPRESSIONS

Most Spanish-speakers consider formalities important. Whenever approaching anyone, try to say the appropriate salutation—good morning, good evening, and so forth. Standing alone, the greeting *hola* (hello) can sound brusque.

Hello. *Hola.*
Good morning. *Buenos días.*
Good afternoon. *Buenas tardes.*
Good evening. *Buenas noches.*
How are you? *¿Cómo está Usted?*
Very well, thank you. *Muy bien, gracias.*
Okay; good. *Bien.*
Not okay; bad. *No muy bien; mal.*
So-so. *Más o menos.*
And you? *¿Y usted?*
Thank you. *Gracias.*
Thank you very much. *Muchas gracias.*
You're very kind. *Muy amable.*
You're welcome. *De nada.*
Good-bye. *Adios.*
See you later. *Hasta luego.*
please *por favor*
yes *sí*
no *no*
I don't know. *No sé.*
Just a moment, please. *Un momento, por favor.*
Excuse me, please (when you're trying to get attention). *Disculpe* or *Con permiso.*
Excuse me (when you've made a mistake). *Lo siento.*
Pleased to meet you. *Mucho gusto.*
Do you speak English? *¿Habla Usted inglés?*
Is English spoken here? *¿Se habla inglés?*

I don't speak Spanish well. *No hablo bien el español.*
I don't understand. *No entiendo.*
How do you say . . . in Spanish? *¿Cómo se dice . . . en español?*
What is your name? *¿Cómo se llama Usted?*
My name is . . . *Me llamo . . .*
Would you like . . . *¿Quisiera Usted . . .*
Let's go to . . . *Vamos a . . .*

TERMS OF ADDRESS

When in doubt, use the formal *Usted* (you) as a form of address.

I *yo*
you (formal) *Usted*
you (familiar) *tu*
he/him *él*
she/her *ella*
we/us *nosotros*
you (plural) *ustedes*
they/them *ellos* (all males or mixed gender); *ellas* (all females)
mister, sir *señor*
missus, ma'am *señora*
miss, young lady *señorita*
wife *esposa*
husband *esposo*
friend *amigo* (male); *amiga* (female)
boyfriend; girlfriend *novio; novia*
son; daughter *hijo; hija*
brother; sister *hermano; hermana*
father; mother *padre; madre*
grandfather; grandmother *abuelo; abuela*

TRANSPORTATION

Where is . . . ? *¿Dónde está . . . ?*
How far is it to . . . ? *¿A cuánto está . . . ?*
from . . . to . . . *de . . . a . . .*
How many blocks? *¿Cuántas cuadras?*
Where (Which) is the way to . . . ? *¿Dónde está el camino a . . . ?*
the bus station *la terminal de autobuses*
the bus stop *la parada de autobuses*
Where is this bus going? *¿Adónde va este autobús?*
the taxi stand *la parada de taxis*
the train station *la estación de ferrocarril*

the boat *el barco* or *la lancha*
the airport *el aeropuerto*
I'd like a ticket to . . . *Quisiera un boleto a . . .*
first (second) class *primera (segunda) clase*
round-trip *ida y vuelta*
reservation *reservación*
baggage *equipaje*
Stop here, please. *Pare aquí, por favor.*
the entrance *la entrada*
the exit *la salida*
the ticket office *la taquilla*
(very) near; far *(muy) cerca; lejos*
to; toward *a*
by; through *por*
from *de*
the right *la derecha*
the left *la izquierda*
straight ahead *derecho; directo*
in front *en frente*
beside *al lado*
behind *atrás*
the corner *la esquina*
the stoplight *el semáforo*
a turn *una vuelta*
here *aquí*
somewhere around here *por aquí*
right there *allí*
somewhere around there *por allá*
street; boulevard *calle; bulevar*
highway *carretera*
bridge *puente*
toll *cuota*
address *dirección*
north; south *norte; sur*
east; west *oriente (este); poniente (oeste)*

ACCOMMODATIONS

hotel *hotel*
Is there a room? *¿Hay cuarto?*
May I (may we) see it? *¿Podría (podríamos) verlo?*
What is the rate? *¿Cuál es la tarifa?*
Is that your best rate? *¿Es su mejor precio?*
Is there something cheaper? *¿Hay algo más económico?*
a single room *un cuarto sencillo*
a double room *un cuarto doble*
double bed *cama matrimonial*

twin bed *cama individual*
with private bath *con baño privado*
hot water *agua caliente*
shower *ducha; regadera*
towels *toallas*
soap *jabón*
toilet paper *papel higiénico*
blanket *cobija*
sheets *sábanas*
air-conditioned *aire acondicionado*
fan *abanico; ventilador*
key *llave*
manager *gerente*

FOOD

I'm hungry *Tengo hambre.*
I'm thirsty. *Tengo sed.*
menu *carta; menú*
order *orden*
glass *vaso*
fork *tenedor*
knife *cuchillo*
spoon *cuchara*
napkin *servilleta*
soft drink *refresco*
coffee *café*
tea *té*
drinking water *agua pura; agua potable*
carbonated water *agua mineral*
bottled uncarbonated water *agua sin gas*
beer *cerveza*
wine *vino*
milk *leche*
juice *jugo*
cream *crema*
sugar *azúcar*
cheese *queso*
snack *antojito; botana*
breakfast *desayuno*
lunch *almuerzo* or *comida*
daily lunch special *comida corrida*
dinner *cena*
the check *la cuenta*
eggs *huevos*
bread *pan*
salad *ensalada*
fruit *fruta*

mango *mango*
watermelon *sandía*
papaya *papaya*
banana *plátano*
apple *manzana*
orange *naranja*
lime *limón*
fish *pescado*
shellfish *mariscos*
shrimp *camarones*
meat (without) *(sin) carne*
chicken *pollo*
pork *puerco*
beef; steak *res; bistec*
bacon; ham *tocino; jamón*
fried *frito*
roasted *asado*
barbecue; barbecued *barbacoa; al carbón*
food to go *comida para llevar; para llevar*
delivery service *servicio a domicilio*

SHOPPING

money *dinero*
money-exchange bureau *casa de cambio*
I would like to exchange travelers
   checks. *Quisiera cambiar cheques de
   viajero.*
What is the exchange rate? *¿Cuál es el
   tipo de cambio?*
How much is the commission? *¿Cuánto
   cuesta la comisión?*
Do you accept credit cards? *¿Aceptan
   tarjetas de crédito?*
How much does it cost? *¿Cuánto cuesta?*
What is your final price? *¿Cuál es su último
   precio?*
expensive *caro*
cheap *barato; económico*
more *más*
less *menos*
a little *un poco*
too much *demasiado*

HEALTH

Help me please. *Ayúdeme por favor.*
I am ill. *Estoy enfermo.*
Call a doctor. *Llame un doctor.*
Take me to ... *Lléveme a ...*

hospital *hospital; clinica medica*
drugstore *farmacia*
pain *dolor*
fever *fiebre*
headache *dolor de cabeza*
stomachache *dolor de estómago*
burn *quemadura*
cramp *calambre*
nausea *náusea*
vomiting *vomitar*
medicine *medicina*
antibiotic *antibiótico*
pill; tablet *pastilla*
aspirin *aspirina*
ointment; cream *pomada; crema*
bandage *venda*
cotton *algodón*
sanitary napkins *Kotex*
birth control pills *pastillas anticonceptivas*
contraceptive foam *espuma
   anticonceptiva*
condoms *preservativos; condones*
contact lenses *pupilentes*
glasses *lentes*
dental floss *hilo dental*
dentist *dentista*
toothbrush *cepillo de dientes*
toothpaste *pasta de dientes*
toothache *dolor de dientes*
delivery service *servicio a domicilio*

POST OFFICE AND COMMUNICATIONS

long-distance telephone *teléfono de
   larga distancia*
I would like to call ... *Quisiera llamar a ...*
collect *por cobrar*
person to person *persona a persona*
credit card *tarjeta de crédito*
post office *correo*
letter *carta*
stamp *estampilla, timbre*
postcard *tarjeta*
airmail *correo aereo*
registered *registrado*
money order *giro*
package; box *paquete; caja*
string; tape *cuerda; cinta*

Internet *internet*
Internet café *ciber café; ciber*
website *página web*
Web search *búsqueda*
link *enlace*
email *correo electrónico*
Skype *Skype*
Facebook *face*

AT THE BORDER

border *frontera*
customs *aduana*
immigration *migración*
tourist card *tarjeta de turista*
inspection *inspección; revisión*
passport *pasaporte*
profession *profesión*
marital status *estado civil*
single *soltero*
married; divorced *casado; divorciado*
widowed *viudado* (male); *viudada* (female)
insurance *seguro*
title *título*
driver's license *licencia de manejar*

AT THE GAS STATION

gas station *gasolinera*
gasoline *gasolina*
unleaded *sin plomo*
fill it up, please *lleno, por favor*
tire *llanta*
tire repair shop *vulcanizadora*
air *aire*
water *agua*
oil; oil change *aceite; cambio de aceite*
grease *grasa*
My ... doesn't work. *Mi ... no sirve.*
battery *batería*
radiator *radiador*
alternator *alternador*
generator *generador*
tow truck *grúa*
repair shop *taller mecánico*
tune-up *afinación*
auto parts store *refaccionería*

VERBS

In Spanish, verbs employ mostly predictable forms and come in three classes, which end in *ar, er,* and *ir.* Note that the first-person (*yo*) verb form is often irregular.

to buy *comprar*
I buy, you (he, she, it) buys *compro, compra*
we buy, you (they) buy *compramos, compran*

to eat *comer*
I eat, you (he, she, it) eats *como, come*
we eat, you (they) eat *comemos, comen*

to climb *subir*
I climb, you (he, she, it) climbs *subo, sube*
we climb, you (they) climb *subimos, suben*

Here are more (with irregularities indicated):

to do or make *hacer* (regular except for *hago,* I do or make)
to go *ir* (very irregular: *voy, va, vamos, van*)
to go (walk) *andar*
to love *amar*
to work *trabajar*
to want *desear, querer*
to need *necesitar*
to read *leer*
to write *escribir*
to repair *reparar*
to stop *parar*
to get off (the bus) *bajar*
to arrive *llegar*
to stay (remain) *quedar*
to stay (lodge) *hospedar*
to leave *salir* (regular except for *salgo,* I leave)
to look at *mirar*
to look for *buscar*
to give *dar* (regular except for *doy,* I give)
to carry *llevar*
to have *tener* (irregular but important: *tengo, tiene, tenemos, tienen*)

to come venir (similarly irregular: *vengo,
viene, venimos, vienen*)

Spanish has two forms of "to be":

to be *estar* (regular except for *estoy,* I am)
to be *ser* (very irregular: *soy, es, somos, son*)

Use *estar* when speaking of location or a temporary state of being: "I am at home." *"Estoy en casa."* "I'm sick." *"Estoy enfermo."* Use *ser* for a permanent state of being: "I am a doctor." *"Soy doctora."*

NUMBERS

zero *cero*
one *uno*
two *dos*
three *tres*
four *cuatro*
five *cinco*
six *seis*
seven *siete*
eight *ocho*
nine *nueve*
10 *diez*
11 *once*
12 *doce*
13 *trece*
14 *catorce*
15 *quince*
16 *dieciseis*
17 *diecisiete*
18 *dieciocho*
19 *diecinueve*
20 *veinte*
21 *veintiuno*
30 *treinta*
40 *cuarenta*
50 *cincuenta*
60 *sesenta*
70 *setenta*
80 *ochenta*
90 *noventa*
100 *cien*
101 *cientiuno*
200 *doscientos*
500 *quinientos*

1,000 *mil*
10,000 *diez mil*
100,000 *cien mil*
1,000,000 *millón*
one-half *medio*
one-third *un tercio*
one-fourth *un cuarto*

TIME

What time is it? *¿Qué hora es?*
It's one o'clock. *Es la una.*
It's three in the afternoon. *Son las tres de la tarde.*
It's 4am. *Son las cuatro de la mañana.*
six-thirty *seis y media*
a quarter till eleven *un cuarto para las once*
a quarter past five *las cinco y cuarto*
an hour *una hora*

DAYS AND MONTHS

Monday *lunes*
Tuesday *martes*
Wednesday *miércoles*
Thursday *jueves*
Friday *viernes*
Saturday *sábado*
Sunday *domingo*
today *hoy*
tomorrow *mañana*
yesterday *ayer*
January *enero*
February *febrero*
March *marzo*
April *abril*
May *mayo*
June *junio*
July *julio*
August *agosto*
September *septiembre*
October *octubre*
November *noviembre*
December *diciembre*
a week *una semana*
a month *un mes*
after *después*
before *antes*

Suggested Reading

The following titles provide insight into the Yucatán Peninsula and the Maya people. A few of these books are more easily obtained in Mexico, but most will cost less in the United States. Most are nonfiction, though several are fiction and great to throw into your carry-on for a good read on the plane, or for when you're in a Yucatecan mood. Happy reading!

ARCHAEOLOGY

Coe, Andrew. *Archaeological Mexico: A Guide to Ancient Cities and Sacred Sites.* Emeryville, CA: Avalon Travel Publishing, 2001.

Coe, Michael D. *Breaking the Maya Code.* New York: Thames and Hudson, 2012. A fascinating account of how epigraphers, linguists, and archaeologists succeeded in deciphering Maya hieroglyphics.

Coe, Michael D. *The Maya.* New York: Thames and Hudson, 2011. A well-illustrated, easy-to-read volume on the Maya people.

Ferguson, William M. *Maya Ruins of Mexico in Color.* Norman, OK: University of Oklahoma Press, 1985. Good reading before you go, but too bulky to carry along. Oversized with excellent drawings and illustrations of the structures of the Maya.

Maya: Divine Kings of the Rain Forest. Cologne: Könemann, 2006. A beautifully compiled book of essays, photographs, and sketches relating to the Maya, past and present. Too heavy to take on the road but an excellent read.

Stephens, John L. *Incidents of Travel in Central America, Chiapas, and Yucatán.* 2 vols. New York: Cosimo Classics, 2008. Good companions to refer to when traveling in the area. Stephens and illustrator Frederick Catherwood rediscovered many of the Maya ruins on their treks that took place in the mid-1800s. Easy reading.

Thompson, J. Eric. *Maya Archaeologist.* Norman, OK: University of Oklahoma Press, 1974. Thompson, a noted Maya scholar, traveled to and worked at many of the Maya ruins in the 1930s.

Thompson, J. Eric. *The Rise and Fall of the Maya Civilization.* Norman, OK: University of Oklahoma Press, 1973. One man's story of the Maya. Excellent reading.

Webster, David. *The Fall of the Ancient Maya.* New York: Thames and Hudson, 2002. A careful and thorough examination of the possible causes of one of archaeology's great unsolved mysteries—the collapse of the Classic Maya in the 8th century.

FICTION

McNay Brumfield, James. *A Tourist in the Yucatán.* Watsonville, CA: Tres Picos Press, 2004. A decent thriller that takes place in the Yucatán Peninsula; good for the beach or a long bus ride.

Sodi, Demetrio M. (in collaboration with Adela Fernández). *The Mayas.* Mexico City: Panama Editorial S.A., 1987. This small book presents a fictionalized account of life among the Maya before the conquest. Easy reading for anyone who enjoys fantasizing about what life *might* have been like before recorded history in the Yucatán.

MEDICAL INFORMATION

Werner, David. *Where There Is No Doctor.* Palo Alto, CA: The Hesperian Foundation, 1992. This is an invaluable medical aid to anyone traveling not only to isolated parts of Mexico but to any place in the world where there's not a doctor (or Internet).

MEXICAN HISTORY AND CULTURE

Díaz del Castillo, Bernal. *The Conquest of New Spain*. New York: Penguin Books, 1963. History straight from the adventurer's reminiscences, translated by J. M. Cohen.

Fehrenbach, T. R. *Fire and Blood: A History of Mexico*. New York: Collier Books, 1995. Over 3,000 years of Mexican history, related in a way that will keep you reading.

Franz, Carl, and Lorena Havens. *The People's Guide to Mexico*. Berkeley, CA: Avalon Travel, 2012. A humorous guide filled with witty anecdotes and helpful general information for visitors to Mexico. Don't expect any specific city information, just nuts-and-bolts hints for traveling south of the border.

Greene, Graham. *The Power and the Glory*. New York: Penguin Books, 2003. A novel that takes place in the 1920s about a priest and the antichurch movement that gripped Mexico.

Meyer, Michael, and William Sherman. *The Course of Mexican History*. New York: Oxford University Press, 2013. A concise one-volume history of Mexico.

Perry, Richard, and Rosalind Perry. *Maya Missions: Exploring Colonial Yucatán*. Santa Barbara, CA: Espadaña Press, 2002. Detailed and informative guide, including excellent hand-drawn illustrations, about numerous colonial missions and structures in the Yucatán Peninsula.

Wolf, Eric. *Sons of the Shaking Earth*. Chicago: University of Chicago Press, 1962. An anthropological study of the indigenous and mestizo people of Mexico and Guatemala.

Wright, Ronald. *Time Among the Maya*. New York: Grove Press, 2000. A narrative that takes the reader through the Maya country of today, with historical comments that help put the puzzle together.

NATURAL MEXICO

Beletsky, Les. *Travellers' Wildlife Guides: Southern Mexico*. Northampton, MA: Interlink Books, 2006. A perfect companion guide if you plan on bird-watching, diving/snorkeling, hiking, or canoeing your way through your vacation. Excellent illustrations.

Heffern, Richard. *Secrets of the Mind-Altering Plants of Mexico*. New York: Pyramid Books, 1974. A fascinating study of many substances, from ancient ritual hallucinogens to today's medicines that are found in Mexico.

PRE-COLONIAL MEXICO

Cortés, Hernán. *Five Letters*. New York: Gordon Press, 1991. Cortés's letters to the king of Spain, telling of his accomplishments and justifying his actions in the New World.

Davies, Nigel. *The Ancient Kingdoms of Mexico*. New York: Penguin Books, 1991. An excellent study of the preconquest of the indigenous peoples of Mexico.

De Landa, Bishop Diego. *Yucatán Before and After the Conquest*. New York: Dover Publications, 2012. This book, translated by William Gates from the original 1566 volume, has served as the basis for much of the research that has taken place in the region.

Nelson, Ralph. *Popul Vuh: The Great Mythological Book of the Ancient Maya*. Boston: Houghton Mifflin, 1974. An easy-to-read translation of myths handed down orally by the Quiche Maya, family to family, until written down after the Spanish conquest.

Internet Resources

CAMPECHE

www.campeche.travel
Official tourism website of Campeche state.

www.culturacampeche.com
Website of Campeche state's office of cultural affairs, including a statewide schedule of events.

www.visitcalakmul.com
Information about visiting Calakmul ruins, other archaeological sites, and surrounding villages; includes listings of guides, ecotourism opportunities, hotels, and more.

CANCÚN

www.cancunmap.com
Excellent source of detailed maps of Cancún, the Riviera Maya, and some inland archaeological zones.

www.cancuntips.com.mx
Online version of Cancún's main tourist magazine, with tons of listings, travel tips, and tourist resources.

CHIAPAS

www.turismochiapas.gob.mx
Official tourism website for the state of Chiapas, with detailed information about sights, cities, and events.

COZUMEL

www.cozumelinsider.com
Good website covering Cozumel, including current tourist information and issues important to locals.

www.cozumelmycozumel.com
Website offering a host of information to travelers and people considering a move to Isla Cozumel, moderated by longtime expats.

www.cozumeltoday.com
Website with articles geared toward travelers; affiliated with *Cozumel Today* magazine.

ISLA HOLBOX

http://the.holboxeno.com
Excellent source of information for Holbox, including an updated schedule of events and goings-on, by day.

www.holboxisland.com
Website focused on Isla Holbox, with information on charter air tours and a handful of other tours and sights.

ISLA MUJERES

www.islamujeres.gob.mx
Official website of the island of Isla Mujeres, including tourist information.

www.islamujeres.info
Excellent resource for the goings-on about Isla Mujeres, including activities, ferry schedules, and even a message board.

www.isla-mujeres.net
Informative website covering Isla Mujeres, with lodging, restaurants, activities, maps, FAQs, coupons, island history, even a Spanish primer.

www.souldeisla.com
Website offering detailed recommendations in Isla Mujeres, from restaurants to wedding planners.

PLAYA DEL CARMEN

www.everythingplayadelcarmen.com
Website with tons of articles, photos, and other info on Playa, plus coupons and package deals.

www.playa.info
Established website with lots of travel planning information to Playa and the Riviera Maya. It also has a popular forum for asking questions and sharing tips.

www.theplayatimes.com
A bimonthly online newspaper that covers, among other topics, arts and culture, area sites, and upcoming events.

PUERTO AVENTURAS
www.puertoaventuras.com
Website with updated information about Puerto Aventuras.

PUERTO MORELOS
www.almalibrebooks.com
Bookstore website that's packed with information about Puerto Morelos; also has listings for short- and long-term rentals.

www.InPuertoMorelos.com
Low-key website operated by the former owners of Alma Libre Bookstore, with info on lodging, activities, and more.

www.puertomorelos.com
Listings of local resorts, eateries, shops, and more, with an option to purchase vacation packages.

TULUM AND THE COSTA MAYA
www.bacalarmosaico.com
Extensive listings of hotels, restaurants, activities, and more in Laguna Bacalar.

www.todotulum.com
Great resource for Tulum encompassing everything from nightlife to real estate.

www.tuchetumal.com
Informative online directory to Chetumal and area sights.

YUCATÁN
www.revistaexplore.com
Website of a tourist magazine that contains excellent coverage of Yucatán state.

www.yucatanliving.com
Award-winning website about living in Mérida and Yucatán state, with helpful travel info like up-to-date event listings.

www.yucatantoday.com
Website of the monthly tourist magazine of the same name. Based in Mérida but contains coverage of all of Yucatán state.

www.yucatan.travel
Official tourism website of Yucatán state.

YUCATÁN PENINSULA (REGIONAL)
www.backyardnature.net/yucatan
Notes and observations by an experienced naturalist about the major plants and animal species in the northern Yucatán Peninsula.

www.cruiseportinsider.com
A good source of information for travelers arriving to the region via cruise ship, including maps and shore excursion descriptions.

www.locogringo.com
Longtime tourism outfit's website includes extensive business listings for the Yucatán Peninsula.

www.travelyucatan.com
Detailed information and practical advice about traveling to and around the Yucatán Peninsula.

Index

List of Maps

Photo Credits

Title page photo: © Liza Prado

All interior photos © Liza Prado, except: page 2 © H.W. Prado; page 6 (top left) © Ravina Schneider; page 7 (bottom left) © Brian Lasenby | Dreamstime.com; pages 10-11 © Brian Lasenby | Dreamstime.com; page 12 © Igor Kiporuk | Dreamstime.com; page 13 (top) © Eddygaleotti | Dreamstime.com; page 15 (top) © Mikhail Dudarev | Dreamstime.com; page 16 (top) © Jonathan Ross | Dreamstime.com; page 17 © Lunamarina | Dreamstime.com; page 27 © Lunamarina | Dreamstime.com; page 32 (left) © Adogslifephoto | Dreamstime.com; page 44 © Gary Chandler; page 47 (bottom) © Gary Chandler; page 102 (top left) © Gary Chandler; page 113 (top) © H.W. Prado; page 121 (top left) © Seadam | Dreamstime.com; (top right) © Darryl Brooks | Dreamstime.com; page 134 (bottom) © Gary Chandler; page 143 © Gary Chandler; page 146 (top right) © H.W. Prado; page 154 (top) © H.W. Prado; page 166 (top left) © Mustang79 | Dreamstime.com; (top right) © Jonmilnes | Dreamstime.com; page 170 (right middle) © H.W. Prado; page 192 (top) © Gary Chandler; page 200 (top left) © H.W. Prado; (top right) © Hoatzinexp | Dreamstime.com; page 208 (right middle) © James Kelley | Dreamstime.com; (bottom) © Filippo Carlot | Dreamstime.com; page 229 (top) © Avrilstyrman | Dreamstime.com; page 279 (top) © Ravina Schneider; page 307 (right middle) © Agami Photo Agency | Dreamstime.com; page 366 (top) © Ravina Schneider; page 383 © Augustin Florian | Dreamstime.com; page 451 (top) © Gary Chandler; (left middle) © Gary Chandler; (right middle) © Gary Chandler

MOON
CAMINO DE SANTIAGO

SACRED SITES,
HISTORIC VILLAGES,
LOCAL FOOD & WINE

BEEBE BAHRAMI

Embark on an epic journey along the historic Camino de Santiago, stroll the most popular European cities, or chase the northern lights in Norway with Moon Travel Guides!

AMALFI COAST

BARCELONA & MADRID

JESSICA JONES

CROATIA & SLOVENIA

EDINBURGH, GLASGOW & THE ISLE OF SKYE

ICELAND

IRELAND

NORMANDY & BRITTANY

NORWAY

PORTUGAL

PRAGUE, VIENNA & BUDAPEST

PROVENCE

ROME, FLORENCE & VENICE

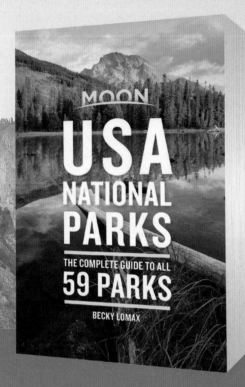

Packed with colorful photos, helpful lists of top experiences, and strategic tips for visiting America's National Parks, this top-selling travel guide is a practical keepsake.

Moon USA National Parks includes a pull-out souvenir map and a designated section to collect each park's stamp.

5 ³/₈" x 8 ³/₈" • 700pp • $24.99 US | $32.49 CAN

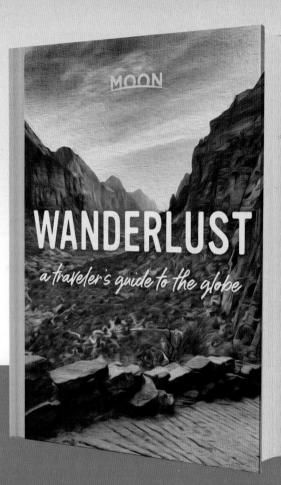

**BUILD YOUR BUCKET LIST
WITH MOON WANDERLUST!**

Find travel inspiration in this handsome
coffee table book full of illustrations and
photos of destinations all around the globe.

10" x 13" Hardcover • 368pp • $40 US | $50 CAN

BAJA
With Los Cabos
JENNIFER KRAMER

CANCÚN & COZUMEL
With Playa del Carmen, Tulum & the Riviera Maya
GERRY PALLANTE & GARY CHANDLER

LOS CABOS
With La Paz & Todos Santos
JENNIFER KRAMER

MEXICO CITY
JULIE MEADE

OAXACA
JUSTIN HENDERSON

PUERTO VALLARTA
With Sayulita & the Riviera Nayarit
MADELINE MILNE

SAN MIGUEL DE ALLENDE
with Guanajuato & Querétaro
JULIE MEADE

TIJUANA, ENSENADA & VALLE DE GUADALUPE WINE COUNTRY
JENNIFER KRAMER

Mexico and Latin America Travel Guides

BELIZE
LEBAWIT LILY GIRMA

CARTAGENA & COLOMBIA'S CARIBBEAN COAST
CAROL REISS

CHILE
with Easter Island
STEPH DYSON

COSTA RICA
NIKKI SOLANO

ECUADOR
& THE GALÁPAGOS ISLANDS
BETHANY PITTS

GALÁPAGOS ISLANDS
TRIP OF A LIFETIME
LISA CHO

MACHU PICCHU
TRIP OF A LIFETIME
RYAN DUBÉ

PATAGONIA
TRIP OF A LIFETIME
Including the Falkland Islands
WAYNE BERNHARDSON

MAP SYMBOLS

≡≡≡	Expressway	⊡	Highlight	✈	Airport	⚲	Golf Course
≡≡≡	Primary Road	○	City/Town	✗	Airfield	🅿	Parking Area
≈≈≈	Secondary Road	◉	State Capital	▲	Mountain	▱	Archaeological Site
▪▪▪	Unpaved Road	◉	National Capital	✦	Unique Natural Feature	♦	Church
- - -	Trail	★	Point of Interest			▯	Gas Station
·····-·	Ferry	●	Accommodation	⟩⟩	Waterfall		
◂━◂━	Railroad	▾	Restaurant/Bar	▲	Park	➴	Dive Site
≡≡≡	Pedestrian Walkway	▪	Other Location	🅣	Trailhead		Mangrove
⊞⊞⊞	Stairs	∧	Campground	⍒	Lighthouse		Reef
							Swamp

CONVERSION TABLES

$°C = (°F - 32) / 1.8$
$°F = (°C \times 1.8) + 32$
1 inch = 2.54 centimeters (cm)
1 foot = 0.304 meters (m)
1 yard = 0.914 meters
1 mile = 1.6093 kilometers (km)
1 km = 0.6214 miles
1 fathom = 1.8288 m
1 chain = 20.1168 m
1 furlong = 201.168 m
1 acre = 0.4047 hectares
1 sq km = 100 hectares
1 sq mile = 2.59 square km
1 ounce = 28.35 grams
1 pound = 0.4536 kilograms
1 short ton = 0.90718 metric ton
1 short ton = 2,000 pounds
1 long ton = 1.016 metric tons
1 long ton = 2,240 pounds
1 metric ton = 1,000 kilograms
1 quart = 0.94635 liters
1 US gallon = 3.7854 liters
1 Imperial gallon = 4.5459 liters
1 nautical mile = 1.852 km

MOON YUCATÁN PENINSULA
Avalon Travel
Hachette Book Group
1700 Fourth Street
Berkeley, CA 94710, USA
www.moon.com

Editor and Series Manager: Kathryn Ettinger
Acquiring Editor: Grace Fujimoto
Copy Editor: Brett Keener
Graphics Coordinator: Suzanne Albertson
Production Coordinators: Suzanne Albertson,
  Lucie Ericksen
Cover Design: Faceout Studios, Charles Brock
Interior Design: Domini Dragoone
Moon Logo: Tim McGrath
Map Editor: Kat Bennett
Cartographer: Kat Bennett
Indexer: Greg Jewett

ISBN-13: 978-1-64049-139-7

Printing History
1st Edition — 1986
13th Edition — November 2019
5 4 3 2 1

Text © 2019 by Liza Prado & Gary Chandler.
Maps © 2019 by Avalon Travel.
Some photos and illustrations are used by
permission and are the property of the original
copyright owners.

Front cover photo: Chichén Itzá © xavierarnau/
GettyImages
Back cover photo: boat dock on Isla Holbox ©
Davitosan | Dreamstime.com

Printed in China by RR Donnelley